A PHILOSOPHY OF EVIDENCE LAW

A Philosophy of Evidence Law

Justice in the Search for Truth

H L HO

OXFORD
UNIVERSITY PRESS

OXFORD
UNIVERSITY PRESS

Great Clarendon Street, Oxford OX2 6DP

Oxford University Press is a department of the University of Oxford.
It furthers the University's objective of excellence in research, scholarship,
and education by publishing worldwide in

Oxford New York

Auckland Cape Town Dar es Salaam Hong Kong Karachi
Kuala Lumpur Madrid Melbourne Mexico City Nairobi
New Delhi Shanghai Taipei Toronto

With offices in

Argentina Austria Brazil Chile Czech Republic France Greece
Guatemala Hungary Italy Japan Poland Portugal Singapore
South Korea Switzerland Thailand Turkey Ukraine Vietnam

Oxford is a registered trade mark of Oxford University Press
in the UK and in certain other countries

Published in the United States
by Oxford University Press Inc., New York

First published 2008

British Library Cataloguing in Publication Data
Data available

Library of Congress Cataloging in Publication Data
Data available

Typeset by Newgen Imaging Systems (P) Ltd., Chennai, India
Printed in Great Britain
on acid-free paper by
Biddles Ltd., King's Lynn, Norfolk

ISBN 978–0–19–922830–0

1 3 5 7 9 10 8 6 4 2

to my parents

General Editor's Preface

This monograph tackles the contested question of how to theorize the law of evidence. The author develops a theoretical approach that draws upon refined concepts of fact, trial, fact-finding, and adjudication, deploying insights from linguistic philosophy, epistemology, and theories of justice. In particular, Chapter 3 delves deep into the epistemology of legal fact-finding, discussing the roles of presumptions, probabilities, and possibilities. The richness of these early chapters then suffuses the application of the theoretical approach to three areas of evidence law, with chapters on standards of proof and their meaning, on hearsay evidence, and on similar fact evidence, using examples from both criminal and civil law. The result is a major exploration of the function and purpose of evidential rules that should command attention from a wide range of criminal justice scholars.

Andrew Ashworth

Preface

The law of evidence has suffered much abuse. Harvey described it as a 'slapdash, disjointed and inconsequent body of rules';[1] Salmond saw it as 'one of the last refuges of legal formalism';[2] Bentham found it to be 'incompetent on every occasion to the discovery of truth, . . . incompetent therefore, on every occasion, to the purposes of justice';[3] and Cross reportedly looked forward to the day when the subject is abolished.[4] There is, so it will be argued, more of value in our common law heritage of evidential rules than the critics allow. Many of the rules express, at the core of their operation, principles integral to the epistemic and ethical justification for the court's findings. The full value of evidence law cannot be seen unless we adopt the perspective of the fact-finder as a moral agent. This is the standpoint of a person with a critical role to play in the trial process. A different perspective is adopted by someone, conveniently characterized as the system engineer, who evaluates the trial and its rules from the outside. The external approach to analysis of evidence law is the dominant one. Although illuminating, the approach is, on its own, inadequate. This monograph makes a case for the indispensability of an internal account. A feature of the account is the focus on trial deliberation. The function and purpose of evidential rules are analysed in terms of their normative application to the process of reasoning towards a verdict. It is a central claim of this book that findings made by the court must be justifiable; they must meet the conjoint demands of epistemic rationality and ethics.

In the main, this study is of the adversarial trial, that tradition of fact-finding that has its origin in the common law. To be sure, there are many differences in evidential rules, as well as legal culture, across common law jurisdictions. Nevertheless, there is, broadly speaking, a family of central features—the core doctrines and concepts—which are shared by trial systems of the Anglo-American model. Three of those features are selected for discussion: the standard of proof, the rule on hearsay evidence, and the rule on similar facts. Occasionally, comparisons will be drawn with the approaches taken by continental systems and international criminal tribunals.

The first two chapters are introductory. Chapter 1 offers an analysis of a number of fundamental aspects of fact-finding: it discusses the role of facts and their

[1] C P Harvey, *The Advocate's Devil* (London: Stevens & Son, 1958) 79.

[2] John W Salmond, *Jurisprudence or the Theory of the Law* (London: Stevens & Haynes, 1902) 597.

[3] Jeremy Bentham, *Rationale of Judicial Evidence*, in John Bowring (ed), *The Works of Jeremy Bentham*, vol 7 (Edinburgh: William Tait, 1843) 206.

[4] As reported by William Twining, *Rethinking Evidence—Exploratory Essays* (Oxford: Blackwell, 1990) 1.

classification and offers a speech act analysis of the act of giving a verdict; it also highlights the major components of trial deliberation as well as the legal techniques of controlling the process. The values and purposes of a trial are examined in Chapter 2. It unpacks the debate on the claim that the trial seeks the truth and explores the connection between truth and justice. The concept of justice as a relational demand, that requires empathic care, is introduced. This is followed by a lengthy treatment of the epistemic aspect of fact-finding in Chapter 3. A belief account of fact-finding is defended, a framework for the acquisition of the relevant beliefs is sketched, and the method and form of deliberation are explored. This chapter is much longer than the others. It was tempting to break it into two to achieve some balance of proportion. But that would be unwise as the sections are all interconnected and should be kept together as a continuous development.

Selected topics of the substantive law of evidence are dealt with in the remaining chapters. Chapter 4 discusses the standard of proof by developing the argument presented in Chapter 3. Relying on the concept of caution, it presses for a variant interpretation of the standard of proof that is, at the same time, compatible with maintaining a categorical distinction between the civil and the criminal standard. Hearsay and similar fact evidence are analysed in Chapters 5 and 6 respectively. The law in these two areas is under much attack for posing technical and unwarranted obstructions to the search for truth. It will be argued to the contrary, that the law reflects our interests in obtaining truth and in doing justice. These are not opposing demands; rather, they act in concert to set legitimate constraints on trial deliberation. The epilogue brings the discussion to a close with a summary of and reflections on the general themes.

Acknowledgements

This book was written over many years. It is based on a doctoral thesis. I am greatly indebted to my supervisors, T R S Allan and Neil Andrews, for their patience and guidance. Thanks also to the examiners, Andrew von Hirsch and Ian Dennis, for their useful comments. Part of the writing was done during a visiting fellowship at the law programme of the Research School of Social Sciences, Australian National University, in 2005. I thank Peter Cane for making the trip possible and to him and his colleagues for making my stay pleasant. Mike Redmayne, whom I met on that visit, generously took time to read many draft chapters. I have benefited greatly from his feedback.

I am grateful to Andrew Ashworth for including this book in the *Oxford Monographs on Criminal Law and Justice* series and for penning the General Editor's Preface. I should also express gratitude for the support of my university and two successive deans, Chin Tet Yung and Tan Cheng Han. The assistance of the staff at C J Koh Law Library was crucial. Luo Ling Ling and Alfian Teo helped me to track down materials and with other tasks.

The editorial team at OUP, including Gwen Booth, Hayley Buckley and Rachel Kemp, were a pleasure to deal with. Nikki Tomlinson was an excellent copy-editor. Valuable comments and suggestions came from the four referees consulted by the Oxford University Press. I hope the final product does not overly disappoint them.

Parts of this book draw from the following articles: 'Justice in the Pursuit of Truth: A Moral Defense of the Similar Facts Rule' (2006) 35 Common Law World Review 51; 'Similar Facts in Civil Cases' (2006) 26 Oxford Journal of Legal Studies 131; and 'What Does a Verdict Do? A Speech Act Analysis of Giving a Verdict', International Commentary on Evidence: vol 4, 2006 : issue 2, article 1, available at: <http://www.bepress.com/ice/vol4/iss2/art1>. I thank the editors and publishers of these journals for allowing me to reuse the materials.

Colleagues who knew about the writing of this book often enquired caringly about its progress, especially in the frantic final stages. I am touched by their gestures. Although (and alas) no longer colleagues, George Wei and Tan Keng Feng continued to provide strong encouragement. I record my appreciation of their friendship.

1

Fact-Finding

Introduction

The aim of this chapter is to lay the foundations for the substantive arguments to come. Fact-finding refers to the task of (i) arriving at and (ii) giving answers to (iii) questions of fact. This statement is not intended as a definition; it merely highlights three central aspects of fact-finding which merit discussion as a prologue to the main arguments. Element (iii) is the focus of Part 1: it considers the role of 'facts' in legal adjudication, examines the legal and evaluative criteria that shape findings of fact, and discusses the conventional classification of facts and findings. Fact-finding has what may be called a public aspect and a deliberative aspect. The public aspect has to do with what is involved in giving a verdict (element (ii)). A verdict is the most general of a finding. As will be seen in Part 2, to give a verdict is to perform a speech act which concurrently bears different illocutionary forces. A different aspect of fact-finding is the process of reasoning by which the court arrives at its conclusions (element (i)). This is the topic of Part 3. It provides a general analysis of trial deliberation and looks at ways in which it is legally controlled. Throughout this study, references will be made to two perspectives of the trial; they correspond to two generally distinguishable approaches to analysis and evaluation. These perspectives and approaches are introduced in Part 4.

1 Fact and Fact-Finding

If fact-finding is about finding answers to questions of fact, it might seem natural for a study of the topic to start by asking 'what is a question of fact?' This is typically framed in a contrastive mode: how is 'a question of fact' different from 'a question of law'? Multifarious legal consequences hang on the choice of characterization. To take just a few examples: it is said that questions of fact are for the jury to decide whereas questions of law are for judges to determine; generally, an appeal can be made on a point of law but not on a finding of fact; unlike a ruling on the law, a finding of fact has no precedential value; and facts must be pleaded but not the law.

It is notoriously difficult to give a unified and logical account of the distinction across such a wide range of applications. Most lawyers see no promise in an a priori analysis and advocate a pragmatic approach based on the usefulness of classifying the question one way or the other.[1] Secondly, it is not true that a question can only be either unequivocally of fact or unequivocally of law: for instance, whether someone is guilty as charged is neither strictly one nor strictly the other.[2] Thirdly, notions about evidence and proof appear to be more basic than the concept of 'question of fact'; while those notions may be used to explicate the concept by defining a question of fact as one that calls for proof and evidence,[3] an attempt to use the concept of 'question of fact' to explicate notions of evidence and proof is unlikely to be fruitful.

For these three reasons, an abstract analysis of 'question of fact' that focuses on its difference from 'question of law' will not serve the present purposes well. It is proposed instead to consider the following three themes on 'fact' in fact-finding: (i) the role of facts in legal adjudication and how that role is connected to notions of justice, (ii) the porosity and substance of the divide between fact and law, and fact and value, and (iii) the logical classification of facts in the traditional vocabulary of evidence law and the variety of findings that can be made. These three topics are discussed in the same order below.

1.1 Role of facts

A distinctive feature of contemporary legal adjudication is its fact-orientation. It is true that disputes in court may not be over facts and often are not; sometimes, cases are argued at first instance on 'agreed facts', and appeal judges deal mainly with questions of law. But, even where the facts are not contested, they are incorporated into the justification for the court's decision. Factual generalizations are embedded in legal rules.[4] Consequently, the adjudication of every dispute under a legal rule is based on what are believed to be, or are taken as, the facts of the case.

[1] Kim Lane Scheppele, 'Facing Facts in Legal Interpretation' (1990) 30 Representations 42; Ronald J Allen and Michael S Pardo, 'The Myth of the Law-Fact Distinction' (2003) 97 Northwestern University L Rev 1769, and 'Facts in Law and Facts of Law' (2003) 7 Intl J of Evidence and Proof 153; John Jackson, 'Questions of Fact and Questions of Law' in William Twining (ed), *Facts in Law* (Wiesbaden: Franz Steiner, 1983) 85. Cf Timothy Endicott, 'Questions of Law' (1998) 114 LQR 292 (offering an analytical approach to the distinction).

[2] Endicott (n 1) 310. Cf Peter Brett, *An Inquiry into Criminal Guilt* (London: Sweet & Maxwell, 1963) 73–74: 'It is often stated that the jury are to decide the facts, while the judge decides the law. This may be true of civil cases, but in criminal matters nothing could be further from the truth. The jury's function in a criminal trial is not merely that of deciding the facts; it is that of deciding guilt.'

[3] For an attempt along this line, see Neil MacCormick, *Legal Reasoning and Legal Theory* (Oxford: OUP, 1978) 86–97.

[4] Hence the maxim *ex facto oritur ius*: 'law is derived from a fact': Max Radin, 'Ex Facto Ius: Ex Iure Factum' in Paul Sayre (ed), *Interpretations of Modern Legal Philosophies—Essays in Honour of Roscoe Pound* (New York: OUP, 1947) 578, 582. Or, more accurately: *per factum cognoscitur ius*: 'by means of a fact, we recognize (or we know) the law': ibid 583.

However, nothing in the logic of dispute resolution says that it must be based on proof of facts. In theory, it is possible for two parties to end their quarrel over who has title to a chattel by tossing a coin. There is the fact that the coin landed in favour of one side. But that fact arose by chance and it determines, rather than proves, entitlement to the chattel. This is a purely procedural way of resolving the dispute.[5] Allocation of the chattel is not based on any principle of substantive justice. Coin-tossing will not do in a modern court of law.[6] As Lord Hope observed in *R v Mirza*:[7] 'A trial which results in a verdict by lot or the toss of a coin, or was reached by consulting an ouija board in the jury room, is not a trial at all.' We object to the arbitrariness of these methods. It is thought that legal decisions should rest on rules, standards, or principles that cut across individual cases. With the introduction of legal standards, rules, and principles, facts enter adjudication. This is as much a logical claim as a historical one: Shapiro reports that the concept of 'fact' originated in law[8] and Milsom attributes the development of law as a system of normative rules to the court's increasing sensitivity to the facts of disputes.[9]

Coin-tossing is a fanciful example. But it is not merely a theoretical possibility for disputes to be settled other than by proof of facts. One legal sociologist tells us of a major divide between adjudicatory forms that are 'fact-oriented' and those that belong to the 'play genres'; the first engage 'processes that "examine evidence" and seek to determine "facts" ' whereas the second 'pursue some symbolic, expressive, or nonrational mode of determining outcome'.[10] A well-known example of the latter, much discussed by legal anthropologists, is the Eskimo song contest where, to put it crudely, disputes are settled by song fights.[11] Indeed, the modern common law form of trial evolved from a form of proof that is not fact-based.

[5] John Rawls, *A Theory of Justice* (revised edn, Oxford: OUP, 1999) 75.

[6] *Re A (Children) (Conjoined Twins: Surgical Separation)* [2001] Fam 147, 203: 'The law cannot say, "Heads I win, tails you lose." ' Much fun was made of Judge Bridlegoose's use of this method in François Rabelais's sixteenth century comic novel *Gargantua and Pantagruel*, translated by Burton Raffel (London: W W Norton & Co, 1990) 354–355, 356–357. But this option is perhaps not as absurd as it seems: Neil Duxbury, *Random Justice—On Lotteries and Legal Decision-Making* (Oxford: Clarendon Press, 1999) especially ch 5.

[7] [2004] UKHL 2, [2004] 1 AC 1118, 1164, para 123. On the infamous use of an ouija board by a jury, see *Young* (1995) 2 Cr App R 379.

[8] Barbara Shapiro, 'The Concept "Fact": Legal Origins and Cultural Diffusion' (1994) 26 *Albion* 227.

[9] S F C Milsom, 'Fact and Law in Legal Development' (1967) 27 University of Toronto L J 1. The same thesis is advanced by Joseph R Strayer, 'The Writ of Novel Disseisin in Normandy at the End of the Thirteenth Century' in his *Medieval Statecraft and The Perspectives of History—Essays by Joseph R Strayer* (New Jersey: Princeton University Press, 1971) ch 1.

[10] Brenda Danet, 'Language in the Legal Process' (1980) 14 Law and Society Rev 445, 491; compare Part IV (D) ('play genres of disputing') with Part IV (E) ('"Fact"-oriented disputing'). On 'play genres', see also Mark Cammack, 'Evidence Rules and the Ritual Functions of Trials: "Saying Something of Something" ' (1992) 25 Loyola of Los Angeles L Rev 783.

[11] eg Max Gluckman, *Politics, Law and Ritual in Tribal Society* (Chicago: Aldine, 1965) 303–313.

In the Middle Ages, issues of right and wrong were not analysed as presenting separate questions of fact and law.[12] A holistic approach was taken instead. As Baker says, medieval forms of proof were 'intended to obviate a human decision on the factual merits of the case'.[13] 'There was no question of going behind [the procedure] into the facts.'[14] The holistic attitude to dispute settlement is reflected, for instance, in the nature of the oath taken by the parties, the secta (the plaintiff's sponsors)[15] and the compurgators (the defendant's oath-helpers).[16] In the oath, an assertion or denial was expressed broadly of the justice of the cause; there was no descending into factual details. A '"true" oath partook of a man's normative evaluation and not simply his belief in the oath's correspondence to an empirical reality'.[17] Indeed, compurgators were not required to have any personal knowledge of the facts underlying the dispute:[18] they swore only 'to the credibility of their chief and the purity of his oath'[19] and have been compared

[12] Mirjan Damaška, 'Rational and Irrational Proof Revisited' (1997) 5 Cardozo J Intl and Comparative L 25, 25–29. Adjudication then proceeded on the basis of 'folklaw' (Harold J Berman, *Law and Revolution—The Formation of the Western Legal Tradition* (Cambridge, Massachusetts: Harvard UP, 1983) ch 1, of 'custom and wise counsel' (J H Baker, *An Introduction to English Legal History* (4th edn, London: Butterworths, 2002) 1; Morris S Arnold, 'Law and Fact in the Medieval Jury Trial: Out of Sight, Out of Mind' (1974) 18 American J Legal History 267, 278–280), and of broad ideas of right and wrong, of what conduct deserves punishment (Rebecca V Colman, 'Reason and Unreason in Early Medieval Law' (1974) 4 *J Intl History* 571, 580; Paul Vinogradoff, *Villainage in England—Essays in English Mediaeval History* (Oxford: Clarendon Press, 1892) 377; see also S F C Milsom, *Historical Foundations of the Common Law* (2nd edn, London: Butterworths, 1981) 39 ('In the whole process the only substantive rules visibly at work are those implicit in the canon of acceptable claims')). There was not then 'Law' in the developed sense of a logical system of rules operating on clearly defined and categorized fact-situations. As Milsom argues, 'legal development consists in the increasingly detailed consideration of facts' and 'the limit at any time is the extent to which the legal process presents the facts for legal handling': S F C Milsom, 'Law and Fact in Legal Development' (1967) 27 University of Toronto LJ 1, 1. See on a similar theme Joseph R Strayer, 'The Writ of Novel Disseisin in Normandy at the End of the Thirteenth Century', in his *Medieval Statecraft and The Perspectives of History* (Princeton, NJ: Princeton UP, 1971) ch 1.

[13] Baker (n 12) 5.

[14] Baker (n 12) 5.

[15] See Frederick Pollock, 'English Law Before the Norman Conquest' (1898) 14 LQR 291, 294; A L Goodhart and H G Hanbury (eds), William Holdsworth, *A History of English Law*, vol 1 (7th edn, London: Methuen, 1956) 300; and Henry C Lea, *Superstition and Force: Torture, Ordeal, and Trial by Combat in Medieval Law* (NY: Barnes & Noble Books, 1996) 81.

[16] Dorothy Whitelock, *English Historical Documents: 500–1042* vol 1 (Oxford: OUP, 1955) 335; Damaška (n 12) 26; Max Rheinstein, *Max Weber on Law in Economy and Society* 227 (Cambridge, Massachusetts: Harvard UP, 1954); and Lea (n 15) 55.

[17] Trisha Olson, 'Of Enchantment: The Passing of the Ordeals and the Rise of the Jury Trial' (2000) 50 Syracuse L Rev 109, 123.

[18] James Bradley Thayer, *A Preliminary Treatise on Evidence at the Common Law—Part I Development of Trial by Jury* (Boston: Little, Brown & Co, 1896) 25; R H Helmholz, 'Crime, Compurgation and the Courts of the Medieval Church' (1983) 1 Law and History Rev 1, 13.

[19] J Laurence Laughlin, 'The Anglo-Saxon Legal Procedure' in H Adams (ed), *Essays in Anglo-Saxon Law* (South Hackensack, NJ: Rothman Reprints, 1972) 183, 297; see also James Appleton Morgan (ed), William Forsyth, *History of Trial by Jury* (2nd edn, Jersey: Frederick D Linn, 1875) 62; and W J V Windeyer, *Lectures on Legal History* (2nd edn, Sydney: The Law Book Co, 1957) 12.

to character witnesses of today.[20] The 'truth' to which they swore carried not purely the intellectual meaning of correspondence to external facts, but, more importantly, the (now unfamiliar) ethical meaning of 'fidelity, loyalty, faithfulness' to the person they were supporting.[21] Similarly, although a judicial duel was held only where there was '[an] affirmative oath of a witness' who 'could swear to what he had seen',[22] the use of a blanket denial meant that no specific point of fact arose for determination.[23] This led one writer to comment that 'the outcome of combat exists independently of the notion of cognitive truth'.[24] The same applies to the test of ordeal. It was believed that God, through His verdict, dispenses such justice as is appropriate in the light of the circumstances, considered as a whole.[25] A party's overall character and reputation were as much at trial as the truth of the allegations made against him.[26]

The outcome of a trial by ordeal, compurgation, or judicial battle was not, strictly speaking, a *proof* outcome, if by 'proof' we mean the proof of facts; it was, rather, the *adjudication* outcome: it marked the termination of the dispute and was not the finding of fact to which rules of law had to be applied to reach the verdict. Alternatively, one could take a looser view of proof and see the result of a medieval mode of proof as simultaneously the proof outcome and the adjudication outcome; these two concepts were, in this context, inextricable. The outcome of adjudication could not be just in the formal, positivist, sense that it was reached by applying correct interpretation of legal rules to true findings of fact: at a time when law and fact were not strictly compartmentalized, this method of analysis was out of place.[27] The justice sought through use of the medieval modes of proof was not grounded in substantive norms operating on the facts of the case; it was based, rather, on submission to and faith in a spiritual power.

[20] R C Van Caenagem, 'Methods of Proof in Western Medieval Law' in his *Legal History: A European Perspective* (London: Hambledon, 1990) ch 4, 77; and Scott Rowley, *The Competency of Witnesses* (1939) 24 Iowa L Rev 482, 485.

[21] Richard Firth Green, *A Crisis of Truth—Literature and Law in Ricardian England* (Philadephia: University of Pennsylvania Press, 1999) ch 1, 101–102.

[22] Milsom (n 12) 39.

[23] S F C Milsom, *The Legal Framework of English Feudalism* (Cambridge: CUP, 1976) 76. The pre-battle procedure of accusal and denial is well captured in medieval literature: eg R Howard Bloch, *Medieval French Literature and Law* (Berkeley: University of California Press, 1977) ch 1, especially 29.

[24] Bloch (n 23) 46.

[25] Paul R Hyams, 'Trial by Ordeal: The Key to Proof in the Early Common Law' in Morris S Arnold *et al* (eds), *On the Laws and Customs of England—Essays in Honor of Samuel E. Thorne* (Chapel Hill: University of North Carolina Press, 1981) ch 4, 111: 'God proclaims a man's guilt or innocence of a particular act in the course of a judgment on the whole man and his soul.'

[26] Green (n 21) 110: '[T]o those small-scale societies which favour the kind of flexible face-to-face justice in which honor and personal reputation are intimately bound up with innocence and guilt, the kind of dispassionate inquiry into fact which we believe to constitute a higher form of jurisprudence will often seem equally repugnant.'

[27] A D E Lewis, 'The Background to Bentham on Evidence' (1990) 2 *Utilitas* 195, 197.

The medieval trial sought divine justice. This is conceptually different from formal justice in the rule-governed and fact-based sense.[28]

In contrast, the conceptual distinction between fact and law is central to contemporary legal analysis. The law does not decide liability or guilt by coin-tossing but according to standards, rules, and principles. If the law adopts the rule that a person who acts in such and such a way is guilty of a crime, the court takes on the task to decide, as a matter of fact, whether the accused acted in that way on the alleged occasion. According to the popular (but, as suggested below, simplistic) model of legal reasoning, the legal conclusion follows from the application of the relevant rule to the facts as found. This reasoning proceeds by way of a deductive syllogism whose major premise is the rule of the form 'if F then C': if the court finds that F (that the accused acted in the manner described by the prosecution), it must further find that C (that the accused is guilty of the crime with which she is charged). C in turns operates as the antecedent of a further rule 'if C then P': if the court finds that C (the accused has committed a crime), the court may or must do P (punish the accused).[29]

On the modern view, legal adjudication has two notionally distinct components: the proof outcome and the adjudication outcome. Is it true that the accused had acted thus and so? This question is legally relevant if the truth of the proposition of fact has legal significance or carries some legal consequence; thus the question is relevant where a finding requires or supports the verdict that the accused is guilty or liable. The answer to the question of fact is the proof outcome while the verdict at the end of the trial is the adjudication outcome. These are theoretically different aspects of adjudication even though they cannot be completely separated[30] and even where, as is typically the case with a jury verdict, the proof outcome is not disclosed. The jury verdict usually proclaims the adjudicatory outcome in general terms that the defendant is guilty or liable, as the case may be, without revealing any specific findings of fact. Nevertheless, the concepts of fact and law should have featured in the analytical construct of the deliberation that led to the verdict. Justice, in a formal legal sense, is about treating people equally according to the law, and since law operates on facts, justice is contingent on factual truth. Whether the law itself is just is, conceptually, a different matter. Truth and justice are, in this way, separable. This understanding of adjudicative reasoning fails to capture the full reality of trial deliberation.

[28] H L Ho, 'The Legitimacy of Medieval Proof' (2004) 14 J of L and Religion 259.

[29] For a much more sophisticated version of this model, see Joseph Horovitz, *Law and Logic—A Critical Account of Legal Argument* (NY: Springer-Verlag, 1972) 148–160.

[30] On this difficulty, see Adrian A S Zuckerman, 'Law, Fact or Justice?' (1986) 66 Boston University L Rev 487, 487–494.

1.2 Fact, law, and value

It is unrealistic for many reasons. To begin with, it fails to acknowledge the complex interplay between law and fact. The court does not look at each separately and then attempt to apply the law to the facts. Not only is the relevancy of facts, and hence the scope of factual inquiry, determined by the law, the relevant law is determined by the facts.[31] Facts and law are considered in tandem and 'adjusted to one another continuously until a result is reached'.[32]

A deeper problem with the account is the oversimplification of its depiction of facts. Facts, as ordinarily understood, refer to observable features of the world. At the primary level, what counts as a fact is a matter of common sense. A 'fact' can be a *state of affairs* (for example, the state of jealousy or insanity), a *process* (a 'going on' like continuous stalking or gradual poisoning), or an *event* (a 'taking place' such as a vehicular collision or an act of stabbing).[33] But facts also include matters which are not usually thought of as directly observable but whose existence we do not regard as any less real for that: an example would be another person's state of mind, which is largely what *mens rea* is about.

The trial, however, does not deal only with facts in one of these primary or brute[34] (physical or mental) senses. A fact, even as ordinarily understood, may be a composite of the physical and the mental. The court often has to answer questions about a person's action. An action is more than overt bodily behaviour; to say that someone acted in a certain way may involve, for example, imputing an intention to her physical movement: bumping into someone is different from shoving her.[35] Even more complex issues often need to be resolved. For example, a ruling is sometimes required on a disputed proposition of probability (such as an alleged 'loss of chance'),[36] on a point of 'counterfactual conditional' (taking the general form 'whether X would have occurred if Y had been the case'),[37] or

31 Scheppele (n 1) 60–61.

32 Paul Chevigny, *More Speech—Dialogue Rights and Modern Liberty* (Philadelphia: Temple University Press, 1988) 165. This interdependency is exhibited in argument: 'The party is asked how the norm can be applicable in the way he claims it is in light of the probable facts, and then he is asked how the facts could be as he claims them to be in light of the norms.' (Ibid.)

33 This classification of facts is taken from Georg Henrik von Wright, *Norm and Action—A Logical Enquiry* (London: Routledge, 1963) 25–26. For a different taxonomy, see John R Searle, *The Construction of Social Reality* (NY: The Free Press, 1995) 120–125.

34 A term popularized by G E Anscombe, 'On Brute Facts' (1958) 18 Analysis 69. It is used here for its evocative value rather than strictly in the sense intended by her.

35 This example is owed to J R Lucas, 'The Ascription of Actions', unpublished, available at <http://users.ox.ac.uk/~jrlucas/ascript.html>.

36 See Chapter 3, Part 2.3.

37 eg Richard A Posner, *The Problems of Jurisprudence* (Cambridge, Massachusetts: Harvard UP, 1990) 204–205; also H L A Hart and Tony Honoré, *Causation in the Law* (2nd edn, Oxford: OUP, 1985) ch XV.

on the prospect of a future occurrence.[38] All of these involve a heavy theoretical element that venture beyond the factual as ordinarily understood.

That a 'question of fact' may raise an issue beyond the primary facts is evident in the legal distinction between 'primary' and 'secondary' facts. More generally, propositions of fact come at different levels of formulation or abstraction and the differentiation is more fine-grained than is suggested by the simple two-fold classification. The proposition that the husband put arsenic in his wife's coffee is basic relative to the proposition that the husband caused the wife's death, which in turn is more basic than the proposition that the husband murdered his wife. At the highest level, a proposition of fact states the 'material facts'; this class of fact is discussed below.

A finding of secondary fact or, as one might also describe it, a finding on a 'mixed question of fact and law', exists at a higher theoretical level than a finding of primary fact. There are different views of what this means; to mention three of them, it is said that findings of secondary facts (i) are inferences drawn from the primary facts;[39] (ii) are compound propositions that incorporate value judgments with the primary findings;[40] and (iii) involve legal classification of the primary facts.[41] A good example is cited by MacCormick: Does artificial insemination by a donor constitute adultery?[42] This question arises even if the primary facts are agreed and, should there be a conflict of evidence, the question remains even when the conflict is resolved. The reason is clear enough: the question can only be answered in the light of one's understanding of the purpose and value of the relevant law and the underlying principles and policies. There may be sound pragmatic reasons for treating a finding on the type of question posed by MacCormick as one of fact—for instance, to control the number of appeals or so that later decisions will not be constrained by the ruling.[43] The important point for our purposes is this: findings of fact at the higher levels will often require theoretical constructions, value judgments and purposive interpretations of the law.

Findings made by the court often bear a theoretical descriptive component. To hold that a contract exists between the parties is not merely to report a perception of a state of affairs; it is to offer a description in legal theoretic terms. A fact often gains sense only from the institutional background. For instance,

[38] William Wilson, 'Fact and Law' in Patrick Nerhot (ed), *Law, Interpretation and Reality—Essays in Epistemology, Hermeneutics and Jurisprudence* (Dordrecht: Kluwer, 1990) 11, 19. Mirjan Damaška, 'Truth in Adjudication' (1998) 49 Hastings LJ 289, 299–300: 'adjudicative fact-finding is not merely a matter of reconstructing historical events. While most facts we seek to establish indeed lie in the past, some exist at the time of inquiry. Still other facts, especially those sought in modern mass litigation, consist of predictions of future occurrences.'

[39] *Benmax v Austin Motor Co Ltd* [1955] AC 370, 373 per Viscount Simonds (a finding of secondary fact is 'an inference from facts specifically found').

[40] Patrick Devlin, *Trial by Jury* (London: Methuen, 1966) 141–144.

[41] MacCormick (n 3) 93–97.

[42] ibid 93.

[43] ibid 93–97; Douglas Payne, 'Appeals on Questions of Fact' (1958) 11 CLP 185, 198–199.

'husband' and 'wife' cannot exist independently of the institution of marriage. Furthermore, the law is full of thick concepts that describe actions in morally loaded language. A classic example is 'murder'. When the jury finds a person guilty of murder, the finding is not intended simply 'to record or impart straightforward information about the facts';[44] it is at the same time to express a value judgment about what happened. The legal lexicon contains countless examples of concepts that blend fact, value, and law: 'negligence', 'reasonable forseeability', 'merchantable quality', 'causation', 'provocation', 'unreasonable conduct', 'dangerous driving', 'recklessness', 'insulting behaviour', 'obscene publication'; these and more do not merely refer to brute features of the physical and mental world. Whether one of these concepts obtains in a particular case is a question of legal proof. An attempt to answer it involves judgment and evaluation. This does not necessarily mean that the fact-finder's own values are called into play. The trier of fact may have to apply legal criteria of the concept which she does not personally endorse.[45]

Fact and law, fact and value, the descriptive and the evaluative, interweave in legal fact-finding and are indissolubly bound.[46] This is not unique to the trial context. Generally, in and outside of the court, any description must inevitably rely on some evaluation. Access to facts is inevitably mediated by one's background assumptions and beliefs. In fashionable idiom, facts are socially constructed and constructed from a worldview.[47] While these observations have sometimes led to overinflated claims about relativism and against the objectivity of truth,[48] they highlight the complexity of the concept of fact and of judgments of fact. But none of these should make us overlook two central requirements: the form of legal decision-making must pass logical muster (a claim that is perfectly compatible

[44] J O Urmson and Marina Sbisà (eds), J L Austin, *How to Do Things with Words* (2nd edn, Oxford: Clarendon Press, 1975) 2.

[45] Carlos E Alchourrón and Eugenio Bulygin, 'Limits of Logic and Legal Reasoning' in Antonio A Martino (ed), *Expert Systems in Law* (Amsterdam: North-Holland, 1992) 7, 16–18.

[46] Karl Olivecrona, *Law as Fact* (2nd edn, London: Stevens & Sons, 1971) 214: 'There is always an element of valuation when a court classifies some event as constituting an "operative" fact. There are no operative facts in nature but only in legal language. Since the law refers to "operative" facts under such names as contract, promise, payment, marriage, etc., alleged facts have to be classified by the courts under such headings. This is a step in the application of the law. It requires something more than ascertaining some facts: these facts have also to be evaluated, with the result that the court either declares them to constitute a contract, a promise, a payment, a marriage, etc., or rejects the proposed classification.'

[47] eg Clifford Geertz, *Local Knowledge—Further Essays in Interpretive Anthropology* (New York: Basic Books, 1983) at 173: 'legal facts are made not born, are socially constructed . . . by everything from evidence rules, courtroom etiquette, and law reporting traditions, to advocacy techniques, the rhetoric of judges, and the scholasticisms of law school education'.

[48] Alvin I Goldman, *Knowledge in a Social World* (Oxford: OUP, 1999) ch 1; Susan Haack, 'Confessions Of An Old-Fashioned Prig' in her *Manifesto Of A Passionate Moderate—Unfashionable Essays* (Chicago: Chicago University Press, 1998) ch 1.

with the rejection of literal formalism)[49] and there are basic facts of the case that the court needs to get correct. This important message is delivered by Bayles:[50]

Of course, judicial decision making is not a simple application of rules and principles to facts. First, finding facts is not a straight-forward descriptive process. Facts must be classified for the application of rules and do not come neatly labeled. Second, many so-called factual questions are matters of evaluation. Determining whether someone was negligent, reasonable, or insane requires judgment and evaluation. Third, even when the facts are clear, it is not always clear what the rules and principles imply. Is a child on a railroad tie extending over a public river on railroad property or not? *Nevertheless, there are core factual matters that one needs to get correct*—that the child was on the tie, that the tie was fastened to railroad property, and so on.

1.3 Classification of facts and findings

Evidence lawyers traditionally classify facts as 'material', 'relevant' or 'irrelevant'. 'Material facts' (which has many other names: 'operative facts', 'dispositive facts', 'ultimate facts', 'facts in issue', and more) are facts that instantiate the legal elements constituting the crime or cause of action or defence in question.[51] It is to the substantive law that one must turn for the *generic* material facts. Thus criminal law sets out the generic elements of different types of crime. Criminal procedure requires *particular* material facts to be specified, albeit briefly, in the criminal

[49] Michael S Moore, 'The Plain Truth about Legal Truth' (2003) 26 Harvard J of Law and Policy 23, 25: 'Contrary to much of the overblown and misdirected rhetoric of the American Legal Realists and their intellectual descendents, a decision in a disputed legal case involves logical deductions. The premises are matters of fact, law, and interpretation, and the conclusion is the proposition describing the decision in the case. What justifies the decision as following from these kinds of propositions is logic... No one can plausibly urge judges or juries to be illogical in their decisions'; Horovitz (n 29) 153 (rejecting the 'view that [a judgment] is neither deductively nor inductively related to the supporting evidence' and arguing that 'a judgment cannot be said to be rationally justifiable by appeal to factual evidence unless it is seen as obtainable, in principle, by an inductive inference followed by a deductive one').

[50] Michael Bayles, 'Principles for Legal Procedure' (1986) 5 Law and Philosophy 33, 40, emphasis added. See also Michael D Bayles, *Procedural Justice—Allocating to Individuals* (Dordrecht: Kluwer, 1990) 116–117.

[51] J L Montrose, 'Basic Concepts of the Law of Evidence' (1954) 70 LQR 527, 536 ('Materiality of evidence signifies that the evidence is concerned with an issue before the court. The question of materiality is not whether the evidence is adequately related to the facts sought to be established thereby, but whether those facts are adequately related to the case made by the party'); Wesley Newcomb Hohfeld, *Fundamental Legal Conceptions—As Applied in Judicial Reasoning* (Westport, Connecticut: Greenwood, 1978) 32: 'Operative, constitutive, causal, or dispositive facts are those which, under the general rules that are applicable, suffice to change legal relations'; James Fitzjames Stephen, *The Indian Evidence Act, With an Introduction on the Principles of Judicial Evidence* (Calcutta: Thacker, Spink & Co, 1872) 9 (facts in issue are disputed facts which 'may by themselves, or in connection with other facts, constitute such a state of things that the existence of the disputed right or liability would be a legal inference from them'), and *Digest of the Law of Evidence* (2nd American edition, NY: George Chase, 1898) 5 ('"facts in issue" means... facts from the establishment of which the existence, non-existence, nature, or extent of any right, liability, or disability asserted or denied in any such case would by law follow'); Graham B Roberts, 'Methodology in Evidence—Facts in Issue, Relevance and Purpose' (1993) 19 Monash U L Rev 68, 69–70.

charge brought against the accused.[52] Likewise, on the civil side, the *generic* material facts are determined by reference to the substantive law. In a claim on a contract, it must be shown that an offer was made, it was accepted, that there was a breach of a term, and so forth. An outline of the *particular* material facts will be set out in the plaintiff's (or claimant's) pleading. For instance, it will stipulate the type of contract that was allegedly made, the nature of the breach that is said to have been committed, and so on. The scope of the factual dispute gains focus through the procedural requirement that the defendant state the allegations she denies or admits or for which she puts the plaintiff (or claimant) to proof.

A proposition of relevant fact is a proposition that is capable of supporting or undermining, directly or in one or more steps and to varying degree, a conclusion on a dispute over a material fact.[53] A proposition of fact is irrelevant if it is incapable of supporting or undermining the conclusion directly or indirectly to any non-negligible degree. For example, it is relevant that the accused's fingerprints were detected at the theft scene (A) because from this, a strong inference may be drawn that the accused was there (B) and, from the latter, a further inference (much weaker than the first and which would have to be conjoined with other facts) could be drawn that he might have been the thief (C). 'Relevant facts' are called 'evidential facts' by Hohfeld. As he says: 'An evidential fact [A in our example] is one which, on being ascertained, affords some logical basis—not conclusive—for inferring some other fact. The latter may be either a constitutive [in our preferred terminology, material] fact [C] or an intermediate evidential fact [B].'[54] (It must be added that this depiction of evidential reasoning is meant only to illustrate the logical structure of the relevancy relation. In actuality, trial deliberation is by no means as linear and one-dimensional as is here suggested. A fuller account is supplied in Chapter 3, Part 3.4.)

Just as facts may be classified for analytical purposes, so may findings of fact. As will be elaborated in Chapter 3, the fact-finder can take one of three doxastic positions on a disputed proposition of fact (p): (i) believe that it is in fact true; (ii) believe that it is in fact false; or (iii) believe neither that it is in fact true nor that it is in fact false. We will call a verdict or finding '*affirmative*' when it is based on the belief that p is in fact true or in fact false as the case may be, and we will call a verdict or finding '*default*' when it is the result of the fact-finder being unable to come to a determinate conclusion either way. A finding is '*positive*' when it is in

[52] The defendant in England sometimes has a statutory obligation to provide a defence statement: Ian Dennis, *The Law of Evidence* (3rd edn, London: Sweet & Maxwell, 2007) 7–8.

[53] For technical definitions, see Rule 401 of the Federal Rules of Evidence (defines relevant evidence to mean 'evidence having any tendency to make the existence of any fact that is of consequence to the determination of the action more probable or less probable than it would be without the evidence'); Stephen, *Digest of the Law of Evidence* (n 51) 5 ('The word "relevant" means that any two facts to which it is applied are so related to each other that according to the common course of events one either taken by itself or in connection with other fact proves or renders probable the past, present, or future existence or non-existence of the other').

[54] Hohfeld (n 51) 34.

favour of the party who has the burden of proving that p, and '*negative*' when it is against her. Henceforth, unless stated otherwise, a reference to a verdict or finding is a reference to a positive verdict or finding.

2 Fact-Finding: A Speech Act Analysis[55]

2.1 Introduction

Fact-finding has a public aspect. A verdict is a conclusion to be arrived at in the privacy of one's mind or a jury room; but when that is done, the verdict must be given in open court. What is it to give a verdict? What does giving a verdict 'do'? By 'verdict' is meant the fact-finder's judgment on the ultimate issue of guilt or liability. The verdict is based directly on findings of material facts and indirectly on findings of relevant facts. Thus at a criminal trial, a guilty verdict of the general form communicates the ultimate finding that the defendant is guilty as charged, which necessarily implies positive findings on fact instantiations of all necessary elements of the crime. In reaching the verdict, the court may, for example, have to decide on an evidential issue of alibi. A guilty verdict implies the rejection of the alibi claim; the court may convict the defendant only if it finds that the defendant, despite her protestation, was at the scene of the crime at the material time.[56] A legal verdict is usually followed by a court directive, such as an order of imprisonment. The directive is authorized by, but not part of, the verdict. Nor are remarks that the judge may make after the verdict is in, or in the course of giving the verdict, part of the content of the verdict. For instance, it is quite usual for the judge to reprimand the defendant after the jury has declared her guilty and before sentence is delivered.

The jury typically returns a general verdict. There is no disclosure of the underlying findings of particular facts.[57] In some jurisdictions, the jury may exceptionally be asked to give a special verdict by stating their findings on specific issues of fact.[58] At a bench trial, judges are expected to be more detailed. As Payne notes:[59]

> Whereas a jury, in returning a general verdict, does not and cannot be compelled to say what are the specific facts to which the relevant legal standard has been applied, a judge

[55] This part is a revised version of my essay, 'What Does a Verdict Do? A Speech Act Analysis of Giving a Verdict', *International Commentary on Evidence*: vol 4, 2006: issue 2, article 1, available at: <http://www.bepress.com/ice/vol4/iss2/art1>.

[56] The present distinction is discussed by Stephen, *The Indian Evidence Act* (n 51) 9–10 where he contrasts 'facts in issue' with 'relevant facts'.

[57] For that reason, the general verdict is criticized for lacking transparency and accountability: eg Lord Justice Auld, *Review of Criminal Courts in England and Wales* (London: HMSO, 2001) ch 11, paras 52–55.

[58] eg the United States Federal Rules of Civil Procedure Rule 49 states: 'The court may require a jury to return only a special verdict in the form of a special written finding upon each issue of fact.' See further Mark S Brodin, 'Accuracy, Efficiency, and Accountability in the Litigation Process—The Case for the Fact Verdict' (1990) 59 Cincinnati L Rev 15.

[59] Payne (n 43) 193.

sitting alone invariably supports his decision by a reasoned judgment in which he sets out the specific facts which he has found to be established, and on which any inference, such as negligence, is based.

Indeed, in *Benmax v Austin Motor Co Ltd*,[60] Viscount Simonds suggested that the judge 'would fall short of his duty if he did not first find the facts and then draw from them the inference of fact whether or not the defendant had been negligent'.

At one level, the giving of a verdict, unlike legal concepts such as right and duty, is directly observable. One can explain what 'giving a verdict' is by pointing to the pronouncement made in the courtroom by the jury or, in the case of a bench trial, the judge, after final deliberation on the contested issues. However, this can only tell us what the verdict denotes in the material world of physical facts; it does not tell us what the verdict connotes in the social world, of which norms, values, and institutions are part. This part explores the connotations of returning a verdict by subjecting it to a speech act analysis. The two most prominent proponents of speech act theory are J L Austin[61] and his intellectual successor John R Searle;[62] while the literature is voluminous, we will draw principally from their writings.

2.2 Constative-performative distinction

Speech act theory is best introduced with a distinction Austin made and subsequently abandoned. Suppose you ask me for the name of this ship. I tell you that it is called *The Queen Elizabeth*. Here, I am *reporting* to you a fact and my statement can itself be true or false. Austin calls this a 'constative'.

Compare this with Austin's famous example: I utter 'I name this ship *The Queen Elizabeth*' as I smash the bottle against its side.[63] The utterance is a central part of my performance of the act of naming the vessel. It is a 'performative utterance'. If all goes well, to say I name this ship 'such and such' *is* to name this ship 'such and such'. Here I am not *reporting the fact* that the ship is called *The Queen Elizabeth*; rather, I am seeking to *make it a fact* that the ship is so named. Unlike in the above example, it is unintelligible to ask whether my naming of the vessel was itself true or false. It does, however, make sense to ask whether

[60] [1955] AC 370, 373. To similar effect, although discussed in the context of a statutory requirement, is the judgment of the Australian High Court in *Fleming v The Queen* (1998) 197 CLR 250, 262–3.

[61] His principal works in this area are 'Performative Utterances' in J O Urmson and G J Warnock (eds), *J L Austin, Philosophical Papers* (3rd edn, Oxford: OUP, 1979) ch 10, and Austin (n 44).

[62] Apart from his book, *Speech Acts—An Essay in the Philosophy of Language* (Cambridge: CUP, 1969), see also John R Searle, 'A Taxonomy of Illocutionary Acts' in K Gunderson (ed), *Language, Mind, and Knowledge* (Minneapolis: University of Minnesota Press, 1975) reprinted in John R Searle, *Expression and Meaning—Studies in the Theory of Speech Acts* (Cambridge: CUP, 1979) ch 1. A concise and accessible introduction to his theory can be found in John R Searle, *Mind, Language and Society—Philosophy in The Real World* (New York: Basic Books, 1998) ch 6.

[63] Austin (n 44) 5–6.

I have *succeeded* in doing what I purported to do *in* saying those words. I may fail for a variety of reasons; my 'performative utterance' or 'speech act' can be, as Austin puts it, 'infelicitous' or 'unhappy' (rather than 'false') in one of several ways.[64] For example, I may lack the authority which I thought I had to christen the ship, in which case, my utterance is an ineffective attempt at naming. While this defect or flaw or hitch leads to a failure to achieve what I set out to achieve in my utterance, it does not make my utterance false.

Similarly, in pronouncing a verdict of guilty or a finding of liability, say for the tort of negligence, the court is not merely reporting that the person has committed the crime for which she was charged or that her conduct breached the civil standard cited by her opponent; the court is also, in the first case, convicting her of that crime, and in the second, declaring the state of legal relation between the parties. While the verdict, in one respect, asserts (if only by implication) propositions about antecedent material facts, it does more; it creates a new and official fact which authorizes further legal actions, such as the imposition of a jail sentence or an award of damages. When the court delivers a verdict or makes a finding, it is not only *describing* or *saying* something; it is also *doing* something *else*. The word 'else' is added because, as Austin came to recognize, '[o]nce we realize that what we have to study is *not* the sentence but the issuing of an utterance in a speech situation',[65] the constative-performative distinction collapses. 'Describing' or 'stating' or 'reporting' is also a form of 'doing'; it is as much performing a speech act as 'promising' is.[66] Further, it is not just statements that can be true or false; the same can be said of some performatives, such as a 'warning'.

2.3 Infelicities and the sincerity condition

Austin sets out an elaborate scheme of ways in which a verbal performance may fail to come off.[67] First, it may misfire and consequently be 'void' or of no effect due to some serious procedural irregularity. One can find many legal examples of this. In the trial context, the defendant does not succeed in 'pleading guilty' if she utters 'Yes, I did it', even though her intention in using those words is clear enough; for a valid plea, she must use the word 'guilty'.[68] Similarly, a verdict can

[64] ibid 14.

[65] Austin (n 44) 139.

[66] See 'the bit where we take it all back': Austin (n 61) 241, 246–251; also Austin (n 44) lecture 11.

[67] Austin (n 44) lectures 2–4.

[68] In a transcript recorded by Pat Carlen, *Magistrates' Justice* (London: Martin Robertson, 1976) 110–111, we see a long exchange between the court and the defendant before the right words were elicited from the latter. A part of the exchange reads:

Magistrate: Do you plead guilty or not guilty?
Defendant: Yes, I did it.
Magistrate: No, I'm asking you whether you plead guilty or not guilty. You must use either the words 'not guilty' or 'guilty'.

misfire and be void. The verdict is properly returned, and consequently has the *force* of a verdict, only when the proper words are uttered by the proper person in the proper manner and under proper circumstances. The jury foreman who tries to deliver the verdict by telephoning the judge will not achieve his objective: the law does not allow him to bring in the verdict in that fashion; typically, he must announce it aloud in the courtroom at the stage of the proceeding when he is formally asked to do so by the clerk. Although it is not the case that the force of all speech acts depends on extra-linguistic conventions, the speech act of giving a verdict certainly does.[69] Anyone with linguistic competence can give a promise. But not anyone with linguistic competence can give a legal verdict.

A performative utterance can go wrong in a second way. Here, unlike in the above instances, the speech act is successfully executed. However, there is what Austin calls an 'abuse of procedure'. Psychological states are expressed in many speech acts. When I make a promise, I express an *intention* to keep it, and when I issue a command, I express a *desire* that it be obeyed.[70] According to Austin, the psychological state expressed by a verdict is *belief*. When the jury foreman utters the verdict in a manner and form that comply with legal procedure, the verdict is validly returned. But something may still be amiss; the verdict may be *insincere*. And that is when the belief state the foreman expresses in the utterance does not correspond with his actual belief state at the point of utterance. So Austin explains:[71]

> 'I find him not guilty—I acquit', said when I do believe that he was guilty. [This act is] not void. I do . . . bring a verdict, though insincerely. Here there is an obvious parallel with one element in *lying*, in performing a speech-act of an *assertive* kind.

Being insincere is a form of infelicity; it is different from being mistaken, which involves making a false statement. An insincere verdict may be true; and conversely, a sincere verdict may be false. Again, to quote Austin:[72]

> [W]e must distinguish really thinking it to be so—for example that he was guilty, that the deed was done by him . . .—from what we think to be so really being so, the thought being correct as opposed to mistaken. (Similarly, we can distinguish really feeling so from what we feel being justified . . .) But thoughts are a most interesting, i.e. a confusing case: there is insincerity here which is an essential element in lying as distinct from merely saying what is in fact false. Examples are thinking when I say 'not guilty' that the deed was done by him . . . But I may in fact be mistaken in so thinking.

[69] Acknowledging as much: P F Strawson, 'Intention and Convention in Speech Acts' (1964) 73 *The Philosophical Review* 439, 443: '[T]he fact that the word "guilty" is pronounced by the foreman of the jury in court at the proper moment constitutes his utterance as the act of bringing in a verdict; and that this is so is certainly a matter of the conventional procedures of the law.'

[70] Searle 1979 (n 62) 4–5.

[71] Austin (n 44) 40.

[72] ibid 41.

The sentence within brackets is significant. Unfortunately, Austin does not pursue the distinction identified in that sentence. He thought that a guilty verdict expresses belief in the defendant's guilt. But the distinction he drew suggests a parallel difference between believing ('really feeling') that the defendant is guilty and believing that one is justified ('feeling justified'), on the evidence adduced at the trial, in judging that he is guilty. One of these psychological states can exist without the other. As will be argued in Chapter 3, Part 1.3, a finding must be based on a detached or 'selfless' belief; this is different from although it will often coincide with a personal or subjective belief.

2.4 Uses of language

2.4.1 Locutionary act and the propositional content of a verdict

The theory of speech act is about the use of language.[73] Austin identifies three important dimensions of such use.[74] First, language is used in performing a *locutionary* act. This is the act of saying something with a certain meaning, where words are uttered with a more or less definite *sense* and *reference*. When I say the bank is broken, I mean bank in the *sense* associated with a river and I mean to *refer* to this river and not that river. My locutionary act fails to 'secure uptake' when you wrongly take me to be announcing that a financial institution has folded. To give a verdict is, in the first instance, to perform the locutionary act of uttering sentences of forms such as 'We find the defendant [not] guilty' or 'We find the defendant [not] liable'. The verdict takes its meaning from the context in which it is given, particularly the applicable substantive law, the charges or pleadings, the conduct of the trial, and the question to which it is uttered in response. One's interpretation of what a verdict says is tied to one's understanding of the psychological state expressed by it. As we saw, Austin claims that a guilty verdict expresses belief. Assume this is correct for the moment. (Some verdicts express further psychological states, the most important of which is the attitude of condemnation or disapproval. On this, more will be said later.) In uttering the word 'guilty' in reply to the question put by the court clerk to the foreman, one could argue that the latter is saying on behalf of the jury something along this line:

> The named defendant, the person who is now standing in the dock, has committed the act he is accused by the prosecution of having committed, and that act amounts to the crime alleged in the charge which has been read before us.

[73] Speech act belongs to the theory of language use (*pragmatics*), which is different from, although related to, the theory of linguistic meaning (*semantics*). For the distinction and relation between them, see Kent Bach, 'Speech Acts and Pragmatics' in Michael Devitt and Richard Hanley (eds), *Blackwell Guide to the Philosophy of Language* (Malden, Massachusetts: Blackwell, 2006).

[74] Austin (n 44) lectures 8–10.

Alternatively, the verdict could be interpreted as an assertion about proof rather than directly about the material facts. On this view, we must add an important qualification which marks a significant difference in what a guilty verdict says:

It is proved according to the law that the named defendant, the person who is now standing in the dock, has committed the act he is accused by the prosecution of having committed, and that act amounts to the crime alleged in the charge which has been read before us.

On yet a third interpretation, the verdict asserts a proposition of probability. This requires the verdict to be read as saying:

It is (very or most) probable that the named defendant, the person who is now standing in the dock, has committed the act he is accused by the prosecution of having committed, and that act amounts to the crime alleged in the charge which has been read before us.

To engage in this process of interpretation is, following a general point made by Searle,[75] to engage in analysing the *propositional content* of a verdict. The first interpretation is defended in Chapter 3, Part 2.4. Here, only a few further remarks need be made in the next paragraph. The main concern of this part of this chapter is with the second aspect of a verdict, its illocutionary forces.

The verdict can be correct or mistaken, depending on whether the proposition it asserts (the propositional content) is true or false. But it would seem that the act of giving a verdict is better judged by other criteria, some of which are not related to the propositional content of the verdict. The jury foreman cannot return a verdict, whatever its content, by telephoning the judge. Other criteria for evaluating the act of giving a verdict have to do with its propositional content. Questions based on content-related criteria include the following: is the court justified on the evidence admitted at the trial in giving the verdict which it did? Is it justified in concluding that the disputed event did occur? Is the judgment supporting the findings of fact sound? And so forth. The court may be justified, in some perfectly intelligible sense of justification, to act as it did in returning a particular verdict even where the content of the verdict is or implies a false proposition.

2.4.2 Illocutionary act and the force and point of a verdict

The locutionary act, as we saw, is the act *of* saying something. There is, secondly, the *illocutionary* act; this is the act performed *in* saying something. We now shift our attention from the *meaning* of a sentence to its *force*. To perform a locutionary act is ipso facto to perform as well an illocutionary act. But a meaningful sentence can be uttered with different forces. To use Searle's example, the sentence 'I am going to do it' has one literal meaning (or propositional content) but can have the force of any one or more of a variety of illocutionary acts; the utterance

[75] Searle disputes Austin's locutionary-illocutionary or meaning-force distinction. As Searle sees it, the real distinction lies between the propositional content of an utterance and its force: John R Searle, 'Austin on Locutionary and Illocutionary Acts' (1968) 77 *The Philosophical Review* 405.

can amount to a promise, a prediction, a threat, a warning, a statement of intention, and so forth.[76] *In* saying something, I am frequently doing something; in our example, I am doing one or more of the following: promising, predicting, threatening, warning, asserting, and so on. Which of these illocutionary acts I perform, or what force my utterance has, will depend on the context in which I speak. It is on the illocutionary forces of a verdict that this part concentrates.

In saying 'I find the defendant (not) guilty' or 'I find the defendant (not) liable', the word 'find' performs the role of, in Austin's terminology, an 'explicit performative verb'.[77] It is what Searle calls an 'illocutionary force-indicating device'.[78] Used in the first person indicative active form, the verb indicates what act the speaker is performing in making that utterance; it tells us how we should take the expressed proposition. The term stands alongside other similar explicit force-indicating devices such as 'promise', 'apologize', and 'warn'. If I say I promise you something, I make it clear to you that you should take what I say with the force of a promise, thus conveying to you my commitment to do as I promised; my utterance is not merely a prediction of what I am likely to do. Unfortunately, the force of the term 'find', as used in the trial context, is nowhere as clear as the force of 'promise', 'apologize', or 'warn'. As will be argued, 'find' bears many dimensions of force.

Searle distinguishes the 'force' of an illocutionary act from its 'point'. A request and a command share the same point of getting someone to do something but they are patently of different forces.[79] Part of the illocutionary point of both a request and a command is to get the addressee to do the act in question; it is to get the world to fit the propositional content of the utterance. Sometimes the direction of fit runs in the opposite direction. When I am reporting to you an incident, I am trying to get the propositional content of my utterance to fit the world as I saw it.[80] The verdict is complex not only because it has multiple illocutionary points, but also because those multiple points do not share one direction of fit. A systematic study of these illocutionary dimensions is conducted in Part 2.5.

2.4.3 Perlocutionary act and illocutionary point: the consequential effect of a verdict

We have thus far discussed two aspects of language use as identified by Austin. First, '*to* say something is to do something' (executing a locution, the act *of* saying something), and secondly, '*in* saying something, we do something' (performing an illocution). Now we come to the third: '*by* saying something, we do something'.[81] The thoughts, feelings, or behaviour of others are frequently

[76] ibid 406–407.
[77] Austin (n 44) 61.
[78] Searle 1969 (n 62) 30.
[79] Searle 1979 (n 62) 3.
[80] ibid 3–4.
[81] Austin (n 44) 109.

affected by our utterances. I may, by the use of language, achieve the consequential effect of *convincing* or *deterring* or *shocking* you. In saying 'Don't do it' (a locutionary act), I could be *advising* you not to do it (an illocutionary act), and if you are *persuaded* by me not to do it, that is the perlocutionary effect of my illocutionary act.[82] My utterance may not achieve the intended effect. It does not when, for example, you refuse to obey my command. The intended effect is one thing, the actual effect is another.

What is the intended consequential effect of a verdict? Specifically, what impact does it aim to have on the 'feelings, attitudes, and subsequent behavior'[83] of the person or persons to whom it is addressed? This is the question that drives some theories of the trial. The purpose of a trial is sometimes derived from a conception of the intended or desired impact of the verdict on its immediate addressee. It is argued that the point of a conviction is not merely to officially record the commission by the defendant of the act alleged in the charge on which she was prosecuted. A conviction typically has the force of condemning or censuring her for that act,[84] and the intended or desired effect of the condemnation or censure is to bring about a sense of shame in her as a first step towards repentance and reform. Taking that to be the intended or desired consequence of a conviction, the criminal trial is then explained or normatively structured by some writers as a process of communication, a moral dialogue with the defendant aimed at getting her to see the wrong she has done.[85] It is a different story with a civil verdict; here, as many lawyers see it, the important point is the authoritative settlement of private disputes. The aim is more ambitious than to contain quarrels in the crude sense of commanding a stop with the threat of sanction; it is to resolve them by persuading the disputants to willingly accept judicial judgments as final and binding. On this view of the perlocutionary effect of a civil verdict, procedural fairness is valuable because it promotes voluntary acceptance of the case outcome.[86]

2.5 The verdict as a speech act: dimensions of its force

This section concentrates on the second of the three dimensions of language use just delineated. A verdict is complex because it has many illocutionary forces, or,

[82] ibid 101–102 and lecture 9.

[83] John R Searle and Daniel Vanderveken, *Foundations of Illocutionary Logic* (Cambridge: CUP, 1985) 11.

[84] The point is that a conviction *itself* expresses criticism of the person's conduct. It is not unusual for the judge to explicitly chastise a person after her conviction in order to bring home the condemnation which is already implicit in the act of conviction.

[85] eg R A Duff, *Trials and Punishments* (Cambridge: CUP, 1986); Antony Duff, Lindsay Farmer, Sandra Marshall and Victor Tadras, 'Introduction: Towards A Normative Theory of the Criminal Trial' in Antony Duff *et al* (eds), *The Trial on Trial—Truth and Due Process*, vol 1 (Oxford: Hart, 2004).

[86] See generally Martin P Golding, *Philosophy of Law* (Englewood Cliffs, New Jersey: Prentice Hall, 1975) ch 6; Tom R Tyler, *Why People Obey the Law* (New Haven: Yale UP, 1990).

on Searle's analysis, many illocutionary points. The difference between 'force' and 'point' was previously noted; although Searle was right that a distinction can be drawn between the two, the difference does not matter very much for present purposes. Hence, they will be used interchangeably; we will include the dimension of 'force' in the 'point' of a verdict, and the dimension of 'point' in the 'force' of a verdict. The basic idea is this: to give a verdict is to perform a variety of speech acts at once. Illocutionary forces can be categorized in many ways. We will follow principally the leading taxonomy offered by Searle.[87]

2.5.1 Declarative aspect of a verdict

To find the defendant guilty or liable is to *assert* a proposition about her guilt or liability: for example, at a criminal trial, that the accused committed the crime with which she is charged and, in the civil context, that the material facts as alleged by the claimant or plaintiff are true. This assertive aspect of a verdict is analysed in the next section. But the finding is not only assertive. The pronouncement of a positive verdict performs an official function. It also *declares* that the defendant *is* guilty or liable as the case may be. This is not a report or description of a past event; it is the creation of a new institutional fact. A new state of affairs is brought into being. The defendant is officially, in the eyes of the law, guilty or liable in virtue of the verdict but not before its delivery.[88] While the facts underlying guilt or liability pre-exist the verdict, the official status of guilt or liability is brought about by the declaration contained in the verdict. It may be true that one has that status and false that the underlying facts are as found by the court.[89] The declaration can exist independently of a verdict. The court may declare a person guilty or liable without having to undertake fact-finding, as when he pleads guilty or consents to have the judgment entered against her. Such cases result in judgments but do not call for any verdict.

The immediate point of the declaration is to turn the content of the material accusations or allegations into official facts by authoritative pronouncement of guilt or liability.[90] This then authorizes and provides the necessary basis and 'immediate reason'[91] for further legal action, such as the imposition of

[87] Searle 1979 (n 62).

[88] John Searle, *Mind, Language and Society* (New York: Basic Books, 1998) 150. Also: D N MacCormick and Zenon Bankowski, 'Speech Acts, Legal Institutions, and Real Laws' in Neil MacCormick and Peter Birks (eds), *The Legal Mind—Essays for Tony Honoré* (Oxford: Clarendon Press, 1986) 128–129; Judith Jarvis Thomson, 'Liability and Individualized Evidence' (1986) 49 Law and Contemporary Problems 199, 213.

[89] Compare Eugenio Bulygin, 'Cognition and Interpretation of Law' in L Gianformaggio and S Paulson (eds), *Cognition and Interpretation of Law* (Turin: Giappiachelli, 1995) 11, 19–20, criticizing Kelsen for suggesting that 'a natural fact, like murder, becomes a legal fact through the pronouncement of the judge'.

[90] Searle 1998 (n 62) 150; MacCormick and Bankowski (n 88) 128–129; Thomson (n 88) 213.

[91] Olivecrona (n 46) 209. See also Hans Kelsen, *Pure Theory of Law* (Berkeley: University of California Press, 1967) 240:

punishment or the award of damages.[92] One citizen can get civil damages from another only if she first gets the court to declare liability on the part of the other by obtaining a verdict against him. In a criminal case, the defendant is presumed innocent prior to the verdict. Her conviction changes this state of affairs. It makes her guilty in the eyes of the law which may now, and only now, punish her. Other legal consequences flow from the official declaration of guilt: many jurisdictions have laws which disqualify a convicted criminal from holding political office, sitting in a jury, acting as a company director, and so on.

Although the facts supporting the verdict are, in the last analysis, primary facts, the official status of guilt or liability, brought about when one is legally certified[93] as guilty or liable, is an extra-linguistic institutional fact. As already noted, anyone can make a promise by simply drawing on the resources of language, and the new fact that is created, a promise, is a linguistic entity.[94] On the other hand, not anyone can anyhow give a verdict. More than the institution of language is needed to do so. The fact that one is a convicted criminal is 'institutional' in the sense that it cannot exist in the absence of certain institutional structures and roles (including courts, judges, and juries), rules (of substantive and procedural law), and conventions (such as the practice of accepting judicial pronouncements as authoritative).[95] It is against this necessary background that the uttering of certain words by a certain person in a certain manner and under certain circumstances can amount to giving a legal judgment.

The declaratory aspect of a judgment is not confined to a declaration of guilt or liability. In jurisdictions where declaratory judgments in the technical sense are available, a judgment may simply declare a person to be in possession of a legal

[T]he legal rule does not say: 'If a certain individual has committed murder, then a punishment ought to be imposed upon him.' The legal rule says: 'If the authorized court in a procedure determined by the legal order has ascertained, with the force of law, that a certain individual has committed a murder, then the court ought to impose a punishment upon that individual.' In juristic thinking the ascertainment of the fact by the competent authority replaces the fact itself that in nonjuristic thinking is the condition for the coercive act.

92 Note, however, that in finding guilt or liability, the court is not thereby committed to imposing punishment or awarding damages. A verdict is, for this reason, not a speech act of the nature of a 'commissive'.

93 cf Zenon Bankowski, 'The Jury and Reality' in Patrick Nerhot (ed), *Law, Interpretation and Reality* (Dordrecht: Kluwer, 1990) 236 (the trial serves the purpose of 'certifying' truth). It is, for the reasons given by Alchourrón and Bulygin (n 45) 13–16, erroneous to equate what is true with what is certified to be true, an error that may arise from confusing finality with infallibility.

94 Searle 1979 (n 62) 7 and 18; John R Searle, 'How Performatives Work' in Daniel Vanderveken and Susumu Kubo (eds), *Essays in Speech Act Theory* (Amsterdam: John Benjamins Publishing, 2001) 99–100.

95 The concept of institutional fact is clearly illustrated by Searle 1969 (n 62) 51: 'it is only given the institution of money that I now have a five dollar bill in my hand. Take away the institution and all I have is a piece of paper with various gray and green markings.' There is much valuable discussion of institutional facts in the context of a trial (eg Bert van Roermund, 'The Instituting of Brute Facts' (1991) 4 Intl J for the Semiotics of Law 279) as well as in the more general legal context (eg Neil MacCormick and Ota Weinberger, *An Institutional Theory of Law—New Approaches to Legal Positivism* (Dordrecht: D Reidel, 1986)).

right without further declaring, as the usual civil verdict does, that any other party has, on the facts, infringed that right. There is yet another class of judgments, known as constitutive judgments, which declare neither a right nor its violation but which, given the satisfaction of certain conditions, brings forth a change in legal relationship or a fresh legal status. Thus a judgment may declare that the parties are no longer married or that a partnership is henceforth dissolved.[96] Such cases may or may not require a trial to determine questions of fact. We will deal neither with declaratory judgments nor uncontested applications for constitutive judgments since neither of them can be accurately described as falling within our specific concern, namely, the type of judgment that is made on a factual issue relevant to an alleged infringement of a legal norm and requiring evidence and proof: in short, a verdict.

2.5.2 *Assertive aspect of a verdict*

While the verdict has an important declarative force, it should not be mistaken for a pure declaration. It has an equally important assertive force. That the verdict has the force of both a declaration and an assertion led Searle to dub it an 'assertive declaration'.[97] The illocutionary point of an assertive is to get the words to fit the world and the sincerity condition is belief.[98] For Searle, the assertion that p expresses the psychological state of believing that p. If it is false that p, one is wrong in asserting that p; and if one does not believe that p when asserting that p, one is insincere.

An example of a pure declarative is a declaration of war. The successful performance of declaring war results in war being declared. A pure declaration of this sort cannot be assessed as true or false. I can fail in my attempt to have a war declared (as when I lack the authority to do so), but if I succeed in declaring a war, then the war is on. As Searle puts it, 'the successful performance guarantees that the propositional content corresponds to the world'.[99] The point of an assertive is to get the words to fit the world: to assert that p where p is true. On the other hand, the point of declaring that p is to bring about p; it is concurrently to get the words to fit the world and to get the world to fit the words. The content of a successful declaration cannot fail to correspond with reality in the way that the content of a successful assertion can fail to match the world. I can successfully assert that a war has broken out when in reality it has not. But it cannot both be the case that I have successfully declared a war and the war is not on. Not only can the propositional content of my assertion be false, I can be insincere in making that assertion. I can lie to you that a war has broken out. But

[96] See the useful discussion in Olivecrona (n 46) 200–202.

[97] Searle 1979 (n 62) 19–20. The ambiguity of the illocutionary force of a verdict was also noted by Austin (n 61) 249–250 and 141–142.

[98] Searle 1979 (n 62) 12–13.

[99] ibid 17.

I cannot lie in declaring a war (although, as noted, I can succeed or fail in having it declared).[100]

If a verdict is nothing more than a declaration, we can only ask if it is valid or not, the answer to which depends on compliance with the necessary procedure for an effective delivery. On both criteria mentioned above, a verdict is not a pure declaration. First, we do evaluate its propositional content in terms of truth and falsity, although we tend to describe the verdict we attack on this score as wrong or mistaken. A verdict that has been validly brought in may yet be criticized for being wrong or mistaken. The propositional content of a verdict fails to match the world when a person is found guilty or liable who in fact is not. Secondly, a verdict, unlike a pure declaration, has a sincerity condition. As we saw, on Austin's interpretation (which, as suggested below, is disputable) the verdict is insincere in the case of jury nullification: the jury acquits the defendant even though it believes him to be in fact guilty. Thus procedural validity is not the only matter of concern about a verdict; there are also important questions of truth and truthfulness.[101]

There is more to a verdict than the declaration, and hence creation, of a new legal fact. A verdict does not create guilt or liability in the way a priest creates a marriage by pronouncing the couple husband and wife.[102] Before the priest makes his pronouncement, the two are not married to each other. On the other hand, that which constitutes the basis of guilt or liability pre-exists the verdict. Indeed, as the term 'fact-*finding*' suggests, the trial involves, as one of many interacting elements, the *discovery* of facts.[103] The verdict not only declares, it also *asserts* propositions about (typically antecedent) facts:[104] the court declares that the defendant *is* guilty or liable *because*, so it asserts, he *did* behave in the alleged manner (or more generally, the facts are as alleged by her opponent). The

[100] cf Searle 1969 (n 62) 65: 'One cannot, for example, greet or christen insincerely, but one can state or promise insincerely.'

[101] Austin long ago recognized this multi-dimensionality: Austin (n 44) 42–43: 'There is a class of performatives which I call *verdictives*: for example, when we say "I find the accused guilty" or merely "guilty"... When we say "guilty", this is happy in a way if we sincerely think on the evidence that he did it. *But*, of course, the whole point of the procedure in a way is to be correct... [W]e may have a "bad" verdict: it may either be *unjustified* (jury) or even *incorrect* (umpire). So here we have a very unhappy situation. But still it is *not* infelicitous in any of our senses: it is not void (if the umpire says "out", the batsman is out; the umpire's decision is final) and not insincere.' See also ibid at 249–250.

[102] Searle 1998 (n 62) 150.

[103] Of course, the trial is neither wholly nor straightforwardly a process of discovery. Trial deliberation is undoubtedly highly complex: for a sophisticated account of 'the intellectual operations the jury must perform on the trial's linguistic practices' (Robert P Burns, *A Theory of the Trial* (Princeton, NJ: Princeton University Press, 1999) 185), see ibid ch VII. This chapter is written from what Burns calls the 'Received View of the Trial'.

[104] Hanna Fenichel Pitkin, *Wittgenstein and Justice* (Berkeley: University of California Press, 1972) 262–263; Antony Duff, Lindsay Farmer, Sandra Marshall and Victor Tadros (eds), *The Trial on Trial—Truth and Due Process*, vol 1 (Oxford: Hart, 2004) 18 ('a trial culminates in a verdict that must surely be understood as asserting (or purporting to assert) a truth about the defendant's guilt or innocence').

assertion of material facts provides the reason for the declaration. To take a simple example, at a murder trial, a guilty verdict necessarily implies a finding that the defendant caused the death of the victim since causing death is an element of murder. A guilty verdict asserts by implication that the defendant did cause the death of the victim. This is a solemn assertion, made under an oath 'to give a true verdict'; it commits the speaker to the truth of what is asserted. The assertion may be mistaken or insincere; accordingly, a verdict may be flawed in either or both ways.

2.5.3 Declaration without corresponding assertion of fact

The declaration contained in a verdict is not necessarily accompanied by a corresponding assertion of fact. One instance of this is where the verdict is a negative one, given against the party bearing the burden of proof. In the nomenclature stipulated at the end of Part 1, a negative verdict or finding can be entered either affirmatively or by default. As traditionally understood, the fact-finder at a civil trial must declare the defendant 'not liable' if she is not persuaded on the balance of probabilities that any of the material propositions of fact essential to the claim is true. It is entirely possible that she is, at the same time, also uncertain that it is false, in which case, she is not justified in asserting that it is false. The law does not require justification for that assertion as a condition for declaring a 'not liable' verdict.[105] Thus a negative verdict in a civil case does not, in itself, imply any assertion that one or more of the material propositions on which the claim rests is false. What can, at best, be implied from a negative finding is the unacceptability of asserting at least one of the material propositions. Of course, and it is beside the present point that, we may have more than a bare verdict to go on; as noted, fact-finders do sometimes reveal the bases of their verdicts and how they have arrived at them.

It is similar on the criminal side. A 'not guilty' verdict declares that the defendant is not guilty; thus, and very importantly, the State cannot punish her on the accusation contained in the charge. A 'not guilty' verdict does not, in itself or without more, amount to an assertion that the defendant is in fact innocent.[106]

[105] *The 'Popi M'* [1983] 2 Lloyd's Rep 235.

[106] Randy E Barnett, *The Structure of Liberty—Justice and the Rule of Law* (Oxford: Clarendon Press, 1998) 206: 'A failure to find a person "guilty" is not the same as a finding of "innocence." When a presumption of innocence has not been overcome by sufficient evidence of guilt, all we know is that there is inadequate evidence to conclude that he is guilty.' Similarly, Duff, Farmer, Marshall and Tadros (n 104) 19: 'surely "not guilty" cannot amount to an assertion of the defendant's innocence, but must rather be read as asserting that he has not been proved to be guilty'. But contrast Damian Cox and Michael Levine, 'Believing Badly' (2004) 33 *Philosophical Papers* 220–221, 309: the authors observe that the judicial system treats 'those not found guilty of an offence as though they were innocent of it'. They claim that while this is 'imperfectly rational behavior' from an epistemic point of view, it is morally justifiable because the 'point of the judicial process is not to arrive at rationally adequate beliefs, but to arrive at a just conclusion'. But the supposed conflict between rationality and morality does not exist if, as the other writers cited before them argue, an acquittal is not an outright assertion of innocence.

That the fact-finder is in reasonable doubt about the defendant's guilt requires that she returns an acquittal. But this is not enough to justify her assertion that the defendant did not commit the crime and a verdict of not guilty should not be read to contain any such assertion. It can only be read generally as a representation that the trier of fact does not accept that the accused is guilty. This may be because she doubts that the accused is guilty or she believes that he is in fact innocent. Since an acquittal can rest on either one of these positions, we cannot tell, on the face of it, whether it is an affirmative or a default verdict.[107] A general verdict of 'not guilty' leaves us in the dark as to whether the jury believes the defendant is in fact innocent or merely has a reasonable doubt about his guilt.[108] Hence, we cannot take an acquittal, of itself, as an assertion that the defendant is innocent.[109]

Of course, the evidence may exonerate the defendant so convincingly that the fact-finder is prepared to assert that he is in fact innocent. But we cannot read that assertion in a general verdict of not guilty in legal systems that permit only one of two options, namely, to find the defendant either 'guilty' or 'not guilty'.[110] To this claim, two clarifications must be added. First, in a legal system, like the Scottish, that permits the third option of returning a 'not proven' verdict, it is reasonable to construe a verdict of 'not guilty' as asserting that the defendant is innocent.[111] Secondly, the verdict may be explained in the judgment delivered at a bench trial, and a reasoned verdict may be required as a rule, as it is in some civil law jurisdictions.[112] In these cases, the court may well take the opportunity in supporting the 'not guilty' verdict to assert that the defendant is in fact

107 That it can be one or the other was noted in *D P P v Shannon* [1975] AC 717, 772. Acquittal is by 'default' where guilt is 'not proven'. 'The verdict "not guilty" includes "not proven",' notwithstanding that English law does not technically recognize a verdict of "not proven": *R v Andrews-Weatherfoil* [1972] 1 WLR 118, 126; *Rutherford v Richardson* [1923] AC 1, 6.

108 *Director of Public Prosecutions v Humphrys* [1977] AC 1, 43.

109 For judicial recognition of this, see *Lewis v Frick* (1914) 233 US 291, 302; *Helvering v Mitchell* (1938) 303 US 391, 397. Note that the claim is merely that an acquittal does not, of itself, amount to an *assertion* of innocence. The defendant, following acquittal, may be treated as if innocent for the purposes of later litigation: eg *Coffee v US* (1886) 116 US 436, 444.

110 As Schiemann LJ put it in *R (Mullen) v Home Secretary* [2002] EWCA Civ 1882 at para 43; [2003] QB 993, 1007, the 'criminal law system... does not provide for proof of innocence' (cf *R (Mullen) v Home Secretary* [2004] UKHL 18 at para 55, [2005] 1 AC 1, 47). This is not true in some jurisdictions. In California, the defendant may, following acquittal, petition for a finding that he is 'factually innocent': see section 851.8 of the California Penal Code.

111 In *McNicol v H M Advocate* (1964) SLT 151, 152, the High Court of Justiciary explained that the 'not proven' verdict 'gives a jury, who have some lingering doubts as to the guilt of an accused and who are certainly on the evidence not prepared to say that he is innocent, the chance to find the charge against him not proven'. See also Samuel Bray, 'Not Proven: Introducing a Third Verdict' (2005) 72 University of Chicago L Rev 1299, 1299–1300: 'Not guilty is for a defendant the jury thinks is innocent; not proven, for a case with insufficient evidence of guilt.'

112 Thomas Weigend, 'Is the Criminal Process about Truth?: A German Perspective' (2003) 26 Harvard J of L and Public Policy 157, 166–167 ('In systems relying on professional judges to find the facts... the court must invariably explain in writing how it arrived at its verdict, and the court must relate the outcome of the case to the evidence presented').

innocent.[113] Here, the assertion of factual innocence is made in statements accompanying the 'not guilty' verdict and is, strictly speaking, not part of the verdict.

A 'not guilty' verdict declares that the defendant is not guilty. Does it declare, more strongly, that the defendant is innocent? The European Court of Human Rights was inclined towards a positive answer in *Sekanina v Austria*:[114]

> The voicing of suspicions regarding an accused's innocence is conceivable as long as the conclusion of criminal proceedings has not resulted in a decision on the merits of the accusation. However, it is no longer admissible to rely on such suspicions once an acquittal has become final.

Does the quashing of a conviction on grounds unrelated to the 'merits of the accusation' also amount to a declaration that the defendant is innocent? One might think that, given the presumption of innocence, a person must be treated for all legal purposes as innocent unless and until proven guilty in court.[115] If this is right, it would seem to follow that a person who has had his conviction quashed for abuse of process should be presumed innocent, and treated in law as having been wrongly convicted. But an application for state compensation by a defendant in precisely that situation was rejected by the House of Lords in *R (Mullen) v Home Secretary*.[116] To obtain compensation under section 133 of the Criminal Justice Act 1988, it must be shown 'beyond reasonable doubt' that the defendant was innocent of the crime with which he was convicted. And this is not shown by the mere fact that the defendant has had his conviction quashed on grounds unrelated to the substance of the case against him.[117]

In another type of situation, it is controversial whether the declaration made in a verdict is accompanied by a corresponding assertion of fact. Sometimes, the law requires the fact-finder to find that p if and so long as q is proved. Rebutable presumptions of law are particularly popular in narcotics legislation. In one typical form of such a presumption, p stands for 'the defendant intended to traffic in a prohibited drug' and q for 'she was in possession of more than a certain quantity of that drug'. The finding that p is implied in a conviction for trafficking, a crime with an intentional element. A conviction for trafficking amounts to a declaration that p. Where, apart from q, there is no evidence of an intention to traffic, it is at least arguable that the court is not sufficiently justified in believing

[113] eg in *R v Fergus* (1994) 98 Cr App R 313, 325, the Court of Appeal, in quashing a conviction, made it a point to announce that 'the conviction was not only unsafe and unsatisfactory but that [the defendant] was wholly innocent'.

[114] (1993) 17 EHRR 221, 235, para 30.

[115] It has been argued that the presumption of innocence is not as expansive as the rhetoric supporting it suggests: Larry Laudan, *Truth, Error, and Criminal Law* (Cambridge: CUP, 2006) 93–96.

[116] [2004] UKHL 18, [2005] 1 AC 1.

[117] For criticisms of this case, see Richard Nobles and David Schiff, 'Guilt and Innocence in the Criminal Justice System: A Comment on *R (Mullen) v Secretary of State for the Home Department*' (2006) 69 MLR 80.

that p and therefore not justified in asserting that p. One could interpret the finding as a declaration that p but not see it as implying or containing the assertion that p. This interpretation might seem better than the theory which construes this case as one where the court is legally compelled to make an assertion of fact for which it knows it lacks sufficient evidence.[118] However, if the conviction does not assert that the person has done certain acts which, together with other elements, amount to the crime with which he was charged, it is difficult to defend and explain the view that the conviction is necessarily wrongful if the person is in fact innocent.[119]

2.5.4 Ascriptive aspect of a verdict

There is a further dimension to the force of a verdict which is connected to both its assertive and declarative aspects. When the court finds the defendant guilty of a crime or liable on a civil claim, it is not merely reporting facts constitutive of the crime or civil claim. The present situation is, of course, unlike the situation where I see that it is raining and tell you that it is. There are at least two complicating factors. First, findings of fact do not merely report that someone has behaved such and so; they often go further in expressing attitudes to that behaviour. This expressive aspect of a verdict is dealt with in the next section. Secondly, and this is the factor that will be discussed here, findings are conclusions drawn from the evidence adduced at the trial, not mere reports of facts directly observed. Those conclusions are reached in a process that involves evaluation. I can look out of the window to see if it is raining. Obviously, the fact-finder is not able in the same way to see for herself what really happened in the case. She has to try to come to a conclusion by weighing the evidence and drawing inferences from it.

Trial deliberation is evaluative in a further sense. We already noted that the conclusion is not purely factual. The finding that there is a binding contract between the parties which one of them has breached integrates a description of observable facts (based on an assessment of the evidence) into a theoretical, non-observable, framework of legal rules, principles, and concepts.[120] As Hart nicely puts it, a judgment is 'a compound or blend of facts and law'.[121] As one might further add, it is also a mixture of facts and values. Mechanical jurisprudence, the depiction of adjudication as a simple deductive application of law to facts, was never more than a straw man. Adjudication involves ascribing legal character to salient facts; it is thus that taking something becomes the criminal act of stealing. This process requires interpretation and the exercise of judgment, not

118 On which see eg Lech Morawski, 'Law, Fact and Legal Language' (1999) 18 Law and Philosophy 461, 465–466: 'in judicial proceedings we are in some circumstances compelled to accept false statements if they follow e.g. from irrebuttable presumptions'.

119 This is further discussed in Chapter 3, Part 1.4 (near the end).

120 See Horovitz (n 29) 151–152.

121 H L A Hart, 'The Ascription of Responsibility and Rights' in A G N Flew (ed), *Essays on Logic and Language* (Oxford: Blackwell, 1951) 145, 146.

only in the characterization of facts but also in picking out the relevant facts to characterize; the two activities run together, one feeding into the other, and both the legal character of facts and the relevancy of facts are controlled by the law.[122] But this only means, and surely no one would deny, that an ascription of legal character to facts is vastly more complicated than a simple perception of fact or a report of the perception; it does not distinguish an ascription from an assertion. To ascribe a legal character to a set of facts is to assert that the set of facts has that legal character.

Thus the ascriptive force of a verdict is not really distinct from its assertive force. The term 'ascription' is only more informative than the term 'assertion' for the term 'ascription' reveals the judgmental or evaluative nature of the assertion that is being made. To put it differently, a high-level finding makes an ascriptive assertion; it is not a straightforward factual assertion of the kind that is a mere report. Indeed, an ascription need not even be a speech act. It stands to an assertion somewhat like how blame stands to an accusation. I can ascribe responsibility to someone or blame her for something without saying it: I can keep it in my heart. But an unuttered assertion does not seem any more intelligible than an unuttered accusation.[123]

It could equally be claimed that when the court publicly ascribes a legal character to a set of facts (for example, the fact of killing, of having the intention to kill and so forth), it is declaring that the set of facts has a particular legal character (it amounts to murder). On this analysis, an ascription again loses its distinctive force. If the jury declares a person guilty of murder by ascribing to her conduct that legal character, so long as the proper procedure was followed, the verdict is valid and the person is a convicted murderer and remains one unless and until the conviction is reversed or quashed by a higher court.

2.5.5 Expressive aspect of a verdict

It may be useful at this point to take stock of the foregoing discussion before pressing ahead. We can ask of a verdict if it is *valid*. Validity requires satisfaction of the conditions for a successful performance of the speech act of declaring a verdict. So it is said, '[O]nly a properly empanelled jury can declare a defendant "Guilty!".'[124] We also evaluate a verdict in terms of truth and truthfulness because, amongst other things, it necessarily, if only impliedly, asserts propositions about the underlying facts. To convict the defendant of murder is, amongst

[122] On the evaluative and normative nature of fact-finding, see Bert van Roermund, *Law, Narrative and Reality—An Essay in Intercepting Politics* (Dorchecht: Kluwer, 1997) ch 4 ('Ascription of Normative Consequences to Facts'); Olivecrona (n 46) 212–215 ('The Element of Valuation'); and on the related difficulty of drawing a bright line between facts and legal norms: Morawski (n 118).

[123] cf John R Searle and Daniel Vanderveken, *Foundations of Illocutionary Logic* (Cambridge: CUP, 1985) 190.

[124] Sanford Schane, introduction to his forthcoming book, *Language and the Law*.

other things, to assert that she caused the death of the deceased; this assertion is either *true* or *false*, and can be made *sincerely* or *insincerely*. Both the determination and the legal characterization of the facts of a case require judgment, which is opened to assessment as *right* or *wrong*. Thus we may ask of a conclusion of fact whether the evidence adduced at the trial was sufficient to justify the finding or assertion that it was the doctor who unplugged the life-support system. So too may we challenge the ascription of legal character to the facts. Even if we know that it was the doctor who pulled the plug, it may yet be unclear under a conceivable system of criminal law whether it is right to call what she did murder.

The question of rightness is related to another: does the doctor *deserve* to be convicted on the charge of murder? Whether a person deserves to be convicted is different from the question of whether she has in fact been (validly) convicted. The latter is concerned with matters such as the proper procedure for effective delivery of the verdict. Whether a person deserves a verdict is also different from whether she deserves the legal consequences of that verdict. Does a person deserve to be convicted is one question; does she deserve the sentence which she got is another. What does it mean to ask whether a person deserves to be convicted? The quick answer is: if she is in law guilty. This answer reduces the question of desert to the questions of truth and rightness. There is arguably more to the question of desert.

'Does the doctor deserve to be convicted?' and 'Has she committed the offence with which she is charged?' pose the same question if we take the view that the doctor deserves to be convicted if and so long as it is right to legally characterize what she did as murder. But it is possible to construe them as different questions. A supporter of jury nullification may well concede that the doctor has, according to the letter of the law, committed a murder and yet insist that this does not provide a conclusive answer to the question of whether she should or must be convicted. Had the doctor acted out of respect and compassion for her patient, she might not be deserving of the opprobrium which comes with being declared a convicted murderer. This concern is not with the ascriptive force of the verdict; we are, after all, supposing the concession that what the doctor did is 'technically' murder. On this interpretation, *pace* Austin, there is no lie in jury nullification;[125] what motivates the acquittal is the recognition of a further force in a murder conviction, an *expressive* force. A guilty verdict does more than declare or assert an ascription of a legal character to the facts; it also communicates the negative attitude that is expressed in that ascription.[126] Conduct to which the character of

[125] For an argument against construing what the nullifying jury does as lying, see Matt Matravers, '"More Than Just Illogical": Truth and Jury Nullification' in Duff, Farmer, Marshall and Tadros (n 104) ch 4.

[126] On the condemnatory aspect of a conviction, see Duff, *Trials and Punishments* (n 85) 108. Tadros argues 'that imposing criminal responsibility expresses moral indignation about the fact that an individual has failed properly to be motivated by the interests of others' (Victor Tadros, *Criminal Responsibility* (Oxford: OUP, 2005) 85; and see further ibid at 79–82).

a crime is ascribed is normally regarded by the State as deserving of a greater or lesser degree of censure. There are many possible reasons why the State would view the conduct in that light: the act which is prohibited may be deemed immoral, anti-social, harmful, costly, or otherwise against public policy; and the force of the negative attitude may range from outrage (for serious crimes like murder and rape) to mild disapproval (for minor offences such as littering).

According to Searle, an expressive has null direction of fit.[127] It seeks neither to get the words to fit the world nor the world to fit the words; rather it presupposes a propositional content to which an attitude is taken. To condemn the doctor for killing her patient *presupposes* that the doctor has killed her patient; but condemning her conduct is different from asserting or declaring that she has done something. What is expressed in a conviction is an attitude of criticism or blame for the act that is, at the same time, declared and asserted in the verdict. Although what the doctor did was murder under positive law, and while that much may be declared and asserted, we may still be reluctant to deplore her action, which is what we will also do if we return a guilty verdict. A conviction is an act of enforcing the law; it comes after the act of bringing a criminal charge and precedes the act of punishment, both of which are also acts of legal enforcement. It may perhaps be said: just as there are laws which, for legitimate extra-legal reasons, the State is reluctant to invoke, and just as legitimate extra-legal factors may lead the State to exercise its discretion not to pursue a prosecution, so too the jury may, on legitimate extra-legal grounds, refuse to enforce a law against a person by holding back from convicting her under it. On this argument, a person may not deserve to have a law enforced against her even where the law, in principle, applies to her case, and one who concedes the latter may yet insist on the former. So far as a guilty verdict expresses an attitude of disapproval,[128] we may ask if that disapproval is deserved. And so far as this disapproval reflects a moral criticism, the conviction calls for moral justification.

Not all verdicts express moral disapproval of past conduct. There may be legal responsibility without moral responsibility. For instance, it is difficult to read condemnation in a conviction of a strict liability offence. Condemnation is also untypical of verdicts in civil cases. Indeed, civil judgments are sometimes awarded against defendants for whom the court has great sympathy. The expressive force of a verdict is contingent on its propositional content. Where the propositional content of a verdict is morally neutral, we would not read any expression of negative attitude into it: an order for eviction does not express outrage at the plight of the poor tenant for having fallen into hard times. The greater the moral gravity of the crime for which a person is convicted, the harsher the disapproval that the verdict may be read to express: a conviction on a charge of rape is more

[127] Searle 1979 (n 62) 15.

[128] Tellingly, 'condemn' is defined in the *Oxford English Dictionary* as synonymous with 'convict'.

condemnatory than a conviction on a charge of petty theft. This is a point to which we must return in our discussion on the standard of proof in Chapter 4.

It is not just the content of a verdict that contributes to its expressive force. The *type* of verdict also matters. As Tadros puts it, 'criminal conviction *per se* has distinctive communicative force'.[129] A single incident may result in both a criminal prosecution and a civil action. The defendant may escape a conviction at the criminal trial and yet be found liable by the civil court. It is generally taken as less serious for a person to suffer a civil judgment than to be convicted of a crime even where the underlying incident is the same for both cases. This is not only because the consequences of a conviction are often more serious than those of a civil judgment (sometimes they are not) but also because a conviction, just in being what it is, usually speaks more badly than a civil judgment may do of the person against whom it is entered. There is a crucial difference between being found liable for assault in a tort action and being found guilty of assault in a criminal prosecution. The verdict in the former is a declaration and assertion of the state of legal relation between the parties, that one has a legal right which the other has violated or that one has breached a legal duty which he owed to the other. On the corrective view, a civil verdict aims to do justice between the parties by restoring their relationship through compensation. But to convict a person of assault is different. Here it may be thought that the aim is to express to the person and the public the State's denunciation of his conduct. A guilty verdict conveys condemnation or disapproval; it tarnishes the agent's life record by branding him a 'convict', an intrinsically opprobrious tag. Compare this with a positive finding made by an English court of a person who is unfit to plead under section 4A of the Criminal Procedure (Insanity) Act 1964. This special finding amounts to a declaration and assertion that he 'did the act or made the omission charged against him'. However, it lacks the additional and distinctive force, which a guilty verdict would have, of further blaming him or holding him responsible for the act or omission.[130]

2.6 Conclusion

A verdict does many things at the same time. It declares legal institutional facts of (non-)guilt or (non-)liability; it asserts propositions of facts pertaining to or constitutive of the alleged guilt or liability; it ascribes legal character to the facts as found; it expresses a psychological state; and, in some cases, it expresses, with greater or lesser force, a negative attitude ranging from strong condemnation to

[129] Tadros (n 126) 75; see also ibid at 80: 'The label "criminal" is appropriate when certain moral attitudes are appropriate in response to the conduct prohibited, and this is to be distinguished from, for example, torts. The label "tortious" may make appropriate some reactive attitudes, but surely not the same kind as are made appropriate by the criminal law.'

[130] *R v H* [2003] UKHL 1, [2003] 1 All ER 497 is, strictly speaking, a logical decision. For broader criticisms, see A J Ashworth [2003] Crim LR 817 (case comment).

mild disapproval of the defendant's past conduct. A verdict can be assessed on many dimensions corresponding to the things that it does; indeed, we should insist that it be defensible on each of those fronts. As a declarative, it can be evaluated as valid or not, and as an assertive, it can be judged as true or false. Further, a verdict can be assessed in terms of right and wrong in its ascription of legal character to the facts of the case. So far as a verdict expresses belief, we demand that it be sincere, and so far as it expresses condemnation, we require that the moral criticism be deserved. The principal aim of this part has been to provide the linguistic resources for clearer discourse on issues surrounding the trial process and a framework within which those issues may be coherently situated.

3 Fact-Finding: The Deliberative Aspect

3.1 Introduction

The law of evidence plays an important role in controlling trial deliberation. This is a central thesis of this book. To set the stage for advancing this claim, it is necessary to understand what trial deliberation is about and how it works. Part 3.2 analyses the deliberative process and identifies its key aspects. Part 3.3 examines the freedom that is allowed in evidential reasoning and the legal techniques that are used to control that freedom.

Much of evidence scholarship focuses on the exclusion of evidence without linking the basis of exclusion to concerns about the legitimacy of factual reasoning. They are treated as largely unrelated. For example, Wigmore divided the principles of evidence, as they are applied to the trial, into two major parts. One part is 'Admissibility,—the procedural rules devised by the law, and based on litigious experience and tradition, to guard the tribunal...against erroneous persuasion';[131] these rules are 'artificial legal rules peculiar to...Anglo-American jury-system'.[132] Another part deals with 'Proof' and is 'concerned with the ratiocinative process of contentious persuasion'.[133] The principles of proof 'represent the natural processes of the mind in dealing with the evidential facts after they

[131] John Henry Wigmore, *The Science of Judicial Proof—as given by Logic, Psychology, and General Experience and illustrated in Judicial Trials* (Boston: Little, Brown and Co, 1937) 3.

[132] ibid 5.

[133] ibid 3. Similarly, see Christine L Boyle and Jesse Nyman, 'Finding Facts Fairly in Roberts and Zuckerman's Criminal Evidence', *International Commentary on Evidence*: vol 2, 2005: issue 2, article 3, at 1, available at: <http://www.bepress.com/ice/vol2/iss2/art3>: 'The Subject of the law of evidence falls into two parts. The most familiar part of the subject is the extensive legal doctrine relating to rules of procedure (such as competence and the examination of witnesses) and the rules of exclusion (such as hearsay). The other part is the fact-finding process, including determinations of relevance and weight, and involving the drawing of inferences.'

are admitted to the jury';[134] '[t]he evidence is in, and the question now is, What is its effect?'[135]

It is misleading to draw such a bright line between the admissibility of evidence and the deliberative process.[136] Many rules of evidence, including rules of admissibility, exist to protect the legitimacy of trial deliberation; they regulate the evaluation of evidence and constrain the manner in which findings of fact are made. The law of evidence can be profitably analysed in the context of trial deliberation. This part introduces a framework for such an analysis. But, first, the meaning and nature of trial deliberation must be explained.

3.2 Aspects of deliberation

Deliberation is a general phenomenon. It is performed in various contexts and on many kinds of question. The present concern is with deliberation conducted at a trial and on questions of fact as broadly construed in Part 1. Unless it appears otherwise, references to 'deliberation' are to 'trial deliberation'. There are a number of aspects to deliberation. Deliberation may be taken to mean (1) the cognitive process in which the fact-finder (2) evaluates the evidence and arguments presented on a disputed allegation of fact (3) in the attempt to make up her mind on what to believe and (4) with a view to deciding whether to find for or against that allegation. Each of these key dimensions of deliberation will be discussed in turn, with the last two under a single heading.

3.2.1 Cognitive process

The term 'deliberation' is sometimes used to refer to an externally identifiable *stage* in the sequence of a trial. After the presentation of evidence and arguments, and hearing the judge's instructions, the jury will retire to deliberate on their verdict. At a bench trial, the judge who chooses not to deliver judgment immediately will, likewise, return to her chamber to consider her decision after hearing the closing submissions of both sides. For present purposes, the term 'deliberation' refers not to a temporal stage of the trial, but to the *cognitive process* whereby the fact-finder decides on findings of fact and the verdict. As a cognitive process, deliberation is an ongoing affair. The fact-finder must not make up her mind before all the evidence is in.[137] However, it is inevitable that she will assess the evidence as the

[134] Wigmore (n 131) 5.

[135] ibid. The distinction was long recognized. In the eighteenth century, Hale made a similar remark when the focus of evidence law was on witness competency: 'It is one thing whether a witness be admissible to be heard, another thing, whether they are to be believed when heard' (quoted in Barbara J Shapiro, *A Culture of Fact—England, 1550–1720* (Ithaca, NY: Cornell UP, 2003) 14).

[136] It is drawn by Thayer as well; according to him, the 'law of evidence . . . excludes matter logically probative' but it 'has no orders for the reasoning faculty': 'Law and Logic' (1900) 14 Harvard L Rev 139, 142.

[137] eg Ninth Circuit Model Civil Jury Instructions, Instruction §1.12 warns the jury thus: 'do not make up your mind about what the verdict should be until after you have gone to the jury room

trial unfolds, forming tentative beliefs about the facts and revising them along the way. Although the final deliberation is conducted in the jury room or sometimes in the judge's chamber, the fact-finder does not begin to think about the evidence only when she retires to consider the verdict.

Trial deliberation as a cognitive process must be distinguished from jury deliberation as a *group activity*.[138] As a group activity, deliberation is observable as the behaviour of individuals interacting with one another whereas, as a cognitive process, deliberation is a 'mental activity'. This activity involves the evaluation of evidence with a view to making up one's mind about what to believe and what to find. To be sure, we cannot fully understand how a jury, as a group, reaches their verdict unless we take account of the interpersonal dynamics that produced the required consensus.[139] Members of the jury are expected to give their views and listen to the opinions of others, and there must be 'discussion, argument and give and take within the scope of [their] oath'.[140] It may be that the jury, which has the advantage of each member bringing to the table their individual set of experience and competency, is more effective in getting the right answer than the judge at a bench trial operating alone.[141] This study is not of the psychology of group interaction and neither does it examine the superiority of plurality decision-making over individual deliberation. Our focus will instead be on the normative rules which regulate deliberation as a cognitive process and which bear on the justification for a finding of fact. Those normative rules should apply to both individual and group deliberation; the rules must be respected by the fact-finder in the course of making up her mind, and, where there is a jury, the rules must also be respected during their discussion on the proper conclusions to draw from the evidence.[142]

to decide that case and you and your fellow jurors have discussed the evidence. Keep an open mind until then.' Available from the official website of the Ninth Circuit: <http://www.ce9.uscourts.gov/>. Similarly, Specimen 55(a) of the UK *Crown Court Bench Book* (available from the website of the Judicial Studies Board at <http://www.jsboard.co.uk/criminal_law/cbb/index.htm>) tells the criminal jury that they 'should avoid reaching concluded views about the case until they have heard all the evidence'.

138 On the group acquisition of a collective belief, see Margaret Gilbert, *On Social Fact* (London: Routledge, 1989) and Frederick F Schmitt, 'The Justification of Group Beliefs' in Frederick F Schmitt (ed), *Socializing Epistemology—The Social Dimensions of Knowledge* (London: Rowman & Littlefield, 1994) ch 12.

139 A point stressed by Mirjan R Damaška, *Evidence Law Adrift* (New Haven: Yale University Press, 1997) 37–40; 'Hearsay in Cinquecento Italy' in Michele Taruffo (ed), *Studi di Vittorio Denti*, vol 1 (Padova: CEDAM: Padova, 1994) 88; and 'Epistemology and Legal Regulation of Proof' (2003) Law, Probability and Risk 117, 119. See also Reid Hastie, Steven Penrod and Nancy Pennington, *Inside the Jury* (Cambridge, Massachusetts: Harvard University Press, 1983) ch 6.

140 *R v Watson & Ors* (1988) 87 Cr App R 1, 8.

141 There is some anecdotal evidence of this in the personal account of jury service by Trevor Grove, *The Juryman's Tale* (London: Bloomsbury, 1998).

142 That deliberation has both a public sense (in our case, as displayed in discussion amongst jurors) and an inner sense (here, as a process of private reflection by each juror) and that the inner sense duplicates or is explainable by analogy with the public sense, see Stuart Hampshire, *Justice is Conflict* (Princeton, New Jersey: Princeton UP, 2000) 7 *et seq*.

3.2.2 Evaluating evidence and arguments

It is natural to think of action as bodily action, and of the mind as a mental state or occurrence. But mental life consists also of acts and activities, many but not all of which enter consciousness. The evaluation of evidence is an exercise that consists of an intricate web of what are sometimes called 'mental acts'. They are performed in the course of assessing the credibility of witnesses, gauging the probative value of evidence, choosing between conflicting accounts, drawing inferences from what are believed to be true, judging testimony for narrative consistency, appraising the overall coherence of each side's version of facts and more. This set of acts, constituting the mental activity of deliberation, is guided by standing attitudes. They are discussed in Chapter 4. Briefly: in civil cases, an impartial attitude must be adopted, whereas at a criminal trial, the fact-finder must take a protective attitude towards the accused; the latter manifests itself in an especially critical orientation towards the prosecution's allegations. More generally, the judge of fact must in all cases approach her deliberative task with the attitude of caution. This is a central theme of Chapters 4 and 5.

In evaluating the evidence, the fact-finder should consider the arguments presented by counsels. These include the 'theory of the case' offered by each side and the attacks made by one side on the theory and evidence offered by the other. The thinking that is carried out in deliberation is partly explicit and partly tacit; it employs overt reasoning, as well as implicit, subconscious or pre-conscious, processes—'heuristics', 'schemas', 'intuitions', 'hunches', and so on.[143] While deliberation is a highly complex psychological process, legal rules typically isolate explicit lines of evidential reasoning for purposes of regulation.[144] The law excludes evidence which it sees as only inviting illegitimate forms of reasoning and regulates deliberation by forbidding the fact-finder from engaging in those lines of objectionable reasoning. This 'atomistic' approach makes sense even though, as is fully acknowledged in Chapter 3, Part 3.4, narrative plays a necessary role in trial deliberation. Being clear on 'the characteristics and effect of individual pieces of evidence on story formation, or on the proof of individual elements of a claim or defense... can help determine the kinds of questions that fact-finders need to answer, and the kind of information on which they should rely in order to answer them'.[145] It is by stepping back from the rush of responses,

[143] eg Daniel Kahneman, Paul Slovic and Amos Tversky (eds), *Judgment under Uncertainty: Heuristics and Biases* (New York: Cambridge University Press, 1982) 129–152; Nancy Pennington and Reid Hastie, 'The Story Model for Juror Decision Making' in Reid Hastie (ed), *Inside the Juror—The Psychology of Juror Decision Making* (Cambridge: CUP, 1993) 192; Marilyn MacCrimmon, 'Developments in the Law of Evidence: The 1989–90 Term: The Process of Proof: Schematic Constraints' (1990) 1 Supreme Court L Rev (2d) 345.

[144] These rules assume 'atomistic' reasoning in contrast to 'holistic' reasoning. On these approaches, see Chapter 3, Part 3.4.

[145] Doron Menashe and Mutal E Shamash 'The Narrative Fallacy', *International Commentary on Evidence*: vol 3, 2005: issue 1, article 3, available at: <http://www.bepress.com/ice/vol3/iss1/art3> at 28–29.

sometimes blind and intuitive, to one's evidence, dissecting thought processes and carefully reducing them to basic steps, that one can catch out habitual and prejudicial assumptions that might otherwise pass unnoticed.

3.2.3 Deciding what to believe and what to find

The fact-finder evaluates evidence and arguments with the view of making decisions at two levels. At the first level, the question is 'what to believe', and at the second level, it is 'what to find'. These aspects of deliberation, and the relation between them, are elaborated in Chapter 3. Some rough observations will suffice for now. In the first instance, the fact-finder will judge what to believe about the disputed allegations of fact on the evidence presented before her. Judgment is a conscious and voluntary process aimed at accepting a proposition only if it is true. 'Acceptance' is often distinguished from 'belief' along the line that 'acceptance' is voluntary and 'belief' is not. The latter is an inner state in which, like it or not, one finds oneself.[146] However, judgment is a kind of acceptance that normally produces a corresponding belief. Our beliefs often come from our judging what to believe. A person who judges that a proposition is true will, unless he is irrational, come to believe that it is true. Note that not every acceptance constitutes a judgment. A person may accept, without judging, that a proposition is true by choosing, or by being disposed, to act on that proposition without believing that it is true.[147] Trial deliberation is a search for possible basis for acceptance in the specific form of a judgment (that is, in the truth-regulated sense). It might be thought that a judgment on a dispute of fact ought usually to determine the finding on that dispute. This view forges a direct connection between the questions at these two levels; in general, the fact-finder must find positively that and only that which she believes to be true. But, as we will see, this is inaccurate. Findings are not always based on the personal or subjective belief about the facts of the case. In general, they must be grounded in a detached form of judgment.

3.3 Freedom and constraints

There is both freedom and constraints in trial deliberation. The freedom consists of the considerable discretion that is given to the fact-finder. Rational observers may reasonably disagree with the findings that she has made. The law allows for such disagreements. Subject to limited scope for interference by higher courts, fact-finders, especially in jury trials, have the last word on issues of fact. Freedom in deliberation supposes that the exercise is voluntary. The exercise is obviously voluntary if it is nothing more than a form of practical deliberation, calling for

[146] eg L Jonathan Cohen, *An Essay on Belief and Acceptance* (Oxford: Clarendon Press, 1992), at 117–125, and 'Should a Jury Say What It Believes or What It Accepts?' (1991) 13 Cardozo L Rev 465.

[147] 'Acceptance' is used in this wider sense by Lehrer, in 'Reason and Consistency' in Keith Lehrer (ed), *Analysis and Metaphysics* (Dordrecht: D Reidel Publishing, 1975) 57–58.

a decision on what to do. But, as just briefly mentioned and as will be argued in Chapter 3, trial deliberation involves the exercise of doxastic judgments. Trial deliberation is voluntary because judgments are voluntary even though beliefs are not. Voluntariness implies choice and choice brings responsibility;[148] this exposes fact-finding to evaluation beyond the criterion of reliability. We do not blame a machine for producing faulty outputs, although we can describe it as unreliable; we do, on the other hand, hold the fact-finder responsible for the judgments and findings she chooses to make. Rules of evidence regulating deliberation are based on normative ideas about what this responsibility entails. It is a theme of this study that the relevant norms are not purely epistemic ones. Practical and moral considerations have complicated and interdependent roles to play.

Responsibility in the exercise of deliberative freedom requires rationality. It is true that the jury is given strong discretion to do their job. However, the law does not, in conferring strong discretion, license plainly irrational judgments of fact.[149] Such judgments are wrong, whether they are discoverable and whether anything should or can be done about it. The constraint of rationality assumes the capacity to employ reasons sensibly and effectively. If we expect the fact-finder to deliberate rationally within the freedom she is accorded, we must see that she is *able* to do so. It is a basic condition that the fact-finder be cognitively competent.[150] There are two related components in cognitive competence. The first is that the fact-finder must possess normal faculties for rational thought and be able to apply ordinary principles of reasoning. Mentally impaired persons are lacking in this regard. The second is that the fact-finder must have a non-minimal amount of life experience and accumulated a non-minimal stock of common knowledge about the world. Children do not meet this qualification. It is for lack of basic cognitive competence, a defect in one or both of its components, that certain persons, including the mad and the very young, are excluded from jury service. Those persons may be described as lacking in (the technical sense of) 'common sense'.[151] Trial deliberation is free insofar as it rides on 'common sense'—on non-expert, rational, reasoning and common knowledge.

[148] Generally, Lorraine Code, *Epistemic Responsibility* (Hanover: Brown University Press, 1987) 51.

[149] Ronald Dworkin, 'The Model of Rules I' (1967) 35 Chicago L Rev 14, 33–34: 'The strong sense of discretion is not tantamount to license, and does not exclude criticism. Almost any situation in which a person acts... makes relevant certain standards of rationality, fairness and effectiveness.'

[150] This condition is examined by L Jonathan Cohen, 'Freedom of Proof' in William Twining (ed), *Facts in Law, Archives for Philosophy of Law and Social Philosophy*, Beiheft No 16 (Wiesbaden: Franz Steiner Verlag, 1983) 1–21.

[151] Common sense can mean a 'power of the mind' or a 'body of beliefs commonly accepted as true': Ronald E Beanblossom and Keith Lehrer (eds), Thomas Reid, *Thomas Reid's Inquiry and Essays* (Indianapolis: Hackett Publishing, 1983) xxvi. According to Price, to exercise common sense is to apply an 'inductive sort of reasonableness' on one's collection of experience: H H Price, *Belief* (London: George Allen & Unwin, 1969) 179. For an extensive list of philosophical interpretations of 'common sense': Louise Marcil-Lacoste, *Claude Buffier and Thomas Reid—Two Common-Sense Philosophers* (Kingston: McGill-Queen's University Press, 1982) 74–75.

Apart from the general demand of rationality that limits the scope for discretion in fact-finding, the law imposes other types and degrees of constraints. Many evidential rules aim to guide or regulate deliberation.[152] They are second-order rules, superimposed on common sense.[153] A rough analogy—and it is no more than that—may be drawn between the law of evidence and a traffic code. Both operate on an activity and are targeted at persons whose competence to carry out that activity is assumed. Traffic rules are, in one respect, driving instructions, and in another, not. They are not driving instructions inasmuch as they do not prescribe what must be done to get the vehicle to move from one point to another. They are driving instructions in the sense that they regulate actions that emanate from the exercise of basic operational skills: they tell drivers where they must not turn, to stop when the traffic light is red, the maximum speed at which they can drive, which side of the road to stay on, and such like. Similarly, it is both true and false that rules of evidence instruct the fact-finder on how to conduct factual reasoning. The fact-finder is assumed competent to evaluate the evidence and is both expected and given general freedom to exercise that competence. She must generally act by her own lights in moving from premises to conclusions. At the primary level, the process of deliberation is simply 'too unruly to obey the lawgiver's rein, too contextual to be captured in a web of categorical legal norms'.[154] However, it can be and is controlled at the secondary level. Various evidentiary rules tell the fact-finder what she must bear in mind or must not do while deliberating. The law steps in when there is a need to advise on facts which are not generally known, or, more significantly, when there is a normative reason to depart from principles of reasoning in daily practical life. A tension is frequently noted between the operation of legal rules of evidence and the manner in which enquiries are usually conducted in everyday contexts.[155] Although many lawyers favour

[152] According to Damaška, *Evidence Law Adrift* (n 139) 8, Anglo-American law of evidence aspires to 'structure the analysis of evidence'. Cf Richard D Friedman, 'Anchors and Flotsam: Is Evidence Law "Adrift"?' (1998) 107 Yale LJ 1921, 1928–1934. On the different ways in which the law impacts on evidential reasoning: Philip McNamara, 'The Canons of Evidence—Rules of Exclusion or Rules of Use?' (1986) 10 Adelaide L Rev 341; Ronald J Allen, 'Structuring Jury Decisionmaking in Criminal Cases: A Unified Constitutional Approach to Evidentiary Devices' (1980) 94 Harvard L Rev 321; Scott Brewer, 'Scientific Expert Testimony and Intellectual Due Process' (1998) 107 Yale LJ 1535.

[153] They aim 'to constrain and control, rather than to facilitate or release, lay cognitive inclinations': Damaška, *Evidence Law Adrift* (n 139) 28. Essentially the same view was expressed long ago by Thomas Starkie, *A Practical Treatise of the Law of Evidence* (2nd edn, London: J & W T Clarke, 1833) 13.

[154] Damaška, *Evidence Law Adrift* (n 139) 20.

[155] As noted in *O'Brien v Chief Constable of South Wales Police* [2005] UKHL 6, [2005] 2 AC 534, 540–1; *R v Kearley* [1992] 2 AC 228, 236; *R v Turner* [1975] 1 QB 834, 841; *John W* [1998] 2 Cr App R 289, 304; cf *R v Apicella* (1985) 82 Cr App R 295, 299; *R v Chandler* [1976] 1 WLR 585, 590. See also: James Bradley Thayer, *A Preliminary Treatise on Evidence at the Common Law* (Boston: Little, Brown and Co, 1898, Rothman reprint 1969) 1–2; Colin Tapper (ed), *Cross and Tapper on Evidence* (11th edn, Oxford: OUP, 2007) 1–2; Damaška, *Evidence Law Adrift* (n 139) 11–12.

fewer evidentiary rules,[156] or less 'technical interferences with ordinary principles of reasoning'[157] as they are inclined to see them, there are often powerful reasons for regulating deliberation. Many rules of evidence, including those to be examined in later chapters, embody values that legitimize trial findings of fact; they are far from mere technicalities.

3.4 Forms of control: advice, regulation, exclusion

Freedom in trial deliberation is relative, the extent of which varies across legal systems and historically.[158] The most stringent form of regulation is the Romano-canonical system of proof. Fact-finding under that system was supposedly controlled by rules stipulating the number of witnesses needed to prove a case and assigning specified weights to different types of evidence[159] although this approach was probably not quite as mechanical as it is sometimes made out

[156] Bentham was probably the most ardent advocate of fewer such rules: see William Twining, *Theories of Evidence: Bentham and Wigmore* (London: Weidenfeld & Nicholson, 1985) 66–75; Gerald J Postema, *Bentham and the Common Law Tradition* (Oxford: Clarendon Press, 1986) 348–350. Cf Stein who argues that 'judicial fact-finding should be thoroughly regulated by law': Alex Stein, 'The Refoundation of Evidence Law' (1996) 9 Canadian Journal of Law and Jurisprudence 279, 285, 'Against Free Proof' (1997) 31 Israel L Rev 573, and *Foundations of Evidence Law* (Oxford: OUP, 2005) ch 4; Menashe and Shamash (n 145), and 'Pass These Sirens By: Further Thoughts on Narrative and Admissibility Rules', *International Commentary on Evidence*: vol 5, 2007: issue 1, article 3,available at: <http://www.bepress.com/ice/vol5/iss1/art3>; Frederick Schauer, 'On the Supposed Jury-Dependence of Evidence Law' (2006) 155 University of Pennsylvania L Rev 165, 194 (arguing that a rule-based approach has the 'advantages of having readily accessible and easily understandable indicators of deeper but harder-to-apply primary considerations').

[157] William Twining, 'Freedom of Proof and the Reform of Criminal Evidence' (1997) 31 Israel L Rev 439, 452. Salmond sees the law of evidence as 'one of the last refuges of legal formalism': John W Salmond, *Jurisprudence or the Theory of Law* (London: Stevens & Haynes, 1902) 597.

[158] The Continental principle of *intime conviction* is sometimes said to free the fact-finder 'from all intersubjectively ascertainable standards': Damaška, *Evidence Law Adrift* (n 139) 21. But this seems an overstatement: Olof Ekelöf, 'Free Evaluation of Evidence' (1964) 8 Scandinavian Studies in Law 47, at 66. Indeed, Barbara Shapiro considers the concept *intime conviction* 'a reasonably close facsimile of [the common law doctrine of] proof beyond reasonable doubt': *Beyond Reasonable Doubt and Probable Cause—Historical Perspectives on Anglo-American Law of Evidence* (Berkeley: University of California Press, 1991), at 247. According to her, even under the less demanding precursor standard—the 'any doubt' test—jurors were not entitled to acquit on frivolous doubts (ibid 21). In Chapter 3, Part 1.3, it is suggested that there is a difference. Fact-finding on the Continental approach is determined by the fact-finder's personal or subjective belief, whereas at common law it turns on a judgmnt of detached or 'selfless' belief.

[159] John H Langbein, *Prosecuting Crime in the Renaissance* (Cambridge, Massachusetts: Harvard University Press, 1974) 238. More fully, see Lorraine Daston, *Classical Probability in the Enlightenment* (Princeton, NJ: Princeton UP, 1988) 41–43 and Arthur Engelman, *A History of Continental Civil Procedure*, translated and edited by Robert Wyness Millar (Boston: Little, Brown & Co, 1927) 41–44. The intricacy of this system led Leibniz to make his famous remark that 'The entire form of judicial procedures is, in fact, nothing but a kind of logic, applied to legal questions' (G W Leibniz, *New Essays on Human Understanding*, translated and edited by Peter Remnant and Jonathan Bennett (Cambridge, Cambridge University Press, 1996) 465).

to be.[160] The common law never took this rigid approach to proof. But it too has developed rules regulating deliberation.[161] There are at least three major techniques of controlling deliberation at common law.

3.4.1 Advice

One of them is 'advice'. At a jury trial, the judge will, in her summing up, instruct the jury on the evidence. The instructions include advice (offered as 'directions') on how they should undertake their task. They can be mandatory[162] or discretionary and are couched in varying degree of severity.[163] Amongst the most strongly worded types of advice is the mandatory common law corroboration warning. The jury is warned that it is dangerous to convict without corroboration. Since the law allows the jury, nevertheless, to convict without corroboration, this instruction counts only as an advice.

Much of the advice given to the jury is in the general interest of rational and fair deliberation. For example, the judge may wish to help the jury to think through a factual issue systematically by setting out, in a comprehensive and logical sequence, the questions they must address. Or she may caution the jury against jumping to conclusions: for instance, the jury may be warned not to infer that the defendant is guilty simply because they believe that she has lied to the police.[164] The jury may also be alerted to certain things that they might otherwise overlook, such as the possibility of collusion amongst witnesses.[165] Where the trial is on an event that happened a long time ago, the judge may alert the jury to the difficulties faced by the defendant in being 'placed at a real disadvantage in putting forward his case'; she may tell them, in fairness, to 'make allowances for the fact that with the passage of time memories fade' and that 'the longer the time

[160] According to Whitman, the Continental medieval judge had more discretion than is usually supposed: James Q Whitman, 'The Origins of "Reasonable Doubt"' (March 1, 2005). *Yale Law School. Yale Law School Faculty Scholarship Series.* Paper 1, available at: <http://lsr.nellco.org/yale/fss/papers/1>, see footnotes 75 to 79 and the associated text. Similarly James Franklin, *The Science of Conjecture—Evidence and Probability Before Pascal* (Baltimore, Maryland: John Hopkins UP, 2001) 19: 'The accusations that the "formal" Continental system of proofs had a "fairly elaborate tariff of gravity" or "strict mechanical rules" should be taken with a grain of salt... The medieval treatises nowhere give the impression of asking judges to depart from normal standards in the interest of keeping to rigid rules.' Reservations to the same effect are expressed by Mirjan Damaška, 'The Death of Legal Torture' (1978) 87 Yale LJ 860.

[161] In this regard, Damaška, *Evidence Law Adrift* (n 139) 19–20 warns that the contrast between common law and Continental systems should not be exaggerated.

[162] One example is the common law practice, equivalent to a rule of law, under which the judge must give the jury a corroboration warning on accomplice evidence: *Davies v DPP* [1954] AC 378, 399. But, in England and Wales, this duty has been abrogated by statute: s 32 Criminal Justice and Public Order Act 1994.

[163] The trend of the 'new forensic reasoning rules' is moving towards more flexibility and less formality: Paul Roberts and Adrian Zuckerman, *Criminal Evidence* (Oxford: OUP, 2004) 482–490.

[164] eg *Crown Court Bench Book* (n 137) specimen direction 27.

[165] eg *R v H* [1995] 2 AC 596, 612.

since an alleged incident, the more difficult it may be for him to answer it'.[166] These directions are based on general standards which are implicit in a rational and fair system of adjudication.

Advice in the form of a communication from judge to jury must be distinguished from advice as a guidance contained in a particular rule or practice. The latter applies even to the judge sitting alone, not in the sense that she has to verbally direct or warn herself but in the sense that she is assumed to know the rule or practice and expected to take heed of its content during deliberation. Sometimes, there is the further requirement that she records the warning in her grounds of decision and state the 'reasons why, notwithstanding the warning or as a consequence of it, a particular verdict is reached'.[167]

Advice is a weak form of control: unlike an order, it calls for reflection rather than strict obedience; it serves to guide reasoning as opposed to regulating it; it is suggestive or cautionary, and, however strongly worded, is not obligatory.[168] On the matter on which advice is given, the fact-finder has the ultimate say. Take the case where legislation permits an adverse inference to be drawn from the defendant's silence.[169] This rule does not obligate the fact-finder to draw the inference; it merely advises the fact-finder of the possibility of drawing it. She is given, as it were, official permission to take the defendant's silence against him *if* she is minded to do so. Another example is section 4(2) of the Civil Evidence Act 1995 in England.[170] It lists a number of factors to which the court may have regard in weighing hearsay evidence. This provision seeks to do no more than make the fact-finder aware of some relevant considerations. The final decision, whether to believe and what weight to accord the hearsay evidence, is hers. The need for advice on factual reasoning is most pressing where common sense is deemed in some way to be an unsafe or inadequate guide to the evaluation of evidence. A good illustration is the *Turnbull* direction.[171] It is issued in the belief that the unreliability of identification evidence is not a matter of common knowledge. This direction does not override the commonsense evaluation of evidence; it seeks rather to inform the exercise of discretion in fact-finding.

[166] eg *Crown Court Bench Book* (n 137) specimen direction 37. See *R v Percival* (1998) The Times 20 July; *Brian M* [2000] 1 Cr App R 49.

[167] *Fleming v The Queen* (1998) 197 CLR 250, 264 (Australian High Court).

[168] eg *R v Mullins* (1848) 3 Cox Cr 526, 531, per Maule J: 'The directions of judges given to juries... are not directions in point of law which juries are bound to adopt, but observations respecting facts, which judges are very properly in the habit of giving, because, with respect to matters of fact, the judge as well as the counsel upon both sides endeavor to assist the jury.'

[169] eg section 196(2) and 123(1) of the Criminal Procedure Code (Cap 68, 1985 Revised ed) (Singapore); section 34 and 35 of the Criminal Justice and Public Order Act 1994 (England).

[170] Section 381(3) of the Criminal Procedure Code in Singapore is to the same effect. There are 'signs of an increasing tendency to develop guidelines relating to the weight of... evidence': Colin Tapper, *Cross and Tapper on Evidence* (11th edn, Oxford: OUP, 2007) 2.

[171] *R v Turnbull* [1977] QB 224.

3.4.2 Regulation

Another way of controlling deliberation is by regulating it. Rules of evidence may instruct the fact-finder on the attitude to adopt in deciding questions of fact, or require her to employ, or refrain from using, specific lines of evidential reasoning. Unlike an advice, a regulation is an order; it is obligatory and prescriptive. A significant feature of a regulation, which sets it apart from an advice, is that it overrides, rather than informs, the exercise of discretion. While an advice is meant to stimulate thinking on the evidence, a regulation imposes a constraint or structure on such thinking. Where the trial is by jury, a regulation, like an advice, is communicated in the form of a jury instruction.

Sometimes, a regulation trumps over lines of factual reasoning that one would ordinarily follow in daily practical life. The trier of fact must abide by a regulation even when she is otherwise inclined to reason differently. Ordinarily, we reason from fact A to fact B only when we judge A to be a good enough reason for believing that B is true. When a presumption of law requires that the fact-finder infer B from A, she must accept that B is true if and so long as she believes that A is true unless and until B is disproved. It matters not whether she thinks A is a good enough reason for believing that B is true. Conversely, when a rule prohibits the inference to B from A, the fact-finder must not reason from A to B even if she is otherwise inclined to think that A supports the inference that B. However convincing she finds the testimony of a witness, if proof of the crime requires corroboration,[172] she cannot convict on the basis of the testimony if there is no corroborative evidence. Sometimes, the regulation may forbid one line of reasoning while leaving another open.[173] For example, the hearsay rule permits the fact-finder to infer from evidence of an out-of-court statement that it was made but not that it is true; and in the case of a joint trial, evidence is sometimes introduced which can be considered only 'against one defendant... which is not admissible against another; for example, statements made by one defendant to the police in the absence of the co-defendant'.[174] Other good examples of such regulations are no longer law. Formerly in England, that a witness[175] at a criminal trial had previously made a statement inconsistent with her testimony could be treated as evidence against her credit but not of the truth of the facts stated;[176] and when the accused was cross-examined on her bad character under s 1(f)(ii) and (iii) of

[172] eg s 13 of the English Perjury Act 1911 (England).

[173] Richard D Friedman (general ed), David P Leonard, *The New Wigmore, A Treatise on Evidence—Selected Rules of Limited Admissibility* (Boston: Little, Brown and Co, 1996) 1:14–1:22, §1.6.1.

[174] *R v M (T)* [2000] 1 WLR 421, 428. Cf *R v Hayter* [2005] UKHL 6, [2005] 1 WLR 605, especially paras 82–83.

[175] If she is the accused, the situation is complicated by rules on admission and confession.

[176] *R v Golder, Jones and Porritt* [1960] 1 WLR 1169, 1171. But now see s 119(1) Criminal Justice Act 2003.

the Criminal Evidence Act 1898[177] the evidence thus elicited could only go to her credibility but not her guilt.[178]

3.4.3 *Exclusion*

'Exclusion' is the third technique of controlling deliberation. It has received more than its fair share of attention. The trial judge is sometimes described as a 'gatekeeper': she decides what testimony or document or other physical objects (call all of them 'information' for short) gets to be admitted as evidence. Upon admission, the information must be taken into account during deliberation. 'Exclusion' can be looked at in a variety of ways. Information may, for one reason or another, be withheld from the jury to keep them ignorant of its existence: the information is *perceptually excluded.* From the party's point of view, exclusion amounts to a *prohibition of proof.* She is prevented from presenting that information to the fact-finder: she cannot, for instance, call or ask a witness to testify to it. Yet another sense of 'exclusion' is *exclusion from use in deliberation* or, more shortly, *exclusion from deliberation.*[179] Sometimes, the information is disclosed to the fact-finder but she is required to refrain from taking it into account in her reasoning. For instance, at a bench trial, the judge often has to make a preliminary ruling on the admissibility of evidence. To be in a position to make that ruling, she will have to know what the evidence is about. If, at the end of the *voir dire*, she decides to exclude the evidence, say of a confession, the confession cannot be proved at the trial. (As noted, exclusion, in one sense, means prohibition of proof.) But there is a further consequence to the ruling: when the judge comes to decide on the verdict, she will have to ignore the confession that she has ruled out. She must not permit the information to influence her decision. The jury is placed in a similar situation when, after inadmissible evidence has been brought wrongly to their notice, the judge instructs them to ignore it altogether.[180]

When information is excluded in the last sense—that is, 'excluded from deliberation'—it is excluded from *all* use in deliberation. As said with reference to the second technique of control, the fact-finder is sometimes permitted to use evidence in one way but not in another. This was described as a case where the law *regulates* evidential reasoning; to describe this as a case where the evidence is

[177] Later renumbered s 1(3)(ii) and (iii) respectively: s 67(1) and schedule 4, Youth Justice and Criminal Evidence Act 1999.

[178] Colin Tapper, *Cross and Tapper on Evidence* (9th edn, London: Butterworths, 1999), 401–403, 410–411, 415–416. Cases have held that the position is now different under s 101 of the Criminal Justice Act: Ian Dennis, *The Law of Evidence* (3rd edn, London: Sweet & Maxwell, 2007) 797.

[179] Exclusion in this sense is not unique to the common law; it was apparently practised even in Roman times: Frank R Herrmann, 'The Establishment of a Rule against Hearsay in Romano-Canonical Procedure' (1995) 36 Virginia J of Intl L 1, 15–16.

[180] She could alternatively order a retrial or, for fear of drawing the jury's attention unnecessarily to the evidence, decide not to comment on it: generally, Roderick Munday, 'Irregular Disclosure of Evidence of Bad Character' [1990] Crim LR 92. Also Damaška, *Evidence Law Adrift* (n 139) 18.

excluded from *some* use in deliberation is likely to produce confusion. It is best not to speak of 'partial exclusion'.[181] Hereafter, any reference to information being 'excluded' or 'excluded from deliberation' means that the trier of fact is not allowed to take the information into account at all.

'Exclusion from deliberation' is more fundamental than 'perceptual exclusion' and 'exclusion as prohibition of proof'. The reason why we exclude a certain matter from the fact-finder's perception or bar a party from adducing it as evidence is because we wish to prevent it from influencing deliberation. 'Perceptual exclusion' and 'exclusion as prohibition of proof' are merely means of enforcing 'exclusion from deliberation'. They are, undoubtedly, very effective means; indeed, they guarantee success: if the jury is kept in the dark about the information by preventing a party from presenting it, it is certain that the information will not figure in their deliberation.

3.4.4 Effectiveness of regulation and of instructions to ignore evidence

It must be noted that the instruction to ignore certain information during deliberation, to put aside what one has already heard or seen, either for all purposes or when deciding on a specified issue, operates principally at the justificatory level.[182] Critics overlook this point when they argue that the fact-finder cannot wipe selected information completely from her mind;[183] performance of this psychological feat, so it is said, is beyond the powers not only of the jury but of anyone.[184] This in turn has encouraged the view that exclusionary rules do not make much sense in bench trials since judges, like all human beings, would not be able to eradicate from their minds information which they have heard but ruled inadmissible.[185] A similar criticism is made of attempts to regulate deliberation; it is unrealistic to expect the fact-finder to perform the 'mental gymnastics'[186] of

[181] In *Ratten v R* [1972] AC 378, 380, Lord Reid drew a distinction between evidence that is 'wholly inadmissible' and that which is 'only partially admissible for a particular purpose'.

[182] Making this point in a different context: Martin P Goldring, 'A Note on Discovery and Justification in Science and Law' in J Roland Pennock and John W Chapman (eds), *Justification Nomos* XXVIII (New York: NYUP, 1986).

[183] In *Krulewitch v United States* (1949) 336 US 440, 453, Justice Jackson of the US Supreme Court commented: 'The naive assumption that prejudicial effects can be overcome by instructions to the jury... all practicing lawyers know to be unmitigated fiction.' See also Damaška, *Evidence Law Adrift* (n 139) 47 *et seq.*

[184] *Nash v United States* (1932) 54 F 2d 1006, 1007, per Judge Learned Hand. A study found judges to be generally not much better than juries in avoiding the influence of inadmissible evidence to which they have been exposed: Andrew J Wistrich, Chris Guthrie and Jeffrey J Rachlinski, 'Can Judges Ignore Inadmissible Information? The Difficulty of Deliberately Disregarding' (2005) 153 University of Pennsylvania L Rev 1251. See also Roderick Munday, 'Case Management, Similar Fact Evidence in Civil Cases, and a Divided Law of Evidence' (2006) 10 Intl J of Evidence and Proof 81.

[185] Kenneth Culp Davis, 'An Approach to Rules of Evidence in Non-Jury Cases' (1964) 50 American Bar Association J 723, 725; Damaška, *Evidence Law Adrift* (n 139) 127–128.

[186] *Nash v United States* (1932) 54 F 2d 1006, 1007; *Robinson v R* [2005] EWCA Crim 3233, [2006] 1 Cr App Rep 480, para 54.

using the evidence only for the permitted purpose, or to rely on it when deciding on one issue (for example, credibility) but not on another (such as guilt).[187]

There is admittedly some force in these criticisms. Even though the fact-finder is told not to be influenced at all by the information to which she has been wrongly exposed, or not to use certain evidence in a specified manner, the possibility of either occurring to some degree cannot be completely ruled out. Her 'disobedience' is not necessarily wilful. The forbidden influence may operate subconsciously. Our doxastic state is not under the sole dominion of reason and we do not consciously acknowledge all the forces that shape our mental life. Even so, it is wrong and cynical to go to the other extreme and deny altogether the effectiveness of instructions to ignore inadmissible information or of rules regulating the use of admitted evidence. Both of them operate at the 'meta-level' of evidential reasoning,[188] impacting on the secondary stage of critical reflection.[189] This is when the fact-finder reviews and scrutinizes, or attempts to 'deconstruct', her first-order beliefs about the facts of the case.[190] She must examine whether her present beliefs can be supported on the admitted evidence. She must ask whether she has allowed herself to be influenced by any forbidden lines of reasoning. If the answer is yes, she must consider revising her views of the facts. She must be satisfied that she can give good and adequate reasons (even if only in general terms) to justify her findings. She must honestly go over the argument she finds in support of her conclusions, to ensure that they respect and comply with the governing evidentiary rules. These expectations of her are neither naïve nor unrealistic. A normal person is able to reflect on her belief and form or revise her judgment in the light of an examination or a re-examination of the underlying justification. The fact-finder is assumed to be capable, as most people are, of introspection and some objectivity. We do have access to our mental life and can exercise a degree of control over it. If the fact-finder is truly unable to follow the law regulating deliberation, for example, where she is privy to extraneous information whose influence she finds impossible to eradicate, the right thing to do is to take her (or in the case of a judge, herself) out of the case.

[187] eg Roselle L Wissler and Michael J Saks, 'On the Inefficacy of Limiting Instructions—When Jurors Use Prior Conviction Evidence to Decide on Guilt' (1985) 9 Law and Human Behavior 37. In the case of a jury trial, it is claimed that a judicial instruction to ignore inadmissible evidence may have a 'backfire effect' where the jurors end up paying greater attention to the evidence than if the judge had said nothing at all: Joel D Lieberman and Jamie Arndt, 'Understanding The Limits of Limiting Instructions' (2000) 6 Psychology, Public Policy and Law 677, 689.

[188] They are 'reasoning about reasoning', on which see generally: Maurice A Finocchiaro, 'Reasoning About Reasoning' in Dov M Gabbay and Hans Jürgen Ohlbach (eds), *Practical Reasoning* (Berlin: Springer, 1996) 167.

[189] On the duty and voluntary nature of critical reflection, see Kihyeon Kim, 'The Deontological Conception of Epistemic Justification and Doxastic Voluntarism' (1994) 54 *Analysis* 282.

[190] 'Second-order beliefs come in many flavors. We believe things about the content of our beliefs, about relationships between beliefs, about how justified our beliefs are, and about why we have certain beliefs': Ward E Jones, 'Explaining Our Own Beliefs: Non-Epistemic Believing and Doxastic Instability' (2002) 111 *Philosophical Studies* 217–249, 220.

Findings of fact should not issue directly from intuitive gut feelings. Insofar as they are supposed to be deliberated conclusions, the findings must be reached by identifying the reasons for views tentatively held about the facts, and by reflecting on the validity and strength of those reasons. This process of evaluation may lead to confirmation of the original views, or it may lead to their abandonment or revision. The fact-finder is likely to experience a conflict between her subjective belief and the finding the law supposedly compels her to make only if the law requires her to reason irrationally or against her moral instincts. However, it is a principal contention of this study that most legal rules on evidential reasoning are based on rational grounds which are sensitive to the special epistemic and moral nature of the trial process. The judge often takes care to explain those grounds to the jury so that they will understand the underlying rationale and come to accept the rules, in the sense of agreeing with them rather than merely feeling bound by them. It is hoped that the jury will internalize those rules or instructions. Internalization is not as problematic as it might seem, as the underlying rationale is likely to appeal to the fact-finder on reflection, particularly when she comes to realize the import and context of her task. There is therefore much less possibility of conflict than is supposed. Conflicts may still arise. However, to the extent that the legal 'constraints' are epistemically and morally sound, it is just as well that some (perhaps unreasonable or unfair) fact-finders are kept from making the findings that they would otherwise have made on reasoning which the law regards as unreasonable or unfair. It is only in these relatively rare cases that the legal constraints are properly speaking constraints.

4 Fact-Finding: Perspectives

Legal fact-finding may be approached from two different angles. For convenience, they will be called external and internal. The external approach is one that is usually taken. Someone who adopts this approach may be described as taking on the perspective of a system engineer. This book introduces a second approach. It requires us to adopt an internal perspective of the trial by assuming the standpoint of the fact-finder as a moral agent. One approach supplements the other; neither alone can reveal the trial in its full complexity. In particular, it is hoped to show that much of value in the law of evidence is lost on the external approach and can only be seen from the internal perspective.

4.1 External perspective of system engineer

Rules of evidence are conventionally viewed from the standpoint of a detached observer of the trial system. The primary concern is that the trial should be regulated such that it will best achieve its goals. Chief amongst the perceived ends is the discovery of the truth in disputes of fact.[191] How likely this goal is achieved is a matter of reliability or accuracy. A verdict is more or less reliable, depending on the accuracy of the trial system which produced it. The accuracy of a trial system is, conceptually, the frequency with which it produces or leads to findings that are correct—or, as Lord Devlin puts it, of the 'percentage of error'.[192]

Many evidential rules are analysed and evaluated in terms of the consequences of their application and of their impact on the outcome of fact-finding. Arguments are made which are typically contingent on the validity of empirical claims about those consequences and impact. For example, one familiar form of justifying an exclusionary rule is to claim that the jury is likely to give the kind of evidence in question more weight than it deserves. Admitting the evidence will ultimately increase the likelihood of the trial producing the wrong conclusions of fact. This style of evaluation takes as its ultimate criterion the correctness of the verdict, and the soundness of the argument depends on whether it is true that the jury is cognitively incompetent as claimed. The trial is studied as a project of naturalized epistemology, one defining characteristic of which is the insistence, roughly speaking, that a theory of legal fact-finding must be continuous with and dependent upon empirical science.[193]

Adjudication is, in Goldman's term, a social practice of 'veritistic epistemology'; the aim is the production of knowledge in the weak sense of true belief.[194] For the analyst who takes this approach, 'a criminal trial is first and foremost an *epistemic* engine, a tool for ferreting out the truth from what will often initially be a confusing array of [conflicting evidence]'.[195] Laudan identifies this as the critical question for evidence law scholars: whether trial systems which 'purport to be seeking the truth [is] well engineered to lead to true beliefs about the world'.[196] A fundamental consideration in evaluating rules of evidence is their effectiveness in guiding the court towards correct outcomes. But this is not the only consideration. First, it is also vitally important, from the systemic point of view, to factor costs into the analysis. For instance, Posner invites us to think 'of a trial as a way of generating information, and the law of evidence as the means of structuring the information search in a way that will (ideally) minimize the sum of error costs

[191] Other objectives are said to include 'inspiring confidence, supporting independent social policies...and tranquilizing disputants': Jack B Weinstein, 'Some Difficulties in Devising Rules for Determining Truth in Judicial Trials' (1966) 66 Col Law Rev 223, 241.

[192] 'Who is at Fault When Injustice Occurs?' in Lord Devlin *et al*, *What's Wrong with the Law?* (London: BBC, 1970) 76.

[193] Brian Leiter, 'Prospects and Problems for the Social Epistemology of Evidence Law' in (2001) 29 *Philosophical Topics* 319; Ronald J Allen and Brian Leiter, 'Naturalized Epistemology and the Law of Evidence' (2001) 87 Virginia L Rev 1491. Cf Mike Redmayne, 'Rationality, Naturalism and Evidence Law' (2003) 4 Michigan State L Rev 849, which prompted a rejoiner: Ronald J Allen and Brian Leiter, 'Naturalized Epistemology and the Law of Evidence: Reply to Redmayne' (2003) 4 Michigan State L Rev 885.

[194] Goldman (n 48) 5; chapter 9 is especially relevant.

[195] Larry Laudan, *Truth, Error, and Criminal Law* (Cambridge: CUP, 2006) 2.

[196] ibid 2.

and the costs of conducting the search itself'.[197] Secondly, truth is pursued for the sake of justice, where justice is primarily understood as the correct application of law to true findings of fact. But against truth and justice must be balanced external values and concerns, typically dressed in the language of 'fairness', 'legitimacy', 'process rights' and 'integrity'.

4.2 Internal perspective of fact-finder as moral agent

The internal analyst adopts the point of view, not of an outside observer of the system as a whole but of a role-player within the system, the fact-finder whose conduct is being regulated by the rules of evidence examined in this monograph. Whereas the traditional, external, approach is outcome- or goal-oriented, the internal approach focuses on the responsibilities of the fact-finder which are attached to her role, and on the demands that the parties are entitled to make on the rationality and morality of her deliberation. Instead of assessing evidentiary rules functionally, as means of achieving specified ends, they are evaluated modally, as constituting features of a rational form of moral engagement between the court and the persons brought before it. This kind of evaluation is conceptual in nature and is founded on normative arguments; it is not contingent on the validity of empirical assumptions connecting means and ends.

To evaluate an evidential rule internally is to seek out its intrinsic value. When a rule has intrinsic value, it has that value, not in virtue of the consequences of its application, but independently of whatever impact its application may have on the decision outcome.[198] This does not mean that we ignore the effect of application altogether for, as Rawls points out, '[a]ll ethical doctrines worth our attention take consequences into account in judging rightness'.[199] What it does mean is that the rightness of a rule is not determined by the consequences that flow from its application but is inherent in the values it expresses. This is a departure from traditional discourse which tends to be dominated by prudential considerations and to concentrate on whether adherence to a particular rule will improve the reliability of the verdict or whether departure from it will increase the proportion of errors in fact-finding.

The general thesis of this study is that epistemic and ethical concerns pertaining to trial deliberation are reflected in the law of evidence. They are related to the claims the person facing a judgment has on the process by which her case is

[197] Richard A Posner, 'Clinical and Theoretical Approaches to the Teaching of Evidence and Trial Advocacy' (2003) 21 Quinnipiac L Rev 731, 737; for his economic views: *Frontiers of Legal Theory* (Cambridge, Massachusetts: Harvard UP, 2001) chs 11 and 12. Cost-efficiency is also stressed by Alex Stein in his analysis of evidence law: *Foundations of Evidence Law* (n 156), especially ch 5.

[198] Michael D Bayles, *Principles of Law—A Normative Analysis* (Dordrecht: D Reidel Publishing, 1987) 29.

[199] Rawls (n 5) 26.

judged and decided. Rules of evidence reflect our conception of justice in the activity of proof and in our tradition of fact-finding. *Pace* Perelman, who said that a challenge to the facts raises a question of truth and not of justice,[200] such a challenge does pose issues not only of truth but also of justice. The court must not only find truth in order to reach a just outcome, it must also do justice in the course of ascertaining the truth.

Various writers have cautioned against the tendency to explain and justify the law of evidence in strictly instrumental terms. They have argued persuasively that some evidential rules, principally those traditionally regarded as side-constraints on the main task of truth determination, are grounded in values that are intrinsic to the fairness, legitimacy, or integrity of the trial. The topics commonly chosen to make good this claim include the privilege against self-incrimination, restriction on the use of improperly obtained evidence, the right of silence, and legal professional privilege.[201] This study hopes to bring the argument to the heart of evidence law, to a selection of major 'mainstream' rules whose avowed purpose is to enhance accuracy.[202] It will be argued that even they cannot be adequately justified or explained consequentially, as rules meant to protect or promote the reliability of trial findings. They embody values that are intrinsic to both the rationality and justice of deliberation. Fact-finding cannot be described wholly in cognitive terms; the enterprise raises internal ethical issues. Infringement of certain evidential rules and standards, including those examined in this book, occasions injustice whether the outcome of the trial is correct or not.

[200] Chaim Perelman, 'Justice and Reasoning' in his *Law, Reason and Justice: Essays in Legal Philosophy*, edited by Graham Hughes (New York: New York University, 1969), reprinted in *Justice, Law and Argument—Essays on Moral and Legal Reasoning* (Dordrecht: D Reidel Publishing Co, 1980) 77.

[201] eg T R S Allan, *Constitutional Justice—A Liberal Theory of the Rule of Law* (Oxford: Oxford University Press, 2001) 77–87, 112–119, 271–277; 'The Concept of Fair Trial' in Elspeth Attwooll and David Goldberg (eds), *Criminal Justice, Archiv Fur Rechts-und Sozialphilosophie*, Beiheft 63 (Steiner Verlag, Franz Stuttgart: 1995); 'Fairness, Truth, and Silence: The Criminal Trial and the Judge's Exclusionary Discretion' in Hyman Gross and Ross Harrison (eds), *Jurisprudence: Cambridge Essays* (Oxford: Clarendon Press, 1992); I H Dennis, 'Reconstructing the Law of Criminal Evidence' [1989] Current Legal Problems 21; 'Instrumental Protection, Human Right or Functional Necessity? Reassessing the Privilege against Self-Incrimination' (1995) 54 CLJ 342, at 375–376, and 'Rectitude Rights and Legitimacy: Reassessing and Reforming The Privilege Against Self-Incrimination in English Law' (1997) 31 Israel L Rev 24; Andrew Ashworth, 'Exploring the Integrity Principle in Evidence and Procedure' in Peter Mirfield and Roger Smith (eds), *Essays for Colin Tapper* (London: LexisNexis, 2003) 107; H L Ho, 'Legal Professional Privilege and the Integrity of Legal Representation' (2006) 9 Legal Ethics 163. For general non-instrumental analysis of aspects of legal procedure, see eg: Duff, *Trials and Punishments* (n 85); T R S Allan, 'Procedural Fairness and the Duty of Respect' (1998) 18 OJLS 497; Gerry Maher, 'Natural Justice as Fairness' in Neil MacCormick and Peter Birks (eds), *The Legal Mind—Essays for Tony Honoré* (Oxford: Clarendon Press, 1986). Cf D J Galligan, *Due Process and Fair Procedures—A Study of Administrative Procedures* (Oxford: Clarendon Press, 1996), especially 78–82, 89–95, 137–140.

[202] They are, in Wigmore's terminology, 'rules of auxiliary tests and safeguards': John Henry Wigmore, *A Treatise on the Anglo-American System of Evidence in Trials at Common Law*, vol 1 (3rd edn, Boston: Little, Brown & Co, 1940) 296.

Conclusion

Four topics were addressed as preliminary matters to our study of the trial. The first topic was 'fact'. Its role in adjudication, its relation to law and value, and the classification of facts were discussed in Part 1. The second and third topics focused on the act of 'finding'. In one sense, a finding of fact is a speech act. As we saw in Part 2, it contains many illocutionary forces. In another sense, fact-finding is a deliberative process. It involves reasoning towards a conclusion, the verdict. Part 3 described the nature of trial deliberation and discussed the variety of techniques the law uses to control the process. Finally, Part 4 dealt with perspectives. Fact-finding can be approached from the outside and evaluated as a system of rules and legal structures. That is the dominant approach. But there is an alternative, one which cannot be ignored without overlooking important aspects of evidence law. The value and purpose of many rules, including those examined in the chapters to come, can be fully appreciated only from the internal point of view, that is, as seen through the eyes of the fact-finder. Discussion of these four topics set the stage for advancing the substantive arguments of this book. But first there is more groundwork to be done in Chapter 2.

2

Truth, Justice, and Justification

Introduction

For many, the trial is about ascertaining the truth. A significant number of others disagree; the basis of and motivation for their disagreement are unpacked in Part 1. Part 2 examines the claim that the trial is a search for the truth. But what does this mean? And why should the court go after the truth? The traditional answers are first examined. From an external standpoint, the relevant criterion is the correctness of the verdict. There is a contingent connection, to which terms like 'accuracy' and 'reliability' refer, between the outcome of fact-finding and truth. Truth is needed so that justice (in the sense associated with 'rectitude of decision') can be done. Part 2 offers different answers from the internal point of view. Here the focus is on the deliberative process. The central issues are questions of justification. Justification has two interdependent aspects: the epistemic and the ethical. The fact-finder has to consider, on the evidence, what to believe about the facts in dispute. She must also be concerned about the morality of the process by which she reaches her verdict. Deliberation must be conducted with justice, conceived as empathic care for the parties. As we will see later, the ethical demand of empathic care affects the epistemic standard that must be applied. In a sentence: it is not only the case that truth is needed to do justice; the court must do justice *in* finding the truth.

1 The Search for Truth

1.1 Opposing views

Commitment to the truth is manifested procedurally at a trial: jurors are sworn to give a true verdict according to the evidence and witnesses are sworn to tell the truth. The truth-seeking function also finds linguistic expression, most clearly in the use of words such as 'proof', 'fact', 'fact-finding', and 'proof of fact'. Ordinarily, to prove something is to show that it is true. In the past, lawyers took 'fact' to mean 'fact in issue'.[1] Nowadays, 'fact' tends to bring to mind what must

[1] Barbara J Shapiro, *A Culture of Fact—England, 1550–1720* (Ithaca, NY: Cornell UP, 2003) traces the history of the concept of fact in law and reports that initially, from as early as the

be done to give a disputed proposition that status: to prove something is to satisfy the trier that it is a fact, equivalently, that it is true. 'Fact-finding' is the exercise of finding the facts, a search for the truth.

Truth, according to Gellner, is the 'first and pre-eminent virtue'; 'anything must be true before it can significantly claim other merits'.[2] Many lawyers hold truth with the same esteem. It is declared by Cory J of the Supreme Court of Canada: 'The ultimate aim of any trial, criminal or civil, must be to seek and to ascertain the truth.'[3] In *Funk v United States*,[4] the United States Supreme Court proclaimed: 'The fundamental basis upon which all rules of evidence must rest—if they are to rest upon reason—is their adaptation to the successful development of the truth.' According to a statement made by Lord Dunedin in the House of Lords, evidence law 'is really nothing more than a set of practical rules which experience has shown to be best fitted to elicit the truth'.[5] In a revised volume of Wigmore's monumental treatise, it is claimed that not 'many...will take seriously the claim that the law of evidence...should have its predominant purpose something other than the search for truth'.[6]

Surely it cannot be gainsaid that the 'basic purpose of a trial is the determination of truth'.[7] And yet many eminent lawyers have begged to differ. Pollock considers it 'the greatest of all fallacies...that the business of a court of justice is to discover the truth'.[8] Maine observed that the 'theory of judicial evidence is constantly misstated or misconceived', that it 'is too often described as being that which it is its chief distinction not to be—that is, as an Organon, as a sort of contrivance for the discovery of truth.'[9] According to Morgan, 'a lawsuit is not...primarily a proceeding for the discovery of truth. It is essentially a proceeding for

sixteenth century, '"fact" in the legal context...did not mean an established truth but an alleged act whose occurrence was in contention' (ibid 11), and 'one of the great changes that occurred over the course of two centuries...was the transformation of "fact" from something that had to be sufficiently proved by appropriate evidence to be considered worthy of belief to something for which appropriate verification had already taken place' (ibid 31).

[2] Ernest Gellner, *Legitimation of Belief* (Cambridge: Cambridge University Press, 1974) 27.

[3] *R v Nikolovski* [1996] 3 SCR 1197, 1206, per Cory J. Similarly, L'Heureux-Dubé J stated in *R v Levogiannis* [1993] 4 SCR 475, 483 that the 'goal of the court process is truth seeking' and stressed in *R v Howard* [1989] 1 SCR 1337 at 1360 that one 'cannot over-emphasize the commitment of courts of justice to the ascertainment of the truth'.

[4] (1933) 290 US 371, 381. See also: *Evidence in Criminal Proceedings: Hearsay and Related Topics*, Consultation Paper No 138, vol 1 (London: HMSO, 1995) para 1.10 ('Rules of evidence have the function of defining the evidence a court may receive in order that it may elicit the truth in relation to any matter in dispute').

[5] *Thompson v R* [1918] AC 221, 226.

[6] Peter Tillers (reviser), *Wigmore on Evidence—A Treatise on the Anglo-American System of Evidence in Trials at Common Law*, vol 1A (Boston: Little, Brown & Co, 1983) 1019.

[7] *Tehan v United States ex rel Shott* (1966) 382 US 406, 416.

[8] Frederick Pollock, *Essays in the Law* (London: MacMillan & Co, 1922) 275.

[9] Henry Sumner Maine, *Village Communities in the East and West—with Other Lectures, Addresses, and Essays* (7th edn, London: John Murray, 1895) 302.

the orderly settlement of a dispute between the litigants.'[10] Lord Wilberforce held in *Air Canada & Ors v Secretary of State for Trade & Anor*[11] that 'the task of the court is to do, and be seen to be doing, justice between the parties... There is no higher or additional duty to ascertain some independent truth.'

How do we make sense of this disagreement? Each side has its case. However, the insights offered by writers of each camp are valid only from the perspective from which they speak and must be understood in the light of the values and concerns which motivate their assertions. Unpacking of the arguments will be done in Parts 2 and 3. The immediate task is to place out of contention three radical views.

1.2 Truth and polemics

Some of those who deny that the trial engages in a search for the truth adopt very controversial positions. Consider this statement:[12]

> [T]he jury is not designed to function as a truth-finder... [It] has a different function—it is meant to be a counterweight to the (supposed) rationality of the fact-finding process. Its purpose is to give the defendant an irrational second chance for an acquittal when an experienced, professional observer would not have a reasoned doubt of the defendant's guilt.

This sweeping dismissal of jurors as irrational is not credible unless it is backed up empirically. After all, anecdotal evidence seems to paint a different picture, suggesting that jurors by and large do take their fact-finding duty rather seriously.[13] The 'professional observer', whatever qualifications that title is supposed to carry, may not have all the evidence that the jury has been exposed to, may not get to see it in the same form as it was presented to them, and does not have to follow the judicial instructions given at the trial. In these circumstances, a difference in the conclusion reached by the jury and the 'professional observer' does not entail that one of them must be irrational. The charge of cognitive irrationality is perhaps directed at human reasoning in general. Studies supporting that charge, first brought to prominence by Kahneman and Tversky,[14] are well known but disputed by some writers.[15] Whatever general lesson one may draw from the

[10] Edmund M Morgan, 'Suggested Remedy For Obstructions to Expert Testimony by Rules of Evidence' (1942–43) 10 University of Chicago L Rev 285, 285. Also: Zechariah Chafee, Jr, Book Review of *A Treatise on the Anglo-American System of Evidence in Trials at Common Law (2nd ed) by John Henry Wigmore* (1924) 37 Harvard L Rev 513, 519.

[11] [1983] 2 AC 394, 438. Similarly, *Islip Pedigree Breeding Centre v Abercromby* 1959 SLT 161, 165.

[12] Thomas Weigend, 'Is the Criminal Process about Truth?: A German Perspective' (2003) 26 Harvard J of L and Public Policy 157, 167.

[13] eg Trevor Grove, *The Juryman's Tale* (London: Bloomsbury, 1998).

[14] Daniel Kahneman, Paul Slovic and Amos Tversky (eds), *Judgment Under Uncertainty: Heuristics and Biases* (Cambridge: Cambridge University Press, 1982) is a classic collection; for a more recent one: Thomas Gilovich, Dale Griffin and Daniel Kahneman, *Heuristics and Biases: The Psychology of Intuitive Judgement* (Cambridge: CUP, 2002).

[15] The most persistent critic is L Jonathan Cohen. His early salvo, 'On the Psychology of Prediction: Whose Is the Fallacy?' (1979) 7 *Cognition*, 385, prompted a reply, Daniel Kahneman

studies and the accompanying debate, nothing in that body of literature suggests a legal design to exploit the alleged cognitive incompetency. The claim that the jury was specifically created to allow criminals an easy escape route seems little more than a provocative postulation.

Denial of the trial's objective of ascertaining truth sometimes takes on a polemical tone, written perhaps with the intention to unsettle more than to inform. An apparent instance is the following:[16]

> Let no one pretend that our system of justice is a search for truth. It is nothing of the kind. It is a contest between two sides played according to certain rules, and if the truth happens to emerge as the result of the contest, then that is pure windfall.

Sometimes, we come to have reasons to believe that a person has been wrongly convicted or found liable. Such knowledge tends to evoke, as it did in the author of the above passage, the feeling that the trial system has failed us. But when we feel that way, it is precisely because we think the system has produced a verdict which does not hold up to its claim of being based on facts. We come to know that those propositions the court declared as true are actually not or we have reasons to doubt that they are. It must be granted for the reasons discussed in Part 2.1 that, in an important sense, 'counsel...are not inquirers; nor is [an adversarial trial] an inquiry into whether the defendant did it';[17] nevertheless, the purpose of trial deliberation *is* to figure out the truth. Polemical statements of the sort quoted above express disappointment at the perceived epistemic inefficacy of the trial system. But the disappointment is intelligible only if the trial has an epistemic function.

1.3 Truth and accessibility

More radical than the views discussed in the previous section is the claim that no trial, however structured, can ever find the truth. The latter view is aired in statements such as the following:[18]

> Since no evidence can provide more than a basis for inferences, which are by definition uncertain (by contrast to deductions, where conclusions follow with certainty from the premises), trials cannot discover absolute truth.

and Amos Tversky, 'On the Interpretation of Intuitive Probability: A Reply to Jonathan Cohen' (ibid 409). This led to a rejoinder, L Jonathan Cohen, 'Whose Is the Fallacy? A Rejoinder to Daniel Kahneman and Amos Tversky' (1980) 8 *Cognition* 89, and a further critique, L Jonathan Cohen, 'Can Human Irrationality be Experimentally Demonstrated' (1981) 4 *The Behavioral and Brain Sciences* 317.

[16] Ludovic Kennedy, *The Trial Of Stephen Ward* (Bath: Chivers Press, 1991) 251.

[17] Susan Haack, 'Confessions Of An Old-Fashioned Prig', in Susan Haack, *Manifesto Of A Passionate Moderate—Unfashionable Essays* (Chicago: Chicago UP, 1998) chs 1 and 13. The more critical observation is delivered in the next sentence, ibid: 'The jury *is*, however, trying to figure out whether the defendant's guilt is established to the required degree by the admissible evidence presented.'

[18] Note, 'The Theoretical Foundation of the Hearsay Rules' (1980) 93 Harvard L Rev 1786, 1787, n 6.

Findings of fact cannot be absolutely true if by that we mean that it is always logically possible that they might be false. Faced with a philosophical sceptic who sets an unusually high standard, I may be forced to concede that I do not know virtually everything that I can, in everyday life, justifiably claim to know. Yet, we are thoroughly familiar with 'commonsense' or 'everyday' certainties.[19] On the classical theory, 'knowledge must concern things that one cannot be wrong about' and demonstrative proof is required.[20] In contrast, the modern conception of knowledge is fallibilist in the sense that 'while we certainly take ourselves to know all sorts of things, and commit ourselves to defending our claims to knowledge', we recognize that we cannot rule out all possibilities of error.[21] In accepting, as we must, the possibility that we might be wrong, we thereby acknowledge the objectivity of truth.[22] The impossibility of establishing demonstrative proof in court is neither here nor there.

Scepticism may, alternatively, take a radical relativistic turn, with claims being made about there being no objective truth, merely constructions of truth from the perspectives of individuals.[23] 'Veriphobia' has been devastatingly criticized by accomplished writers such as Goldman and Haack.[24] It is only necessary to make some brief remarks here. That primary facts exist as external realities is a basic assumption that renders the purpose of a trial intelligible.[25] To take an objective view of primary facts is not to ignore the complex interdependency of fact and value, fact and law, discussed in Chapter 1, Part 1.2. Further, if we abandon the concept of objective truth, we may also have to surrender 'any claim to be able to talk of "mistakes" or "errors" or "miscarriages of justice" or "wrongful convictions"'.[26] Even if this is putting it overly strong,[27] it is difficult to see how the disavowal of objective truth would not at least diminish our ability to

[19] Distinguishing the absolute and commonsense certainties: Christopher Hookway, *Scepticism* (London: Routledge, 1990) 132–133.

[20] Michael Williams, *Problems of Knowledge—A Critical Introduction to Epistemology* (Oxford: OUP, 2001) 38.

[21] ibid 41.

[22] Michael P Lynch, *True to Life—Why Truth Matters* (Cambridge, Massachusetts: MIT Press, 2004) 10–11, 22.

[23] On the many kinds of relativism: Haack, 'Reflections on Relativism: From Momentous Tautology to Seductive Contradiction' in Haack (n 17) ch 9, 149–166.

[24] Alvin I Goldman, *Knowledge in a Social World* (Oxford: OUP, 1999) ch 1; Haack (n 17) ch 1. Taking a middle course, Simon Blackburn, *Truth—A Guide for the Perplexed* (London: Allen Lane, 2005) argues that there are both bad arguments that must be rejected and useful lessons to be drawn from the debate.

[25] Mirjan R Damaška, *Evidence Law Adrift* (New Haven: Yale University Press, 1997) 95, and 'Truth in Adjudication' (1998) 49 Hastings L J 289, 290, 296–301.

[26] William Twining, 'Hot Air in the Redwoods, a Sequel to the Wind in the Willows' (1988) 86 Michigan L Rev 1523, 1544, and 'Some Scepticism about Some Scepticism' in *Rethinking Evidence—Exploratory Essays* (2nd edn, Cambridge: CUP, 2006) 99. The former was a response to Kenneth W Graham, Jr, '"There'll Always Be An England": The Instrumental Ideology of Evidence' (1987) 85 Michigan L Rev 1204, 1211.

[27] As Nicolson argues: 'Truth, Reason and Justice: Epistemology and Politics in Evidence Discourse' (1994) 57 MLR 726, 729–734.

condemn conviction and punishment of the innocent with the force that does justice to the victim.[28]

Contrary to what the name suggests, the impossibility of discovering the (objective) truth is not the contention of 'fact-sceptics' like Jerome Frank.[29] Frank did not deny that the trial should aim at finding the truth; instead, he was very much concerned that it should, and advocated reforms to that end.[30] His writings on the subject were more iconoclastic than sceptical; he was especially keen to destroy the false images of certainty and predictability that shrouded fact-finding and to highlight the elements therein of subjectivity and chance. It was against complacency that he fought his battles. This 'sceptic' was a man of great faith and hope, as revealed, for instance, towards the end of his essay, provocatively entitled 'Facts are Guesses'. The 'defense of grave miscarriages of justice,' he wrote, 'is legitimate only if they are inevitable—that is, only if everything practical has been done to avoid such injustices'. Unfortunately, many cases of injustice were the result of 'needless defects in the court-house methods of getting at the facts'. These methods must be reformed. We should not, he stressed, 'demand perfection. Perfect justice lies beyond human reach. But the unattainability of the ideal is no excuse for shirking the effort to obtain the best available.'[31] To Frank, as to many others, the discovery of truth is an aspiration that gives the trial its direction and meaning.[32]

Analysis of legal fact-finding does not need to draw on any deep theory of truth.[33] It suffices to adopt the commonsense or classical view.[34] Something is true if and only if it corresponds to reality, has objective existence in the external

[28] See generally Daniel A Farber and Suzanna Sherry, *Beyond All Reason—The Radical Assault on Truth in American Law* (New York: Oxford University Press, 1997) ch 5, and on the point of unfairness to the victims, see especially ibid 96, 116, 117.

[29] Zenon Bankowski, 'The Value of Truth: Fact Scepticism Revisited' (1981) 1 LS 257, 260.

[30] Justice Douglas of the United States Supreme Court applauded Frank for the 'crusading spirit' with which he advocated 'sweeping changes to alleviate the deficiencies in the means by which we sort out the innocent from the guilty': foreword to Jerome Frank and Barbara Frank, *Not Guilty* (London: Panther, 1961) 7–8.

[31] Jerome Frank, *Courts on Trial—Myth and Reality in American Justice* (New Jersey: Princeton University Press, 1973 ed) 35–36; discussed in Twining, 'Some Scepticism about Some Scepticism' (n 26) 109–112.

[32] eg Twining, 'Hot Air in the Redwoods, a Sequel to the Wind in the Willows' (n 26) 1544; D J Galligan, *Due Process and Fair Procedures—A Study of Administrative Procedures* (Oxford: Clarendon Press, 1996) 5.

[33] Susan Haack, 'Truth, Truths, "Truth" and "Truths" in the Law' (2003) 26 Harvard J of L and Public Policy 17, 19: 'Crucial as they are to justice, the factual claims at issue in legal proceedings are usually straightforwardly true or else false, and should cause no special unease about truth or objectivity. If they sometimes do, perhaps it is the result in part of a confusion of what *is* true with what is *known* or *proven* to be true, and in part of immersion in the adversary system, which can give people the idea that there must always be two sides to every question, that it is arrogance to suppose that we can ever really know the truth, that there are always grounds for doubt, that all we can do is to give due consideration to rival "truths"...'

[34] To understand that inquiry is an attempt to discover the true answer to a question, 'no elaborately articulated theory of truth is needed': Susan Haack, 'Epistemology Legalized: Or, Truth, Justice and the American Way' (2004) 49 American J of Jurisprudence 43, 45.

world, independently of what we say or believe.[35] Aristotle puts it pithily: 'to say of what is not that it is not, or of what is that it is, is true'.[36] This study is interested in epistemological issues arising in the context of trial deliberation. Questions in epistemology are of belief and knowledge. They are different from metaphysical and ontological questions about existence and being, of what it is to be true.[37] A fact is true whether anyone believes it; and not everything we believe is true.

To say that the idea of correspondence is at the heart of the ordinary understanding of truth is not to say that it is or ought to be the general criterion according to which the court makes findings of fact. The statement that it is true that A killed B is perfectly intelligible as an assertion that, in reality, A did kill B; but how is the court to see that A really did kill B? It can scarcely be suggested that verification of correspondence be a general legal condition for accepting something as a fact. Many accounts of evidential reasoning are on offer. There are plenty of resources from which to draw in building an account that applies to trial deliberation; we may turn to theories based on ideas such as coherence,[38] plausibility,[39] 'foundherentism',[40] inference to the best explanation, and abductive reasoning.[41] All of these theories are compatible with the meaning of truth as correspondence.[42]

1.4 Truth and sincerity

The truth-seeking function of the trial faces challenge from another quarter, from the suggestion that the court should ensure, not so much that the verdict speaks the truth, but that the public believes that it does. This appears to be radical subtext of an argument made by Nesson in an article which is well-known amongst evidence scholars.[43] According to Nesson, the value of many rules of evidence

[35] This is the 'classical realist account of truth': Laurence Bonjour, *The Structure of Empirical Knowledge* (Cambridge, Massachusetts: Harvard University Press, 1985) 4.

[36] Quoted in Haack (n 34) 45.

[37] A D Woozley, *Theory of Knowledge—An Introduction* (London: Hutchinson's University Library, 1949) 133–134; John Searle, *Mind, Language and Society* (New York: Basic Books, 1998) 5.

[38] eg D N MacCormick, 'The Coherence of a Case and The Reasonableness of Doubt' (1980) 2 Liverpool L Rev 45; Dan Simon, 'A Third View of the Black Box: Cognitive Coherence in Legal Decision Making' (2004) 71 University of Chicago L Rev 511.

[39] Nicholas Rescher, *Plausible Reasoning—An Introduction to the Theory and Practice of Plausibilistic Inference* (Amsterdam: Van Gorcum, 1976); Douglas Walton, *Legal Argumentation and Evidence* (Pennsylvania: Pennsylvania State University Press, 2002) chs 4 and 6.

[40] Susan Haack, *Evidence and Inquiry* (Oxford: Blackwell, 1995) ch 4.

[41] John R Josephson and Susan G Josephson, *Abductive Inference—Computation, Philosophy, Technology* (Cambridge: Cambridge University Press, 1994) ch 1 and appendix B; John R Josephson, 'On the Proof Dynamics of Inference to the Best Explanation' (2001) 22 Cardozo L Rev 1621; David A Schum, 'Species of Abductive Reasoning in Fact Investigation in Law' (2001) 22 Cardozo L Rev 1645.

[42] Making this point, but more generally: John Searle (n 37) 32; Alfred Schutz, *Reflections on the Problem of Relevance* (New Haven: Yale University Press, 1970) 136.

[43] Charles Nesson, 'The Evidence or the Event? On Judicial Proof and the Acceptability of Verdicts' (1985) 98 Harvard L Rev 1357. He pursues this theme in a number of later articles: 'Reasonable Doubt and Permissive Inferences: The Value of Complexity' (1979) 92 Harvard L Rev

lies in procuring and preserving public acceptance of a positive verdict;[44] they protect the appearance of truth in the material propositions of fact on the basis of which the defendant is declared guilty or liable.

Public order is secured only when there is general compliance with the law. The trial, as 'a drama that the public attends and from which it assimilates behavioral messages',[45] should send the message that will best achieve that objective. It should preach: 'You did the thing enjoined by the law; therefore, you will pay the penalty,'[46] and not say: 'We will convict and punish you only if your violation is proved by due process of law.'[47] The former encourages people 'to conform [their] conduct to the behavioral norms embodied in the substantive law', whereas the latter 'invites people to act not according to what...is lawful, but according to what they think can be proved against them'.[48] Accordingly, the verdict should be represented 'not as a statement about the evidence presented at trial, but as a statement about...what happened'.[49] The general thrust of Nesson's argument seems to be this: the more it generally seems that fact-finding is accurate and law enforcement is effective, the more the public will follow the law. There is thus a strong social interest in creating an image of certainty in the application of legal norms.

Take, for instance, Nesson's discussion on the hearsay doctrine. Requiring the original source of evidence to stand as a witness gives citizens who are not at the trial a reason for thinking that the court has greater access to the truth than they have. This, in turn, may persuade them to defer to its judgment.[50] But it may also have the opposite effect. Hearsay evidence is generally considered to be relevant. The public may be less inclined to accept the verdict if they see that the court did not take relevant evidence into account. The better view, according to Nesson, is that the hearsay law reflects 'the legal system's concern for the *continuing* acceptance of the verdict'.[51] Its long-term stability is protected by preventing 'jurors from basing a verdict on the statement of an out-of-court declarant who might later recant the statement and discredit the verdict. Cross-examination of a declarant

1187, 1195; 'Agent Orange Meets the Blue Bus: Fact-finding at the Frontier of Knowledge' (1986) 66 Boston University L Rev 521, 532; 'Constitutional Hearsay: Requiring Foundational Testing and Corroboration Under the Confrontation Clause' (1995) 81 Virginia L Rev 149. Nesson's thesis is applied by Carl F Carnor, 'Daubert and the Acceptability of Legal Decisions' (2005) 5 J of Philosophy, Science and Law, available at: <www.psljournal. com/archives/all/cranor.cfm>.

[44] A similar point was made by Henry Hart and John T McNaughton, 'Some Aspects of Evidence and Inference in the Law' in Daniel Lerner (ed), *Evidence and Inference* (Illinois: The Free Press, 1958) 48, 52–53.

[45] Nesson, 'The Evidence or the Event? On Judicial Proof and the Acceptability of Verdicts' (n 43) 1360.

[46] ibid.

[47] ibid.

[48] ibid.

[49] ibid 1358.

[50] ibid 1372–1373.

[51] ibid 1373. Original emphasis.

minimizes the risk that a verdict will be undercut by ensuring that the declarant cannot easily recant his statement.'[52] Various exceptions to the exclusionary rule can, he suggests, be explained in the same way. For example, it is doubtful that dying declarations are inherently reliable. The better explanation for admitting them is that they 'pose little risk of destabilizing the judgment. There is virtually no chance that the declarant will later come forward to discredit a verdict based on his statement.'[53] This comes dangerously close to prioritizing the concealment of error above the discovery of truth.

Issues can be taken, as a number of writers have done, with various assumptions Nesson makes in his argument.[54] But there is a more fundamental objection. Recognizing how radical his proposal was, he made these contemplative remarks in his conclusion:[55]

> [S]hould the search for truth ever be compromised to enhance the acceptability of verdicts and thus the power of the law's substantive message? Should the appearance of justice ever be more important than actual justice? These questions are difficult to approach, much less to answer... To argue that the search for truth may be compromised in order to enhance the power of the law's substantive message is to force us to confront an unsettling choice and to make an argument that is in some sense inherently unsatisfying.

Nesson adopts an external standpoint. He takes de facto public acceptance of the truthfulness of trial verdicts as a condition that facilitates stable and effective governance. So far as this statement goes, it must be correct. But it does not go very far. Overlooked are the rightful expectations and demands of citizens. The government lacks good faith, is worthy of neither respect nor allegiance, if it cares more about appearing to speak to the people truthfully than to actually do so. While it will take an elaborate argument to show how truthfulness is 'built intrinsically into the relations between the government and the people', the claim is perfectly uncontroversial that liberal democracy is founded to some extent on a relationship of trust between the two.[56] The policy for which Nesson has sympathy would appear to endorse, even promote, that breach of trust.

There is a critical difference between the *acceptability* of a verdict and its *acceptance*, corresponding to the difference between 'legitimacy' in the normative sense

[52] ibid.

[53] ibid 1374.

[54] eg Ronald J Allen, 'Rationality, Mythology, and the "Acceptability of Verdicts" Thesis' (1986) 66 Boston L Rev 541; Neil B Cohen, 'The Costs of Acceptability: Blue Buses, Agent Orange, and Aversion to Statistical Evidence' (1986) 66 Boston L Rev 563; Roger C Park, 'The Hearsay Rule and the Stability of Verdicts: A Response to Professor Nesson' (1986) 70 Minnesota L Rev 1057.

[55] Nesson, 'The Evidence or the Event? On Judicial Proof and the Acceptability of Verdicts' (n 43) 1391.

[56] Bernard Williams, *Truth and Truthfulness: An Essay in Genealogy* (Princeton: Princeton UP, 2002) 210. He suggests that the pursuit of truth in the political sphere is ultimately aimed at 'destroying representations that have the effect of keeping people' in situations where they are 'in the unrecognized power of another' (ibid at 231). Lynch (n 22) ch 10 offers a briefer defence of the value of truth in liberal democracy.

according to which the legitimacy of a judicial decision 'provides a prima facie moral obligation for citizens to obey' it, and 'legitimation' in the sociological, Weberian sense, which 'asks a causal question about how the legal system induces belief in its authority and compliance with its laws'.[57] Acceptance denotes a social fact. Acceptability, on the other hand, is a normative claim that must be backed by good argument.[58] The focus of Nesson's analysis is the public acceptance of verdicts. But it is far more important that verdicts be truly acceptable. It is intrinsically unjust to find a person liable or guilty when she is not. We want the court to be genuine in its quest for truth, and to do justice to the persons whose case is before it. A court that worries more about having its mistakes uncovered has lost sight of its first duties.

De facto public acceptance of trial verdicts should not be treated as an end in itself, however much procurement of such acceptance may serve the interests of government. After their conviction, the Birmingham Six brought a civil action against the police for assault. The same allegations about the assault had been made but were dismissed at a *voir dire* by the judge presiding at the criminal trial. In the Court of Appeal, Lord Denning held that the civil action should be stopped. These were some factors that influenced his decision:[59]

> If the six men win, it will mean that the police were guilty of perjury, that they were guilty of violence and threats, that the confessions were involuntary and were improperly admitted in evidence, and that the convictions were erroneous. That would mean that the Home Secretary would have either to recommend they be pardoned or he would have to remit the case to the Court of Appeal... This is such an appalling vista that every sensible person in the land would say: 'It cannot be right that these actions should go any further.'

Whatever Lord Denning might have meant to say, it best illustrates our point to give the passage an uncharitable interpretation: 'Suspicion about the truth of the allegations should not be pursued lest it casts doubt on the justice of the convictions. It might uncover facts which undermine public trust in the criminal justice system, and it is all important to avoid the serious and undesirable repercussions that would follow the collapse of confidence in the judiciary.' It is easier to fall into such thoughts if one goes along with the subtext of Nesson's message that securing public acceptance of verdicts is the primary aim. The danger is that it may blind us to the need to dispense individual justice.[60] Political strategizing is no business of the trial court. Its primary concern must be the acceptability of the verdict it delivers.

[57] Ken Kress, 'Legal Indeterminacy' (1989) 77 California L Rev 283, 285.

[58] Ota Weinberger, 'Legal Validity, Acceptance of Law, Legitimacy. Some Critical Comments and Constructive Proposals' (1999) 12 Ratio Juris 336, 346.

[59] *McIlkenny v Chief Constable of West Midlands Police Force* [1980] 1 QB 283, 323.

[60] Note (n 18) 1814.

By projecting ourselves into the place of the fact-finder, we see an entirely different picture from the one that we have been discussing. The juror does not see herself as an accomplice in some manipulative scheme of public relation. Some quick comments will do at this juncture to sketch roughly the arguments to come; elaboration, refinements, and qualifications will be made in Chapter 4. A positive finding asserts its propositional content. To find positively that p is to assert that p. When a person makes an assertion, she invites others to take her word for it, with the implicit assurance that she can be trusted. She thereby makes herself responsible for the truth of what she tells us. That responsibility is especially great in the context of legal fact-finding. The fact-finder has sworn to give a true verdict according to the evidence. She is well aware of the gravity of the verdict and of the consequences for others. Responsibility for the truth calls for the exercise of due effort and care in the evaluation of evidence. The fact-finder must conscientiously satisfy herself of the presence of good enough justification for believing a disputed proposition. Briefly, where she finds positively that p without judging that one is justified in believing that p, she tells a lie or, at least, has conveyed a misrepresentation.

2 External Analysis

We have examined three positions which either reject or under-prioritize truth-finding as the purpose of the trial. Each lacks merit. But much more is said by others in support of their claim that the trial is not a search for the truth. And, unlike those whose views were just criticized, they have a case. But so do those who apparently take an opposite view. This part attempts to unpack the debate from the external and internal perspectives introduced in Chapter 1. As we will see, there is much talking past each other.

2.1 Impediments to the search for truth

Opposition to the claim that the ascertainment of truth is a primary purpose of the trial is sometimes targeted at features of the adversarial system. On this reading, disavowal of the truth-seeking function is not as subversive as the positions reviewed in Part 1. It is pointed out that the fact-finder in an adversarial trial has a passive role. She has neither duty nor power to 'enter into an investigation of [her] own'.[61] It is up to the parties to procure evidence, to decide what part of it to adduce before the court, and how to present it. When it is unclear on the proffered evidence where the truth lies, it is generally outside the power of the fact-finder to search, or to direct others to search, for further evidence that would clear

[61] R W Fox, *Justice in the Twenty-First Century* (London: Cavendish Publishing, 2000) 10. See also Frederick Pollock, *Essays in the Law* (London: MacMillan & Co, 1922) 275.

her doubt. The parties are also responsible for the formulation of their respective cases. They control the pleadings and hence the scope of their dispute: 'litigants are sovereign in determining what is in issue between them'.[62] 'The event that underlies the cause of action is therefore not examined from all factual aspects that are material in terms of substantive law.'[63] The fact-finder has only to hear the submissions and evidence presented by both sides, and to answer such specific questions of fact as are properly put before her. The court is not interested in the 'whole truth' because:[64]

> Facts which are neither stipulated nor alleged and proved, and facts which remain undisclosed... do not exist as far as the judge is concerned, who aims at establishing only that relative truth which is attainable within the limits set by the procedural acts of the parties.

The fact-finder may not get to hear relevant evidence because it is inadmissible[65] or because the witness, for one reason or another, cannot be brought before the court on the day of the trial.[66] Crucial evidence may be withheld for strategic reasons, or it may simply be unprocurable, or 'the truth may lie with witnesses whom neither side is prepared to lead'.[67] The objective of each adversary is to win the courtroom struggle, for the sake of which tactics are often employed 'that distort or suppress the truth, for example, concealing relevant witnesses, withholding information that would help the other side, preparing witnesses to affect their testimony at trial (coaching), and engaging in abusive cross-examination'.[68]

[62] Damaška, 'Truth in Adjudication' (n 25) 304. It follows that, at an adversarial trial, a case cannot be disposed on a point that was not pleaded: eg *Yew Wan Leong v Lai Kok Chye* [1990] 2 Malayan LJ 152 (decision of the Malaysian Supreme Court).

[63] Damaška, 'Truth in Adjudication' (n 25) 304. A related point is made by H L A Hart, 'The Ascription of Responsibility and Rights' in A G N Flew (ed), *Essays on Logic and Language* (Oxford: Blackwell, 1951) 145, 155: 'the Judge's function is... in a case of contract to say whether there is or is not a valid contract, upon the claims and defences actually made and pleaded before him and the facts brought to his attention, and not on those which might have been made or pleaded. It is not his function to give an ideally correct legal interpretation of the facts, and if a party... through bad advice or other causes fails to make a claim or plead a defence which he might have successfully made or pleaded, the judge in deciding in such a case, upon the claims and defences actually made, that a valid contract exists has given the right decision.'

[64] Max Rheinstein, *Max Weber on Law in Economy and Society* (Cambridge, Massachusetts: Harvard University Press, 1954) 228.

[65] Weigend (n 12) 168: '[Exclusionary rules] limit the pool of (relevant) information available to the decision-maker and thus reduce the chances that the verdict will be based upon a completely "true" finding of facts.'

[66] ibid 160: 'Because the [adversarial] system excludes from the court's view everything that cannot be introduced as evidence on the day set for the trial, the "truth" is based only on the relatively small array of material then available, and valuable information will be ignored because one or both parties cannot present it at the right time in the legally prescribed manner. The adversarial system, at least in the form practiced in the Anglo-American world, therefore does not lead to the discovery of "true" truth but of an artificially generated set of facts euphemistically called "procedural truth".'

[67] *Islip Pedigree Breeding Centre v Abercromby* 1959 SLT 161, 165; this was the situation in *Alrich Development Pte Ltd v Jumabhoy* [1994] 3 SLR 1.

[68] John H Langbein, *The Origins of Adversary Criminal Trial* (Oxford: OUP, 2003) 1.

One party may for whatever reason choose not to challenge an allegation made by his opponent, indeed, even if she knows it to be false. Where an allegation is uncontested, the fact-finder must render her verdict on the assumption that it is true.[69] In an adversarial system, the judge's role is not unlike that of 'a referee in a football match'; she 'is not expected to take positive steps to ensure that truth and justice prevail' but only to see that the trial is 'fairly conducted'.[70] For Summers, 'the judicial proceeding may be characterized less as a search for substantive truth than as a search for a definite winner'.[71]

Some of these claims are exaggerated. For instance, not all exclusionary rules obviously undermine the accuracy of fact-finding. Many of these rules profess to exclude evidence on grounds of unreliability. It is true that unreliability is often not the only objection. For example, the inadmissibility of evidence obtained by torture is defensible as an expression of abhorrence for such conduct; still, unreliability is a concomitant reason for the exclusion.[72] Admittedly, not all exclusionary rules are based on the concern about unreliability,[73] and exclusionary rules that are based on this concern sometimes throw out evidence which is actually reliable.

Exaggerated or not, the critics' claims add up to a compelling case. Both defenders and critics of the adversarial system[74] typically adopt the standpoint of the system engineer: they attend to the structural features of the trial, observe the distribution of powers and duties within the process, and dispute over matters such as the debilitating effect of certain features on the discovery of truth. Many aspects of the adversarial system are apparently truth-obstructing; whether the degree of truth-obstruction can nonetheless be justified and whether the system ought to be re-engineered to make it less adversarial are separate questions. The external viewpoint is undoubtedly an enlightening one; it shows that, at the systemic level, there are difficulties in claiming that the trial, in its adversarial form, aims at truth.

[69] David P Derham, 'Truth and the Common Law Judicial Process' (1963) 5 Malaya L Rev 338, at 344–349; Louis Waller (ed), *Derham, Maher and Waller, An Introduction to Law* (7th edn Sydney: LBC Information Services, 1995) ch 10.

[70] A W Brian Simpson, general introduction to John H Langbein, *The Origins of Adversary Criminal Trial* (Oxford: OUP, 2003) v.

[71] Robert S Summers, 'Formal Legal Truth and Substantive Truth in Judicial Fact-Finding—Their Justified Divergence in Some Particular Cases' (1999) 18 Law and Philosophy 497, 506.

[72] Goldman (n 24) 31, citing the historical study by John H Langbein, *Torture and the Law of Proof* (Chicago: Chicago University Press, 1977).

[73] Guido Calabresi, 'The Exclusionary Rule' (2003) 26 Harvard J of Law and Public Policy 111 at 111 (noting that the law sometimes excludes 'evidence whose validity or "truthfulness" is unaffected or actually increased as a result of how it was gathered' because 'the method of obtaining the evidence ostensibly violates constitutional or other legal commands').

[74] The literature they have generated is vast. For a much cited debate: Marvin E Frankel, 'The Search For Truth: An Umpireal View' (1975) 123 University of Pennsylvania L Rev 1031; Monroe H Freedman, 'Judge Frankel's Search for Truth', ibid 1060; H Richard Uviller, 'The Advocate, the Truth, and Judicial Hackles: A Reaction to Judge Frankel's Idea', ibid at 1067. For a book-length treatment: William T Pizzi, *Trials without Truth* (NY: NYU Press, 1999).

However, not all significant aspects of the trial can be seen from the external perspective. A different and important picture emerges when one takes the fact-finder's point of view. A juror is neither party nor privy to truth-obstructing tactics and manoeuvres. Even if the adversarial features highlighted above show the system to be half-hearted in its pursuit of the truth, the fact-finder is committed to that pursuit.[75] When all the evidence is in and all has been said, she must decide the case. Her duty then is to deliver a true verdict according to the evidence. Broadly speaking, trial deliberation aims at true findings that can be justified on the evidence.

Against this contention, one might argue that the trier of fact does not need to know where the truth lies in order to decide on a question of fact. In a criminal case, she must enter an acquittal so long as she is in reasonable doubt about the guilt of the accused. At a civil trial, she must give judgment against a party so long as that party fails to discharge his burden of proof.[76] To be in doubt, or to be unpersuaded, that an allegation is true is not to know that it is false.[77] But these observations apply only to a negative finding or verdict. Chapter 3, Part 1.3 takes the position, roughly stated for now, that the fact-finder is justified in giving a positive finding or verdict only if one is justified in believing the truth of its propositional content. We care about justification for belief because we care about the truth.[78] The internal analysis focuses on justification.

2.2 Inadequacy of procedural justice

Verdicts might well be shown to be false by evidence which was not brought before the court. This possibility led Lord Wilberforce to hold in *Air Canada & Ors v Secretary of State for Trade*[79] that so long as the court makes its findings 'in accordance with the available evidence and the law, justice will have been fairly done'. We can demand from the court the fair dispensation of justice; but we misunderstand the purpose and nature of the trial if we expect it to produce the objective truth. On this view, truth is not essential for justice. Or, as Viscount Kilmuir puts it, 'justice comes before truth'.[80]

Lord Wilberforce and Viscount Kilmuir seem to equate justice with fair process. This is a construal of justice that judges, conscious of the fallibility of legal

[75] Haack (n 17) ch 1, 13.

[76] This is the basis for the assertion in J D Heydon (ed), *Cross on Evidence* (5th Australian edn, Sydney: Butterworths, 1996) 239 that: 'It is plainly wrong to tell the jury—even in a civil case, but certainly in a criminal one—that it is for them to decide where the truth lies.' Similarly, but confining himself to the civil context: Damaška, 'Truth in Adjudication' (n 25) 304.

[77] *Hickman v Peacey* [1945] AC 304, 318; Viscount Kilmuir, 'Introduction, The Migration of the Common Law' (1960) 76 LQR 41, 42–3.

[78] Lynch (n 22) 26.

[79] [1983] 2 AC 394, 438.

[80] (1960) 76 LQR 41, 43.

fact-finding, and anxious not to attract undue criticisms, are especially keen to spread. Lord Devlin joined the two judges in spreading the message:[81]

> Provided that he has been given a fair trial and that the judge has been seen to be careful and impartial, a plaintiff who has been wrongly disbelieved, painful though it may be, ought not to feel that he has been the victim of injustice.

But surely the plaintiff (and, all the more so, a defendant who has been convicted of a crime she did not commit) has every right to feel aggrieved.[82] The trial is not a system of pure procedural justice;[83] the justice of the verdict must be judged, in part, by a criterion independent of the procedure. A party is unjustly treated if and when the court withholds from her substantive entitlements under the law, however unintentional the error;[84] and generally worse is the plight of the innocent who has been wrongly convicted. That someone has had a fair trial may justify our insistence that she accepts an adverse verdict in the absence of reason to doubt the court's findings. But we are not entitled to maintain that stance towards her once we realize that some crucial part of the material findings was false; we now have to acknowledge that there was a miscarriage of justice. A refusal to acknowledge this is not totally callous, for one may still have sympathy for the party. This sentiment, however, is not essentially different from the sort one would feel for the sufferer of some natural disaster which is free of human causation. The person against whom a verdict is wrongly given is the victim of an injustice; it misses an essential force of her grievance to dismiss her plight as a mere misfortune.[85] The harm she has suffered was intentionally inflicted through a chain of human agency that includes the decision to find her guilty or liable. That decision is wrong whenever it is based on a material falsehood. Truth is, in

[81] Lord Devlin, 'Who is at Fault When Injustice Occurs?' in Lord Devlin *et al*, *What's Wrong with the Law?* (London: BBC, 1970) 71. Echoing a similar view: Blackburn (n 24) 30.

[82] George Schedler, 'Can Retributivists Support Legal Punishment' (1980) 63 *The Monist* 51, 191: 'If human systems of punishment could be said to be just merely because they have various procedural safeguards in them, then those who are worst off under them would still have to admit that justice had been done. But it would be ludicrous, for example, to try to convince a woman who had been imprisoned for a crime she did not commit that such a theory has plausibility.' Likewise, David M Paciocco, 'Balancing the Rights of the Individual and Society in Matters of Truth and Proof: Part II—Evidence about Innocence' (2002) 81 Canadian Bar Review 39, 44 writes: 'When we recognize a wrongful conviction we, quite rightly, consider it to be an inexcusable tragedy. It is no answer to the factually innocent to say, "Well. Even though you are factually innocent it is fair to leave you convicted because the law was applied with perfection during your trial."'

[83] cf Weigend (n 12) 168: 'In adversarial systems, truth is ultimately a procedural concept... To the extent that substantive truth is regarded as elusive, the fairness of proceedings becomes the main foundation of the verdict's legitimacy, and any result that has been found in conformity with procedural rules becomes acceptable.'

[84] Making this point in the criminal context: R A Duff, *Trials and Punishments* (Cambridge: Cambridge University Press, 1986) 107–108; John Rawls, *A Theory of Justice* (revised edn, Oxford: Oxford University Press, 1999) 75.

[85] While the difference between an injustice and a misfortune is commonly recognized, they cannot be separated by 'a simple and stable rule': Judith N Shklar, *Faces of Injustice* (New Haven: Yale UP, 1990) 2.

the sense to be explained in Chapter 3, Part 1.4, the standard of correctness for a positive verdict. Lord Wilberforce and company would, one suspects, in substance agree with this. When they chose to speak differently, to equate justice with fair process, it was with an agenda: to stress, quite rightly, that the court is not necessarily to be blamed whenever a verdict turns out to be an error.

2.3 Truth as aspiration: accuracy and reliability

Many critics of the adversarial system urge for reform to remove or mitigate its truth-obstructing features. In making that call, they are endorsing rather than disputing the truth-seeking function of the trial since their complaint is that the trial system is not, in this regard, as effective as it should be. The critics typically take an outsider perspective. Their evaluation is outcome-oriented, with the focus on the capacity of the system to get the facts right. Since the trial is structured by rules of evidence, those rules are assessed according to their impact on that capacity. Fact-finding, we are told, should strive for 'accuracy'.[86] Morgan, for instance, suggests that the court should try to get 'as close an approximation of the truth as is possible'.[87] This is a puzzling statement. The suggestion makes sense if we are, say, trying to judge how old or heavy a person is. 'Accuracy' is a measure of proximity to the truth. The closer the estimate is to the real age or weight, the nearer it approaches correctness. But a positive finding by the court carries a categorical assertion. It is not an estimate. It is either true or false. As Hoernlé puts it (in a different context):[88] 'If falsity means simply exclusion from, or incompatibility with, an objective order, then a miss, as the proverb has it, is as good as a mile—or, rather, it is as bad.' I am not guilty of murder if I did not kill the victim, however close I came to finishing him off.

The reference to 'accuracy' when speaking of a finding of fact must be to the likelihood of its truth, and not how close it is to the truth. If this is right, we would arguably do better to speak of 'reliability' instead. On the other hand, 'accuracy' seems to convey better than 'reliability' the idea that uncovering the actual facts is the goal. A person is praised for being reliable, not accurate, when she is trusted to get the job done. Reliability implies functional efficacy. It has a wider usage than the word 'accuracy'. Accuracy is linked specifically to truth. The insistence on accuracy renders salient the truth-seeking function of the trial; perhaps this is

[86] eg Ronald Dworkin, 'Principle, Policy, Procedure' in *A Matter of Principle* (Cambridge, Massachusetts: Harvard University Press, 1985) ch 3.

[87] Edmund M Morgan, 'Hearsay Dangers and the Application of the Hearsay Concept' (1948) 62 Harvard L Rev 177, at 184–185. Similarly, Jack B Weinstein, 'Alternatives to Hearsay Rules' (1968) 44 FDR 375, 376 ('what we are trying to do at a trial is to get as close an approximation to the truth as practicable'), and 'Some Difficulties in Devising Rules for Determining Truth in Judicial Trials' (1966) 66 Columbia L Rev 223, 242: speaks of the 'approximation of the facts'. Also Weigend (n 12) 163: speaks of the trial process seeking 'closest approximation to the truth'.

[88] R F Alfred Hoernlé, 'Notes on Professor J S Mackenzie's Theory of Belief, Judgment and Knowledge' (1918) 27 *The Philosophical Review* 513, 515.

why 'accuracy', despite the apparent inappropriateness, is commonly used as an evaluative criterion.

A verdict is more or less reliable depending on the reliability of the trial system which produced it. In assessing the latter, a wide array of systemic features may fall under scrutiny, including institutional allocation of the fact-finding role (the principal question being whether to assign it to the judge or the jury), forms of evidential reasoning (which is controlled by legal rules), and trial procedure (dealing, for example, with permissible approaches to and scope of witness examination). The greater our confidence in the reliability of a trial system, given the features which it has, the greater our confidence in the reliability of the verdicts it produces. In theory, the reliability of the system can be determined inductively by investigating the ratio of correct findings to mistaken ones in a random sample of cases; this is, as Lord Devlin puts it, to look at the 'percentage of error'.[89] The results of this kind of study give an estimate of the trial system's propensity to produce the correct outcome. How good an estimate it is will depend partly on how large the number of cases that were investigated. But this approach cannot work unless it is possible to implement an independent method of investigating and verifying the correctness of findings in the sample cases. The practical possibility of devising such a method is highly doubtful; as Diamond observes, 'we cannot compare... verdict with some gold standard of truth because no such dependable standard exists'.[90]

As is suggested in Part 3 below, the concern about reliability translates into a different set of questions on the internal analysis. We can ask of a particular verdict whether it could be justified on the evidence presented at the trial. More than that, the actual reasoning by which the fact-finder reached her verdict, if disclosed, can be judged for its epistemic soundness. Even if the actual reasoning is not disclosed, it is still entirely meaningful to step into the shoes of the fact-finder and assess the justification that is provided by the evidence for the verdict. Here, the question is not whether the verdict could be justified but whether, to one's mind, the verdict is justified by the evidence.

Of first importance to the system engineer is that 'trial and appellate process are designed to reduce to the minimum the occasions when a person is convicted

[89] Devlin (n 81) 76.

[90] Shari Seidman Diamond, 'Truth, Justice, and the Jury' (2003) 26 Harvard J of L and Public Policy 143 at 150. Cf Goldman (n 24) 291–292. See also Bruce D Spencer, 'Estimating the Accuracy of Jury Verdicts' (2007) 4 J of Empirical Legal Studies 305, providing a technical statistical estimate of error rate in jury cases based on the rate at which judges would agree with the outcomes. However, as Lawrence Solum observed of a follow-up paper by Spencer: '[I]mpartial observers without independent knowledge of the underlying facts (unfiltered by the trial) have no basis for determining whether the process actually results in correct outcomes. Measuring correctness always requires an independent and neutral factual investigation—something that is missing from this data.' (Remark made on 29 June 2007 in his blog: <http://lsolum.typepad.com/legaltheory/2007/06/spencer-on-wron.html>.)

of a crime which he did not commit'.[91] It is thought that the reliability of the trial system, in this quantitative sense, can be improved by putting more resources into the administration of justice. But there is no escaping from the economic truism that resources are scarce and there are competing demands on them. Society cannot afford the 'most accurate' procedure possible (what would that be?) and must settle for less.[92] Our commitment to getting the truth, so it is urged, goes only so far as the level of reliability that we are able to afford. This view is perfectly reasonable. However, it carries the risk that the ascertainment of truth may come to be seen only as an ideal, in theory dispensable under the weight of competing social interests.

There is a crucial sense in which getting at the truth is not merely an aspiration but a positive requirement in fact-finding. Looking at the task from the fact-finder's perspective, her job is to figure out the truth. Subject to the qualifications and refinements that are made in Chapter 3, she is justified in returning a positive verdict only if she judges that one is justified in believing, on the evidence proffered in court, that the material propositions supporting the verdict are true. This principle expresses a commitment to truthfulness that is binding on the fact-finder. Further, truth is the standard of correctness for a positive finding; the standard is absolute in the sense that the finding is wrong whenever and just because it is false.

2.4 Justice as rectitude

On the external approach, truth is desired, but not for its own sake; it is so that 'justice' may be done. The reference to 'justice' in this context is traditionally to a conception of it that is often called 'justice as rectitude'; this conception is diametrical to the view discussed above of justice as procedural fairness. 'The law cannot say, "Heads I win, tails you lose".'[93] Cases must be decided on merits, and the merits, if any, are to be found in the facts. A distinctive feature of the modern form of legal adjudication is its foundation in rules and facts.[94] Arguably, every legal rule posits, or can be stated in terms of, general facts.[95] A claim deserves to

[91] *R (Mullen) v Home Secretary* [2002] EWCA Civ 1882, para 33; [2003] QB 993, 1005, per Schiemann LJ.

[92] If nothing else, there must be limits to the scope of enquiry: *Attorney-General v Hitchcock* (1847) 1 Exch 91, 105. See also R W Fox, 'Expediency and Truth-Finding in the Modern Law of Evidence' in Enid Campbell and Louis Waller (eds), *Well and Truly Tried—Essays on Evidence in Honour of Sir Richard Eggleston* (Sydney: Law Book Co, 1982) 175; Alfred Bucknill, *The Nature of Evidence* (London: Skeffington, 1953) 70, 76–77.

[93] *Re A (Children) (Conjoined Twins: Surgical Separation)* [2001] Fam 147, 203. But this option is perhaps not as absurd as it seems: Neil Duxbury, *Random Justice—On Legal Lotteries and Legal Decision-Making* (Oxford: Clarendon Press, 1999) especially ch 5.

[94] Chapter 1, Part 1.1.

[95] Or 'type-facts', as Radin calls them: "Ex Facto Ius: Ex Iure Factum", chapter XXVIII in Paul Sayre (ed), *Interpretations of Modern Legal Philosophies—Essays in Honour of Roscoe Pound* (New York: Oxford University Press, 1947) 585.

succeed under a legal rule only if its factual predicate or antecedent is instantiated. The facts necessary to support the claim, if disputed, must be proved. For example, if the legal rule is that the first in time prevails, the claimant, to succeed in his claim on a property, must prove that she was in possession of it before her opponent. Justice, in the sense of giving a person her due under substantive law, is contingent on the material facts obtaining: a verdict for the claimant is just only if the court has got it right in finding that the claimant had prior possession. As Lord Denning wrote, the object of the trial judge 'above all, is to find out the truth, and to do justice according to law'.[96] Doing justice, in this narrow sense, is applying substantive law correctly to true findings of facts. This is the basic idea in Bentham's conception of the ultimate end of procedure which he called 'rectitude of decision'.[97] Conceiving justice as rectitude locates justice outside of fact-finding, a point neatly encapsulated in Perelman's statement: 'If the challenge is to the facts that are alleged, then we are concerned with truth and not with justice.'[98]

2.5 Truth as primary, but not absolute, goal

The claim, it should be noted, is that a primary aim of the trial is the ascertainment of truth. One who makes this claim may yet acknowledge, if not insist, that other values (those 'external to proof'[99] or, as it is sometimes called, 'collateral

[96] *Jones v National Coal Board* [1957] 2 QB 55, 63. And again, *Harmony Shipping v Davis* [1979] 3 All ER 177, 180–181.

[97] On this concept: William Twining, *Theories of Evidence: Bentham and Wigmore* (London: Weidenfeld & Nicholson, 1985) 88 *et seq*; and on its wide acceptance as the primary objective of the trial: William Twining, 'The Rationalist Tradition of Evidence Scholarship' in *Rethinking Evidence—Exploratory Essays* (2nd edn, Cambridge: CUP, 2006) 35.

[98] Chaim Perelman, 'Justice and Reasoning' in his *Law, Reason and Justice: Essays in Legal Philosophy*, edited by Graham Hughes (New York University, 1969), reprinted in *Justice, Law and Argument—Essays on Moral and Legal Reasoning* (D Reidel Publishing Co, 1980) 77.

[99] The distinction between values internal to proof and those external to it is made by D J Galligan, 'More Scepticism about Scepticism' (1988) 8 OJLS 249, 255, corresponding to which is the distinction Wigmore draws between 'rules of probative policy' and 'rules of extrinsic policy': John Henry Wigmore, *A Treatise on the Anglo-American System of Evidence in Trials at Common Law*, vol 1 (3rd edn, Boston: Little, Brown & Co, 1940) 296. Divisions may be drawn within the category of external values. For instance, the externality may be more or less remote from the defining purpose of proof: according to Weigend (n 12) 170, some external 'interests (for example, excluding evidence obtained by means of illegal wiretaps) pertain to the overriding concern of keeping the criminal process fair, while others (for example, avoiding revelation of state secrets) are completely foreign to the purpose of the criminal process'. Another example is the line drawn by David M Paciocco, 'Balancing the Rights of the Individual and Society in Matters of Truth and Proof: Part II—Evidence about Innocence' (2002) 81 Canadian Bar Review 39 at 50, between 'subordinated evidence' (which is excluded 'because of competing policy interests or... principles') and 'practical exclusion' (where evidence is disallowed because of 'practical interests related to the conduct of the trial'). Rules of practical exclusion are intended, in the language of Bentham, to 'minimize vexation, expense and delay': David M Paciocco, 'Evidence About Guilt: Balancing the Rights of the Individual and Society in Matters of Truth and Proof' (2001) 80 Canadian Bar Rev 431, 438.

values'[100]) and, in a criminal case, rights of the accused,[101] have to be respected in pursuing that end.[102] For instance, an accused person cannot be compelled to testify even if putting him in the witness box is likely to shed light on the case. Some have argued that forcing him to speak violates his privacy.[103] It is a matter of contention whether our regard for this value should prevail over our regard for the truth; and it is a matter of contention only because we are mindful that '[t]ruth, like all other good things, may be loved unwisely—may be pursued too keenly—may cost too much'.[104] Since the claim is that the pursuit of truth is the main goal, and not that it is the absolute or all-overriding end,[105] it involves no contradiction to admit to the legitimacy of 'side-constraints' on that enterprise.[106] Thus Wigmore had no difficulty accommodating 'rules of extrinsic policy' within a scheme which places the ascertainment of truth at the centre of the trial agenda.[107] Whether a constraint is legitimate would depend, it is often said, on the balancing of competing values.[108]

[100] Damaška, 'Truth in Adjudication' (n 25) 301.

[101] Andrew Ashworth, 'Excluding Evidence as Protecting Rights' [1977] Crim LR 723; Richard C C Peck, 'The Adversarial System: A Qualified Search for the Truth' (2001) 80 Canadian Bar Rev 456; *Williams v Florida* (1970) 399 US 78, 113–114, per Black J.

[102] As these writers are careful to stress: D J Galligan, *Due Process and Fair Procedures—A Study of Administrative Procedures* (Oxford: Clarendon Press, 1996) 7, 12, 51, 79, 81, and Galligan (n 99) 255; Goldman (n 24) 284–285; Damaška, 'Truth in Adjudication' (n 25) 301: 'Quite obviously, . . . truth-conducive values cannot be an overriding consideration in legal proceedings: it is generally recognized that several social needs and values exercise a constraining effect on attempts to achieve fact-finding precision. Various lists have been compiled of these countervailing considerations: privacy and human dignity, the demand for stability in decisionmaking, and cost figure prominently among them. There is no agreement, however, on what precisely should be included in the list, and how these "collateral" values should be balanced against the desire for accuracy in fact-finding.'

[103] eg D J Galligan, 'The Right of Silence Reconsidered' [1988] CLP 69, 88–91; Robert S Gerstein, 'Privacy and Self-Incrimination' (1970) 80 *Ethics* 87.

[104] *Pearse* v *Pearse* (1846) 1 De G & Sm 12, 28 (statement made in context of legal professional privilege). Weigend (n 12) 167 reports a dictum by the German Federal Court of Appeals that 'it is not a principle of criminal procedural law that the truth should be sought at any price'.

[105] Rawls (n 84) 486.

[106] eg Andrew Ashworth, 'Concepts of Criminal Justice' (1979) Crim LR 412 (claims that the general justifying aim of the administration of criminal justice is to detect, convict, and sentence the guilty and identifies various qualifiers to the pursuit of that aim, amongst them, principles of fairness).

[107] Wigmore (n 99) 296: 'Extrinsic policies' are 'policies which override the policy of ascertaining the truth by all available means'.

[108] *Elkins v US* (1960) 364 US 206, 233; Wigmore (n 99) 296; J J Spigelman, 'The Truth Can Cost Too Much: The Principle Of A Fair Trial' (2004) 78 Australian LJ 29. On difficulties in the concept of 'balancing': eg Gerry Maher, 'Balancing Rights and Interests in the Criminal Process' in Antony Duff and Nigel Simmonds (eds) *Philosophy and the Criminal Law, Archives for Philosophy of Law and Social Philosophy*, Beiheft No 19 (Wiesbaden: Franz Steiner Verlag, 1984) 99; John Cottingham, 'Weighing Rights and Interests in the Criminal Process' in Duff and Simonds (ibid) 109; Andrew Ashworth and Mike Redmayne, *The Criminal Process* (3rd edn, Oxford: Oxford University Press, 2005) at 30–32, 40–43, 45–48.

3 Internal Analysis

3.1 Introduction

This section takes an internal perspective, that of the person whose duty is to deliberate on findings of fact and ultimately the verdict.[109] From her point of view, truth and justice are values embedded in issues of justification; otherwise put, a positive verdict or finding must be defensible epistemically and morally. These two aspects of justification are introduced below. The epistemology of fact-finding is more fully considered in Chapter 3. Following that, in Chapters 4 to 6, it will be shown how ethical demands commingle with epistemic concerns in selected areas of evidence law. Epistemic and moral norms, so it will be argued, are implicit or expressed in many legal rules regulating fact-finding.

3.2 Epistemic justification

The fact-finder must have adequate epistemic justification for her findings. Chapter 3 argues that a positive finding of fact must be based on belief in its propositional content. The finding is not justified where the underlying belief is not. In this study, justification is construed in the internal sense. Belief in the propositional content of a positive finding must be internally justified; put differently, fact-finding aims at beliefs that are internally justified. But that is not all that it aims at. Externally, truth is the standard of correctness for belief and, hence, for the positive finding that is grounded on that belief. Fact-finding aims at beliefs which are internally justified *and* true: this is almost as good as saying that it aims at knowledge. These claims about justification, belief, truth, and knowledge are introduced below and further examined in Chapter 3.

3.2.1 Internal epistemic justification

The internal justification for the belief underlying a positive finding is evaluated from the perspective of the fact-finder. She faces this key normative question in the course of deliberation: Given the evidence available on this disputed proposition of fact, is one justified in judging it true? (Notice the reference to 'one'. There is a difference between a truly *subjective* first-personal statement, 'I judge and therefore believe that p is true', and a *detached* first-personal statement, 'I judge that one would be justified in believing that p'. The latter statement is

109 As such, an internalist epistemic approach is taken. Contrast the externalist approach adopted by Goldman (n 24) who offers an accuracy-centered analysis of legal fact-finding: ch 9, especially 283. For a general comparison of the two approaches: George Pappas, 'Internalist vs. Externalist Conceptions of Epistemic Justification', *The Stanford Encyclopedia of Philosophy (Spring 2005 Edition)*, Edward N Zalta (ed), online: The *Stanford Encyclopedia of Philosophy*, <http://plato.stanford.edu/archives/spr2005/entries/justep-intext/>.

also subjective but only to the extent that the judgment is subjective. This important point is developed in Chapter 3. It will be glossed over here.) Three senses of justification may be distinguished. Two of them are, loosely speaking, subjective and the third is objective. All of them are first-personal in the very narrow sense that the availability of justification is limited by the evidence made available to the epistemic agent, in our case, the fact-finder. This is not a set of settled terminology. 'Justification' has different meanings for different philosophers; as Wedgwood observed, an element of stipulation is unavoidable.[110] Our labels are merely convenient devices to point at certain distinctions. Some will probably think that better names could have been chosen.

When we say that the fact-finder is subjectively justified in believing a proposition in the first-personal sense, we mean, to begin with, that a good enough rational argument concluding in the proposition believed exists on the evidence that she has. Following Feldman (but not strictly), a 'good enough rational argument' exists only where there is justification for believing its premises and for believing that the premises are properly connected to the conclusion, and where the argument is not defeated by other background beliefs of the fact-finder.[111] Given the social context of the trial, the argument must also pass some inter-subjective cognitive standard that is acceptable across a wide enough section of the relevant community.[112] A further condition must also obtain. This condition can be set at two levels. At the stronger level, she must have come to believe the proposition by that argument and would, were she asked to show justification, give it in support of her belief.[113] Call this '*strong-subjective justification*'. Alternatively, we need not require that the argument must have actually influenced her belief but merely that she would, if her attention were properly drawn to the argument, offer or accept it as justification for her belief.[114] Call this '*weak-subjective justification*'. It is *objectively* justified for the fact-finder to believe a disputed proposition in the first-personal sense if a good enough rational argument exists on the evidence available to her; the argument may be beyond her grasp and it need

[110] Ralph Wedgwood, 'Contextualism about Justified Belief', forthcoming, available at his website: <http://users.ox.ac.uk/~mert1230/papers.htm>. For a critical analysis of five different senses of epistemic justification, see Jonathan Sutton, *Without Justification* (Cambridge, Massachusetts: MIT Press, 2007) 14–41.

[111] Richard Feldman, 'Good Arguments' in Frederick F Schmitt (ed), *Socializing Epistemology—The Social Dimensions of Knowledge* (London: Rowman and Littlefield, 1994) ch 8, 176–179.

[112] On inter-subjective justification, see Stewart Cohen, 'Knowledge and Context' (1986) 83 *J of Philosophy* 574, 577 and 'Knowledge, Context, and Social Standards' (1987) 73 *Synthese* 3, 5–7.

[113] David B Annis, 'A Contextualist Theory of Epistemic Justification' (1978) 15 *American Philosophical Quarterly* 213, 217; Jules L Coleman, 'Rational Choice and Rational Cognition' (1997) 3 Legal Theory 183, 186–187.

[114] Kent Bach, 'A Rationale for Reliabilism' (1985) 68 *The Monist* 246, 256; Robert Hambourger, 'Justified Assertion and the Relativity of Knowledge' (1987) 51 *Philosophical Studies* 241, 267, n 10.

neither have led her to the belief nor be one that she could construct or would offer to justify her belief.[115]

The fact-finder must aim at findings that are justified in the strong subjective sense. Justification in either the second or third sense is not good enough. On the external view of the trial discussed above, accuracy or reliability is the pivotal value, and what seems ultimately to matter is that the conclusion is correct. The external objection to irrational reasoning is that it increases the chances of error in the outcome of deliberation. A particular verdict may be correct even though it was produced by irrational reasoning. In such a case, one might say that no harm was done after all. But one should insist that something has gone wrong: the fact-finder has failed to discharge her duty properly in not deliberating as she ought to. It is wrong to find the defendant guilty by consulting an ouija board[116] or by the toss of a coin.[117] It is wrong even if the verdict happens to be correct and even where rational support for belief in his guilt exists on the evidence admitted in court. In those circumstances, the verdict is justifiable in the third sense of justification; the evidence ignored by the fact-finder is objectively strong enough to entitle or permit her to hold the belief in guilt. It is also possible for the belief to be justifiable in the second sense: perhaps the fact-finder would, if her attention were later drawn to it, come to recognize the rational support for the verdict in the admitted evidence. Even though the belief is justifiable in either the second or third senses, she is not justified in holding that belief where justification is understood in the first sense.[118] That alone is ground for criticism. Rationality is a demand in fact-finding that cannot be completely identified with the demand of reliability or accuracy.[119]

To be justified in the strong-subjective sense in believing that p, the epistemic agent must hold the belief in consequent of perceiving a connection between evidence and conclusion, a connection that is capable of constituting a good enough rational argument for the belief. Trial deliberation is a context in which we expect

[115] In Firth's terminology, a belief may be 'propositionally warranted' (it is warranted *for* the person to believe the proposition) even where it is not 'doxastically warranted' (the fact-finder is not warranted *in* believing the proposition, for example, where his underlying reasoning is irrational): Roderick Firth, 'Are Epistemic Concepts Reducible to Ethical Concepts?' in Alvin I Goldman and Jaegwon Kim (eds), *Values and Morals—Essays in Honor of William Frankena, Charles Stevenson, and Richard Brandt* (Dordrecht: D Reidel, 1978) 215, 218.

[116] cf *Young* (1995) 2 Cr App R 379.

[117] *R v Mirza* [2004] UKHL 2, [2004] 1 AC 1118, 1164.

[118] Tyler Burge, 'Content Preservation' (1993) 102 *The Philosophical Review* 457, 458–459.

[119] David Christensen, *Putting Logic in its Place—Formal Constraints on Rational Belief* (Oxford: Clarendon Press, 2004) 1 writes: '[T]hough the dimensions of accuracy and rationality may well be linked, they are evidently not the same. A fool may hold a belief irrationally—as a result of a lucky guess, or wishful thinking—yet the belief might happen to be accurate. Conversely, a detective might hold a belief on the basis of careful and exhaustive examination of all the available relevant evidence—in a paradigmatically rational way—and yet the evidence might happen to be misleading, and the belief might turn out to be way off the mark.'

the agent to have proper reasons for her beliefs. Annis makes this general observation which is relevant to the present point:[120]

> Consider a case where relative to an issue-context we would expect *S* to have reasons for his belief that *h*. Suppose when asked how he knows or what his reasons are he is not able to do it for some of the evidence. We may not be able to articulate all our evidence for *h* but we are required to do it for some of the evidence. It is not enough that we have evidence for *h*; it must be *taken* by us as evidence and this places us 'in the logical space of reasons, of justifying and being able to justify what one says.'

It is true that in our daily lives, relatively few of our factual beliefs are acquired with critical self-consciousness. Many of them simply dawn upon us; they are not the product of any conscious judgment. Reflective introspection is unlikely to reveal all the factors which caused a belief or all the evidential justification for it. But in the trial context, the verdict cannot be delivered directly from the unreflective gut feelings of the fact-finder. She must arrive at her beliefs about the facts of the case by deliberation. Deliberation is a process that engages reasoning, wherein the agent is required to examine the justification for believing the disputed proposition; it involves analysis of evidence and a conscious and critical evaluation of arguments for and against that belief.[121] In short, deliberation is an activity of justifying belief in the propositional contents of the findings under consideration. Pappas captures the basic idea thus:[122]

> [O]ne is justified in believing *p* only if one *has justified* the belief that *p*. Justifying a belief... is an activity in which one adduces evidence or reasons in favor of the belief.
>
> [B]eing justified in believing that *p* is a state one achieves by working things out, reasoning through some sequence of evidentiary steps and then drawing a conclusion that counts as the justified belief. When one engages in reasoning of this type one is aware of the steps through which one reasons and, *inter alia*, also aware of the justifiers that serve to support one's conclusion.

It can hardly do for the fact-finder to convict the defendant on gut feelings, with the opaque claim that she can just see, or she just knows, that he is guilty.[123] The fact-finder must identify the grounds for her views and evaluate them. For sure, there are limits on the degree to which she can articulate her reasoning and identify the details of her justification. First, deliberation is normatively complex. As noted in Chapter 1, Part 1.2, fact-finding involves evaluation and constructive interpretation; it incorporates legal and value judgments within factual

[120] David B Annis, 'A Contextualist Theory of Epistemic Justification' (1978) 15 *American Philosophical Quarterly* 213, 217; the quote within the quote is from Wilfred Sellars, *Science, Perception and Reality* (London: Routledge and Kegan Paul, 1963) 169.

[121] 'Evaluation', as Dewey says, is 'a distinctly intellectual operation. Reasons, and grounds one way or the other have to be sought for and formulated': John Dewey, *Logic: The Theory of Inquiry*, edited by Jo Ann Boydston (Carbondale: Southern Illinois UP, 1991) 174.

[122] George Pappas (n 109) in the first and penultimate paragraph of Part 7 respectively, summarizing one strand of argument that has been advanced in favour of internalism. Original italics.

[123] Larry Laudan, *Truth, Error, and Criminal Law* (Cambridge: CUP, 2006) 42–43.

judgments. Secondly, deliberation is psychologically complex. Inward reflection, however diligently conducted, is unlikely to expose all the influences that caused the beliefs the fact-finder has about the facts of the case. Sometimes she may not be able to reconstruct in detail the argument for such a belief. For example, the Canadian Supreme Court observes that:[124]

> there may be something about a person's demeanor in the witness box which will lead a juror to conclude that the witness is not credible. It may be that the juror is unable to point to the precise aspect of the witness's demeanor which was found to be suspicious, and as a result cannot articulate either to himself or others exactly why the witness should not be believed. A juror should not be made to feel that the overall, perhaps intangible, effect of a witness's demeanor cannot be taken into consideration in the assessment of credibility.

However, acknowledgment of these complexities does not force us to concede the futility of any attempt at critical self-reflection. It is reasonable to suppose that the fact-finder, as with any normal human being equipped with rational faculties, is capable of articulating the bases of her beliefs most of the time and at least in general terms.

Burns attacks the 'received view of the trial' which depicts a value-free process of discovering facts and fitting them in categories pre-defined by the substantive law. This view, according to him, perpetuates a form of 'mechanical jurisprudence' at the trial level.[125] He offers a rich and complex theory of the trial as a rhetorical event. However, unease arises when Burns claims that '[t]he jury's final form of understanding is a literally *indescribable* grasp of facts, norms, and possibilities for action'.[126] Should we not want and expect the fact-finder to be as explicit as she can be about her grounds and reasoning? Pritchard alerts us to the danger of subconscious prejudice: 'A juror might find . . . that his "grounds", when exposed to the clear light of day, are, if genuine grounds at all, inadequate to justify the belief that he instinctively formed.'[127] It is only in making determinate our claims that we can engage in rational discussion and if the trial is, as Burns says, the 'crucible of democracy', the point of deliberation (whether conducted in the jury room or in the fact-finder's mind) is to articulate the reasoning and evaluate the grounds for a verdict going one way or the other. Of course, Burns does not mean to celebrate inscrutability. But the jury's ability to be explicit, and the

[124] *R v Lifchus* (1997) 150 DLR (4th) 733, 744. Elizabeth Fricker, 'Against Gullibility' in Bimal Krishna Matilal and Arindam Chakrabarti (eds), *Knowing From Words* (Dordrecht: Kluwer Academic Publishers, 1994) 150 makes the same observation but insists that 'the subject's beliefs must not be opaque to her'; she must be able to defend her credibility judgment by defending her capacity to tell whether the speaker (witness) is sincere or not.

[125] Robert Burns, 'The Distinctiveness of Trial Narrative' in Antony Duff, Lindsay Farmer, Sandra Marshall and Victor Tadros (eds), *The Trial on Trial—Truth and Due Process*, vol 1 (Oxford: Hart, 2004) ch 9, 162.

[126] ibid 160, 169 (emphasis added); see also ibid 176.

[127] Duncan Pritchard, 'Testimony' in *Truth and Due Process* (n 125) ch 7, 120.

value of explicitness, in trial deliberation should not be underestimated. What is it to be explicit? Here is Adler:[128]

> To be explicit is to articulate or formulate or express what has been implicit. Explicitness highlights and clarifies claims, assumptions, or commitments, while increasing the visible range of beliefs with which any particular belief must cohere. In articulating, formulating, or expressing, we bring beliefs forward as claims, rather than as elements in the background of our understanding. Hazy thoughts are forced into the mold of definite statements... The reconstruction of an argument into an ordered set of premises and conclusion, where premises are broken down to simple statements and inferences (or subconclusions), is a paradigm of explicitness.

Explicitness helps to force out from obscurity fallacious reasoning, questionable assumptions, unsubstantiated conclusions, unfair prejudices, and other wrongs and defects that might otherwise go undetected in trial deliberation.[129]

Justifying belief in the internal sense is justifying to oneself. This private process has a public counterpart. The latter occurs when a juror defends her beliefs about the facts in issue before her fellow jurors and when a judge explains her findings in the course of giving the grounds of her judgment. Plainly, the claim that the fact-finder must justify her belief in the content of her positive finding is not undermined by the lack of transparency: that the jury does not have to give reasons does not mean that they do not need to reason or to have reasons.[130] It is true that the observer who has no access to how the jury actually reasoned can only judge their findings in terms of objective justification. And even where the reasoning actually used by the fact-finder is disclosed and it is not one we agree entirely with, there may be reasons to let the verdict stand. It would, however, be a mistake to take what we are prepared to let pass for the standard at which the fact-finder should aim. Deliberation aims at belief that is justified in the strong subjective sense. Hereafter, references to epistemic justification should be interpreted in that way unless otherwise stated.

3.2.2 Truth as the external standard of correctness

The 'first-person' perspective, just considered, stands in contrast to the external, 'third-person', perspective. The latter is a 'privileged' or 'idealized' perspective in that facts are accessible from that standpoint which might be unknown to the

[128] Jonathan Adler, *Belief's Own Ethics* (Cambridge, Massachusetts: MIT Press, 2002) 87.

[129] Laudan (n 123) 38–44 makes a parallel argument for jurors to identify the reasons for their doubts. In the larger picture, 'the rejection of intuitionism is', as Andrew Altman, 'Legal Realism, Critical Legal Studies, and Dworkin' (1986) 15 *Philosophy and Public Affairs* 205, 218, tells us 'firmly rooted in a commitment to the rule of law ideal. That ideal requires that legal decisions be the outcome of reasoning that can be reconstructed according to principles which can be articulated and understood.'

[130] cf Weigend (n 12) 166 ('the jury does not even have to strive toward a verdict based on the "truth" as it emerged at the trial, because the jury is not required to give reasons for its verdict and thus is not answerable to anyone regarding the rationality of its decision').

subject. Whereas the first-person perspective is concerned with the rationality of believing a proposition, the third-person perspective centres on the truth of the proposition.[131] The belief is correct only if the proposition is true. This is one way of describing the distinction: to hold an unjustified belief is a cognitive *fault* whereas to hold a justified belief that, unbeknownst to the agent, is false, is not a cognitive fault but a cognitive *defect*.[132]

Internal epistemic justification has to do with the rationality of the process by which a person arrives at her belief in the light of the evidence that she has; as so understood, the justification is independent of the truth or falsity of the belief.[133] It is irrational to judge that a witness is telling the truth, and, consequently to believe her testimony, on the bad reasoning that she has dark hair and every person with dark hair is absolutely honest. This criticism stands even if the witness did in fact give her testimony accurately and sincerely.[134] Now take the converse case. Suppose a malicious liar goes into the witness box and asserts that she saw the accused commit the crime in question. The fact-finder appraises her testimony in an entirely rational and responsible manner. But the witness is just too good an actor. The fact-finder is, understandably, duped. There is a good enough rational argument for believing the testimony that can be gathered from a range of factors: the witness appears confident and honest, her story hangs together, she comes out well under cross-examination, and so forth. The fact-finder is justified in believing the witness even though her testimony is actually false.[135] There is nonetheless an important sense in which she is wrong to hold that belief. As will be suggested in Chapter 3, truth is the standard of correctness for a belief. The fact-finder is not at fault; it is reasonable for her to believe the witness; and she is blameless for holding that belief. Despite all that, her belief, being false, is defective. While she can justify her *believing* what she did, her *belief* is not justified from a third-person perspective. Our third person is given to know what the first person does not: that the witness is lying.

[131] Paul Helm, *Belief Policies* (Cambridge: Cambridge University Press, 1994) 21; Bach (n 114) 251.

[132] Jim Edwards, 'Burge on Testimony and Memory' (2000) 60 *Analysis* 124, 128–129. Yet another way of putting this is to use Pollock's terminology and say that, in the latter case, the belief is justified but not warranted: John L Pollock, 'How to Reason Defeasibly' (1992) 57 *Artificial Intelligence* 1, 5.

[133] See Angus Ross, 'Why Do We Believe What We Are Told?' (1986) 28 *Ratio* 69, 83–84; Catherine Z Elgin, 'Word Giving, Word Taking' in Alex Byrne, Robert Stalnaker, and Ralph Wedgwood (eds), *Fact and Value—Essays on Ethics and Metaphysics for Judith Jarvis Thomson* (Cambridge, Massachusetts: MIT Press, 2001) 106; Jules L Coleman, 'Rational Choice and Rational Cognition' (1997) 3 Legal Theory 183, 183, n 2. Broadly similar is Lehrer's distinction between 'personal' and 'verific' justification: Keith Lehrer, 'Personal and Social Knowledge' (1987) 73 *Synthese* 87, 88–89.

[134] Duff (n 84) 115; Ronald J Allen and Gerald T G Seniuk, 'Two Puzzles of Juridical Proof' (1997) 76 Canadian Bar Rev 65, 78.

[135] As Peter Lipton says, 'those who rely on testimony but are not completely gullible must make the realist's distinction between belief and truth': 'The Epistemology of Testimony' (1998) 29 *Studies in History and Philosophy of Science* 1, 6–7.

Arguably, the ultimate aim of fact-finding is to know the facts of the case, which means at least having justified and true beliefs about those facts. This argument is explored in Chapter 3. Justification in the strong subjective sense is required for knowledge. But, on the usual analysis, knowledge is more than justified true belief.[136] Suppose in the last example the accused did what our malicious liar said she saw him do. While the witness thought she was giving false testimony, it turns out to be true after all. As in the earlier example, the fact-finder is justified in believing the testimony and in believing therefore that the accused is guilty as charged. That belief is true. Yet, it is only a matter of luck that she got the verdict right. She did not *know* that the accused is guilty.

3.3 Ethics of justice

At a trial, values other than truth have to be respected, not simply as subsidiary considerations, but as values which are internal to the nature and purpose of fact-finding. This section introduces the general theme. Variations of the theme are played out in Chapters 4, 5 and 6. Those chapters examine, respectively, the standard of proof, the hearsay rule, and the similar facts rule. Trial deliberation faces moral constraints. Chapter 2 described deliberation as a mental activity. Deliberative acts involve matters as diverse as the use of reasoning, the drawing of inferences, the exercise of judgment, and the adoption of a particular guiding attitude in deciding questions of fact. It will be argued that these are all proper subjects of moral evaluation. This claim is made with regards to mental actions taken during deliberation. The claim is not directed at external actions taken after deliberation. Suppose the jury has come to a verdict. They re-enter the courtroom and declare the accused guilty as charged. This act of convicting the accused is unjust if she is not in fact guilty. Or take the case of jury nullification. Some claim that the act of acquitting the defendant, despite belief in his guilt, is in certain situations morally defensible. Just as the public act of convicting or acquitting someone is subject to moral appraisal, so too are the means by which the outcome is physically secured. When it becomes known that the police have extracted by torture the confession on which the prosecution relies, we condemn their action as morally reprehensible.

Unlike these clear cases of conduct that are open to ethical appraisal, it is far from obvious what it means to talk about justice in, or the morality of, trial deliberation. A finding of fact is reached by reasoning. Reasoning is an activity. At a trial deliberation, reasoning culminates in a judgment of fact. A judgment, as Chapter 3 elaborates, is a mental act over which the agent has control; it is the precursor of belief, which itself is involuntary. Assume for the sake of discussion that the law is straightforward and, as the fact-finder, I know that I must publicly

[136] As demonstrated by Edmund L Gettier, 'Is Justified True Belief Knowledge' (1963) 23 *Analysis* 231.

declare the accused guilty of a crime if and only if I judge and believe that she is guilty of it. I also know that such a declaration would have significant adverse impact on her. According to a theme explored in Chapter 4, justice conceived as empathic care requires that I exercise sufficient caution in deliberation on her guilt. The moral concept of caution also explains the law's attitude towards hearsay evidence. Where the original source of the statement is not available for cross-examination, and her trustworthiness is unknown, it is incautious to take the statement at face value. This general sentiment is developed more fully in Chapter 5. Caution in deliberation is a moral virtue when it is exercised out of respect and concern for the person whose case is being judged.

The scope for ethical evaluation gets more complicated in other aspects of deliberation. It is morally wrong for counsel to argue in court that the defendant must have done it again just because he is a very bad person, the sort who would do this kind of terrible thing. Say we agree that, in advancing this argument (call it 'the offensive reasoning'), counsel insults the personal dignity of the defendant. It is also wrong, perhaps more so, for the judge to publicly use or endorse the offensive reasoning, either in what she says to the jury or in her grounds of judgment. Public speeches made by lawyers and judges at trials are, without much problem, subject to the constraints of morality, and, in this case, what they say is morally offensive. But it does not straightforwardly follow that moral constraints should similarly apply to trial deliberation. Suppose I am the sole judge of fact. The offensive reasoning occurs in the privacy of my mind. I allow it to influence my conclusion that the accused is guilty. I return a guilty verdict. The evidence is strong enough, without the offensive reasoning, to justify the conviction. I do not tell anyone my reliance on the offensive reasoning. Have I acted unjustly towards the accused? Does my deliberation fall short morally? A positive answer is offered in Chapter 6.

The conception of justice that is drawn upon in an internal analysis is different from the external view of justice as rectitude. A party has not merely a right that the substantive law be correctly applied to objectively true findings of fact, and a right to procedure that is rationally structured to determine the truth; she has, more broadly, a right to a just verdict, where justice must be understood to impose ethical demands on the manner in which the court conducts the trial, and importantly, on how it deliberates on the verdict. Findings of fact must be reached by a form of inquiry and process of reasoning that are not only epistemically sound but also morally defensible. Justice, on this view, is not a static concept; it is, following Kamenka:[137]

> not so much an idea or an ideal as an activity and a tradition—a way of doing things, not an end-state... As an intellectual activity, the activity and judgement of justice carry with them the ethic of discourse and enquiry.

[137] Eugene Kamenka, 'What is Justice?' in Eugene Kamenka and Alice Erh-Soon Tay (eds), *Justice* (London: Edward Arnold, 1979) 14.

Rawls considers the criminal trial as an exemplification of 'imperfect procedural justice', where there is an independent criterion for the desired outcome but no feasible way of guaranteeing it. 'The desired outcome is that the defendant should be declared guilty if and only if he has committed the offense with which he is charged.' He contrasts this with a system of 'pure procedural justice', as is found, for example, in a fair gamble: here, 'there is no independent criterion for the right result: instead there is a correct or fair procedure such that the outcome is likewise correct or fair, whatever it is, provided that the procedure has been properly followed'.[138]

While the distinction drawn by Rawls is an important one, the trial does not aim purely at the first type of justice. Elements of both 'imperfect procedural justice' and 'pure procedural justice' must be structured into any legitimate system of legal fact-finding.[139] For sure, we want the defendant to be declared guilty if and only if she has committed the alleged crime for which she stands charged. But, as Rawls would certainly agree, that is not all we desire of the trial.[140] The concept of a just verdict cannot be completely isolated from the concept of reaching a verdict justly;[141] in Duff's words: 'the justice... of a judicial decision is in part a matter of the justice of the process by which it was reached'.[142] We do not merely want the court's positive findings to be true. We also require, in both criminal and civil cases, justification for those findings. This claim presupposes a vision of a trial, set out and defended by various writers, as a process that seeks to justify an adverse decision to the person against whom it is taken.[143] We cannot reasonably expect her to accede fully to the moral authority of that finding, whether it be true or not, if it was reached by an unjust reasoning. Injustice occurs when deliberation is conducted with insufficient regard for her dignity or inadequate concern for her

[138] Rawls (n 84) 74–75.

[139] Those who favour this view include: David Resnick, 'Due Process and Procedural Justice' in J Roland Pennock and John W Chapman (eds), *Due Process, Nomos* XVIII (New York: New York University Press, 1977) 212–214; T R S Allan, *Constitutional Justice—A Liberal Theory of the Rule of Law* (Oxford: Oxford University Press, 2001) 206, 77–87; Duff (n 84) especially ch 4; Gerry Maher, 'Natural Justice as Fairness' in Neil MacCormick and Peter Birks (eds), *The Legal Mind—Essays for Tony Honoré* (Oxford: Clarendon Press, 1986) 103, 112, n 24; Laurence H Tribe, 'Trial by Mathematics: Precision and Ritual in the Legal Process' (1971) 84 Harvard L Rev 1329, 1381.

[140] In a satirical piece that defends standards of fair trial, G E M Anscombe and J Feldman, 'On the Nature of Justice in a Trial' (1972) 33 *Analysis* 33, 35 remarked: '"[C]ourt of justice" is not the same thing as "committee for nailing criminals". Similarly, "convicting" means more than a group in power being satisfied on good evidence of the guilt of someone, and using the powers of the state to clobber him.'

[141] This point is frequently made in discussion on the moral legitimacy of a conviction: eg, Ian Dennis, *The Law of Evidence* (3rd edn, London: Sweet & Maxwell, 2007) 49–58; Andrew L T Choo, *Abuse of Process and Judicial Stays of Criminal Proceedings* (Oxford: OUP, 1993) 13–14; Nick Taylor and David Ormerod, 'Mind the Gaps: Safety, Fairness and Moral Legitimacy' [2004] Crim LR 267.

[142] R A Duff, 'The Limits of Virtue Jurisprudence' in Michael Brady and Duncan Pritchard (eds), *Moral and Epistemic Virtues* (Oxford: Blackwell, 2003) 199, 205.

[143] Allan (n 139) 77–87; Duff (n 84) introduction and ch 4.

interests.[144] This is a normative, and not an empirical or a psychological, claim; what matters is not whether the person would accept the finding, but whether we are entitled to say that she ought to, given how it was made. The court must strive, in the manner in which it reaches the verdict, to acquire the moral authority to say to the parties that they should accept it, even or especially when it affects them adversely. This is not to promote justice and fairness as means of obtaining de facto acceptance of the verdict; if that be our goal, we need only to promote the appearance of justice and fairness. It is at once far simpler and more powerful to say: the fact-finder ought to be just and fair to the parties because, as a person, she ought to care about justice and fairness to her fellow human beings.[145]

In his beautifully written book, Gaita spoke of justice beyond fairness. Justice as humanity is more basic than concerns for fairness. Unless the humanity of a person is recognized, her claim for an equal distribution of goods and opportunities cannot register; and when a person protests against injustice, her plead is for something much more fundamental than fairness.[146] It runs deep in us to have our personhood fully acknowledged by others, that they see us as equally capable of pain and happiness, joy and suffering. Only a sense of empathy or, more powerfully, love[147] will make us see the inherent preciousness of a person, and it is only then that we can talk about her inalienable rights and dignity. Unconditional respect is due to the most heinous of wrongdoers; they still deserve to be kept 'amongst us as our fellow human beings'.[148] According to Gaita, criminals must be brought to justice for two important reasons. We owe it to the victims to have the wrongs done to them acknowledged by the community. We also owe justice to the criminals. The concern 'for justice as the acknowledgment that all human beings are owed inalienable respect goes deep in our system of criminal justice'. Gaita writes:

> The insistence that even the most foul criminals are owed unconditional respect, that even they belong to the constituency in which they may intelligibly press claims for fair treatment and due process, is the acknowledgment of our human fellowship with them. Our insistence that they be granted due process is an expression of justice that is deeper than anything that can be captured by the notions of proper procedure or fairness. Justice Laudan, the judge presiding over the trial of Adolf Eichmann in Jerusalem, was moved to say, against those who wished the trial to be no more than a show trial, that it had only one purpose, and that was to do justice. He meant, amongst other things, that it had

[144] That injustice betokens want of respect or lack of concern: J R Lucas, *On Justice* (Oxford: Clarendon Press, 1980) 7.

[145] cf Joseph Raz, 'Law by Incorporation' (2004) 10 Legal Theory 1 at 2–3.

[146] Raimond Gaita, *A Common Humanity: Thinking about Love and Truth and Justice* (London: Routledge, 2000) 81.

[147] For W G Maclagan, respect as an absolute valuation of a person is grounded in love 'not as a romantic passion but as Agape, an energy of the rational will': 'Respect for Persons as a Moral Principle—II' (1960) 35 *Philosophy* 289, 289; this claim is examined by him in 'Respect for Persons as a Moral Principle—I' (1960) 35 *Philosophy* 289 at 204 *et seq.*

[148] Gaita (n 146) xvi.

to do justice to Eichmann for Eichmann's sake because it was owed to him as a human being. This is the most sublime aspect of our legal tradition.[149]

To acknowledge the humanity in the accused person is of course not to excuse her wrongdoing. Nor does the acknowledgment diminish our ability to judge, as severely as it is appropriate, the moral gravity of her deed.[150] It should, however, stop us from succumbing to the brute instinct of vengeance.

Gaita's conception of justice as humanity finds strong resonance with Dubber's account of the sense of justice. For Dubber, the sense of justice, understood as the 'basic capacity for empathic interpersonal role taking',[151] is 'the prerequisite for judicial decision making as well as for jury deliberation'. In the trial context, the sense of justice refers to 'the ability and willingness [of the fact-finder] to recognize others [in particular, the parties and victims] as equal and rational persons and treat them as such, by placing oneself in their shoes and experiencing life situations from their point of view'.[152] It is through reflection and the conceptualization of another person as a fellow moral being, someone with equal capacity for autonomy as oneself, that one comes to have respect for her and want to treat her in accordance with that respect. Such respect obviously does not preclude us from punishing her. What the sense of justice does demand, however, is that 'we may not remove her from the realm of justice altogether'.[153] Even a psychopath 'does not deserve to be disposed of as a mere object'.[154]

Slote similarly views justice as a form of, as we may put it, other-regarding affective attitude. He has over the years developed a relational theory of 'ethics as empathic caring'. In his own words, 'the actions of individuals [should be evaluated] in terms of whether they express, exhibit, or reflect empathically caring motivation, or its opposite, on the part of individuals'.[155] The action of a selfish person, or an action that is motivated by self-interest, is not necessarily unethical. An act is wrong only if it expresses or exhibits or reflects an uncaring attitude towards others. Clearly, a charity donation cannot be described in these terms. Yet, a selfish person may make a large donation merely to gain fame.[156] The ethical constraint is therefore only a negative one. The empathy of which Slote speaks is not confined to the feelings that the person we care about actually

[149] ibid 10–11. See also ibid 54.
[150] ibid xiii–xiv.
[151] Markus Dirk Dubber, *The Sense of Justice—Empathy in Law and Punishment* (NY: NYU Press, 2006) 148.
[152] ibid 75.
[153] ibid 99.
[154] ibid 101.
[155] Michael Slote, *The Ethics of Care and Empathy* (London: Routledge, 2007) 94. His earlier works on this topic include *Morals From Motive* (Oxford: OUP, 2001) ch 4 ('Justice as Caring') and 'Autonomy and Empathy' (2004) 21 *Social Philosophy and Policy* 293.
[156] Slote, *The Ethics of Care and Empathy* (n 155) 32–33.

experiences. It extends to the feelings she *would* have if we did certain things or if certain things happened.[157]

One might think that caring is in tension with respect: a parent who imposes restrictions on a child out of caring concern undermines her autonomy and is in that sense disrespectful of her. One might also think that caring is inconsistent with justice. Justice may require that I fail a student whose happiness and future I care about.[158] However, empathic caring, as Slote means it, is compatible with—indeed, it makes sense of—respect for autonomy and a particular conception of justice. Caring includes empathy, and genuine cases of disrespect are cases of failure of empathy, the non-cognizance of another person's real wants, fears, and individuality.[159] Slote acknowledges that the ethics of empathic caring is inconsistent with the traditional liberal approach to justice.[160] Liberalism recognizes greater individual rights against non-interference than would be acceptable on Slote's theory. But the ethics of empathic caring 'can develop a plausible view of justice... all of its own'.[161] For example, he argues that, in the case of hate speech, the harm it can cause is the main matter to which the moral agent should be empathically sensitive. This, however, is not the important lesson we want to draw from his discussion. The important lesson is how empathic caring is an important dimension of justice.

These theories provide valuable insights into the trial, but only when it is viewed from the internal perspective. We must place ourselves in the role of the fact-finder as a moral agent standing in relation to the person whose case she is empowered to dispose. Justice in trial deliberation requires that she acknowledges the humanity of that person (Gaita), exercises a sense of justice (Dubber), and responds to her with empathic care (Slote). In short, the trier of fact must appreciate, from the position of that person, the value of respect and concern. A verdict should be given against her only when it can be justified on grounds that she ought reasonably to accept. The standard of proof and evidential reasoning used in reaching the verdict must express adequate respect and concern. As will be argued more fully in later chapters, to be overly dismissive of a party's case, to jump to conclusions against her, to be unbothered by the potential defeasibility of an adverse inference from hearsay evidence, to assume from her unsavoury past that she has done it again because she is the sort of bad person who would do this sort of thing are each, in their own ways, acts of disrespect and unconcern, amounting even, as in the last example, to a failure to acknowledge her moral autonomy. It does not matter, or perhaps it makes it worse, that the party does

[157] ibid 15.

[158] This example was given by N Athanassoulis in his online review of Slote's *Morals from Motives* (2004) Notre Dame Philosophical Reviews, available at: <http://ndpr.nd.edu/review.cfm?id=1245>.

[159] Slote, *The Ethics of Care and Empathy* (n 155) ch 4.

[160] ibid ch 5.

[161] ibid 2.

not know that she has been unjustly treated (jury deliberation, after all, is usually kept secret): she has objectively suffered moral harm.[162] The moral frame of mind does not obtain comfort in the security against being found out; justice requires full empathy, an 'imaginative reconstruction'[163] of how the party would feel *if* she were to find out. The fact-finder ought to care to find the truth because she ought morally to respect and care for the person standing before the court. In this sense, the trial is not only about accuracy; it is, more importantly, about affirming a common humanity.

Conclusion

The externalist wants to reduce the frequency of outcome errors to a level compatible with the efficient allocation of resources and an adequate protection of competing values and rights. Some of those who take this approach sometimes treat justice as purely a procedural matter; they lose sight of the injustice inherent in finding someone liable or guilty who in fact is not. Others at the opposite end relate truth to justice as rectitude; such a view fails to give due recognition to process values. The internal perspective offers a different account. The search for truth is a search for epistemic justification for belief in the disputed propositions of fact. Justice must be done within the process of reaching the verdict. In the conduct of deliberation, the judge of fact must be sufficiently motivated by empathic care for the person who is the target of an adverse finding.

[162] The objectivity of moral harm is stressed in a different connection by Ronald Dworkin, 'Principle, Policy, Procedure' in his *A Matter of Principle* (Cambridge, Massachusetts: Harvard University Press, 1985) ch 3, 80.

[163] This term is used and the idea analysed by Lawrence Blum, 'Compassion' in Amélie Oksenberg Rorty (ed), *Explaining Emotions* (Berkeley: University of California Press, 1980) ch 21, 509–513.

3

Epistemology of Legal Fact-Finding

Introduction

As we saw in Chapter 2, the claim is often made, and sometimes challenged, that the trial engages in a search for the truth. As a social institution, the system of legal adjudication certainly has other or more complicated aims. To name a few alternatives, it has been suggested that the trial seeks 'to secure the peaceful settlement of social conflict';[1] serves the communicative function of persuading 'the person whose conduct is under scrutiny of the truth and justice of its conclusions';[2] and has the objectives of 'inspiring confidence, supporting independent social policies...and tranquilizing disputants'.[3] Further, critics have highlighted many (especially adversarial) features of the trial system which cast doubt on whether it is designed to find the truth; at any rate, the system, they argue, is not well-engineered to produce true outcomes. Be all that as it may, there is a sense in which the trial seeks the truth. This much becomes clear when we put ourselves in the place of the fact-finder. Seen from her perspective, the purpose of trial deliberation *is* to figure out the truth. This chapter examines the epistemic function of fact-finding from the internal point of view. The argument unfolds in a discursive fashion, with elaborate foundations laid at the beginning, rough views put forth tentatively, which are then gradually modified and refined as the discussion proceeds. This style undoubtedly taxes the reader's patience. But there seems no better way to present the set of disparate theories and views which we will cover as a connected thread of argument.

[1] Henry M Hart Jr and John T McNaughton, 'Some Aspects of Evidence and Inference in the Law' in Daniel Lerner (ed), *Evidence And Inference* (Glencoe, Illinois: Free Press, 1958) 52.

[2] R A Duff, *Trials and Punishments* (Cambridge: CUP, 1986) 116. See also Antony Duff, Lindsay Farmer, Sandra Marshall and Victor Tadras, 'Introduction: Towards A Normative Theory of the Criminal Trial' in Antony Duff *et al* (eds), *The Trial on Trial—Truth and Due Process*, vol 1 (Oxford: Hart, 2004); T R S Allan, *Constitutional Justice—A Liberal Theory of the Rule of Law* (Oxford: OUP, 2001) 81 *et seq*.

[3] Jack B Weinstein, 'Some Difficulties in Devising Rules for Determining Truth in Judicial Trials' (1966) 66 Columbia L Rev 223, 241.

1 Epistemic Foundations

1.1 Assertion

Jurors must swear or affirm that they 'will faithfully try the defendant and give a true verdict according to the evidence'.[4] This duty, stated as a rule of fact-finding, is our starting point of analysis:

R: The fact-finder must 'give a true verdict according to the evidence'.

Just as the jury is required to give a true verdict according to the evidence, the judge sitting at a bench trial is required to do the same. 'Fact-finder' in R refers as much to the jury as to the judge sitting as the sole decider of fact.

What is it to require the fact-finder 'to give a true verdict according to the evidence'? A positive verdict rests on the propositions which constitute or are otherwise essential to the legal case of the side bearing the burden of proof. These propositions may or may not be contested at the trial. Often, only some of them are in dispute. The duty of the fact-finder can be rendered more specific by substituting in R 'finding on a disputed proposition' for 'verdict':

R*: The fact-finder must give a true *finding on a disputed proposition* according to the evidence.

Chapter 1, Part 2, gave an analysis of a finding or verdict as a speech act with multiple illocutionary forces. This chapter focuses only on the assertive aspect. To find that p is, amongst other things, to assert that p:

FA: In finding that p, the fact-finder asserts that p.

In FA, 'finding' refers to a positive finding; for reasons stated in Chapter 1, a negative finding usually lacks a corresponding assertive force. Sometimes, what is found and asserted is a very general proposition, to the effect that the defendant is liable on the claim that has been brought against her or that the defendant is guilty as charged. This is typically the case at a jury trial: the verdict given by a jury is usually a general one. But, exceptionally, the jury is called upon to return a special verdict where it is required to answer specific questions.[5] For bench trials, it is common for judges to state particular findings in their grounds of judgment.[6]

[4] *R v Mirza* [2004] UKHL 2, [2004] 1 AC 1118, 1175; Practice Direction [2002] 1 WLR 2870, para 42.4.

[5] On the forms that a special verdict can take: Mark S Brodin, 'Accuracy, Efficiency, and Accountability in the Litigation Process—The Case for the Fact Verdict' (1990) 59 U of Cincinnati L Rev 15, 84. The author argues for greater use of 'fact verdict'.

[6] See Douglas Payne, 'Appeals on Questions of Fact' (1958) 11 CLP 185, 193; *Benmax v Austin Motor Co Ltd* [1955] AC 370, 373.

At the general level, the assertion contained in a verdict is not an assertion of brute fact. 'He committed murder' and 'He stabbed the deceased to death' are very different propositions. As already noted in Chapter 1, Part 1, the first is much more complex than the second, blending as it does fact and value, fact and law. Nevertheless, Bayles was right to observe of legal decisions that 'there are core factual matters that one needs to get correct'.[7] If the fact-finder is wrong on the fact that the accused stabbed the deceased, she is wrong on the finding that he committed murder. A positive verdict (of guilt) or general finding (of liability) implies certain specific findings and assertions of 'core factual matters'. It is on those findings and assertions that this chapter concentrates.

For the moment, p in FA will be treated simply as a proposition of core fact. Two complications will be addressed later. First, there is the problem considered in Part 2.4 of how best to understand p, whether as a proposition of fact or a proposition about the proof of that fact ('proposition of proof') or a proposition about the probability of the truth of the proposition of fact ('proposition of probability'). Secondly, as will be suggested in Part 3 below, triers of fact adopt a holistic approach to trial deliberation. They do not treat propositions as discrete entities but as parts of broader hypotheses about the case. The plausibility of a hypothesis is judged as a whole and relative to the plausibility of competing hypotheses.

1.2 Knowledge

It has come to be widely accepted amongst epistemologists that an assertion always carries a claim of knowledge.[8] When I assert that p, I necessarily imply that I know that p or represent myself as knowing that p.[9] Three arguments have been cited in support of this view.[10] First, it is common to challenge assertions with objections such as 'But you don't know that'. This objection makes sense only if knowledge is at least implied in an assertion. Secondly, if I have just bought a ticket in a lottery about which I know nothing suspicious, it is usually improper for me to assert that I will lose. The simplest explanation for this is that I do not know that I will lose, however high the probability that I will lose. If I knew that I would lose, I would not have bought the ticket. Thirdly, suppose someone says,

[7] Michael Bayles, 'Principles for Legal Procedure' (1986) 5 Law and Philosophy 33, 40.

[8] For a survey of competing theories of assertion, including the knowledge account: Matt Weiner, 'Norms of Assertion' (2007) 2 *Philosophy Compass* 187.

[9] eg Peter Unger, *Ignorance—A Case For Scepticism* (Oxford: Clarendon Press, 1975) ch VI; Timothy Williamson, *Knowledge and Its Limits* (Oxford: OUP, 2002) ch 11; Michael Slote, 'Assertion and Belief' in Jonathan Dancy (ed), *Papers On Language And Logic—The Proceedings Of The Conference On The Philosophy Of Language And Logic* (Keele: Keele University Press, 1979) 177; Keith DeRose, 'Assertion, Knowledge, and Context' (2002) 111 *The Philosophical Rev* 167; John Hawthorne, *Knowledge and Lotteries* (Oxford: OUP, 2004) 23–24; Jason Stanley, *Knowledge and Practical Interests* (Oxford: OUP, 2005) 10–11.

[10] These arguments are attributed to Williamson and discussed by Jonathan Sutton, 'Stick to What You Know' (2005) 39 Noûs 359, 374–375 and *Without Justification* (Cambridge, Massachuetts: MIT Press, 2007) at 44.

'It's raining but I don't know that it's raining.'[11] It may well be the case that at time t, it is both raining and the subject does not know that it is raining. So, the sentence would appear free of logical inconsistency. Yet, it is extremely odd for a person to utter such a statement. That the statement strikes us as strange is best explained by a knowledge account of assertion. It is odd to make this statement because it contains a pragmatic contradiction.[12] In asserting that it is raining, the subject represents herself to know that it is raining. But, in the second conjunct, she denies having any such knowledge.[13]

According to Williamson, it is a constitutive rule of an assertion that one must assert p only if one knows p. Call this KA, the knowledge account of assertion:

KA: One must assert that p only if one knows that p.

This is a constitutive rule in the sense that it governs every performance of the act of assertion. KA does not imply that one fails to make an assertion where one lacks the relevant knowledge. Williamson accepts, as he must, that assertions are often made in violation of KA. That KA is often infringed does not show that it is false; after all, many rules are often broken. What Williamson claims is that it is always wrong to assert that p where one does not know that p. The norm in KA arises from the specific nature of assertion and the wrong in question is not a moral wrong. While it is morally wrong to cheat at a game, this is possible only because the game is constituted by rules which are themselves non-moral. Maradona is accused of having cheated in scoring that controversial World Cup goal because there is a rule against deliberate handball; the rule itself is non-moral. Analogously, KA is a non-moral rule that makes possible moral wrongs such as insincere assertions or lies.[14] KA may be imported into the trial context via this earlier thesis:

FA: In finding that p, the fact-finder asserts that p.

From FA and KA, we arrive at this conclusion:

KF: The fact-finder must find that p only if she knows that p.

KF (the knowledge account of a finding of fact) finds general support in the views taken by those who place knowledge at the centre of legal fact-finding. For example, Pardo claims that: 'The trial is fundamentally an epistemological event.

[11] G E Moore, *Commonplace Book 1919–1953* (London: Allen & Unwin, 1962) 277 (giving the different example: 'Dogs bark, but I don't know that they do').

[12] What makes this a pragmatic contradiction is that the 'inconsistency arises not from what you are claiming but from the fact that you are claiming it': Kent Bach, 'Speech Acts and Pragmatics' in Michael Devitt and Richard Hanley (eds), *Blackwell Guide to the Philosophy of Language* (Oxford: Blackwell, 2006) 147, 147.

[13] Unger (n 9); Williamson (n 9) 253.

[14] Williamson (n 9) 240.

We want jurors and judges to know.'[15] Similarly, Tadros and Tierney argue that 'a defendant ought only to be convicted of a criminal offence if it is known that he is guilty of that offence'.[16] Duff tells us to 'see the verdict as a claim to knowledge: in convicting the defendant the court claim to know that he is guilty'.[17] In the New Zealand Court of Appeal case of *R v Wanhalla*,[18] Hammond J suggests that judges 'were concerned to articulate how one "knows" something for legal purposes' when formulating the instruction on the criminal standard of proof.

KF is likely to strike many as overly demanding. The resistance to KF is understandable since it is easy to overestimate the difficulty with which knowledge is acquired and there is a tendency to wrongly equate it with (absolute) certainty.[19] These mistakes are noted in the discussion to come. In any event, there is an apparently less demanding account of assertion and fact-finding that relies on 'justified belief' instead of 'knowledge'. Another reservation about KF is that it is clearly too simplistic. Elaboration in terms of its core components is needed to bring out the complexities of trial deliberation and its legal regulation.

1.3 Belief

There are two broad strategies for working out an apparently less radical and yet richer account of assertion and fact-finding. One is to focus on the internal component of KA. On the traditional view, a person knows that p only if (i) she believes that p, (ii) she is justified in believing that p, and (iii) p is true.[20] In most cases, one knows p when these three conditions are satisfied. Exceptionally, a Gettier complication prevents this from happening.[21] Suppose a malicious liar has unwittingly given true evidence, with the intention of framing the defendant. She claims that she saw him commit the crime. But she is lying. Unknown to her, the material part of her testimony is true: the defendant did commit the crime. The witness is so convincing in the witness box that the fact-finder comes to believe, and is justified in believing, her testimony. Whilst the fact-finder

[15] Michael S Pardo, 'The Field of Evidence and the Field of Knowledge' (2005) 24 Law and Philosophy 321, 321. The claim is repeated in Michael S Pardo, 'Testimony', forthcoming in (2007) 82 Tulane L Rev, draft available at: <http://papers.ssrn.com/s013/papers.cfm?abstract_id=986845>.

[16] Victor Tadros and Stephen Tierney, 'The Presumption of Innocence and the Human Rights Act' (2004) 67 MLR 402. Tadros, in a separate paper, reiterated the claim that a 'conviction is warranted...only if knowledge that the defendant perpetrated the offence is demonstrated': 'Rethinking the Presumption of Innocence' (2007) 1 Crim L and Philosophy 193, 209.

[17] Duff, *Trials and Punishments* (n 2) 115.

[18] [2007] 2 NZLR 573, para 141.

[19] On the common error of this way of thinking: Michael P Lynch, *True to Life—Why Truth Matters* (Cambridge, Massachusetts: MIT Press, 2004) especially ch 2.

[20] Williamson (n 9) does not subscribe to the standard analysis of knowledge. For him, knowledge is a primitive concept (a 'factive mental state') which cannot be analysed in terms of more basic epistemic components. But his knowledge account of assertion (KA) can stand independently of his radical take on knowledge.

[21] Edmund Gettier, 'Is Justified True Belief Knowledge' (1963) 23 *Analysis* 121.

(i) believes that the accused is guilty, (ii) is justified in having that belief (in the sense that it is rational to believe the testimony), and (iii) it is true that the accused is guilty, most would not attribute to the fact-finder knowledge of the defendant's guilt. The reason, as conventionally understood, has to do with this: we do not know that p if p is true merely by chance. In the example, it was accidental that the witness's testimony was true, and it was even more of a fluke that the fact-finder's belief in the accused's guilt was true. It is controversial what else is required for knowledge in addition to the three requirements. One philosopher remarks that 'the project of repairing the JTB [justified true belief] account of knowledge in response to Gettier's counterexamples... is about as degenerative a research programme as one could wish for'.[22] The hope for a conjunctive analysis of knowledge has diminished; any attempt to analyse the concept by laying down its necessary and sufficient conditions is now considered by many as futile.[23] It is enough for present purposes to delineate, as we have done, some core aspects of knowledge.

The knowledge rule may be seen as having an internal component (comprising elements (i) belief and (ii) justification) and an external component (consisting of element (iii) truth). Roughly speaking, belief is a matter of the mind; truth is a matter of the external world. The internal component of KA is the rule that tells the subject when it is proper to make an assertion. From her point of view, the facet of KA that regulates the practice of assertion is captured in this 'justified belief rule for assertion':

JBRA: One must assert p only if one (i) believes and (ii) is justified in believing p.

It is possible to argue that JBRA is not merely the internal component of KA: it *is* KA. This may be supported by reducing KA to two fundamental norms about belief: first, 'one must assert p only if one believes p', and, secondly, 'one must believe p only if one knows p'.[24] A more radical view, offered by Sutton, is simply that justified belief is knowledge.[25] We will pursue a less controversial strategy for developing a less demanding account of assertion. This is to substitute for KA a belief-centred rule of assertion. Lackey challenges KA in a forthcoming article.[26] She claims that knowledge cannot be what is required for proper assertion because 'there are cases in which a speaker asserts that *p* in the absence

[22] Alexander Bird, 'Justified Judging' (2007) 74 *Philosophy and Phenomenological Research* 81, 82.

[23] Peter Unger, 'The Cone Model of Knowledge' (1986) 14 *Philosophical Topics* 125. As Antti Karjalainen and Adam Morton, 'Contrastive Knowledge' (2003) 6 *Philosophical Explorations* 74, 76, observe: 'no one would now begin a paper on knowledge by simply laying down necessary and sufficient conditions for "S knows that p" and then going on with the assurance that what these conditions picked out was knowledge'.

[24] Jonathan Sutton, *Without Justification* (n 10) 44.

[25] Argued at length in Sutton, *Without Justification* (n 10).

[26] Jennifor Lackey, 'Norms of Assertion', forthcoming in *Noûs*, available at her homepage: <http://www.niu.edu/phil/~lackey/research.shtml>.

of knowing that *p* without being subject to criticism.' She gives this example: Martin, who is just beginning to see through the racist nature of the beliefs he was brought up with, is a juror at the trial of a black man charged with raping a white woman:

> ...After hearing the relatively flimsy evidence presented by the prosecution and the strong exculpatory evidence offered by the defense, Martin is able to recognize that the evidence clearly does not support the conclusion that the defendant committed the crime...In spite of this, however, he can't shake the feeling that the man... is guilty... Upon further reflection, Martin begins to suspect that such a feeling is grounded in the racism that he still harbors, and so he concludes that even if he can't quite come to believe that the defendant is innocent..., he nonetheless has an obligation to present the case to others this way... [A]fter leaving the courthouse, [a friend asks Martin] whether the "guy did it." Despite the fact that he does not believe, and hence does not know, that the defendant... is innocent, Martin asserts, "No, the guy did not rape her."

We are given that Martin recognizes 'that the evidence clearly does not support the conclusion that the defendant committed the crime'. This must mean that Martin knows that he does not know that the defendant is guilty. Hence, it would be wrong for Martin to tell his friend, 'Yes, the guy did rape her.' This conclusion is consistent with KA. But Martin tells his friend instead, 'No, the guy did *not* rape her.' On Lackey's analysis, this assertion violates KA because Martin does not believe, and hence does not know, the proposition which he asserts. Nevertheless, Martin is not wrong to make the assertion; indeed, she thinks that he deserves praise rather than criticism because he is 'able to transcend his own racism and thereby offers an assertion that is both true and epistemically flawless'. Lackey proposes the following 'reasonable to believe norm of assertion' in place of KA:

> RTBNA: One should assert that p only if (i) it is reasonable for one to believe that p, and (ii) if one asserted that p, one would assert that p at least in part because it is reasonable for one to believe that p.

The value of Lackey's paper lies in providing insights that must be taken on board in developing any belief-centred account of assertion as a basis for a theory of legal fact-finding. Some elaborations of RTBNA are in order before addressing its legal application.

It is convenient to start with the second limb. Condition (ii) of RTBNA is meant to exclude assertions from qualifying as proper where the reasonableness of a speaker's assertion that p is wholly disconnected from the reasonableness of the belief that p. Imagine a criminal trial where the admitted evidence is so strong that it is reasonable for one to believe that the accused is guilty as charged. Condition (i) of RTBNA is satisfied. I find (equivalently, assert) that she is guilty. But my belief in her guilt is based entirely on prejudice, motivated wholly by my intense dislike of her as a person after learning of the many outrageous crimes she had committed on other occasions. I jump to the conclusion that she is guilty of the present crime without bothering much with the evidence adduced at the trial. My assertion infringes condition (ii) of RTBNA and is improper.[27]

Lackey pegs the standard of reasonableness in condition (i) of RTBNA to that of justified belief, such that 'it is reasonable for S to believe that p only if S has epistemic support that is adequate for S's justifiedly believing that p were S to believe that p on that basis'. Condition (i) may therefore be revised to read 'one should assert that p only if (i) one would be justified in believing that p'; and, with a corresponding alteration to condition (ii), we have this modified version of RTBNA:

RTBNA*: One should assert that p only if (i) *one would be justified in believing that p*, and (ii) if one asserted that p, one would assert that p at least in part because *one would be justified in believing that p under (i)*.

Condition (i) of RTBNA* might appear to come close to JBRA. However, they are different in at least one crucial respect. Whereas JBRA requires the asserter to personally believe that p, condition (i) of RTBNA* does not. The latter requires only that one would be justified in believing p (in the sense that it is reasonable for one to believe that p): the asserter need not herself hold that belief. In other words, RTBNA and RTBNA* permit what Lackey calls 'selfless assertions', an example of which, according to her, is the assertion Martin made to his friend in the case stated earlier.[28]

We now turn to the legal application of RTBNA*. RTBNA* gains its relevance in the legal context from this earlier claim:

FA: In finding that p, the fact-finder asserts that p.

Taken together, FA and RTBNA* produce this obligatory rule; call this the 'belief account of fact-finding':

BAF: The fact-finder must find that p only if (i) one would be justified in believing that p, and (ii) if one found that p, one would find that p at least in part because one would be justified in believing that p under (i).

If the above is right, the fact-finder is at a common law trial required to make findings of fact according to her judgment of what 'one would be justified in believing'. Often this will be the same as what the fact-finder personally believes. But this is not always the case. There are two potential causes of a divergence between 'selfless' and 'personal' beliefs. We must therefore allow that in finding

[27] The problem of prejudice is examined more closely in Chapter 6.

[28] But it is not absolutely clear that Martin actually lacks the relevant belief. I raise some problems with Lackey's analysis of this hypothetical in 'The Epistemic Basis of Legal Fact-finding' (2007) 1 *The Reasoner*, issue 2, 5; cf Déirdre M Dwyer, 'Knowledge, Truth and Justification in Legal Fact Finding' (2007) 1 *The Reasoner*, issue 4, 5. Both are available at <http://www.thereasoner.org/>.

that p, the fact-finder may only be making a selfless assertion that p. These causes were explored in Chapter 1, in the discussion on trial deliberation. First, in deciding what to believe of a factual dispute, the judge at a bench trial must ignore any evidence which she has perceived but ruled inadmissible, and, in a jury trial, the jury must remove from their consideration inadmissible evidence to which they have been mistakenly exposed. Since the fact-finder is sworn to give a true finding of fact *according to the evidence*, she is obligated to consider the admitted evidence presented before her. It is often added that she must *only* consider such evidence.[29] While there is little harm in saying this, the statement cannot be taken literally. To take it literally would require exclusion even of general background knowledge about the world.[30] Without this knowledge, fact-finding cannot get off the ground. It is impossible, for example, to impute a motive for a crime without relying on background beliefs about human psychology. But the trier of fact is not allowed to rely on *all* of her pre-existing stock of knowledge. To give the clearest example, she cannot draw on personal knowledge of the defendant; indeed, possession of such personal knowledge is a ground for disqualification from hearing the case.

There is a second cause of the possible divergence of 'selfless' and 'personal' beliefs. Trial deliberation is regulated by the law and the fact-finder is prohibited from applying certain lines of evidential reasoning to particular types of evidence. Instances of such regulation are closely examined in the later chapters on standard of proof, hearsay evidence, and similar fact evidence. In the light of these two causes, BAF requires some emendations. The revised version is shown below, with the effects of legal regulation in italics:

BAF*: The fact-finder must find that p only if (i) one would be justified in believing *sufficiently strongly* that p *if one were to take into account only the admitted evidence, ignore any inadmissible evidence to which one might have been exposed, and avoid reliance on any line of evidential reasoning that the law might forbid in the case at hand*; and (ii) if one found that p, one would find that p at least in part because one would be justified in believing that p under (i).

This is quite a mouthful. For convenience and at the price of some inaccuracy, we will frequently refer to the above more shortly thus: 'the fact-finder must find that p only if one would be justified in believing that p within the terms of BAF*'.

[29] *Goold v Evans & Co* [1951] 2 TLR 1189, per Denning LJ ('It is a fundamental principle of our law that a judge must act on the evidence before him and not on outside information'); Manual of Civil Model Jury Directions issued by the United States Courts for the Ninth Circuit (2007) §1.7, available under the 'Publications' area of the Ninth Circuit's website at <http://www.ce9.uscourts.gov> ('In reaching your verdict, you may consider only the testimony and exhibits received into evidence... Anything you may have seen or heard when the court was not in session is not evidence. You are to decide the case solely on the evidence received at the trial').

[30] Arguably, such beliefs play the role of evidence understood in the broader sense that is 'not just limited to cases in which one has a specific datum to which to point': G C Stine, 'Skepticism and Relevant Alternatives, and Deductive Closure' (1976) 29 *Philosophical Studies* 249, 259. If such beliefs count as evidence, they are not evidence 'presented at the trial'.

There are nine points to be made by way of elaboration. The first four are brief ones. *First*, BAF* applies only to a positive finding of fact. To return a negative verdict such as an acquittal, one need not judge that one would be justified in believing that the accused is innocent; it is enough to judge that there is a reasonable doubt about her guilt. *Secondly*, the 'belief' that figures in BAF* is of the categorical kind. It is the concept employed in standard epistemology and refers to the mental state necessary for knowledge. As we will see in Part 2.5 below, there is a second kind of belief known as 'partial belief' that is preclusive of knowledge. *Thirdly*, the belief must be strong enough to satisfy the relevant standard of proof; exactly what this means will be examined in Chapter 4.

Fourthly, whether there is sufficient justification for a finding will depend on the evidence adduced at the trial. In the *Wagon Mound* cases,[31] two separate claims were made for losses suffered in consequence of a fire caused by the same oil spillage. A question that had to be decided was whether the defendant could reasonably be expected to have known that the oil was capable of being set afire when spread on water. The courts reached contrary conclusions in the two cases. Although the findings were contradictory, both were justified. This is because the justification for each finding must be assessed relative to the evidence presented at the respective trial and, as the Privy Council observed in the later case, the evidence adduced at the two trials was significantly different.[32]

Fifthly, BAF* assumes the existence of legal rules on the admissibility and use of evidence. While such rules do exist in common law trial systems, they purportedly do not exist or, at any rate, are less noticeable, in those Continental systems which claim to adhere to the principle of 'free proof'.[33] In the latter jurisdictions, it would not be surprising that verdicts are required to reflect the personal beliefs of the fact-finder rather than 'selfless beliefs'. The French concept of 'intime conviction' is a case in point. Under article 353 of the French Criminal Code, the trial judge has strong discretion in fact-finding. The provision emphasizes most vividly the personal nature of the belief that is needed for a conviction:[34]

[31] *Overseas Tankship (UK) Ltd v Morts Dock and Engineering Co Ltd (The Wagon Mound)* [1961] AC 388; *Overseas Tankship (UK) Ltd v The Miller Steamship Co Pty* [1967] AC 617. I thank Jane Stapleton for alerting me to the relevance of these cases.

[32] *Overseas Tankship (UK) Ltd v The Miller Steamship Co Pty* (n 31) 640.

[33] Freedom of proof has various meanings. It is used here in the second and third senses (which are two aspects of free deliberation) identified by William Twining, *Rethinking Evidence—Exploratory Essays* (2nd edn, Cambridge: CUP, 2006) 232, n 65.

[34] This English translation is from <http://195.83.177.9/code/liste.phtml?lang=uk&c=34&r=3966>, the website of the French Government. Thanks to Helene Marie Nicole Dreux-Kien for the reference. The Spanish Constitutional Court has felt the need to impose some objectivity on the test of 'judgement according to conscience': Jordi Ferrer Beltrán, 'Legal Proof and Fact Finders' Beliefs' (2006) 12 Legal Theory 293, 295, n 4; and see further, ibid 300, n 12. Some rationality constraint is perhaps also contained within the practice of discourse: Eric Landowski, 'Truth and Veridiction in Law' (1989) 2 Intl J for the Semiotics of Law 29, 38–39 ('the so-called theory of "free" evaluation . . . eventually subordinates the judge to an intersubjective system of belief control which itself ultimately depends on a narrative and discursive grammar of social discourse').

The law does not ask the judges to account for the means by which they convinced themselves; it does not charge them with any rule from which they shall specifically derive the fullness and adequacy of evidence. It requires them to question themselves in silence and reflection and to seek in the sincerity of their conscience what impression has been made on their reason by the evidence brought against the accused and the arguments of his defence. The law asks them but this single question, which encloses the full scope of their duties: are you inwardly convinced?

Sixthly, that the fact-finder believes that p does not in itself make it proper for her to find that p. The belief must be one that is justifiable under condition (i) and, as required by condition (ii), the finding that p must be made in part because the belief that p is so justifiable. A belief is not justifiable under condition (i) if it is irrational (as would be the case if it was, for example, acquired from reading tea leaves) or is based on inadmissible evidence or is arrived at by a legally forbidden reasoning. Further, a finding, although justifiable in the required sense, is also wrong if it was not motivated at all by the belief that it was so justifiable, as happened in our earlier example of a conviction based on nothing more than a feeling of revulsion for the defendant.

Seventhly, BAF* permits a finding to be made without the fact-finder personally believing the content of the finding. Such a finding is not necessarily insincere. Admittedly, BAF* injects an element of detachment in fact-finding. But the fact-finder is committed to finding only what she believes a person who follows BAF* would be justified in judging to be true. In this regard, a comparison may be made with rules which stipulate when the judge may withhold a case from being put to a jury for lack of minimal sufficiency of evidence or when the appellate court is empowered to interfere with trial findings.[35] These circumstances tend to be narrowly framed. For example, the United States Supreme Court has held that the test for reviewing a conviction is 'whether, after viewing the evidence in the light most favorable to the prosecution, *any* rational trier of fact *could* have found proof of guilt beyond a reasonable doubt'.[36] The reviewing court does not look into the reasoning actually employed by the jury in reaching its factual conclusion.[37] A review judgment as to what any rational person *could* have found is entirely different from a judgment as to what one *would* find were one to take BAF* seriously. The review court does not commit itself at all to the finding it allows to stand. In contrast, the trier of fact commits herself to the findings

[35] For an overview of the law in these areas, see Vern R Walker, 'Epistemic and Non-epistemic Aspects of the Factfinding Process in Law', Journal of Philosophy, Science and Law 5 (2005) 6–8, available at <http://www.psljournal.com/archives/all/walkerpaper.cfm>.

[36] *Jackson v Virginia* 443 (1979) US 307, 324, second italics added.

[37] Thus, in *Delk v Atkinson* (1981) 665 F 2d 90, 98, n 13, the United States Court of Appeals, Sixth Circuit held:

The question whether the evidence is constitutionally sufficient is of course wholly unrelated to the question of how rationally the verdict was actually reached. Just as the standard announced today does not permit a court to make its own subjective determination of guilt or innocence, it does not require scrutiny of the reasoning process actually used by the factfinder—if known.

that she makes (albeit within the terms of BAF* rather than in the simple first-personal sense).

BAF* does not dispense with sincerity altogether because the fact-finder is permitted to find that p only if condition (ii) is satisfied, and it is satisfied only if, in finding that p, she does so in part *because* she judges and consequently believes, at the higher level, that one would be justified in believing that p under condition (i). The fact-finder who holds the meta-level belief but not the personal belief that p is not strictly speaking insincere in finding that p. Such a finding certainly does not constitute a lie since the fact-finder does not set out to deceive in asserting that p. However, it is wrong for the fact-finder to find that p where she does *not* believe that the belief that p is justifiable in the sense required by condition (i). Where the finding is made in the knowledge that she lacks that meta-belief, her finding is at best insincere. And sincerity matters. If the fact-finder finds that p without believing that one would be justified in believing that p within the terms of BAF*, she misrepresents her opinion on the truth of p, or worse still, her finding is a lie.[38] It is unjust of a court to declare a person liable or guilty on the basis of a misrepresentation or a lie.

Eighthly, BAF* applies in most but not all cases. Condition (i) of BAF* instructs the fact-finder to ignore such inadmissible evidence to which she might have been exposed and avoid those lines of reasoning, if any, which the law forbids from being applied to the evidence adduced at the trial. These instructions are negative ones; the fact-finder is expected, subject to those caveats, to judge what propositions of fact one would be justified in believing on the evidence properly admitted in court. Exceptionally, the law renders irrelevant this doxastic judgment. It dictates the finding that the fact-finder must make. Consider the corroboration requirement. Let it be that the fact-finder is entirely convinced by a witness; she strongly believes his testimony that p. No evidence is produced to even remotely suggest that p is false. Even though she strongly believes that p, she is prevented from finding that p if it needs to be corroborated and there is no evidence to support the witness's testimony. The fact-finder's doxastic judgment is overridden. The most often cited instance of a law requiring corroboration in England is section 13 of the Perjury Act 1911. It prevents a person from being convicted of perjury 'solely upon the evidence of one witness as to the falsity of any statement alleged to be false'; if the witness's testimony is the only evidence that is available, an acquittal must be returned however strongly the fact-finder believes the testimony.

BAF* is also displaced by another legal device. The validity of rebuttable presumptions of law, within important limits set by constitutional or human rights laws, is recognized in virtually all developed jurisdictions. The broad structure of such a presumption runs as follows: the fact-finder must presume and find that X (let us say intention to traffic) where Y (for example, possession of more

[38] cf Unger (n 9) 261–262.

than a stipulated quantity of prohibited drugs) is proved and remains unrebutted. Suppose that the seized drug exceeds the stipulated quantity but is not large enough to make it beyond reasonable doubt that the drugs were held for the purpose of trafficking and not for personal consumption. If Y is proved, and X is not rebutted, the presumption compels the fact-finder to find that X even where it is not justifiable, on Y alone, to believe that X. While Y may provide a reason for believing that it is possible or likely that X is true,[39] one presumes X just where one judges that Y is not good enough reason on its own for believing that X is in fact true. Here, BAF* is displaced on practical grounds. The policy justifying a presumption of law of the present kind is, rightly or wrongly, often couched in terms of our interest in securing convictions, with emphasis placed on the gravity of the social ill that is sought to be contained.[40]

BAF* has no role to play at all where there is no need for trial deliberation. Where a conviction follows a guilty plea or a civil judgment is entered by default, a declaration of guilt or liability is made by the court without it having to resolve any dispute of fact and, therefore, without it having to deliberate on what to believe of the facts in dispute. As Spencer tells us: 'In English law..., the effect of a guilty plea is to oblige the court to convict, whether or not it believes the accused is really guilty—something which is a considerable derogation from the principle that the court should convict only those persons of whose guilt it is convinced.'[41]

Leaving aside the room for pragmatic considerations that epistemic contextualism and interest-relative accounts of knowledge and justified belief allow (topics for Chapter 4), BAF* is essentially an epistemic rule. A presumption of law, on the other hand, is a practical rule; it deals with the question 'what to do' rather than 'what (it is reasonable for one) to believe'. Following the analysis of Shah and Velleman, considered in detail below, I regard p as true both when I believe that p and when I presume that p. But when I presume that p, I regard p as true for practical purposes, and this is different from regarding p as true in the nature of a

[39] Arguably, Y must offer such a reason if it is to raise a presumption that X. For Leibniz, a presumption is more than a conjecture: 'to *presume* something is not to accept it *before* it has been proved, which is never permissible, but to accept it *provisionally* but not groundlessly, while waiting for a proof to the contrary'. G W Leibniz, *New Essays on Human Understanding*, edited by Peter Remnant and Jonathan Bennett (Cambridge: CUP, 1996) bk IV, ch xiv, 457 (italics original). For discussion of Leibniz's views on presumption, see Robert Merrrihew Adams, *Leibniz—Determinist, Theist, Idealist* (Oxford: OUP, 1994) ch 8

[40] eg *Ong Ah Chuan v PP* [1980–1981] Singapore L Rep 48, 62 (Privy Council decision on appeal from Singapore): '[Rebuttable] [p]resumptions [of law] are a common feature of modern legislation concerning the possession and use of things that present danger to society like addictive drugs, explosives, arms and ammunition'; *PP v Yuvaraj* [1969] 2 Malayan LJ 89, 92 (Privy Council decision on appeal from Malaysia): 'The policy which underlies [the presumption of law in] s 14 of the Prevention of Corruption Act 1961 is, in their Lordships' view, clear...Corruption in the public service is a grave social evil which is difficult to detect, for those who take part in it will be at pains to cover their tracks.'

[41] J R Spencer, 'Evidence' in Mireille Delmas-Marty and J R Spence (eds), *European Criminal Procedures* (Cambridge: CUP, 2002) ch 11, 621.

belief. The practical nature of a presumption is highlighted by Ullmann-Margalit and Margalit:[42]

> The point of a presumption (that p) ... is practical, not theoretical. One presumes that p in order to act on it, in a situation where the decision as to which action to take depends on whether or not p is the case. One is to enter p as a premise into one's pertinent piece of practical deliberation and to proceed as if it were true ... The question of whether or not the person actually believes that it is true does not arise.

Ninthly, BAF* takes justified selfless belief as the aim of a positive verdict or finding of fact. Against this, one might argue that the objective of trial deliberation is to get the truth, to find that p if and only if p. But truth cannot be all that is aimed at. If I flip a coin to decide a verdict, there is a 50 per cent chance of hitting the truth. Suppose I do hit the truth. I find and assert that the accused is guilty and it is true that the accused is guilty. No one could reasonably regard my assertion as proper since it was based on nothing more than a lazy and irresponsible guess. Truth is not all that matters. On the other hand, truth does matter. Justified belief is not all that trial deliberation aims at either. We want a positive verdict or finding of fact to be both justified and *correct*. Suppose the defendant was convicted on evidence which was such that it was reasonable for one to believe, and hence one would be justified in believing, that she is guilty, thus satisfying condition (i) of BAF*, and suppose further that condition (ii) was also satisfied. As it turns out, the evidence against the defendant was fabricated and she is innocent. She was wrongfully convicted. It is beside the point that we cannot blame the court for having wrongfully convicted her. As a matter of fact, we do think it wrong to find a person guilty (or, for that matter, liable) where she is not, however reasonable and blameless we think the court was in arriving at its verdict.

A knowledge-based account of fact-finding easily explains why the conviction itself was wrongful. According to KF, the fact-finder must find positively that p only if she knows that p. It is impermissible to assert what is false even though one is blameless or acts reasonably in asserting it.[43] In our hypothetical scenario, the guilty verdict violated KF. The court found and asserted that the defendant was guilty when it did not know that she was guilty, and the court did not know that she was guilty because she was not. In contrast, BAF* appears to lack the resources to explain why the conviction itself was wrongful. And we do say and want to say that the conviction was wrongful.[44] Is there any way of adding truth

[42] Edna Ullmann-Margalit and Avishai Margalit, 'Holding True and Holding as True' (1992) 92 *Synthese* 167, 171.

[43] Williamson (n 9) 256.

[44] Glanville Williams, 'A Short Rejoinder' [1980] Crim LR 103, 104, n 1: '[S]ome lawyers assert that if all the rules of law, evidence and procedure have been applied and an innocent man is nevertheless convicted, there is no miscarriage of justice. I do not accept this language, and would regard it as ostrich-like. There is a miscarriage of justice whenever an innocent man is convicted.' David M Paciocco, 'Balancing the Rights of the Individual and Society in Matters of Truth and Proof: Part II—Evidence

as a normative criterion on to BAF* without ending up with KF? If we say that the fact-finder must find that p only if (i) one would be justified in believing that p within the terms of BAF* *and* (ii) p is true, is that not, in effect, coming close to saying that the fact-finder must find that p only if she *knows* that p? It may still be possible to hold back from the strong claim that knowledge is required for a positive finding by, as it were, embedding truth as a normative standard within BAF*. One possibility is to exploit the idea that a belief is correct if and only if it is true.[45] Unfortunately, this argument is not at all easy to construct. An attempt at such an argument is made in the next section by relying on a normative theory of doxastic deliberation offered by Shah and Velleman. As much can be obtained from their theory, it will be discussed at length. It is unclear that the argument can fully succeed.

1.4 Truth

Shah and Velleman address the long-standing controversy over the voluntariness of belief. According to one view, we cannot believe at will.[46] Beliefs, so it is said, are not under our direct control. I look out of the window and I see rain. My belief that it is raining follows my perception immediately. I did not acquire that belief from any evaluation of evidence. Neither did I decide to have that belief. I cannot decide to believe otherwise, however much I want the sun to be out. Of course, I can choose to act as if I believe that it is not raining (I can lie to you about the weather), I can choose to imagine that it is not raining (by daydreaming of a sunny day), and I can choose to do something which will indirectly[47] change the belief I know I have (by getting myself hypnotized into believing that the day is fine).[48] It still remains that I cannot believe that it is not raining by simply choosing to believe it there and then.[49]

about Innocence' (2002) 81 Canadian Bar Rev 39, 43–44 is of the same opinion: 'When we use that term [ie, wrongful conviction], we do not refer to those who are factually guilty but who have been given imperfect trials. We refer to those who are factually innocent, including those to whom the procedures have been applied with perfection.'

45 This view is defended by a number of philosophers, including: Shah and Velleman, whose article is discussed later in the text; Peter Railton, 'Truth, Reason, and the Regulation of Belief' (1994) 5 *Philosophical Issues* 71, 74 ('It is . . . distinctive and *constitutive* of belief not only that it represents its content as true, but that it takes itself to be correct only if that particular content really is true'); and Ralph Wedgwood, 'The Aim of Belief' (2002) 16 *Philosophical Perspectives* 267 (maintaining that a belief is correct if and only if the proposition believed is true).

46 eg Bernard Williams, 'Deciding to Believe' in his *Problems of the Self—Philosophical Papers 1956–72* (Cambridge: CUP, 1973) ch 9.

47 Analogously, while I can indirectly make my heart beat faster by going for a run, I cannot directly control my heart rate in the same way I control my arm movement: Ullmann-Margalit and Margalit (n 42) 179.

48 In the last case, until I succeed in deluding myself, I do not believe it yet, and when I do come to believe it, the belief is (as one could say) something that happened to me.

49 There are rare cases where it seems that the subject can choose to adopt a belief. One is where an athlete wills herself to believe that she will win the race, knowing that her having that belief

While there is clearly a sense in which we cannot decide *to* believe something just like that, there is also a sense in which we are certainly capable of deciding *that* something is true.[50] We often wonder whether to believe what we are told or who to believe. Such questions run through the fact-finder's mind as she listens to the evidence being given at a trial. Surely it is possible to reason and make up one's mind on what or who to believe. How do we reconcile the seemingly obvious possibility of doxastic deliberation with the apparent involuntariness of belief? Shah and Velleman offer a convincing solution.[51]

A belief can arise without deliberation: recall the example of seeing rain and believing that it is raining. But not all beliefs arise spontaneously or non-consciously or unintentionally in this fashion. Some beliefs are acquired through doxastic deliberation.[52] I am in a windowless room and someone tells me that it is raining outside. I ask myself whether to *believe* her. To be able to ask that question, I must have a concept of belief. I exercise that concept in deliberating whether to believe what she tells me. I weigh the evidence and engage in reasoning. I cannot think why she would lie to me, and I see a wet umbrella in her hand, a fact I take to corroborate her testimony. I judge that she is telling me the truth and come to affirm and consequently to believe that it is raining outside.

Truth figures, descriptively and normatively, in the concept of belief. To accept that p is to regard or treat p as true; it involves the disposition to behave as if p were true.[53] But acceptance is the generic attitude shared by cognitive attitudes. While belief that p involves acceptance that p, one also accepts that p where one assumes or imagines or supposes that p. Belief is different from these other

increases the chances of victory. But this is 'just a special case of the common situation in which beliefs are (partially) under our control because the set of facts which make them true or false are under our control (I can come to have the belief that the light is on by flipping the light switch)': Neil Levy, 'Doxastic Deliberation' (2007) 155 *Synthese* 127, 137.

[50] On the distinction between 'deciding to believe that p' and 'deciding that p is true', see Stuart Hampshire, *Thought and Action* (London: Chatto and Windus, 1982) 158; contrast Matthias Steup, 'Doxastic Voluntarism and Epistemic Deontology' (2000) 15 *Acta Analytica* 25, 36.

[51] Nishi Shah and David J Velleman, 'Doxastic Deliberation' (2005) 114 *The Philosophical Rev* 497. This article builds on Nishi Shah, 'How Truth Governs Belief' (2003) 112 *The Philosophical Rev* 447 and is developed further in Nishi Shah, 'A New Argument for Evidentialism' (2006) 56 *The Philosophical Quarterly* 481. For other defences of doxastic voluntarism, see Carl Ginet, 'Deciding to Believe' in Matthias Steup (ed), *Knowledge, Truth, and Duty* (New York: OUP, 2001) ch 4 and Steup (n 50) (both papers draw on examples of courtroom trials).

[52] The distinction between belief as a non-voluntary or primitive mental state or disposition ('primary belief') and belief as a mental state that is produced by some form of deliberation is drawn by many philosophers: D H Mellor, 'Consciousness and Degrees of Belief' in D H Mellor (ed), *Prospects For Pragmatism—Essays In Memory Of F P Ramsey* (Cambridge: CUP, 1980) ch 7 ('plain' or 'first order belief' versus 'assent' or 'conscious belief'); Ronald B de Souza, *How to Give a Piece of Your Mind: or, the Logic of Belief and Assent* (1971) 25 *Rev of Metaphysics* 52 ('confidence' or subjective probability versus 'belief' proper); Daniel C Dennett, 'How to Change Your Mind' in his *Brainstorms: Philosophical Essays On Mind And Psychology* (Sussex: Harvester Press, 1981) ch 16 ('belief' versus 'opinion'); L Jonathan Cohen, *An Essay On Belief And Acceptance* (Oxford: OUP, 1992) ch 1 ('belief' versus 'acceptance').

[53] Shah and Velleman (n 51) 498.

cognitive propositional attitudes because only an acceptance that is, at least to some extent, regulated for truth is a belief; in forming, revising, and abandoning a belief, 'one responds to evidence and reasoning in ways that are designed to be truth-conducive'.[54] I can suppose or assume or imagine that p—accept that p, say, for the sake of argument or idle fun—even where I know that the evidence is against p. The same cannot be said of belief. Being regulated for truth is part of the concept of belief. A cognitive attitude can be properly *described* as a belief only if it is regulated for truth. This is not to deny that beliefs can be influenced also by extra-evidential considerations.[55] An attitude generated in part by wishful thinking or prejudice may be a belief nonetheless.

The concept of belief is also governed *normatively* by the standard of truth. Shah and Velleman build their case on the observation that doxastic deliberation inevitably gives way to factual inquiry. If we ask ourselves 'whether to believe that p',[56] our mind turns necessarily and naturally to the question 'whether p'. The answer to the latter factual question determines the answer to the former deliberative question, and the only way of answering the deliberative question is to answer the factual one. How do we explain this? The best explanation is that truth is contained in the concept of belief as the standard of correctness.[57] Doxastic deliberation employs the concept of belief. To decide whether to believe that p is to decide whether to have that cognitive attitude towards p that is conceived as the belief that p, and it is because the concept of belief is governed by the normative standard of truth that 'whether to believe that p' inevitably gives way to 'whether p'. So, in deliberating on what to believe, one is already committed to using truth as the standard of correctness. That truth is the normative standard governing the concept of belief means that it is correct to believe that p if and only if p is true. The same standard does not apply to other cognitive attitudes towards p. It is not wrong to assume or suppose or daydream that p just because p is false. It is, on the other hand, wrong to judge and consequently believe that p if p is false.

[54] ibid.

[55] Pragmatic consideration may exert an influence where the belief is acquired other than by doxastic deliberation, and it may also exert an implicit or unacknowledged influence in doxastic deliberation. For elaboration, see Shah, 'A New Argument for Evidentialism' (n 51) 489–490.

[56] This is different from the question of whether it *benefits* me to believe something. A non-believer may immerse herself in religious practices in the hope that she will be mentally conditioned into believing God. While the desire for salvation prompts her to take steps towards attaining the relevant belief, the desire is not a reason for believing that God exists. Whether to believe something is different from whether it is desirable to believe it. The 'doxastic question whether to believe that *p*' should not be confused with the 'practical question whether to bring about the belief that *p*': Shah, 'A New Argument for Evidentialism' (n 51) 498. The relation between practical and theoretical reasoning is further explored in Chapter 4 on Standard of Proof.

[57] The connection between belief and truth cannot be established by simply pointing out that to believe something is to believe it true. We could also say that to wish something is to wish it true, but obviously, we do not apply to wishes the same normative standard we apply to beliefs: we do not say that it is correct to wish that p if and only if p is true: Shah and Velleman (n 51) 497.

One deliberates whether to believe that p by engaging 'in reasoning that is aimed at issuing or not issuing in one's believing that p in accordance with the norm for believing that p'.[58] Where doxastic deliberation yields a belief, it does so via a judgment. The judgment is bound by the same norm that governs the belief: 'a judgment, like a belief, is correct if and only if its content is true'.[59] To judge that p is to commit the mental act of affirming p with the aim of doing so only if p is true. It is possible to accept p without this aim. There is no such aim, for example, when we merely suppose or assume or imagine that p. My belief that p is an attitude towards p, a mental *state* wherein p is represented as true. My judgment that p is a cognitive mental *act* of putting forward p in my mind and presenting it as true. It is strictly speaking the judgment that is the object of doxastic deliberation. The mental state or cognitive attitude of believing that p arises simply and non-inferentially from the cognitive mental act of judging that p. I come to *believe* that you are telling me the truth from *judging* that you are telling me the truth. This transition is a perfectly common phenomenon even though it is ineffable how the judgment (the act of affirming a proposition) induces the belief (the standing affirmative attitude towards the proposition).

What are we then to make of the claim that belief is involuntary or that we cannot believe at will? This claim captures the important insight that one cannot believe arbitrarily by judging arbitrarily. If you accept that p arbitrarily, without aiming to accept that p only if p is true, you are not seeking to judge p and therefore you are not deliberating whether to believe that p. One who reasons on what to believe is conceptually bound to have this aim. A person is not deliberating whether to believe p if she is unresponsive to evidence for or against p; she is not judging p if she is not aiming to accept p only if p is true. This is not to deny that one can arbitrarily accept p, by, for example, assuming or conjecturing that p. However, where reasoning is not aimed at getting the truth-value of p right, the reasoning, whatever else it may be, is not conducted with a view to judging p. That this is so does not mean that we cannot reason about what to believe. Doxastic deliberation is possible even though we cannot decide to believe arbitrarily.

Shah and Velleman distinguish the deliberative question 'whether to believe that p' from the factual question 'whether I do believe that p'. The latter can be interpreted in one of two ways, as 'whether I do *already* believe that p' or 'whether I *now* believe that p'. The first directs me to search my mind for an existing belief on p; the latter requires me to make up my mind on whether to believe p with a view to self-ascription of that belief. Only the latter is of interest for present purposes. I ascertain 'whether I do now believe that p' by asking 'whether to believe that p', or more accurately, 'whether to judge that p', which in turn is potentially transparent to the question 'whether p'. Where I judge that p, and yet fail to come to know that I believe that p, I am being irrational.

[58] ibid 502. [59] ibid 503.

In some cases, I find that I already accept tentatively that p, for example, as a suspicion. (We will return to this important cognitive state when we discuss partial belief in connection with probability.) Where I find such an antecedent acceptance of p, but do not believe that p or do not believe it yet, I can ascertain whether I do now believe that p by deciding whether to accord my pre-existing acceptance the status of a belief. I do so by subjecting my pre-existing acceptance to the regulation of truth, and by applying to it the standard of truth as the standard of correctness. The process of regulating my pre-existing acceptance for truth may be inconclusive and I may thus be reluctant to elevate that acceptance to the status of a belief. In short, I may decide not to believe but to continue to classify my acceptance as at best a suspicion. My deliberation is equally complex where I find an antecedent belief that p but decide to reopen the question whether p in a way that puts at risk my acceptance of p as a belief. When I do so, I reduce my acceptance to the status of a hypothesis and keep my acceptance open to further testing for truth. Here, as before, the question is not whether to believe p *tout court* but whether to accord my acceptance that p the status of a belief or to accord it the lower status of a mere suspicion or hypothesis.

The fact-finder does not retire to consider the convict with a clean mental slate. A fact-finder who pays attention to the evidence as it is being given would invariably have formed tentative views or impressions on issues such as accuracy, reliability, and trustworthiness. She undertakes doxastic deliberation as the trial proceeds, even if she does not consciously pose to herself the question 'whether to believe' the evidence and even if she does not come (indeed she must not come) to any firm conclusion just yet. One juror captures this phenomenon surprisingly well in a report on his personal experience: 'as the evidence unfolds one achieves a more regulated judgment'.[60] It is true that the fact-finder must 'keep an open mind' at this stage. That is best interpreted as an instruction to always be ready and willing to reconsider and change any impressions that she might have formed before all the evidence is in. Whatever cognitive attitudes she brings into the final stage of deliberation must remain subject to revision.

At that final stage, she must ask herself: what do I believe about the facts of the case? A 'selfless' form of the question is required by BAF*: would one be justified in believing that such and such an allegation is true, leaving aside such evidence and reasoning as may be excluded by the law? It is likely that the two questions will in fact be run together in actual deliberation. For example, the fact-finder may retire to consider the verdict with a pre-existing acceptance of the testimony of a witness in the weak form of a suspicion that it is true. For the moment, she accepts his testimony only as a hypothesis; she is not prepared to believe it just yet until she has had the chance to go over all the evidence more carefully, to see, for instance, how his testimony holds up against all that she has seen and heard at

[60] Account by Alan Wykes in Dulan Barber and Giles Gordon (eds), *Members of the Jury* (London: Wildwood House, 1976) 142.

the trial. She is expected to apply the injunction to ignore any inadmissible evidence to which she might have been exposed and to eschew such forbidden lines of reasoning as the admitted evidence might invite. She must decide, in the light of that injunction, whether one would be justified in according her pre-existing acceptance of the witness's testimony the status of a belief or to continue to regard it as still a hypothesis.

In the kind of situation just described, there is considerable 'latitude in whether to regard one's acceptance as a belief',[61] and there can be pragmatic reasons for or against regarding it as such. These reasons 'have to do primarily with what is at stake'.[62] As Shah and Velleman say:[63]

> The question whether one believes that *p* is here a question of whether to accord one's acceptance of *p* the status of belief, and hence a question of whether *to* believe it rather than merely suspect or hypothesize it. And when the question is whether to believe that *p* rather than merely suspect or hypothesize it—given that one somehow accepts it—the answer may depend on the relative costs of belief versus suspicion rather than on the truth value of *p*.

The authors' theory is therefore compatible with epistemic contexualism and interest-relative accounts of knowledge and justified belief, theories to which we will return in Chapter 4 on Standard of Proof.

As we have seen, Shah and Velleman claim that a belief is correct if and only if it is true. How can this claim about the correctness of belief be connected to the propriety of a finding or an assertion of fact? Just because it is correct to *believe* that p if and only if p is true does not mean that it is correct to *find* or *assert* that p only if p is true. To get us to the latter conclusion, we need some rule to the effect that one must find or assert only what one believes. This is where BAF* comes in. To recall: the fact-finder must find that p only if one would be justified in believing that p within the terms of BAF*.

Following Shah and Velleman, the reference to 'belief' in BAF* should be read in the first instance as a 'judgment'. That one would be *justified* in judging and consequently believing that p does not entail that one is *correct* to believe that p. The belief that p is correct if and only if p is true. One might try to argue that truth is *presupposed* in BAF* as an independent standard of correctness because the norm is contained in the concept of belief that is exercised in trial deliberation. However, the argument cannot be that straightforward. To begin with, the concept of belief used in BAF* is the more complicated one of 'selfless belief'.

[61] Shah and Velleman (n 51) 514.

[62] ibid 517 where the authors further explain: 'Sometimes the costs of continuing active testing of a cognition would be high if it were true, whereas the costs of postponing further tests would be low if it were false. One then has pragmatic reason to accord the cognition the status of belief. In other cases, the costs of failing to find counterevidence, if it existed, would be high, or those of continuing to look for it, if it didn't exist, would be low. One then has pragmatic reason for hypothesizing rather than believing.'

[63] ibid 517–518, and see also ibid endnote 39.

But this complication can be accommodated. The concept of 'belief' is part of the concept of 'selfless belief'. If p is false, it is incorrect for me to believe that p. My belief that p is incorrect, however justified I am in believing it. Equally, if p is false, one's belief that p is incorrect, however justified one is in believing it. Since one must find that p only if one would be justified in believing p (within the terms of BAF*, more on which below), the finding is incorrect if the belief is incorrect. Call this 'TSC': truth is the standard of correctness for a finding of fact; here as before, 'finding' refers only to a positive finding.

There are two other and related problems with this argument. First, as noted, the trier of fact does not simply deliberate whether to believe *tout court* the disputed propositions. She may find herself already accepting the proposition, and what she must finally decide is whether to accord her acceptance the status of a belief or a hypothesis. As Shah and Velleman say, this decision is opened to pragmatic influences. It would seem therefore that the correctness of the decision cannot turn on truth alone. This problem is difficult to overcome. This is perhaps a possible response: in according one's acceptance the status of a belief, one finally comes to believe the disputed proposition. While pragmatic considerations impact on the rationality of deciding to believe a disputed proposition, the correctness of a belief once held is determined by truth alone.[64]

Secondly, trial deliberation appears at first blush to be constrained by rules that are based on extra-epistemic considerations. However, on closer inspection, those 'constraints' on evidentiary reasoning are mostly rules that, by and large, aim to make one's belief epistemically justifiable. (This is true in the case of the hearsay rule and the similar facts rule, as will be argued in Chapters 5 and 6 respectively.) There are only a few exceptions that obviate epistemic judgment, such as the doctrine of corroboration and presumptions of law, and they operate in few cases. It seems therefore still possible to argue that the norm of truth is contained in the concept of belief that figures in BAF* and that one's belief, and the consequential finding, that p is generally correct only if p is true.

It is tempting to go further. Can it be said: even if the finding that p is driven solely by a legal presumption, it is incorrect if p is false? Take our earlier example. Suppose someone is convicted of drug trafficking on the basis of a legal presumption that he intended to sell or distribute the drugs that were found on him. The evidence, let us assume, is insufficient to justify the belief that he had such intention. As it turns out, the accused is in fact innocent. Unless we say that his conviction communicates an assertion that he committed the crime, it is very difficult to see how the conviction was wrongful. Here is an argument that might work: we can perhaps insist that his conviction does communicate the assertion of guilt by separating the conditions for making a finding of fact and the illocutionary force of that finding. The legal presumption calls the fact-finder to convict the accused even if she does not judge that one would be justified in believing that he

64 This is near to the point raised by Wedgwood (n 45) 274.

had the intention to traffic: BAF* is displaced. However, the finding is communicated and received as an assertion of guilt rather than merely as a declaration that the accused is hereby presumed guilty. If this is right, the assertion of guilt, like all assertions, is regulated by RTBNA*: hence, one should assert that p only if, amongst other things, one would be justified in believing that p. If p is false, the belief that p is incorrect (TSC). Consequently, if p is false, the assertion that p is also incorrect. This allows us to say of our example that the finding of guilt *qua* an assertion of guilt is incorrect.

The standard of *correctness* in TSC is independent of the standard of *justification* required by BAF*. A finding that is justified under BAF* may yet be incorrect or false, and an incorrect or false finding may nonetheless be justified under BAF*. TSC and BAF* serve different functions. TSC is an evaluative criterion that is applied from a third person perspective on the outcome of trial deliberation, where the falsity of a positive finding necessarily makes the finding wrong. BAF* functions instead as a regulative rule; it guides the fact-finder in the process of deliberation, setting the standard for a justified finding that operates from her point of view. A theory that combines BAF* and TSC is certainly more elaborate than the knowledge account of fact-finding. But it is unclear how they are significantly different. It is doubtful that they are different if BAF* and TSC are combined as linked elements such that the ultimate aim is somehow to obtain truth *through* justified belief. We may thus say that the *ultimate* aim of trial deliberation is *knowledge*, understood to mean the aim of producing a positive finding that satisfies BAF* in a way that also satisfies TSC, whereas the *immediate* aim of trial deliberation is *justified belief* of the type required by BAF*.

2 Belief and Probability

2.1 Belief and fact-finding

Part 1 provided a belief-centred account of trial deliberation and fact-finding. The role of belief in fact-finding finds some support in the cases. In *Sargent v Massachusetts Accident Company*,[65] the Supreme Court of Massachusetts insisted that to make a positive finding there must be 'actual belief in its truth'. In the Australian High Court case of *Briginshaw v Briginshaw*,[66] Dixon J held that

[65] (1940) 307 Mass 246, 250. Followed in *Smith v Rapid Transit* (1945) 317 Mass 469, 470. See also *Anderson v Chicago Brass Co* (1906) 127 Wis 273, 280 where the Supreme Court of Wisconsin held: 'It is well settled by a long series of decisions in this court that the party upon whom rests the burden of proof does not lift that burden by merely producing a preponderance of evidence... In order to entitle himself to a finding in his favor his evidence must not only be of greater convincing power, but it must be such as to satisfy or convince the minds of the jury of the truth of his contention.'

[66] (1938) 60 CLR 336, 361–2. This is described as the 'predominant position in Australian case law' in *Seltsam Pty Ltd v McGuiness* (2000) 49 NSWLR 262, 284, providing a long citation of cases

'when the law requires the proof of any fact, the tribunal must feel an actual persuasion of its occurrence or existence before it can be found'. In England,[67] Lord Scarman appeared to have taken a similar view in *R v Home Secretary, ex p Khawaja*[68] when he commented that facts 'must be proved to the satisfaction of the court'; in the earlier case of *Re the Estate of Fuld, decd (No. 3)*,[69] he had similarly insisted that 'the conscience of the court... must be satisfied by the evidence'. However, the idea that fact-finding is determined by belief faces considerable resistance. For example, Murphy J declared his opposition unequivocally in the Australian High Court case of *TNT Management Pty Ltd v Brooks*:[70] 'The requirement of belief is inconsistent with, and has no place in a system which applies the balance of probabilities as the standard of proof.' Academics are divided on the issue, with the supporters of the belief requirement somewhat in the minority.[71] Unfortunately, it is not always clear exactly what the opponents are claiming and on what grounds they rest their opposition.

There are at least five possible objections to a belief-centred account of fact-finding. The first objection draws attention to the fact that the law imposes on the fact-finder the duty to decide on the verdict. This implies that she can choose what verdict to give. Since beliefs are beyond one's control, if beliefs determine her verdict, she lacks that choice.[72] It should be clear by now that this argument is unsound. As we have seen in Part 1.4 above, the involuntariness of belief is reconcilable with the clear possibility of deciding what to believe. Judgments, which produce beliefs, are within our control.

The second objection is that the law does not require the verdict to reflect the *personal* beliefs of the fact-finder. Sbisà, for example, wrote:[73]

> what is relevant is the fact that the decision, that the judge has to take, has to be related to the evidence provided and the arguments exposed in the trial, while his/her personal

and academic writings, in addition to which, see Australian Law Reform Commission Interim Report No 26, *Evidence*, vol 2 (Canberra: Australian Government Publishing, 1985) ch 16.

[67] For the English position, see Mike Redmayne, *Standards of Proof in Civil Litigation* (1999) 62 MLR 167, 177–178; Rosemary Pattenden, *The Risk of Non-Persuasion in Civil Trials: The Case Against a Floating Standard of Proof* [1988] Civil Justice Quarterly 220, 224–225.

[68] [1984] 1 AC 74, 114.

[69] [1968] P 675, 686.

[70] (1979) 53 Australian LJ Rep 267, 271, per Murphy J. See also the English Court of Appeal decision in *The Brimnes* [1975] 1 QB 929, 968, 970, cf 951. The probabilistic reasoning used in both decisions is criticized by Mark Ockelton, *How to be Convinced*, (1980) 2 Liverpool L Rev 65, 70–72.

[71] Those who explicitly reject the requirement include Alan D Cullison, 'Probability Analysis of Judicial Fact-Finding: A Preliminary Outline of the Subjective Approach' (1969) 1 U of Toledo L Rev 538, 569–576; James Brook, 'Inevitable Errors: The Preponderance of the Evidence Standard in Civil Litigation' (1982) 18 Tulsa LJ 79, 89 *et seq*. Contrast William Trickett, 'Preponderance of Evidence, and Reasonable Doubt' (1906) 10 *The Forum* 75, 80; Fleming James Jr, 'Burdens of Proof' (1961) 47 Virginia L Rev 51, 53–54.

[72] Cohen (n 52) 121; Beltrán (n 34) 298–299.

[73] Marina Sbisà, 'Response to P J van den Hoven' (1988) 1 International Journal for the Semiotics of Law 47 at 8.

beliefs do not have to be so related. Thus, the counsel's argumentation can aim at influencing, and indeed influence, the decision of the judge without (aiming at) influencing his/her beliefs.

This view is echoed by Raz:[74]

> The whole system of law and enforcement via courts and tribunals is based on acceptance of presumptions, like the presumption of innocence, and on accepting verdicts based on evidence presented in court, while ignoring all other evidence. Juries and judges are not required to believe that the accused is guilty or innocent. They are only required to accept and pronounce verdicts which are correct according to the evidence before them.

A related objection has it that allowing a verdict to rest on personal beliefs is to endorse 'an absolutely subjective notion of proof'.[75] The answer to all of these challenges can already be found in BAF*. As we may recall, BAF* relies on the concept of 'selfless belief' rather than 'personal belief' and insists that one must be justified in believing the relevant proposition.

Thirdly, and this was also raised earlier, it may be pointed out that trial deliberation is heavily regulated by the law.[76] The court has often to decide its verdict on non-cognitive grounds. Admittedly, BAF* is subject to qualifications; Part 1.3 identified instances where BAF* is displaced or has no application. But those are exceptional cases. It is also true that evidentiary rules impose 'constraints' on trial deliberation. Those 'constraints' are not as tight as we might suppose, operating mainly as negative rules, and they have a strong epistemic character in the sense that their main aim is to instruct the fact-finder to form judgments that are epistemically justifiable. For example, as will be argued in later chapters, rules that exclude reliance on certain inferences from hearsay evidence and evidence of previous misconduct are centrally (although not wholly) concerned with the rationality of belief.

The fourth and fifth objections are based on an argument of probability. Critics of the belief requirement insist that fact-finding is based on probabilities and not belief.[77] This criticism is understandable since legal standards of proof, especially the civil standard, are often described in the language of probability. However, the probability argument trades on a confusion of epistemic justification (BAF*) with truth as the standard of correctness (TSC). The positive finding that p is correct only if p is true. But, so it is said, we can never be absolutely certain that

[74] Joseph Raz, 'Reasons: Practical and Adaptive' (July 2007) Oxford Legal Studies Research Paper No 12/2007, draft available at SSRN: <http://ssrn.com/abstract=999870>.

[75] Beltrán (n 34) 297.

[76] Cohen (n 52) 122–123; Beltrán (n 34) 297.

[77] On the supposed distinction between the 'belief' approach and the 'probability' approach: K J Carruthers, 'Some observations on the Standard of Proof in Marine Insurance Cases with Special Reference to the "Popi M" Case' (1988) 62 Australian LJ 199; D H Hodgson, 'The Scales of Justice: Probability and Proof in Legal Fact-finding' (1995) 69 Australian LJ 731; Richard M Eggleston, *Evidence, Probability And Proof* (2nd edn, London: Weidenfeld & Nicolson, 1983) 130–137.

p is true. Therefore, we should not demand that the fact-finder be absolutely certain that p before finding positively that p. To find positively that p, she need not believe that p is true; it suffices if she believes that p is probably true. It follows that she is justified in making that finding so long as she is justified in believing that p is probably true. The degree of probability need only be more than 0.5 in a civil case. It has to be much higher at a criminal trial to secure a guilty verdict; but, even so, it need not reach 1, a figure which represents certainty.[78]

On closer inspection, this argument intertwines two different arguments. The objection to a belief-centred account of fact-finding is based on two distinct grounds. According to one version of the probability argument, there is no quarrel with the role of belief in fact-finding. After all, 'probability' and 'belief' are not mutually exclusive bases for findings of fact. Even if one has to decide on probabilities, one still has to decide on the basis of one's belief about the probabilities. Indeed, on one view, probability *is* belief. As we will see, of the various theories of probabilities, only that which conceives probabilities in terms of degrees of belief could plausibly serve as the legal basis for deciding questions of fact. If trial deliberation is not based on belief, it is difficult to see what else it could be based on. (Knowledge, as noted, is an alternative. But those who reject belief as the basis of fact-finding are unlikely to accept knowledge either; at least, it is hard to see why they would.) The probability argument, on the first interpretation, is directed at the propositional content of a finding. It consists of the claim that the content of a finding is not a proposition of fact but a proposition of probability. To justify a finding, the fact-finder needs only to believe, and be justified in believing, in the relevant proposition of probability. This argument is examined further and refuted in Part 2.4.

Unlike the first version of the probability argument, the second version accepts that the propositional content of a finding is factual. Here, the dispute is not over the propositional content of a finding but over the attitude the trier of fact must have towards the proposition contained in her finding. The opponents argue that the belief that p should not be a condition for the finding that p because this sets the standard of proof at or near absolute certainty.[79] The fact-finder need not believe categorically that p in order to find that p; it suffices that she believes to a

[78] '[A]s it seldom happens that absolute certainty can be obtained in human affairs, therefore reason and public utility require that Judges and all mankind, in forming their opinions of the truth of facts, should be regulated by the superior number of probabilities on the one side and on the other': per Lord Mansfield, *The Douglas* case, quoted by Best J in *R v Burdett* (1820) 4 B & Ald 95, 122.

[79] Ralph K Winter, 'The Jury and the Risk of Nonpersuasion' (1971) 5 Law and Society Rev 335, 339; Brook (n 71) 92; J P McBaine, 'Burden of Proof: Degrees of Belief' (1944) 32 California L Rev 242, 250; Edmund M Morgan, *Some Problems of Proof under the Anglo-American System Of Litigation* (Westport, Connecticut: Greenwood Press, 1956) 84.

sufficiently high degree that p.[80] The latter belief is of the kind commonly called partial belief. Advocates of a Bayesian approach to analysing legal fact-finding place partial belief at the centre of their analysis. To put it roughly, to have only a partial belief that p is to think 'probably p', where probably qualifies not the proposition p but the subject's attitude towards p. This argument is discussed in Parts 2.5 and 2.6, where the position is taken that fact-finding in general requires categorical belief. 'Categorical' should be understood in the sense of 'categorical distinction', as when it is said that one either believes p or does not believe p. Unfortunately, the name may lead one to think, mistakenly, that to believe categorically that p is to be (absolutely) certain that p, a cognitive state considered near impossible to attain, especially under sceptical challenge. In fact, as we will see, categorical beliefs are commonplaces and come in varying strengths.[81]

Once it is seen that neither of the two versions of the probability argument stands, a first step can be taken towards solving a well-known paradox of legal proof. This is the undertaking of Part 2.6. A preliminary matter must first be dealt with. The next section prepares the ground for subsequent arguments by examining the philosophical foundations of probability.

2.2 Theories of probability

There are many theories of probability: of what it is and how it is measured. To qualify as a theory of probability, the theory must satisfy the mathematical rules known as the probability calculus.[82] Different theories of probability offer different interpretations of that calculus. While the mathematical component is open to a variety of interpretations, it is itself uncontroversial.[83] There is, unfortunately,

[80] One may object to deciding questions of fact on the basis of belief for exactly the opposite reason. To find someone guilty of a crime (p), it is not good enough to merely believe that p, in the sense of thinking that p is likely or probable; one must be sure that p is true. The intuitive idea underlying this objection is in fact the source of the belief-centred account of fact-finding that is developed in this chapter; as so interpreted, the 'objection', far from offering resistance to that account, actually supports it.

[81] Nicholas Rescher, *Dialectics—A Controversy-Oriented Approach to the Theory of Knowledge* (Albany: State University of New York Press, 1977) 91 distinguishes between 'categorical certainty' and 'practical or effective certainty'. He distinguishes between the 'certainty' in 'absolutistic sense of logical infallibility' and 'certainty' as 'the realistic concept that underlies our actual, real-life processes of argumentation and reasoning'; 'we must be certain of what we know, but the "certainty" that must attach to knowledge-claims need not be absolutistic in some way that is in principle unrealizable. It must be construed in the sense of *as certain as can reasonably be expected in the circumstance*' (ibid 90).

[82] For an accessible introduction to the probability calculus: Brian Skyrms, *Choice and Chance—An Introduction to Inductive Logic* (4th edn, Belmont, CA: Wadsworth, 2000) ch VI.

[83] As Maria Carla Galavotti, *Philosophical Introduction to Probability* (Stanford, CA: CSLI Publications, 2005) 12 tells us: 'The mathematical properties of probability, in fact, hold quite independently of the interpretation attached to it'; and ibid 54, she cautioned 'that the mathematical features of probability can and should be kept separate both from its applications and the foundational and philosophical issues connected with it'.

no fixed nomenclature, and the taxonomies offered by different writers tend to vary somewhat.[84] It is convenient to start with this classification by Gillies:[85]

1. The *logical* theory identifies probability with degree of rational belief. It is assumed that given the same evidence, all rational human beings will entertain the same degree of belief in a hypothesis or prediction.
2. The *subjective* theory identifies probability with the degree of belief of a particular individual. Here it is no longer assumed that all rational human beings with the same evidence will have the same degree of belief in a hypothesis or prediction. Differences of opinion are allowed.
3. The *frequency* theory defines the probability of an outcome as the limiting frequency with which that outcome appears in a long series of similar events.
4. The *propensity* theory... takes probability to be a propensity inherent in a set of repeatable conditions. To say that the probability of a particular outcome is p is to claim that the repeatable conditions have a propensity such that, if they were to be repeated a large number of times, they would produce a frequency of the outcome close to p.

Gillies separates these four theories into two classes. The last two theories are grouped together in the *objective* category. Both the frequency theory and the propensity theory share an objective view of probability, according to which, probability is a fact, a 'human-independent' feature of the 'objective material world'.[86] A clear instance is the application of probability to radioactivity. The 'probability of a particular isotope of uranium disintegrating in a year'[87] exists as a matter of physical fact whether anyone knows or believes it.

Mellor prefers the nomenclature 'physical probability' to 'objective probability'. A reason for this is that logical probability, which Gillies excludes from his objective category, is also objective, albeit not in Gillies's sense of being part of the material world but in the sense that it has a logically derived value. Two persons cannot both be right if they give different values to the logical probability of the same hypothesis relative to the same set of evidence. Unlike subjective probability, logical probability is not a matter of personal opinion.

For Gillies, logical and subjective theories of probability belong together in the *epistemological* camp. Subjective probability is also known as personal probability. The term 'logical probability' is not used by Mellor, who prefers instead to talk of 'epistemic probability'. For him, 'epistemic probability' is the kind of probability that measures how far evidence supports or undermines a hypothesis about the world, and this, on one view, tells us how justified it is for one to

[84] See, generally, Paul Humphreys, 'Probability, Interpretations of' in Edward Craig (ed), *Routledge Encyclopedia of Philosophy* (London: Routledge, 1998) vol 7, 701–705; Donald Gillies, *Philosophical Theories of Probability* (London: Routledge, 2000); Skyrms (n 82) ch VII; Alan Hájek, 'Interpretations of Probability', entry in *Stanford Encyclopedia of Philosophy* available at: <http://plato.stanford.edu/entries/probability-interpret> (2003); D H Mellor, *Probability—A Philosophical Introduction* (London: Routledge, 2005); Galavotti (n 83).

[85] Gillies (n 84) 1.

[86] ibid 2.

[87] ibid 2.

believe the hypothesis given the evidence. To call the probability 'logical' supposes that there is a logical relation between evidence and hypothesis. This view is much discredited; 'many philosophers now deny that epistemic probabilities measure a confirmation relation, logical or otherwise, between hypotheses and evidence'.[88] Nevertheless, the term 'logical probability' is well-established and we will use it alongside 'epistemic probability' to refer loosely to the kind of probability that measures the degree of rational belief in a hypothesis that is justified or constrained by a body of evidence. The label 'epistemological probability' will be reserved for the broad category that encompasses both logical/epistemic probability and subjective probability.

For some philosophers, only one of the theories of probability is right. There is only one correct concept of probability. But there is much to be said for the tolerance exhibited in the pluralist stance.[89] Pluralists recognize the validity of each of the different theories but accord them different spheres of operation. Epistemological theories of probability are deemed appropriate for the social sciences, including the study of legal trials, while objective interpretations are considered better suited for the natural sciences.[90]

2.2.1 *Physical probability*

The propensity theory is newer and less established than the frequency theory. Propensity is, on one conception, the disposition of a set of repeatable conditions to produce a frequency of a type of outcome ('long-run propensity') and, on another conception, the disposition of a particular set-up to produce a type of outcome on a particular occasion ('single case propensity'). As Hájek has noted, propensities are categorically different things depending on which conceptions one adopts. On the first view, a fair die has a strong disposition to land '3' with

[88] Mellor (n 84) 88.

[89] Frank Plumpton Ramsey, 'Truth and Probability' in *The Foundations of Mathematics and Other Logical Essays* (London: Routledge & Kegan Paul, 1931) ch VII, 157 ('the difference of opinion between statisticians who for the most part adopt the frequency theory of probability and logicians who mostly reject it renders it likely that the two schools are really discussing different things, and that the word "probability" is used by logicians in one sense and by statisticians in another'); Rudolp Carnap, *Logical Foundations of Probability* (2nd edn, London: University of Chicago Press, 1962) 19 (arguing that 'there are two fundamentally different concepts for which the term "probability" is in general use'. There is Probability$_1$, 'a logical, semantical concept', which 'is the degree of confirmation of a hypothesis *h* with respect to an evidence statement', and Probability$_2$, a factual or empirical concept, which is as a form of relative frequency; Ian Hacking, *The Emergence of Probability* (Cambridge: CUP, 1975) 12 (distinguishing between 'statistical' probability, 'concerning itself with stochastic laws of chance processes' and 'epistemological' probability which is 'dedicated to assessing reasonable degrees of belief in propositions quite devoid of statistical background').

[90] See Gillies (n 84) 3 and ch 8. Galavotti (n 83) at 235: 'It seems undisputable that epistemic probability has a role to play in the realm of the social sciences where personal opinions and expectations enter directly into the information used to support forecasts, forge hypotheses and build models... Conversely, the frequency interpretation, due to its empirical and objective character, has long been considered the natural candidate to account for the notion of probability occurring within the natural sciences.' See also ibid 238.

long-run frequency of 1/6 and the value 1/6 does not measure the propensity. On the second view, 1/6 is the measure of the propensity to land '3' and this disposition, unlike on the first view, is a weak one.[91]

There are many versions of the frequency theory. The general idea may be illustrated with a familiar example: suppose an urn contains ten marbles. They are identical except that two are black and eight are white. I am to draw one out of the urn at random. What is the probability that I will draw a white marble? On the frequency theory, the probability in this case is conceived as the colour ratio that would theoretically emerge from an infinite series of trials using the same chance set-up (known as the hypothetical 'limiting relative frequency'). If, upon repeating the exercise a thousand times, with the marble thrown back in after each draw, we find that the number of times a white marble is chosen to the number of times a black marble is drawn is in the proportion of 8:2, we can conclude that the estimated probability of drawing a white marble is 0.8. This figure is conditional on a set of events, the empirical 'collective' consisting of the thousand trials.

2.2.2 *Epistemological probability*

Whereas objective or physical probabilities are features of the world, epistemological probabilities are features of beliefs about the world. The subjective theory treats probability as the degree of actual belief held by a particular person, whereas the logical or epistemic theory analyses probability as the degree of rational belief in a hypothesis that is justified by the evidence.

On the logical or epistemic theory, probability is linked to what one *should* believe. The degree to which it is rational to believe in a hypothesis is conditional on what is known. Probability, on this theory, measures the extent to which a body of evidence confirms or disconfirms a hypothesis. For proponents of the logical theory, this probability relation is (as the name implies) a logical one, although obviously not of the deductive sort. Not all theories of confirmation are probabilistic. On some views, the degree to which evidence confirms a hypothesis is not quantifiable and not subject to the probability calculus. In Part 3, a non-probabilistic theory, applicable in the context of trial deliberation, is sketched.

On the subjective theory, the probability of a proposition is, generally speaking, the degree to which a given person, the subject, believes it to be true. The degree of her belief is reflected in her willingness to act on the proposition, and a theoretical way of measuring that willingness is by the lowest odds she would accept in betting that the proposition is true. The computation is sometimes based on betting quotients instead of odds. The betting quotient is N/(M+N) where the odds offered are N:M on A. Other things being equal, the higher the betting quotient (or lower the odds) she would accept, the stronger her belief. This is true on the condition that our hypothetical bet is not influenced by other considerations; we

[91] Hájek (n 84): see discussion under heading 3.4.

assume, for example, that the subject 'could afford the bet, wanted to win it, and had no other interest in whether A is true'.[92] Most importantly, it is assumed that the subject is coherent in her beliefs. Her beliefs are incoherent if, for example, they lead her at the same time to accept both my bet of 3:1 odds on p (she will pay me three dollars if p, and I will pay her one dollar if not-p) and my bet of 2:1 odds on not-p (she will pay me two dollars if not-p, and I will pay her one dollar if p). A 'Dutch Book' can be made against her in such a case; whichever the outcome (p or not-p), she is bound to lose money on the bets taken as a whole.[93] If it turns out that p, she wins one dollar on the first bet but loses two on the second; and if turns out that not-p, she loses three dollars on the first bet and wins only two on the second. Adherence to this coherence condition ensures that the subject's degrees of belief conform to the probability calculus.

Although subjective probability is a matter of personal opinion, there is, in Bayes's theorem, an objective method of revising one's degree of subjective belief with the introduction of additional evidence. The subjective Bayesian[94] begins with a degree of personal belief as the prior or initial probability. Bayes's theorem is a mathematical formula for deriving the posterior or final probability from a quantitatively precise computation of the impact of new evidence on the prior probability. In its simplest form,[95] one's belief is updated by 'conditionalizing' on the new evidence, a process that involves, roughly speaking, multiplying the prior odds of the hypothesis by the 'likelihood' ratio, a technical term for the value obtained by dividing the probability of the evidence, given that the hypothesis is true by the probability of the evidence, given that the hypothesis is false. Many scholars of evidence law have tried to use Bayesian theory to cast light on legal proof,[96] attracting criticisms and resistance from some academics[97]

[92] Mellor (n 84) 67.

[93] This example is taken from Roy Weatherford, *Philosophical Foundations of Probability Theory* (London: Routledge & Kegan Paul, 1982) 221–222.

[94] Note that Bayesianism has also been embraced by some of those who take an objectivist view. Galavotti (n 83) 51 and 225.

[95] This qualification is important not only because the mathematical details can get extremely technical, but also because there are purportedly as many as 46,656 varieties of Bayesian theories: I J Good, *Good Thinking—The Foundations of Probability and Its Applications* (Minneapolis, MN: University of Minnesota Press, 1983) ch 3.

[96] A P Dawid, 'Bayes's Theorem and Weighing of Evidence by Juries' in Richard Swinburne (ed), *Bayes's Theorem* (Oxford: OUP, 2002) ch 4; and Philip Dawid, 'Probability and Proof', Appendix II to Terence Anderson, David Schum and William Twining, *Analysis of Evidence* (2nd edn, Cambridge: CUP, 2005), available only online at: <http://www.cambridge.org/catalogue/catalogue.asp?isbn=9780521673167&ss=res>. See also Bernard Robertson and G A Vignaux, *Interpreting Evidence—Evaluating Forensic Science in the Courtroom* (Chichester, West Sussex: Wiley, 1995).

[97] For an overview of the controversies, see Paul Roberts and Adrian Zuckerman, *Criminal Evidence* (Oxford: OUP, 2004) at 120–132; Roger C Park and Michael J Saks, 'Evidence Scholarship Reconsidered: Results of the Interdisciplinary Turn' (2006) 47 Boston College L Rev 949 at 988–995. Much of the debate can be found in these collections: (1986) 66 Boston University L Rev, issues 3 and 4 (containing papers presented at a symposium on Probability and Inference in the Law of Evidence); (1991) 13 Cardozo L Rev, issues 2 and 3 (containing papers presented at a symposium on 'Decision and Inference in Litigation'); (1997) 1 Intl J of Evidence

and judges.[98] A field of literature is generated that has come to be called 'New Evidence Scholarship'.[99] The title is a little misleading as scholars have engaged in probabilistic analysis of legal cases since the seventeenth century (indeed, the pioneers of mathematical probability were inspired by proof in law[100]) and there has always been academic interest in subjecting legal evidence to probabilistic analysis.[101]

2.2.3 *Differences and relationship*

We have seen how objective probability is different from epistemological probability. The first group of theories takes probability as a feature of the external world while the second treats probability as a matter of belief. In the second group, the critical difference between logical/epistemic probability and subjective probability is that the latter is a matter of subjective opinion whereas the former is not. The following are further distinctions that can be drawn amongst the four theories of probability, with accompanying illustrations:

(i) *Subjective probability is different from objective probability*: suppose I know that a coin is biased but not in which way. What is the probability of it landing heads? For all I know, the coin could equally land heads as tails, and in a sense I am as inclined to believe one outcome as I am the other. My actual credence in the coin landing heads may be said to be 0.5. But the objective probability of it landing heads is not 0.5 since the coin is biased in one direction.[102]

(ii) *Subjective probability is different from logical or epistemic probability*: in the above example, my actual credence in the coin landing heads is 0.5. But the logical or epistemic probability of it landing heads is not 0.5. I know the coin is biased and I am ignorant of the direction of bias. Logical or epistemic probability cannot be derived from ignorance.[103] P and not-p do not have equal logical or epistemic probabilities just because the available evidence tells me nothing about how probable they are.

and Proof (special issue on 'Bayesianism and Juridical Proof' edited by Ronald J Allen and Mike Redmayne). Though out-of-date, mention must be made of these classic monographs: L Jonathan Cohen, *The Probable and the Provable* (Aldershot: Gregg Revivals, 1991 reprint, first published in 1977); Eggleston (n 77).

[98] eg *R v Adams* [1996] 2 Cr App R 467, 481; *R v Doheny and Adams* [1997] 1 Cr App R 369, 375; *R v Adams (No 2)* [1998] 1 Cr App R 377, 384–5.

[99] Richard Lempert, 'The New Evidence Scholarship: Analyzing the Process of Proof' (1986) 66 Boston University L Rev 439; John D Jackson, 'Analysing the New Evidence Scholarship: Towards a New Conception of the Law of Evidence' (1996) 16 OJLS 309; Park and Saks (n 97) 984–997.

[100] eg Lorraine Daston, *Classical Probability in the Enlightenment* (Princeton, NJ: Princeton University Press, 1988) 14; Hacking (n 89) ch 10.

[101] John Tozer, 'On the Measure of the Force of Testimony in Cases of Legal Evidence' (1849) 8 *Transactions of the Cambridge Philosophical Society* 143.

[102] Gillies (n 84) 21; a somewhat similar example is given by Mellor (n 84) 12.

[103] Mellor (n 84) 12, 27–29 and 85.

(iii) *Logical or epistemic probability is different from objective probability*: I toss an ordinary coin and I see clearly that it has landed on its edge. It is rational for me to believe what I clearly see. Whereas the chance or objective probability of the coin landing on its edge is miniscule, the epistemic probability of it having landed on its edge, given my perceptual evidence, is extremely high.[104]

(iv) *Logical or epistemic probability is relative to evidence whereas subjective probability and objective probability are not*: as noted, objective or physical probability exists as a fact of the material world whether anyone is aware of it. It is also not relative to evidence. Neither is subjective probability. My actual credence in p may be based on no more than a groundless hunch.[105] Logical or epistemic probability, on the other hand, is essentially conditional: it expresses the relation between a hypothesis and the evidence which supports or undermines it.[106]

(v) *Logical or epistemic probability is different from objective probability in not being empirical*: as Mellor puts it, 'empirical data cannot provide evidence for or against [epistemic probabilities] by making hypotheses about their values more or less probable'.[107] It is true that the epistemic probability of the proposition that 'the objective probability of p is x' may have to be revised with the introduction of a new piece of evidence. But the new piece of evidence is not evidence for or against the proposition of the epistemic probability itself. The proposition that the epistemic probability of A is x relative to evidence B remains as it is with the introduction of a new piece of empirical evidence C. C cannot support or undermine, or render more or less probable, that proposition of epistemic probability since that proposition expresses a relation only between A and B. What the introduction of C does is to provide the basis for a *distinct* proposition of epistemic probability, namely, that the epistemic probability of A is y relative to evidence B and C. An important lesson on legal fact-finding can be drawn from this. If all that a positive finding of fact expresses is a proposition of epistemic probability, a finding of guilt cannot be shown to be false by any post-conviction introduction of newly discovered exculpatory evidence. That we *do* think of the conviction as wrongful suggests that we do not read a finding of fact as merely expressing a proposition of epistemic probability. As will be argued in Part 2.4, findings of fact assert propositions of fact.

Although epistemological probability is categorically different from objective probability, the first may be based on the second. Statistical probability informs epistemological probability so far as one's belief about the probability of a singular

[104] Example borrowed from Mellor (n 84) 11.
[105] ibid 65.
[106] ibid 80–82.
[107] ibid 82.

event rests on the probability of an event of that type occurring within the relevant reference class. However, an epistemological probability is still epistemological even when it is based on statistical probability. That an epistemological probability is objectively based does not mean that it is no longer epistemological. Where I know that p has an objective probability and nothing else about p, the degree of my actual belief in p, and the degree of rational belief that I should have in p, may well share the same *value* as the objective probability of p. Even so, these probabilities are not of the same kind. One can exist without the other. My subjective probability may be based on the wrong objective probability; and since logical probability does not entail the truth of the evidence on which it is conditional, it is possible for logical probability to be conditional on evidence (in this case, of objective probability) that is, in fact, false.[108] Howson and Urbach remind us of the 'subtle distinction between the values of a probability being objectively based and the probability itself being an objective probability'.[109] More generally, objective probability can exist even if no one is aware of it and, conversely, a belief need not be based on any knowledge of objective probability. Where, as would typically be the case, the objective probability forms only part of the body of available evidence, the other evidence may make it rational to have a belief with a probability value that is entirely different from the objective probability. This remark by Keynes is as amusing as it is pertinent:[110]

> To a stranger the probability that I shall send a letter to the post unstamped may be derived from the statistics of the Post Office; for me those figures would have but the slightest bearing upon the question.

2.3 Trial and probabilities

Since the uncertainty that the scientist seeks to explore is 'the result of randomness or indeterminism in the world itself',[111] it is only fitting that her work is guided by a theory of probability that treats probability as a feature of the material world that she is investigating. But the uncertainty that faces us at a trial is 'the result of the incompleteness and inadequacy of our knowledge'.[112] It is natural that we should be tempted to turn to an epistemological theory of probability for management of that kind of uncertainty. The frequency theory of probability deals with mass phenomena and repetitive events. It does not apply easily to singular non-repeatable incidents. For such cases, probability has to be conceived in epistemological terms. Since trials typically concern singular events, *if* deliberation is

[108] ibid 34.

[109] Colin Howson and Peter Urbach, *Scientific Reasoning: The Bayesian Approach* (La Salle, Illinois: Open Court, 1989) 228. See also Gillies (n 84) 119–120.

[110] John Maynard Keynes, *A Treatise on Probability* (London: Macmillan, 1948) 322. Quoted by Gillies (n 84) 122; see also ibid 183 and Mellor (n 84) 85.

[111] Weatherford (n 93) 249.

[112] ibid 249.

guided by probability (which will be disputed), it follows that we should, in the usual case, take an epistemological view of the operative probability.[113]

Assume for the moment that factual questions have to be decided at a trial on the basis of epistemological probabilities. What this means is that the fact-finder must make a positive finding only if she believes to a sufficiently high degree that the propositional content of that finding is true.[114] One might try to absorb both epistemological interpretations by attributing them different significance in the trial process. The subjective theory highlights the *power* which is bestowed on the judge of fact while the logical or epistemic theory emphasizes the *responsibility* which in consequence lies upon her. The subjective theory permits differences of opinion. People may, on the same evidence, reasonably differ in the views they take of the facts of the case.[115] If probability is read subjectively, for the purposes of the trial, a contested proposition is more probably true than false if and so long as the fact-finder believes to a greater degree that it is true than that it is false; and, conversely, it is more probably false than true if and so long as she believes it to be false to a greater extent than she believes it to be true. This discretion comes with responsibility. Insofar as 'probability' is the degree of rational belief in a hypothesis relative to the evidence, the injunction to decide according to probability is an injunction to search the evidence for confirmation or disconfirmation of the hypothesis. The fact-finder must be rational in determining how strongly the evidence supports the disputed factual allegation.[116] She must entertain only that degree of belief that it is rational, on the evidence, to entertain in the truth of the disputed allegation.

Nothing that has been said is meant to suggest that the concept of objective probability is alien to the trial process. Clearly, it is not. Objective probability can play at least two important and different roles. First, evidence is commonly given of objective probabilities at a trial.[117] For instance, statistical information is often included in expert testimony. When a DNA scientist testifies on the random occurrence ratio of a match, the probability of which she speaks is objective.[118] In this and similar situations, the fact-finder has to take into account evidence of objective probability in deliberation on what to believe about the facts of the

[113] As observed by Mellor (n 84) 10–11.

[114] As recognized by Richard A Posner, *The Problems of Jurisprudence* (Cambridge, Massachusetts: Harvard UP, 1990) 212; Vern R Walker, 'Preponderance, Probability and Warranted Factfinding' (1996) 62 Brooklyn L Rev 1075, 1102–1104; Gudmund R Iversen, 'Operationalizing the Concept of Probability in Legal-Social Science Research' (1971) 5 Law and Society Rev 331, 332.

[115] eg *Henry Walters* [1969] 2 AC 26, 30.

[116] Weatherford (n 93) 130: logical probability theory 'has a *regulative* relation to people's thoughts—it doesn't describe the way they actually do think, it describes how they must think if they are to think correctly'.

[117] cf s 10, Civil Evidence Act 1995 (England): actuarial tables prepared by the Government Actuary's Department are admissible in evidence for the purpose of assessing general damages for future pecuniary loss.

[118] This ratio is based on statistics contained in the relevant DNA database: *Gordon* (1995) 1 Cr App R 290, 295.

case.[119] However, to return to the important point made in the previous section, while epistemological probability may be based on or influenced by evidence of objective probability, that it is so based or influenced does not mean that it is not epistemological.

Although the court may rely on evidence of objective probability in arriving at the epistemological probability of the disputed proposition of fact, it is not *necessary* to have such evidence. As Mellor says, evidence about the hypothesis that the butler committed the crime 'need not give [it] any chances, ie physical probabilities, to which [its] epistemic probabilities can be equated';[120] a witness who testifies to having caught the butler red-handed is not giving evidence *of* objective probability (even if there is some sort of objective probability that a person with her properties and in her position would tell the truth). The witness is giving testimony of knowledge acquired non-inferentially from perception. Perception is not probabilistic evidence (indeed, it is not evidence at all, being a direct source of knowledge) even though we can talk of the probability of perceptual mistake.[121]

Neither is objective probability *sufficient* for a positive finding of fact. This is a controversial claim and it will be defended more fully later. In real cases, there will invariably be other evidence adduced in the case which may make 'any chance that the butler *would* do the crime... differ from the epistemic probability that he *did* do it'.[122] But let us suppose the unrealistic scenario that only evidence of objective probability is available. On its own, this evidence can only justify a finding of probability. However, as is argued in the next section, what a finding asserts is a proposition of fact, not a proposition of probability. What is needed, on the probabilistic account of fact-finding, is a sufficiently high degree of belief in the proposition of fact. There is a difference between believing that p has objective probability of x and having a degree of belief, with the probability of x, that p. In Mellor's view:[123]

[119] Sometimes, the evidence is wrongly used. Much publicized instances include *People v Collins* (1968) 438 P 2d 33 in the United States (David McCord, 'A Primer for the Nonmathematically Inclined on Mathematical Evidence in Criminal Cases: *People v Collins* and Beyond' (1990) 47 Washington and Lee L Rev 741); the Sally Clark scandal in the United Kingdom (Richard Nobles and David Schiff, 'Misleading Statistics Within Criminal Trials—the Sally Clark Case' (2005) 2 *Significance* 17); the case against Lucia de B in the Netherlands (Ronald Meester, Marieke Collins, Richard Gill and Michiel van Lambalgen, 'On the (ab)use of statistics in the legal case against the nurse Lucia de B' (2006) 5 Law, Probability and Risk 233).

[120] Mellor (n 84) 88.

[121] It is often said that all evidence is ultimately 'statistical' or 'probabilistic': eg Laurence Tribe, 'Trial by Mathematics: Precision and Ritual in the Legal Process' (1971) 84 Harvard L Rev 1329, 1330, n 2; Richard A Posner, 'An Economic Approach to the Law of Evidence' (1999) 51 Stanford L Rev 1477, 1508; Frederick Schauer, *Profiles, Probabilities and Stereotypes* (Cambridge, Massachusctts: Harvard UP, 2003) 103; Jonathan J Koehler, 'The Probity/Policy Distinction in the Statistical Evidence Debate' (1991) 66 Tulane L Rev 141, 143 and n 11; *US v Veysey* (n 197). This is questionable: see Williamson (n 9) 252 where, in discussing the claim that 'virtually all empirical knowledge has a probabilistic basis', he draws an illuminating distinction 'between the causal and evidential senses of the word "basis"'.

[122] Mellor (n 84) 88.

[123] Mellor (n 84)11.

it is not sufficient for the defence to show that the *chance* of the butler being the murderer was low, as indeed it might have been. (Suppose for example he was chosen at random from hundreds of would-be assassins.) That is irrelevant: what matters is the probability relative to the evidence before the court that the butler *was* the murderer. It is that epistemic probability which the prosecution needs to show is high enough to justify a guilty verdict and the defence needs to show is not so.

The justification for using a particular definition of reference class (the would-be assassins) is highly problematic.[124] Even if we can solve the reference class problem, the naked statistical evidence can, on its own, establish only that there is a certain objective probability that the butler, being the type of person that falls within the reference class, *would* do such a thing. The objective probability that the butler *did* commit the crime is either one (if he did it) or zero (if he did not). There can however be an epistemological probability of the proposition that the butler committed the crime: the statistical evidence may lead to or justify a certain degree of belief that the butler did it. This kind of belief is often called 'partial belief'. A partial belief warrants the assertion that something is probable; only a categorical belief can warrant an assertion of fact.[125] More will be said on this in Part 2.5, when we examine in greater detail the differences between the two types of belief.

There is a further and somewhat controversial role that objective probability may play apart from its role as evidence at a trial. Exceptionally, a claim is based on what seems to be a proposition of objective probability rather than of fact. For example, where a party is not given the opportunity to present herself in the final round of a competition and sues in contract to recover compensation for the 'loss of a chance' of receiving a prize, she does not have to prove that she would in fact have won but only that there was some real probability of her winning.[126] This type of case and those analogous to it are controversial. It is often unclear what interpretation of probability is being taken, in what sense it is objective, and highly debatable, especially in the context of medical negligence, whether the law ought to allow recovery on mere proof of a probability such as a 'loss of chance of cure'.[127] It is more common at the pre-trial and review stages to find

[124] See the debate in the following: Mark Colyvan, Helen M Regan and Scott Ferson, 'Is it a Crime to Belong to a Reference Class?' (2001) 9 *J of Political Philosophy* 168; Peter Tillers, 'If Wishes Were Horses: Discursive Comments on Attempts to Prevent Individuals from Being Unfairly Burdened by their Reference Classes' (2005) 4 Law, Probability and Risk 33; Ronald J Allen and Michael S Pardo, 'The Problematic Value of Mathematical Models of Evidence' (2007) 36 J of Legal Studies 107. See also the forthcoming special issue on the reference class problem in (2007) 11 Intl J of Evidence and Proof, issue 4.

[125] See V H Dudman, 'Probability and Assertion' (1992) 52 *Analysis* 204; Williamson (n 9) 248 ('Probabilistic evidence warrants only an assertion that something is probable').

[126] The classic case is *Chaplin v Hicks* [1911] 2 KB 786.

[127] For a sample of the enormous literature, see Helen Reece, 'Losses of Chances in the Law' (1996) 59 MLR 188; David Hamer, '"Chance would be a Fine Thing": Proof of Causation and Quantum in an Unpredictable World' (1999) 23 Melbourne University L Rev 557; Jane Stapleton, 'Lords a'leaping Evidential Gaps' (2002) 10 Torts LJ 276 and 'Loss of Chance of Cure from

applications based on propositions framed as probabilities or likelihoods. For instance, the prosecution is required to prove 'probable cause' for the issuance of a search warrant;[128] a party seeking discovery of a document has to prove that the document is 'likely' to support her case;[129] and in a petition to have a conviction set aside on the ground of prejudice caused by ineffective legal assistance, it must be shown that there is a 'reasonable probability that, but for counsel's unprofessional errors, the result of the proceeding would have been different'.[130] It is difficult to see how an objective interpretation can be taken of probability in these applications; only the epistemological interpretation seems suitable.

2.4 Propositional content

It is unusual for a case to rest merely on a proposition of probability. Most of the time, the ultimate propositions requiring proof are of facts (understood broadly). In the usual case, a positive finding asserts a proposition of fact. For example, in a conviction for murder, the guilty verdict asserts, *inter alia*, that the defendant caused the death of the victim. The question 'whether the defendant caused the death of the victim' is treated in law as a question of fact, although it is not purely factual; some value judgment is involved as well. The difficulty of separating fact and value was alluded to in Chapter 1, Part 1.2, and need not detain us further, because what we want to highlight is the distinction between an assertion of a proposition of fact (understood broadly) and an assertion of the probability of the truth of that proposition of fact ('assertion of probability' for short).

There are three alternative readings of a finding that one could take, all of which should be rejected. First, one might claim that a finding asserts a proposition of objective probability. In rare cases, it is sufficient to prove propositions of probability; this possibility was already acknowledged. It cannot be ruled out that a finding of liability in such cases may amount only to an assertion of objective probability. However, as a general proposition, this claim is clearly unsound.

Cancer' (2005) 68 MLR 996; Chris Miller, 'Loss of Chance in Personal Injury: A Review of Recent Development' (2006) 5 Law, Probability and Risk 63.

128 *Brinegar v US* (1949) 338 US 160, 175: 'In dealing with probable cause,...as the name implies, we deal with probabilities.' But the degree of probability necessary to satisfy the probable-cause standard is said to be incapable of precise definition or quantification; what is needed is a reasonable ground for belief in guilt: *Maryland v Pringle* (2003) 540 US 366, 370–371.

129 eg *Three Rivers DC v Bank of England* [2002] EWCA Civ 1182, paras 21–22, 30–33; [2003] 1 WLR 210, 221–222, 224–226. In this case, the English Court of Appeal held that the term 'likely' 'does not carry any necessary connotation of "more probable than not". It is a word which takes its meaning from context.' It may appear from the context of the statute or regulation in which the term appears that only a 'modest threshold of probability' is intended: ibid para 22.

130 *Strickland v Washington* (1984) 466 US 668, 698. The United States Supreme Court added that a reasonable probability is 'a probability sufficient to undermine confidence in the outcome' (ibid). This standard was applied to a different situation in *United States v Copeland* (2005) 369 F Supp 2d 275. Judge Weinstein held that, in the circumstances of the case, proof of a 20 per cent probability of prejudice was sufficient for the petition to succeed (ibid 287–288).

The assertion made in a guilty verdict is that the defendant caused the victim to die and not that it is objectively probable that she caused the victim to die. This, as we saw, was Mellor's view. It is nicely echoed by a juror reflecting on her jury service:[131]

> The jury is not asked to decide whether Mr X is... probably a thief. They are asked to decide whether the prosecution has proved that, on this occasion, there *was* a theft and Mr X was the one responsible.

Trials deal mostly with disputed propositions of past events. It is not very meaningful to talk of the objective probability of an event that has already occurred. The value can only be one (if the alleged event did happen) or zero (if it did not happen); it is difficult to see how it can have any intermediary value.[132] Since the finding that p has objective probability of one is tantamount to the finding that p, a positive finding expresses a proposition of fact after all. Of a past event, only probability conceived epistemologically, it seems, can have an intermediary value. One can believe in varying degrees, ranging from one to zero, that something did or did not happen.

Could it then be argued, as a second alternative, that a finding of fact expresses a proposition of epistemological probability? On this argument, the finding of guilt asserts either a proposition about the degree of the fact-finder's personal belief that the defendant in fact caused the victim to die (if a subjective interpretation is taken of probability) or a proposition about the degree to which it is rational to believe that the defendant committed the crime on the evidence adduced before the court (if one adopts an epistemic theory of probability). Neither view is tenable. Both carry this unacceptable implication: the finding can never be shown to be wrong so long as, *at the time of returning the guilty verdict*, the fact-finder holds the relevant belief (on the first reading), or the evidence available to her *at the trial* rationally supports the relevant belief (on the second reading). A finding that merely asserts a proposition of epistemological probability is immune to challenge by any post-conviction discovery of empirical evidence, however strongly it exonerates the defendant. The fresh evidence does not show that the relevant subjective belief was lacking at the time of conviction, and, to repeat an earlier point, the epistemic probability of guilt relative to the body of evidence adduced at the trial is not rendered more or less probable by the introduction of evidence discovered *after* the trial. All that it does is to introduce a distinct epistemic probability, one that is relative to a different body of evidence, larger than the set available at the trial.

Another problem with the second view is that it confuses the content of the proposition that is asserted with what Austin calls the sincerity condition for a

[131] See the account by Penelope Wallace in Dulan Barber and Giles Gordon (eds), *Members of the Jury* (London: Wildwood House, 1976) 131.

[132] Don Fallis, 'Goldman on Probabilistic Inference' (2002) 109 *Philosophical Studies* 223, 229–230.

speech act.[133] As we saw in Chapter 1, Part 2.3, psychological states are expressed in many speech acts. The second view treats partial belief as the psychological state expressed by a verdict. It then makes the mistake of reading that psychological state into the content of the proposition that is asserted.

A third alternative to the claim that a finding asserts a proposition of fact is that it asserts a proposition about the proof of that proposition of fact (briefly, 'proposition of proof'). The finding that p, so it is said, asserts that it has been proved that p. But this merely raises the question of the circumstances in which the fact-finder may conclude that p is proved, that is to say, of when the fact-finder may find that p. BAF* was developed in Part 1 as our answer to that question. To return to the point of the previous paragraph, we must be careful to distinguish the conditions under which a finding is allowed and the content of the proposition that is asserted by the finding. BAF* states the conditions that permit the finding that p; what p contains is a separate matter on which BAF* is silent. Indeed, we explicitly left it for further consideration in our earlier discussion.

There are positive reasons for favouring the view that positive verdicts or findings assert factual propositions. First, it squares perfectly with what they actually say. The jury pronounces the defendant guilty (or liable); the jury does not pronounce her probably guilty (or liable). A categorical form of expression is used, amounting to an outright assertion. Secondly, the view is also consistent with how the law acts on the verdict. The treatment that follows the verdict is usually just as categorical. With rare exceptions, an all-or-nothing approach is taken. The punishment that follows a conviction is not apportioned according to the established probability of guilt, and rarely are civil damages apportioned according to the established probability of liability.[134] The first and second reasons are not conclusive since one can choose not to speak or act in accordance with one's belief; the force of the first and second reasons lies in the undesirability of such disjuncture.[135] There is a loss of integrity when the court's speech and action are

[133] See Chapter 1, Part 2.3.

[134] This 'all-or-nothing' approach is taken 'throughout the world': Frederick Schauer, *Profiles, Probabilities and Stereotypes* (Cambridge, Massachusetts: Harvard UP, 2003) 89–90. Contrast Hendrik Lando, 'The Size of the Sanction Should Depend on the Weight of the Evidence' (2005) 1 Rev of Law and Economics 277 who offers the radical proposal that criminal sanctions be apportioned according to the weight of the evidence against the accused persons. Richard Foley, 'The Epistemology of Belief and the Epistemology of Degrees of Belief' (1992) 29 *American Philosophical Quarterly* 111 claims this kind of apportionment is impractical. He notes that juries:

'are not given option of delivering numerically precise judgments. They cannot, for example, judge that it is likely to degree 0.89 that the defendant is guilty. There is nothing in principle that precludes a legal system from allowing such calibrations and then adjusting the punishment to reflect the degree of belief that the jury has in the defendant's guilt. But in fact there is no legal system of this sort and for good reasons. Any such system would be horribly unwieldy.' (Ibid 123.)

[135] Such disjuncture is implied in statements like this dictum from Lord Diplock in *Mallet v McMonagle* [1970] AC 166, 176: 'In determining what did happen in the past a court decides on the balance of probabilities. Anything that is more probable than not it treats as certain.' This seems to suggest that the court may act *as if* something is true even where it does not believe it to be true. See also *Malec v J C Hutton Pty Ltd* (1990) 169 CLR 638, 642–3: 'If the probability of the event having

inconsonant with its actual belief. Thirdly, the State should be allowed to punish the defendant for a crime only if the court is justified in asserting that the accused did, in fact, commit it. As we will see, greater responsibility is assumed in making that assertion of fact than in making a mere assertion of probability.[136] If the court is not prepared to assert, and to assume responsibility for asserting, that the defendant is in fact guilty as charged, it should not convict her on the charge. A parallel argument applies to civil judgments. Although they are not seen as punitive, civil judgments acquire bite only when located within the coercive framework of the law.[137] Unless the State is in a position to assert that the defendant is in fact liable, thereby making itself both accountable for the truth and responsible for any error, it lacks the authority to treat her as liable.

2.5 Two concepts of beliefs

In Part 1.3, it was argued that to find that p, one must be justified in believing that p within the terms of BAF*. In Part 2.3, it was argued that those who claim that questions of fact are decided on probabilities at a trial must, for this purpose, rely on an epistemological theory of probability. On the probabilistic view, to find that p, one must believe to a sufficient degree that p where the concept of belief is different from that deployed in BAF*. The latter kind of belief is commonly known as 'categorical'. Either one believes p or one does not. To be more accurate, three doxastic positions are available:[138] in addition to believing p, one can believe that p is false, which is to disbelieve p, or suspend judgment about p, thus neither believing nor disbelieving p.[139] On the other hand, in defining probability as a *degree* of belief, the epistemological theory presupposes that one can believe something to a greater or lesser extent; this kind of cognitive attitude is called '*partial* belief'.

2.5.1 Partial belief

When 'belief' and cognate terms are used in ordinary speech, the reference is usually to the cognitive attitude of partial belief rather than categorical belief. The

occurred is greater than it not having occurred, the occurrence of the event is treated as certain; if the probability of it having occurred is less than it not having occurred, it is treated as not having occurred.'

[136] Parts 2.5.1 and 2.5.2 below.

[137] Even H L A Hart, who provided a compelling case against the sanction theory of law, appeared to have conceded as much: *The Concept of Law* (2nd edn, Oxford: Clarendon Series, 1994) 27–28.

[138] See James Fitzjames Stephen, *A General View Of The Criminal Law Of England* (London: Macmillan, 1863) 239; C J Misak, *Truth And The End Of Inquiry—A Peircean Account Of Truth* (Oxford: Clarendon Press, 1991) 49.

[139] Suspending judgment is more than neither believing nor disbelieving p. If p never crosses my mind, I neither believe nor disbelieve it. Even something incapable of having any mental state, such as a rock, can have the property of neither believing nor disbelieving that p: Wedgwood (n 45) 272.

attitude of partial belief, as we will shortly see, is closely related to the attitude of suspicion. Ordinarily, one says that one believes that p when one merely has a partial belief or suspects that p. It is common, when one finds evidence lacking in some respect, to say: 'I don't really *know* that such and such is the case, but I *believe* that it is.' The kind of belief which is thus reported is preclusive of knowledge. A claim to know offers an assurance or guarantee of sorts. It implies the claim that one cannot, practically speaking, be wrong. It is incoherent (or trivial) to say: 'I know but I can (or could) be wrong.'[140] On the other hand, one's claim to 'mere' belief acknowledges, indeed emphasizes, the real possibility of error. Ordinarily, to say 'I believe' is akin to saying 'I think', 'I suppose', or 'in my opinion'.[141] In saying that we 'merely' believe p, we alert our listener to a perceived inadequacy—a falling short or incompleteness—in our evidence, and in doing that, we disclaim knowledge of p. With that disclaimer, we disavow or at least lessen our commitment to, and therefore responsibility for, the truth of p.[142]

A similar effect is achieved by the use of the adverb 'probably', as when we say: 'probably p'.[143] We issue this implicit disclaimer to limit our responsibility to those likely to rely on our statement when the evidence does not give us the assurance needed to bear the burden of asserting outright that p is true. As was argued in Part 1, when one asserts that p, one implies knowledge of p, and when one knows that p, one believes categorically that p (more fully, that p is in fact true). In everyday conversation, we eschew the categorical or strict usage of 'belief' in its various forms. To say that one believes that p is often to deny any claim to knowledge of p; it is to indicate, instead, that one occupies a qualified doxastic position with respect to p.[144] One believes that 'probably p' in the sense that one partially believes p or believes p to a certain degree.

Partial belief in p justifies the assertion that 'probably p'. This is not equivalent to the assertion that 'p has a certain objective probability'. Ordinarily, when someone holds a degree of belief in something (such as, to use Christensen's

[140] J L Austin, 'Other Minds' in J O Urmson and G J Warnock (eds), *Philosophical Papers* (3rd edn, Oxford: OUP, 1979) 76, 98. Austin's views are defended by Mark Kaplan, 'If You Know, You Can't be Wrong' in Stephen Hetherington (ed), *Epistemology Futures* (Oxford: Clarendon Press, 2006) and echoed by Rescher (n 81) 91.

[141] cf Slote (n 9) 182–184.

[142] A J Ayer, *The Problem of Knowledge* (London: Macmillan & Co, 1956) 17–18 used 'believe' in this sense when he wrote: 'To say that I know something is the case... is... to vouch for the truth of the whatever it may be... If my credentials do not meet the usual standards, you have the right to reproach me. You have no right to reproach me if I merely say that I believe, though you may think the less of me if my belief appears to you irrational.'

[143] 'Probability' is looked at from this angle by: Stephen Toulmin, *The Uses Of Argument* (Cambridge: Cambridge UP, 1958) ch 2; J N Findlay, 'Probability without Nonsense' (1952) 2 *Philosophical Quarterly* 218; Neil Cooper, 'The Concept of Probability' (1966) 16 *British J for the Philosophy of Science* 226; John King-Farlow, 'Toulmin's Analysis of Probability' (1963) 29 *Theoria* 12; J R Lucas, *The Concept of Probability* (Oxford: OUP, 1970) chs 1 and 2.

[144] cf Sutton (n 24) 64: 'Utterances of the form "I believe that *p*" and similar forms ("I think that *p*", "p, I believe", "I think so", etc.) often, I suggest, do not express belief in the proposition that *p*. They express, rather, a belief that *p* is probable (more likely than not, perhaps).'

example, that Jocko cheated on Friday's test), it is fanciful to think that the agent must have in mind some proposition about reference class or propensity.[145] In its epistemological sense, probability does not reside in the content of the believed proposition, as objective probability does;[146] it is, rather, a measure of the extent of belief in a proposition. The statement 'probably p' is thus ambiguous. It can be the exterior analogue of either a partial belief in p or of a categorical belief in the objective probability of p.

Can we really believe something only partially? Many philosophers are of the view that believing to degree x that p (or having the partial belief in p of the probability value x) is not the same as believing (categorically) that the probability of p is x.[147] If partial belief in a proposition does not mean a categorical belief in a proposition of probability, what does it mean? This is mysterious to some philosophers.[148] Mellor, while acknowledging the inconclusiveness of the view that beliefs come by degrees,[149] quickly adds: 'Against this on-off (categorical) view of belief must be set the evident possibility of *doubting* A.' Mellor observes that doubting A comes 'by degrees that seem to reflect degrees of belief in A'.[150] He gave the telling example of tossing a coin that is known to be either two-headed or two-tailed. Without knowing whether the coin is one or the other, our credence in it landing heads is 1/2, as is our credence in it landing tails.[151] This does not mean that we believe the objective probability of it landing heads, or for that matter, tails, is 1/2 (the objective probability is either one or zero); what this seems to mean is that we are as *inclined* to believe in one outcome (heads up) as in the other (tails up). Partial belief it seems is an inclination to categorical belief but falling deliberately short of it.

Mellor also suggests that subjective credence may be based on a mere hunch.[152] This is just as telling as his example. For it suggests that a partial belief is a *suspicion*. Recall the contrast Shah and Velleman drew between 'suspicion' and 'belief'. To suspect that p is to accept p tentatively, as still open to revision, treating p not as a fact but as a hypothesis that is subject to further testing for truth. In calling a suspicion a belief, we are perhaps committing the error to which Hampshire

[145] David Christensen, *Putting Logic in its Place: Formal Constraints on Rational Belief* (Oxford: Clarendon Press, 2004) 19–20.

[146] David Owens, *Reason Without Freedom—The Problem Of Epistemic Normativity* (London: Routledge, 2000) 144 must have had the latter in mind when he wrote: 'that we can think p more or less likely... would be a point about the *content* of the belief, not about its *strength*'.

[147] eg Ramsey (n 89) 187–188 ('The pretensions of some exponents of the frequency theory that partial belief means full belief in a frequency proposition cannot be sustained'); Helen Beebee and David Papineau, 'Probability as a Guide to Life' (1997) 94 *J of Philosophy* 217, 218 ('believing to degree 0.9 that the coin will land heads is not the same as (fully) believing that in some objective sense its probability of heads is 0.9').

[148] For example, Sutton (n 24) 12, who takes a categorical view of belief, finds talk of 'degree of belief' hard to understand.

[149] Mellor (n 84) 66.

[150] Mellor (n 84) 12. See also ibid 65–66.

[151] ibid 12.

[152] ibid 65.

has alerted us; we may be confusing the thinking that p as a mere datum of consciousness, reported in the autobiographical statement that 'the thought that p is true occurs to me now', and believing that p in the strong sense of thinking that p which one is ready to assert as true.[153] Be that as it may, 'the view that belief comes by degrees... is widely held'.[154] It is pedantic to deny that there is such a thing as partial belief. People certainly talk as if there is such a thing. We will take it that believing (to a greater or lesser degree) that p is suspecting (more or less strongly) that p, or being (more or less) inclined to believe categorically that p while consciously withholding oneself from that categorical belief.

2.5.2 Categorical belief

Categorical belief is belief in the strict sense. According to the standard analysis of knowledge discussed in Part 1, belief is a condition for knowledge. This kind of belief is not of the partial kind for, as just observed, partial belief is preclusive of knowledge. The kind of belief necessary for knowledge is categorical.[155] If one knows that p, one believes categorically that p. One cannot know p without categorically believing it. One believes categorically that p when one judges that p is, in fact, true. And in saying that one believes that p, one expresses commitment to that judgment. Only categorical belief that p justifies the outright assertion that p.[156] The outright assertion that p commits the speaker to the truth of what is asserted.

That commitment is not undertaken in every instance of saying something. When I read aloud to a blind person the sentences of a newspaper article, I am not vouching for the truth of the report. Asserting a proposition is not the same as merely uttering a sentence expressing that proposition; one can say something without asserting it.[157] When a person asserts that p, she invites others to take her word for it, with the implicit assurance that her word can be trusted.[158] To assert a proposition, as Peirce noted long ago, 'is to make oneself responsible for its truth'.[159] The responsibility is especially great when one makes a solemn

[153] Stuart Hampshire, *Freedom of the Individual* (London: Chatto and Windus, 1975) 101–102.

[154] Mellor (n 84) 66.

[155] Christensen (n 145) 13: 'Knowledge has typically been seen as belief-plus-certain-other-things... [M]ainstream epistemologists of various persuasions have typically employed a binary model of belief.'

[156] Jonathan E Adler, *Belief's Own Ethics* (Cambridge, Massachusetts: MIT Press, 2002) 235.

[157] Even a parrot is capable of that: G E Moore, 'Saying That P' in *Commonplace Book 1919–1953* (London: George Allen, 1962) ch 15.

[158] Catherine Z Elgin, 'Word Giving, Word Taking' in Alex Byrne, Robert Stalnaker and Ralph Wedgwood (eds), *Fact And Value—Essays On Ethics And Metaphysics For Judith Jarvis Thomson* (Cambridge, Massachusetts: MIT Press, 2001) ch 5. The same has been said of a claim of knowledge: Ayer (n 142) 13; J L Austin, 'Other Minds' (1946) 20 *Supplementary Proceedings of the Aristotelian Society* 148, 171.

[159] Charles Hartshorne and Paul Weiss (eds), *Collected Papers Of Charles Sanders Peirce* (Cambridge, Massachusetts: Harvard UP, 1934) vol 5, 384. I am grateful to Susan Haack for referring me to this quotation. Peirce's view is echoed by Charles Fried, *Right and Wrong* (Cambridge,

assertion in a finding formally made in a court of law;[160] the fact-finder does 'not merely invite reliance on [her] finding, [she] acts in awareness that reliance will follow'.[161]

Confusion arises because '[i]ronically, a sentence of the form "I believe that *p*" is sometimes used to convey precisely that one does *not* believe that *p*, strictly speaking'.[162] The categorical nature of the belief is made clear in the more explicit statement 'I believe that p is in fact true'. Expression of commitment to the categorical judgment that p carries a responsibility for the truth of p that is greater than when one claims merely 'probably p'.

One can believe categorically that p more or less strongly. The strength of a categorical belief is measured by its tenacity: how strongly one believes categorically that p is a matter of how difficult it is to persuade one to abandon that belief.[163] On a view that has a sizeable group of adherents, this notion of belief strength is not numerically quantifiable by a mathematical measurement that abides by the probability calculus.[164] On the one hand, it is claimed that evidential reasoning is too 'subtle and complex'[165] to be formally captured by Bayesian analysis, and, on the other, it is said that probabilistic reasoning is too complicated for human beings to handle, requiring as it does the assignment and updating of probabilities in an 'exponential' combination of evidential propositions.[166] More will be

Massachusetts: Harvard UP, 1978) 56–57: 'To make an assertion is to give an assurance that the statement is true...An assertion may be seen as a kind of very general promise; it is a promise or assurance that the statement is true.'

[160] Peirce made a similar point in relation to testifying under oath: (n 159) 386.

[161] Judith Jarvis Thomson, 'Liability and Individualized Evidence' (1986) 49 Law and Contemporary Problems 199, 213.

[162] Sutton (n 24) 64.

[163] Owens (n 146) 144; Gilbert Harman, *Change in View* (Cambridge, Massachusetts: MIT Press, 1986) 22.

[164] For Keynes, probabilities are usually not numerically quantifiable; we can at best compare one probability with another. Sometimes, they are not even comparable: Keynes (n 110) 27–28; Gillies (n 84) 33–35; Mellor (n 84) 16. For a defence of Keynes's comparative approach to probability: Jochen Runde, 'Keynes After Ramsey: In Defence of *A Treatise on Probability*' (1994) 25 *Studies in History and Philosophy of Science* 97. It could be that Keynes's view of probability was influenced by what he saw in the law. (Cf Jan Dejnožka, *Bertrand Russell on Modality and Logical Relevance* (Aldershot: Ashgate, 1999) ch 10, noting legal influence on his theory of relevance.) In his *A Treatise on Probability*, Keynes referred to Bentham's writings on judicial evidence (Keynes (n 110) 20), discussed legal cases (ibid 24–27), and paid tribute to that 'set of practical men, the lawyers' who 'have been more subtle in [the handling of probabilities] than the philosophers' (ibid 24). Contrast Atiyah, *Pragmatism and Theory in English Law* (London: Stevens & Sons, 1987) 135–136: 'Lawyers must rely a great deal, in the process of proof, on probability, but they are generally extremely weak on probability theory, preferring to depend on the very unreliable intuition and common sense of the plain man.'

[165] Susan Haack, *Defending Science—Within Reason: Between Scientism and Cynicism* (New York: Prometheus, 2003) 75. Haack has on many occasions expressed 'reservations about the epistemological usefulness of the mathematical theory of probabilities': see the literature cited in 'On Logic in the law: "Something, but not All"' (2007) 20 Ratio Juris 1, 16, n 62.

[166] Harman (n 163) ch 3; Robert Nozick, *The Nature of Rationality* (Princeton, NJ: Princeton UP, 1993) 96 ('The task of assigning probabilities to each and every well-formed statement and combination of statements is overwhelming'); Stewart Cohen, 'Knowledge, Assertion, and

said on the strength of categorical belief and about how one comes to hold such a belief in Part 3.

2.5.3 *Illustration*

To illustrate some of the preceding comments, suppose I am to draw at random a marble from an urn. I know that the urn contains eight white marbles and two black ones. I believe that:

[1] The probability that the marble I will draw is white is 0.8.

[1] is a categorical proposition of probability.[167] (For the sake of discussion, assume away any conceptual difficulties and treat [1] as uncontroversial.) I believe [1] categorically. My categorical belief in [1] is based on my categorical belief in other propositions including the proposition that the urn contains ten marbles, that eight of them are white, two of them are black, and that each stands an equal chance of being drawn. I can also say, albeit with less precision:

[2] It is likely that the marble I will draw is white; or

[3] The marble I will draw will probably be white.

Like [1], [2] and [3] are also probability propositions. Since I know and therefore believe each of them to be true, I can sincerely make the following statements:

[4] '*I believe* the probability that the marble I will draw is white is 0.8;'

[5] '*I believe* it is likely that the marble I will draw is white'; or

[6] '*I believe* the marble I will draw will probably be white.'

The word 'believe' in [4] to [6] is used in the strict or categorical sense: in saying 'I believe', I am reporting my categorical judgment on the truth of the relevant proposition. The kind of belief that is reported is necessary for knowledge. In each case, I could just as well have said, and it would perhaps be clearer for me to

Practical Reasoning' (2004) 14 *Philosophical Issues* 482, 487 ('"[K]nowledge" talk can be viewed as a heuristic for simplifying reasoning. If we had a considerably greater capacity for storing and computing evidential probabilities, we could do all our reasoning by relying just on the probabilities. But given our actual capacities, we rely on [a] rough and ready, imprecise notion of knowledge, and allow as a rule of thumb, that when you know P, you can appeal to P in reasoning'). Making the same point in the context of legal proof: Craig R Callen, 'Notes on a Grand Illusion: Some Limits on the Use of Bayesian Theory in Evidence Law' (1982) 57 Indiana Law Journal 1 at 10–15. Ralph Wedgwood, 'Contextualism about Justified Belief', forthcoming, draft available at <http://users.ox.ac.uk/~mert1230/papers.htm>, suggests (ibid n 4) that 'part of the reason for our having [categorical] beliefs is that reasoning with partial beliefs is enormously more complicated than reasoning with simple outright beliefs'.

167 Richard I Aaron, 'Feeling Sure' (1956) 30 *Supplementary Proceedings of the Aristotelian Society* 1, 11 ('Every statement of the kind "It is probable that p" is a second order statement which is itself categorical'); Robert Hambourger, 'Justified Assertion and the Relativity of Knowledge' (1987) 51 *Philosophical Studies* 241, 243: 'to say that *P* is probable is to assert outright, and so to affirm, a claim about probabilities'.

say, 'I know' instead of 'I believe'. Unlike in the examples below, I am not using the words 'I believe' to qualify my doxastic position.

Given my antecedent set of beliefs, my knowledge and understanding of how things stand, I do not categorically believe that:

[7] 'The marble I will draw will be white.'

Notice that [7] is not a proposition of probability but a proposition of future fact. If I use 'belief' in the same strict or categorical sense as it is used in [4] to [6], I will now have to say:

[8] '*I do not believe* that the marble I will draw will be white.'

[8] is not equivalent to the statement that '*I disbelieve* that the marble I will draw is white'. Non-belief (in the negative sense of withholding categorical acceptance) of a proposition is different from disbelief (in the sense of outright rejection) of that proposition. In the sense in which 'believe' is used in [8], I neither believe nor disbelieve the proposition that the marble I will draw will be white. But, ordinarily, in the situation under consideration, one would say:

[9] '*I believe* that the marble I will draw will be white.'

Importantly, 'believe' has a whole new meaning in [9]. Here, I am not merely attributing or ascribing a belief to myself; rather, I am qualifying my doxastic position in relation to the proposition in question.[168] The qualification is more prominent when the phrase 'I believe' is used parenthetically, thus:

[9a] 'The marble I will draw will, *I believe*, be white.'

This is merely to change the structure of the sentence; the content of [9] and [9a] remains the same. In ordinary conversation, we tend to speak in the manner of [9] or [9a] and not [8]. Whereas in [4] to [6], 'believe' is used in the categorical sense, in [9] and [9a] it is used in the partial sense. The proposition in [9] and [9a] could just as well be expressed with the statement, 'I *suspect* that the marble I will draw will be white.' But in [4] to [6], I do not merely suspect the truth of the relevant propositions; I know and therefore categorically believe them to be true. If 'believe' in [9] were given the same meaning as 'believe' in [8], [9] would plainly contradict [8]. For [9] to be consistent with [8], 'believe' as used in [9] must mean something different from the same word appearing in [8]. This variation in the use of 'believe' mirrors two qualitatively different cognitive attitudes.

2.5.4 Differences and relationship

This section attempts to clarify the differences and relationship between partial and categorical beliefs.[169] What sets them apart has not to do with the

[168] Slote (n 9) 182.

[169] The general concept named 'categorical belief' here (a term which is also used by writers such as Daniel Hunter, 'On the Relation between Categorical and Probabilistic Belief' (1996)

thoroughness of deliberation. One can be as hastily formed or as carefully deliberated as the other. Neither has it to do with the strength of believing a proposition. Both categorical and partial beliefs can vary in strength, although different notions of strength apply to each of them. Roughly speaking, and putting it tentatively, the strength of one's partial belief in p refers to how strongly one suspects that p is in fact true, whereas the strength of one's categorical belief in p is the degree of tenacity with which one holds on to the view that p is in fact true. Adding to the confusion, both notions of strength can be and have been described as a degree of confidence in p.

The first two features that set apart these two concepts of belief have been noted. If, as de Souza has suggested, belief can be viewed either through the theory of action or through epistemology,[170] one may say that categorical belief is knowledge-oriented, whereas partial belief is action-oriented. As mentioned, categorical belief is the psychological state necessary for knowledge whereas partial belief is the psychological state that excludes knowledge. The value of partial belief lies in practical reasoning, as a tremendously important guide to action. We are often willing and have no choice but to take calculated risks, to act on the basis that p without knowing—that is, without believing categorically—that p. To believe that probably p is, to borrow King-Farlow's words, to 'deem it worthy, in appropriate conditions, to act upon' p, 'granted certain subjective utility conditions'.[171]

Secondly, it is proper to assert categorically that p only when one believes categorically that p. It is improper to assert categorically that p when one merely believes that probably p. When one holds only a partial belief in p (equivalently, merely suspects that p), it is proper only to assert that probably p. As White points out, asserting that 'probably, p' is not asserting that p in a guarded or qualified way; it is a guarded or qualified alternative to asserting that p.[172]

Thirdly, when one believes that probably p (that is, believe p to a degree quantifiable by a probability value, say x), one also believes that probably not-p (that is, believe not-p to the degree quantifiable by the probability value of (1-x)). One believes only partially that p because one apportions one's credence over both

30 *Noûs* 75, 75) is also called by many other names: eg 'flat-out belief' (Michael E Bratman, *Intention, Plans, And Practical Reason* (Cambridge, Massachusetts: Harvard UP, 1987) 36–37); 'all-or-nothing belief' (Harman (n 163) 22); 'dogmatic belief' (Radu J Bogdan, *Belief—Form, Content And Function* (Oxford: OUP, 1986) 15); 'full belief' (Adler (n 156) especially chs 9 and 10). The distinction presently drawn between 'categorical' and 'partial' beliefs is also generally referred to by other sets of opposing terms: eg 'belief tout-court' versus 'degrees of belief' (Brian Weatherson, 'Can We Do Without Pragmatic Encroachment?' (2005) 19 *Epistemology* 418, 420); 'degrees of belief' versus 'belief simpliciter' (Foley (n 133)); 'simple outright belief' versus 'mere partial belief' (Wedgwood (n 166)); 'binary belief' versus 'graded belief' (Christensen (n 145)); 'full belief' versus 'partial belief' (Adler (n 156) especially chs 9 and 10).

170 de Souza (n 52) 55.

171 King-Farlow (n 143) 23.

172 Alan R White, *Modal Thinking* (Oxford: Blackwell, 1975) 69.

p and not-p.[173] This distributive property explains why this type of belief is called 'partial belief'. No similar equivocation exists in the case of believing categorically that p: here, one believes that in fact p.[174] The subject affirms the proposition believed while rejecting (more or less strongly) all competing propositions which are inconsistent with it. To believe that in fact p is to judge that, among the relevant alternatives, p alone is true. The nature and structure of categorical belief are further clarified in Part 3 below.

It is irrational for a person, at the same time, to believe categorically that p and to believe categorically that not-p because one would thereby be committing oneself at once to two doxastic positions that are contradictory. However, it is sometimes perfectly rational to suspend or withhold categorical belief (by suspending or withholding categorical judgment) and believe neither that p nor that not-p; to hold a partial belief is to enter this agnostic state,[175] to be uncommitted to either of these positions. The notion of suspending belief (or more accurately, suspending judgment) applies to a categorical belief but not to a partial belief. The strength of the kind of belief measured by epistemological probability can carry a value anywhere along the continuum from 0 to 1. One does not lack a belief conceived probabilistically when one sits perfectly on the fence so to speak; rather, one has a partial belief with the exact probability value of 0.5.[176] This subjective spread of credence may come about when one can detect no evidence for p and also no evidence for not-p. But in that situation, one is neither justified

[173] Wedgwood (n 166): 'There seems to me to be a brute difference between a *simple outright belief* in a proposition, and a *mere partial belief* in that proposition. A partial belief is a mental state in which one "hedges one's bets", by placing some positive credence both in the proposition in question and in other incompatible propositions; a simple outright belief, on the other hand, is a mental state in which one simply believes the proposition, without really apportioning one's credence between the proposition and any incompatible propositions at all. This difference cannot be captured simply by the fact that I am more confident in the propositions in which I have a simple outright belief than in the propositions in which I have a mere partial belief. Even though I am more confident that 1 + 1 = 2 than I am that Dushanbe is the capital of Tajikistan, I do not really have a merely partial belief that Dushanbe is the capital of Tajikistan. I simply believe it. Admittedly, I might retreat to a mere partial belief if I were likely to suffer heavy costs for having an incorrect belief about the capital of Tajikistan; but except in that special case, I have a simple outright belief that Dushanbe is the capital of Tajikistan.'

[174] As George I Mavrodes, 'Belief, Proportionality, and Probability' in Michael Bradie and Kenneth Sayre (eds), *Reason And Decision* (Ohio: Bowling Green State University, 1981) 58, 59 claimed, this 'is not equivalent to believing that [p] has a chance of being true, that it may possibly be true, that it has a certain probability of being true, or anything of the sort'.

[175] Susan Haack calls this 'can't-tell agnosticism', in contrast to 'plain agnosticism' where one fails to investigate the evidence: '"The Ethics of Belief" Reconsidered' in Lewis Hahn (ed), *The Philosophy Of R M Chisholm* (Chicago: Open Court, 1997) ch 5, 135.

[176] de Souza (n 52) 54–55 ('For the Bayesian, whenever I believe that p (to some degree d) I also believe ~p (to a degree 1-d). But for the non-Bayesians I normally believe p only if I do not believe ~p. Furthermore, there is for the Bayesian no such thing as the suspension of belief, which for the non-Bayesian consists in neither believing p nor believing ~p'); Hunter (n 169) 87 ('a proposition whose subjective probability is 0.5 is not a borderline case of a belief, but is a clear case of a non-belief').

in believing categorically that p nor in believing categorically that not-p.[177] A person who suspends categorical belief (and therefore neither believes nor disbelieves p) does not have a belief with zero probability value: a person who assigns zero probability to p can hardly be said to have no belief about p; on the contrary she disbelieves p and her disbelief is extreme.[178]

The fourth feature that distinguishes between the two kinds of belief is really just another dimension of the third. It was mentioned at the outset of this section that both partial and categorical beliefs can vary in strength and it is not any difference in strength that separates them. Their relationship cannot be explained with reference to a probability threshold. A categorical belief is not a partial belief that happens to have crossed a particular threshold of probability (x); it is not the case that one believes categorically that p when one's degree of confidence in p is greater than x. Any value that might be selected for x would seem arbitrary.[179] Secondly, the threshold view leads to a situation where one must believe categorically the independent premises of a deductive argument because one's degree of confidence in each of them is greater than x, but one does not believe categorically the conclusion because the product of the probabilities of the premises is less than x.[180] Thirdly, that we withhold categorical belief in p (or more accurately, that we do not judge that p) even when we know the probability of p to be extremely high suggests that it is not any perceived failure to cross some probabilistic threshold that stops us from forming a categorical belief. While I personally believe, and it is rational for me to believe, that it is supremely improbable that my single ticket in a million-ticket lottery will be the winner, I do not believe categorically and would not be justified in believing categorically that I will in fact lose.[181] Suppose the threshold view is right. One cannot imagine the probability of any ordinary proposition of fact being higher than the probability of my one-in-a-million ticket losing. By any reasonable setting of the threshold, the probability of losing surely surpasses the threshold. We must therefore say that I believe categorically that my ticket will lose. In that case, we must also say that I believe categorically that every other ticket will also lose since the probability of losing for each of

[177] Susan Haack, *Defending Science—Within Reason: Between Scientism and Cynicism* (New York: Prometheus, 2003) 75: 'the probability of p and the probability of not-p must add up to 1, but if there is insufficient evidence either way, neither a claim nor its negation may be warranted to any degree'.

[178] Risto Hilpinen, 'Some Epistemological Interpretations of Modal Logic' in G H von Wright (ed), *Logic and Philosophy* (The Hague: Martinus Nijhoff, 1980) 19, 20.

[179] Robert Stalnaker, *Inquiry* (Cambridge, Massachusetts: MIT Press, 1984) at 91; Foley (n 133) 112.

[180] This assumes that the premises are independent. The conclusion is unacceptable because the person who accepts it has 'to either have credences that [are] not supported by her evidence, or credences that [are] incoherent': Weatherson (n 169) 421.

[181] Dana K Nelkin, 'The Lottery Paradox, Knowledge, and Rationality' (2000) 109 *The Philosophical Review* 373.

them similarly exceeds the threshold. But this is inconsistent with my categorical belief that one ticket will be the winning one.[182]

The feature distinguishing the two types of belief is in the kind of doxastic position one takes. To hint again of the theory that will be developed in Part 3: the categorical belief that p comes from the judgment that in fact p, and the judgment is made when one considers p 'perfectly possible' and rejects, more or less forcefully, all the relevant hypotheses competing with p. The acceptance of p is elevated from that of a hypothesis to that of a categorical belief.

The person with only a partial belief in p, who believes probably p, does not judge categorically that p. But withholding full acceptance of p does not mean outright rejection of p. A person who believes that probably p considers the evidence inadequate to justify acceptance that p is in fact true, or for that matter, in fact false; and when she applies the adverb 'probably' to p, she is warning her audience as much.[183] But the evidence, to her mind, does justify tentative acceptance of p as a possible basis of practical deliberation. The acceptance is tentative because she holds it open to further testing and revision, as a more or less well-grounded hypothesis. However well-grounded it is, a hypothesis is not a fact.

It is possible to switch from one kind of belief to the other. I believe *tout court* that I locked the door on my way out. I do not partly believe that I locked the door and partly believe that I did not. If you ask me whether I have locked the door, my reply is simply 'Yes, I did'. I do not equivocate and say 'I probably did'. But suppose you challenge my assertion and thereby my categorical belief. You remind me that I have forgotten to lock the door in the past. I think you have a point and begin to doubt whether I did lock the door after all. Here is a situation where, following the description of Shah and Velleman, I downgrade my pre-existing acceptance of a proposition from the status of a belief to the status of a suspicion or hypothesis; to use the present terminology, my belief that I have locked the door has switched from one that is categorical to one that is only partial. The switch can easily go in the other direction, as when one's doubt is removed upon further reflection or receipt of new evidence: if I telephone my neighbour to check on my door and she tells me, after checking, that it is locked, my partial belief reverts to a categorical one.

Although we can switch from one to the other, the two kinds of belief are mutually exclusive: one cannot, at the same time, both believe categorically that p and believe partially that p. If one believes that in fact p, one does not believe that probably p, and vice versa. If a person only believes that probably p, she does not, at the same time, believe that p is, in fact, true. Return to our lottery example. Let there be a lottery, about which, to my knowledge, there is nothing out of the ordinary. If I hold only one of many lottery tickets that have been

[182] Many have made this point: eg Mark Kaplan, *Decision Theory as Philosophy* (Cambridge: CUP, 1996) 95.

[183] J O Urmson, 'Parenthetical Verbs' (1952) 61 *Mind* 480, 485, 495; Toulmin (n 143) 89–90.

issued, I am justified in believing that most probably I will not win. But I do not believe, and I am not justified in believing, however weakly, that in fact I will not win.[184] If I have that categorical belief, I would not have bought the ticket in the first place and would not continue to hang on to it while awaiting the results. As will be argued later, what stands in the way of the categorical belief that I will lose is my inability to eliminate the possibility of me winning the lottery. The statistical probability of winning, however small, is nevertheless distinct and real.

2.6 Proof paradox

The groundwork is done for taking a first step towards solving a well-known paradox of legal proof. This paradox is set in the context of civil litigation. But the reasoning used to solve it should also apply, and apply with greater force, to criminal trials. Hopefully, even if the argument is found unpersuasive in civil cases, it may yet be accepted for criminal proof.

At a civil trial, the received view has it that the standard of proof is 'on the balance of probabilities' or, more accurately, 'over the balance of probabilities' or 'on the preponderance of probabilities'. This has been taken to mean that a proposition is proved if and so long as its probability is established at more than 0.5.[185] A puzzle arises on this probabilistic interpretation of the civil standard. One can think of situations where, on the evidence, there is a more than 0.5 probability that p is true and the evidence clearly does not justify a positive finding that p. The paradox comes in many versions. For ease of reference, two of them are quoted in full below. The first, the gatecrasher scenario, is given by Cohen:[186]

> [I]t is common ground that 499 people paid for admission to a rodeo, and that 1,000 are counted on the seats, of whom *A* is one. Suppose no tickets were issued and there can be no testimony as to whether *A* paid for admission or climbed over the fence. So by any plausible criterion of mathematical probability there is a .501 probability, on the admitted facts, that he did not pay. The mathematicist theory would apparently imply that in such circumstances the rodeo organizers are entitled to judgement against *A* for the admission-money, since the balance of probability... would lie in their favour. But it seems manifestly unjust that *A* should lose his case when there is an agreed mathematical probability of as high as .499 that he in fact paid for admission... [T]here is something wrong somewhere. But where?

[184] Dudman (n 125) 205; George I Mavrodes, 'Intellectual Morality in Clifford and James' in Gerald D McCarthy (ed), *The Ethics Of Belief Debate* (Atlanta, Georgia: American Academy of Religion, 1986) 205, 210 (using the example of drawing a card randomly from a stack).

[185] For instance, in *Davies v Taylor* [1974] AC 207, 219, Lord Simon said that 'the concept of proof on a balance of probabilities... can be restated as the burden of showing odds of at least 51 to 49 that such-and-such has taken place or will do so'.

[186] Cohen (n 97) 75; see also 270–271.

Thomson sets out another version of the paradox, the cab scenario:[187]

> Mrs Smith was driving home late one night. A taxi came towards her, weaving wildly from side to side across the road. She had to swerve to avoid it; . . . in the crash, she suffered two broken legs. Mrs Smith therefore sued the Red Cab Company . . . [T]here are only two cab companies in town, Red Cab (all of whose cabs are red) and Green Cab (all of whose cabs are green), and of the cabs in town that night, six out of ten were operated by Red Cab. [Mrs Smith did not see the colour of the taxi which hit her car.] If we believe Mrs Smith's story, and are aware of no further facts that bear on the case, then we shall think it .6 probable that her accident was caused by a cab operated by Red Cab . . . Is it right that Mrs Smith win her suit against Red Cab? The standard of proof in a tort suit is 'more probable than not,' which is plausibly interpretable as requiring only that the plaintiff establish a greater than .5 probability that the defendant (wrongfully) caused the harm. But most people feel uncomfortable at the idea of imposing liability on Red Cab on such evidence as Mrs Smith here presents. Why? That is the problem.

All commentators are quick to treat as uncontroversial the statistical or mathematical probability of A being a gatecrasher and of the accident-causing cab being red. An objective interpretation of probability appears to be taken, as a measurement of modal chances or metaphysical possibilities.[188] On a set of equally possible cases, the probability of an outcome (that the person we pick at random is a gatecrasher or the cab which caused the accident was red) is the ratio of possible cases with that outcome (the number of gatecrashers or the number of red cabs on the road) to the total number of possible cases (the total number of people in the stadium or the total number of cabs on the road).[189]

Since, in each scenario, there is only evidence of objective probability to be had on the crucial issue, it seems to be assumed that the epistemological probability must share the same value as the relevant objective probability.[190] The epistemological probability of the proposition that A gatecrashed in the first scenario and that a red cab caused the accident in the second would then exceed the value of 0.5. Yet, the intuition shared by most people is that judgment should not be entered against the defendant.[191] According to Posner, that the plaintiff

[187] Thomson (n 161) 199–200. This version is based loosely on *Smith v Rapid Transit Inc* (1945) 317 Mass 469, and discussed in *Herskovits v Group Health Cooperative* (1983) 664 P 2d 474, 490; *Hotson v East Berkshire HA* [1987] 1 AC 750, 789.

[188] Mellor (n 84) 22–23, 44.

[189] Despite the criticisms the classical conception of probability has attracted, it continues 'to be the working theory of the ordinary person': Weatherford (n 93) 74.

[190] This assumption is questioned by David Kaye, 'Paradoxes, Gedanken Experiments and the Burden of Proof: A Response to Dr Cohen's Reply' [1981] Arizona State LJ 635, 637. The epistemological probability may be lower than the objective probability if account is taken of the plaintiff's failure to produce other, non-statistical, evidence. This failure 'suggests that the evidence would not have supported [the] plaintiff's claim'. But this challenge can be met by simply adding the additional fact to both scenarios that no other evidence can be found.

[191] But a few have argued against intuition: eg Daniel Shaviro, 'Statistical Probability Evidence and the Appearance of Justice' (1989) 103 Harvard L Rev 530, criticized by Craig R Callen, 'Adjudication and the Appearance of Statistical Evidence' (1991) 65 Tulane L Rev 457.

should win is 'a conclusion almost no legal professional accepts';[192] Nesson and Brilmayer have separately suggested that the judge would not even allow such cases to go to the jury;[193] and Stein, finding the 'imposition of liability... strikingly counterintuitive', thinks that in the gatecrasher scenario, 'virtually every judge would rule in A's favour on a motion of direct dismissal'.[194]

From the external perspective, it may seem obvious that the law ought to allow recovery on a simple calculation of utility. After all, in the gatecrasher scenario, 'to deny recovery would increase unnecessarily the number of errors in the long run. Holding each spectator liable for trespass will result in 501 correct decisions and 499 incorrect decisions. Disallowing liability will result in only 499 correct decisions but 501 incorrect ones.'[195] But Posner has pointed out that the alternative to allowing the thousand trials to proceed is not to allow any of the cases to go to trial. Choosing the first option over the second will only result in a few additional correct decisions. The social benefits to be had from that small additional number of correct decisions may not exceed the social costs of conducting a thousand trials.[196]

Other arguments are available from the external perspective of the system engineer. Some writers try to explain or justify denying recovery from this standpoint by locating their objections in economic or social consequences of giving judgment for the plaintiff in the two scenarios. They raise considerations such as ensuring overall accuracy of the trial system, minimizing errors in the long run, providing incentives for desired behaviour by the parties, allocating resources efficiently, and promoting acceptance of verdicts. A sample of their arguments appears below:

- A likely explanation for the poverty of evidence presented by the plaintiff is that she did not carry out adequate investigation into the facts. The court should not waste its resources on a party who neglects to conduct a sufficient search for better evidence. Dismissal of the case would send out the right message and encourage diligence in case preparation.[197]
- '[W]here individualized evidence is likely to be available—evidence which would typically permit better estimates of the probabilities than can be had

192 Posner (n 121) 1509.

193 Charles Nesson, 'The Evidence or the Event? On Judicial Proof and the Acceptibility of Verdicts' (1985) 98 Havard L Rev 1357, 1379; Lea Brilmayer, 'Second-Order Evidence and Bayesian Logic' (1986) 66 Boston University L Rev 673, 675.

194 Alex Stein, *Foundations of Evidence Law* (Oxford: OUP, 2005) 77 and 78 respectively.

195 Brilmayer (n 193) 676.

196 Posner (n 121) 1510.

197 ibid 1509, and writing in his judicial capacity: *US v Veysey*, No. 01–4208, 2003 US App LEXIS 12934, at *14 (7th Cir, 26 June 2003), and *Howard v Wal-Mart Stores Inc* (1980) 160 F 3d 358, 360. Richard W Wright, 'Causation, Responsibility, Risk, Probability, Naked Statistics, and Proof: Pruning the Bramble Bush by Clarifying the Concepts' (1988) 73 Iowa L Rev 1001, 1055 criticizes this argument for not explaining 'why the plaintiff, rather than the defendant, is being charged with failure to supply other types of evidence'.

from background statistics alone—plaintiffs should be forced to produce it. In the long run, fewer mistaken verdicts should result under this rule of law.'[198]

- If the law were to allow Mrs Smith to succeed, the general upshot would be that the company with the greater number of cabs plying the street would always be liable for unexplained accidents. This gives neither of the companies the incentive to be careful. The result is 'as inefficient as it is unfair'.[199]
- 'Although the defendant probably caused the plaintiff's injury, the fact finder cannot reach a conclusion that the public will accept as a statement about what happened... What is crucial... is that the public cannot view whatever statement the factfinder makes as anything other than a bet based on the evidence... Because the judicial system strives to project an acceptable account about what happened,... the plaintiff's evidence is insufficient, notwithstanding the high probability of its accuracy.'[200]

As the literature cited in the footnotes indicate, these arguments are controversial and have attracted compelling criticisms. It is unnecessary to take a stand on the controversy as the present aim is to illuminate, and argue from, a perspective to legal fact-finding that is wholly distinct from that taken by participants of the debate. The proposed solution to the paradox 'talks past' the arguments of both sides.

A second group of writers points to the moral implications of holding the defendant liable in the two scenarios. For example, it is said:

- '[I]deas of justice probably explain why many regard naked statistical evidence as insufficient to justify imposing liability on [Red Cab] Company... In matters of justice, people ordinarily do not think statistically. They see justice not as a phenomenon to be maximized over the long run, but as an ideal to be realized in each case. If a [cab] company is to be punished, it should be for what its driver did and not for having more [cabs] on the road than its competition.

[198] David Kaye, 'The Laws of Probability and the Law of the Land' (1979) 47 University of Chicago L Rev 34, 40. For extensive critique: Brilmayer (n 193) 677–678.

[199] Tribe (n 121) 1350. Similarly, see Suzanne Scotchmer, 'Rules of Evidence and Statistical Reasoning in Court' in Peter Newman (ed), *The New Palgrave Dictionary Of Economics And The Law*, vol 3 (London: Macmillan Reference, 1998) 389, 391–392 and Posner (n 121) 1510. Posner's version of this argument is challenged by Richard Lempert, 'The Economic Analysis of Evidence Law: Common Sense on Stilts' (2001) 87 Virginia L Rev 1619, 1671–1672 (criticizing Posner for pushing his argument 'to the point of silliness', ibid 1671), and by Ronald J Allen and Brian Leiter, 'Naturalized Epistemology and the Law of Evidence' (2001) 87 Virginia L Rev 1491, 1526 (accusing Posner of 'rootless theorizing', ibid 1521). Taking Posner's argument on its own terms, it is all too easy for Red Cab company to turn the table against Green Cab company by withdrawing just enough cabs from service so that the number of green cabs on the road exceeds the red ones. See the reply by Richard A Posner, 'Comment on Lempert on Posner' (2001) 87 Virginia L Rev 1713, 1713, n 7.

[200] Nesson (n 193) 1379.

With naked statistics, it seems as if the [cab] company is being punished for its dominant position.'[201]

- 'If the system's overriding aim were to discover the truth more often than not, then the percentage of paying patrons would constitute an evidential fact that is pertinent to the business of the court. Even if the defendant himself was not in fact a gatecrasher, he perhaps ought to lose in the suit against him in order to maintain a stochastic probability of success for the system as a whole.' But the business of the court is to deal 'out justice between individual adversaries on the particular occasion' and not to try 'to fulfil stochastic norms of their own.'[202]
- 'A person who deliberately runs his life in such a way as not to commit torts or break contracts is not to be put at risk by the probative procedures of the system just because he falls into a category of which the majority happen to be tort-feasors or contract-breakers. Otherwise the courts in such a case are not dealing out justice between individual adversaries on the particular occasion, but trying to fulfil stochastic norms of their own.'[203]
- 'In the rodeo case, a decision against the defendant... would be analogous to corporate punishment, as the judgment will rest on nothing but the defendant's membership of a group most of whose members did not pay. As a principle for the imposition of responsibility, corporate punishment is characterized by the assumption that it is justified to hold an entire social group responsible for the transgressions of its individual members. Our moral and legal values strongly resist this principle because it fails to acknowledge that the individual is entitled to judgment on his own actions.'[204]
- '[W]hen we infer that the defendant acted like a majority of the people in the stadium..., we treat him as someone randomly selected from the crowd, who can be assumed to have engaged in the modal behavior. When we infer that the defendant caused this accident because he caused a majority of prior accidents or owned a majority of cabs, we treat his present misconduct as inferable from his past, or his accident rate from his ownership rate. In many contexts, these would be reasonable inferences to make in the absence of other information. But they are felt to be inconsistent with the law's commitment to treat the

[201] Lempert (n 199) 1669.

[202] L Jonathan Cohen, 'On Analyzing the Standards of Forensic Evidence: A Reply to Schoeman' (1987) 54 *Philosophy of Science* 92, 94. Contrast Alf Ross, 'The Value of Blood Tests as Evidence in Paternity Cases' (1957) 71 Harvard L Rev 466, 482–483, whose argument (that the result of blood tests should be treated as conclusive evidence of non-paternity) proceeds exactly from the 'overriding aim' described by Cohen.

[203] Cohen (n 202) 94.

[204] A A S Zuckerman, 'Law, Fact or Justice' (1986) 66 Boston University L Rev 487, 499.

> defendant as an autonomous individual, free to determine and alter his conduct at each moment.'[205]

There is a more basic, and non-moral, sense in which it would be wrong to find the defendant liable in either of the scenarios. To re-use two analogies: the rules of a game, which are themselves non-moral, make possible the immoral wrong of cheating; similarly, it is possible to lie only because an assertion is regulated by non-moral rules stipulating when it is proper to make an assertion. One may wholeheartedly accept that there are some moral objections to finding the defendant liable in both scenarios. But those objections must be viewed against the non-moral constitutive rule of fact-finding. The alleged moral wrongs presuppose but do not consist of a violation of that rule. Violation of that rule is a more fundamental wrong.

The case was earlier presented for taking this as the constitutive rule: the fact-finder must find that p only if one would be justified in believing that p within the terms of BAF*. It was argued that the concept of belief in BAF* is of the categorical kind. In the two scenarios, the probabilistic evidence does not justify the categorical belief that p (that A was a gatecrasher or that the cab which knocked into Mrs Smith's car was red): this is intuitively obvious but more work is done in Part 3 to explain why it is so. The probabilistic evidence may justify the categorical belief that the objective probability of p exceeds 0.5, or it may justify a partial belief in p of the same probability value (if the epistemological probability is based on the objective probability): but neither is good enough to make it proper to find that p. If one only believes partially that p, or if one believes categorically that there is an objective probability of p, it is proper only to assert 'probably, p' or 'it is probable that p'. But the finding that p asserts that p, a proposition of fact and not probability. It is improper to assert that p if one is not justified in believing categorically that p.

Let it be given instead that nine hundred persons did not pay to watch the rodeo and only one hundred did. The objective probability that A was a gatecrasher, as we may suppose, is now 0.9. This information causes X (who has no other evidence) to believe to a correspondingly high degree that A did not pay for his entrance. It is rational for X to accept a bet, if the odds are good enough, that A did not hold a ticket.[206] Taking a calculated risk, X accepts the bet. He utters, as he throws down money on the table, 'I say A was a gatecrasher!' That X believes this to be probably true is inferable from his action. But he does not know and therefore does not believe the proposition to be in fact true. No one who is aware that gambling is going on can sensibly take X to be asserting that A was a

[205] David T Wasserman, 'The Morality of Statistical Proof and the Risk of Mistaken Liability' (1991) 13 Cardozo L Rev 935, 943.

[206] This assumes that there is an available method of finding out conclusively whether or not it is true: cf L Jonathan Cohen, 'Subjective Probability and the Paradox of the Gatecrasher' [1981] Arizona State LJ 627, 630; Kaye (n 190) 642.

gatecrasher (saying is not the same as asserting[207]) nor hold X responsible for the truth of the proposition. The statistical information alone does not justify the assertion because it does not justify the kind of belief required of knowledge.[208] A court that has only such statistical evidence is in no better position than X. It lacks justification to find that the defendant did not pay for his entrance because it lacks justification to assert the same; and it lacks justification to make that assertion because it lacks justification for believing categorically that the defendant was a gatecrasher.[209]

To avoid an over-reading of this argument, a reminder is in order. Remember that the ultimate propositions that must be proved to succeed in a claim are determined by the substantive law. As previously noted, sometimes it is only necessary to prove a proposition of probability (for example, a 'loss of chance'), and many pre-trial applications (such as for an interim restraint order) require only partial belief in the claim, that is to say, the belief that the claim will probably succeed at the trial.[210] The substantive law may also make it sufficient to prove certain statistical facts, for example, by assigning liability on the basis of 'market share' as seen in *Sindell v Abbott Laboratories*.[211] What we see here is not the introduction of a novel evidentiary principle. This analysis by Callen is clearly right:[212]

> *Sindell* relied on statistical information to alter the burden of persuasion. It recognized the need for more flexibility of decisionmaking standards in situations in which information must necessarily be lacking. *It did so, however, as a result of adaptation of substantive doctrine to address a particular problem.* It does not follow from *Sindell* that courts should treat any given piece of evidence as sufficient to support a verdict.

The proposed solution to the paradox encounters a serious objection that must be overcome if the solution is to be at all persuasive. Imagine an alternative situation where, in lieu of statistical evidence yielding a 0.9 probability of liability, we have a witness testifying that she saw A furtively climbing over the stadium fence just before the show began. Another witness claims that A told her that she had no ticket. This is the sort of evidence that could justify the categorical belief that A did not pay for his entrance: whether it does justify the belief will depend

[207] Unger (n 9) 267; Williamson (n 9) 249.

[208] Slote (n 9) 178–179; Williamson (n 9) 246; Dudman (n 125).

[209] That statistical evidence alone cannot justify a positive finding of fact is recognized in some cases (eg *Byers v Nicholls* (1987) 4 New Zealand Family L Rep 545, 551–2: 'even a high mathematical probability does not translate into a forensic certainty') and is defended by Wright (n 197) 1049–1067; cf *S v McC; W v W* [1972] AC 24, 41–2. However, in the English case of *Adams* [1996] 2 Cr App R 467, 469–470, it was held that DNA evidence alone may be sufficient to establish guilt. This seems inconsistent with the model direction given in *Doheny and Adams* [1997] 1 Cr App R 369, 375, which implicitly requires other evidence to justify singling the defendant out from the class narrowed down by the DNA evidence: cf *Adams No 2* [1998] 1 Cr App R 377, 384–5 (conviction apparently in absence of such other evidence).

[210] *Cream Holdings Ltd v Banerjee* [2004] UKHL 44, [2005] 1 AC 253, para 22.

[211] (1980) 607 P 2d 924.

[212] Callen (n 191) 491–492.

on matters such as the credibility of the witnesses, how strongly their testimony, if accepted, support the belief,[213] and more broadly, as will be explained, the eliminability of alternative hypotheses that are available on the evidence. The probability of mendacity or innocent error on the part of the witnesses may well be higher than 0.1. The court is prepared to give judgment against A on the basis of the testimonial evidence but not on the basis of the statistical information alone. How is this defensible when the testimonial evidence is, in some sense, less reliable than the statistical evidence?[214]

Fact-finding is unlike betting on the truth; it is not about acting on probabilities.[215] To bet that the defendant did not pay for his entrance is not to assert that he did not pay for his entrance. On the other hand, to find the defendant had gatecrashed is ordinarily to assert that he had gatecrashed. While the statistics may justify the belief that the defendant had probably committed trespass (a partial belief), it does not justify the belief that he had in fact committed trespass (a categorical belief). The latter is necessary for a finding of liability.

There is a special repugnance in finding a person liable on the sole basis of statistics. Such information alone cannot justify the belief that he is in fact liable. Of course, if we hold a person liable on the basis of oral evidence and in the belief that he is in fact liable, we can still be wrong.[216] But in the first case, we saw an inadequacy in the evidence and we intentionally subjected the defendant to an open risk of injustice: we gamble on the facts at his expense.[217] In the second case, we feel safe enough to dismiss the risk of injustice for the only reasonable conclusion to be drawn from the evidence is that the defendant did not purchase a ticket: if we err in this judgment, the error is of the kind that no human being and no system of trial can completely avoid.[218]

Ross once argued that blood tests should be treated as conclusive or legally irrebuttable proof of non-paternity because, overall, fewer mistakes will be

[213] That we frequently fail to keep the first two factors apart is noted by David A Schum, 'Comment' (1986) 66 Boston University L Rev 817, 820, and 'Probability and the Processes of Discovery, Proof, and Choice' (1986) 66 Boston University L Rev 825, 856.

[214] Frederick Schauer, *Profiles, Probabilities and Stereotypes* (Cambridge, Massachuetts: Harvard UP, 2003) 93–96; Alan M Dershowitz, *Reasonable Doubts: The Criminal Justice System and the OJ Simpson Case* (NY: Touchstone, 1997) 40; Ferdinand Schoeman, 'Statistical vs. Direct Evidence' (1987) 21 *Noûs* 179; Steven C Salop, 'Evaluating Uncertain Evidence with Sir Thomas Bayes: A Note for Teachers' (1987) 1 *J of Economic Perspectives* 155; Shaviro (n 191) 539–542.

[215] Posner (n 114) 215.

[216] Following Sutton (n 24) 7–14, the first may be described as a case of 'known unknown': we know that we do not know that the person is liable (although we may be justified in believing that he is probably liable). The second may turn out to be an 'unknown unknown' situation: we think we know that the defendant is liable, and if we are wrong about that, we do not know that we do not know that he is liable.

[217] Mary Dant, 'Gambling on the Truth: The Use of Purely Statistical Evidence as a Basis for Civil Liability' (1988) 22 Columbia J of L and Social Problems 31, 42–47.

[218] Tribe (n 121) 1372–1373, 1374–1375. In *R (Mullen) v Home Secretary* [2002] EWCA Civ 1882, para 33; [2003] QB 993, 1005, Schiemann LJ described this as 'an inescapable fact of human life'.

committed by the judicial system with this rule than without.[219] It is both descriptively false and normatively wrong to claim that fact-finders decide or ought to decide verdicts from the systemic point of view by applying reasoning aimed at delivering the largest proportion of correct outcomes in the long term. The duty of a fact-finder is and ought to be to do justice in the immediate case before her. Waldron makes a general point in another context that is very relevant here: 'outcomes to individuals matter and... aggregate justifications are in their very nature unsatisfactory because they treat outcomes to individuals as sort of incidental side effects, rather than the essence of the issue'.[220]

3 Structure of Trial Deliberation

3.1 Shackle's model of categorical belief

This section offers a tentative analysis of categorical belief, the concept pivotal to the theory advanced. A rudimentary sketch will be made of the structure of this kind of belief; we will try to answer the question: how does one judge whether (in fact) p? Since categorical belief does not entail absolute certainty,[221] there is the further question to be answered: what does the strength of categorical belief measure? When one comes, in consequence of the judgment that p, to believe that p, what does one's degree of confidence in p reflect? Clues to the answers can be found by examining a number of different, yet connected, theories. While these theories cannot be fully assimilated, each in its own way illuminates salient features of categorical belief and of its strength; on many of those features, the explanatory force of the theories converge.

Price highlights two aspects to believing that p.[222] One is 'preference'; the other is 'confidence'. Combining his views with those of Shah and Velleman discussed above, the two aspects may be stated thus:

(i) To believe (or more accurately, judge) that p is, in the first place, to choose p over some other propositions; it is to reject or dismiss the proposition(s) that compete against p for truth-regulated acceptance.

(ii) To believe (or more accurately, judge) that p is, in addition to (i), to be sufficiently confident that p.

[219] Ross (n 202) 482–483, discussed by Richard A Wasserstrom, *The Judicial Decision—Toward a Theory of Legal Justification* (Stanford, California: Stanford UP, 1961) 164–165.

[220] Jeremy Waldron, 'Does Law Promise Justice?' (2001) 17 Georgia State University L Rev 759, 779.

[221] Adler (n 156) especially ch 10. As he puts it: 'One can be entitled to a full belief without having unqualified confidence in that belief' (ibid 250); 'full belief is compatible with variations in confidence (with diminished confidence corresponding to doubt)' (ibid 254). Arguments against the view of categorical belief as certainty are also presented by Christensen (n 145) 21–22 and Kaplan (n 182) 91–93.

[222] H H Price, *Belief* (London: George Allen & Unwin, 1969).

The first aspect—preference—flows from the dogmatic nature of belief. It is irrational to judge that, in fact, both p and q, where q is an instance of not-p. If one believes that in fact q, one cannot at the same time believe that in fact p. One does not believe that in fact p where one does not find good reason to prefer p to q. But believing that p is more than preferring p to its contradictories. There is a further element which the first aspect, (i) above, fails to capture. To judge that p is, in the first place, to single p out from the propositions that compete for truth-regulated acceptance; and p is not open for truth-regulated acceptance if it is not, to use a phrase explained later, 'perfectly possible'. Suppose the fact-finder finds p, an explanation offered for an event, fanciful and q, a competing hypothesis, even more absurd. Of the two, p is less implausible than q and so, for what it is worth, she prefers p to q. But she must reject both since neither is plausible enough. She thinks that the truth must lie elsewhere, although she does not know where.[223]

We do not consider in the abstract whether to believe categorically that p is true. The choice between p and not-p is a choice between p and some other proposition or hypothesis which instantiates not-p.[224] We invariably assess p against its contradictories, whether they figure explicitly or not in our mind. Suppose I have gone away for a year and missed out on an entire season of football. I hear from a friend that team o has won the league championship. In believing my source and that team o is the champion, it is in a sense true that I am choosing the proposition that team o has won (p_o) to the proposition that it has not (not-p_o). But I choose p_o only because I prefer it to the proposition that some other team has carried the trophy; I choose p_o over the propositions p_q, p_r, p_s... that team q, r ,s... respectively has emerged as ultimate victors.[225] When we contemplate not-p, what we have in mind are these contradictory propositions (p_q, p_r, p_s...) taken as whole. Similarly, at a trial, when the fact-finder believes that a certain event occurred in a certain way, it is because he prefers that account to all of the contradictory explanations or hypotheses that compete for truth-regulated acceptance.

A heuristic model that advances understanding of these two aspects of doxastic judgment can be extracted from a theory developed by Shackle. The theory is on decision-making under uncertainty and intended for application in the field of economics. The focus will be on those parts of it that can be used to construct a general framework of categorical belief acquisition that shows how such a belief can vary in strength. The methodology Shackle offers, to borrow

[223] The classic illustration is *The 'Popi M'* [1983] 2 Lloyd's Rep 235; on which see Carruthers (n 77).

[224] Richard Swinburne, *Faith and Reason* (Oxford: OUP, 1981) 7: 'Belief-that is relative to alternatives; and where this is not realized or where the alternatives are not clearly specified, a man who expresses belief may not be saying anything very clear.'

[225] ibid 4–6.

the words of a different author, is 'non-computational',[226] 'at bottom qualitative and comparative rather than quantitative and mathematical',[227] and reflects 'a more basic... level of analysis than the calculus of probability'.[228] Shackle's theory revolves around the idea of 'possibility' (which is measured by 'potential surprise') as opposed to 'probability'. His theory is one of a group of avowedly non-probabilistic accounts of reasoning, other members of which include theories of 'plausible reasoning',[229] 'abductive reasoning',[230] and, perhaps, 'inference to the best explanation'.[231]

Unlike mathematical 'probability', Shackle's concept of 'possibility' is 'non-metrical'; the assignment of 'possibilities' is not governed by 'rules for arithmetic operations'.[232] By '(im)possibility', Shackle does not mean 'logical (im)possibility'. For him, 'possible' means 'intuitively or subjectively possible, possible in the judgement of a particular individual at a particular moment';[233] when a person makes a possibility judgment, he is making 'a statement about his own mind and thoughts, not, except indirectly, about the objective and external world'.[234] The degree of possibility[235] ranges from perfect possibility to impossibility; it can be expressed in terms of the degree of 'potential surprise' ('the surprise we *should* feel if the given thing *did* happen'[236]) and is the inverse measure of the extent of

[226] Nicholas Rescher, *Plausible Reasoning—An Introduction To The Theory And Practice Of Plausibilistic Inference* (Amsterdam: Van Gorcum, 1976) 59.

[227] ibid 38; see also ibid 17.

[228] ibid 59.

[229] The non-probabilistic nature of plausible reasoning is stressed by Rescher (n 226) especially ch 4 and at 59, and by Douglas Walton, *Legal Argumentation And Evidence* (Pennsylvania: Pennsylvania State University Press, 2002) especially 108–114.

[230] eg John R Josephson and Susan G Josephson, *Abductive Inference—Computation, Philosophy, Technology* (Cambridge: Cambridge University Press, 1994) 26–27 and appendix B (doubting that mathematical probabilities have much of a role to play in the analysis of abductive reasoning).

[231] eg Gilbert Harman, who coined this phrase in 'The Inference to the Best Explanation' (1965) 74 *The Philosophical Review* 88, rejects probabilistic reasoning as the basis of a reasoned change of view 'because of a combinatorial explosion such reasoning involves': Harman (n 163) 10, and, more fully, ibid ch 3. Cf Peter Lipton, *Inference to the Best Explanation* (2nd edn, London: Routledge, 2004) ch 7 who believes that inference to the best explanation is compatible with Bayesian probability.

[232] As noted by Hamblin in his expansion on Shackle's work: C L Hamblin, 'The Modal "Probably"' (1959) 68 *Mind* 234, 234.

[233] G L S Shackle, *Decision, Order And Time In Human Affairs* (2nd edn, Cambridge: CUP, 1969) 54. There are many kinds of possibility and that which Shackle has in mind is similar to what Gibbs calls 'natural possibility': Benjamin Gibbs, *Real Possibility* (1970) *American Philosophical Quarterly* 340, 340–343 (1970).

[234] Shackle (n 233) 67.

[235] Arguably, it would be more accurate to speak (as does Hamblin (n 232)) of 'plausibility' rather than 'possibility'. White (n 172) 60, in distinguishing probability and possibility, points out that, strictly speaking, there cannot be degrees of possibility; something is either possible or it is not.

[236] In contrast to 'actual' surprise, which is 'a feeling occasioned by an actual rather than an imagined happening': Shackle (n 233) 68.

disbelief.[237] 'Possibility' and 'potential surprise' presuppose our ability to form judgments about what *can* (as opposed to *will*) happen.[238]

> If a man feels that, should his knowledge and understanding remain as they are, the occurrence of a given thing would not surprise him in the slightest degree, we may say that, for him, that thing is perfectly possible.[239]

The perfect possibility of a hypothesis is the lack of any discernible real obstacle to it becoming or being true.[240] As another author puts it, something is perfectly possible for me if nothing of which I am aware that 'is…or has been actual is incompatible with the actuality of that thing'.[241] More plainly, Runde writes: 'An hypothesis *H* is perfectly possible if and only if the truth of *H* is consistent with the actor's stock of knowledge.'[242] Background beliefs and the capacity of imagination play necessary roles in judgments of possibility.[243] That which is judged perfectly possible is assigned zero degree of potential surprise. 'Zero potential surprise expresses zero disbelief':[244] when the possibility of a hypothesis is judged perfect, the degree of disbelief in it is zero.[245]

Contrariwise, if a person feels that a proposition is certainly wrong, he can be said to judge it as impossible. 'The occurrence of something hitherto judged impossible would cause a man a degree of surprise which is the greatest he is capable of feeling.'[246] That which is judged impossible is completely disbelieved and is assigned the absolute maximum degree of surprise. In between these two extremes, there are corresponding degrees of possibility and of potential surprise that may be ranked as 'mild', 'moderate', 'considerable' and so forth.[247]

[237] The connection between belief and surprise was also recognized by Price (n 222) 275–278. He wrote, ibid 276: 'if a person *is* surprised when a proposition *p* is falsified, this is about the strongest evidence we can have that he did, until then, believe the proposition for some period of time; and the degree of his surprise is about the strongest evidence we can have concerning the degree of his belief'.

[238] Shackle (n 233) 67.

[239] ibid 67.

[240] The hypothesis is 'entirely unobstructed, wholly free, within [our] thought, of any threatened interference': G L S Shackle, 'The Bounds of Unknowledge' in Stephen F Frowen (ed), *Business, Time And Thought—Selected Papers Of G L S Shackle* (London: Macmillan Press, 1988) 60, 86; see also 63, 64, 66.

[241] Gibbs (n 233) 340 (definition of 'natural possibility').

[242] Jochen Runde, 'Shackle on Probability' in Peter E Earl and Stephen F Frowen (eds), *Economics as an Art of Thought—Essays in Memory of G L S Shackle* (London: Routledge, 2000) 225.

[243] Moacir dos Anjos Jr and Victoria Chick, 'Liquidity and Potential Surprise' in Peter E Earl and Stephen F Frowen (eds), *Economics as an Art of Thought—Essays in Memory of G L S Shackle* (London: Routledge, 2000) 242, 251: 'What is deemed possible is conditioned by the agent's remembered experiences and by the elements which stimulate his imagination.'

[244] Shackle (n 233) 74.

[245] Shackle (n 240) 63.

[246] Shackle (n 233) 68.

[247] ibid 112. This is not to say that the interval can be calibrated in the manner of a scale: G L S Shackle, 'Decision' (1986) 13 *J of Economic Studies* 58, 60.

Shackle gives this example:[248]

Show me a hat-box, assuring me that it contains some kind of hat. I know no reason why the hat should not be a bowler; but equally I know of nothing which suggests that it cannot be a straw, or again that it may not be a soft felt. Zero potential surprise can be assigned to each of an unlimited number of rival, mutually exclusive, hypotheses all at once.

There is a crucial difference between this example and our marbles-in-an-urn example in Part 2.5.3. In Shackle's example, we have no information at all about the kind of hat that is in the box, whereas in our earlier example, we know that the marbles in the urn are either white or black and that the white marbles outnumber the black ones by eight to two. In Shackle's example, it is perfectly possible that the hat is a bowler, as well as that it is a straw, felt, and what not, and we would not be in the least surprised if it turns out to be any one of these. By 'potential surprise', Shackle means the surprise which runs *counter* to our expectation. This is different from the surprise that is felt upon encounter of *novelty*, or the *unexpected*.[249] The surprise we may feel upon discovery of an unthought-of kind of hat in the box is of the second, not the first, kind.

It is unclear whether Shackle would reach the same conclusion on possibility in the marbles-in-an-urn example as in the hat example.[250] The better view is that the two examples are materially different. In the marbles example, I would be much less surprised if the marble I draw turns out to be white than if it turns out to be black. Consequently, I assign a greater possibility to drawing a white marble than to drawing a black one. I do not judge it perfectly possible that the marble I will draw is white. I know that the urn contains both white and black marbles, and my knowledge and understanding of the world, including objective chances, makes me think that the two black marbles in the urn are potential obstacles to drawing out a white marble. Nothing of which I am aware allows me to rule out that potentiality. I thus refrain from judging categorically that the marble I will draw will in fact be white. The judgment of perfect possibility that the drawn

248 Shackle (n 233) 69–70.

249 G L S Shackle, *Imagination And The Nature Of Choice* (Edinburgh: Edinburgh UP, 1979) 88.

250 Shackle would on Runde's following interpretation of his views (n 242) 226: 'Compare the toss of a fair coin with the toss of a fair die. The outcomes of a head and an ace are both perfectly possible on Shackle's definition, although the respective probabilities are different.' J L Ford, *Choice, Expectation and Uncertainty—An Appraisal of G L S Shackle's Theory* (Oxford: Martin Robertson, 1983) 72 has an opposite interpretation of Shackle's position: '[T]o those critics who have argued that it is logically possible to assign zero degrees of potential surprise to two hypothetical outcomes whilst contending that the one is more likely to occur than the other, Shackle's reply is immediate and clear. To hold that the one outcome is more likely than the other must imply that there is an obstacle in the way of the other outcome's occurring. Therefore, it must be assigned a higher degree of potential surprise than the one outcome.'

marble will be white is 'incongruous or incompatible with the essential nature of things and their existing particular state'.[251]

To judge and consequently believe categorically that p is in fact true, it is not enough to judge that p is perfectly possible. Where both of two competing hypotheses are perfectly possible, a rational person would not believe that one or the other is, in fact, true. In the hat example, we would not believe that the box in fact contains a bowler; whilst we think that it is perfectly possible that it contains a bowler, we also think that it is perfectly possible that it contains some other kind of hat. We cannot believe that it is, as a matter of fact, true that both p and q, where q is a contradictory of p. To believe that p, we must not only think that p is perfectly possible, we must also think that none of its contradictories is perfectly possible. How strongly one believes that p in that situation will depend on the possibility of p relative to the possibility of the strongest of the contradictories.

The gatecrasher and cab scenarios are like the marbles-in-an-urn example. Given our knowledge of the composition of paying and non-paying spectators in the audience and of red and green cabs plying the street at the relevant time, it does not strike us as perfectly possible that A is a gatecrasher or that the cab which caused the accident was red, for exactly the same reason that we do not judge it perfectly possible that the marble I will draw is white, or for that matter, black. While the evidence justifies the belief that it is more probable than not that A watched the show for free, it does not justify the belief that this was in fact the case. It is admittedly more possible that A is a gatecrasher than that he is not, but neither strikes us as perfectly possible: A, after all, was picked at random from the crowd and so he could be one of the 499 people who had paid for their entrance. In the light of what we know and understand about the world, we discern the real possibility of obstacle to it being true that he was a trespasser. The cab scenario is open to a similar analysis. We understand that any one of the cabs in town that night could have caused the accident and we know there were green cabs operating in town that night: our awareness of these facts prevents us from assigning perfect possibility to the hypothesis that a red cab caused the accident, as the possibility that the cab was green is alive. This is not to deny the relevance of statistical evidence. Shackle freely admits that 'statistical frequencies are... amongst the materials out of which... judgements [on potential surprise] arise'.[252] In view of the statistics, it is rational to believe that the possibility of the accident being caused by a red cab is greater than the possibility of it being caused by a green cab: but it still remains that neither is perfectly possible.

Shackle is emphatic in rejecting the identification of perfect possibility with perfect certainty.[253] He distinguishes 'possibility' from 'probability', making it very clear at the same time that information on objective probability may

[251] Shackle (n 233) 74, and also ibid 87–88.
[252] ibid 72; see also *Re J S (Declaration of Paternity)* (1981) 2 Fam L Rep 146, 151.
[253] Shackle (n 233) 70–71.

influence one's judgment of possibility.[254] Possibility, unlike probability, is a non-distributional uncertainty variable. In using possibility as an uncertainty variable, we are neither confined to a closed list of alternative hypotheses nor constrained to assign values in a way that must sum up to unity. Perfect possibility is by no means equivalent to a probability of one. Possibility and probability can be mapped on to each other only in a 'purely arbitrary and artificial' way.[255] To say that it is perfectly possible that the hat is a bowler is not to say that it is certain that it is a bowler. We are not in the least certain that it is a bowler because we think that it is also perfectly possible that it is some other kind of hat. There is no limit to the number of such other alternatives that we may also judge perfectly possible, and we need not revise our judgment of possibility as more alternatives come to mind. A probabilistic analysis, on the other hand, presupposes an exhaustive list of rival hypotheses and requires that the sum of probability values given to them add up to one; the result is that every hypothesis must have a probability value of less than one, and the value of at least one hypothesis has to be lowered with each addition of a rival.[256]

When we believe categorically that p, the strength of our belief is bounded by the degree of possibility we attribute to the most possible of the competing hypotheses. We cannot be certain that p, even though we think p is perfectly possible, so long as we assign some (albeit less than perfect) possibility to one or more of p's contradictories. The degree of a person's belief in p can be expressed 'by means of the potential surprise he assigns to the least (potentially) surprising rival hypothesis'.[257] To use an earlier example, if I believe that team o has won the league championship, this idea carries for me zero potential surprise, and a greater than zero degree will be attributed to the contradictory, considered as a set, that it has not won. This set comprises the specific contradictory hypotheses that team q, r, s... has won instead. To these I will attach varying degrees of potential surprise, judged according to factors such as my assessment of the current strengths of the teams, and the lowest amongst these 'will then project upon the contradictory as a whole its own degree of potential surprise'.[258] The higher the degree of potential surprise that is projected on the contradictory as a whole, the stronger the belief that team o has won.[259] Thus beliefs that are categorical can yet vary in strength; one can believe more or less strongly that a proposition is in fact true.

254 ibid 72, 113. Cf Runde (n 242) 221–222 and n 8.

255 Shackle (n 233) 113.

256 Shackle (n 247) 59, and Shackle (n 240) 65–66. See also Rescher (n 226) 15–16, 31 (drawing similar distinction between 'plausibility' and 'probability').

257 Shackle (n 233) 71.

258 ibid 73.

259 Judge Posner had some such relationship in mind when he said in *Spitz v Commissioner* (1992) 954 F 2d 1382, 1384 (7th Circuit): 'the plausibility of an explanation depends on the plausibility of the alternative explanations'. On relative plausibility theory, see below.

Three features of Shackle's analysis of belief strength need to be emphasized. First, as others have pointed out, the strength of belief is not a matter of the intensity of any feeling. As Ramsey says, 'the beliefs which we hold most strongly are often accompanied by practically no feeling at all; no one feels strongly about things he takes for granted'.[260] Shackle must not be accused of equating the strength of belief with the intensity of any actual feeling. It is important to note that he relies on the notion of 'potential' surprise. I believe categorically and take for granted that the armchair I am sitting on is an armchair. I do not experience any feeling, intense or otherwise, for the truth of that proposition. But *if* the chair should turn out to be a giant tortoise in disguise, I *would* be hugely surprised.

Secondly, other writers have suggested that the strength of a categorical belief has to do with its 'tenacity': the more difficult it is to make the subject change her mind, the stronger is her belief.[261] This conception of strength is compatible with Shackle's analysis. How strongly one believes categorically that p depends on how close to being perfectly possible one thinks the alternative hypotheses are. The weaker the discerned obstacle to the truth or realization of an alternative hypothesis, the less it takes by way of new evidence and argument to overcome it, to persuade one that the competing hypothesis is perfectly possible after all. When one is persuaded, one abandons the categorical belief that p since, in one's eyes, p is no longer the only hypothesis that is perfectly possible. The notion of tenacity may be said to be related to the notion of confidence thus: the greater the confidence one has in p, the more tenaciously one holds on to the categorical belief that p.

Thirdly, Shackle's theory is not prescriptive. It was not his intention to 'devise a decision rule which, if properly used, will generate "optimal" decisions'.[262] His theory is largely descriptive, although, as with any descriptive theory of human reasoning, it involves some idealization and thus has a normative element.[263] When applied to trial deliberation, his theory helps us to understand the method by which a rational fact-finder settles on categorical beliefs about the facts of the case, a method which doubles as a framework for justifying those beliefs, and also to understand how the beliefs can vary in strength.

In summary and to take stock of where we are at: The discussion in this section followed up on the contention that the fact-finder must find that p only if one would be justified in believing that p within the terms of BAF*. The belief needed for this purpose is of the categorical kind. A model has just been outlined that is

[260] Ramsey (n 89) 169.

[261] Owens (n 146) 144; Harman (n 163) 22.

[262] Frank H Stephen, 'Decision Making Under Uncertainty: In Defence of Shackle' (1986) 13 *J of Economic Studies* 45, 45.

[263] Harman (n 163) 7 ('normative and descriptive theories of reasoning are intimately related. For one thing, ... it is hard to come up with convincing normative principles except by considering how people actually do reason, which is the province of a descriptive theory. On the other hand it seems that any descriptive theory must involve a certain amount of idealization, and idealization is always normative to some extent').

suggestive (and no more than that) of the general method by which one arrives at a categorical belief and that tries to make sense of the strength of that belief. Shackle's theory indirectly explains how positive findings of fact are made at a trial by casting light on how one generally comes to believe categorically that p. His model of categorical belief (henceforth 'SMCB') is anchored in these principles: (i) one believes categorically that p when one judges that p is perfectly possible and none of its contradictories is also perfectly possible; and (ii) the strength of one's belief that p reflects inversely the degree of possibility one conceives of the strongest of those contradictories.

SMCB complements BAF* by providing a theory of the belief component in the latter. These two theories, as integrated, will be called SMCB-BAF*. In the sections to follow, parallels will be drawn between SMCB-BAF* and other theories. The similarities lend corroborative support to the SMCB-BAF*. More importantly, the parallel theories provide important insights which help us to sharpen BAF* and SMCB.

3.2 Relevant alternatives theory

SMCB resembles the relevant alternatives theory of knowledge ('RATK'). This is not surprising given that categorical belief is a component of knowledge. RATK is not *a* theory as such but a family of theories; different proponents offer different versions of a broadly common analysis of knowledge. An understanding of RATK and of the difficult issues it raises helps us to make important adjustments to SMCB and BAF*.

The basic idea at the core of RATK is thus stated by its leading proponents: Dretske claims that knowledge is 'an evidential state in which all relevant alternatives (to what is known) are eliminated';[264] Lewis defines knowledge such that 'S knows that p [if and only if] S's evidence eliminates every possibility in which not-P—except for those possibilities that we are properly ignoring';[265] and, for Goldman: 'A person knows that p... only if the actual state of affairs in which p is true is distinguishable or discriminable by him from a relevant possible state of affairs in which p is false. If there is a relevant possible state of affairs in which p is false and which is indistinguishable by him from the actual state of affairs, then he fails to know that p.'[266] The similarity between RATK and SMCB is clear enough: to know or believe categorically that p, one must be able to rule out alternatives to p. RATK faces three difficulties; these are difficulties that SMCB will also have to address.

264 Fred Dretske, 'The Pragmatic Dimension of Knowledge' (1981) 40 *Philosophical Studies* 363, 367.

265 David Lewis, 'Elusive Knowledge' (1996) 74 *Australasian Journal of Philosophy* 549, 554.

266 Alvin I Goldman, 'Discrimination and Perceptual Knowledge' (1976) 73 *Journal of Philosophy* 771, 774.

First, what counts as an alternative or a competing hypothesis? One answer is: q is an alternative or competing hypothesis to p if and only if they cannot both be true at the same time. If the defendant was at home watching television with her family at the material time, she could not be the one who started the fire at the site of arson. But one proposition may undermine another without their being mutually exclusive: the proposition that the defendant has no motive to commit a crime and the proposition that she committed the crime are not contradictory. Nevertheless, the defendant's lack of motive counts as a non-conclusive reason against believing that she is guilty. A workable concept of an alternative or competing hypothesis will have to be complex enough to deal with such cases. The key is to recognize the multiplicity of levels at which a hypothesis may be formulated and be of relevance, and this recognition can come about only when a hypothesis is seen as a narrative, a complex of propositions rather than a singular proposition of fact. Two competing hypotheses may yet have much in common. This observation is pursued in the next section.

The second difficulty is in defining relevance. Not every logical or theoretical possibility qualifies as an alternative; otherwise, and if epistemic deductive closure holds, no knowledge of the external world is possible. That I do not know that I am not a (handless) brain-in-a-vat would seem to entail that I do not know that I have a pair of hands. I can know that I have a pair of hands only if I can rule out the alternative possibility that I am a brain-in-a-vat. The philosophical sceptic points out that I cannot rule out that alternative since all the experiences that I have are consistent with me being a brain-in-a-vat. Knowledge that I have hands can be defended by insisting that, in everyday contexts, the alternative of me being a brain-in-a-vat is simply irrelevant. That alternative is overly fanciful, an unreal possibility, too remote to worry about. To know that p, one does not have to rule out all possible alternatives to p; one needs only to rule out those alternatives which are relevant. This immediately raises the problem of distinguishing alternatives that are too speculative from those that deserve our attention. Philosophers have found it 'exceedingly difficult to capture the distinction between relevant and irrelevant alternatives in a precise criterion'.[267]

Lewis offers a number of rules to determine relevance. One is the 'rule of actuality': 'The possibility that actually obtains is never properly ignored; actuality is always a relevant alternative.'[268] Another is the 'rule of resemblance': 'Suppose one possibility saliently resembles another. Then if one of them may not be properly ignored, neither may the other.'[269] He uses this to explain why, in the lottery example, we do not know (or, as we may also say,[270] why we do not believe categorically) that the person holding the ticket has not won: 'For every ticket, there

[267] Stewart Cohen, 'Skepticism, Relevance, and Relativity' in Brian P McLaughlin (ed), *Dretske and His Critics* (Oxford: Blackwell, 1991) 32.

[268] Lewis (n 265) 554.

[269] ibid 556.

[270] Relying on Nelkin (n 181).

is the possibility that it will win. These possibilities are saliently similar to one another: so either every one of them may be properly ignored, or else none may. But one of them may not properly be ignored: the one that actually obtains.'[271] This argument applies equally to the gatecrasher and cab scenarios: the possibility that A did not pay for his entrance saliently resembles the possibility that he did; and the possibility that a red cab caused the accident saliently resembles the possibility that it was a green cab which caused the accident. We cannot ignore one possibility without ignoring the other, and we cannot ignore both because one of them actually obtains. In the lottery example as in the two scenarios, there are relevant alternatives which cannot be ignored.

The problem of deciding the relevancy of an alternative hypothesis constantly arises in legal fact-finding. At a criminal trial, a defence will not be put to the jury and will not be considered at all unless there is some 'evidence that, if believed, and on the most favourable view, could be taken by a reasonable jury to support the defence'.[272] This doctrine ensures that time is not wasted on bare postulations of entirely speculative defences. Similarly, not every factual hypothesis deserves consideration. The following is an amusing first-hand account of jury deliberation in a shoplifting case where one juror drove the author, a fellow juror, to despair:[273]

> [I]n the jury room one man reacted to the concept of 'reasonable doubt' as if it were a challenge to his ingenuity. It meant, he insisted, that we were to see if we could think of any possible alternative explanation of events, and he could—somebody had 'planted' the garment in the girl's bag. It was pointed out to him that even the defence had not put forward this explanation. That didn't matter, he said, perhaps they hadn't thought of it. There MUST be reasonable doubt if you could construct another theory, after all, it wasn't physically impossible, was it? It was now pointed out to him that although it wasn't physically impossible, his explanation was not based on a single scrap of evidence. Who did he think had done the 'planting', the store detective? 'A person or persons unknown,' said the odd man out, proudly. He could not be shaken. He saw himself now, it seemed, in the role of Sherlock Holmes, not of juror.

The failure of this juror to restrain his imagination and worry only about hypotheses founded on the evidence makes him a parody of the heroic juror number eight in *Twelve Angry Men*. As the courts have constantly emphasized in the context of the criminal standard of proof, a reasonable doubt is not established by raising a merely conceivable hypothesis inconsistent with guilt. Alternative possibilities which are 'fantastic and unreal',[274] 'fanciful',[275] 'mere conjecture[s]',[276]

[271] Lewis (n 265) 557.

[272] G Williams, 'The Logic of "Exceptions"' [1988] CLJ 261, 265, relied upon by Lord Hope in *R v Lambert* [2002] 2 AC 545, para 84.

[273] Alan Wykes in Dulan Barber and Giles Gordon (eds), *Members of the Jury* (London: Wildwood House, 1976) 76.

[274] *Green v The Queen* (1971) 126 CLR 28, 33 (Australian High Court).

[275] *PP v Selvakumar Pillai s/o Suppiah Pillai* [2004] 4 SLR 280, para 51 (Singapore High Court).

[276] *Peacock v The King* (1911) 13 CLR 619, 661 (Australian High Court).

or 'illusory'[277] do not deserve attention. Although the jury is entitled to consider an alternative factual hypothesis even if it was not put forward by counsel at the trial,[278] the jury is not allowed to engage in wild speculation. In *Mancini v DPP*, the House of Lords gave the example of 'a case in which no evidence has been given which would raise the issue of provocation' and stressed that, in such circumstances, it is not for 'the jury to speculate as to provocative incidents, of which there is no evidence and which cannot be reasonably inferred from the evidence'.[279] The point is captured by Tan[280] in this statement approved by the Singapore Court of Appeal in *Took Leng How v PP*:[281] where a doubt 'cannot yet concretely be articulated in relation to the evidence in the case, it remains an untested hypothesis and may be rejected'.

The third difficulty with RATK lies in the notion 'elimination'. To know that p, one must be able to eliminate or rule out all relevant alternatives to p. According to SMCB, to acquire the categorical belief that p, one must judge p perfectly possible and the competing hypotheses less than perfectly possible. I do not believe categorically that A was a gatecrasher or that the cab which caused the accident was red because I judge both hypotheses as less than perfectly possible. And I come to that judgment because I am unable to rule out the alternative possibility that A did pay for his entrance or that the cab was green. The evidence must be such as to justify singling out for acceptance one hypothesis of facts establishing guilt or liability and to justify ruling out all relevant competing hypotheses against guilt or liability; it is perhaps this idea that lies behind the oft-heard protest that statistical evidence is not (sufficiently) 'specific' or 'particularized'.[282] What the protesters could mean is that evidence good enough to secure a positive verdict must point specifically to guilt or liability in the manner just described. The evidence available in the two scenarios does not provide the necessary type of reasoning or explanation that would do the job. As will be argued later, what is needed is a causal type of reasoning or explanation.

How lacking in plausibility or possibility must a competing hypothesis be before it may be eliminated? As will be suggested in Chapter 4, there is no fixed or absolute standard; much will depend on what is at stake. In a serious criminal case, an alternative hypothesis to guilt cannot be safely dismissed so long as it is

[277] *Tang Kin Seng v PP* [1997] 1 SLR 46, paras 95–6 (Singapore High Court).

[278] *Mancini v DPP* [1942] AC 1, 7.

[279] ibid 12.

[280] Tan Yock Lin, *Criminal Procedure*, vol 2 (Singapore: LexisNexis, 2005) ch XVII, para 2952.

[281] [2006] SGCA 3; [2006] 2 SLR 70, para 29.

[282] eg *United States v Shonubi* (1993) 998 F 2d 84, 86, 89; *United States v Shonubi* (1997) 103 F 3d 1085, 1089–1093 (both are decisions of the United States Court of Appeals for the Second Circuit); Brilmayer (n 193) 675; Cohen (n 97) 271; Glanville Williams, 'The Mathematics of Proof' [1979] Crim LR 297, 305; Stein (n 194) ch 3.

'more than a fanciful possibility';[283] the plausibility of an alternative hypothesis must be much higher if it is to defeat proof in a run of the mill civil claim.

3.3 Relative plausibility theory

In a series of well-known articles, Allen puts forth a 'relative plausibility theory' of legal fact-finding.[284] His theory has had impact on the law in the United States, having been cited by Judge Posner in a number of cases before the Court of Appeals for the Seventh Circuit.[285] Allen gave this summary of his views in an article he co-wrote with Leiter:[286]

> The critical insight of the relative plausibility theory is that legal fact finding involves a determination of the comparative plausibility of the parties' explanations offered at trial rather than a determination of whether discrete elements are found to a specific probability. In civil cases the factfinder is to identify the most plausible account of the relevant events, whereas in criminal cases the prosecution must provide a plausible account of guilt and show that there is no plausible account of innocence.

There is agreement between relative plausibility theory and SMCB-BAF* that trial deliberation involves assessment of the relative plausibility or possibility of competing hypotheses. But there are material differences quite apart from differences in the premises of the theories and reasoning on which they are based. For instance, Allen advocates different approaches for civil and criminal trials. Generally speaking,[287] the civil court must decide according to the relative plausibility of the stories offered by both sides in support of their respective cases, whereas the criminal court must not only find the prosecution's case plausible

[283] *Nadasan Chandra Secharan v PP* [1997] 1 Singapore L Rep 723, para 89 (Singapore Court of Appeal).

[284] Including Ronald J Allen, 'The Nature of Juridical Proof' (1991) 13 Cardozo L Rev 373, 'A Reconceptualization of Civil Trials' (1986) 66 Boston University L Rev 401, and 'Factual Ambiguity and a Theory of Evidence' (1994) 88 Northwestern University L Rev 604.

[285] *Spitz v Commissioner* (1992) 954 F 2d 1382, 1384–5; *United States v Beard* (2004) 354 F 3d 691, 692–3; *Anderson v Griffin* (2005) 397 F 3d 515, 521.

[286] Allen and Leiter (n 199) 1527–1528. See also Ronald J Allen, 'A Reconceptualization of Civil Trials' (n 284) 436 ('The objective of a criminal trial is not to choose among stories of the parties. Rather it is to determine whether or not the only plausible explanation of the event in question is that the defendant is guilty as charged… [T]he government [is required] not only [to] establish its own case but [also] to negate any reasonable explanations of the relevant affairs consistent with innocence'); Ronald J Allen, 'The Nature of Juridical Proof' (n 284) 413 ('The state must disprove every story consistent with innocence. If, after hearing all the evidence, a juror concludes that there is a plausible scenario consistent with innocence, then the juror should vote for acquittal'). Others have taken similar positions: see eg Larry Laudan, *Truth, Error, and Criminal Law* (Cambridge: CUP, 2006) at 82–83. For a different theory that explains legal proof in terms of comparison of hypotheses: Lennart Aqvist, 'Towards a Logical Theory of Legal Evidence: Semantic Analysis of the Bolding-Ekelof Degrees of Evidential Strength' in Antonio A Martino (ed), *Expert Systems in Law* (Amsterdam: North-Holland, 1992) 67.

[287] Leaving aside important ambiguities in the relative plausibility theory noted by Dale A Nance, 'Naturalized Epistemology and the Critique of Evidence Theory' (2001) 87 Virginia L Rev 1551 at 1575–1588.

but must also be able to reject as implausible all other accounts of innocence. SMCB-BAF*, on the other hand, offers a unified theory of trials. Civil cases are not decided by a relative judgment as to which of the hypotheses offered by the parties is the more plausible; if neither hypothesis is plausible enough, even if one is less implausible than the other, judgment should be given against the party carrying the burden of proof.[288] The structure of deliberation is the same for both civil and criminal trials; the difference lies in the 'standard of proof' that operates within that structure, a difference that is explained in Chapter 4 as an attitudinal one. On the contextualist approach briefly mentioned above, where less is at stake at a civil trial than in a criminal case (which is not always so), proof should be easier to establish in the former than in the latter: it should take less by way of evidence and argument to eliminate the competing hypotheses in the first than in the second case.[289]

These differences aside, both theories share the basic conception of legal proof as a matter of constructing and comparing the possibility (or plausibility) of competing hypotheses, ending in the question whether one is justified in believing (or treating) any of them as the true (or most plausible) account. This is by no means a novel approach. The basic idea can be found in old evidence treatises, case authorities from across the spectrum of common law jurisdictions, and even from international tribunals. Examples from these sources are cited below to show the broad support they give to the conception of legal proof shared by both theories; differences in the details need not detain us as they do not detract from the commonality of the core idea.

In England, the notion that proof requires elimination of all reasonable alternative hypotheses goes back a long way and can be found in evidence treatises of the nineteenth century.[290] The best statement of this view is in Wills's classic treatise on circumstantial evidence:[291]

> In order to justify the inference of guilt, the inculpatory facts must be incompatible with the innocence of the accused, and incapable of explanation upon any other reasonable hypothesis than that of his guilt.

[288] See earlier discussion, at n 223. Cf Allen and Leiter (n 199) 1531. Underlying this position is the view that civil liability should be imposed only when the court is in a position to assert that the plaintiff is in fact entitled to his legal claims. Cf Ronald J Allen, 'Constitutional Adjudication, the Demands of Knowledge, and Epistemological Modesty' (1993) Northwestern University L Rev 436, 454: 'constitutional litigation is not a question of deciding whether some proposition is true or false; it is a question of resolving contrasting explanations. The structure of litigation is not whether one party should win or lose but instead whether one party should win rather than another.'

[289] Chapter 4 argues for a variant standard of proof and against a categorical distinction between the criminal and civil standards.

[290] eg John Pitt Taylor, *A Treatise on the Law of Evidence as Administered in England and Wales* vol 1 (7th edn, London: Maxwell, 1878) 84: The jury 'must decide, not whether these facts are consistent with the prisoner's guilt, but whether they are inconsistent with any other rational conclusion; for it is only on this last hypothesis that they can safely convict the accused'.

[291] William Wills, *An Essay on the Principles of Circumstantial Evidence*, edited by Alfred Wills (6th edn, London: Butterworth, 1912) 311.

A further way, Wills explained:[292]

> Every other reasonable supposition by which the facts may be explained consistently with the hypothesis of innocence must... be rigorously examined and successively eliminated; and only when no other supposition will reasonably account for all the conditions of the case can the conclusion of guilt be legitimately adopted.

Wills cited as authority a statement reportedly made by Lord Chief Baron Macdonald in *R v Patch*[293] that 'the jury must be satisfied that there is no rational mode of accounting for the circumstances other than the conclusion that the prisoner is guilty'. In *Hodge's case*, Alderson B instructed the jury that, before they could find the prisoner guilty on the basis of circumstantial evidence, they must be satisfied 'not only that those circumstances were consistent with his having committed the act, but they must also be satisfied that the facts were such as to be inconsistent with any other rational conclusion than that the prisoner was the guilty person'.[294] This has come to be called the 'rule in *Hodge's case*' and is taken to have laid down the 'legal requirement... that no inference can be drawn against an accused unless it is the only reasonable inference'.[295] A leading modern text on English evidence law describes this rule as 'traditional' and 'orthodox'.[296]

On the civil side, a similar approach was taken in *Sweeney v Coote*.[297] An injunction was sought to restrain the defendant from conspiring with others to injure the plaintiff in her business and employment. The action failed for lack of adequate proof. According to Lord Loreburn, a positive finding of conspiracy is not one that the court will make 'by a light conjecture'. The allegation 'must be plainly established. It may, like other conclusions, be established as a matter of inference from proved facts, but the point is not whether you can draw that particular inference, but whether the facts are such that they cannot fairly admit of any other inference being drawn from them.'[298]

In Canada, the test formulated by Wills was adopted in *Sankey v R*.[299] In this case, MacDonald CJA stressed that the evidence need not rule out all possible hypotheses against the finding of guilt. Otherwise, no conviction could

[292] ibid 312.

[293] Surrey Spring Assizes, 1805, As reported in Wills (n 291) 313–314.

[294] (1838) 2 Lew CC 227, 228. Similarly, *R v Onufrejczyk* [1955] 1 QB 388, 394.

[295] *Tang Kwok Wah, Dixon v Hong Kong Special Administrative Region* [2002] HKCU 40, para 61. Ibid para 25, it was held that the rule in *Hodge's case* went 'to the standard to which the prosecution must prove its case' and did not 'lay down how the jury must always be directed in order to make them understand how to apply that standard' (see also ibid para 61). There is no such mandatory requirement in England (*McGreevy v Director of Public Prosecutions* (1973) 57 Cr App R 424), Hong Kong (*Tang Kwok Wah, Dixon v Hong Kong Special Administrative Region* [2002] HKCU 40), or Trinidad and Tobago (*Daniel and others v Trinidad and Tobago* [2007] UKPC 39, para 43).

[296] Roberts and Zuckerman (n 97) 366 and 367 respectively.

[297] [1907] AC 221.

[298] ibid at 222.

[299] [1927] 4 DLR 245, 247–8 (British Columbia Court of Appeal). The decision was reversed by the Canadian Supreme Court but not on this point: ibid 267.

ever be obtained on circumstantial evidence, as in every case 'many other hypotheses might be conjured up . . . consistent with the prisoner's innocence'. The court would entertain only those hypotheses which are reasonable.[300] As we have seen, an exculpatory hypothesis which is entirely speculative and lacking in evidential support is treated in law as irrelevant, posing no obstacle to a conviction.

The views expressed by Wills have also been followed in India.[301] The law commission gave this summary of the law on proof as contained in the Indian Evidence Act:[302]

> In civil cases, there are usually two versions of the facts. The court, on the basis of the evidence adduced before it, chooses that version which it thinks is more probable, that is, it will accept that version which a prudent man will act upon the supposition that exists. If there is no defence version, the court can take that fact into consideration in concluding that the plaintiff's version of the facts exists. In conceivable cases, the court can reject both versions as false.
>
> But in a criminal case, whether or not there is a defence version the court must be satisfied that a reasonable alternative version is *not possible*, because, if it is possible, a prudent man will not act upon the supposition that the prosecution version exists. He will act on the supposition that the alternative version exists.

In the United States, the same general principles were enunciated by Greenleaf long ago: 'In civil cases, it is sufficient if the evidence, on the whole, agrees with and supports the hypothesis, which it is adduced to prove; but in criminal cases, it must exclude every other hypothesis but that of the guilty of the party.'[303] With more elaboration, he argued that the force of circumstantial evidence depends on its[304]

> sufficiency to exclude every other hypothesis but the one under consideration. Thus, the possession of goods recently stolen, accompanied with personal proximity in point of time and place, and inability in the party charged, to show how he came by them, would seem naturally, though not necessarily, to exclude every other hypothesis, but that of his guilt. But the possession of the same goods, at another time and place, would warrant no such conclusion, as it would leave room for the hypothesis of their having been lawfully purchased in the course of trade.

[300] ibid 246.

[301] eg *State of Rajasthan v Kheraj Ram* [2003] 3 LRI 692 (decision of the Indian Supreme Court).

[302] Law Commission of India, 185th Report on Review of the Indian Evidence Act, 1872, March 2003, 24, available at: <http://www.lawcommissionofindia.nic.in/reports.htm>. Emphasis is original.

[303] Simon Greenleaf, *A Treatise on the Law of Evidence*, vol 1 (5th edn, Boston: Little & Brown, 1850) 19.

[304] ibid 16.

This view remains valid in the United States; it is unmistakably echoed in the *Corpus Juris Secundum*:[305]

[P]roof beyond a reasonable doubt is such proof as precludes every reasonable hypothesis except that which it tends to support, and is proof which is wholly consistent with the guilt of the accused, and inconsistent with any other rational conclusion.

The law in Singapore and Malaysia is largely the same. In the leading case of *Sunny Ang v PP*,[306] the Malayan Federal Court found this jury direction given by the trial judge to be 'perfectly adequate':

The... question to which I must draw your attention is that the question in this case, depending as it does on circumstantial evidence, is whether the cumulative effect of all the evidence leads you to the irresistible conclusion that it was the accused who committed this crime. Or is there some reasonably possible explanation such, for example—'Was it an accident?'... [Does the circumstantial evidence, taken together,] lead you to the irresistible inference and conclusion that the accused committed this crime? Or is there some other reasonably possible explanation of those facts?

This so-called *Sunny Ang* test (also known as the 'only reasonable inference test'[307]) was adopted by the Singapore Court of Appeal in *PP v Oh Laye Koh*[308] with these comments:

[T]he test propounded in *Sunny Ang v PP* [is] that before circumstantial evidence can secure an accused's conviction, it must lead inevitably and inexorably to one conclusion and one conclusion only: the accused's guilt. In other words, the circumstantial evidence, taken in its totality, must lead to the irresistible inference and conclusion that the accused committed the crime. In such a case, the prosecution would not have proved its case beyond a reasonable doubt if there existed, in the mind of the court, any other reasonably possible explanation for the events in question.

305 *Corpus Juris Secundum*, vol 23, *Criminal Law*, §1502 (available on Westlaw; database updated June 2007). This rule is supported by many cases. It is said to be 'elementary' (*Powers v Commonwealth* (1970) 211 Va 386 at 388), 'axiomatic' (*State v Sivri* (1994) 231 Conn 115, 131) and 'well settled' (*Wooden v Commonwealth* (1915) 117 Va 930, 935). For a recent State authority, see *Molina v Commonwealth* (2006) 47 Va App 338, 369. For Federal authorities, see *Tinsley v US* (1930) 43 F 2d 890, 897–898 (Circuit Court of Appeals of the Eighth Circuit), the cases cited by Allen and Leiter (n 199) 1532–1534, and Ronald J Allen and Michael S Pardo, 'The Problematic Value of Mathematical Models of Evidence' (2007) 36 J of Legal Studies 107, 136, n 39.

306 [1966] 2 Malayan LJ 195, 198.

307 *PP v Chee Cheong Hin Constance* [2006] SGHC 9; [2006] 2 Singapore L Rep 24, para 84.

308 [1994] 2 Singapore L Rep 385, 391. The test was also applied by the Singapore Court of Appeal in *Nadasan Chandra Secharan v PP* (n 283) paras 84–86 (ibid para 85: 'The question before us is simply this: Does the cumulative evidence drive one inevitably and inexorably to the one conclusion and one conclusion only, that it was the appellant who intentionally caused the death of the deceased? Or is there some other reasonably possible explanation of the facts connecting the appellant to the murder?') and by the Singapore High Court in *PP v Selvakumar Pillai s/o Suppiah Pillai* [2004] 4 Singapore L Rep 280, paras 50–52.

The 'only reasonable inference' test is settled law in Hong Kong as well. In the leading authority of *Kwan Ping Bong v R*,[309] Lord Diplock held that the inference of guilt 'must be compelling—one (and the only one) that no reasonable man could fail to draw from the direct facts proved'.

The same approach prevails in Australia. Her High Court has used these slightly different formulations to describe essentially the same quality circumstantial evidence must possess to justify a conviction: (i) 'guilt should not only be a rational inference but should be the only rational inference that could be drawn from the circumstances';[310] (ii) 'the circumstances must be such as to be inconsistent with any reasonable hypothesis other than the guilt of the accused';[311] (iii) 'the inference of guilt [must be] the only inference which... could rationally [be] draw[n] from the circumstances';[312] (iv) there must be 'no other explanation than guilt [that] is reasonably compatible with the circumstances';[313] (v) the conclusion of guilt must be the 'only rational inference that the circumstances... enable [the jury] to draw';[314] (vi) 'the evidentiary circumstances must bear no other reasonable explanation';[315] and (vii) there must be no 'other inference consistent with innocence [that] is reasonably open on the evidence'.[316]

The Privy Council hearing an appeal from the Court of Appeal for Eastern Africa in the case of *R v Sharmpal Singh* took a similar position when it opined:[317]

> [T]he Crown not only had to dispose of the defence set up but had also to prove that the evidence adduced by the prosecution was consistent only with murder... [T]he inability of the medical evidence to speak with precision about the degree of force used, together with other circumstances of the case..., opened up both manslaughter and accident as alternative possibilities requiring consideration.

[309] [1979] Hong Kong L Rep 1, 5. This case has been cited on many occasions in Hong Kong; a recent example is *Hong Kong Special Administrative Region v Sung Pak Lun* [2006] HKCU 1491 (Hong Kong Court of Appeal). The correctness of the principle laid down by Lord Diplock was considered 'undoubtedly correct' and 'incontrovertible' in *Tang Kwok Wah, Dixon v Hong Kong Special Administrative Region* (n 295) paras 5 and 61 respectively.

[310] *Shepherd v The Queen* (1990) 170 CLR 573, 578.

[311] *Peacock v The King* (1911) 13 CLR 619, 634. This principle has received repeated endorsement in later High Court cases: eg *Knight v The Queen* (1992) 175 CLR 495, 509–510; *Barca v The Queen* (1975) 133 CLR 82, 104.

[312] *Plomp v The Queen* (1963) 110 CLR 234 at 252.

[313] ibid 243; followed by the Singapore High Court in *PP v Chee Cheong Hin Constance* (n 307) para 84.

[314] *Plomp v The Queen* (n 312) 252, cited in *Barca v R* (1975) 133 CLR 82, 104 and *Cutter v R* (1997) 143 ALR 498, 502.

[315] *Martin v Osborne* (1936) 55 CLR 367, 375, cited in *Cutter v R* (1997) 143 ALR 498, 510.

[316] *Shepherd v R* (n 310) 579, cited in *Cutter v R* (n 314) 512.

[317] [1962] AC 188 at 195. Relying on this passage, the High Court of Singapore in *PP v Ow Ah Cheng* [1992] 1 Singapore L Rep 797, 805 ruled that the prosecution had failed to prove that the accused had committed murder because 'the evidence adduced was not consistent only with murder'.

The same approach is adopted by the International Criminal Tribunal for the Former Yugoslavia. In *Prosecutor v Sefer Halilovic*, the Trial Chamber held that guilt[318]

> must be established beyond reasonable doubt... It must be the *only* reasonable conclusion available. If there is another conclusion which is also reasonably open from that evidence, and which is [as] consistent with the [innocence of the accused as with his or her guilt], he or she must be acquitted.

As this long list of examples shows, there are plenty of legal authorities for the comparative and eliminative approach to fact-finding which characterizes both SMCB-BAF* and the relative plausibility theory.

3.4 Narrative model of trial deliberation

BAF*, as framed, suggests that fact-finding involves isolated judgments on the truth of singular propositions of fact. This does not accurately describe the psychological realities of trial deliberation.[319] In actual practice, 'evidence is evaluated not as isolated pieces, but rather in large cognitive structures, most familiarly in the form of narratives, stories or global accounts'.[320] As Justice Souter remarked, evidence 'has force beyond any linear scheme of reasoning, and as its pieces come together a narrative gains momentum'.[321] Fact-finders adopt an approach that is generally and for the large part 'holistic' rather 'atomistic'.[322] Certainly, litigation lawyers present their cases as if triers of fact reason in this way. All advocacy texts highlight the practical necessity of having a 'case theory in order to run a trial'[323] and teach that persuasion of the jury can

[318] Judgment dated 16 November 2005 (available at <http://www.un.org/icty/cases-e/index-e.htm>) at para 15, quoting from the *Celibici* Appeal Judgment, para 458.

[319] Ronald J Allen, 'The Narrative Fallacy, the Relative Plausibility Theory, and a Theory of the Trial,' *International Commentary on Evidence*: vol 3 (2005): issue 1, article 5, available at: <http://www.bepress.com/ice/vol3/iss1/art5>, at 1: 'juridical proof largely involves ordinal estimations of complete explanations of events rather than cardinal determinations of discrete elements'. Martin Kusch, *Knowledge by Agreement—The Programme of Communitarian Epistemology* (Oxford: Clarendon Press, 2002) 81 warns us to 'be suspicious of... Bayesian treatment of testimony assessment' as 'credibility and plausibility (of evidence and witnesses) are not the sort of things that are best thought of in discrete quantities', citing the English Court of Appeal decision in *R v Adams* [1996] 2 Cr App R 467, 481.

[320] Dan Simon, 'A Third View of the Black Box: Cognitive Coherence in Legal Decision Making' (2004) 71 University of Chicago L Rev 511, 560.

[321] *Old Chief v US* (1997) 519 US 172, 187.

[322] For discussion on these two different approaches, see M A Hareira, 'An Early Holistic Conception of Judicial Fact-Finding' [1986] The Juridical Review 79; Mirjan Damaška, 'Atomistic and Holistic Evaluation of Evidence: A Comparative View' in David S Clark (ed), *Comparative and Private International Law—Essays in Honor of John Henry Merryman on his Seventieth Birthday* (Berlin: Duncker & Humblot, 1990) 91.

[323] Andrew Palmer, *Proof and the Preparation of Trials* (Pyrmont NSW: Lawbook, 2003) 43. Similarly, Michael S Pardo, 'Juridical Proof, Evidence, and Pragmatic Meaning: Toward

only be achieved by telling a coherent story about what happened and, better yet, why it happened.

The holistic approach is supported by findings of psychologists who show that juror decision-making proceeds by constructing stories or narratives out of the evidence presented at the trial.[324] Stories are developed from the central action identified in the criminal charge or pleadings. This central action serves as the basic framework onto which substance is added by drawing inferences from the surrounding events, establishing a web of relationships that is complex due not only to the intricacy of the support network but also to the varied nature of the connections that may call to be established, including those that are causal, motivational, and intentional. The evidence presented at the trial is interpreted in the light of the fact-finder's general background beliefs about the world, including her opinion of what counts as a good story. Usually, more than one interpretation fits the evidential data more or less well. The fact-finder must judge whether any one of the stories stands out as free of explanatory hitches and is sufficiently deserving of acceptance as the true account. This selection is made within the framework of the available legal options (for example, it may be open to find the defendant guilty either of murder or of a lesser offence) and by transposing features of the stories to the attributes of each legal option; to do this, the fact-finder must have some understanding of what it takes to factually instantiate the essential elements of the crimes.

Many useful insights can be drawn from the storytelling literature. One was already acknowledged: judgments of plausibility are rendered not on propositions of fact viewed individually and in isolation. This is certainly not to say that the fact-finder will never have to ask whether a particular proposition of fact is true; it is however to claim that the truth of any particular proposition of fact will have to be assessed in the context of a larger hypothesis or story or narrative account.[325] For the purposes of BAF*, p will therefore take different forms (a specific proposition, a fragment of a story, the story taken as a whole, a sub-plot of the story, and so on) according to the level and angle of critical assessment that is being undertaken; and there will be a great deal of 'to and fro' between the different levels and angles in the course of trial deliberation.

Evidentiary Holism' (2000) Northwestern University L Rev 399, 404 observes that 'trial advocacy scholarship embraces the story model'.

[324] The established scholarship in this area includes W Lance Bennett and Martha S Feldman, *Reconstructing Reality in the Courtroom—Justice and Judgment in American Culture* (New Brunswick: Rutgers University Press, 1981); Nancy Pennington and Reid Hastie, 'Evidence Evaluation in Complex Decision Making' (1986) 51 *Journal of Personality and Social Psychology* 242; Nancy Pennington and Reid Hastie, 'A Cognitive Theory of Juror Decision Making: The Story Model' (1991) 13 Cardozo L Rev 519.

[325] Pardo (n 323) 401: 'A holistic theory...does not eliminate the need for atomistic analysis; rather, it shows that any such analysis is dependent upon the holistic theory under which it proceeds.'

Hypotheses are formulated at different levels and from different angles too. There is the main storyline and there are the sub-plots.[326] At the higher levels, for one hypothesis to be an alternative to another, they need not be completely different: indeed, it is hard to imagine that they will ever be completely different. As Allen and Jehl noted, 'the stories told by the parties will often be highly similar, differing in only a few salient factual respects'.[327] The factual dispute tends to be 'localized', narrowed down to a few factual issues or even one alone. On the contested issues, the trial will be fought by presenting competing lower-level hypotheses to support the respective versions of the truth. At the lowest level, one hypothesis is an alternative to another only if they cannot both be true on the disputed issue.

The second insight provided by the narrative theory is that we must refine our understanding of 'justification' in the context of BAF*. The fact-finder must find that p only if one would be *justified* in believing that p within the terms of BAF*. Justification imports a legal substantive element at the highest level in the sense that a judgment on the justification for the finding that the defendant is guilty of murder requires an understanding of the legal meaning of murder, and the evaluation of that judgment will have to be assessed partly in terms of the correctness of that understanding. Here, fact and value, fact and law, are inextricably meshed. At the lowest level, however, the finding will be one of 'brute' fact; for example, that the defendant added rat poison to his wife's cocoa. The justification for this lowest level finding is essentially epistemic, and BAF* applies with least complication and is primarily aimed at this level.

The third gain from understanding the holistic nature of trial deliberation is related also to the notion of 'justification'; it provides us with the resources to make broad-based assessment of the plausibility of a hypothesis. According to SMCB, one believes categorically in a hypothesis when one judges that it is perfectly possible and none of its contradictories is also perfectly possible. The hypothesis must have the quality of 'uniqueness',[328] a point well stressed in many of the legal quotations in the previous section. To recall, when we say that a hypothesis (p) is perfectly possible but not any of its contradictories, what we mean is that, in the circumstances of the case, we judge that (i) p is so possible that we would not be in the least surprised if it turns out to be true, and (ii) we would be surprised to some degree or other if any relevant alternative hypothesis should turn out to be true. As was previously suggested, all of the relevant alternative hypotheses must be so lacking in possibility that, in the circumstances of the case, we feel safe enough to

[326] Bernard S Jackson, *Law, Fact and Narrative Coherence* (Liverpool: Deborah Charles, 1988) 85: 'We have in the trial not simply a single story, but a set of stories. The act of testifying of each individual witness is a story in itself.'

[327] Ronald J Allen and Sarah A Jehl, 'Burdens of Persuasion in Civil Cases: Algorithms v. Explanations' (2003) 4 Michigan State L Rev 893, 937.

[328] Compare Pennington and Hastie, 'A Cognitive Theory of Juror Decision Making: The Story Model' (n 324) 528.

dismiss them. The nature and consequences of the finding that p determine how lacking in possibility the relevant alternative hypotheses must be to make it safe enough to rule them out. We will assume that 'possibility' and 'plausibility' are interchangeable concepts and that the criteria for 'plausibility' discussed below apply to 'possibility' as well.

Many factors are relevant to the assessment of plausibility. This assessment can be made independently of the evidence adduced at the trial. Any internal contradiction found within a story[329] will be fatal and will make the story implausible unless the contradiction can somehow be explained away or rendered insignificant. A hypothesis that is not internally contradictory may nevertheless be considered inherently unbelievable or difficult to believe when certain of its essential features cannot be easily reconciled with our general knowledge about 'the ways in which human beings behave, or how the world operates'.[330] The plausibility of a hypothesis can also be judged against the evidence. A hypothesis is implausible or not perfectly plausible if, in certain essential respects, it contradicts or is otherwise inconsistent with a part of the accepted evidence (including what it implies) or with an accepted inference from the evidence. A suggestion to this effect was made by the House of Lords in *McGreevy v Director of Public Prosecutions*[331] when it observed that 'if a fact which [the jury] accept is inconsistent with guilt or may be so, they [can] not say that they [are] satisfied of guilt beyond all reasonable doubt'. All of the factors discussed in this paragraph identify rather specific obstacles to full plausibility.

The plausibility of a hypothesis can be judged by a further set of criteria that are relatively vague. First, the greater the portion of the evidence a story is able to account for (or, as we may say, the degree of 'coverage'), the higher its plausibility.[332] The more it leaves unexplained, the less convincing it is. Secondly, the 'completeness' of a story contributes to its plausibility. A story is less persuasive the more gaps it has.[333] That is why the motive for committing a crime is factually relevant even though it 'is not a pre-requisite of guilt'.[334] Being able to account

[329] Contrast this with the strategy of putting contradictory stories as alternatives ('my client wasn't there; and if he was, then he didn't do it'). On the wisdom of this strategy, see Palmer (n 323) 51–52.

[330] ibid 50.

[331] (1973) 57 Cr App R 424, 436. A similar point was also noted by the Privy Council in *Teper v R* [1952] AC 480, 498; according to Lord Normand: 'It is... necessary before drawing the inference of the accused's guilt from circumstantial evidence to be sure that there are no other co-existing circumstances which would weaken or destroy the inference.'

[332] Pennington and Hastie, 'A Cognitive Theory of Juror Decision Making: The Story Model' (n 324) 527–528.

[333] *Old Chief v US* (n 321) 189, per Justice Souter: 'People who hear a story interrupted by gaps of abstraction may be puzzled at the missing chapters, and jurors asked to rest a momentous decision on the story's truth can feel put upon at being asked to take responsibility knowing that more could be said than they have heard.' This observation intertwines two related problems: gaps in the story (account of what happened) and gaps in the body of evidence (presented to support the given account). The latter is discussed below.

[334] *Nadasan Chandra Secharan v PP* (n 283) para 81 (Singapore Court of Appeal).

for the motive adds to the completeness and hence plausibility of the story; but not being able to provide a motive is not a bar to finding the defendant guilty.[335] A third criterion of plausibility is coherence.[336] The coherence of a story is more than consistency in the weak sense of non-contradiction of the component parts; it is the added quality of the individual elements integrating well together to yield a smooth and convincing narrative of events.

Fourthly, the plausibility of a hypothesis increases with the degree of positive support it receives from the evidence. A holistic view must be taken of evidential support for a hypothesis. As the Australian High Court put it in *Shepherd v The Queen*,[337] 'the probative force of a mass of evidence may be cumulative, making it pointless to consider the degree of probability of each item of evidence separately'. Evidential support has at least five aspects, as discussed in Part 3.5 below.

3.5 Concept of evidential support

The extent to which evidence supports a hypothesis depends, in the first place, on how credible the evidence is: for example, is this witness telling the truth? If the evidence is found credible, a second factor is the sufficiency of the reason or ground it gives for believing the hypothesis: accepting that what the witness says is true, how does that support the hypothesis? The difficulty is that neither of these questions can be answered in the abstract: thus whether this witness is telling the truth will often depend on whether other witnesses are telling the truth; and what and how strong a reason or ground an accepted piece of evidence gives for believing an aspect of a hypothesis will depend on how well it integrates explanatorily with the reasons and grounds offered by other accepted evidence in support of that and other features of the hypothesis.[338]

How strongly the evidence supports a hypothesis depends, thirdly, on the extent to which the significant features of the hypothesis are anchored in the evidence. While reliance on background beliefs is inescapable when constructing a story from a body of evidence that is usually 'fragmentary, incomplete, ambiguous, and inconsistent',[339] a hypothesis cannot, in any of its crucial aspects, be grounded in a mere supposition or assumption. As Twining cautions, there is

[335] As the Singapore High Court held in convicting the accused in *Public Prosecutor v Chee Cheong Hin Constance* (n 307) para 112: 'The law recognises that often the reason for a killing is so securely concealed within an accused's mind that it may well be unfathomable. This is one such case.'

[336] For a sample of the literature, see Neil MacCormick, 'The Coherence of a Case and the Reasonableness of Doubt' (1980) 2 Liverpool LR 45, *Legal Reasoning and Legal Theory* (Oxford: Clarendon Press, 1978) 90–93; 'Notes on Narrativity and the Normative Syllogism' [1991] 4 Int J for the Semiotics of Law 163, 167–168; Bernard S Jackson (n 326) 58–60; Simon (n 320).

[337] (1990) 170 CLR 573 at 580.

[338] Susan Haack's analogy of solving a jigsaw puzzle is apt: *Evidence and Inquiry* (Oxford: Blackwell, 1993) ch 4.

[339] Simon (n 320) 549.

a danger that a narrative might be 'used "to sneak in" irrelevant or improper considerations, to conceal or divert attention from gaps or weaknesses in an argument'.[340]

Evidential support is, fourthly, a function of the 'comprehensiveness of evidence'.[341] By this is meant something along the line of Keynes's concept of 'weight of evidence'.[342] Weight in the Keynesian sense is popularly interpreted to mean the quantum of evidence on which a probability assessment is made. However, as Runde has argued, it is more accurate to describe 'weight as the balance of the relevant knowledge and relevant ignorance or equivalently, the degree of completeness of the information on which a probability is based'.[343] There is no correlation between epistemological probability and weight; epistemological probability could go up, down, or remain as it is as weight increases with more evidence being introduced.[344]

The problem of incomplete evidence is faced in virtually every form of factual investigation; it confronts inquirers from archaeologists to historians to detectives. The trier of fact in an adversarial trial is no exception, although, unlike the others, she is not strictly speaking an inquirer in at least this respect: she does not go after the evidence; the evidence is given to her. The body of evidence adduced at a trial will invariably contain gaps. The extent of gaps is a factor to be taken into account by the trier of fact in assessing the plausibility of a hypothesis.[345]

[340] William Twining, *Rethinking Evidence—Exploratory Essays* (2nd edn, Cambridge: CUP, 2006) 319. The normative issues that this danger raises are discussed by Doron Menashe and Mutal E Shamash 'The Narrative Fallacy,' *International Commentary on Evidence*: vol 3 (2005): issue 1, article 3, available at: <http://www.bepress.com/ice/vol3/iss1/art3>.

[341] Thinking about the evidence seems to involve a higher order belief about the evidence and it is controversial whether comprehensiveness of evidence can be factored into the probability calculus. See L Jonathan Cohen, 'The Role of Evidential Weight in Criminal Proof' (1986) 66 Boston University L Rev 635; David Kaye, 'Do We Need a Calculus of Weight to Understand Proof Beyond a Reasonable Doubt?' (1986) 66 Boston University L Rev 657; Brilmayer (n 193); Nils-Eric Sahlin, 'On Higher Order Beliefs' in Jacques-Paul Dubucs (ed), *Philosophy of Probability* (Dordrecht: Kluwer Academic Publishers, 1993) ch 2, 13. It would seem that Keynes had comprehensiveness of the available evidence in mind when he spoke of 'weight', a concept he thinks should be distinguished from probability; this is reflected, for instance, in his statement: 'New evidence will sometimes decrease the probability of an argument, but it will always increase its "weight" ': (n 110) 71; Jochen Runde, 'Keynesian Uncertainty and The Weight of Arguments' (1990) 6 *Economics and Philosophy* 275; Barbara Davidson and Robert Pargetter, 'Guilt Beyond Reasonable Doubt' (1987) 65 *Australasian J of Philosophy* 182 (linking 'weight of evidence' to 'resilience' of a probability assessment).

[342] Davidson and Pargetter (n 341) argue that evidence must have sufficient Keynesian weight to justify a conviction. This thesis drew responses from Nancy J Dunham and Robert L Birmingham, 'On Legal Proof' (1989) 67 *Australasian J of Philosophy* 479, and Stephen Cohen and Michael Bersten, 'Probability Out of Court: Notes on "Guilt Beyond Reasonable Doubt" ' (1990) 68 *Australian J of Philosophy* 229. Evidential 'weight' plays a major role in Stein's theory; he uses the concept to explain the proof paradoxes: (n 194) 80–91.

[343] Runde (n 242) 231; and more fully, Runde (n 341).

[344] Adler (n 156) 251.

[345] Jack B Weinstein and Ian Dewsbury, 'Comment on the Meaning of "Proof Beyond a Reasonable Doubt" ' (2006) 5 Law, Probability and Risk 167, 169, noting that, on the standard charge, the jury is asked to consider the 'lack of evidence', thus alerting the jury to consider the

In forming our beliefs, we have to and do take into account the extent of our ignorance. The reasoning employed in trial deliberation is defeasible or of a 'non-monotonic' nature, 'meaning that it can be defeated by new incoming premises that have the effect of overturning the inference'.[346] An important implication flows from this: if the trier of fact is aware that the available evidence adduced in support of a hypothesis is significantly incomplete, that too much of relevance is as yet hidden from her, that 'there is a significant chance that there is a better explanation'[347] for the event in question, she would not be justified in believing that the hypothesis is true.[348] The evidence provided in the gatecrasher and cab scenarios is supposed to consist wholly of statistical information; by any standard, the evidence is seriously incomplete.

The present consideration seems not to be purely epistemic; it seems to have a moral dimension. Consider an analogy with the work of a detective.[349] After some investigation, the evidence points to Y being the culprit. But the detective has other leads which she can pursue and she is aware that they may tell her more about the case, generating other and more plausible hypotheses of who did it and how and why the person did it. The detective acts irresponsibly if, in her haste to close the file, she ignores those leads and settles on the belief that Y is in fact the culprit. Even if this is the most likely hypothesis on the evidence that she has gathered, it is still, in the circumstances, wrong of her to believe that Y is guilty. The wrong, it seems, is both epistemic and moral.[350]

The detective should, as it were, have dug deeper into the case to prepare a more secure evidential foundation for her conclusion. As it stands, her believing that Y was the culprit is not sufficiently safeguarded from epistemic defeasibility. The detective is conscious of the risk that further information exists, knowledge of which may rebut or undercut the justification for her conclusion.[351] She is

'weight' or 'thinness' of the evidence adduced by the prosecution. This was said in reply to the concern voiced by James Franklin, 'Case Comment—*United States v Copeland*, 369 F Supp 2d 275 (EDNY 2005): Quantification of the "Proof Beyond Reasonable Doubt" Standard' (2006) 5 Law, Probability and Risk 159, 161–163 that evidence which establishes guilt to a high probability may nevertheless lack 'weight' in the Keynesian sense.

346 Walton (n 229) 110.

347 Josephson and Josephson (n 230) 15.

348 *Old Chief v US* (n 321) 189. This notion of 'comprehensiveness of evidence' is explored by philosophers who examine the relevance of self-awareness of ignorance in the reasoning process; eg Gilbert Harman argues that 'reasoning always involves essentially the implicit acceptance of the proposition that there exists no unpossessed evidence of a certain sort against the conclusion of that reasoning'. ('Reasoning and Evidence One Does Not Possess' (1980) 5 *Midwest Studies in Philosophy* 163, 165.) He proposes a principle of reasoning which 'tells one not to accept a conclusion unless one is justified in accepting the proposition that there is no obtainable undermining evidence against that conclusion' (ibid 166).

349 A similar example is used by Swinburne (n 224) 50 and David B Annis, 'A Contextualist Theory of Epistemic Justification' (1978) 15 *American Philosophical Quarterly* 213, 218.

350 On the relationship between epistemic and ethical appraisals, see Haack (n 175).

351 Briefly, information *rebuts* a conclusion if it shows the conclusion to be false and *undercuts* it if it shows that an inference to the conclusion is, after all, not warranted by the evidence. What is attacked in the first case is the conclusion, and in the second, the connection between the premises

blameworthy in dismissing that risk if she did so out of hastiness or sloth. Further, her action on that belief is morally culpable. She harms Y by charging him with the crime; and by not pursuing a more thorough investigation before doing so, she displays an irresponsible disregard for Y and his interest.[352]

In the gatecrasher and the cab scenarios, the fact-finder is in a position similar, though not identical, to the detective's. There is at least one major difference. While the detective has the task of conducting physical investigation, the fact-finder in an adversarial setting has neither the power nor the duty to track down evidence. Nevertheless, the general principle with which we are concerned applies equally to the deliberation of both: evidence in support of a hypothesis needs to be sufficiently comprehensive to justify believing it. Much of what was said in the detective example applies to the two scenarios. As there are too many important questions yet to be explored, to settle on the belief that A did not pay to watch the show, or that a red cab had caused the accident, would be 'jumping to conclusion'.[353] Not only is this belief epistemically unsound, the fact-finder is blameworthy in holding it if she did so out of epistemic laziness or negligence. Further, such inadequacy of effort and caution in deliberation shows a lack of due respect and concern for the defendant. The intertwining of epistemic and ethical considerations here is complex and it is unclear that they are separable.

There is a fifth aspect to evidential support. The evidence must support a hypothesis capable of providing a causal or explanatory account of the event in question before she is justified in accepting the hypothesis as in fact true. Some sort of causal explanation for an event seems necessary for knowledge of it and categorical belief that it happened.[354] As Nelkin has suggested, 'one must be able

and the conclusion: John L Pollock, 'Epistemology and Probability' (1983) 55 *Synthese* 231, 233; *Contemporary Theories of Knowledge* (Totowa, New Jersey: Rowman & Littlefield, 1986) 38–39; 'Defeasible Reasoning' (1987) 11 *Cognitive Science* 481, 485; 'The Building of Oscar' (1988) 2 *Philosophical Perspectives* 315, 319; 'A Theory of Defeasible Reasoning' (1991) 6 *Intl J Of Intelligent Systems* 33, 34; 'How to Reason Defeasibly' (1992) 57 *Artificial Intelligence* 1, 2–3.

[352] cf *Ribemont v France*, Application no 15175/89, judgment of the European Court of Human Rights dated 10 Feb 1995: at a press conference, state official and senior police officers held out the applicant as an instigator of a murder. Upon his discharge, the applicant claimed successfully that the State had violated his right to be presumed innocent under article 6(2) of the European Convention of Human Rights.

[353] As Sahlin (n 341) 19 puts it in his discussion of a broadly similar example, 'one is somewhat worried about what one does not know. Crucial pieces of evidence or information may be missing and have thus not been presented at the trial.' He argues that 'the degree of epistemic reliability is not mirrored in our assessment of how likely or unlikely a hypothesis is' (ibid 18). In deciding on the verdict, the fact-finder must be guided not only by his assessment of the probability of its truth given such knowledge as he has, he must also reflect on the reliability of that assessment by considering how complete or adequate his knowledge is (ibid 15).

[354] 'The basic idea is that one has knowledge when one's belief is causally connected to the facts in the right way... S knows p if and only if the fact p is causally connected in an appropriate way with S's believing p': Earl Conee and Richard Feldman, "Evidentialism" in their *Evidentialism—Essays in Epistemology* (Oxford: Clarendon Press, 2004) 280. Contrast the causal theory of verdicts offered by Roy Sorensen, 'Future Law: Prepunishment and the Causal Theory of Verdicts' (2006) 40 *Noûs* 166.

to postulate a causal or more broadly explanatory connection between one's belief and the object of belief' if one is to be rational in holding that belief.[355] Thomson similarly argues that to justify a belief that p, our 'reason for believing that p is true must ensure, or *guarantee*, that p is true'.[356] (How confident we are that we have such a reason is a separate matter relating to the strength of belief.) Imagine, she tells us, that Bert has bought five lottery tickets, and that altogether a hundred of them were sold. The lottery, let us further postulate, is known not to be rigged. On the evidence, the objective probability that Bert will lose the lottery is .95: so we would believe that he would probably lose. But we are not justified in believing that he will, as a matter of fact, lose.[357] This is because, according to Thomson, our 'reason for believing that Bert will lose the lottery does not in any way guarantee that Bert will lose it'.[358]

This point sits comfortably with Shackle's requirement of perfect possibility: the evidence does not give us reason to think that it is perfectly possible that Bert will lose. On the evidence that we have, and on our understanding of the situation, including the belief that each of the hundred tickets stands a chance of winning, it is common sense to concede some, however slight, possibility to the hypothesis that the winning ticket is one of the five that Bert holds. Consequently, our understanding of the situation stands in the way of our believing that it is perfectly possible that Bert will lose. It is irrational to hold this belief on the basis of our knowledge of objective probability alone. This knowledge does not help us to understand why he will lose, and if he has lost, why he has lost.[359] The probability is neither a cause of nor an explanation for the loss. Suppose he wins; when we hear of this, we would still believe the event to be objectively improbable: it is just one of those things that happen against the odds. The probability of Bert losing, so we may say, does not provide us with a reason for the belief that he will lose which is sensitive to the truth.[360] And, as was argued, it is part of the concept of belief that an acceptance must be regulated for truth. For largely the same reason, the statistical probability alone does not in either the gatecrasher or the cab scenario justify the relevant belief. Mere membership of a reference class is neither a cause of nor an explanation for the alleged behaviour (gatecrashing) or event (road accident).[361]

When will the evidence justify a categorical belief? Consider Thomson's counter-example, as slightly modified:[362] suppose we see the ticket seller tear up and

[355] Nelkin (n 181) 399.

[356] Thomson (n 161) 208.

[357] This example is given in ibid 207–208.

[358] ibid 208.

[359] Judith Jarvis Thomson, 'Remarks on Causation and Liability' (1984) 13 *Philosophy and Public Affairs* 101, 130, 132.

[360] Nelkin (n 181) 396–401.

[361] The same observation is made in connection with discriminatory legislation and practices by Joel Feinberg, *Harm to Others* (Oxford: OUP, 1984) 201.

[362] Thomson (n 161) 208.

throw away Bert's ticket stubs. They will therefore not be in the pool from which the winner, so we understand, will be drawn. Now we have evidence which provides us with a reason for believing that Bert will, as a matter of fact, lose. With the destruction of the stubs, Bert stands no chance at all of winning. Some sort of causal connection is present here which was absent in the earlier example: while we can say, after the event, that tearing up of the ticket stubs caused Bert to lose the lottery, we cannot sensibly say the same of his having bought five lottery tickets.

It cannot be emphasized enough that on neither Thomson's nor Shackle's account does categorical belief mean absolute certainty. Such a belief can be held more or less strongly. Consider again the modified gatecrasher scenario where one witness testifies to having seen A climbed over the stadium fence and another testifies that A had admitted to being a gatecrasher. This is the kind of evidence that may (but does not necessarily) justify the belief that A did not, in fact, pay for his entrance; a causal story can be constructed from the evidence. The story may come be accepted as true with greater or less confidence. On the evidence, it is perfectly possible that A did not pay for his entrance. That he was gatecrashing is the best explanation for his behaviour, and it 'is the appeal to explanation, over and above any appeal to probability, that is important when a person comes to know a nonprobabilistic conclusion'.[363] Given that he has made an admission and given the strange manner in which he chose to enter the stadium, we would not be in the least surprised if he was in truth a trespasser. No obstacle is encountered in our way of thinking that this was, in fact, the case; nothing in the evidence contradicts or is inconsistent with the hypothesis. But it is still possible that he was not a trespasser. Perhaps he had bought a ticket but simply wanted to avoid walking a long distance to reach the stadium gate; climbing the stadium fence was just a convenient shortcut. Or perhaps the witness who testified to A's admission misheard what A told her or has an axe to grind against A. But the witness is not hard of hearing, she sat next to A, and they are strangers to each other. Our background experience and knowledge, including knowledge of human nature and normal social behaviour, lead us to judge as low the possibility of the alternative hypotheses; none of them is perfectly possible and we would be very surprised if any of them were true. The strength of our belief that the defendant had in fact gatecrashed on the show varies inversely with the degree of possibility we assign to the strongest of the competing hypotheses, for example, that he was just too lazy to walk to the entrance or that he is being framed. We cannot be absolutely certain of that belief so long as we feel unable to dismiss all competing hypotheses as impossible. In this way, one can believe that a hypothesis is, in fact, true even though one is not absolutely certain that it is.

[363] Gilbert Harman, 'Knowledge, Inference and Explanation' (1968) 5 *American Philosophical Quarterly* 164, 167. Dant (n 217) 54–58 argues that evidential reasoning at a trial should proceed by drawing an inference to the best explanation, and that such reasoning is unavailable where evidence is purely statistical.

Conclusion

The trial—or more specifically, trial deliberation—seeks the truth. It seeks the truth *via* justified belief in the facts of the case. That is the immediate and general aim. To the extent that truth is the standard of correctness for a positive verdict or finding, the ultimate aim, one could say, is knowledge. An attempt was made to formulate the constitutive rule of a positive finding. It was argued that the fact-finder must find that p only if one would be justified in believing that p within the terms of BAF*. The concept of belief that operates in this connection is the concept of categorical belief. This is different from the concept of partial belief. The judge of fact settles on her categorical factual beliefs about the case within a framework which involves comparing and eliminating hypotheses. A sketch of this framework was offered as an alternative to probabilistic analysis of fact-finding. Cases are not disposed on probability assessments; this denial of its dispositive role is compatible with acknowledgment of its other uses in legal fact-finding.

4

Standard of Proof

Introduction

The standard of proof is usually analysed and evaluated from an external viewpoint. Part 1 identifies the three main features of this approach. Each of them is problematic. Part 2 suggests that the problems can be resolved by taking the internal perspective. From that perspective, it can be seen that there are two aspects to the standard of proof. In one aspect, it refers to the caution that must be exercised in making a positive finding. The evidence must be able to justify a strong enough categorical belief in the truth of the disputed allegation, where what is strong enough is a function of the seriousness of both the content of the allegation and the consequences of accepting that it is true. On this variant interpretation of the standard of proof, the standard is tied to the gravity and consequences of particular findings of fact. The need for caution has moral underpinnings; it is motivated ultimately by concern and respect for the person to whom the finding is adverse. In the second aspect, the standard of proof is about the distribution of caution in trial deliberation. It is here that there exists a difference in kind between the civil standard and the standard to which the prosecution is held: the former instructs the fact-finder to be impartial whereas the latter requires her to take a protective attitude towards the defendant when deliberating on her guilt; the first is grounded in the principle of equality and the second in the demand for accountability by the state for the harm it seeks to inflict on citizens.

1 External Analysis

1.1 Characteristics

It is traditional to take an external approach in analysing the standards of proof. This approach has three notable features. Although not every lawyer will agree or agree fully with each of the features as described, the description should be familiar enough to be regarded as not far from the dominant understanding. First, the external approach focuses on the degree of the fact-finder's belief or confidence in the truth of a disputed proposition or, more broadly, factual hypothesis (p) after she has examined and weighed the evidence. This will be referred to as the 'end-state' of evidential evaluation. On this approach, the standards have nothing to say on the process leading to that end-state.

Secondly, it views standards of proof as decisional thresholds. If the fact-finder's degree of belief in the truth of p (or, more technically, if the subjective probability of p) crosses a certain level, she must accept it; otherwise, she must reject it. As a decisional threshold, the standard of proof has a default and a regulatory function. The first does not often come into play whereas the second governs every finding of fact. In its default function,[1] a standard of proof stipulates how a question of fact must be answered in the 'exceptional case' where 'a judge conscientiously seeking to decide the matter before him [is] forced to say "I just do not know" ';[2] or, as Viscount Dunedin puts it, where the trier of fact is unable to come to any 'determinate conclusion' on the issue.[3] A court that faces this difficulty is expected nevertheless to give its decision there and then, and unequivocally. The law requires that it finds against the party carrying the burden of proof on the ground that she has failed to prove her case to the required standard.[4] As a default rule, the standard of proof has been described as a 'tie-breaker'.[5]

In its regulatory function, the standard of proving p is the minimum degree to which the fact-finder must believe (in the partial sense) that p to find that p. It is the benchmark against which she must measure her confidence in p, quantifiable as a probability value, at the conclusion of her evaluation of the evidence. In most cases, the fact-finder would be able to come to a 'determinate conclusion' in the sense that it would be clear to her whether the threshold set by the relevant standard has been crossed. Of course, to say that the satisfaction of a standard is clear is not to say that the standard does not apply: it is to say exactly the opposite. As a regulatory rule, the standard of proof is not confined to marginal or difficult cases. Every finding of fact is regulated by a standard of proof.

There is a further aspect to the second feature. On the received understanding, standards of proof are fixed and predetermined: one standard applies to all cases within the relevant category, and the decisional threshold operating in each category does not vary with the circumstances of individual cases. In general, (1) civil cases must be decided on the 'balance of probabilities' and (2) guilt in criminal

[1] Steve Wexler, 'Burden of Proof, Writ Large' (1999) 33 U of British Columbia L Rev 75, 75–76; Barbara D Underwood, 'The Thumb on the Scales of Justice: Burdens of Persuasion in Criminal Cases' (1977) 86 Yale LJ 1299, 1300–1301; Richard H Gaskins *Burdens of Proof in Modern Discourse* (New Haven: Yale UP, 1992) 3–4, 29.

[2] *Morris v London Iron Co* [1988] QB 493, 504, per May LJ. The exceptional nature of this method of deciding the case, to be used only in the last resort, was stressed by the Court of Appeal in *Cooper v Floor Cleaning Machines Ltd and Anor*, Times Law Reports, 24 October 2003 and *Stephens & Anor v Cannon & Anor* [2005] EWCA Civ 222, Times Law Reports, 2 May 2005.

[3] *Robbins v National Trust Co* [1927] AC 515, 520. Followed in *Dingwell v J Wharton (Shipping) Ltd* [1961] 2 Lloyd's Rep 213, 216.

[4] eg *Hickman v Peacey* [1945] AC 304, 318.

[5] *US v Gigante* (1994) 39 F 3d 42, 47.

cases must be proved 'beyond reasonable doubt'. Call them, respectively, the 'civil standard' and the 'criminal standard'.[6] In most common law jurisdictions, there are only these two standards.[7] (Exceptionally, as in the United States, there is a third and intermediate standard of 'clear and convincing evidence'.[8] But this will be ignored as it does not alter the substance of the present analysis.) What distinguishes the civil and the criminal standard is that proof must be established to a higher probability under the second than the first.[9]

The third feature of the external approach is a methodological assumption underlying traditional evaluation of the level at which the law ought to peg the probability threshold. On the external approach, this normative question is essentially a matter of social policy, where the standard of proof is treated as a means of attaining desired ends. (This third feature is distinct from the latter aspect of the second feature discussed in the preceding paragraph. It is possible to take an instrumental view while arguing against a fixed standard; one could maintain, for example, that the instrumental function is most effective if the standard is allowed to vary suitably from case to case.)[10]

A common argument proceeds thus: we want to convict the guilty and also desire to avoid convicting the innocent. Raising the criminal standard leads to both a lowering of the probability of convicting the innocent (sometimes called a false positive or type I error) and an increase in the probability of acquitting the guilty (sometimes called a false negative or type II error); conversely, lowering the standard will advance the objective of catching the guilty but will be detrimental to the protection of the innocent. We should aim for optimal trade-off between these two general goals.[11] 'The optimal standard of proof... should balance the social cost of false convictions... against the social cost of false acquittals',[12] and further, against the costs of errors must be weighed the costs of installing

[6] The latter is a term of convenience. It is slightly misleading: the criminal standard is not the sole standard applicable in a criminal trial; where the accused carries the burden of proof, as she sometimes does on some issues, the standard is often said to be similar to the civil standard: *R v Swaysland* [1987] BTLC 299, 307–8; *Carr-Briant* [1943] KB 607, 612; *PP v Yuvaraj* [1970] AC 913, 921.

[7] There are no other (intermediate) standards in England (*Re H (Minors)* [1996] AC 563, 587; *R (N) v Mental Health Review Tribunal* [2005] EWCA Civ 1605, [2006] QB 468, 497), Australia (*Briginshaw v Briginshaw* (1938) 60 CLR 336, 361), or Scotland (*Mullan v Anderson* [1993] SLT 835, 842, 846 and 851).

[8] eg *US v Fatico* (1978) 458 F Supp 388, 404–5.

[9] *Re H (Minors)* (n 7) 587; *Miller v Minister of Pensions* [1947] 2 All ER 372, 374.

[10] eg Erik Lillquist, 'Recasting Reasonable Doubt: Decision Theory and The Virtues of Variability' (2002) 36 University of California Davis L Rev 85 offers an expected utility model of decision theory that requires the standard of proof to vary according to 'the costs and benefits of accurate and inaccurate verdicts in a particular case' (ibid 194).

[11] cf Alan Wertheimer, 'Punishing the Innocent—Unintentionally' (1977) 20 *Inquiry* 45.

[12] Thomas J Miceli, 'Optimal Prosecution of Defendants Whose Guilt Is Uncertain' (1990) 6 J of Law, Economics, and Organization 189, 196.

procedures to reduce the rate of errors.[13] A judicial sample of this thinking can be found in these remarks of Harlan J in *Re Winship*:[14]

The standard of proof influences the relative frequency of these two types of erroneous outcomes [namely (i) the error of finding an innocent person guilty or a defendant liable who in fact should not have been found liable and (ii) the error of acquitting a guilty person or finding a defendant not liable who in fact should have been found liable]. If, for example, the standard of proof for a criminal trial were a preponderance of the evidence rather than proof beyond a reasonable doubt, there would be a smaller risk of factual errors that result in freeing guilty persons, but a far greater risk of factual errors that result in convicting the innocent. Because the standard of proof affects the comparative frequency of these two types of erroneous outcomes, the choice of the standard to be applied in a particular kind of litigation should, in a rational world, reflect an assessment of the comparative social disutility of each.

In *R v Muller*,[15] the need to secure a greater rate of convicting the guilty in order to maintain 'law and order' prompted Pollock CB to warn jurors not to be overly demanding of the evidence necessary to support a conviction: they should be prepared to convict on that degree of certainty with which they conduct important practical affairs in their own lives. 'To require more would be really to prevent the repression of crime, which it is the object of criminal courts to effect.' On the other hand, if the legal system appears to convict even the innocent, its legitimacy—or 'public confidence' in the trial as an institution—would be undermined.[16] Raising the decisional threshold increases the risk of acquitting the truly guilty whereas lowering it increases the risk of convicting the truly innocent. Each entails its own set of costs and we must decide how best to trade off one against the other. The law must 'pitch the required degree of probability at a level that will ensure the conviction of a high proportion of the guilty and at the same time keep the risk of convicting the innocent acceptably low'.[17] Our interest in the effectiveness of crime control has to be weighed against our interest in ensuring public confidence in the legal system.[18]

On this line of thinking, standards of proof are evaluated as instruments of policy. Inasmuch as social policies have to respond to changing conditions and

[13] See eg Alex Stein, *Foundations of Evidence Law* (Oxford: OUP, 2005) 14; see also the literature cited ibid n 28 and ch 5.

[14] (1970) 397 US 358, 371. See also *R v Pahuja* (1988) 49 SASR 191, 204, per Cox J: the law should 'pitch the required degree of probability at a level that will ensure the conviction of a high proportion of the guilty and at the same time keep the risk of convicting the innocent acceptably low'.

[15] (1865) 4 F & F 383, note (a).

[16] *Re Winship* (n 14) 364.

[17] *R v Pahuja* (1988) 49 SASR 191, 204. Similarly: *US v Fatico* (n 8) 411.

[18] Henry L Chambers Jr, 'Reasonable Certainty and Reasonable Doubt' (1998) 81 Marquette L Rev 655, 656–657, 700; Jon O Newman, 'Beyond "Reasonable Doubt"' (1993) 68 New York U L Rev 979, 981; Ernest van den Haag in Reiman and van den Haag, 'On the Common Saying that it is Better that Ten Guilty Persons Escape than that One Innocent Suffer: *Pro* and *Con*' (1990) 7 *Social Philosophy and Policy* 226, 245.

circumstances, standards of proof should similarly keep up with the times. Thus it has been suggested that 'as society's interest in crime control changes, society's assessment of the proper balance between erroneous convictions and erroneous acquittals may change';[19] some go even further, advising that we should lower the standard of proof for the prosecution when the crime rate is high, and raise it when the crime rate is down.[20] How easy a conviction is secured, so it is claimed, has fluctuated in the course of history. It is 'a question of degree, varying according to time and place' how far the law can afford to be generous to the accused.[21] Allen observes that the presumption of innocence (with which the criminal standard, as we will see, is linked) 'had not fully developed until the nineteenth century was well advanced'.[22] He notes:[23]

> that four hundred years ago in all criminal trials of which we have any record, the dice were loaded heavily against the accused. The presumption of innocence was not only absent from, but antagonistic to, the whole system of penal procedure. How and why have we come to hold the contrary view so strongly...?

The answer, he suggests, is to be found not in ethics but 'in the profound change which has taken place in the organization of society'.[24] A society yet to develop an effective bureaucracy for social control, and which lacks institutions for policing and criminal investigation, is likely to wish for more decisive state intervention in containing lawlessness and disorder. 'Only when society is emancipated from fear—only when it can rely, *in the main*, on its organized protective forces—dare it give suspected persons the benefit of the doubt';[25] 'it is only when there is a reasonable and uniform probability of guilty persons being detected and convicted that we can allow humane doubt to prevail over security'.[26] 'The quality of justice,' he warns us, must not be 'strained by unreflective cliché'; the rightful place of the presumption of innocence is 'somewhere between the elevating impulse of compassion and the unlovely necessity of self-protection'.[27]

Clearest examples of the treatment of standards of proof as instruments of policy appear in economic analyses of their operation. In relation to the civil

[19] Note, '*Winship* on Rough Waters: The Erosion of the Reasonable Doubt Standard' (1993) 106 Harvard L Rev 1093, 1095.

[20] A suggestion made to that effect by Ernest van den Haag in Reiman and van den Haag (n 18) 241.

[21] James Fitzjames Stephen, *A History of the Criminal Law of England*, vol 1 (London: Macmillan & Co, 1883) 354.

[22] Carleton Kemp Allen, 'The Presumption of Innocence' in his *Legal Duties—And Other Essays in Jurisprudence* (Oxford: Clarendon Press, 1931) 273. It is doubtful that Allen is right. Record of the principle that in 'doubtful cases one ought rather to save than to condemn' can be found in '*Mirror of Justices*, written no later than 1290 AD': Lloyd E Moore, *The Jury: Tool of Kings—Palladium of Liberty* (Cincinnati: W H Anderson, 1974) 26.

[23] Allen (n 22) 271.

[24] ibid 271–272.

[25] ibid 272.

[26] ibid 287.

[27] ibid 294.

standard, a typical argument is that it 'should be set at a level which will ensure optimal deterrence of tortious conduct (ie it should not under-deter, increasing the number of accidents, but nor should it over-deter, increasing the cost of safety measures and encouraging potential victims to be careless)'.[28] In the criminal context, Posner suggests that the high standard for proof of guilt acts as an incentive for public prosecutors to bring to trial only those who are 'clearly guilty', thus lowering the overall risk of the criminal system producing false convictions.[29] When 'crime rates rise faster than prosecutorial resources', it is a feasible option to reduce the 'procedural advantages of the defendant' (including, presumably, a lowering the criminal standard) if 'society wants to maintain the same balance between the probabilities of convicting the innocent and of acquitting the guilty'.[30]

1.2 Critique

Each of the three characteristics of the traditional mode of analysis identified above poses difficulties. The first, as we may recall, is the focus on the end-state of evidential evaluation. A standard of proof fixes the necessary and sufficient degree of belief or confidence the fact-finder, upon evaluation of the evidence, must have in the truth of p to find that p. This ignores how that state of belief came to be. As the Canadian Supreme Court said of the instruction to jurors to convict when they are 'sure' or 'certain' of guilt:[31]

> [S]tanding alone[, it] is both insufficient and potentially misleading. Being 'certain' is a conclusion which a juror may reach but, it does not indicate the route the juror should take in order to arrive at the conclusion.

The court should be concerned with the rationality of belief and not merely with its strength. What matters, as Laudan argues, is not only the state of mind of jurors but, more importantly, how they arrived at that state. As he puts it: 'The firmness of a belief, that is, the depth of one's conviction in it, does nothing to settle whether the belief is rational or founded on the evidence';[32] and it is

[28] Mike Redmayne, 'Standards of Proof in Civil Litigation' (1999) 62 MLR 167, 172, n 19. The standard of balance of probabilities has been defended as efficient in providing maximal incentives to take care in avoiding liability for negligence: Dominique Demougin and Claude Fluet, 'Preponderance of Evidence' (2006) 50 *European Economic Review* 963, and 'Deterrence versus Judicial Error: A Comparative View of Standards of Proof' (2005) 161 *J of Institutional and Theoretical Economics* 193.

[29] Richard A Posner, 'An Economic Approach to the Law of Evidence' (1999) 51 Stanford L Rev 1477, 1506.

[30] ibid 1506. Cf Tone Ognedal, 'Should the Standard of Proof be Lowered to Reduce Crime?', (2005) 25 Intl Rev of Law and Economics 45, warning that the lowering of the criminal standard to increase conviction rate has a potential trade-off in its impact on the comparative incidence of serious and minor crimes.

[31] *R v Lifchus* (1997) 150 DLR (4th) 733, 745.

[32] Larry Laudan, 'Is Reasonable Doubt Reasonable?' (2003) 9 Legal Theory 295, 304.

'crucial to insist that beliefs in guilt, if they lead to conviction, must be rationally well founded'.[33] Suppose the fact-finder is genuinely sure that the defendant is guilty. But her certainty came from consulting an ouija board.[34] If she convicts the defendant on this basis, has she not incorrectly applied the standard of proof? And does that not demonstrate that the justification for a finding of fact is not to be found purely in the end-state of deliberation: it must also depend, must it not, on the rationality of the reasoning which led to that end-state?

One could try to respond to this criticism, and defend the end-state interpretation of the standard of proof, by stressing that the degree of belief it requires, whilst a necessary condition, is insufficient for a proper conviction. Strictly speaking, as one could argue, the ouija board user had correctly applied the standard of proof since she was sure of the defendant's guilt. What she had violated was the separate norm of rationality which stands in the background of every trial deliberation. It is an unspoken requirement implicit in every trial that the fact-finder must decide on the verdict in a rational fashion. But the problem with this argument is that we want to say that rationality is a *legal* requirement; and it is difficult to see how we are conceptually compelled to hive off this requirement from the legal concept of standard of proof and unclear what we stand to gain from doing so. The argument advanced in this chapter stands to gain if the standard of proof is understood as imposing the rationality requirement because it may then be read to contain a standard of caution. It is rational to be appropriately cautious in judging a dispute of fact. The standard of proof, in virtue of its rationality requirement, contains the demand that appropriate caution be exercised in fact-finding.

The second feature of the external analysis identified above was that it viewed standards of proof as decisional thresholds. There are a number of difficulties with this view. First, consider the civil standard. Conventional wisdom has it that 'a balance of probabilities means more likely than not or more probable than not'.[35] If the usual interpretation of this is right, it would seem to follow that any probability that exceeds 0.5 will satisfy the civil standard: 'The balance must be tipped by the defendant, no more.'[36] As seen in Chapter 3, this interpretation leads to unacceptable conclusions; an argument was made in favour of a belief account of fact-finding, according to which, the fact-finder must find that p only if one would be justified in believing that p within the terms of BAF*. *Briginshaw*

[33] ibid 305. It is a separate debate whether the juror needs to identify and articulate the reason for her doubt: Laudan, ibid at 306–310; contrast Steve Sheppard, 'The Metamorphoses of Reasonable Doubt: How Changes in the Burden of Proof Have Weakened the Presumption of Innocence' (2003) 78 Notre Dame L Rev 1165, 1213–1214.

[34] cf *Young* (1995) 2 Cr App R 379.

[35] *R v Swaysland* (n 6) 299, 308. Also: *Re H (Minors)* (n 7) 586; *The 'Popi M'* [1985] 2 All ER 712, 718.

[36] *R v Swaysland* (n 6) 306.

v Briginshaw[37] is instructive on this score. A petition for divorce was filed on the ground of adultery. The trial judge dismissed it for this reason:[38]

I do not know what to believe. I have been very troubled... I have done my best to decide, but the petitioner must satisfy me that his story is true. I think I should say that if this were a civil case I might well consider that the probabilities were in favour of the petitioner, but I am certainly not satisfied beyond reasonable doubt that the evidence called by the petitioner should be accepted.

On appeal to the Australian High Court, it was held that the standard of proof was the civil standard. The appeal was nevertheless dismissed. On the view that the trial judge had taken of the evidence, the civil standard was not discharged. It is insufficient for the fact-finder to believe that it is more likely than not that the allegation is true; he must believe that the allegation is, in fact, true. Dixon J concluded, from reading what the trial judge had said as a whole, that the latter 'had not formed an actual belief that the adultery took place, although he thought that possibly he might consider that the probabilities disclosed by the evidence were greater in favour of that conclusion than against it'.[39] This fails to satisfy the civil standard of proof because:[40]

when the law requires the proof of any fact, the tribunal must feel an actual persuasion of its occurrence or existence before it can be found. It cannot be found as a result of a mere mechanical comparison of probabilities independently of any belief in its reality.

The conventional understanding of the criminal standard is also problematic. It is a common observation that 'beyond reasonable doubt' is virtually impossible to define.[41] Trial judges are constantly warned against saying too much about it to the jury.[42] Sometimes, they are advised to avoid using the phrase altogether.[43] Definition is elusive because of a misconception of the definiendum. The criminal standard is traditionally conceived as a predetermined decisional threshold

[37] (1938) 60 CLR 336.

[38] ibid 337.

[39] ibid 359–360.

[40] ibid 361; see also 349, 350–351, 353–354.

[41] *Ching* (1976) 63 Cr App R 7, 11. Apparently, jurors find the phrase confusing: R Matthews, Lynn Hancock and Daniel Briggs, *Jurors' Perceptions, Understanding, Confidence and Satisfaction in the Jury System: a Study in Six Courts*, Research Development and Statistics Directorate of UK Home Office Online Report 05/04 (2004) at 38, available at: <http://www.homeoffice.gov.uk/rds/pdfs2/rdsolr0504.pdf>.

[42] eg *Henry Walters* [1969] 2 AC 26, 30; *Ching* (n 41) 10; *R v Hepworth & Fearnley* [1955] 2 QB 600, 603. Many writers too have argued against defining 'beyond reasonable doubt': Frank Bates, 'Describing the Indescribable—Evaluating the Standard of Proof in Criminal Cases' (1989) 13 Crim LJ 330; Note, 'Reasonable Doubt: An Argument Against Definition' (1995) 108 Harvard L Rev 1955.

[43] They are advised to tell the jury instead that, to convict, they must be 'sure' or 'completely (or fully or thoroughly) satisfied': *R v Kritz* [1950] 1 KB 82, 89; *Summers* (1952) 36 Cr App R 14, 15; *R v Hepworth and Fearnley* [1955] 2 QB 600, 603–4; *Re J S (Declaration of Paternity)* (1981) 2 FLR 146, 151. But the 'time-honoured formula' of proof beyond reasonable doubt was favoured by Lord Scarman in *Ferguson v The Queen* [1979] 1 All ER 877, 882.

that applies uniformly to all criminal trials. For it to be operational in this way, we must know what the benchmark is and how it is to be applied: is the threshold set, across the board, at 85 per cent probability, or 95 per cent, or 99 per cent...?[44] And what is it to be 85 per cent confident, or 95 per cent confident, or 99 per cent confident?[45] When those who support the threshold view are asked to quantify the legal threshold, their usual reaction is to postulate a figure which they then conveniently assume to be correct in the rest of their analyses.[46] It may be possible to come up with a theoretical answer as to what the threshold ought to be by performing some utility calculation with appropriate assumptions;[47] and it may be that the standard, if coarsely defined, is operational insofar as one is able by introspection of one's mental state to form vague impressions of personal confidence. But there is no consensus on how best to quantify the minimum degree of confidence, even if only roughly as a band of probabilities. In surveys where respondents are forced to come up with a number, their answers range over a considerable spectrum.[48] More importantly, the probabilistic threshold is nowhere stated in the law and there is strong judicial hostility to any attempt at probabilistic quantification of the standard.[49] In *R v Cavkic*,[50] the New Zealand Court of Appeal held that the trial judge should have told the jury, in response to a question about the probabilistic value of reasonable doubt,

[44] When asked, judges and laypersons give very different answers to this question: Stephen E Fienberg, *The Evolving Role of Statistical Assessments as Evidence in the Courts* (New York: Springer-Verlag, 1989) 201–204; Joseph L Gastwirth, *Statistical Reasoning in Law and Public Policy: Tort Law, Evidence and Health* (Boston: Academic Press, 1988) 700–702; Lillquist (n 10) 111–117.

[45] Larry Laudan, *Truth, Error, and Criminal Law* (Cambridge: CUP, 2006) 77–78 questions the intelligibility of these questions.

[46] eg Frederick Schauer and Richard Zeckhauser, 'On the Degree of Confidence for Adverse Decisions' (1996) 25 J of Legal Studies 27, 33–34; *Brown v Bowen* (1988) 847 F 2d 342, 345–6; *Branion v Gramly* (1988) 855 F 2d 1256, 1263, n 5.

[47] eg David Hamer, 'Probabilistic Standards of Proof, Their Complements and the Errors that are Expected to Flow from Them' (2004) 1 University of New England LJ 71.

[48] This is shown in the result of a survey conducted in the United Kingdom of members of the public, magistrates, and criminal justice professionals: Michael Zander, 'The Criminal Standard of Proof: How Sure is Sure?' (2000) 150 NLJ 1517. See also the earlier survey conducted by John Warwick Montgomery, 'The Criminal Standard of Proof' (1998) 148 NLJ 6837. Significant variations were also found in responses to similar surveys conducted in New Zealand (Warren Young, Neil Cameron and Yvette Tinsley, *Juries in Criminal Trials—Part Two—A Summary of the Research Findings*, in New Zealand Law Commission Preliminary Paper 37, vol 2 (Wellington, 1999) para 7.16) and in the United States (Rita James Simon and Linda Mahan, 'Quantifying the Burdens of Proof—A View from the Bench, the Jury, and the Classroom' (1971) 5 Law and Society Rev 319; C M A McCauliff, 'Burdens of Proof: Degrees of Belief, Quanta of Evidence, or Constitutional Guarantees?' (1982) 35 Vanderbilt L Rev 1293; Harry D Saunders, 'Quantifying Reasonable Doubt: A Proposed Solution to an Equal Protection Problem' (December 7, 2005) Bepress Legal Series, Working Paper 881, available at: <http://law.bepress.com/expresso/eps/881/>; *US v Fatico* (n 8) 409–411; *US v Hall* (1988) 854 F 2d 1036, 1044; *Vargas v Keane* (1996) 86 F 3d 1273 (see judgment of Judge Weinstein)).

[49] See authorities cited by Peter Tiller and Jonathan Gottfried, '*United States v Copeland*, 369 F Supp 2d 275 (EDNY 2005): A Collateral Attack on the Legal Maxim That Proof Beyond A Reasonable Doubt is Unquantifiable?' (2006) 5 Law, Probability and Risk 135, 135–137.

[50] (2005) 12 VR 136, para 229.

'not to approach their task by reference to some calculation of percentages'. The same court noted in a different case that no 'sensible judge would ever attempt to put a mathematical value on what constitutes proof beyond reasonable doubt'.[51] As was argued in the last chapter, questions of fact are decided on the basis of categorical beliefs. A categorical belief cannot be thought of simply as a partial belief that exceeds a certain value of probability. Common criticisms are that any value we select for the probabilistic threshold would seem arbitrary and that implementation of the threshold view raises problems such as that of conjunction.[52] Not surprisingly, we find similar criticisms reproduced in discussion of legal proof.[53]

Some think that it is impossible to put a figure on the strength of belief required for proof.[54] To try to quantify the 'reasonableness' of doubt, said Stephen, is like 'trying to count what is not number, and to measure what is not space':[55] 'We cannot say no man shall be convicted unless there are six pounds or eight yards of evidence against him.'[56] This led him to a wholly subjective interpretation of the criminal standard. The true principle, he suggested, is 'to estimate the value of evidence entirely by the effect which it does in fact produce upon the minds of those who hear it'.[57] Hence, 'the amount of evidence necessary for a conviction is that amount of evidence, be it greater or less, which will place twelve jurymen in a state of certainty'.[58] As one critic points out, this means, remarkably, that the jury can never be wrong![59]

The problem of fixing the threshold is a false one; it cannot be solved but must be dissolved. Although we may take issues with Stephen, he was generally right to be scornful of the idea that evidence must weigh up to some quantitative measure which it is the job of the standard of proof to demarcate. For Packer, the criminal standard is suggestive of an 'adjudicative mood'.[60] It is more accurate to say that it refers to an attitude. As will be argued in Part 2, the standard of proof should be interpreted as an instruction to the fact-finder on the attitude that she must adopt

[51] *R v Wanhalla* [2007] 2 NZLR 573, para 42.

[52] See discussion in Chapter 3, Part 2.5.4.

[53] On the problem of arbitrariness or subjectivity, see Laudan (n 45) 77–78; and on the problem of conjunction, see L Jonathan Cohen, *The Probable and the Provable* (Aldershot: Gregg Revivals, 1991 reprint, first published in 1977) ch 5, and Ronald J Allen and Sarah A Jehl, 'Burdens of Persuasion in Civil Cases: Algorithms v. Explanations' (2003) Michigan State L Rev 893.

[54] *Briginshaw v Briginshaw* (n 7) 343; William Wills, *An Essay on the Principles of Circumstantial Evidence*, edited by Alfred Wills (5th edn, London: Butterworth & Co, 1902) 9.

[55] James Fitzjames Stephen, *A General View of the Criminal Law of England* (London: Macmillan & Co, 1863) 262.

[56] James Fitzjames Stephen, 'The Characteristics of English Criminal Law' (1857) Cambridge Essays 1, 27.

[57] ibid.

[58] ibid 28. Similarly, *Green v R* (1972) 126 CLR 28, 32–33: 'A reasonable doubt is a doubt which the particular jury entertain in the circumstances. Jurymen themselves set the standard of what is reasonable in the circumstances.'

[59] Wills (n 54) 266.

[60] Herbert L Packer, *The Limits of the Criminal Sanction* (Stanford: Stanford UP, 1968) 137.

when deliberating on the verdict. It is, in one aspect, about the caution she must exercise in making her findings. To draw a rough analogy: if you ask me to drive fast, it is intelligible for me to ask, 'How fast?' and it is equally intelligible for you to respond with a quantitative answer, if only as a rough indication of the speed you desire. But if you ask me to drive cautiously, it makes no sense for me to ask, 'How cautiously?' and expect you to give me a quantitative reply, even as an estimate. What caution requires of a formula one racer is very different from what it requires of the driver of a busload of young children. The demands of due caution depend on the context.

The third feature of the conventional mode of analysis is the evaluation of standard of proof as a means of achieving some social ends. Where the threshold should be set is a question of policy; it involves balancing competing social interests, minimizing economic costs of errors, maximizing overall utility, and so forth. This kind of approach stands in danger of overlooking the intrinsic injustice of a wrong verdict. In late eighteenth-century England, the 'widespread feeling that crime was a growing problem and was not being sufficiently rigorously prosecuted'[61] led Paley, the Archdeacon of Carlisle, to admonish juries for their 'overstrained scrupulousness, or weak timidity'.[62] He pleaded:[63]

> The security of civil life... is protected chiefly by a dread of punishment. The misfortune of an individual [to be wrongly convicted] cannot be placed in competition with this object... [W]hen certain rules of adjudication must be pursued... in order to reach the crimes with which the public are infested; courts of justice should not be deterred from the application of these rules, by *every* suspicion of danger, or by the mere possibility of confounding the innocent with the guilty. They ought rather to reflect, that he, who falls by a mistaken sentence, may be considered as falling for his country.

This call provoked widespread criticisms. Best called it 'inhuman'.[64] Wills branded it an 'execrable doctrine'.[65] Romilly responded with a scathing critique.[66] It is easy to understand why so many were appalled by Paley's comments. He is

[61] Barbara Shapiro, *Beyond Reasonable Doubt and Probable Cause—Historical Perspectives on Anglo-American Law of Evidence* (Berkeley: U of California Press, 1991) 220.

[62] William Paley, *The Principles of Moral and Political Philosophy* (Dublin: Exshaw *et al*, 1785) 318.

[63] ibid 321–322. France had a similar advocate in Siméon-Denis Poisson. Writing in 1837, he argued that the jury should not decide 'upon the actual guilt or innocence of the accused, but rather on whether public security was better served by a conviction or an acquittal' and that 'the true criterion of judicial success was the security of the society at large, rather than the danger of erroneous conviction in individual cases'. Lorraine Daston, *Classical Probability in the Enlightenment* (Princeton, NJ: Princeton UP, 1988) 362 and 304 respectively.

[64] W M Best, *A Treatise on Presumptions of Law and Fact with the Theory and Rules of Presumptive or Circumstantial Proof in Criminal Cases* (London: Hodges and Smith, 1844) 291. Another critic was the reporter of *R v White* (1865) 4 F & F 383, note (a).

[65] Wills (n 54) 268.

[66] Samuel Romilly, *Observations on the Criminal Law of England as it Relates to Capital Punishments, and on the Mode in which it is Administered* (London: T Cadell & W Davies, 1810) 72–76.

dismissive of, and even appears to deny, the injustice of a false conviction. This is evident in the absurdity of his military analogy. As Best commented:[67]

> the ... soldier [who dies] in defence of his country ... falls with honour, his memory is respected ... ; while the [innocent who has been wrongly convicted] has not even the sad consolation of being pitied, but sees himself branded with public ignominy.

The soldier is not a victim of injustice in the way the innocent convict is. An important distinction is drawn by Murphy: while it is admirable for a person to sacrifice himself for a noble cause, it is altogether a different matter for me to choose to sacrifice him for the good of others.[68] As Wills said in his reply to Paley: 'Justice never requires the sacrifice of a victim.'[69] The conviction of an innocent person, however unintentional, whatever the supposed social benefits, is intrinsically unjust. Any argument that ignores this moral fact is dangerously flawed.

For all that, there is an inescapable element of truth in Paley's argument. Every legal system, however legitimate, is practically certain to produce some wrongful convictions.[70] Hopefully, such errors are highly exceptional. But we cannot pretend they never happen, and given human fallibility, they cannot be completely ruled out in any workable system of trial. If it is unjust to convict the innocent, is it not also unjust to support an institution that we know will result, even though exceptionally, in miscarriages of justice? This question assumes wrongly that we should place on the same moral plane the deliberate framing of a targeted individual and the unwitting punishment of a person mistakenly believed to be guilty, the latter being merely an unintended consequence of institutional imperfection.[71] Consider this parallel example. The authority does not intend to bring about deaths by building a highway even though it knows before the construction that it is statistically certain that some fatal accidents will occur on it.[72] Similarly, we do not deliberately set out to punish the innocent when we create a criminal justice system even though we know that some miscarriages are bound to happen. In neither case can it

[67] Best (n 64) 292. Cf Mirko Bagaric and Kumar Amarasekara, 'The Errors of Retributivism' (2000) 24 Melbourne U L Rev 124, 141–143, who argue that convicting a man of a crime we know he did not commit is 'no more horrendous' than difficult decisions taken in war times, such as asking soldiers to fight and die in defence of their country.

[68] Jeffrie G Murphy, 'The Killing of the Innocent' in his *Retribution, Justice, and Therapy—Essays in the Philosophy of Law* (Dordrecht: D Reidel, 1979) 18.

[69] Wills (n 54) 268.

[70] In *R (Mullen) v Home Secretary* [2002] EWCA Civ 1882, para 33; [2003] QB 993, 1005, Schiemann LJ described this as 'an inescapable fact of human life'. See also Glanville Williams, *The Proof of Guilt* (3rd edn, London: Stevens & Sons, 1963) 190; Michael Philips, 'The Inevitability of Punishing the Innocent' (1985) 48 *Philosophical Studies* 389; Alan Wertheimer (n 11). In theory, conviction of the innocent can be prevented by not convicting anyone at all. But that is obviously impractical.

[71] Michael S Moore, 'Justifying Retributivism' (1993) 27 Israel L Rev 15, 20.

[72] This example is based on that given by Murphy (n 68) 13. Also useful is the seatbelt example given by Wertheimer (n 11) 52–54.

truthfully be said that we have 'sacrificed' the lives or interests or rights of a targeted few as a means of attaining some greater good for society as a whole. As Duff rightly stresses, when a miscarriage of justice occurs, 'it occurs *despite* our intention and our efforts to avoid it'.[73]

Undoubtedly, we should take great measures to avoid wrongful convictions. There is a limit to the efforts that can be taken, given competing demands for limited resources. Dworkin and others have argued that, while a person has a right not to be convicted if innocent, she does not have the right to the most accurate fact-finding system possible, however much it may cost.[74] But the central point remains that the trial system should never *aim* at convicting the innocent. This point finds specific expression in the requirement of the general principle defended in Chapter 3: the fact-finder must not find the defendant guilty unless she judges that one would be justified in believing that he is guilty within the terms of BAF*. This principle expresses an internal commitment not to sacrifice justice at the altar of utility.

2 Internal Analysis

2.1 Introduction

The difficulties with traditional discourse on the standard of proof cannot be overcome without a fundamental revision of our understanding of the concept. Part 2 seeks to bring about this revision by engaging in an internal form of analysis that is different on each of the features identified of the external approach: here, we will assume an internal (not external) perspective, focus on the process (not end-state) of evidential evaluation, explain the standard as an instruction on deliberative attitude (not as a decisional threshold), and treat it as an expression of epistemic principles, rooted in a view of justice as empathic care and respect (not as instruments of social policy).

The argument to be pursued picks up on this general principle which was defended in Chapter 3: the fact-finder must find that p only if one would be justified in believing that p within the terms of BAF*. It is a term of BAF* that the belief must be sufficiently strong. That is to say, the fact-finder must have sufficient confidence in p. The required level of confidence depends on the caution she must exercise in the context of the case at hand. She must exercise such caution as

[73] R A Duff, *Trials and Punishments* (Cambridge: CUP, 1986) 159.

[74] For Dworkin, a person does however have the two related rights: the 'right to procedures justified by the correct assignment of importance to the moral harm (of a wrongful verdict) the procedures risk, and a related right to a consistent evaluation of that harm in the procedures afforded them as compared with the procedures afforded others in different... cases': Ronald Dworkin, 'Principle, Policy, Procedure' in his *A Matter of Principle* (Cambridge, Massachusetts: Harvard UP, 1985) ch 3, 93. See also Wertheimer (n 11).

is commensurate with the seriousness of what is said of, and at stake for, the party who is affected by her finding. Underlying this claim is the premise that the court must treat the party with due respect and concern.

Two proposals will be advanced. First, 'standard of proof' should be interpreted as 'standard of caution'.[75] Caution in the context of trial deliberation is a propositional attitude, a critical frame of mind that comes in shades of resistance to persuasion on the truth of a disputed allegation. The degree of resistance should increase with one's awareness of the gravity of the allegation and of the consequences of judging it true. As the standard of proof (that is, caution) rises, the greater the confidence the fact-finder must have in p to justify her finding that p. In this sense, the standard of proof is a variant standard.

Secondly, it will be argued that the deliberative attitude must vary with the kind of dispute presented by the case at hand. There must be the right distribution of caution. It is here that we can find a difference in kind between the civil and the criminal standards. The civil standard requires the fact-finder to be equally open-minded in determining the truth of one party's hypothesis (p) as in determining the truth of his opponent's allegation (q), where p and q are inconsistent or contradictory. The underlying idea is that she must treat both sides equally. She must not be more disposed, or more ready or willing, to accept p than q for that would be treating the side alleging p more favourably than the side alleging q; and the same holds the other way round. In the usual case, BAF* applies symmetrically to both parties.

In contrast, the criminal standard instructs the fact-finder to adopt a 'protective attitude' in deliberation; in general, where p is a proposition supporting a guilty verdict, she must find that p only if she judges that one would be justified in believing that p within the terms of BAF*. On the other hand, BAF* does not apply to any alternative hypothesis (q) that supports a 'not guilty' verdict. So long as the fact-finder *suspects* that q is true, so that a reasonable doubt is cast on the hypothesis of guilt, she must acquit the defendant. This asymmetrical treatment is based on the value judgment that it is a greater kind of wrong to convict the innocent than to acquit the guilty.

2.2 Standard of caution

2.2.1 Context and caution

The variant nature of 'standard of proof', understood as 'standard of caution', comes from the context-dependency of caution. A useful starting point for development of this view is an observation made by Allen. He finds it 'difficult to

[75] cf James Fitzjames Stephen, *A General View of the Criminal Law of England* (2nd edn, London: Macmillan, 1890) 183. Referring to the criminal standard, he wrote: 'Its real meaning, and I think its practical operation, is that it is an emphatic caution against haste in coming to a conclusion adverse to a prisoner.' Approved in *Briginshaw v Briginshaw* (n 7) 352.

know what real meaning is to be attached' to the statement that 'in a civil case a preponderance of probabilities is sufficient, but in a criminal case the prisoner's guilt must be proved beyond all reasonable doubt'.[76] He says:[77]

> I apprehend that a judge who directed a jury in an action for damages, 'You need not be as careful in arriving at your conclusions as if you were trying a criminal case', would considerably startle the legal world and the public; . . . I know of no authority for the proposition that their duty is any less when property, and not life or liberty, is at stake.

Allen does not explain what he means by carefulness on the part of the jury. It may be that he is thinking of how the jury attends to the evidence and the effort they take to scrutinize it, which effort may be judged in terms of criteria such as thoroughness and diligence. Was the fact-finder sufficiently attentive during the trial, meticulous in going over the evidence, alert to possible grounds for believing or disbelieving a witness, conscientious in trying to 'piece things together', and so forth? Or did she 'forego or unduly shorten the act of hunting, inquiring . . . because of mental sloth, torpor, impatience to get something settled'?[78]

Arguably, the 'standard of proof' has nothing to do with the standard of care as just construed. A rebuttal to Allen is possible even if we accept the traditional view of a standard of proof as a probability threshold for deciding issues of fact. Consider the grading of student essays: the standard of proof is somewhat like the mark that separates a pass from a failure. How carefully the examiner must read an essay does not turn on the percentage point at which a pass is set. A rebuttal is also possible if, as is argued, 'standard of proof' means 'standard of caution'. 'Care' (in the narrow sense imputed to Allen) and 'caution' operate at different levels. The fact-finder must search the evidence with care for possible reasons to believe or disbelieve p. But whether the reasons she has found are good enough to justify believing sufficiently strongly that p for the purposes of BAF* depends on the epistemic standard that those reasons must satisfy and the strength of belief they must support; what qualify as good enough reasons is contingent on the degree of caution she must, in the circumstances, exercise in finding positively that p.

Even if this distinction between caution and care is put aside, and we assume that they are equivalent notions, there is still an ambiguity in Allen's argument. It is always wrong to act incautiously. But what constitutes cautious behaviour depends on the circumstances of action. Caution cannot be judged by a single factor or on a common scale, independently of context. A person driving at ninety kilometres per hour on a clear stretch of traffic-free highway is not acting less

[76] Carleton Kemp Allen, 'The Presumption of Innocence', in his *Legal Duties—And Other Essays in Jurisprudence* (Oxford: Clarendon Press, 1931) 253, 287.

[77] ibid 288.

[78] John Dewey, *How We Think—A Restatement of the Relation of Reflective Thinking to the Educative Process* (Boston: D C Heath, 1933) 16.

cautiously than a person who drives at forty kilometres per hour on a narrow and crowded street; speed alone is not determinative. One should drive cautiously at all times. But what constitutes cautious driving depends on the circumstances.

We should agree with Allen that the trier of fact must always act cautiously, whether the trial is civil or criminal. But this does not mean that the demands of caution must remain the same despite contextual differences. The greater the stake involved in a finding of fact, the stronger must be the supporting evidence and the more difficult it must be to persuade her to make that finding; conversely, the lesser the stake, the lower the standard to be met. The employment of different standards in two cases does not alone mean that the fact-finder is acting less cautiously in one case than in the other. This is as wrong as it is to say that whenever two persons drive at different speeds, the faster driver is *necessarily* acting with less caution than the slower one. In a sense, where two persons exercise the caution appropriate to their respective contexts, neither is acting more cautiously than the other. But it remains true to say that the higher the risk of harm there is in one's action, the greater the caution that one must exercise to avoid that harm while so acting.

2.2.2 Context and confidence

Caution in fact-finding requires that the fact-finder finds positively that p only if she judges that one would be justified in believing that p within the terms of BAF*. The degree of confidence in p should not be mistaken for the intensity of feeling or emotion towards p.[79] One may be completely unexcited by something of which one is utterly convinced. As explained previously, the degree to which a person believes that p is the tenacity with which she holds on to the point of view that p is true, and refers to how difficult it would be to make her change her mind or withdraw commitment to that point of view. Stephen phrased the idea well: 'degrees of belief are degrees rather of stability than of intensity'; the stronger belief 'is far more firmly lodged than the [weaker], and would be less easily dispossessed'.[80]

The strength of belief necessary to justify a positive finding of fact is context-dependent; more specifically, it must be commensurate with the seriousness of what the finding says about a party and the consequences for her of that finding. Respect for that person and care for her welfare are virtues we expect the fact-finder to exhibit. Crucially, these virtues operate *within* epistemology. Epistemic and moral considerations do not stand in opposition but intertwine to make a

[79] cf John Henry Wigmore, *A Treatise on the Anglo-American System of Evidence in Trials at Common Law*, vol 9 (3rd edn, Boston: Little, Brown & Co, 1940) 325 ('intensity of human belief').

[80] James Fitzjames Stephen, *A General View of the Criminal Law of England* (London: Macmillan & Co, 1863) 245.

combined case for a variant standard of proof. The sections to follow seek to make good these claims.

2.2.3 *Theoretical and practical reasoning generally*

It is worth clarifying at the outset what the present argument is not about. It is not about taking the external perspective of the system engineer and evaluating the organizational design of the legal system. For instance, there are undoubtedly practical reasons for distributing different types of cases amongst the many tiers and branches of courts and tribunals that exist in developed jurisdictions. Efficiency in resource allocation and cost-reduction in dispute settlement are some of the practical reasons for channelling minor disputes to 'small claims tribunals'. Neither is the present argument about the structures of the trial system or of the legal process more generally. Again, it is undeniable that these matters are shaped by practical considerations.[81] The doctrine of *res judicata* and limitations on appeal on questions of fact are obvious examples. Consider also how constraints on resources affect the range of evidence that the court will allow to be adduced. The judge has the duty to divert the trial process from paths of enquiry that are unlikely to yield anything or much that is of significance. Since judicial resources are limited, the worth of their expenditure must be addressed. Probative force is a matter of degree. It shades imperceptibly out of existence. Not every proposition of fact that is treated as legally irrelevant completely lacks probative value:[82] sometimes, the proposition simply has too little probative value to merit investigation, given the costs of doing so.[83] The lack of (sufficient) probative value is in itself generally harmless and not, on its own, ground for exclusion. However, it is wasteful of judicial resources to allow proof of an unprobative or insufficiently probative proposition.[84] Our

[81] As rightly observed by Colin Tapper, 'Trends and Techniques in the Law of Evidence' in Birks (ed), *Pressing Problems in the Law, vol 1, Criminal Justice and Human Rights* (Oxford: OUP, 1995) 13 at 33, economic constraints 'determine many aspect[s] of criminal procedure and evidence, from the order of presenting evidence, to the use of estoppels and other means to prevent the relitigation of matters once they have been determined. Similar considerations dominate the rules relating to the matters which may be appealed, and the procedures for dealing with the admission of fresh evidence on an appeal.'

[82] '[I]t is as idle to enquire as it is impossible to say whether the evidence was rejected . . . because it was altogether irrelevant, or merely because it was too remotely relevant': Colin Tapper (ed), *Cross and Tapper on Evidence* (11th edn, Oxford: OUP, 2007) 74.

[83] Peter Tillers (reviser), John Henry Wigmore, *Wigmore on Evidence—A Treatise on the Anglo-American System of Evidence in Trials at Common Law*, vol 1A (Boston: Little, Brown & Co, 1983) 973, note to §28.

[84] In many jurisdictions, the court has a general discretion to exclude evidence on the ground that it would waste time: eg s 403 of the United States Federal Rules of Evidence and s 135(c) of the Australian Evidence Act 1995.

interest in efficiency justifies exclusion.[85] In the oft-quoted remark of Rolfe B in *Attorney-General v Hitchcock*:[86]

> If we lived for a thousand years instead of about 60 or 70, and every case was of sufficient importance, it might be possible, and perhaps proper ... to raise every possible inquiry as to the truth of statements made.

The present argument is not about the practical factors that direct and mould trial proceedings; it is about the encroachment of practical (or pragmatic) considerations on trial deliberation. Practical factors impinge much more directly and visibly on the *rationality of inquiry*, centring on such outward activities as discovery, adduction, and challenging of evidence, than they do on the *rationality of belief*, pertaining to its acquisition, revision, or abandonment, on the evidence that is already admitted.[87] Trial deliberation is essentially a theoretical (or epistemic) exercise, the analysis of which cannot be fruitfully engaged without taking the viewpoint of the agent. As a rough distinction, practical reasoning is reasoning about what to do; theoretical reasoning is reasoning about what to believe. The reasoning a driver uses in deciding whether to take a safer route or a more scenic one is largely practical; she must choose between her interests or desires. The reasoning she uses in determining which of two routes is safer or more beautiful is ultimately theoretical; she is seeking the truth on the matter.[88]

2.2.4 *Justice and justification in fact-finding*

There are two possible kinds of justification for a finding of fact. One is practical, the other is epistemic. Leaving aside for later discussion complications about their interconnection, it may be said of practical justification that it treats the finding that p as an action which can be appraised independently of the truth of p, and, of epistemic justification, that it treats the finding that p as the acceptance of p in the belief that it is true.[89] Appreciation of this difference can perhaps help to

[85] According to Bentham, it is proper to exclude irrelevant evidence, not because its exclusion incurs no costs but because we thereby avoid the vexation, expense, and delay which would have attended its production (Jeremy Bentham, *Rationale of Judicial Evidence* in John Bowring (ed), *The Works of Jeremy Bentham*, vol 7 (Edinburgh: W. Tait, 1843) Book IX, Part I, ch 1, 343). As William Twining noted (*Theories of Evidence: Bentham and Wigmore* (London: Weidenfeld & Nicholson, 1985) 68, n 7), to Bentham, 'the exclusion of irrelevant ... evidence is *justified* rather than strictly *required*'. See also Geoffrey R Stone, 'The Rules of Evidence and the Rules of Public Debate' [1993] The U of Chicago Legal Forum 127, 129: 'the primary reason for excluding immaterial or irrelevant evidence is that its presentation is a waste of time. If the evidence proves nothing in dispute, why take the time at trial to hear it? Because judicial time and resources are limited, it is costly to hear evidence that serves no constructive purpose. Hence, we toss it out.'

[86] (1847) 1 Exch 91, 105.

[87] John David Owens, 'Does Belief Have an Aim?' (2003) 115 *Philosophical Studies* 283, 288.

[88] These examples are based on those given by Gilbert Harman, 'Practical Aspects of Theoretical Reasoning' in Alfred R Mele and Piers Rawling (eds), *The Oxford Handbook of Rationality* (Oxford: OUP, 2004) ch 3, 45.

[89] M Jamie Ferreira, *Scepticism and Reasonable Doubt—The British Naturalist Tradition in Wilkins, Hume, Reid, and Newman* (Oxford: OUP, 1986) 21, 53–54, 72, 183–186; Brian Carr,

resolve a dispute on whether questions of fact should be decided in court in the same way that decisions are made out of court. On the one side we have judges like Lord Diplock who think that the task of determining guilt is no more esoteric than 'applying to the evidence adduced at the trial the common sense with which [fact-finders] approach matters of importance to them in their ordinary lives'.[90] Similarly, Lord Chief Baron Pollock is reported to have told the jury: 'If the conclusion to which you are conducted be that there is that degree of certainty in the case that you would act upon it in your own grave and important concerns, that is the degree of certainty which the law requires, and which will justify you in returning a verdict of guilty.'[91] On the other side we have cases like *R v Lifchus*,[92] where the Canadian Supreme Court held that 'beyond reasonable doubt' is not an 'ordinary' concept and that it is inappropriate when applying it to employ the reasoning that one uses in making practical decisions, even those that are of utmost importance in one's life. Ginsburg J took a similar position in the United States Supreme Court case of *Victor v Nebraska*.[93]

Judges in the second camp may be interpreted as insisting, and they would be right to insist, that practical rationality does not govern legal fact-finding in the same way as it does choices of action people make outside the courtroom. The 'domestic analogy' was rejected by the New Zealand Court of Appeal with the observation that such choices are often 'influenced by elements of speculation, hope, prejudice, emotion'.[94] In our daily lives, we frequently act, as we must, amidst uncertainty by taking calculated risks.[95] For instance, a person may choose to undergo life-threatening surgery (which certainly qualifies as a 'grave and important' matter) even though she does not believe that the operation will in fact succeed. Her choice is rational if she knows that imminent death is even more likely were she to forego the operation.

Should a trial verdict be decided similarly by assessing risks and weighing likely costs against potential good of acting on different options? The issue is the familiar one posed by critics of utilitarianism.[96] To borrow, with some modifications, McCloskey's example:[97] a judge is presiding at a racially explosive criminal

'Knowledge and Its Risks' (1982) 82 *Proceedings of the Aristotelian Society* (New Series) 115, 123–124.

[90] *Henry Walters* [1969] 2 AC 26, 30. Also: *Ferguson v The Queen* [1979] 1 All ER 877, 881. Cf *Gray* (1973) 58 Cr App R 177, 183; *R v Hepworth and Fearnley* [1955] 2 QB 600, 603.

[91] *Reg v Manning and Wife* (1849), quoted in Wills (n 54) 269. The judge repeated his views in *R v Muller* (1865) 4 F & F 383, n (a). Cf *Brown v R* (1913) 17 CLR 570, 596.

[92] (1997) 150 DLR (4th) 733, 741–2.

[93] (1994) 511 US 1, 23 *et seq.*

[94] *R v Adams*, CA 70/05, 5 September 2005; see also *R v Wanhalla* [2007] 2 NZLR 573, paras 56, 131–134 and 166.

[95] *Victor v Nebraska* (n 93) 24. Similarly, *Brown v R* (1913) 17 CLR 570, 585, 586, 594–5.

[96] H J McCloskey, 'A Note on Utilitarian Punishment' (1963) 72 *Mind* 599; J J C Smart and Bernard Williams, *Utilitarianism—For and Against* (Cambridge: CUP, 1973) 98.

[97] H J McCloskey, 'An Examination of Restricted Utilitarianism' (1957) 66 *The Philosophical Rev* 466, 468–469.

trial. She knows the defendant is innocent. She also knows that an acquittal is very likely to lead to riots by lynching mobs which will result in death to many people. The consequences are far worse if the accused is acquitted than if he is convicted and punished; disutility in the loss of many innocent lives outweighs the disutility in the wrongful imprisonment of one man. (Assume there is no risk of any remoter costs that raises doubt about this conclusion, such as the risk of the frame-up coming to light and undermining public confidence in the judiciary.)[98] There is greater good in the overall outcome if the judge declares the man guilty. But the judge who convicts wholly on this reasoning has fallen short of an ethically and epistemically sound deliberation.

First, consider the ethical aspect: one must be remarkably hard-hearted to think only of utility. In a discussion of belief and reasonable doubt, Stephen said that 'the wisdom of belief, in any particular instance, is a question of the balance of advantages'.[99] It would be almost barbaric to judge the wisdom of a conviction in the same way. The defendant's claim to justice, even if not decisive, has independent and fundamental relevance. A common line of challenge to utilitarianism is that it fails to take moral cognizance of the injustice intrinsic in the conviction and punishment of the innocent.[100] To decide a defendant's fate purely on utilitarian costs analysis is to deny him respect as a person; it is to treat him 'as a means in one's calculations of what would be good for others'.[101]

At the other end, moral absolutism is just as difficult to embrace. It is difficult to deny the possibility of situations in which it is morally permissible, perhaps even obligatory, to commit an unjust act.[102] Extreme circumstances are conceivable that could make it correct to convict and punish an innocent person. However, a person with humane sensibility will take this tragic step only with much anguish and regret, and, after the event, she would feel a deep sense of guilt. There is a frightening moral callousness in the judge who sees no dilemma and is prepared to punish an innocent defendant so long as there is, to quote Stephens again, a 'balance of advantages'.[103] We must recognize the wrong we do 'if there is to be anything that can count as a sense of common humanity'

[98] The relevance of such potential costs was stressed by T L S Sprigge, 'A Utilitarian Reply to Dr McCloskey' (1965) 8 *Inquiry* 264, 275–280.

[99] James Fitzjames Stephen, *A History of the Criminal Law of England* (London: Macmillan & Co, 1883) 260.

[100] eg C L Ten, *Crime, Guilt and Punishment* (Oxford: Clarendon Press, 1987) at 32–36. Anscombe sees no point in arguing with someone who, in advance, is willing to contemplate the option of lawfully killing the innocent; for her, that person simply has a corrupt mind: G E M Anscombe, 'Modern Moral Philosophy' (1958) 33 *Philosophy* 1, 17, n 1.

[101] Murphy (n 68) 18.

[102] For a retributivist who accepts as much, see H J McCloskey, 'Utilitarian and Retributive Punishment' (1967) 64 *The J of Philosophy* 91, 102.

[103] A committed utilitarian might simply bite the bullet and insist that it is morally right to convict an innocent person if, overall, this produces less misery than an acquittal. See humorous entry in Daniel Dennett (ed), *The Philosophical Lexicon*, available at: <http://www.blackwellpublishing.com/lexicon/#O>:

between us and the person we harm.[104] In a morally adequate deliberation, one will have to struggle with the grave injustice of framing an innocent person, acting only if forced by overwhelming reasons and never just on a preponderance of utility. There ought to be far greater resistance to injustice than utilitarianism would appear to allow.[105]

Next, consider the epistemic aspect. While the verdict certainly has practical effects, trial deliberation is not a form of practical reasoning. The fact-finder's job is not to decide whether, all things considered, it is *right* to convict the defendant. It is her job to determine whether it is *true* that the defendant is guilty; the jury, after all, is sworn to give a true verdict according to the evidence. Trial deliberation is essentially a form of theoretical reasoning, although, as we shall see, pragmatic considerations encroach upon it. A verdict is, in one aspect, assertive, and deliberation on the verdict is an epistemic exercise in the sense of involving the mental act of judging where the truth lies. To find the defendant guilty is, amongst other things, to assert that he is guilty, and, according to the principle (BAF*) defended previously, the fact-finder is justified in finding him guilty only if she believes that one would be justified in believing in his guilt within the terms of BAF*. Short of this, the fact-finder must return an acquittal. Ordinarily, to convict someone we know to be innocent, or, in circumstances where we judge that one would not be justified in believing him to be guilty for the purposes of BAF*, is to tell a lie.[106] The defendant suffers a special insult to his dignity when his wrongful conviction is deliberate.[107]

This additional insult is not inflicted in a mistaken conviction. But the victim of an innocently incurred wrongful conviction suffers injustice nonetheless. A wrongful conviction, whether deliberate or mistaken, constitutes an injustice

outsmart, v. To embrace the conclusion of one's opponent's *reductio ad absurdum* argument. 'They thought they had me, but I outsmarted them. I agreed that it *was* sometimes just to hang an innocent man.'

This entry is named after J J C Smart, in a reference to his argument in Smart and Williams (n 96) 69–73. In fairness to Smart, he was fully sensitive to the injustice involved and accepted the result unhappily and with reluctance. More disturbing is the discussion in Mirko Bagaric and Kumar Amarasekara, 'The Errors of Retributivism' (2000) 24 Melbourne U L Rev 124, 141–143.

[104] Raimond Gaita, *A Common Humanity—Thinking about Truth, Love and Justice* (London: Routledge, 2000) 51.

[105] See Saul Smilanksy, 'Utilitarianism and the "Punishment" of the Innocent: The General Problem' (1990) 50 *Analysis* 256; McCloskey (n 102) 102–103 (the good that comes out of it must be 'sufficiently great to override the stringent demands of the duty of justice'); Igor Primoratz, *Justifying Legal Punishment* (New Jersey: Humanities Press, 1989) at 61.

[106] This point is about a conviction as an assertion of guilt and not about the meaning of punishment; it is therefore different from the argument made by A M Quinton, 'On Punishment' (1954) 14 *Analysis* 133, 137 that it is a kind of lie to call the infliction of suffering or harm on someone you know to be innocent 'punishment'. Cf Matt Matravers, '"More than Just Illogical": Truth and Jury Nullification', in Antony Duff *et al* (eds), *Truth and Due Process* (Oxford: Hart, 2004) ch 4 (suggesting that jury nullification does not necessarily involve a lie).

[107] Dworkin (n 74) ch 3: 'there is a special injustice in knowingly and falsely claiming that someone has committed a crime. That is, among other things, a lie' (ibid 79); 'the deliberate act involves a lie and therefore a special insult to the dignity of the person' (ibid 84).

to the defendant just in virtue of it being false that he committed the crime for which he has been officially condemned. Leaving aside the possibility of special cases (such as detention without trial or under an administrative order, which is strictly speaking, not punishment[108]), a person cannot be legally punished by the State for a crime of which he has not been convicted. A practical purpose of conviction is to authorize punishment. To convict an innocent person is to give the green light to her unjust punishment. Insofar as it is unjust to punish an innocent person, it is also unjust to intentionally bring about that punishment. In this sense, conviction of the innocent is, for want of a better phrase, instrumentally unjust.

But the conviction is not only instrumentally unjust. Dworkin argues that there is a moral cost intrinsic to every erroneous verdict. The person convicted of a crime which he did not commit suffers a 'moral harm', as does the person held liable in tort, say, for driving negligently 'when in fact he was not behind the wheel'.[109] This kind of harm is an objective concept; it arises simply in virtue of the injustice of being wrongly found guilty or liable, whether the victim knows or cares about the injustice. Moral harm is additional to whatever 'bare harm' the person may suffer as a result of the verdict, for example, in being forced to pay damages or in the loss of liberty. However, we should avoid over-abstraction. Shklar portrays our sense of injustice as an innate sentiment, which is primary and universal: 'normal human beings can tell when they have been affronted'.[110] A conviction expresses moral condemnation. It 'is far more than a formal step preceding the imposition of punishment; it is, in itself, a record of social disgrace'.[111] The defendant suffers an affront when publicly blamed for something he did not do. This is true even if the blame was mistaken and the insult cuts especially deep if it were a lie.

This 'injustice in *judgment*', as Feinberg calls it,[112] 'consists precisely in the falsity of the derogatory allegation', in not being 'truly... judged in matters that are relevant to our esteem'.[113] Such grievance exists independently of the injustice of wrongful *punishment*. The accused's grievance for being falsely judged remains even 'if his sentence is suspended and no further hardship is imposed upon him'.[114] Two separate points can be made. First, there can be unjust punishment without any (unjust) conviction, as when an all-powerful monarch uses the State apparatus to punish a subject, not for infringing any criminal law, but simply for

[108] For historical examples: Markus Dirk Dubber, 'The Criminal Trial and the Legitimation of Punishment' in Antony Duff *et al* (n 106) ch 5, 88–92.

[109] Dworkin (n 74) 92.

[110] Judith N Shklar, *The Faces of Injustice* (New Haven: Yale UP, 1990) 90.

[111] Peter Brett, *An Inquiry Into Criminal Guilt* (London: Sweet & Maxwell, 1963) 36.

[112] Joel Feinberg, 'Noncomparative Justice' (1974) 83 *The Philosophical Rev* 297, 302 calls this the 'injustice of judgment'.

[113] ibid 325. See also Duff (n 73) 108–109.

[114] Feinberg (n 112) 302.

incurring her displeasure.[115] Secondly, there can be an unjust conviction without any (unjust) punishment. This is possible at least in theory and real cases may come close enough. For example, a person may be convicted but let off punishment on the grounds of exceptional mitigating circumstances[116] or, if sentenced, she may subsequently be pardoned in a show of official mercy. However, even where she is spared punishment, the defendant can rightly feel aggrieved at having her official record blackened with a crime she did not commit. It is the intrinsic injustice of a wrongful conviction that sometimes moves the relatives of the victim to fight to clear her name even after she has passed away; and it is refusal to accept this particular kind of injustice that leads some victims to refuse application for pardon because that implies admission to guilt. The more opprobrious the finding that has been wrongly made against a person, the more enraged she is entitled to feel at the injustice suffered. There is greater injustice in being wrongly blamed for child abuse than for jaywalking.

According to Dworkin, civil litigants as well as criminal defendants have 'a right to procedures justified by the correct assignment of importance to the moral harm the procedures risk'.[117] This right, he stresses, 'is the right that a particular importance be attached to the risk of moral harm, not a right to a particular, independently describable, overall level of accuracy in adjudication'.[118] But how exactly do we attach sufficient importance to the risk of moral harm? From the standpoint of an external observer, the degree of importance we attach to the injustice of a wrongful verdict may be seen in how much we are prepared to pay for increased accuracy in our trial procedure. Dworkin's moral costs approach, as Bayles has rightly noted, 'is still an instrumentalist one. Legal procedure is simply a means to achieving proper outcomes,'[119] where what is 'proper' includes the avoidance of moral harm.

But the importance of avoiding injustice can be given an internal construal, by taking the viewpoint of the fact-finder. How much importance she attaches to avoiding injustice is manifested in the caution she exercises in the process of deliberating on the facts and verdict. Justice *in* fact-finding requires that she treats the accused with due respect and concern in the course of her deliberation.[120] It is an ethical failure on her part to make a finding adverse to the accused without the degree of caution commensurate with the seriousness of (i) the allegation that

[115] H J McCloskey, 'The Complexity of the Concepts of Punishment' (1962) 37 *Philosophy* 307, 319–320.

[116] A P Simester and W J Brookbanks, *Principles of Criminal Law* (2nd edn, Wellington: Brookers, 2002) 4: noting sometimes 'offenders are discharged without receiving any sentence for their wrongdoing'.

[117] Dworkin (n 74) 93.

[118] ibid 95–96.

[119] Michael Bayles, 'Principles for Legal Procedure' (1986) 5 Law and Philosophy 33, 48, repeated (but not verbatim) in his *Procedural Justice—Allocating to Individuals* (Dordrecht: Kluwer, 1990) 125.

[120] For an example of such treatment, but of a civil party: *Bater v Bater* [1951] P 35, 36.

has been made against him and (ii) the consequences for him in her acceptance of the allegation.[121] In *R (N) v Mental Health Review Tribunal*,[122] the English Court of Appeal made it very clear that both of these factors must be taken into account in applying the civil standard of proof. In principle, they should also be relevant in criminal cases.

The seriousness of an allegation will be as evident to the judge as to the jury. But the same cannot be said of the seriousness of the consequences if the allegation is accepted. Jurors would not know exactly what legal sanction is likely to follow if they return a positive verdict. Although it is possible that they might learn something of the consequences from the judge's instruction or from counsel's submission, there is no general requirement that they be told. Nevertheless, the jury should have some general idea of how serious the consequences are likely to be: no legal expertise is needed to know that punishment is very light for petty shoplifting whereas a conviction for sexual abuse will be followed by a lengthy imprisonment. Grove speaks with first-hand authority as he reflects on his jury service in a kidnapping case:[123]

> Jurors are meant to concentrate on their verdicts, not speculate on sentences. *But of course they do and they would scarcely be human if they did not*... I wondered how we would all be feeling were ours a murder case and capital punishment still in force.

2.2.5 *Theoretical and practical reasoning in trial deliberation*

Consider this contrasting pair of examples. You are thinking of employing someone to look after your children. It comes to your attention that the candidate you have in mind was previously suspected of having molested a minor. The police could not find strong enough evidence to charge her in court. Should you still hire her? That is a practical question about what you should do. Is the allegation true? That is a theoretical question about what you should believe. You can know what to do even if you cannot make up your mind what to believe. The evidence strikes you as insufficient to justify believing that she had, in fact, molested a child. But you are entitled to err on the safe side and protect your children from the risk of possible harm. You may turn her away, exercising your right to choose whom to hire. You do not owe the candidate the same obligations that you would owe her if you were a juror having to decide whether she did molest the child in the alleged previous incident. It would not do for the jury to declare her guilty on mere suspicion. To convict the accused of a crime is not a practical matter of

[121] What varies is the degree of caution, not truth. Contrast Robert S Summers, 'Formal Legal Truth and Substantive Truth in Judicial Fact-Finding—Their Justified Divergence in Some Particular Cases' (1999) 18 Law and Philosophy 497, 506: 'truth varies with standards of proof, and standards of proof vary with what is at stake'.

[122] *R (N) v Mental Health Review Tribunal* (n 7) 497–500.

[123] cf Trevor Grove, *The Juryman's Tale* (London: Bloomsbury, 1998) 150. Emphasis added.

risk management.[124] It is, in part, to *assert* that she had committed the crime. More than that, it is to *condemn* her action, to express deep moral disapproval of the way she had behaved.[125] To find that she is guilty is also to *declare* that she is guilty for the purposes of imposing punishment. She suffers injustice on multiple counts if she is wrongly convicted. Being innocent, she does not deserve to be blamed for the alleged action, she does not deserve the court's reproach, and she does not deserve to be punished.

While trial deliberation is not wholly an enterprise of risk management, it has necessarily a practical element. Both theoretical reasoning and practical reasoning are engaged. Deliberation is practical in the sense that it aims at a decision on *what to do*: should we *declare* the defendant guilty or liable? We know that our finding of guilt or liability will likely result in legal sanctions befalling her. The deliberation is theoretical in the sense that it addresses questions about *what to believe*, and therefore what to *assert* about the facts of the case. The fact-finder must consider, for example, whether the witnesses are trustworthy and whether the contested allegations are true. The practical aspect of trial deliberation is dependent on the theoretical aspect because, in general, the fact-finder must decide what verdict to declare on the basis of her beliefs about the facts of the case.

Conversely, the practical aspect impinges on the theoretical aspect by affecting the amount of justification needed for judging as true, and thus believing, a contested proposition of fact. This claim concerns the role of practical interests in the formation of epistemically rational beliefs. It has nothing to do with cases of practically motivated beliefs which are epistemically irrational. A person may have pragmatic reason for wanting to believe something. It may be pragmatically rational for a mother to practise self-deception and believe, against the evidence, that her son is innocent of a crime if, by doing so, she is relieved of great emotional pain. All things considered, she is perhaps better off that way. Still, it is epistemically irrational for her to believe that her son is innocent given the

[124] This is not to say that the law and legal process are never in the business of risk management. Preventive detention under legislations such as the Singapore Internal Security Act (Cap 143, 1985 Rev Ed, which was invoked recently against suspected militant extremists: 'Self-radicalised Law Grad, 4 JI Militants Held', *The Straits Times*, June 9, 2007) is meant as a pre-emptive measure, to avoid the risk of anticipated harm. But the point is precisely that such a detention is not authorized by a trial. Other, more insidious, forms of legal risk management exist. One example is the introduction of the device of Anti-Social Behaviour Order in the United Kingdom, criticized by A P Simester and Andrew von Hirsch, 'Regulating Offensive Conduct through Two-Step Prohibitions' in Andrew von Hirsch and A P Simester (eds), *Incivilities: Regulating Offensive Behaviour* (Oxford: Hart, 2006) ch 7. Another example is the criminalizing of some activity which is not in itself wrong but which indicates that some wrong has probably occurred: Frederick Schauer and Richard Zeckhauser, 'Regulation by Generalization' (2007) 1 *Regulation and Governance* 68.

[125] Duff (n 73) 108. Also Brett (n 111) 36: 'A judgment of conviction for a crime... imports a condemnation for moral fault'; and, correspondingly, ibid 205: 'the overriding principle [is] that we must be able to blame the defendant for what he did if we are to convict him'.

weight of evidence against it.[126] That believing in her son's innocence will bring much-needed solace is not an epistemic reason for believing that her son is innocent; it is not a consideration that makes the belief more likely to be true.[127]

To return to the divergence of judicial views noted earlier, it is unlikely that either Lord Diplock or Chief Baron Pollock were really saying that the court need not believe in the positive findings it makes. When they implied that fact-finding involves a calculation of risk of the sort people are generally familiar with, they were probably alluding to the fact that we draw inferences, form factual judgments, and claim knowledge all the time in everyday affairs, and that, to do these, it is only common sense not to look for logical demonstration but to demand of the evidence a degree of cogency that suits what is at stake and the objects and purposes of our enquiries.[128] The same may generally be said of trial deliberation. At a trial, the decision to find positively that p on the ground that it is true requires an evaluation of the sufficiency of evidence, which, for the finding to be justified, must be sensitive to the import and consequences of doing so. Importantly, the import and consequences must be reached through empathy with the person who stands to be affected by the finding. The instruction to imagine how one would decide a matter of great importance to oneself is a reminder of how important the verdict is to the person who stands to be affected by it. Evidence of a factual proposition is always logically inconclusive in that it does not entail the truth of the proposition. However strong the evidence seems to be, and however strongly we believe in the truth of that which the evidence supports, we have, in every case, to concede that our belief might be false. But not every logical possibility of falsehood should deter a positive finding.[129] We have to decide whether a possibility should be taken as real or dismissed as unworthy of consideration, posing no genuine obstacle to a claim of knowledge, given what is at stake. As Carr says:[130]

[126] The conflict between practical and epistemic rationality is noted in Richard Foley, *The Theory of Epistemic Rationality* (Cambridge, Massachusetts: Harvard UP, 1987) at 211.

[127] Gilbert Harman, *Reasoning, Meaning and Mind* (Oxford: Clarendon Press, 1999) 102. For further discussion on the relation between theoretical and practical reasoning, see by the same author, 'Practical Aspects of Theoretical Reasoning' in Alfred R Mele and Piers Rawling (eds), *The Oxford Handbook of Rationality* (OUP, 2004) ch 3, 45–56, and 'Internal Critique: A Logic is Not a Theory of Reasoning and A Theory of Reasoning is Not a Logic' in Dov M Gabbay and Hans Jurgen Ohlbach (eds), *Studies in Logic and Practical Reasoning*, vol 1 (Amsterdam: Elsevier Science, 2002) 171.

[128] It was from this insight that 'common sense' philosophers started propounding the concepts of 'moral certainty' and 'proof beyond reasonable doubt' in the seventeenth century: Shapiro (n 61) especially 28; Ronald E Beanblossom and Keith Lehrer (eds), *Thomas Reid's Inquiry and Essays* (Indianapolis: Hackett Publishing, 1983) 252–253, 270.

[129] As courts like to say, the law deals only with 'real doubt' (*Brown v R* (1913) 17 CLR 570, 596), not doubts which are 'imaginary or frivolous' (*R v Lifchus* (n 31) 744–5). For further discussion: Chapter 3, Part 3.2.

[130] Carr (n 89) 120.

> [W]e *have* to make up our minds about matters for which the evidence one way or the other is logically inconclusive, and the question of just *how* inconclusive our standards for warranted firm belief *can afford to be* must rest on the kind of risks that are taken by our acquiring those firm beliefs.

These intuitive ideas have received serious attention from philosophers recently and it is worthwhile to explore their arguments at some length.

2.2.6 Scepticism

Epistemic contextualism is motivated by the challenge of scepticism. Radical scepticism invokes hypothetical scenarios of which this is a famous example: suppose it is possible to keep alive a brain in a vat. Through electro-chemical stimulation, the brain-in-a-vat experiences an external world exactly as a normal person would. If all of the phenomenal evidence I have of an external world is consistent with the fact that I am just a brain-in-a-vat, how do I know that I am not a brain-in-a-vat? It would seem that I cannot rule out this possibility. And if I cannot rule out this possibility, then I do not really know that I am not a brain-in-a-vat. If I am a bodiless-brain-in-a-vat, I do not have hands. If I do not know that I am not a brain-in-a-vat, it would seem to follow that I do not know that I have a pair of hands. Just as I cannot rule out the possibility that I am just a brain-in-a-vat, I cannot rule out the possibility that my hands do not really exist. If radical scepticism is right, we hardly know anything at all, not even such mundane facts as that I have a pair of hands. But surely I know that I have hands, and indeed much else besides.

This version of scepticism is 'global' in the sense that the totality of our beliefs is called into question by the possibility that all the evidence that we have or could have that we are not brains-in-a-vat is compatible with our being brains-in-a-vat. Suppose a limited case of scepticism, where only a specific belief is called into question.[131] The moderate sceptical claim is that the kind of evidence that you happen to have for that particular belief does not rule out the possibility that it is false. (The radical sceptic goes much further. She claims that the possibility of your belief being false cannot be rejected on the basis of *any* evidence.)[132] This is a well-known example of a moderate sceptical hypothesis.[133] You are at a zoo, standing in front of an enclosure with a sign indicating that the animal on display is a zebra. You see that the animal, standing a distance away, looks exactly like a zebra: it is of the right size, has black and white strips, and so forth. You claim to

[131] David Annis, 'A Contextualist Theory of Epistemic Justification' (1978) 15 *American Philosophical Quarterly* 213, 214.

[132] Stewart Cohen, 'How to be a Fallibilist' (1988) 2 *Philosophical Perspectives: Epistemology* 91, 111.

[133] This example was invented by Fred I Dretske, 'Epistemic Operators' (1970) 67 *J of Philosophy* 1007, 1015–1016.

know that the animal is a zebra. Denote this as follows, taking p as the proposition that the animal you see is a zebra:

(1) Kp

You also know that if the animal on display is a zebra, it cannot be some other kind of animal, say a mule. Knowledge that it is a zebra (p) entails knowledge that it is not a mule. Thus letting q stand for the proposition that the animal on display is not a mule:

(2) $K(p \rightarrow q)$

Since you know that the animal is a zebra, on the so-called principle of closure,[134] it follows from (1) and (2) that you know that the animal is not a mule:

(3) $[Kp \,\&\, K(p \rightarrow q)] \rightarrow Kq$

But the sceptic asks: how do you know that the animal is not, in reality, a mule painted with black and white strips and otherwise so cleverly disguised that anyone standing where you are would think that it is a zebra? Even though this is very unlikely to be the case, it cannot be ruled out completely. You cannot be absolutely certain that the animal is not actually a mule: for all you know, that could be true. Under sceptical pressure, you are forced to concede that you do not really *know* that the animal is not a mule, retreating to the weaker stance that you only have good reasons to *believe* that it is *improbable* that the animal is a mule:

(4) $\neg Kq$

But I know that the animal is a zebra only if I know that it is not a mule. Since I do not know that it is not a mule, then, following from (2) and (4), by *modus tollens*, I do not know that it is a zebra after all:

(2) $K(p \rightarrow q)$
(4) $\neg Kq$
Therefore (5) $\neg Kp$

We end up denying a piece of ordinary knowledge; the conclusion in (5) contradicts (1). The sceptic denies (1): she denies that we know that the animal is a zebra. But if the sceptic is right, we cannot truthfully claim to know many of the things that we ordinarily claim to know, and we speak falsely on the many occasions in our everyday lives when we purport to have knowledge. Some philosophers see

[134] According to which, knowledge is closed under known entailments: if you know p and you also know that p entails q, then you know q.

the way out in denying the closure principle (3) instead.[135] But that position has relatively little purchase and may be ignored.[136] Epistemic contextualism offers a different way out.

2.2.7 Epistemic contextualism[137]

Contextualism offers this diagnosis of the problem. In the context of a philosophical discussion on scepticism, an extremely high epistemic standard is employed. It seems that absolute certainty is required. Under that standard, you cannot claim to know that the animal is a zebra unless the evidence entails the truth of your belief that it is a zebra. When you are engaged with the sceptic, it is true to deny (1). But in an ordinary context, the epistemic standard is very much lower. S's epistemic position with respect to p need not be as strong as is required by the sceptic. You can claim to know that the animal is a zebra even where your evidence does not rule out all conceivable possibilities of error. There are different interpretations of epistemic strength. On one conception of epistemic strength, your evidence is strong enough where, roughly speaking, alternative hypotheses, such as the one about the animal being a painted mule, are just too fanciful to be taken as relevant or as live possibilities. It is true, in the context of an ordinary conversation, to assert (1) (that you know that the animal is a zebra).

The basis of epistemic contextualism is semantic.[138] What proposition is expressed by the sentence 'S knows that p' (or, to put it differently, what this sentence means or its 'semantic content') depends on the context in which the sentence is used. Suppose the question is whether S knows a particular proposition of fact (S knows that p) at a particular time (t) and in a particular world (w). Referring to S at t and in w, one person (A) may say that S knows that p whereas another person (B) may say that S does not know that p. Contextualism allows that A's claim and B's denial that S knows p may both be true. This possibility arises because sentences employing the word 'know' (and cognate terms) may

[135] Seminal discussions include Dretske (n 133) and Robert Nozick, *Philosophical Explanations* (Oxford: Clarendon, 1981) 204–211.

[136] eg Richard Feldman, 'Skeptical Problems, Contextualist Solutions' (2001) 103 *Philosophical Studies* 61, 64 says denial of the closure principle is 'among the least plausible ideas to gain currency in epistemology in recent years'.

[137] For an introduction to (the problems in) epistemological contextualism, see Keith DeRose, 'Contextualism: An Explanation and Defense' in John Greco and Ernest Sosa (eds), *The Blackwell Guide to Epistemology* (Oxford: Blackwell, 1999) ch 8; Michael Brady and Duncan Pritchard, 'Epistemological Contextualism: Problems and Prospects' (2005) 55 *The Philosophical Quarterly* 161; the debate between Earl Conee and Stewart Cohen in 'Is Knowledge Contextual' in Matthias Steup and Ernest Sosa (eds), *Contemporary Debates in Epistemology* (Oxford: Blackwell, 2005) ch 2.

[138] Some critics argue that the contextual constraints on knowledge attribution are conversational rather than semantic: the context affects when it is proper to *say* that 'S knows that p', and not whether it is *true* that 'S knows that p': Keith Lehrer, 'Sensitivity, Indiscernibility and Knowledge' (2000) 10 *Philosophical Issues* 33, 33–34.

have different semantic content, expressing different propositions in the light of the circumstances in which they are uttered.

According to epistemic contextualism, 'know' is indexical. The meaning of the sentence in which the verb is used is sensitive to the context of its usage.[139] Take an uncontroversial example of an indexical, 'I'. A may say: 'I am tired.' B may say: 'I am not tired.' Obviously, it is possible for both statements to be true because 'I' has a different referent in each sentence. Where the sentence is used by A, 'I' means 'A' whereas in B's context of use, it means 'B'. Analogously, in our example where A says 'S knows that p' and B says 'S does not know that p', both statements may be true because 'know' may have different semantic content in each statement. As used by A, 'knows' means 'knows according to the epistemic standard that applies in A's context', whereas, as used by B, 'knows' means 'knows according to the epistemic standard that applies in B's context'.

This supposes that 'know' is gradable. An analogy is often drawn with the adjective 'tall'.[140] What proposition is expressed by a sentence employing 'tall' depends on the context of its utterance. It may be true both for A to say, in the context of a conversation about John's potential to be a jockey, that 'John is tall' and for B to say, in the context of a discussion about John's potential to be a professional basketball player, that 'John is not tall', even though both A and B are referring to the same person at the same time. John is tall according to a standard that applies in one context of description but not tall according to a higher standard that applies in a different context of description: he is tall for a jockey but not tall for a professional basketball player. Similarly, the meaning of the sentence 'S knows that p' is context sensitive. The gradability of the predicate 'know' allows the same sentence employing 'know', when uttered in different contexts, to express different strengths of epistemic relation between S and p. S counts as knowing p in a particular context only if S's epistemic position with respect to p is good enough to satisfy the standard for knowledge that operates in that context. Just as, in our example, contextual differences allow one to say that 'John is tall' and another to say, of the same person at the same time, that 'John is not tall', differences in the context of knowledge attribution may similarly make it true for A to claim that S knows that p and for B to deny that S knows that p even where both A and B are referring to S at t and in w.

If A knows that S knows that p, then A knows that p. Suppose little is at stake for A that p is true (that is, little is at stake for A that S knows that p, and is, as such, a source of knowledge that p). A may properly accept that S knows that p on the evidence that S has. If it matters a lot to a different person, B, whether p is true (that is, it matters a lot to B whether S knows that p, and is a source of

[139] Challenged by Wayne A Davis, 'Are Knowledge Claims Indexical?' (2004) 61 *Erkenntnis* 257–281; Brian Weatherson, 'Questioning Contextualism' in Stephen Hetherington (ed), *Aspects of Knowing—Epistemological Essays* (Amsterdam: Elsevier, 2006) ch 9.

[140] Contrast Jason Stanley, 'On the Linguistic Basis for Contextualism' (2004) 119 *Philosophical Studies* 119, 123–130.

knowledge that p), B may properly deny that S knows that p, given S's evidence. The epistemic standard for knowledge attribution (the epistemic standard according to which a third person (A or B) can truly assign knowledge to the subject (S)) differs according to the practical features that are present or salient to the third person (A or B) in the context in which she deliberates on whether to make that ascription. The higher the epistemic standard, given the context in which the third person is deliberating whether to assign knowledge that p to S, the stronger is the evidence S must have for that person to say that S knows that p, or to put it more generally, the stronger must be S's epistemic position with respect to p. So, holding S's circumstances fixed, it may be true for the knowledge-attributor whose stake is low to say that S knows that p and also true for a different knowledge-attributor whose stake is high to say that S does not know that p. The higher the stake involved in the context in which it is said that S knows, the higher the epistemic standard that the evidence must satisfy. In a philosophical discussion on scepticism, an extremely high epistemic standard is in use. In that setting, it is true to say that I do not know that I am not a brain-in-a-vat. The epistemic standards are much lower and much easier to meet in quotidian contexts. Outside the philosophy classroom, it is surely true to say that I know that I have hands: indeed, to question my knowledge of that fact is hardly intelligible. Cohen describes contextualism as a 'good news, bad news' theory: 'The good news is that we have lots of knowledge...; the bad news is that knowledge... [is] not what [it is] cracked up to be.'[141]

It may help to concretize this discussion with a well-known example given by Cohen to illustrate the intuitive appeal of epistemic contextualism. While this example exploits a clear contrast between a high standard case and a low standard case, he is not suggesting that there are only two possible standards, one high and the other low. Just as there are numerous possibilities of contextual differences, and numerous variations in the seriousness of what is at stake, so there are numerous gradations of epistemic standards.

The airport case[142]

Mary and John are at the L.A. airport contemplating taking a certain flight to New York. They want to know whether the flight has a layover in Chicago. They overhear someone ask a passenger Smith if he knows whether the flight stops in Chicago. Smith looks at the flight itinerary he got from the travel agent and responds, 'Yes I know—it does stop in Chicago.' [It matters little to Smith whether this is true or not.] It turns out that Mary and John have a very important business contact they have to make at the Chicago airport. Mary says, 'How reliable is that itinerary? It could contain a misprint. They could have changed the schedule at the last minute.' Mary and John agree that Smith doesn't really *know* that the plane will stop in Chicago. They decide to check with the airline agent.

[141] Stewart Cohen, 'Contextualism Defended' in Matthias Steup and Ernest Sosa (eds), *Contemporary Debates in Epistemology* (Oxford: Blackwell, 2005) 56, 61–62.

[142] Stewart Cohen, 'Contextualism, Skepticism, and the Structure of Reasons' (1999) 13 *Philosophical Perspectives* 57 at 58, with the words within brackets added.

The point of this example is that the truth value of a knowledge ascription depends on the 'standard of knowledge' that applies in the context of ascription. There are different ways of conceptualizing 'standard of knowledge'. On the internalist analysis advanced by Cohen, the standard is located in epistemic justification:[143] to know that p in a particular context, one's evidence or reasons for believing that p must be strong or good enough for that context.[144]

Wedgwood offers a fuller contextualist account of 'justified belief'.[145] He notes that there are in fact two distinct epistemic goals which require balancing from case to case. They are (i) having an outright belief in p if p is true and (ii) not having an outright belief in p if p is false. ('Outright belief' is another name for the kind of belief called 'categorical' in Chapter 3.) For a rational agent, the greater she values (ii) more than (i), the stronger the justification she will require for believing p outright; and where the justification is not strong enough, she will either suspend judgment on p (that is, neither believe p outright nor disbelieve p outright) or have only a partial degree of belief in p. Any standard of justified belief that she chooses to use is, from the strictly epistemic point of view, equally legitimate. For Wedgwood, practical considerations are not part of the meaning of 'justified belief' but part of the context that determines which proposition is communicated by sentences of the form 'S is justified in believing p'. Such a sentence can express any of a number of propositions about how much justification S has for p. Which of these propositions is expressed depends on the proposition the speaker intends to communicate in uttering that sentence. In uttering the sentence, the speaker may be focusing on the practical situation of someone who might believe that p. This person could be the speaker herself or S or someone else. Call that person X. The proposition the speaker intends to express is one about how much justification S has for p, such that a belief in that proposition could guide a rational believer in X's situation in forming and revising her belief

143 '[J]ustification is a predicate that can be satisfied to varying degrees and that can be satisfied *simpliciter*... [H]ow justified a belief must be in order to be justified *simpliciter* depends on the context. And since justification *simpliciter* is a component of knowledge, ascriptions of knowledge will likewise be context sensitive': Stewart Cohen, 'Contextualism Defended: Comments on Richard Feldman's Skeptical Problems, Contextualist Solutions' (2001) 87 *Philosophical Studies* 87 at 88. Cohen's major pieces in this area include Cohen (n 132) and (n 142). For a briefer version, see his 'Contextualism and Skepticism' (2000) 10 *Philosophical Issues: Skepticism* 94.

144 On Cohen's account, the standard of evidence or reason is determined by the context, such as the interest at stake for, and the salience of error possibilities to, the knowledge attributor. Very roughly, a person knows p in context C only where there is good enough reason to justify her belief that there is no alternative to p that is relevant in C. See Stewart Cohen (n 132) especially at 101–103 (explanation of 'relevance'), and also his: 'Skepticism, 'Relevance, and Relativity' in Brian P McLaughlin (ed), *Dretske and His Critics* (Oxford: Blackwell, 1991) ch 2; and 'Contextualist Solutions to Epistemological Problems: Scepticism, Gettier, and the Lottery' (1998) *Australasian J of Philosophy* 289. There are other interpretations of strength of epistemic position: eg Keith DeRose offers an externalist version in 'Solving the Skeptical Problem' (1995) 104 *The Philosophical Review* 1 and 'Knowledge, Assertion and Lotteries' (1996) *Australasian J of Philosophy* 568.

145 Ralph Wedgwood, 'Contextualism about Justified Belief', forthcoming, draft available from his webpage: <http://users.ox.ac.uk/~mert1230/papers.htm>.

in p. The correct standard of justified belief is the one that is favoured by the correct conception of the practical considerations (such as needs, purposes, and values) that are at stake in X's situation, and the statement 'S is justified in believing p' is true if and only if S's belief in p meets this particular standard.

To modify the airport case, suppose Mary said instead: 'Smith is not justified in believing that the flight will stop in Chicago.' In uttering that sentence, she has in mind her and her husband's common practical situation and not Smith's. Mary's interest in Smith is as a potential informant (or testimonial source of knowledge) on whether the flight will stop in Chicago. The proposition Mary intended to communicate in her statement is one about how much justification Smith has for the proposition that the flight will lay over in Chicago, such that a belief in that proposition could guide a rational believer *in the couple's situation* in forming and revising her belief in that proposition. It is very important to Mary and her husband that Smith is right; a lot is at stake for them. A high standard of justified belief is favoured by a correct conception of their practical situation. Given the weakness of the evidence available to Smith, the justification for believing his testimony (taking it as a source of knowledge) on the Chicago stopover falls below that standard. In the circumstances, Mary's statement that 'Smith is not justified in believing that the flight will stop in Chicago' is true.

2.2.8 Interest-relative accounts of knowledge and justified belief

For some philosophers, such as Jason Stanley[146] and John Hawthorne,[147] practical interests play a part in determining a person's possession of knowledge: as Hawthorne puts it, one's 'practical environment' makes a difference to what one knows.[148] But they disagree that the truth value of a knowledge ascription is context sensitive. It is not the practical interests of the knowledge attributor but those of the subject or those that are salient to her that count; and they count in the sense that they affect her epistemic position. So, in the airport case, whether Smith knows that the flight will stop in Chicago depends in part on what practical interests Smith has in the stopover. Since we have supposed that little is at stake for him, the epistemic standard is low. If his evidence is good enough to satisfy that low standard, then it is true that Smith knows that the plane will land in Chicago. Why then does it seem counter-intuitive to claim it is wrong for Mary to say that Smith does not know this, on the evidence that Smith has, when Mary

[146] Jason Stanley, *Knowledge and Practical Interests* (Oxford: OUP, 2005) ch 5.

[147] John Hawthorne, *Knowledge and Lotteries* (Oxford: Clarendon, 2004) ch 4, making a case for 'sensitive moderate invariantism', sometimes referred to as 'Subject Sensitive Invariantism'. For spirited replies by contextualists: Stewart Cohen, 'Knowledge, Speaker and Subject' (2005) 55 *The Philosophical Quarterly* 199 and 'Knowledge, Assertion, and Practical Reasoning' (2004) 14 *Philosophical Issues: Epistemology* 482; Keith DeRose, 'The Ordinary Language Basis for Contextualism, and the New Invariantism' (2005) 55 *The Philosophical Quarterly* 172 and 'The Problem with Subject-Sensitive Invariantism' (2004) 68 *Philosophy and Phenomenological Research* 346.

[148] Hawthorne (n 147) 176.

has a lot at stake in the layover? According to Hawthorne, this is because of the human psychological 'tendency to overproject our own lack of knowledge to others'.[149] Stanley prefers a different strategy: it seems counter-intuitive only because we naturally recognize that what Mary really cares about is whether Smith would know of the Chicago stopover were he in Mary's practical situation, and the answer to that question is 'no'.[150]

Fantl and McGrath offer a parallel argument for epistemic justification.[151] Whether a person is justified in believing a proposition depends on whether she has good enough evidence to know that proposition; and whether her evidence is good enough to justify her belief will depend on how much is at stake for her in the truth of the proposition.[152] In the airport case, assuming that Mary and Smith have the same evidence of the flight stopping in Chicago, consisting only of the itinerary supplied by Smith's travel agent, Fantl and McGrath would allow the possibility that Smith is justified in believing that the stopover will occur (because he has little at stake in it) and Mary is not (because her stake is much higher).[153] Whether a person is justified in believing a proposition cannot be a matter of evidence alone.[154] It is not necessarily the case that, if two persons have

[149] ibid 163. He offers another argument (ibid 159–160): if Mary were to assert that Smith knows that the plane will stop in Chicago, it would imply that she knows it will stop there. Since, on Hawthorne's interest-relative theory, she does not know that the plane will stop there, she cannot assert that Smith knows it. This argument is criticized by Stanley (n 146) 99 for its failure to explain why Mary *can* assert that Smith does *not* know the fact.

[150] Stanley (n 146) 101–103.

[151] Jeremy Fantl and Matthew McGrath, 'Evidence, Pragmatics, and Justification' (2002) *The Philosophical Review* 67.

[152] Others have similarly suggested that the rational belief that p is sensitive to what is at stake for the subject in p: eg Robert Nozick, *The Nature of Rationality* (Princeton, NJ: Princeton UP, 1993) 96–98; Christopher Hookway, *Scepticism* (London: Routledge, 1990) 139: 'the amount of evidence we require in support of an hypothesis before we can describe it as justified may reflect the degree of support that is required before we can feel that we are acting responsibly when we act upon it. This promises to explain some of the relativities involved in our concept of justified belief: the greater the disaster if our actions fail to achieve their purpose, the more evidence we require before we regard the belief as properly justified; the greater the risks attaching to inaction, the readier we are to act on limited evidence.'

[153] In technical terms, they (n 151) argue for this 'pragmatic necessary condition of epistemic justification': PC: 'S is justified in believing that p only if it is rational for S to prefer as if p', where 'it is rational for S to prefer as if p' means: for any states of affairs A and B, S is rational to prefer A to B, given p, if and only if S is rational to prefer A to B, in fact. In our example, for the states of affairs A (board the flight without seeking further evidence of the Chicago stopover) and B (not board the flight until one has obtained such further evidence), S is rational to prefer A to B, given p (ie prefer the state of the world where she does A and p is true to the state of the world where she does B and p is true), if and only if S is rational to prefer A to B, in fact (given that not much is at stake, it is in fact rational to take the flight without taking the trouble of seeking further evidence). However, if much is at stake, as it is for Mary, it would not be rational in fact to prefer A to B and so S would not be justified in believing p.

[154] Contrast the defence of evidentialism put up by Earl Conee and Richard Feldman, 'Evidentialism' in *Evidentialism—Essays in Epistemology* (Oxford: Clarendon Press, 2004), 296: to know p, one's belief that p must satisfy the justification condition, which they conceive 'along the lines of the legal standard for conviction in criminal cases, proof beyond reasonable doubt'. One must, *inter alia*, have 'strong reason' to believe p. As the authors candidly admit, their account

the same evidence relating to p, one is justified in believing p if and only if the other is too: thus 'evidentialism' is false. The practical context in which p is an issue for the subject plays a necessary role in determining what evidence is strong enough to justify her belief that p.

Weatherson makes a significant modification to the theory of Fantl and McGrath.[155] It is not our state of confidence (or 'degrees of belief') but our belief (or 'belief *tout court*') that is pragmatically sensitive. In the airport case, despite one having more at stake in the matter than the other, Smith and Mary are, if they have the same set of evidence, justified in having the same degree of confidence in the proposition that the flight will land in Chicago. However, given that much less is at stake for Smith than for Mary, the first may be justified in believing the proposition whereas the second is not. On this view, the practical interests of the epistemic agent matters, not to the degree of confidence in a proposition that she is justified in having (a question of epistemology),[156] but to the degree of confidence that is necessary, given her practical context, for it to qualify as a belief in the proposition (a question of the philosophy of mind). Thus Weatherson agrees with Fantl and McGrath, but for different reasons, that evidentialism is false. Evidentialism is false in this sense: it is not the case that if two subjects have the same degree of confidence in p, one must believe *tout court* that p if and only if the other does too.

2.2.9 The ethics of epistemology

The theories surveyed in the last two sections have this in common: they emphasize the relevance of practical interests or stakes. They differ, however, on the person whose interests or stakes are relevant and how those interests or stakes are relevant. For the contextualists, whether it is true for a person (the knowledge-attributor) to say that someone (the subject) knows p is not solely a matter of what evidence the subject has for or against p; it depends also on extra-evidential factors, particularly the practical importance to the knowledge-attributor of that knowledge. For Wedgwood, practical interests affect the truth value of the

'leaves many important questions about the strength of evidence unanswered'; in particular, it 'leaves open exactly how strong those reasons must be'. It is difficult to see how the requisite strength of epistemic justification can be answered in the abstract, free from the context in which knowledge of p is in issue. As David Owens, *Reason Without Freedom—The Problem of Epistemic Normativity* (London: Routledge, 2000) 25 observes: 'A reasonable belief will be forthcoming only when I have sufficient evidence in *p*'s favour to warrant belief in *p*. And how are evidential considerations alone to determine when I have sufficient evidence?' He argues, ibid at 27: '[W]here and when I form a view as to whether *p* is true will be determined by my sense of how important the issue is, what the consequences of having a certain belief on the matter would be and how much of my limited cognitive resources I ought to devote to it before reaching a conclusion.'

155 Brian Weatherson, 'Can We Do Without Pragmatic Encroachment?' (2005) 19 *Philosophical Perspectives* 417, 434–436.

156 Similar comment is made by Conee and Feldman (n 154) 103–104. They are against epistemic contextualism. For them, practical factors do not contribute to whether a person is well enough justified to have knowledge but to her readiness to attribute knowledge.

statement that someone is justified in believing p. The practical interests that count are those of the person who might believe p, the one the maker of the statement is focusing on as she makes the statement. For proponents of interest-relative accounts, whether the subject knows p or is justified in believing p depends on the practical interests of the subject herself. Weatherson argues that the stakes determine the degree of confidence in p that the subject must have for her state of confidence in p to amount to the belief *tout court* that p.

Despite these differences, all sides will often reach the same result in cases of self-attribution of knowledge or justified belief,[157] where it is one's own practical situation that one is mindful of. In such cases, I am both the knowledge-attributor and the subject; the question is not 'Is someone else justified in believing p?' but 'Am I justified in believing p?' Epistemic contextualism and the interest-relative accounts are agreed that, in such cases, the epistemic standard varies with what is at stake for me in the truth of p. Or, following Weatherson, one justifiably believes that p only where one is justified in having a degree of confidence in p that is sufficiently strong, and whether it is sufficiently strong is determined by one's practical situation.

The previous chapter defended this rule of fact-finding:

BAF*: The fact-finder must find that p only if (i) one would be *justified* in believing *sufficiently strongly* that p if one were to take into account only the admitted evidence, ignore any inadmissible evidence to which one might have been exposed, and avoid reliance on any line of evidential reasoning that the law might forbid in the case at hand, and (ii) if one found that p, one would find that p at least in part because one would be justified in believing that p under (i).

As we have just seen, different writers assign different roles to practical interests in their respective accounts of knowledge or justified belief. The most straightforward account of the impact of practical interests in BAF* is to claim that the greater the stakes, the stronger the categorical belief needed for finding that p. What is meant by the strength of categorical belief was explored in Chapter 3. Another strategy is to locate the relevance of stakes in setting the justification needed for believing categorically that p. This may be done by insisting that the higher the stakes, the more it will take by way of evidence to rule out the relevant alternative hypotheses.[158] It matters not for our purposes whether practical

[157] As noted, eg by Keith DeRose, 'The Problem with Subject-Sensitive Invariantism' (2004) 68 *Philosophy and Phenomenological Research* 346, 347.

[158] On the more popular contextualist interpretation of the relevant alternatives theory of knowledge, the context determines the range of alternatives that are relevant. The view taken above takes the second contextualist approach noted by Feldman in this passage: 'According to the relevant alternatives theory, a person knows a proposition to be true if and only if the person can rule out all relevant alternatives to the proposition. Since what counts as all the relevant alternatives to a proposition can vary with context, what the person can correctly be said to know varies with context. It's also possible to blame the context sensitivity on the phrase "rule out". It may be that considerations that are sufficient to rule out an alternative in one context do not count as sufficient

interests affect the standard of epistemic justification or the necessary strength of belief; they probably affect both. We will speak loosely in the discussion that follows and use 'epistemic standard' as a term that is neutral on all these possible readings. The important lesson, on any of these readings, is simply this: practical interests bear on the standard of caution in fact-finding.

There is, however, a problem that cannot be so conveniently left aside. Recall the argument just made: in cases where I am ascribing to myself knowledge of p or justified belief in p, the relevant standard varies with what is at stake for me in the truth of p. Even if this argument is right, it does not carry us far enough. It at best establishes that, in finding that p, for example, that the defendant is guilty, the fact-finder must take into account *her own* practical interests in the truth of p. But does the fact-finder have any personal practical interests in the truth of p? It is the defendant who clearly has a lot at stake. Another problem with applying epistemic contextualism and interest-relativity to trial deliberation is that they tend to focus on prudential interests. The key element of the context exploited in the airport case was self-interest: Mary has much to lose if the flight does not stop over in Chicago. In contrast to that example, it is not immediately obvious what prudential interests the fact-finder has in getting the facts rights. However, as a number of writers have noted, we do sometimes peg the relevant standard to the practical situation of someone else, and none of the theories we have examined precludes the trier of fact from adopting as her own the interests of the persons whose case is before her.[159] But why should she care about those persons?

The answer is that justice requires it. This can be seen only when we adopt the perspective of the fact-finder as a moral agent, and consider the motivation and affective attitude that characterizes a virtuous judge of fact. The *self-interested* fact-finder may have some practical interests in getting the truth: the realization that one has sent an innocent person to jail is likely to be painful to a juror and errors cannot be good for the career and reputation of the judge assigned to conduct bench trials. What motivates the *virtuous* trier of fact is an ethical interest in being correct. A verdict has practical significance and consequences. For example, it may authorize or potentially lead to official imposition of state-enforced sanction on the defendant.[160] Further, the allegations the court is asked to accept will often speak very badly of the one against whom they are made. On one view, the justice of an action depends on whether it exhibits or reflects

to rule it out in another' (Richard Feldman, 'Skeptical Problems, Contextualist Solutions' (2001) 103 *Philosophical Studies* 61, 65).

[159] Related to the present point, see Keith DeRose, 'The Problem with Subject-Sensitive Invariantism' (2004) 68 *Philosophy and Phenomenological Research* 346, 349: 'There's nothing in contextualism to prevent a speaker's context from selecting epistemic standards appropriate to the subject's context, even when the subject being discussed is no party to the speaker's conversation.'

[160] Stephen (n 56) 26: 'an English criminal trial may be considered as the discussion of the question: shall we grant the prosecutor's demand that the prisoner may be punished?'

a motivation of empathic care.[161] It is easiest to see what this involves in the setting of a personal relationship. Suppose someone tells you that your friend has behaved deplorably on some occasion. If the allegation goes against your close understanding of your friend's character, you have an *epistemic* reason to disbelieve (or at least not believe) the allegation. Quite apart from this, your sense of loyalty may call for you to trust your friend and to stand by her. It may be argued that the norms of friendship provide you *ethical* reasons to be sceptical of the allegation or even to judge it false.[162] But these ethical reasons cannot be conclusive without damaging epistemic rationality; you are blinded by your loyalty if it commits you, in advance, *never* to judge as true anything bad about your friend however the evidence stacks up against her. While ethical norms may conflict with epistemic norms,[163] the two do not always clash head-on. Ethical considerations may infiltrate, rather than oppose, one's epistemic judgments. Your friendship with the person whose reputation is being disparaged could be seen as constituting a feature of the context which sets your epistemic standard; it should need stronger evidence and argument to persuade you of the truth of an allegation made against your friend than if it was made against a complete stranger. But so far as you stray from the epistemic standard of disinterested objectivity, and apply one corrupted by partiality, is it still not the case that you are epistemically irrational or irresponsible?[164]

The argument can be turned around. Roughly speaking, it is not that there are unique moral reasons to be epistemically partial when judging the truth of unsavoury statements made about our friends; rather, we ought, in this regard, to treat strangers (more) like friends. We can take that step only by respecting the common humanity that binds us to all others. A sharpened sense of empathy should make us see that the harm of a false accusation is as real when suffered by a stranger as when suffered by someone close to us. This generalization allows the development of a relational theory of justice with an affective characteristic. Justice is about caring for another as guided from her standpoint, establishing a relationship that is sensitive to her feelings, needs, and interests. In the domain of private morality, I am unjust to you when my action towards you is not motivated by sufficient concern about your feelings and welfare. In the public sphere, an institution treats a citizen unjustly when it deals with her in a disrespectful or

[161] On the relation between justice and empathic care: Michael Slote, *The Ethics of Care and Empathy* (London: Routledge, 2007) chs 1 and 4, 'Autonomy and Empathy' (2004) 21 *Social Philosophy and Policy* 293, and 'The Justice of Caring' (1998) 15 *Social Philosophy and Policy* 171; Scott D Gelfand, 'The Ethics of Care and (Capital) Punishment (2004) Law and Philosophy 593; Susan Moller Okin, 'Reason and Feeling in Thinking About Justice' (1989) 99 *Ethics* 229.

[162] Damian Cox and Michael Levine, 'Believing Badly' (2004) 33 *Philosophical Papers* 209, 222, 223.

[163] The possibility of this conflict is noted by Conee and Feldman (n 154) 2, 101–102, 112. Simon Keller goes so far as to argue that friendship sometimes requires epistemic irresponsibility: 'Friendship and Belief' (2004) 33 *Philosophical Papers* 329.

[164] For such a view, see Keller (n 163); Sarah Stroud, 'Epistemic Partiality in Friendship' (2006) 116 *Ethics* 498.

disinterested fashion. At a trial, the fact-finder knows that her findings will have adverse effects. Justice requires her to discharge her function with empathic care. She needs to see things from the perspective of the one who stands to be harmed by the finding she proposes to make and appreciate the importance to him that she gets it right. Caring for him means caring to know the truth about his case.[165] The fact-finder must be conscious of the insult the person can rightly feel if she is dismissive of his plea or hasty in accepting an allegation that casts him in disrepute. The more there is at stake for him in a verdict, the stronger the belief or justification that is required to give that verdict. A lack of respect and concern for the person is expressed in the want of caution in reaching findings adverse to him; it is manifested in the inadequacy of evidence to meet the epistemic standard that ought to apply, given the degree of harm he is likely to suffer in or from those findings.

If a person is aware that the action that will follow her epistemic judgment will harm others, she owes it to those others to ensure that her belief meets an epistemic standard that is suitably demanding. The more serious the harm is, the higher the epistemic standard she must apply. A scientist needs more by way of evidence to justify her belief and certification that an experimental infant vaccine is safe than to justify her belief and certification that a newly invented rat poison is effective.[166] Similar considerations apply in trial deliberation. The fact-finder must not reach factual conclusions as easily at a trial as she does in everyday affairs where little is at stake in her beliefs and assertions. As Austin once remarked, 'the presence of the hat [in the hall], which would serve as proof of it's owner's presence [at home] in many circumstances, could only through laxity be adduced as a proof in a court of law'.[167] Indeed, there is a *continuum* of epistemic standards, and not just one standard that is high and another that is low, in and outside of the forensic setting. Justice demands that the epistemic standard at a

[165] See generally Linda Zagzebski, 'Epistemic Value and the Primacy of What We Care About' (2004) 33 *Philosophical Papers* 353 (arguing that 'epistemic values arise only from something we care about. It is caring that gives rise to the demand to be epistemically conscientious': ibid 376–377).

[166] Annis (n 131) 215 ('The importance (value or utility) attached to the outcome of accepting *h* when it is false or rejecting *h* when it is true is a component of the issue-context. Suppose the issue is whether a certain drug will help cure a disease in humans without harmful effects. In such a situation we are much more demanding than if the question were whether it would help in the case of animals'); Richard Rudner, 'The Scientist *Qua* Scientist Makes Value Judgments' (1953) 20 *Philosophy of Science* 1, 2: 'since no scientific hypothesis is ever completely verified, in accepting a hypothesis the scientist must make the decision that the evidence is *sufficiently* strong or that the probability is *sufficiently* high to warrant the acceptance of the hypothesis. Obviously our decision regarding the evidence and respecting how strong is "strong enough", is going to be a function of the *importance*, in the typically ethical sense, of making a mistake in accepting or rejecting the hypothesis.' Ibid 3: 'how great a risk one is willing to take of being wrong in accepting or rejecting the hypothesis will depend upon how seriously in the typically ethical sense one views the consequences of making a mistake.'

[167] J L Austin, 'Other Minds' in J O Urmson and G J Warnock (eds), *J L Austin, Philosophical Papers* (3rd edn, Oxford: OUP, 1979) 76, 108.

trial varies with the gravity of the particular case. The more serious is the allegation or the larger the stake, the greater the caution that must be exercised in deliberation. This is a requirement of justice as empathic care in the relationship between the judge and the party over whom she has authority. For some, the caring attitude in terms of which justice is presently conceived is a basic moral virtue and is intrinsically good. For others, it is the relationship cultivated by empathic concern that is of value.[168] The lesson to be learnt, on either view, is the meaning and importance of being a virtuous judge of facts. A virtuous judge appreciates the moral weight of her task; she reaches her verdict against a person, not with reckless disregard, but with sensitivity to the harm she is bringing onto him and respect for his dignity.[169] Justice as care is also related to an important purpose of the trial. The court aims to arrive at findings in a manner which will entitle it to the moral claim that they should be accepted, with all the consequences that follow. The court is not entitled to this claim if it reaches its findings in a cavalier manner, as is evident when conclusions are drawn with manifest insufficiency of caution.

The greater is the stake in being correct on p, the greater the caution that must be exercised in finding that p; the greater the caution that must be exercised, the higher the epistemic standard that must apply. To insist on the practice of greater caution is to insist on the application of a higher standard of proof. The party against whom an adverse finding is made on evidence that is manifestly inadequate, relative to the standard of caution that is appropriate, is entitled to feel that the court did not value him sufficiently and did not care enough about his interests. He has suffered injustice, understood, following Lucas, as 'an affront which belittles the worth of the man who suffers it'.[170] A trial that is unjust has failed in its purpose, as an enterprise aimed at securing the moral authority to insist that its decision ought to be accepted. Although the phrase 'moral certainty' has gone out of fashion, it is particularly apt as an expression of the legal standard of proof. The poignancy of the phrase is lost once its message is reduced only to the mundane observation that absolute or logical certainty is not required for a criminal conviction.[171] On

[168] See the debate between Michael Slote, 'Caring Versus the Philosophers' (1999) *Yearbook of the Philosophy of Education*, available at: <http://www.ed.uiuc.edu/EPS/PES-Yearbook/1999/slote.asp> (29 August 2005) and Nel Noddings, 'Two Concepts of Caring' (1999) Yearbook of the Philosophy of Education, available at: <http://www.ed.uiuc.edu/EPS/PES-Yearbook/1999/noddings.asp> (29 August 2005).

[169] A related message is conveyed by Whitman in his historical study of the criminal standard of proof. He observes that 'we have forgotten how morally fearsome the act of judging is'. A conviction should only be made 'in a spirit of humility, of duteousness, of fear and trembling about our own moral standing'. 'Instructing jurors forcefully that their decision is "a *moral* one" about the fate of a fellow human being, is, in the last analysis, the only meaningful way to be faithful to the original spirit of "reasonable doubt".' James Q Whitman, 'The Origins of "Reasonable Doubt"' (March 1, 2005). *Yale Law School. Yale Law School Faculty Scholarship Series*. Paper 1. <http://lsr.nellco.org/yale/fss/papers/1>, Part IX, Conclusion. To appear in his forthcoming book: *The Origins of Reasonable Doubt: Theological Roots of the Criminal Trial* (Yale UP).

[170] J R Lucas, *On Justice* (Oxford: Clarendon Press, 1980) 7.

[171] The 'original point of speaking of a probability as a "moral" or "practical" certainty... is that it is strong enough to *act* on without hedging one's bets in view of the theoretical possibility of error': Robert Merrihew Adams, *Leibniz—Determinist, Theist, Idealist* (New York: OUP, 1994)

a richer, if unhistorical,[172] reading of the phrase, it states the imperative of moral justification in a conviction; the court must show due care for the defendant by employing an epistemic standard that is sufficiently high relative to what is at stake for him in its findings.

The present conception of justice is internal to trial deliberation. It suggests a sense in which ethics operate within epistemology.[173] Take a counter-example. Jurors are known to act in disregard of the truth and to acquit the defendant because they find the law under which he is charged so objectionable that they refuse to enforce it. Some consider such action morally and politically justified.[174] But the arguments relied upon in this connection are often based on considerations unrelated to epistemological concerns. In contrast, the claim advanced in this chapter, as indeed in this book as a whole, is that the justice of a finding of fact requires that it be both epistemically and morally justified. These two elements do not oppose one another. They are mutually reinforcing strands, intertwining to form a common thread of justification.

2.2.10 A variant standard of proof

The discussion has concentrated on philosophy thus far. It will now be brought to the legal materials. The received view is that there are two standards of proof and what sets them apart is that proof of guilt must be established to a higher probability than proof of a civil claim.[175] If, as is suggested, the standard of proof has to comport with the seriousness of the factual allegation and of the consequences in accepting it as true, the received view is coherent only if a criminal conviction is, of its nature, necessarily more serious than a finding of civil liability.

Characteristically, civil liability lacks the stigma of a criminal conviction. A criminal conviction blames the defendant for his action whereas a civil judgment

198. According to James Franklin, *The Science of Conjecture—Evidence and Probability Before Pascal* (Baltimore, Maryland: John Hopkins UP, 2001) 69, the term 'moral certainty' was first used around 1400 by Jean Gerson with reference to the principle expressed by Aristotle in *Nicomachean Ethics* that one should only demand as much precision as the nature of the subject admits.

[172] Larry Laudan, 'Is Reasonable Doubt Reasonable?' (2003) 9 Legal Theory 295, 297 notes that, during the Enlightenment, Locke and Wilkins 'dubbed this sort of certainty "moral" not because it had anything to do with ethics and morality but to contrast it with the "mathematical" certainty traditionally associated with a rigorous demonstration'.

[173] This location of ethics within epistemology is different from the general debate on the 'ethics of belief' first started by W K Clifford and William James: see generally the collection of essays in Gerald D McCarthy (ed), *The Ethics of Belief Debate* (Atlanta, Georgia: American Academy of Religion, 1986). The distinction and relationship between ethical and epistemic appraisals are analysed by Susan Haack, '"The Ethics of Belief" Reconsidered' in Lewis Hahn (ed), *The Philosophy of R M Chisholm* (La Salle: Open Court, 1997) ch 5.

[174] eg Paul Butler, 'Racially Based Jury Nullification: Black Power in the Criminal Justice System' (1995) 105 Yale LJ 677. Cf Lord Justice Auld, *Review of the Criminal Courts of England and Wales* (London: HMSO, 2001) 173–176.

[175] *Miller v Minister of Pensions* (n 9) 374; *Bater v Bater* (n 120) 37; *Hornal v Neuberger Products Ltd* [1957] 1 QB 247, 258; *Davis v Davis* [1950] P 125, 127–8.

aims at compensation for loss.[176] Civil liability does not imply blameworthiness. Economists are fond of treating damages as prices or 'money extracted for doing what is permitted'.[177] In some civil ('hard') cases, findings of fact are made against defendants whom we feel deserve sympathy rather than blame. It is also true that a criminal conviction usually carries graver consequences than a civil verdict; being imprisoned is worse than having to pay compensation (assuming not too great a disparity in the length of imprisonment and the size of compensation).

However, to justify a *categorical* distinction in the criminal and civil standards of proof, it has to be shown that *every* criminal case is more serious than *any* civil case. This is difficult to accept. First, a civil finding may speak just as badly of a party as may a criminal verdict of an accused;[178] indeed, sometimes it speaks worse: to be found to have intentionally killed someone, and therefore liable for the tort of battery,[179] is far more serious than to be found guilty of petty shop-lifting. In civil litigation, it is common for allegations to be made against the defendant of action that is more or less blameworthy; examples come easily to mind: unconscionable conduct, exploitation, coercion, duress, fraud, bad faith, discriminatory practices, illegal transactions, 'turning a blind eye', negligence, and so forth.

Secondly, a civil trial may share the expressive function of a criminal prosecution. This is clearly the case where a civil action is based on an alleged crime committed by the defendant.[180] In *Mullan v Anderson*,[181] the wife and children of the man allegedly killed by the defender brought a civil action against him for damages. The judges noted that while the action did not have 'criminal consequences', it had 'criminal connotations' for 'the pursuers [were] seeking to establish that the defender murdered the deceased'. An equally clear case is the award of exemplary or punitive damages; such damages are meant as punishment, meted out to mark the court's disapproval of the defendant's conduct.[182] The censure thus conveyed is not much different from the censure communicated in an imposition of a criminal fine. Even in ordinary private law actions, where no crime is alleged and no punitive damages sought, it is not uncommon to find judges rebuking parties for their bad behaviour.

[176] On the blame element in a conviction, see Andrew von Hirsch, *Censure and Sanctions* (Oxford: Clarendon, 1993). On the difference between the expressive function of a conviction and a civil verdict, see Chapter 1, Part 2.5.5.

[177] Robert Cooter, 'Prices and Sanctions' (1984) 84 Columbia L Rev 1523, 1523.

[178] It has been noted that a civil verdict does not necessarily have less 'moral force' than a criminal verdict: Anonymous, 'Some Rules of Evidence—Reasonable Doubt in Civil and Criminal Cases' (1876) 10 American Law Review 642, 648–649.

[179] eg *Halford v Brookes*, The Times, 3 October 1991, [1992] PIQR P175; *Mullan v Anderson* (n 7).

[180] On 'civil prosecution' and the need for safeguards in such cases: Jane Stapleton, 'Civil Prosecutions—Part 1: Double Jeopardy and Abuse of Process' (1999) 7 Torts LJ 244 and 'Civil Prosecutions—Part 2: Civil Claims for Killing and Rape' (2000) 8 Torts LJ 15.

[181] (n 7) 839, 847.

[182] *Rookes v Barnard* [1964] AC 1129, 1228; *W v W* [1999] 2 NZLR 1, 3.

Thirdly, the consequences of a civil finding may outweigh those of a finding of guilt: judgment sums for serious torts exceed fines imposed for minor offences. This is an objective fact. Subjectively, in the eyes of the affected person, more may be at stake in a civil than in a criminal trial. In *Hornal v Neuberger Products Ltd*, Morris LJ remarked:[183]

> In some criminal cases liberty may be involved; in some it may not. In some civil cases the issues may involve questions of reputation which can transcend in importance even questions of personal liberty. Good name in a man or woman is 'the immediate jewel of their souls'.

For all these reasons, it is difficult to justify a categorical difference in the standard of caution for civil and criminal cases; the standard in both contexts should be determined on the same broad principle.[184] There must be as many 'standards of proof' as there are material differences in the circumstances of cases—or, more accurately, there should only be one standard, a variant one. As Lord Stowell held in *Loveden v Loveden*:[185] 'The only general rule that can be laid down upon the subject is, that the circumstances must be such as would lead the guarded discretion of a reasonable and just man to the conclusion.'[186] The argument advanced here receives some support from those judges who have openly confessed to 'difficulty in understanding how there is or there can be two standards'[187] and is consistent with the observation made by some judges[188] that 'the choice between the two standards is not one of great moment. It is largely a matter of words.'

The language in which the criminal standard is expressed is open-textured. What standard is imported by the phrase 'proof beyond reasonable doubt' depends on what is meant by reasonable, and it is only rational to determine what

183 (n 175) 266.

184 G H L Fridman, 'Standards of Proof' (1955) 30 Can Bar Rev 665, 670.

185 (1810) 2 Hagg Con 1, 3. 'Men will pronounce without hesitation that a person owes another a hundred pounds on evidence on which they certainly would not hang him': Wills (n 54) 267, n (n); cf 269–272.

186 It seems that the legal standard of proof in some civil jurisdictions is a floating one of the sort suggested here. Michele Taruffo, 'Rethinking the Standards of Proof" (2003) 51 American J of Comparative Law 659 at 669 tells us that in 'France, Italy and Spain, there simply are no fixed standards of proof, since the evaluation of proofs is left to the free discretion of the judge'. Another writer claims: 'In Continental European law, no distinction is made between civil and criminal cases with regard to the standard of proof. In both, such a high degree of probability is required that, to the degree that this is possible in the ordinary experience of life itself, doubts are excluded and probability approaches certitude' (Heinrich Nagel, 'Evidence', entry in *Encyclopaedia Britannica* under the heading 'Burden of Proof', retrieved on 12 October 2005 from *Encyclopaedia Britannica Premium Service:* <http://www.britannica.com/eb/article-9109441>).

187 *R v Hepworth and Fearnley* [1955] 2 QB 600, 603. In *R v Murtagh and Kennedy*, Hilberry said, during the hearing of argument, that he could not see the difference between the onus of proof in a civil and criminal case: 'If a thing is proved, it is proved': The Times, 24 May 1955, quoted in Ockelton, (1980) 2 Liverpool L Rev 65, 67.

188 *R v Home Secretary, ex p Khawaja* [1984] 1 AC 74, 112. To the same effect: *Bater v Bater* (n 120) 36 ('more a matter of words than anything else'); *B v Chief Constable of Avon and Somerset Constabulary* [2001] 1 WLR 340, 354 ('the difference... is... largely illusory'); Alfred Bucknill, *The Nature of Evidence* (London: Skeffington, 1953) 59.

is reasonable with reference to the context. The concept of 'proof beyond reasonable doubt' originated in the seventeenth century as an intellectual response to scepticism, a response that was built on the Aristotelian precept that the demand on proof must suit the subject matter.[189] Since criminal cases differ in both the gravity of charges and the range of punishment, there is no basis for applying to all of them a uniform standard of caution. After a thorough review of empirical studies, one author concludes that, in fact, jurors do not apply a fixed standard across the board but vary, from case to case, the amount of proof they need for a conviction.[190] There is, as argued above, moral reasons for this flexibility: the court fails to show sufficient care for the accused when it finds him guilty of murder with no greater evidential justification than it would require for a conviction on speeding. Judges have often acknowledged that the strictness of proof must be commensurate with the seriousness of the crime.[191] For instance, Holroyd J said in *Re Hobson*:[192] 'The greater the crime the stronger is the proof required for the purpose of conviction.'

Given the broad texture of the term 'reasonable', it is not obvious why the so-called criminal standard should not apply to civil cases as well.[193] At a civil trial, the fact-finder is justified in giving a positive verdict only if she is satisfied of the truth of the underlying facts, but 'if a court has to be satisfied, how can it at the same time entertain a reasonable doubt'?[194] Judge Learned Hand once noted that there is no real distinction between 'the evidence which should satisfy reasonable men, and the evidence which should satisfy reasonable men beyond reasonable doubt'.[195] A similar view was taken by Bucknill LJ in *Bater v Bater*: 'To be satisfied and at the same time to have a reasonable doubt seems to me to be an impossible state of mind.'[196] Indeed, in the same case, Denning LJ accepted that 'the phrase "reasonable doubt" can be used as aptly in a civil case... as in a criminal case'.[197]

[189] *Nicomachean Ethics* 1.3; Theodore Waldman, 'Origing of the Legal Doctrine of Reasonable Doubt' (1959) 20 *Journal of the History of Ideas* 299, 306–307; M Jamie Ferreira, *Scepticism and Reasonable Doubt—The British Naturalist Tradition in Wilkins, Hume, Reid, and Newman* (Oxford: Clarendon Press, 1986) 34, see also 19, 22, 198.

[190] Lillquist (n 10) 111–117.

[191] *Bater v Bater* (n 120) 37; *R v Hampshire County Council, ex p Ellerton* [1985] 1 WLR 749, 758. Many older authorities are discussed in Wills (n 54) 269–271.

[192] (1823) 1 Lewin 261, 261.

[193] Clermont and Sherwin claim, and are disturbed, that civil disputes are judged by a standard similar to the criminal standard in civil-law countries: Kevin M Clermont and Emily Sherwin, 'A Comparative View of Standards of Proof' (2002) The American J of Comparative Law 243, and see also Kevin M Clermont, 'Standards of Proof in Japan and the United States' (2004) 37 Cornell Intl LJ 263. But the accuracy of this claim is challenged by Michele Taruffo, 'Rethinking the Standards of Proof' (2003) 51 The American J of Comparative Law 659.

[194] *R v Home Secretary, Ex p Khawaja* (n 188) 113.

[195] *US v Feinberg* (1944) 140 F 2d 592, 594.

[196] (n 120) 36.

[197] ibid 37.

The European Court of Human Rights ('the European Court') has regularly applied the standard of proof beyond reasonable doubt when hearing claims made by individuals against states for breach of Convention rights.[198] It has been argued a number of times before the European Court that this standard is unreasonably high, given the difficulties the applicant faces of obtaining proof in such cases.[199] According to one submission, the standard should be brought down from 95 per cent probability or more, which is said to be the threshold of proof beyond reasonable doubt, to around 75 per cent probability.[200] Such arguments have been rejected as misconceived on two counts. First, they are mistaken about the character of the cases with which the European Court has to deal: 'its task is to rule on State responsibility under international law and not on guilt under criminal law'.[201] Accordingly, 'its use of "beyond reasonable doubt" should not be confused with the criminal standard of proof'[202] as understood under domestic laws. Secondly, the arguments are based on a misunderstanding of what the European Court means by 'proof beyond reasonable doubt'. In Strasbourg jurisprudence, that standard is fluid and context-driven. As was noted in the judgment of the First Section in *Nachova & Ors v Bulgaria*:[203] 'It has been the Court's practice to allow flexibility, taking into consideration the nature of the substantive right at stake and any evidentiary difficulties involved.' This view was strongly reiterated by the Grand Chamber when the case was brought before it:[204]

> In the proceedings before the Court, there are no procedural barriers to the admissibility of evidence or pre-determined formulae for its assessment. It adopts the conclusions that are, in its view, supported by the free evaluation of all evidence... [T]he level of persuasion necessary for reaching a particular conclusion and, in this connection, the distribution of the burden of proof are intrinsically linked to the specificity of the facts, the nature of the allegation made and the Convention right at stake. The Court is also attentive to the seriousness that attaches to a ruling that a Contracting State has violated fundamental rights.

[198] eg *Ireland v United Kingdom* (1978) 2 EHRR 25, para 161; *Adali v Turkey*, Application no 38187/97, 31 March 2005, paras 216, 219.

[199] eg *Nachova v Bulgaria*, Application nos 43577/98 and 43579/98, 6 July 2005, decision of the Grand Chamber, para 140.

[200] ibid paras 153, 514.

[201] ibid para 166. See also *Adali v Turkey*, Application no 38187/97, 31 March 2005, para 216: 'the responsibility of a State under the Convention... is not to be confused with the criminal responsibility of any particular individuals'.

[202] *Napier v Scottish Ministers*, 2005 SLT 379, para 17. Ibid at para 19, the Court of Session observed that 'taken in its context, the formula "proof beyond reasonable doubt" as used by the European Court has a wholly different significance from its use in criminal trials in Scotland'.

[203] Application nos 43577/89 and 43579/98, para 166 (26 February 2004). Judgment of the First Section.

[204] (n 199) para 147.

The civil standard is equally open to, and has been given, a contextualist interpretation. Although it is commonly said that the standard of proof 'on the balance of probabilities' applies uniformly to all civil cases, courts have conceded that there can be variations within this standard. There is no shortage of judicial statements to this effect; judges have said that:

- the 'more serious the allegation, the higher the required standard of proof';[205]
- the 'civil standard is a flexible standard to be applied with greater or lesser strictness according to the seriousness of what has to be proved and the implications of proving those matters';[206]
- the 'standard of proof required by a cautious and responsible tribunal will naturally vary in accordance with the seriousness or importance of the issue';[207]
- the 'seriousness of an allegation made' and 'the gravity of the consequences flowing from a particular finding are considerations which must affect the answer to the question whether the issue has been proved';[208]
- 'the court will require the high degree of probability which is appropriate to what is at stake',[209] 'proportionate to the nature and gravity of the issue'[210] and 'commensurate with the occasion';[211]
- an 'allegation [that is] of a serious character... requires a corresponding degree of satisfaction as to the evidence';[212]
- 'the nature and gravity of an issue necessarily determines the manner of attaining reasonable satisfaction of the truth of the issue'.[213]

These statements appear to support a variant standard of proof. However, according to a view which has considerable history and currency, they do not. It is said that they can be reconciled with the position that the standard stays fixed at the

[205] *Yogambikai Nagarajah v Indian Overseas Bank* [1997] 1 SLR 258, 269 (Singapore Court of Appeal). This case was cited by the Singapore High Court in *Vita Health Laboratories Pte Ltd v Pang Seng Meng* [2004] 4 SLR 162, 174 for the principle that 'the graver the allegation the higher the standard of proof incumbent on the claimant'. Again, in *Tang Yoke Kheng v Lek Benedict* [2005] 3 SLR 263, 271, the Singapore Court of Appeal held: 'the graver the consequences, the more severe the requirement for proof ought to be'.

[206] *B v Chief Constable of Avon and Somerset Constabulary* [2001] 1 WLR 340, 353–4.

[207] *Briginshaw v Briginshaw* (n 7) 343–4. Also *Serio v Serio* (1983) 4 FLR 756, 763; *The 'Zinovia'* [1984] 2 Lloyd's Rep 271, 272.

[208] *Briginshaw v Briginshaw* (n 7) 361–2. Also: *Helton v Allen* (1940) 63 CLR 691, 701, 712.

[209] *R v Home Secretary, ex p Khawaja* (n 188) 113; see also ibid 124.

[210] ibid 97. Similarly, *Hornal v Neuberger Products Ltd* (n 175) 258; *Blyth v Blyth* [1966] AC 643, 669; *R v Hampshire County Council, ex p Ellerton* (n 191) 757, 759; *Lawrence v Chester Chronicle & Associated Newspapers Ltd*, The Times, 8 February 1986 (judgment of May LJ).

[211] *Bater v Bater* (n 120) 37.

[212] *R v Home Secretary, ex p Khawaja* (n 188) 105. Also *Re M (A Minor)* [1994] 1 FLR 59, 67. Similarly, Cartwright J in the Canadian Supreme Court case of *Smith v Smith* [1952] SCR 312, 331–2 held that satisfaction of the civil standard of proof 'must depend on the totality of the circumstances on which... judgment is formed including the gravity of the consequences'.

[213] *Wright v Wright* (1948) 77 CLR 191, 210.

point of balance of probabilities. The flexibility is said to lie only in the *application* of the standard.[214] Evidence has to be judged against one's background understanding of the world; it is impossible for the fact-finder to approach evidence without any pre-existing beliefs. Some things will appear to her inherently more probable than others. If she believes that fraud is less common than carelessness, it would and should take more to persuade her, on the balance of probabilities, that an allegation is true if it is one of fraud than if it is one of negligence. The standard of proof is not higher in the first case than in the second: in each, to accept the allegation, the fact-finder need only to believe that it is more likely true than not; to describe it in terms of probabilities, the benchmark remains at 0.5.

This argument has been advanced in various forms. A nineteenth-century writer observed that an allegation of an exceptional act has 'an immense antecedent *im*probability to be got over, and subdued by proof', whereas an allegation of an occurrence of a common event attracts 'an antecedent probability' of truth.[215] In Bayesian terms, whether the evidence is sufficient to carry the probability of p beyond 0.5 depends on the 'prior probability' of p.[216] In *Thomas Bates & Son v Wyndham's Ltd*,[217] Buckley LJ claimed: 'In every case the balance of probability must be discharged, but in some cases that balance may be more easily tipped than in others.' Morris LJ conveyed the same point in *Hornal v Neuberger Products Ltd*[218] when he said that 'the very elements of gravity [are] a part of the whole range of circumstances which have to be weighed in the scale when deciding as to the balance of probabilities'. In *Re H (Minors)*,[219] Lord Nicholls explicitly denied 'that where a serious allegation is in issue the standard of proof required is higher. It means only that the inherent probability or improbability of an event is itself a matter to be taken into account when weighing the probabilities and deciding whether, on balance, the event occurred.' Slade LJ was equally adamant in *R v Hampshire County Council, ex p Ellerton*:[220] 'the concept of the flexible standard of proof... is *not* that it involves proof on (say) a 51–49 balance of probabilities in some cases and (say) a 75 to 25 balance in others... [It] is simply that the relative seriousness of the allegation is a relevant factor

214 *R (N) v Mental Health Review Tribunal* (n 7) 497–498.

215 *R v White* (1865) 4 F & F 383, n (a). Similarly: *Cross and Tapper* (n 82) 171; David Hamer, 'The Civil Standard of Proof Uncertainty: Probability, Belief and Justice' (1994) 16 Sydney LR 506, 512–513; Zelman Cowen and P B Carter, *Essays on the Law of Evidence* (Oxford: OUP, 1956) 252–253, 254.

216 Bernard Robertson, 'Criminal Allegations in Civil Cases' (1991) 107 LQR 194, 195; Hamer (n 215) 512.

217 [1981] 1 All ER 1077, 1085. Also: *In re Dellow's Will Trusts* [1964] 1 WLR 451, 454–5; *Re Cleaver (deceased)* [1981] 2 All ER 1018, 1024.

218 (n 175) 266.

219 [1996] AC 563, 586.

220 (n 191) 759. In the same case, May LJ took a different view (ibid 758) but he apparently changed his mind in *Lawrence v Chester Chronicle & Associated Newspapers Ltd*, The Times, 8 February 1986. See also *Neat Holdings Pty Ltd v Karajan Holdings Pty Ltd & Ors* (1992) 110 ALR 449, 450; *R (N) v Mental Health Review Tribunal* (n 7) 498.

(on occasions a highly relevant factor) in considering whether or not the civil burden of proof on the balance of probabilities has been discharged in any given case.' Lord Hoffman said it most clearly in the Hong Kong case of *Aktieselskabet Dansk Skibsfinansiering v Brothers & Ors*:[221] 'the court is not looking for a higher degree of probability. It is only that the more inherently improbable the act in question, the more compelling will be the evidence needed to satisfy the court on a preponderance of probability.'

These judges are right that the fact-finder's pre-existing beliefs about, and background understanding of, the world will affect her judgment on the sufficiency of evidence and the truth of p. The argument for a flexible standard of proof is that the standard of evidential justification to support a finding must vary with the significance and consequences of that finding for the party it affects. Some critics have pointed out that the connection between the moral gravity of a conduct and its frequency of occurrence cannot be assumed. It requires empirical support, which is lacking.[222] Contrary to the view expressed by the judges referred to in the preceding paragraph, other judges have held that the degree of probability required for proof fluctuates from case to case.[223] It does not stay fixed at 0.5. Lord Denning was clear on this in *Bater v Bater*:[224]

> [I]n civil cases, the case may be proved by a preponderance of probability, but there may be *degrees of probability* within that standard. The degree depends on the subject-matter. A civil court, when considering a charge of fraud, will naturally require for itself *a higher degree of probability* than that which it would require when asking if negligence is established... *In some cases 51 per cent would be enough, but not in others.*

A number of law lords spoke in similar terms in *R v Home Secretary, ex p Khawaja*; for example, Lord Scarman said: 'The flexibility of the civil standard of proof suffices to ensure that the court will require *the high degree of probability* which is appropriate to what is at stake.'[225] A similar position was taken by the Canadian Supreme Court in *R v Oakes*: '[w]ithin the broad category of the civil standard, there exist *different degrees of probability* depending on the nature of the case'.[226] While it is not entirely helpful to employ the language of probability, statements such as these suggest, contrary to the position held on the other side, that the standard of proof is not uniform and not fixed at a certain level; in the words of Lord Denning, 'there is no absolute standard'.[227]

[221] [2001] 2 BCLC 324, 329.

[222] Redmayne (n 28) 184–185; Robertson (n 216) 195.

[223] For discussion of the two approaches: Redmayne (n 28) 176–177.

[224] [1951] P 35, 37. Emphasis added. See also: *Blyth v Blyth* [1966] AC 643, 669 ('the degree of probability depends on the subject-matter'); *R v Hampshire County Council, ex p Ellerton* (n 191) 757 ('*degrees of probability* within' civil standard).

[225] (n 188) 113 (emphasis added); also ibid 97 and *Slattery v Mance* [1962] Lloyd's Rep 60, 63.

[226] [1986] 1 SCR 103, 137. Emphasis added.

[227] *Bater v Bater* (n 120) 37.

2.2.11 *Opposition to a variant standard*

Why is there such judicial ambivalence? What is it in a variant interpretation of the standard of proof that appeals to some judges and makes others oppose the idea? We will start with the possible reasons for the opposition. The first objection to the interpretation may be briefly disposed of. It might be feared that the contextualist interpretation licenses careless treatment of less serious cases. This fear, as we saw in Part 2.2.1, is groundless. On the narrow understanding of 'care' as having to do with diligence in attending to the evidence and evaluating it, the concept of 'care' is different from the concept of 'caution'. The contextualist interpretation does not challenge, descriptively nor normatively, the statement of Morris LJ in *Hornal v Neuberger Products Ltd*[228] that 'no court and no jury would give less careful attention to issues lacking gravity than to those marked by it'.

Secondly, the argument in favour of a predetermined and fixed standard of proof is sometimes driven by the objection to tying the standard externally to clearly extra-epistemic considerations. Thus Lempert writes:[229]

> [W]e do not... adjust the burden to track the benefits to society of correct convictions. We do not, for example, decrease the government's burden of proof when it prosecutes highly publicized cases, even if convictions in these cases are likely to have substantially greater deterrent effects than convictions of unknown people for run-of-the-mill crimes.

This is an apt and valid observation. It is objectionable to use the standard of proof merely as a means of attaining some larger social benefits. The likelihood of conviction should not depend on external circumstances unconnected with the defendant's blameworthiness for the crime with which she is charged. Suppose we lower the standard of proof as the crime rates go up and as social interests in crime control become more pressing.[230] This makes the chances of conviction fortuitous; it is unjust to judge a 'defendant who happened to come to trial at a time when the relative cost of false conviction was high... by a lower standard than an equally reprehensible defendant who came to trial in different circumstances'.[231] But none of these is advocated in the theory advanced in this chapter; on the contrary, the theory is offered precisely in opposition to instrumental analysis. A contextual standard of proof is tied to complementary epistemic and moral considerations which operate within fact-finding.

Thirdly, Macaulay noted in the early part of the nineteenth century that, sometimes, when the jury was not completely satisfied of the accused's guilt in relation

[228] (n 175) 266.

[229] Richard O Lempert, 'The Economic Analysis of Evidence Law: Common Sense on Stilts' (2001) 87 Virginia L Rev 1619, 1664.

[230] Reiman and van den Haag (n 18) 241.

[231] Michael L Davis, 'The Value of Truth and the Optimal Standard of Proof in Legal Disputes' (1994) 10 J of Law, Economics, and Organization 343, 351.

to a serious crime, it would simply convict him of a lesser offence.[232] He is rightly critical of this approach. The fact-finder should care equally to do justice whether the trial is of a 'petty' or of a 'serious' crime. It is unjust to convict the accused without categorical belief in his guilt, however light the crime with which he is charged. As we insisted in Chapter 3, there must be evidence of the kind capable of justifying categorical belief; if not, the prosecution's case must fail, and nothing in the argument offered in this chapter is intended to save it.[233] But it is only rational that the standard of justification for categorical belief should vary with the circumstances, and where to set the standard is an issue that cannot be avoided. The fact-finder must deliberate on the verdict with appropriate caution by demanding the standard of epistemic justification that suits the context, taking into account the stakes involved.

A fourth possible objection to the contextualist approach is that it creates uncertainty.[234] The standard of proof is linked to the burden of persuasion: it is a target which the party bearing the burden seeks to meet. This target, it might be argued, should be clearly fixed and known beforehand;[235] the resulting certainty helps the parties to prepare for the trial and to assess whether they have a good enough case to pursue. But it is difficult to see what certainty lies in the formula that proof be established on the 'balance of probabilities'. After all, and contrary to what the formula seems to imply, it is all too obvious that the satisfaction of this test is not determined by 'mere mechanical comparison of probabilities'.[236] It is never easy to predict how the fact-finder will judge the evidence and litigants would not know beforehand what evidence would eventually emerge at the trial.[237] Most crucially, there is little left of the supposed certainty once it is accepted, as it is even by some of those who maintain that the standard is fixed, that the balance of probabilities may be tipped more easily in some cases than in others.

The fifth objection is this: if people are to be treated equally, anyone who brings a civil claim should have it judged by the same standard of proof as applies to everyone else's; similarly, all persons charged before a criminal court should have their guilt determined by a common standard.[238] This argument treats 'standard of proof' as a probability threshold and confuses equal treatment with being treated as an equal. To be treated as an equal is not equivalent to receiving the same distribution of some goods or burdens; it means to be treated with the same

[232] Thomas Babington Macaulay, *The Critical and Historical Essays Contributed to the Edinburgh Review by Lord Macaulay*, vol 1 (10th edn, London: Longman, 1860) 143.

[233] Pressing a similar point: Carr (n 89) 120.

[234] *Re H (Minors)* (n 7) 587; *R v Hampshire County Council, ex p Ellerton* (n 191) 761; *Mullan v Anderson* (n 7) 842. See also Cowen and Carter (n 215) 252.

[235] Rosemary Pattenden, 'The Risk of Non-Persuasion in Civil Trials: The Case Against a Floating Standard of Proof' [1988] Civil Justice Quarterly 220, 230–231.

[236] *Briginshaw v Briginshaw* (n 7) 361.

[237] Redmayne (n 28) 181–182.

[238] McCauliff (n 48) 1334–1335. Cf Redmayne (n 28) 183–184.

respect and concern.[239] In legal fact-finding, equality in the second sense does not call for—actually, it calls against—the employment of a predetermined and inflexible threshold of subjective probability in all cases. On the proposed interpretation of the 'standard of proof' as a 'standard of caution', there is technically only one standard: at every trial, a level of caution must be exercised which is commensurate with the stake involved for the person whose case is being judged, and this is done by applying a suitably high standard of evidential justification. The contextualization of evidential justification is itself a dictate of equality; litigants are treated with equal respect and concern when their cases are treated with the degree of caution that is appropriate to each of them.

Lastly, the view that the criminal standard has to be different from the civil standard may be traced to the deeply felt belief that there is and ought to be a material difference in the approach to determining facts in civil and criminal cases. The concept of standard of proof has two aspects. Insofar as it is about the degree of caution to be exercised in fact-finding, there is no difference *in kind* in the standards applicable in civil and criminal trials. But there is a further aspect to the concept. It concerns the distribution of caution, which is the topic of the next section. A difference in kind (as opposed to degree) in deliberative attitude is to be found in this second aspect.

2.3 Distribution of caution

2.3.1 Difference in attitude

A hint of the difference can be found in *Davis v Davis*.[240] At the trial, the judge proceeded on the basis that the allegation of cruelty on which the divorce petition was based had to 'be proved with the same degree of strictness as a crime is proved in a criminal court'.[241] The Court of Appeal held that this amounted to a misdirection. Denning LJ stressed that there 'is a considerable difference between the standard of proof required in criminal cases and in civil cases';[242] the criminal 'standard is a proper safeguard to persons accused in criminal cases; but, if applied in divorce cases, it may mean unjustly depriving an injured party of a remedy which he ought to have'.[243]

This passage stresses a crucial difference between the deliberative attitude required in a criminal case and that which is proper in the civil context. The criminal standard of proof 'safeguards' the accused against wrongful conviction by instructing the fact-finder to deliberate in a manner that gives overriding importance to the risk of a false finding of guilt: in effect, she should be more

239 Ronald Dworkin, *Taking Rights Seriously* (London: Duckworth, 1977) 227.
240 [1950] P 125.
241 ibid 127–8.
242 ibid 128.
243 ibid 129.

cautious in accepting an allegation supportive of conviction than one which undermines the conclusion of guilt. On the other hand, in a civil adjudication, the fact-finder is expected to treat both parties with equal respect and concern; this was in essence Lord Denning's point when he highlighted the need to consider the interests of one party alongside that of her opponent. While deliberation on guilt requires caution to be weighted in favour of the accused, deliberation in a civil trial generally requires the court to be equally cautious in accepting an allegation in favour of either party. This distinction has to do with the *distribution*, rather than *degree*, of caution, and it is in the distribution of caution that we can find valid substance to the claim that there are two distinct standards of proof, the criminal and the civil.

2.3.2 The impartial attitude

A civil litigation involves a dispute between persons in their private dealings. The law is committed to treating them as equals in the adjudication of their dispute. The standard of proof 'on the balance of probabilities' is an expression of this commitment.[244] It instructs the fact-finder to be impartial: in her deliberation on the verdict, she must give equal consideration to the dignity and interests of each of the parties.[245] A false finding will usually inflict equal moral harm whichever side is the victim.[246] The court must take the versions of facts presented by both sides with the same seriousness, out of equal respect and concern for each party.[247] Therefore, as a general rule, the fact-finder must exercise the same degree of caution in finding that p, a hypothesis put forward by the plaintiff or claimant in support of her case, as in accepting that q, a contradictory hypothesis offered by the opponent in support of her defence.

What this means is that the same epistemic standard must be used in relation to either of the hypotheses. This requirement may be construed as follows, using the framework developed in Chapter 3: the court should accept a hypothesis only

[244] A connection between the civil standard and equal treatment of parties is noted by many: David Kaye, 'The Error of Equal Error Rates' (2002) 1 Law, Probability and Risk 3, 6–7; James Brook, 'Inevitable Errors: The Preponderance of the Evidence Standard in Civil Litigation' (1982) 18 Tulsa Law Journal 79, 85–86; Hamer (n 215) 509, 513; Redmayne (n 28) 171–172.

[245] For formulation of egalitarianism in terms of a principle of equal consideration of human interests: Stanley I Benn, 'Egalitarianism and the Equal Consideration of Interests' in J Roland Pennock and John W Chapman (eds), *Nomos IX: Equality* (New York: Atherton Press, 1967) 61.

[246] Ronald Dworkin, 'Principle, Policy, Procedure' in his *A Matter of Principle* (Cambridge, Massachusetts: Harvard UP, 1985) ch 3, 89 (but also noting that this is not always true); Thomas C Grey, 'Procedural Fairness and Substantive Rights' in J Roland Pennock and John W Chapman (eds), *Due Process, Nomos*, XVII (New York: NY U Press, 1977) 182, 185 ('There is no greater justice in an error one way than the other. Accordingly, procedural fairness requires that the facts be found by a preponderance of the evidence').

[247] That the civil standard of proof expresses the value of equality is judicially recognized, eg, by the Supreme Court of the United States in *Herman & MacLean v Huddleston* (1983) 459 US 375, 390: 'A preponderance-of-evidence standard allows both parties to "share the risk of error in roughly equal fashion." (Citing *Addington v Texas* (1979) 441 US 418, 423.) Any other standard expresses a preference for one side's interests.'

if, to begin with, it judges it to be perfectly possible or plausible; if the hypotheses offered by both sides are perfectly possible or plausible, neither should be accepted. If only one is perfectly possible or plausible, it will be accepted only if all relevant alternative hypotheses are so lacking in possibility or plausibility that it is safe enough to rule them out. Putting this differently, one must be sufficiently confident that the accepted hypothesis is true, and how much confidence is required depends on what is at stake. The court must take the same approach and use the same epistemic standard in judging a disputed hypothesis, whichever side it favours.

The parties' right to be treated equally in the way just described is in addition to their right to the proper level of caution. Suppose the fact-finder decides on the truth by flipping a coin. She is in a hurry and does not care whether she gets the facts right or wrong. Her action does not violate the parties' right to equal treatment inasmuch as she is not biased either way. However, she has, in failing to put any rational effort into reaching a correct verdict, violated their right to have their claims treated with proper caution. The parties' claims must be given equal *and* due consideration.

When the fact-finder finds the case of either side equally possible or plausible, the instruction to be impartial as contained in the civil standard does not tell her how she should decide, and decide she must. She needs a further instruction on how to break this impasse. There is, as we have noted, a default aspect to the standard of proof which directs the fact-finder, in such a situation, to find against the side bearing the burden of proof. Lord Brandon observed in *The 'Popi M'*[248] that '[n]o judge likes to decide cases on burden of proof if he can legitimately avoid having to do so'. There are two possible explanations for the reluctance to decide 'by default'. The first is that the fact-finder is conceding failure in the execution of her task, the discovery of truth. Secondly, the principle of impartiality appears to be compromised: where the court does not know what or whom to believe, it would be acting partially if it nevertheless accepts the version of the facts presented by one side. We should, however, resist viewing the default function of the civil standard as a sort of pragmatic 'let-out', the operation of which involves the sacrifice of principle to practical necessity. The better view is that the default principle is itself a principle of justice, based on the idea that if a party wishes the court to impose liability on another, it is only 'right' that she should have to prove the facts necessary to justify that imposition.

'Right', here, has a moral sense. The basic idea is that we do not and should not think the worst of people we care about. We ought instead to be charitable in the judgments we make of others in our community, thinking ill of them only if

[248] [1985] 2 All ER 712, 718. See also: Brian MacKenna, 'Discretion' (1974) 9 The Irish Jurist (NS) 1, 10.

there is justification for doing so. Nance has made an argument along this line, which, in the quote below, he couches in deontological terms:[249]

> Our duty to respect others entails a duty to presume their compliance with serious social obligations... [T]o presume that someone has breached his or her duty fails to accord that person the dignity associated with the status of *membership* in the community that is governed by the norms whose breach is at issue. It fails to accept the person as reasonably committed to the good of the community for which those norms exist, since reasonable commitment entails by-and-large compliance with the community moral duties.

This gives value and substance to a well-known evidential maxim. It is variously formulated; for instance, it is said: 'he who asserts must prove', 'the party asserting the affirmative of a proposition must prove it', and 'a party is not required to prove a negative'.[250] As a practical guide to allocating the burden of proof, this maxim is useless since 'any proposition can be recast to change its form from positive to negative, or conversely'.[251] However, it makes sense if construed as the legal instantiation of the wider moral principle that 'one ought to presume, until sufficient evidence is adduced to show otherwise, that any given person has acted in accordance with serious social obligations'.[252] On this principle, a sort of presumption of innocence applies even in civil cases.[253] Wills subscribes to the same view as Nance. For Wills, the rule which places the burden 'on the party who asserts the existence of any fact which infers legal accountability' is founded on 'evident principles of justice'; specifically, 'No man can be justly deprived of his social rights without proof that he has committed some act which legally involves forfeiture of them. The law... regards every man as legally innocent until the contrary is proved.'[254]

2.3.3 *The protective attitude*

Unlike the purpose of a civil adjudication, '[i]n a prosecution, the Court is not adjusting rights between two persons'.[255] At a criminal trial, the court holds the prosecution to account by demanding that they satisfy the fact-finder of the guilt of the accused. The chief purpose of scrutinizing the prosecution's evidence, and thus the primary role of the fact-finder, is to protect the accused against wrongful conviction. A *protective attitude* must be adopted when determining the truth

[249] Dale A Nance, 'Civility and the Burden of Proof' (1994) 17 Harvard J of Law and Public Policy 647, 653.

[250] The maxim finds statutory expression in section 103 (1) of the Singapore Evidence Act (Cap 97, 1997 rev ed): 'Whoever desires any court to give judgment as to any legal right or liability, dependent on the existence of facts which he asserts, must prove that those facts exist.'

[251] Nance (n 249) 663.

[252] ibid 648.

[253] ibid 689.

[254] William Wills, *An Essay on the Principles of Circumstantial Evidence*, edited by Alfred Wills (6th edn, London: Butterworth, 1912) 304–305.

[255] *Hurst v Evans* (1916) 1 KB 352, 357, per Lush J.

of the prosecution's case.[256] It is sometimes said that the fact-finder should be 'biased' in favour of the accused.[257] This description is harmless if all that is meant is differential treatment. But 'bias' has a derogatory meaning because it usually implies that the differential treatment is unwarranted. To be biased in favour of the accused is either to be 'overly' dismissive of the evidence against her or to be 'too' receptive to arguments supporting her acquittal. The adverbs 'overly' and 'too' indicate a deviation from the proper standards of deliberation. But if we accept, as we should, that the trier of fact ought to be more disposed to reject the case of the prosecution than that of the defence, it would be wrong to accuse a fact-finder who is thus disposed of being 'too' dismissive of the first or 'overly' receptive of the second. We should not then say that she is 'biased', for it implies that she is acting improperly whereas, in our judgment, she is not.

What the protective attitude requires is that the fact-finder adopts a deliberative posture of scepticism towards the prosecution's case. She should be much less disposed to judge as true a factual hypothesis p, where p supports a guilty verdict, than to reject a factual hypothesis q where q undermines conviction. She must accept p only if she believes that one would be justified in believing that p within the terms of BAF*, one of which terms requires the belief in p to be sufficiently strong. The required degree of confidence in p will, if the argument of this chapter is right, vary with the stakes involved. On the other hand, to accept q, she need not judge that one would be justified in believing q at all; it is enough that she *suspects* that q is true, judging it to have enough plausibility to cast a reasonable doubt on p. Thus where a trial turns on the testimony of the accused against the testimony of the prosecution's principal witness, it is a misdirection to inform the jury that they have to choose between the two. This is because the jury 'do not have to believe that the accused is telling the truth before he is entitled to be acquitted';[258] they must acquit the accused, notwithstanding that they do not believe his testimony if they 'are left in reasonable doubt by it' or 'on the basis of the [other] evidence [they] do accept, [they] are not convinced beyond reasonable doubt of his guilt'.[259] The criminal court has the primary task of protecting the accused from a wrongful conviction. It is not only consistent with but also a natural part of this protective role to acquit in the event of doubt about guilt. The deliberative attitude required of the fact-finder at a criminal trial is distinctly asymmetrical.

[256] cf Chambers (n 18) especially 673, linking the criminal standard with the fact-finder's duty to address the prosecution's case with a 'skeptical mindset'.

[257] Thus Barbara D Underwood suggests, metaphorically, that the fact-finder must put a thumb on the defendant's side of the scales of justice: 'The Thumb on the Scales of Justice: Burdens of Persuasion in Criminal Cases' (1977) 86 Yale LJ 1299, 1299, 1306–1307. The protective attitude is related to the presumption of innocence, and it is said there is an intrinsic element of bias in a presumption: Edna Ullman-Margalit, 'On presumption' (1983) 80 *Journal of Philosophy* 143, 146.

[258] *R v E* (1996) 89 Australian Crim Rep 325, 330.

[259] *R v W(D)* [1991] 1 SCR 742, 758.

This asymmetry is based on the belief, expressed typically in the form of a numerical ratio, that it is (*n* times) worse to risk conviction of the innocent than to risk acquittal of the guilty.[260] Call this the 'moral judgment'. The criminal standard is 'inextricably linked'[261] to the presumption of innocence in the sense that both are based on the moral judgment.[262] That much is uncontentious. But whether the moral judgment is itself justifiable is a different matter on which only a few words need be offered here. It is unclear how precise an argument can be articulated in its support. Grey explains that 'while it is important as a matter of public policy (or even of abstract justice) to punish the guilty, it is a very great and concrete injustice to punish the innocent'.[263] But, as a justification for the moral judgment, it is vague and raises more questions than it tries to answer. Or we might attempt to draw some justification out of Dworkin's claim that the accused if innocent has a right to acquittal, but the State does not have the corresponding right to conviction if he is guilty.[264] However, as Harris says, 'this asymmetry of rights in the context of the criminal law is something Dworkin never explains'.[265] The validity of the moral judgment was the subject of a debate between Reiman and van den Haag.[266] Reading it brings to mind Hampshire's remark that: 'In moral and political philosophy one is looking for adequate premises from which to infer conclusions already and independently accepted because of one's feelings and sympathies.'[267] Even if we are unable to articulate fully or reach agreement on 'adequate premises' for the moral judgment, it is incontrovertible that 'feelings and sympathies' for it are deep and widespread.

Conclusion

The full importance of the standard of proof cannot come into sight if one sticks to an external viewpoint. There are serious shortcomings in the traditional way

[260] Reiman and van den Haag (n 18) 227. The numerous permutations of the ratio and their sources are extensively documented by Alexander Volokh, 'n Guilty Men' (1997) 146 U of Pennsylvania L Rev 173.

[261] *R v Lifchus* (n 31) 743. In *Re Winship* (n 14) 363, the United States Supreme Court held that the standard of proof beyond reasonable doubt 'provides concrete substance for the presumption of innocence'.

[262] This is true of our modern understanding. But a historical argument is made by Whitman (n 169) that the criminal standard 'was never designed to protect the accused'. It originated as an assurance to jurors of the safety of their souls if they should choose to convict the accused. 'In its original form, it had nothing to do with maintaining the rule of law..., and nothing like the relationship we imagine to the values of liberty.'

[263] Grey (n 246) 185.

[264] Ronald Dworkin, 'Hard Cases' in his *Taking Rights Seriously* (London: Duckworth, 1977) 100.

[265] J W Harris, *Legal Philosophies* (2nd edn, London: Butterworths, 1997) 201.

[266] (n 18). Vidar Halvorsen adds his voice to the debate in 'Is it Better that Ten Guilty Persons Go Free Than that One Innocent Person be Convicted?' (2004) 23 Criminal Justice Ethics 3.

[267] Stuart Hampshire, *Justice is Conflict* (Princeton: Princeton UP, 2000) xiii.

of looking at the standard of proof. This chapter has argued for a different interpretation, one that focuses on the ethics and epistemology of trial deliberation. The argument draws on considerations internal to the trial, with emphasis on the assertive, declarative, and expressive aspects of positive findings of fact. To find that p is to assert that p. For the assertion to be justified, the court must judge that one is justified in believing sufficiently strongly that p is true (within the terms of BAF*), which means that there must be strong enough evidential support for this belief. A finding of fact also has declarative force; as an official declaration, a positive verdict opens the way for the imposition of legal sanction. The fact-finder knows that her decision carries consequences for the parties. Further, moral disapproval of a party's conduct is often expressed in findings made by the court. The fact-finder must therefore conduct her deliberation with three values foremost in mind: truth, respect, and concern. She must do justice to the person who will be affected by her decision. Justice requires integrity: so she should assert that p only if she believes that one would be justified in believing that p (within the terms of BAF*). It also demands humanity: so any decision that she takes against a party must be reached with the amount of caution that reflects due respect for him and appropriate concern for his interests. Exercising the right degree of caution is what the standard of proof is about. Understood as a 'standard of caution', the standard of proof should vary from case to case.

The distribution of caution raises a separate issue. Corresponding to two types of distribution are two kinds of attitudes. The first is the 'attitude of impartiality'. In a civil case, the fact-finder must treat the parties equally, and therefore, on a particular issue, she should be equally disposed to accept the allegations made by either of them. At a criminal trial, she must assume a 'protective attitude' towards the accused: more caution should be exercised in finding against than for him. This asymmetry is grounded in the value judgment that it is a greater wrong to convict the innocent than to acquit the guilty. The difference in the civil and criminal standards, therefore, reflects a fundamental difference in the kind of attitude the trier of fact must assume in deliberation.

5

Hearsay

Introduction

The last two chapters considered general aspects of trial deliberation. Chapter 3 looked broadly at how the fact-finder goes about judging questions of fact. It offered a description of the methodological framework within which that task is carried out and an analysis of the rule by which findings are generally regulated. It was argued in Chapter 4 that fact-finding must be conducted with the right attitude. In particular, caution should be exercised in sufficient degree and with the right distribution: fact-finding must be approached impartially in civil litigation and with a protective attitude towards the accused in criminal cases. From these matters of generality, the focus will now shift to specific forms of evidential reasoning. Certain types of evidence are given special legal treatment. This chapter considers hearsay evidence; the next will deal with evidence of 'similar facts'.

An external view is typically taken of the hearsay rule. Considered of central importance is the effect the rule has on the capacity of the trial system to produce correct verdicts. This kind of analysis focuses on causal links between the empirical assumptions on which the rule rests and the effectiveness of the trial as a mode of inquiry. It will be argued in Part 1 that there are deficiencies in this approach. Only when we depart from the standpoint of the system engineer, and analyse the rule from an internal perspective, can it be seen that at play are principles intrinsic to the legitimacy of fact-finding. Part 2 seeks to make good this claim. Two related explanations will be offered for the hearsay rule. The first is derived from the logic of epistemology and the second from the practice of epistemology. As discussed in Chapter 3, in finding that p, the court is, amongst other things, asserting that p, and it is justified in asserting that p only if one would be justified in believing that p within the terms of BAF*. The hearsay rule stems firstly from the demand for epistemic justification for believing p on the basis of a reported statement (or, more precisely, a 'testimony') that p. Secondly, the rule expresses concern about the defeasibility of the epistemic justification for inferring p from evidence of a person's word or conduct, a concern that arises from her unavailability for courtroom examination. Underlying the need for epistemic justification and for assurance of its non-defeasibility is a consideration that impinges on the fact-finder as a moral agent: such caution must be exercised in drawing an adverse finding against a person as adequately reflects due respect and concern for her. The hearsay rule exemplifies the requirement that trial deliberation meets the mutually reinforcing demands of rationality and justice.

1 External Analysis

Debate on the hearsay rule centres typically on the consequences of its application, in particular, its impact on the court's ability to get the facts right. It is thought that the rule protects against fact-finding errors. Two arguments are frequently made in support of this contention: first, that the rule is necessary because of the jury's incompetence in evaluating hearsay, and secondly, that it is the corollary of certain trial procedures designed to ensure a high frequency of correct verdicts.[1] Both rest on assumptions that are revealing when questioned.

1.1 Incompetence of jury

We have it on as great an authority as Thayer that the common law system of evidence is the 'product of the jury system ... where ordinary, untrained citizens [act] as judges of fact'.[2] This is said to explain particularly well why we have the hearsay rule.[3] For example, in *R v Bedfordshire*, Lord Campbell CJ commented: 'Hearsay evidence is to be excluded, as the jury might often be misled by it.'[4] Jurors are untrained in the evaluation of evidence. Admission of hearsay evidence incurs the risk of the jury giving it more weight than it objectively deserves.[5] The reason for exclusion is not that the evidence is logically irrelevant but that it might

[1] A different and novel argument is made by Dale A Nance, 'The Best Evidence Principle' (1988) Iowa L Rev 227. He claims that the hearsay exclusionary rule gives lawyers an incentive to produce 'the epistemically best, reasonably available evidence' (ibid 272). (See also by the same author, 'Understanding Responses to Hearsay: An Extension of the Comparative Analysis' (1992) Minnesota L Rev 459, and Michael L Seigel, 'Rationalizing Hearsay: A Proposal for a Best Evidence Hearsay Rule' (1992) 72 Boston University L Rev 893.) But the amount of incentive offered by the hearsay rule may be questioned given that it has so many exceptions. As Brian Leiter, 'Prospects and Problems for the Social Epistemology of Evidence Law' (2001) 29 *Philosophical Topics* 319, 322 observes, although 'on its face, the hearsay doctrine is a rule of exclusion, in reality it is a rule of admission'. Further, the incentive effect can in theory be achieved even without an exclusionary rule, as when judges simply 'make it clear that, as a matter of policy, they will put much more weight on direct evidence': Walter Sinnott-Armstrong, 'Which Evidence? A Response to Schauer' (2006) 155 U of Pennsylvania L Rev 129, 131.

[2] James Bradley Thayer, *A Preliminary Treatise on Evidence at the Common Law* (Boston: Little, Brown and Co, 1898) 509.

[3] James Bradley Thayer, 'Bedingfield's Case—Declarations as a Part of the Res Gesta' in his *Legal Essays* (Boston: Boston Book Company, 1908) 207, 265; R W Baker, *The Hearsay Rule* (London: Isaac Pitman & Sons, 1950) 7.

[4] (1855) 4 El & Bl 535, 541.

[5] William Wills, *An Essay on the Principles of Circumstantial Evidence*, edited by Alfred Wills (5th edn, London: Butterworth & Co, 1902) 266; Baker (n 3) 21.

exert undue influence on the jury.[6] Epistemic paternalism is at play: 'The courts apparently feel that jurors cannot be counted on to discount hearsay testimony adequately. So they substituted their own wisdom for that of the jurors.'[7] Given that the rule reflects distrust in the jury's cognitive skills, there is no, or less, need for it as the population from which jurors are drawn becomes more educated,[8] and also when fact-finding is conducted by an expert, a judge.[9]

The historical soundness of this explanation has been challenged.[10] But the origin of the rule is not of present concern. To justify the rule is not the same as explaining how it came to be,[11] and what interests us is the justificatory force of the argument. The force of the argument would appear to be seriously undermined by the fact that the hearsay rule is not confined to jury trials.[12] One may try to explain this away as an untidy but quite common phenomenon of a legal rule transcending the limits of its historical rationale.[13] But to pass the position off as an anomaly is to concede that the argument cannot fully justify the rule. The force of a justification must not, however, be confused with its scope. One can subscribe to the force of an argument, taken on its merit, even as one denies its applicability to the case in hand. It is thus that one is able to point to the fact that a court or tribunal sits without a jury as a reason why it should not be bound by the rule;[14] this stance presupposes that fear of jury incompetence is indeed our motivation for excluding hearsay evidence.

The jury argument is, in the following ways, an external one. It conceives and assesses the hearsay rule as a means to an end. The central plank of the argument is the empirical claim that most jurors are unable to weigh hearsay evidence correctly. Around this premise, a complex set of calculation grows. The focus is on the causal impact of regulating a trial by that rule on the likelihood of truth in the

6 *Berkeley Peerage* case (1811) 4 Camp 401, 415.

7 Alvin I Goldman, 'Epistemic Paternalism: Communication Control in Law and Society' (1991) 88 *The Journal of Philosophy* 113, 119.

8 H A Hammelmann, 'Hearsay Evidence, A Comparison' (1951) 67 LQR 67, 68.

9 *Berkeley Peerage* case (n 6) 415; Kenneth Culp Davis, 'An Approach to Rules of Evidence in Non-Jury Cases' (1964) 50 American Bar Association J 723, 725, and 'Hearsay in Nonjury Cases' (1970) 83 Harvard L Rev 1362, 1365–1366; Leo Levin and Harold K Cohen, 'The Exclusionary Rules in Nonjury Criminal Cases' (1971) 119 U of Pennsylvania L Rev 905, 928–929.

10 Edmund M Morgan, 'The Jury and the Exclusionary Rules of Evidence' (1936) 4 U Chicago L Rev 247, especially 252–256; Frank R Herrmann, 'The Establishment of a Rule Against Hearsay in Romano-Canonical Procedure' (1995) 36 Virginia Journal of International Law 1; T P Gallanis, 'The Rise of Modern Evidence Law' (1999) 84 Iowa L Rev 495, 503, 551. Cf Baker (n 3) 9–10.

11 Mirjan R Damaška, *Evidence Law Adrift* (New Haven: Yale UP, 1997) 3.

12 John MacArthur Maguire, *Evidence—Common Sense and Common Law* (Chicago: The Foundation Press, 1947) 15.

13 Generally: *DPP v Shannon* [1975] AC 717, 765; O W Holmes, *The Common Law* (London: Macmillan, 1911) 5.

14 *Wright v Tatham* (1837) 7 Ad & E 313, 389, per Baron Parke ('Some greater laxity may be permitted in a Court which adjudicates both on the law and on the fact, and may be more safely trusted with the consideration of such evidence than a jury'); Kenneth Culp Davis, 'Hearsay in Nonjury Cases' (1970) 83 Harv L Rev 1362; Law Reform Committee, Thirteenth Report, *Hearsay Evidence in Civil Proceedings*, Cmnd 2964 (1966) 4, 6.

findings of fact the court produces. We must weigh the potential consequences of having and not having the rule. Since, according to the argument, hearsay evidence is excluded in spite of its relevance, the exclusion may deny the fact-finder of valuable probative information. This negative effect can be tolerated only if it is offset by a greater gain: the admission of hearsay must do more harm than good for the discovery of truth.[15] A trial system that is governed by the hearsay rule will, in the long run, be more reliable than one that is not so regulated only if the chances of obtaining truth in the verdict are greater with the rule than without.

At the heart of this analysis, we find an empirical assumption that is also the supposed problem: jurors are generally not competent to handle hearsay evidence. This assumption is certainly questionable. Experimental studies face methodological hurdles and their results are inconclusive.[16] Seeing the assumption as an indictment on the intelligence of ordinary folk, some writers suggest that it is traceable to an elitist 'contempt felt in past centuries by upper-class English judges for lower-class jurors',[17] and that it 'reflects an eighteenth-century class arrogance sorely out of place in today's society'.[18] Without denying that some element of snobbery is involved,[19] this account takes the jury argument at its worst. It must possess some merits to have had such a long grip on lawyers' perception of the rule. Why should we distrust the jury's ability to evaluate hearsay

[15] Law Reform Committee, Thirteenth Report (n 14) 4; Edmund M Morgan, 'Hearsay Dangers and the Application of the Hearsay Concept' (1948) 62 Harvard L Rev 177, 185.

[16] eg Richard F Rakos and Stephan Landsman, 'Researching the Hearsay Rule: Emerging Findings, General Issues, and Future Directions' (1992) 76 Minnesota L Rev 655; Margaret Bull Kovera, Roger Park and Steven D Penrod, 'Jurors' Perceptions of Eyewitness and Hearsay Evidence' (1992) 76 Minnesota LR 703; Peter Miene, Roger Park and Eugene Borgida, 'Juror Decision Making and the Evaluation of Hearsay Evidence,' (1992) 76 Minnesota L Rev 683. According to Roger Park, 'Visions of Applying the Scientific Method to the Hearsay Rule' (2003) Michigan State L Rev 1149, 167: 'it is difficult to draw broad, general inferences from the empirical literature about the impact of hearsay evidence'. See also Roger C Park and Michael J Saks, 'Evidence Scholarship Reconsidered: Results of the Interdisciplinary Turn' (2006) 47 Boston College L Rev 949 for a comprehensive survey of empirical studies relating to hearsay evidence and their limitations. The authors note (ibid 975) that some studies reveal 'jurors to be quite capable of heavily discounting hearsay testimony as compared to firsthand witness testimony', whereas in other studies, 'the jurors credited the hearsay as much as they did firsthand testimony. It is not always clear what the right or ideal response should be to the hearsay testimony, in contrast to the testimony of the firsthand witness.'

[17] Andrew L-T Choo, *Hearsay and Confrontation in Criminal Trials* (Oxford: Clarendon Press, 1996) 34–35, citing S Landsman and R F Rakos, 'Research Essay: A Preliminary Empirical Enquiry Concering the Prohibition of Hearsay Evidence in American Courts' (1991) 15 Law and Psychology Rev 65, 70.

[18] Paul S Milich, 'Hearsay Antinomies: The Case for Abolishing the Rule and Starting Over' (1992) 71 Oregon L Rev 723, 772.

[19] A law lord, Patrick Devlin, wrote extra-judicially in *Trial by Jury* (London: Methuen, 1966) 140 that the jury is better than the trained judge at assessing the credibility of a lay witness because jurors hear the witness as one who is as ignorant as they are whereas the judge, who 'regards so much as simple that to the ordinary man may be difficult, may fail to make enough allowance for the behaviour of the stupid'!

evidence? Do lay persons not, after all, have ample experience in handling hearsays in their daily lives?[20]

One response to this is that hearsay should not be received at a trial in the same way one tends to handle it in everyday affairs. There are significant disparities in the circumstances of the making of such statements, and there is a risk that jurors will treat hearsay in the legal context more favourably than they ought to.[21] In many of our ordinary dealings, we take what we are told at face value, and it is at least arguable that often we are justified in doing so. But it would be irresponsible for the fact-finder to do the same during trial deliberation in the face of a conflict of evidence on disputed facts. She owes a duty to the disputant who will be harmed if an allegation is accepted to exercise caution in accepting it. What caution requires is positive and sufficiently strong justification for accepting the truth of the allegation.

Hearsay evidence fails to provide enough of the necessary assurance. To be justified in believing a statement the truth of which is contested, the trier of fact must have positive evidence of the trustworthiness of its maker. In the normal case where the maker does not testify, the court would not have before it evidence relating to her trustworthiness and, consequently, would lack justification for relying on her statement. This explanation locates the reason for the rule in the special epistemic situation of a trial. In that context, there is an unusually heavy responsibility to be right in what one believes, and therefore an especially critical attitude must be taken towards hearsay evidence. This argument is pursued in Part 2. It allows an explanation that is capable of drawing some of the sting out of the charge of elitism. The law requires hearsay to be treated differently to how it is often received outside the court. If the judge is indeed better at handling hearsay evidence than the juror, it is not because the judge is innately more intelligent than the lay person; it is that, of the two, the judge, by reason of her office and professional training, can understand better the need to obey the law or will feel greater compulsion[22] to do so.[23]

1.2 Procedural safeguards: oath and cross-examination

The second conventional argument concentrates on the procedure for giving and challenging legal testimony—call this the 'testimonial procedure'. In general,

[20] *R v Gilfoyle* [1996] 3 All ER 883, 902; George F James, 'The Role of Hearsay in a Rational Scheme of Evidence' (1940) 34 Illinios L Rev 788, 794; Lewis Edmunds, 'On the Rejection of Hearsay' (1889) 5 LQR 265, 268, 273.

[21] Roger Park, 'A Subject Matter Approach to Hearsay Reform' (1987) 86 Michigan L Rev 51, 60–61; Thomas Starkie, *A Practical Treatise of the Law of Evidence* (2nd edn, London: J & W T Clarke, 1833) 15–16.

[22] If nothing else, because her career prospects and professional reputation are at stake.

[23] *Wright v Tatham* (1838) 7 Ad & E 313, 375 (jury 'unaccustomed to consider the limitations and restrictions which legal views upon the subject would impose'); Jennifer Mnookin, 'Bifurcation and the Law of Evidence' (2006) 155 University of Pennsylvania L Rev 135, 144–145; Richard D Friedman, 'Anchors and Flotsam: Is Evidence Law "Adrift"?' (1998) 107 Yale LJ 1921, 1943.

the witness must present and identify herself publicly in court, give her evidence under solemn conditions, swear (or affirm solemnly) to tell the truth, and answer all questions put to her in the awareness that she can be prosecuted for perjury if she lies. Each of these factors helps to induce the witness to speak carefully and sincerely; and the greater the care and sincerity, the greater the accuracy of her testimony. Another advantage in calling a person to the witness box is that her demeanour while in it may cast light on her credibility. More importantly, by appearing as a witness, she makes herself available for cross-examination. This allows the opponent a chance to (a) expose the insincerity of the witness, (b) clarify ambiguity in her use of language, (c) test her memory on the subject of her testimony, and (d) challenge the accuracy of her perception of the events in question.[24] Cross-examination is, in Wigmore's dramatic phrase, 'the greatest legal engine ever invented for the discovery of truth'.[25]

In a hearsay situation, the original maker of the statement is absent from the trial. If we allow her 'testimony' to be introduced, as it were, by proxy, through the mouth of another, we would lose such assistance to the search for truth and such protection against falsehood, as we might otherwise gain by calling her as a witness.[26] The soundness of this argument is contingent on the validity of empirical assumptions about the link between the hearsay rule and the trial outcome. An instrumental view is taken of the rule: it is seen as a means of ensuring a factually correct verdict.

Two features of the testimonial procedure have been especially emphasized in this connection.[27] They are the non-taking of oath and the absence of the opportunity of cross-examination. Many commentators find the second to be far more persuasive than the first:[28] it is often pointed out that the oath cannot be the decisive factor because testimony given under oath in one proceeding is still considered as hearsay in another.[29] There is general agreement that the primary

[24] Various writers have built theories of hearsay around these four 'testimonial infirmities': Laurence H Tribe, 'Triangulating Hearsay' (1974) 87 Harvard L Rev 957; Michael H Graham, '"Stickperson Hearsay": A Simplified Approach to Understanding the Rule Against Hearsay' [1982] University of Illinois L Rev 887.

[25] John Henry Wigmore, *A Treatise on the Anglo-American System of Evidence in Trials at Common Law*, vol 5 (3rd edn, Boston: Little, Brown & Co, 1940) 29. Similarly: A F Ravenshear, 'Testimony and Authority' (1899) 8 *Mind* (New Series) 63, 76 ('the most powerful weapon conceived for exposing falsification').

[26] *Teper v R* [1952] AC 480, 486.

[27] For comprehensive discussion of the rule's rationale: Wigmore (n 25) §1362–1364; Choo (n 17) chs 1 and 2; Baker (n 3) chs 2 and 4; Edmund M Morgan, *Some Problems of Proof Under the Anglo-American System of Litigation* (Westport, Connecticut: Greenwood Press, 1956) 106–140, and Morgan (n 15) 179–185.

[28] Wigmore (n 25) 7, for example, wrote that the oath 'is merely an incidental feature customarily accompanying cross-examination, and that cross-examination is the essential and real test required by the rule'.

[29] *R v Hawkins* (1996) 111 CCC (3d) 129, 153; Choo (n 17) 29–31; Ian Dennis, *The Law of Evidence* (3rd edn, London: Sweet & Maxwell, 2007) 663.

justification for the rule is that a hearsay statement cannot be tested, and have its true probative worth exposed, by cross-examination.[30]

It is worthwhile to mention two fallacies, not because the flaws are difficult to detect—on the contrary, they are obvious—but because it will help us to avoid premature truncation of analysis. First, it is often said that hearsay evidence is unreliable because it is not subjected to cross-examination. This statement is misleading at best. Cross-examination is an option and we do not expunge the evidence of a witness just because a party chooses not to cross-examine her. The objection to hearsay evidence is to the lack of an *opportunity* to cross-examine the maker of the original statement. Secondly, the loss of this opportunity cannot be interpreted merely as the loss of an *aid* in the search for truth. If this is all it means, it cannot possibly justify the exclusion of hearsay evidence. To exclude evidence on the ground alone that the fact-finder cannot evaluate it as well as she could evidence that has been exposed to cross-examination makes little sense—almost as little sense as a hungry person refusing food for the reason that it is not as nutritious as it could be.[31] The advisory committee to the United States Federal Rules of Evidence once remarked, 'when the choice is between evidence which is less than best and no evidence at all, only clear folly would dictate an across-the-board policy of doing without'.[32] A positive objection to admission is needed to justify the exclusion. To pursue our example: if the food is harmful to one's health, rather than merely deficient in nutrition, this would be a positive reason for even a starving person to reject it.

The positive objection to admitting hearsay evidence can be found by subjecting the rule to an internal analysis. From that point of view, it can be seen that there are two related aspects to the objection. First, the testimonial procedure, which includes but is not confined to the procedure of cross-examination, is devised to *create* evidence relating to the witness's trustworthiness. In a hearsay situation, the original maker of the statement does not enter the witness box. Thus the testimonial procedure cannot be brought to bear on her to bring out evidence relating to her trustworthiness. In the clearest case to which the rule applies, neither is such evidence available from any other source. Without positive evidence of her trustworthiness, the fact-finder lacks epistemic justification for believing her statement. Secondly, even where some such evidence is available, the lack of the opportunity to cross-examine the original maker of the statement may remain a live concern. Important questions may be left unanswered about

[30] *Anderson v US* (1974) 417 US 211, 220; Wigmore (n 25) 1, 3, 7, 9, 202; Morgan (n 15); Morgan (n 27) 106–140; and Edmund M Morgan, *Basic Problems of Evidence*, vol 2 (Philadelphia: American Law Institute, in collaboration with American Bar Association, 1957) ch 9, especially 211–221; John MacArthur Maguire, *Evidence—Common Sense and Common Law* (Chicago: The Foundation Press, 1947) 15, 17–18.

[31] Park and Saks (n 16) 976–977. It is assumed here that live testimony is not available.

[32] Federal Rules of Evidence, Art VII, advisory committee note.

the defeasibility of the inference that is sought to be drawn from her word or conduct. These lines of argument are further developed in Part 2.

1.3 Reliability

We have just considered two arguments that are traditionally offered in support of the hearsay rule. They have this in common: both treat the rule as a means of ensuring the 'reliability' of the trial system. 'Reliability', on this view, refers to the propensity of the system to produce factually correct verdicts. As so understood, 'reliability' is an empirical issue; it is judged by the proportion of disputes that are correctly determined to those that are wrongly decided. But the problem is how one knows that a verdict or finding of fact is *actually* correct or wrong.[33] There are of course isolated cases where we can be certain one way or the other; for example, we can be sure that the accused was falsely convicted of murder when, after the trial, the alleged victim turns up well and alive.[34] But such unequivocal cases are exceptional.[35] It seems impossible, without methodological circularity, to devise a system of verifying conclusively the correctness of the run of verdicts, and this is what is needed to establish, as a fact, the extent to which the trial system is on the whole reliable.[36]

Instead of analysing reliability externally, as a property of the trial system, it can be viewed, alternatively, from the perspective of the agent working within the system. The interest, on the latter approach, is in the normative demands she must meet which are internal to the fact-finding enterprise. In the external sense, reliability is contingent on empirical truths: it involves a study of the psychology of the trier of fact and the central question is whether exposing her to hearsay evidence will increase the likelihood of outcome error in the present case or in the long run. On the internal conception, the reliability of hearsay evidence is about the propriety of relying on hearsay, about the justifiability of using it as the basis of an inference; it raises the issue of whether such evidence justifies belief in

[33] Neil MacCormick, *Legal Reasoning and Legal Theory* (Oxford: Clarendon Press, 1978) 87: 'we can only be *sure* that a mistake *was* made if we think that we found some *unquestionably* reliable way of establishing present truths about past states of affairs; and sometimes those who have least confidence of the law's methods seem to have remarkable faith in their own'.

[34] As allegedly happened in a medieval incident recounted by Peter the Chanter to show the unreliability of the ordeal: John W Baldwin, 'The Intellectual Preparation for the Canon of 1215 Against Ordeals' (1961) 36 *Speculum* 613, 629. But such incidents happen in modern times too: eg James Morton, 'No Body of Evidence', *The Times* (London), 3 June 2003.

[35] But Lord Steyn expressed greater optimism in *R (Mullen) v Home Secretary* [2004] UKHL 18 at para 55, [2005] 1 AC 1, 47: 'Sometimes compelling new evidence, eg a DNA sample, a forensic test result, fingerprints, a subsequent confession by a third party who was found in possession of the murder weapon, and so forth, may lead to the quashing of a conviction. The circumstances may justify the conclusion beyond reasonable doubt that the defendant had been innocent.' Alvin I Goldman, *Knowledge in a Social World* (Oxford: OUP, 1999) 291–292 is as optimistic.

[36] Eleanor Swift, 'A Foundation Approach to Hearsay' (1987) 75 California L Rev 1339, 1350, 1351–1352; cf Goldman (n 35) 291–292.

the truth of what is reported at 'second-hand', and the focus is on how a responsible and rational person would appraise the evidence, given her existing stock of knowledge and understanding of the world. Hearsay evidence is excluded not so much on the basis that it is unreliable (in the sense that admitting it will probably lead the fact-finder astray) as that its reliability is unknown to her (in the sense that information is lacking, or that there are as yet unexplored aspects of the evidence that have to be explored, to justify the claim that the report is true).[37]

2 Internal Analysis

The external conception of reliability is not of any immediate help to the trier of fact. To be of direct use to her, 'reliability' would have to be re-thought in normative terms, such that the focus is on what is needed to justify the acceptance and use of evidence. The preceding discussion has alluded briefly to two related problems with establishing such justification in connection with hearsay. First, the non-appearance of the original source of the statement (S) in court often deprives it of evidence needed to justify inferring the truth of what S said (p) from the fact that S said it. To justify this kind of reliance on S's statement, sufficient information about her trustworthiness with respect to p is needed, and, where our first objection holds, the information is lacking. Secondly, even if we have some such information, the non-availability of S for questioning before the court may leave the justification for the inference we are seeking to draw from her word or action too vulnerable to defeat. Where either of these problems exists, we do not have enough assurance that the inference is true, and the degree of assurance we require is reflective of the respect and concern we have for the person against whom the inference is drawn. These two threads to our account of the hearsay rule will be called, respectively, the 'testimonial argument' and the 'defeasibility argument'.

2.1 The testimonial argument

2.1.1 Testimony

The concept central to the first thread of our account is 'testimony'. Giving testimony in court ('legal testimony') is a special instance of a much wider social practice.[38] We convey and acquire knowledge all the time by telling and

[37] Drawing distinction along similar line: Mary Morton, 'The Hearsay Rule and Epistemological Suicide' (1986) 74 Georgetown LJ 1301, 1307, 1310.

[38] For discussion of testimony in the trial context, see Duncan Pritchard, 'Testimony' in Antony Duff, Lindsay Farmer, Sandra Marshall and Victor Tadros (eds), *The Trial on Trial—Truth and Due Process* (Oxford: Hart, 2004) ch 6; Michael S Pardo, 'Testimony', forthcoming in Tulane Law Review, draft available at: <http://ssrn.com/abstract=986845>.

asking, or, to employ a heavier expression, by giving and receiving testimony.[39] The general term 'testimony' will be used in the broader sense which encompasses both legal testimony and testimony rendered outside the trial process. Where and only where, to avoid confusion, it is necessary to highlight the fact that only the ordinary and non-legal sense of testimony is intended, the term in its various forms will be denoted with an asterisk: testimony*, testify*, and so forth.

This section briefly sketches the paradigm case[40] of testimonial communication. Our attention will be confined to ordinary 'lay' testimony. Since this chapter does not deal with opinion evidence, philosophical issues on expert testimony will not be discussed. Testimony can be considered from the side of giving it or from the side of receiving it.[41] First, consider the former, the act of testifying.[42] Call the actor 'the testifier'. To testify is to communicate factual information, the truth of which the recipient is invited to accept on the word of the testifier. There must be a specific communicative intention. (This point, as we will see, is especially relevant to the topic of 'implied assertions'.) One has not testified to p merely because one has, by word or conduct, led another to believe that p. Suppose S departs hastily when H tells her that police officers are nearby, asking questions about a recent crime. S has not, by her action, testified* to her involvement in the crime even though H might have suspected as much from her conduct. S did not intend to convey that information to H. To testify* that p, it is not enough for S to intend, by her word or action, to get H to believe that p. S must, in addition, intend that H come to that belief through recognizing, and on the basis, that this is what S wants her to believe. For example, I casually draw your attention to my liking of a particular object in order to get you to see that it will do nicely as my birthday gift (that p). I did what I did with the intention of making you believe that p; but I cannot be said to have testified* that p since I did not intend that you should see through what I was really trying to do. The central or standard elements of the necessary communicative intention may be stated thus:[43] for S to testify to H that p, S must intend that H (i) sees that S believes

[39] Amongst the first to note the prevalence of this practice and to analyse it was David Hume in his *Enquiries Concerning Human Understanding And Concerning The Principles Of Morals*, edited by L A Selby-Bigge and P H Nidditch (3rd edn, Oxford: Clarendon Press, 1975) (1777) 111–112.

[40] It is paradigmatic in the sense that the described transaction qualifies as a testimonial communication on any account of testimonial communication. There are many testimonial models and the one sketched here would no doubt be considered by some as too narrow in some respects: eg David Owens, 'Testimony and Assertions' (2006) 130 *Philosophical Studies* 105; Jennifer Lackey, 'The Nature of Testimony' (2006) 87 *Pacific Philosophical Quarterly* 177.

[41] That, for a complete analysis, testimony has to be examined from both sides, see Ravenshear (n 25) 70 *et seq;* Catherine Z Elgin, 'Word Giving, Word Taking' in Alex Byrne, Robert Stalnaker and Ralph Wedgwood (eds), *Fact and Value—Essays on Ethics and Metaphysics for Judith Jarvis Thomson* (Cambridge, Massachusetts: MIT Press, 2001) ch 5.

[42] C A J Coady, *Testimony—A Philosophical Study* (Oxford: Clarendon Press, 1992) ch 2; Peter J Graham, 'What is Testimony?' (1997) 47 *The Philosophical Quarterly* 227; D H Mellor, 'Telling the Truth' in D H Mellor (ed), *Ways of Communicating* (Cambridge: CUP, 1990) 81.

[43] Which is an adaptation of the definition of 'meaning' given by H P Grice, 'Utterer's Meaning and Intentions' (1969) 78 *The Philosophical Rev* 147, 151, a concept first examined by him in

that p and sees that S intends H to believe that p, and (ii) believes that p on the basis of (i).

This does not mean that testimony must be explicit. It can be implicit in at least two ways: by either indirect or implied meaning. An example of the first is where we agree on a coded language so that when I tell you that p, I mean that, and testify* *indirectly* to, q. As for the second, suppose I tell my housemate that I am hungry and she replies: 'There are some sandwiches on the kitchen table.' This statement *implies* that I may help myself to the food. The invitation is clear enough even though it was not said explicitly that I may eat the sandwiches, nor was the offer literally entailed by what was said.

We turn now to the receipt of testimony. A person (H) hears an utterance by S.[44] For this to be a paradigm case of H believing S's testimony, H must, to begin with, understand S to be performing a speech act of the kind which may be described as 'asserting that p' or 'attesting to p' or 'telling the truth (or fact) about p'; and, further, H must understand what S is saying and referring to.[45] On one view, strictly speaking, H must recognize that S made her utterance intending H to believe that p, and to believe that p on the basis of this recognition.[46] When H believes S's testimony, she believes S is telling the truth. There are two aspects to this belief. First, H believes that S is saying what S believes to be true. Secondly, H believes that what she takes S to be saying (p) is true.[47] For H to believe S's testimony, she must believe in both senses and in such a way as to connect the two. To believe S's testimony that p is to believe that p *through* S's testimony: it is to accept as true what S asserts for the reason that she has asserted it.[48]

To believe p as a result of hearing S's testimony is not the same as believing S's testimony that p. There is a difference between acquiring belief *through* testimony (believing what someone tells us in consequent of judging her trustworthy) and

'Meaning' (1957) 66 *The Philosophical Rev* 377. For other Grice-inspired analyses of testimony, see Richard Moran, 'Getting Told and Being Believed' in Jennifer Lackey and Ernest Sosa (eds), *The Epistemology of Testimony* (Oxford: OUP, 2006) ch 12; Edward S Hinchman, 'Telling as Inviting to Trust' (2005) 70 *Philosophy and Phenomenological Research* 562. The 'intention to assert' requirement in Rules 801(a) and (c) of the US Federal Rules of Evidence may be read in terms of the present analysis.

[44] S need not speak to H. H may overhear S's testimony to someone else and believe it: Michael Welbourne, 'Testimony, Knowledge and Belief' in Bimal Krishna Matilal and Arindam Chakrabarti (eds), *Knowing From Words* (Dordrecht: Kluwer Academic Publishers, 1994) 297, 302–303.

[45] Elizabeth Fricker, 'The Epistemology of Testimony' (1987) 61 *Supplementary Proceedings of the Aristotelian Society* 57, 69 *et seq*; Michael Welbourne, 'The Community of Knowledge' (1981) 31 *Philosophical Quarterly* 302, 308–311.

[46] This mirrors the communicative intention essential for testifying: see above. But contrast Jennifer Lackey, 'The Nature of Testimony' (2006) 87 *Pacific Philosophical Quarterly* 177.

[47] James F Ross, 'Testimonial Evidence' in Keith Lehrer (ed), *Analysis and Metaphysics* (Dordretch: R Reidel, 1975) 35, 40.

[48] cf Michael Welbourne, 'The Transmission of Knowledge' (1979) 29 *The Philosophical Quarterly* 1, 5: 'For me to believe you *is* for me to suppose that I have learnt (come to know) that *p* from you.'

acquiring it *from* a testimonial act, as when I come to believe that S has a cold from noticing the nasal tone of her voice.[49] Or, I may infer that S is agitated from the way she speaks, for instance, when I notice the distress in her voice.[50] That S points to a giraffe and calls it an elephant will lead me to believe that she does not know what an elephant is. In these three cases, I acquire my belief *from* testimony*, not *through* it.[51] I did not believe that S had a cold or was agitated or that she does not know what an elephant is by believing her testimony*. I did not form my belief on the basis of the *content* of S's testimony*; rather, I infer it from her testimonial *act*.[52] This does not mean that in every case where I believe p upon perceiving someone's testimony that p, I believe p through her testimony. If a person pretending to be dead were to shout out 'I am alive' as I try to take her pulse, I would accept that she is, indeed, alive: what we have is a situation where S testifies* that p, and I, upon hearing it, accept that p. But I accept that p not through believing her testimony* (although I have to admit I agree with it[53]); rather, it is because I take the fact that she speaks as proof that she is alive.

In summary: (a) for a person to give testimony, she must make a statement with a specific communicative intention with the elements described above; and (b) for a person to receive testimony *as testimony*, she must respond to it in a certain way. In the latter, she must accept p through believing S's testimony that p, and this must be distinguished from inferring that p merely in consequent of perceiving S's testimonial act; in the first case, but not in the second, the person may be described as relying on, or receiving, S's statement 'testimonially'.

2.1.2 Operation of the hearsay rule

When lawyers say that a 'question of hearsay only arises when the words are relied on "testimonially"', the use of that term may be understood in the sense just described.[54] The quotation is taken from the judgment of Lord Wilberforce in

[49] This example is taken from Robert Audi, 'Testimony, Credulity, and Veracity' in Lackey and Sosa (n 43) ch 1, 26–27.

[50] *Ratten v R* [1972] AC 378.

[51] Robert Audi, 'The Place of Testimony in the Fabric of Knowledge and Justification' (1997) 34 *American Philosophical Quarterly* 405, 410, nn 13, 14; Sanford C Goldberg, 'Testimonially Based Knowledge from False Testimony' (2001) 51 *The Philosophical Quarterly* 512, 512.

[52] Jennifer Lackey, 'Knowing from Testimony' (2006) 1 *Philosophy Compass* 432, 433.

[53] G E M Anscombe, 'What is it to Believe Someone?' in C F Delaney (ed), *Rationality and Religious Belief* (Notre Dame: University of Notre Dame Press, 1979) 141, 144–145; cf Welbourne (n 48) 4, 5.

[54] In the United States, the concept of 'testimonial' was recently used to mark out the ambit of the right of confrontation protected under the Sixth Amendment of her Constitution. The Supreme Court held in *Crawford v Washington* (2004) 541 US 36, 53–4 that the provision barred 'admission of testimonial statements of a witness who did not appear at trial unless he was unavailable to testify, and the defendant had had a prior opportunity for cross-examination'. For further discussion: H L Ho, 'Confrontation and Hearsay: a Critique of Crawford' (2004) Intl J of Evidence and Proof 147. The Supreme Court in this case and in *Davis v Washington* (2006) 126 S Ct 2266 declined to give a general definition of 'testimonial statement'. What is clear is that the concept of 'testimonial' that applies for the purposes of the right of confrontation is infiltrated by special constitutional

Ratten v R.[55] In this case, the disputed evidence was of a telephone call made by a female from a house wherein a woman was allegedly murdered by the accused. The caller had asked the operator for the police in a distressed voice. This evidence was considered relevant in two ways. First, it contradicted the accused's assertion that no call, apart from his, was made from the house during the relevant period. Secondly, it showed that the woman was in a state of fear, thus undermining the accused's claim that the gun from which the fatal shot was fired had gone off by accident. In requesting for the police, the woman was not testifying* to the operator: 'I am making a telephone call' or 'I am fearful'. The operator could hear for herself, and did not need to be told, that the woman was making a telephone call. The operator could also tell from the woman's voice that she was fearful; while justification for this belief was gained *from* hearing her speak, it was not gained *through* believing what she had said. The court held that the evidence was not hearsay. This is because, to quote Lord Wilberforce again: 'A question of hearsay only arises when the words are relied on "testimonially", i.e. as establishing some fact narrated by the words.'[56]

The hearsay rule, in substance, forbids a way of using or reasoning on hearsay evidence.[57] It is important to separate the import of the rule from the techniques of enforcing it. The ban on the forbidden reasoning is enforced by exclusion of hearsay evidence where the evidence is not offered for any other use that is legitimate. Where it has some legitimate use, the evidence is admitted; and sometimes, hearsay evidence which lacks any legitimate use is inadvertently admitted: in both cases, the ban is enforced not by exclusion but by regulating deliberation on the evidence, that is, by requiring the fact-finder to refrain from reasoning on the evidence in the forbidden way.[58] To describe the hearsay rule as the rule that excludes hearsay evidence is to confuse the rule with the technique of enforcing it.

concerns and is different from the ordinary concept of 'testimony'. Take, for instance, this ruling of the Supreme Court in *Davis v Washington* (ibid 2273): 'Statements are nontestimonial when made in the course of police interrogation under circumstances objectively indicating that the primary purpose... is to enable police assistance to meet an ongoing emergency.' There is nothing in the ordinary concept of 'testimony' that prevents one from telling facts in an ongoing emergency. It is highly doubtful that philosophical discussion of testimony can illuminate this area of constitutional law in the same way it can the general hearsay rule. Cf Michael S Pardo, 'Testimony', forthcoming in Tulane Law Review, draft available at: <http://ssrn.com/abstract=986845>.

[55] *Ratten v R* (n 50) 387, per Lord Wilberforce; see also John Henry Wigmore, *Evidence in Trials at Common Law*, vol 5, James H Chadbourn revision (Boston: Little, Brown and Co, 1974) 3, § 1362: 'the hearsay rule... signifies a rule rejecting assertions, offered testimonially, which have not been in some way subjected to the test of cross-examination'.

[56] (n 50) 387.

[57] It is, as McNamara puts it, a 'rule of use' rather than a 'rule of exclusion': Philip McNamara, 'The Canons of Evidence—Rules of Exclusion or Rules of Use? (1986) 10 Adelaide L Rev 341.

[58] Mirjan Damaška, 'Hearsay in Cinquecento Italy' in Michele Taruffo (ed), *Studi di Vittorio Denti*, vol 1 (Padova: CEDAM, 1994) 59, 87; McNamara (n 57) 351, 352; *R v Glasby* (2000) 115 Australian Crim Rep 465, 479, 481.

The most often cited statement of the form of reasoning forbidden by the common law hearsay rule came from the Privy Council in *Subramaniam* v *PP*:[59]

Evidence of a statement made to a witness by a person who is not himself called as a witness . . . is hearsay and inadmissible when *the object of the evidence is to establish the truth of what is contained in the statement.* It is not hearsay and is admissible when it is proposed to establish by the evidence, not the truth of the statement but the fact that it was made.

The common law definition is mirrored in the United States Federal Rules of Evidence. Rule 802 excludes hearsay evidence, and hearsay is defined in Rule 801 (c) as:

a statement, other than one made by the declarant while testifying at the trial or hearing, *offered in evidence to prove the truth of the matter asserted.*

The objection is not to a defect in the evidence as such, but to what the party adducing the evidence ('the proponent') intends to do with it. She is not allowed to persuade the fact-finder to rely on the court-of-court statement testimonially; the law forbids the fact-finder from relying on the statement in that way. Evidence (E) of someone (S for 'speaker' or 'source of information') having asserted something ('p' to stand for 'proposition') is inadmissible where:

(a) E is either documentary evidence or legal testimony which is produced or given at a trial by someone other than S (call that person W);
(b) the proponent wants the fact-finder, on the basis of E, to accept that S had testified* that p, and as a further step, to accept that p by believing S's testimony* (this entire chain of reasoning will be called 'the hearsay inference'); and
(c) there is no other line of legally permissible reasoning that the proponent wants the trier of fact to apply to E.

Where the evidence is not adduced for the purpose of inviting the fact-finder to draw the hearsay inference (see (b) above), it will not be excluded under the hearsay rule. It is not adduced for that purpose where the fact that S had said that p is in itself material or relevant. The classic example is the utterance of a threat in a case of duress. The accused claims that she committed the crime only because a third party had threatened to harm her if she refused to obey his order.[60] Evidence of the utterance of that threat is admissible. It is admissible despite being evidence 'of a statement made to a witness by a person who is not himself called as a witness'. Evidence of the threat is not adduced to prove the truth of the proposition

[59] [1956] 1 WLR 965, 970. Emphasis added. A formulation close to the common law definition is adopted in Singapore: *Soon Peck Wah v Woon Che Chye* [1998] 1 Singapore L Rep 234, 244; Jeffrey Pinsler, *Evidence, Advocacy and the Litigation Process* (Singapore: LexisNexis, 2003) 72. However, there are significant departures from the common law definition in s 115 of the Criminal Justice Act 2003 of England and Wales: see Dennis (n 29) 699–705.

[60] *Subramaniam v PP* (n 59).

asserted in it. The hearsay rule kicks in only when the hearsay inference is sought to be drawn from the evidence. That the threat was made is itself relevant because it provides a rational basis for fear; it matters not whether there was truly an intention to carry out the threat or whether it would in fact have been carried out.

It can often be unclear whether the proponent is seeking to rely on the hearsay inference. A classic example of an especially problematic case is *R v Rice*.[61] To prove that Rice had travelled on a particular flight, the prosecution sought to introduce evidence that one of the used tickets collected from the passengers on that flight had his name on it. The ticket was held not to be hearsay and was admitted in evidence. One might argue that the ticket contained a testimony*. Suppose I put my initials on a piece of personal property, say a ring. My intention may be to tell whoever finds it that it belongs to me.[62] Similarly, so one could argue, the person who printed the name on the ticket intended to tell the relevant airline and airport employees that the ticket belonged to Rice. But this is a disanalogy. A ring does not become mine just because I put my initials on it; the ticket, on the other hand, is arguably Rice's just because it has his name. Printing his name on the ticket was constitutive of making the ticket his; it was not to report the fact that the ticket had been issued to him. A clearer example of a constitutive document is a contract. No one would think of excluding it as hearsay evidence in an action brought by one contracting party against the other. The document does not record the fact that the parties had previously entered into a contract; the document *is* their contract.

It is irrelevant what assertion the ticket-issuer intended to make when she issued the ticket; what was relevant was the fact that the ticket carried Rice's name. How is this fact relevant? It may be inferred that Rice was on the flight from this series of premises: that the used ticket was collected from a passenger on the particular flight; that it was written out in the name of Rice; and that, usually, only a person whose name appears on a ticket is allowed to board the plane.[63] Whether this argument is valid will depend on certain facts about domestic air travel administration. In any event, it is unnecessarily elaborate. Had a contractual document carrying Rice's name been found left in the plane at the end of the flight, it would undoubtedly have been treated as relevant and admissible. The same analysis is applicable as straightforwardly to the ticket.

2.1.3 Personal knowledge requirement

An epistemic objection to the hearsay inference exists where, by reason of S's absence from the trial, the trier of fact lacks justification for believing her

[61] [1963] 1 QB 857.

[62] Compare the discussion of this example by Paul S Milich, 'Hearsay Antinomies: The Case for Abolishing the Rule and Starting Over' (1992) 71 Oregon L Rev 723, 730–732.

[63] Admittedly, the strength of this inference was weakened by the fact that the ticket bore an additional name (Moore) and by the prosecution's case that someone else (Hoather) had used the seat booked for that person: (n 61) 871.

testimony* that p. Notice that this immediate objection is to reliance on S's testimony* and not reliance on W's legal testimony. (Recall that W is the courtroom witness.) There is no question of relying on W's legal testimony that p because, as we are assuming, W did not herself perceive p. Under the 'personal knowledge' rule, W is allowed to testify only to that of which she has personal knowledge. The law treats W as not knowing that p because W did not perceive p herself. Therefore W cannot legally testify to p.

Suppose W heard S say that she (S) saw the accused commit the crime in question. As just said, a witness at a trial is permitted to testify only to matters that she had directly perceived and thus knows to be true.[64] W did not see the commission of the crime and therefore cannot testify that the accused did it. Why does the court allow W to testify to p only if she knows that p? This question will be considered first from the point of view of the testifier. It is absurd for a person to assert that p and at the same time disavow knowledge of p.[65] W's testimony would not make any sense if she were to tell the court simply and in the same breath: 'The accused did it but I do not know that the accused did it.' If W accepts that she does not know that the accused committed the crime, she should not assert that as a fact.

The personal knowledge rule is also justifiable from the perspective of the fact-finder, the person who is asked to receive the testimony. As elaborated in Chapter 3, trial deliberation aims immediately at justified belief and ultimately at knowledge. Testimony is adduced as a potential source of knowledge. Unless W knows that p, the fact-finder cannot gain knowledge that p by believing W's testimony that p, not even when p is true.[66] To reuse the example first given in Chapter 2, Part 3.2.2: suppose a malicious liar has unwittingly given true evidence, and, because of the way she gave it, the fact-finder believes, and is justified in believing, her. Even though the fact-finder is justified in believing that the accused is guilty, and her belief is true, she cannot be said to *know* that the accused is guilty. The reason has to do with this: we do not know that p if p is true merely by chance.[67] In our example, it was accidental that the witness's testimony was true, and it was even more of a fluke that the fact-finder's belief in the accused's guilt was correct.[68] If W knows not that p, her testimony that p is not a source, not even a

[64] Wigmore (n 25) 9 and vol 2, 762–768; Kenneth S Broun *et al* (eds), *McCormick On Evidence*, vol 1 (6th edn, St Paul, Minnesota: West Publishing, 2006) 47–51; *Johnson v People's Cab Co* (1956) 386 Pa 513, 515. This common law requirement has taken statutory form: eg s 62, Evidence Act of Singapore (Cap 97, 1997 rev edn); Rule 602, Federal Rules of Evidence of the United States.

[65] eg Robert Hambourger, 'Justified Assertion and the Relativity of Knowledge' (1987) 51 Philosophical Studies 241, 251–22. See further Chapter 3, Part 1.2.

[66] This is the dominant view: eg Michael Dummett, 'Testimony and Memory' in Bimal Krishna Matilal and Arindam Chakrabarti (eds), *Knowing From Words* (Dordrecht: Kluwer Academic Publishers, 1994) 251, 264. This is disputed by some philosophers; for a recent challenge: Sanford Goldberg, 'Testimonial Knowledge through Unsafe Testimony' (2005) 65 *Analysis* 302.

[67] Bernard Williams, *Descartes—The Project of Pure Enquiry* (London: Penguin, 1978, reprinted 1990) 44–45.

[68] Audi (n 51) 409.

potential source, of knowledge that p. The personal knowledge requirement can thus be understood as flowing logically from the fact that the trial is ultimately a knowledge-seeking enterprise.

Suppose, when pressed for clarification, our hypothetical W elaborates: 'S told me that the accused did it. But I did not see it for myself, so I do not know that the accused did it.' In testifying, the speaker invites the hearer to accept as true what she says on the basis of her saying so.[69] W is inviting the court to take it at her word that S said such and such. But she is anxious that the court does not hold her responsible for the truth of the proposition that the accused did it; she does not think that she can justifiably claim to know this. While W feels able to testify to what S said, W does not believe that she is in a position to testify—to give *her* word—that the accused committed the crime. Since she is not testifying to that fact, there is no question of finding guilt through believing her testimony.

The personal knowledge requirement and the hearsay rule, while conceptually independent, are operationally linked.[70] When W testifies in court that S told her that the accused perpetrated the crime for which she is standing trial (that 'S testified* that p'), W is not thereby testifying to p: she is not telling us, giving her word, that p is true. W is testifying only to S's testimony*, namely, the fact that S told her that p, and it is of *that* fact, not p, that W had personal perception. W knows by unmediated perception that S told her that p. W's legal testimony that S told her that p therefore satisfies the personal knowledge requirement.[71] But W's legal testimony is irrelevant, and can be excluded on that ground alone, unless the fact-finder is allowed, upon believing W's testimony that S had testified* that p, to believe S's testimony* and accept that p is true. If the fact-finder is allowed to do this, W's evidence would be indirectly relevant. But she is not allowed to do this because of the hearsay rule.[72] That rule prevents W's legal testimony on S's testimony* from being received and used as evidence of p. Consequently, W's legal testimony can serve no useful purpose at the trial; that S had testified* that p is, in itself, a legally irrelevant fact.[73]

Why does the hearsay rule forbid the fact-finder from finding that p through believing S's testimony* that p? One reason rests on this general epistemic principle: to be justified in believing S's testimony* that p, one must be justified in

[69] Elgin (n 41) 98.

[70] Baker (n 3) 16–17; *McCormick on Evidence* (n 64) vol 1, 48 and vol 2, 131. Historically, the latter might have descended from the former: Thayer (n 2) 518–519.

[71] See note of the Advisory Committee on Rule 602 of the United States Federal Rules of Evidence.

[72] Thayer (n 3) 270–271; Colin Tapper (ed), *Cross and Tapper on Evidence* (11th edn, Oxford: OUP, 2007) 591.

[73] It is relevant if, in addition, we have some basis for thinking that S spoke the truth, but that cannot be assumed. It is fallacious to make that assumption as it begs the question of whether p is true: Clifton B Perry, 'Hearsay, Nonassertive Conduct and *Petitio Principii*' (1991) *Intl J of Applied Philosophy* 45.

believing that S is trustworthy with respect to p. The defence of this principle follows.

2.1.4 *Justification for believing testimony*

Our discussion is now brought back to general principles. To be justified in believing S's testimony, H must be justified in believing not just that S is speaking honestly, but also that the state of affairs is as S reports it. The latter depends not just on S's veracity, but also on her epistemic 'competence' with respect to p. In theory, if S is competent with respect to p, then if S asserts sincerely that p, p is true.[74] S's competence depends on many factors. They include the accuracy of her memory and expression of p, her freedom from bias or unconscious influences in acquiring and conveying the knowledge that p, her opportunity or means for knowing that p, and her capacity and skill relative to p.[75] Together, S's sincerity and competence constitute her trustworthiness or credibility. These two terms are interchangeable, but, for consistency, only the first will be used hereafter. When H believes S's testimony, H is taking S's word as the basis for believing p, or for believing p more strongly than before. For H to defend her belief that p, it is inadequate for her merely to cite the fact that S said so:[76] where that belief is gained through S's testimony, it is necessary for H to add that S is trustworthy on the topic.[77]

2.1.5 *Duty of critical judgment*

The trier of fact is justified in believing S's testimony that p only if she has *positive reason* to believe that S is trustworthy with respect to p. As we will see, this requirement emanates from the special nature of the trial context and is implicit in the duty of deliberation. Where, by reason of S's absence from the trial, there is no evidence of her trustworthiness, the trier of fact would not be justified in believing through S's testimony* that p. She is not entitled to *assume* that S is trustworthy.

This 'inferentialist view', as Pritchard calls it,[78] is not self-evident. Indeed, the contrary 'default view'[79]—that there is no smoke without fire—has a strong intuitive appeal. When S tells us that p, it is natural to suppose, in the absence of grounds for suspicion, that S knows that p. It is perfectly rational to treat

[74] Following Elizabeth Fricker, 'Against Gullibility' in Bimal Krishna Matilal and Arindam Chakrabarti (eds), *Knowing From Words* (Dordrecht: Kluwer Academic Publishers, 1994) 125, 147.

[75] This list is borrowed from Ravenshear (n 25) 70–74.

[76] Jonathan Barnes, 'Socrates and The Jury: Paradoxes in Plato's Distinction Between Knowledge and True Belief (II)' (1980) 54 *Supplementary Proceedings of the Aristotelian Society* 193, 199, 200.

[77] But, ordinarily, we do not bother to state explicitly the latter: D M Armstrong, *Belief, Truth and Knowledge* (Cambridge: Cambridge University Press, 1973) 81.

[78] Pritchard (n 38) 101–102.

[79] ibid.

testimony as having some initial plausibility.[80] We have got our starting point wrong. That S told us that p is in itself a reason (albeit a prima facie reason) for believing that p. Positive reason is only needed to justify *dis*belief in S's testimony, not belief in it.[81] Some lawyers are attracted to this view. For instance, Baker, in his critique of the hearsay rule, reminds us that the 'statements of third persons are acted upon in the practical affairs of everyday life without the slightest hesitation or suspicion'.[82]

This is a false parallel. First, that we act on the word of others does not necessarily imply that we believe their testimony; after all, we may have no choice but to accept what they say, or we may consider it prudent to act on it or not worth the while to check it out.[83] We take risks when we act, as we often must, amidst uncertainty. However, relying on testimony as a guide to practical action is different from accepting testimony in the belief that it is true.[84] At a trial, the fact-finder aims ultimately at knowledge, to reach a positive finding that satisfies both the standard of justified belief (as contained in BAF*) and truth (as stipulated in TSC);[85] her task is not mere risk management, at least not in any straightforward or crude sense.

Secondly, even if it is true that we often believe what we are told, it is still an open question whether it is because we usually *assume* that others are trustworthy or that, most of the time, we *judge* them to be so. If the notion of judging testimony* seems strained in the ordinary context, it may simply be, as some writers have suggested, that we are not conscious of much that goes on (perhaps instantaneously or automatically) in our mind and that we are more discerning in the reception of testimony* than we realize.[86]

Thirdly, the analogy between ordinary affairs and trial proceedings is misplaced. We sometimes feel, to some degree, obligated socially[87] and morally[88] to trust what our neighbours tell us. For some philosophers, testimony is not a mere communication of belief; it offers, as a defining feature, an assurance of truth, an invitation to trust. In refusing to take someone's word for it, we slight the

[80] As argued by George F James, 'The Role of Hearsay in a Rational Scheme of Evidence' (1940) 34 Illinios L Rev 788, 792.

[81] J L Austin, 'Other Minds' (1946) 20 *Supplementary Proceedings of the Aristotelian Society* 148, 154.

[82] Baker (n 3) 14.

[83] Jonathan E Adler, 'Testimony, Trust, Knowing' (1994) 91 *J of Philosophy* 264, 274.

[84] For this reason, it is beside the point that 'most momentous actions, military, political, commercial and of every other kind, are daily undertaken on hearsay evidence': Ernest Jerome Hopkins (ed), Bierce Ambrose, *The Enlarged Devil's Dictionary* (London: Penguin, 2001) 176.

[85] See the defence of BAF* and TSC in Chapter 3, Part 1.

[86] Peter Lipton, 'The Epistemology of Testimony' (1998) 29 *Studies in History and Philosophy of Science* 1, 25; Mellor (n 42) 92; Adler (n 83) 274–275; Frederick Schmitt, 'Justification, Sociality and Autonomy' (1987) 73 *Synthese* 43, 64.

[87] H H Price, *Belief* (London: George Allen & Unwin, 1969) 114; Lorraine Code, *Epistemic Responsibility* (Hanover: Brown University Press, 1987) 172; Welbourne (n 45) 303.

[88] Price (n 87) 114–115.

person.[89] However, it is all too plain that the fact-finder is under no such constraints to believe testimony presented at a trial.

On the contrary, and this is the fourth point, it would be irresponsible for the fact-finder to assume the truth of the evidence she receives. It may be that people more often than not tell the truth and that testimony is usually correct. Even so, this does not carry us very far. Indeed, Fricker argues that this alone can never justify—not even in relation to mundane testimony—the presumption that a testifier is trustworthy on the subject of her testimony and, derivatively, the belief that her testimony is true.[90] Many disagree that it is always gullible to receive testimony uncritically.[91] But even they would concede that it could, in certain circumstances, be doxastically irresponsible for the fact-finder to assume that the testifier is trustworthy.[92] As McDowell says:[93]

> A person sufficiently responsible to count as having achieved epistemic standing from someone else's words needs to be aware of how knowledge can be had from others, and rationally responsive to considerations whose relevance that awareness embodies. That requires his forming beliefs on the say-so of others to be rationally shaped by an understanding of, among other things, the risks one subjects oneself [or others] to in accepting what people say.

Chief amongst the considerations to which the fact-finder must be responsive is the fact that her acceptance of a material allegation advanced at the trial is detrimental, in more ways than one, to the party against whom it is made. Justice in deliberation demands general sensitivity to the types of harm which would be inflicted by a positive finding should the allegation be false. A harmful finding should only be made with the degree of caution that shows sufficient respect for the affected person and adequate concern for his welfare. There is, accordingly, an ethical obligation to adopt a sufficiently critical attitude towards testimony adduced in support of the allegation. It is also epistemically rational to be critical. That the allegation is disputed, the testimony under challenge, or other inconsistent evidence exists ought to raise suspicion. Additionally, certain features of the witness, including her relationship with others involved in the case, may make salient the possibility that her testimony is biased, mistaken, exaggerated, a lie, or otherwise inaccurate; one or more of these risks will often be brought home to the fact-finder during cross-examination in an attack on the witness's credibility.[94]

[89] Moran (n 43); Hinchman (n 43).

[90] (n 45) 76. Similarly: Leslie Stephen and Frederick Pollock (eds), Clifford, William Kingdon, 'The Ethics of Belief' in his *Lectures and Essays*, vol 2 (London: Macmillan, 1879) 177, 189.

[91] eg Christopher J Insole, 'Seeing Off the Local Threat to Irreducible Knowledge by Testimony' (2000) 50 *The Philosophical Quarterly* 44, especially 51.

[92] eg Tyler Burge, 'Content Preservation' (1993) 102 *The Philosophical Review* 457, 468, 484; Dummett (n 66) 261.

[93] John McDowell, 'Knowledge by Hearsay' in his *Meaning, Knowledge and Reality* (Cambridge, Massachusetts: Harvard UP, 1998) 414, 434–435 (words in square brackets added).

[94] As Anthony Quinton noted, evidence is presented to the fact-finder under arrangements that 'explicitly presume' 'the liability of witnesses to lie, to be simply misinformed or to use words in

It is epistemically unsound and ethically irresponsible, in the trial context, for the fact-finder to take testimony on simple trust.

Against this, it might be said that the fact-finder is justified in taking the default view because witnesses are placed under oath. The fact that perjury is punishable provides a prima facie reason to believe that witnesses will be sufficiently motivated to tell the truth.[95] But, as Pritchard rightly points out, what we have in the threat and fear of legal sanctions are independent non-testimonial grounds for believing the witnesses.[96] In refusing to take the sincerity of witnesses for granted and insisting that they be placed under oath before they testify, the law is actually adopting the inferentialist position.

The need for positive reason to believe testimony is implicit in its legal status as *evidence* through which one may acquire belief in its content;[97] otherwise put, it is implicit in the fact-finder's duty of deliberation. Many have argued, *pace* Fricker, that in much of our daily affairs, testimony has a different epistemological role; often, we presume that the testifier is trustworthy: I ask for the time, you tell me, and I believe you, just like that, without deliberation.[98] When it is presumed that S is trustworthy on the matter of p and therefore that p is true, S's testimony serves as a simple transmission of knowledge rather than as a potiential source or ground of knowledge.[99] We take S's word on trust, on faith; and we claim to know that p directly on her authority.[100] On the other hand, when we want to be positively satisfied of S's trustworthiness before believing her testimony, we are treating her testimony as putative evidence of p;[101] we accept S's testimony, not by receiving it indiscriminately, but only when it passes our critical evaluation as a candidate for justified belief. This is how the fact-finder should

an unusual way': 'Authority and Autonomy in Knowledge' in his *Thoughts and Thinkers* (London: Duckworth, 1982) ch 8, 67.

[95] The presumption was urged by Gilbert in an earlier age when the oath generally had greater significance than it has today: 'there is that Sanction and Reverence due to an Oath, that the Testimony of one Witness naturally obtained Credit; unless there be "stronger" appearance of probability to the contrary' (Capel Lofft (ed), Lord Chief Baron Gilbert, *The Law of Evidence*, vol 1 (Dublin: Byrne, Moore, Jones and Rice, 1795) 287).

[96] Pritchard (n 38) 119.

[97] As we saw, this use of evidence of testimony is different from the case where a belief is acquired *from* (rather than *through*) the evidence.

[98] eg David Christensen and Hilary Kornblith, 'Testimony, Memory and the Limits of the *A Priori*' (1997) 86 *Philosophical Studies* 1, 6–7.

[99] Dummett (n 66) 264.

[100] For accounts along this line: Dummett (n 66); Zeno Vendler, 'Telling the Facts' in Peter A French, Theodore E Uehling, Jr and Howard K Wettstein (eds), *Contemporary Perspectives in the Philosophy of Language* (Minneapolis: University of Minnesota Press, 1979) 220, 227; John Hardwig, 'Epistemic Dependence' (1985) 82 *The Journal of Philosophy* 335, particularly 344–349.

[101] It is so treated by Coady (n 42) 42 *et seq*; cf Graham (n 42). The distinction between the two ways of viewing testimony is noted by the latter, 231–232, as by: Anscombe (n 53) 151; Welbourne (n 48) 8–9 and (n 45) 311–312; Burge (n 92) 484; Edward Craig, *Knowledge and the State of Nature* (Oxford: Clarendon Press, 1990) 40, 43–44.

receive testimony at a trial.[102] If she has evidence, and is sufficiently satisfied, of S's trustworthiness with respect to p, she possesses ground for believing that p on S's word, and it is only when this is the case that she is justified in accepting S's testimony as a basis for believing p. Notice that the belief is not based wholly on S's testimony; it is also based on evidence and belief about S.[103] Critical reflection is expected and inferences must be made prior to reaching the justified belief that p. The trier of fact must be satisfied of adequate grounds to support, at each step, the inference from S's testimony that S believes that p, and from there that p is true: the first step depends on S's sincerity in asserting that p and the second on S's competence with respect to p.[104]

2.1.6 Significance of not following testimonial procedure

This is what we have established as a general principle: the trier of fact is not justified in believing a testimony that p unless she has positive evidence of the testifier's trustworthiness in relation to p. The testimonial procedure is devised precisely to create such evidence. Its application is valuable in three respects. First, the act of testifying in court has intrinsic evidential value. By the act itself, the witness commits heavily to the truth of her testimony. To give legal testimony, a person must appear before the court, identify herself publicly, take the oath, asseverate that such and such is true, and expose herself to possible punishment for perjury. That a person has come forward and vouched for the truth of p in this way and under these circumstances must count as some evidence that her belief that p is real and strong.

Secondly, the act of testifying is also significant from a behavioural point of view. Assessment of a person's trustworthiness is ordinarily done by exercise of 'folk psychology', which is sensitive in diverse ways to more personal cues than can be exhaustively listed. Demeanour is commonly treated as evidence of trustworthiness; many signs relating to a person's trustworthiness are said to be detectable only from a face-to-face encounter.[105] The fact-finder relies on a variety of indicators, including 'style, paralinguistic cues, and nonverbal behavior to reach a decision about a witness's credibility'.[106] All of these are lost if the fact-finder has no perceptual contact with the maker of the statement, as would be the case when evidence of that statement is given by someone else. However, the

[102] As Audi (n 51) 406 observed. To repeat, the present concern is with testimony of facts, not expert opinion. Clearly, the fact-finder's duty of critical judgment is much more complicated when it comes to scientific or opinion evidence. That topic falls outside the ambit of this chapter.

[103] Robert Audi, 'Testimony, Credulity, and Veracity' in Lackey and Sosa (n 43) ch 1, 26.

[104] That the inference is indirect and goes via S's belief: Mellor (n 42), 89.

[105] *Creamer v Bivert* (1908) 214 Mo 473; 113 S.W. 1118, 1120–1121; *National Labor Relations Board v Dinion Coil Co* (1952) 201 F 2d 484, 487–490; *Clarke v Edinburgh Tramways Co* 1919 SC (HL) 35, 36–7; *Powell v Streatham* [1935] AC 243, 256; Jerome Frank, *Courts on Trial—Myth and Reality in American Justice* (New Jersey: Princeton UP, 1973 edn) 21.

[106] William O'Barr, *Linguistic Evidence—Language, Power, and Strategy in the Courtroom* (San Diego: Academic Press, 1982) 42 (this section is written by John M Conley).

significance of demeanour evidence must not be overstated; its actual value is a matter of dispute. Also, how much influence demeanour evidence actually has on trial deliberation must not be exaggerated. What a witness says is likely to be a better indicator and to have a greater impact on our assessment of her trustworthiness than how she looks, speaks, or behaves in the witness box.[107]

The value of bringing a witness in court comes, thirdly, from the information we can get from her. During examination-in-chief, the witness will invariably testify not only to the proposition (p) that is immediately relevant or material, but also to the surrounding circumstances and background facts. This allows the plausibility of the specific allegation p to be judged against the coherence of the witness's account as a whole, together with the other evidence presented in the case.[108] Cross-examination tends to challenge weaknesses in the story told in chief. Effective responses to those challenges will deepen the justification for accepting that p; conversely, failure to rise to those challenges may undermine or undercut such justification.[109]

When we assess a person's trustworthiness, we do not only judge her physical capacities and skills, such as the power of her perceptual faculties, the accuracy of her communication, and the ability to form correct judgments on the matter at hand. We also engage in rationalization of her behaviour. This process involves deciphering the workings of her mind. She is ascribed a certain mental state in the light of which her testimony is explained; a possible belief, motive, intention, or desire is imputed to her for testifying as she did.[110] We infer p through S's testimony that p when the most coherent account of why S said that p is that she believes p and p is true.[111] The more background information that is available, the better we are able to draw this 'inference to the best explanation'. Numerous things are of interest in this connection. It is of value to know if S is related to the parties, the significance of that relation, whether she stands to lose or gain from the outcome of the case, how she came to be involved in it, the situation she was in when she allegedly observed that p, relevant aspects of her disposition and character, and so on. It is also important to see whether she is able to tell, unprompted

[107] Brian MacKenna, 'Discretion' (1974) 9 The Irish Jurist (NS) 1, 10; Olin Guy Wellborn III, 'Demeanor' (1991) 76 Cornell L Rev 1075. Even if live testimony does not enhance credibility judgments, it does not follow, as Wellborn is careful to add, that it does not have 'overall positive value'. For instance, he noted that the requirements of live testimony 'may well deter dishonest witnesses': ibid at 1092. Contrast James P Timony, 'Demeanour Credibility' (2000) 49 Catholic University L Rev 903, supporting 'the use of demeanor... as a factor in determining witness credibility' (ibid 906) and arguing that '[i]rrespective of its potential pitfalls..., demeanor evidence is still one of the best guides to judging a witness's credibility' (ibid 920).

[108] The holistic nature of evidential evaluation was discussed in Chapter 3, Part 3.4.

[109] However fully the witness 'may harmonise his tale with all he knows, it is extremely unlikely that an exhaustive cross-examination would not bring to light some conflict with matters not known to the witness, although known to others': Ravenshear (n 25) 76.

[110] Jack Lyons, 'Testimony, Induction and Folk Psychology' (1997) 75 *Australasian J of Philosophy* 163, 170–176.

[111] Lipton (n 86) 27–29; Adler (n 83) 274–275.

by leading questions, a story that 'hangs together', to observe how she tells it, her behaviour, and the persuasiveness of her response when challenged. This is why calling S to recount her story personally before the court, getting her to provide background information, and subjecting her to searching cross-examination are so crucial. When S does not stand as a witness, the fact-finder may simply not know enough to justify acceptance of her trustworthiness or to defend such acceptance;[112] consequently, knowledge of p cannot be obtained through S's testimony.[113]

(A slight digression from the main argument: Where S stands as a witness, the fact-finder may, from a judgment of her performance in court, come to believe her testimony or disbelieve her testimony categorically. But the belief need not be categorical. If evidence of S's trustworthiness is equivocal, the fact-finder may withhold from believing S's testimony categorically and merely believe it to a certain degree. In that event, the degree to which she is justified in believing S's testimony depends on the strength of the available evidence of S's trustworthiness.)

2.1.7 Evaluation of the testimonial argument

It may be asked: if, as the testimonial argument suggests, there is a rational basis for objecting to uncritical and unwarranted drawing of the hearsay inference, should not every rational system of trial have a hearsay rule? Why then is there no such rule in Continental jurisdictions? Indeed, many common law countries have embarked or are thinking of embarking on statutory relaxation of the rule.[114] Is this statutory assault not indicative of loss of faith in the rule by even common law lawyers? Lastly, why have international and war crimes tribunals not felt any need to have a hearsay rule even when, one would have thought, their interests in legitimacy are especially great? Has the testimonial argument exaggerated, if not plainly misrepresented, the significance of the hearsay rule?

As stressed earlier, we must be careful to differentiate the import of the hearsay rule from the exclusionary method of its enforcement. Once this distinction is kept in mind, it will be seen as an oversimplification the claim that civil law jurisdictions allow free admission and use of hearsay evidence. In fact, a number of writers have shown that the hearsay doctrine developed on the

[112] cf *Blastland* [1986] AC 41, 54, per Lord Bridge: hearsay evidence is excluded due to 'the great difficulty… of assessing what, if any, weight can properly be given to a statement by a person whom the [fact-finder has] not seen or heard and which has not been subject to any test of reliability by cross-examination'.

[113] The kind of knowledge in question has been called 'discursive'. On justification and defensibility as conditions of discursive knowledge, see Keith Lehrer, 'Testimony and Trustworthiness' in Lackey and Sosa (n 43) ch 7.

[114] For a survey of this trend relating to criminal trials, see The Law Reform Commission of Hong Kong Consultation Paper, *Hearsay in Criminal Proceedings*, November 2005, available at: <http://www.hkreform.gov.hk>, ch 5.

European continent long before it emerged at common law.[115] What is true is that, in Continental legal systems, the doctrine seldom[116] takes the form of an exclusionary rule; it is embodied generally in broad principles relating to the legitimate use of hearsay evidence in establishing proof or, sometimes, more concretely, in rules that provide when and to what extent such evidence can be used to support findings of fact.[117] This preference is understandable: exclusion of evidence is not a suitable option, as the absence in civilian jurisdictions of a sharp division between the roles of judge and fact-finder makes it difficult to shield the fact-finder from the evidence; on the other hand, the technique of regulating the use of evidence is particularly appropriate because, first, the judge has the power to track down the source of the hearsay statement and to investigate the trustworthiness of that source, and secondly, the requirement that she gives detailed reasons for her decision allows a higher court to check on the soundness of her assessment and use of hearsay.[118] The concern about the epistemic justification for reliance on hearsay in legal fact-finding is certainly not unique to the common law. While the manner in which that concern is addressed differs from country to country, most systems of trial, whether of the civil or common law tradition, subscribe to some degree and in some form to the underlying norms. As Damaška puts it, although the players and their instruments are not the same, the normative scores are similar.[119]

For much the same reason, the growing trend to reduce the rigour of or abolish the hearsay rule does not undermine our argument. This trend stems from dissatisfaction with the technique of excluding hearsay evidence. There is a perception that this technique is overly blunt, often leaving out evidence even where the fact-finder would have been able to judge the trustworthiness of the out-of-court declarant on the statement that she had allegedly made. The tide against the exclusionary technique does not necessarily reflect a diminished concern

[115] Herrmann (n 10); Damaška (n 58), and 'Of Hearsay and Its Analogues' (1992) 76 Minnesota L Rev 425; Hammelmann (n 8) 68–69.

[116] But a rule of exclusion is not without precedent: Ulla Jacobsson, 'Hearsay Testimony in Sweden' (1973) 17 Scandinavian Studies in Law 129, 144–146.

[117] For instance, when witnesses with first-hand knowledge of the facts are available, the court is expected to call them rather than rely on hearsay evidence; and, on some matters, hearsay evidence must be corroborated: Damaška (n 58) 70, and (n 115) 439–441; Heinrich Reiter, 'Hearsay Evidence and Criminal Procedure in Germany and Australia' (1984) 10 Monash L Rev 51, 55; Jacobsson (n 116) 130; J R Spencer, 'Orality and the Evidence of Absent Witnesses' [1994] Crim LR 628, 641, 642, n 68, and 'Evidence' in Mireille Delmas-Marty and J R Spence (eds), *European Criminal Procedures* (Cambridge: CUP, 2002) ch 11, 619 ('According to German case law, hearsay evidence is normally insufficient on its own to found a conviction: it must be corroborated by other evidence of a more reliable type).'

[118] Damaška (n 58) 85 and (n 117) 427–428; Jeremy A Blumenthal, 'Shedding Some Light on Calls For Hearsay Reform: Civil Law Hearsay Rules In Historical And Modern Perspective' (2001) 13 Pace International L Rev 93, 113–115. But according to Spencer, 'Evidence' (n 117) 623–624: 'the French judge, though bound to list the facts that he finds proved, has no duty to explain how he assessed the evidence on which these findings of fact are based'.

[119] Damaška (n 58) 84.

about the use of hearsay evidence, a concern to which that technique is merely one response. For instance, no lawyer could possibly think that the abolition of the hearsay rule under the Civil Evidence Act 1995 liberated the fact-finder from all constraints on how she may reason on hearsay. Section 4(1) of the Act requires that the court, in evaluating the weight of hearsay evidence, '*shall* have regard to any circumstances from which any inference can reasonably be drawn as to the reliability or otherwise of the evidence'. As Carter said of this provision: 'Nothing could be broader, more bland or so incontrovertible.'[120] It is unfortunate that, in stating the principle so widely, the section fails to identify the precise problem with hearsay evidence. Nevertheless, the condition for reliance on the hearsay inference is implicit in the general principle expressed in section 4(1): the inference that p is 'reasonable' only if it is epistemically justifiable, and it is not epistemically justifiable for the fact-finder to infer that p unless she has some basis on which she can assess, with justification, that S is trustworthy with regards to p.

The common law hearsay rule has also been statutorily relaxed on the criminal side. In England and Wales, section 114(1)(d) of the Criminal Justice Act 2003 confers on the court discretion to admit hearsay if it is 'satisfied that it is in the interests of justice for it to be admissible'. Similarly, section 3(4) of the South African Law of Evidence Amendment Act 1988 gives the court discretion to admit hearsay evidence 'in the interests of justice'. Under these statutes, the discretion must be exercised by taking into account the reliability of the original source or the probative value of the evidence.[121] It is difficult to see how the court can reach a favourable conclusion on the issues of reliability and probative value unless it is satisfied of the trustworthiness of the out-of-court maker of the statement. What has been discarded is merely the rigidity of the law.

It is also true that international courts or tribunals and national courts created with the involvement of the international community (such as the International Criminal Court, the Iraqi Special Tribunal, the Special Court for Sierra Leone, the International Tribunal for the Former Yugoslavia, and its sister tribunal for Rwanda) do not exclude hearsay evidence as a rule. Does this show that the hearsay rule is a quirk of common law, unrecognized by international standards of procedural fairness, and dispensable even when it is especially important to secure the legitimacy of a trial? Four reasons support a negative answer. First, it is not cynical to suspect that some of the rules of some these institutions were influenced by political motives; outcries of 'victor's justice' and 'show trials' are familiar enough. The prosecution might have been allowed to rely freely on hearsay evidence for the sake of political expediency, out of steadfast determination to

[120] P B Carter, 'The Hearsay Rule: Retreat or Rationalisation' in Charles Sampford and C A Bois (eds), *Sir Zelman Cowen—A Life in the Law* (St Leonards, New South Wales: Prospect Media, 1997) 29, 36.

[121] Section 114(2)(e) Criminal Justice Act 2003; s 3(1)(c)(iv) Law of Evidence Amendment Act 1988.

obtain convictions.[122] Secondly, the liberal admission and use of hearsay evidence at some international trials, most infamously those conducted by the Nuremberg and Tokyo tribunals, has been fiercely criticized.[123] It would be perverse, without more, to recommend the practice of those special tribunals to ordinary courts.

Whereas the first and second points are sceptical of the use of hearsay evidence by some of these special judicial bodies, the third and fourth observations point to possible factors that excuse their lax attitude towards such evidence. These factors, however, do not apply to domestic courts. The third point is this: courts and tribunals specially created in consequent of political disasters face problems unique to the kind of cases with which they have to deal. 'Cases of mass violations of human rights and international humanitarian law, such as genocide, war crimes, and crimes against humanity, present exceptional . . . logistical challenges.'[124] This is due to the vast number of victims, witnesses, and incidents involved. Speaking from personal judicial experience, Wald noted:[125] 'It is often necessary to present evidence on the events leading up to the outbreak of hostilities to set the stage for the particular incidents that gave rise to the alleged war crimes.' Further, due to how war crimes are defined, proof may be required of 'the existence of an international armed conflict, a nexus between the illegal acts alleged and an armed conflict, the occurrence of a systematic or widespread campaign against civilians . . . , or an intent to destroy a religious, ethnic, or racial group'.

Whereas proof in the typical municipal trial is of 'a single discrete incident', the job of international and special tribunals is more like 'documenting an episode or . . . era of national or ethnic conflict'.[126] These tribunals also undertake much broader social functions than normal courts do. They are expected, among other things, to contribute 'to the restoration and maintenance of peace',[127] to help in 'establishing historical facts', and to make 'societies come face to face with

[122] See the controversies surrounding the trial of Saddam Hussein by the Iraqi Special Tribunal: Gregory S McNeal, 'Unfortunate Legacies: Hearsay, Ex Parte Affidavits and Anonymous Witnesses at the IHT', *International Commentary on Evidence*: vol 4, 2006: issue 1, article 5, available at: <http://www.bepress.com/ice/vol4/iss1/art5>.

[123] See Virginia Morris and Michael Scharf, *The International Criminal Tribunal for Rwanda*, vol 1 (Irvington-on-Hudson, NY: Transnational, 1998) 13–14; written submission of Michael Scharf before the United States House Armed Services Committee, Hearing on Standards of Military Commissions and Tribunals, 26 July 2006, available at: <http://armedservices.house.gov/comdocs/schedules/07–26-06ScharfTestimony.pdf>, 3–4.

[124] Special Report of the United States Institute of Peace, 'Building the Iraqi Special Tribunal—Lessons from Experiences in International Criminal Justice', June 2004, available at: <http://www.usip.org/pubs/specialreports/sr122.pdf>, 1.

[125] Patricia M Wald, 'To "Establish Incredible Events by Credible Evidence": The Use of Affidavit Testimony in Yugoslavia War Crimes Tribunal Proceedings' (2001) 42 Harvard Journal of International Law 535, 536.

[126] ibid 536–537.

[127] Almiro Rodrigues and Cécile Tournaye, 'Hearsay Evidence' in Richard May *et al* (eds), *Essays on ICTY Procedure and Evidence in Honour of Gabrielle Kirk McDonald* (The Hague: Kluwer, 2001) ch 23, 296–297.

the past'.[128] To conduct an inquiry of such large scope and for such broad purposes, it is neither wise nor feasible to ignore all information that is not conveyed by personal testimony.[129] It must also be noted that some of the international tribunals lack coercive power. This makes evidence gathering difficult enough as it is. The difficulty is aggravated by the fact that crimes against humanity are carried out on a wide scale, involving displacements of population, where victims are often afraid to step forward to testify or have fled and disappeared.[130] 'To adopt strict rules on admissibility of evidence in these circumstances would complicate the task of [such tribunals] tremendously.'[131] Thus one could argue that the unique nature of the job to be done, coupled with the special circumstances in which it must be carried out, excuse reliance by these unusual institutions on hearsay evidence.[132]

Fourthly, most international tribunals have merely rejected the rigidity of the common law exclusionary rule. They have in fact embraced the spirit of the testimonial argument offered above. Although hearsay evidence is not always excluded, neither is it always admitted. Whether it is admissible depends on its relevancy and probative value. In *Prosecutor v Tadić*,[133] the Trial Chamber of the International Criminal Tribunal for the Former Yugoslavia held that, in assessing the probative value of hearsay, the court must examine the 'truthfulness, voluntariness, and trustworthiness of the evidence'. It must do so by looking at 'the circumstances under which the evidence arose as well as the content of the statement'. In one case, the Appeals Chamber found the hearsay evidence 'so lacking in terms of the indicia of reliability' that it was held to be non-probative and

[128] Dominic McGoldrick, 'War Crimes Trial Before International Tribunals: Legality and Legitimacy' in R A Melikan (ed), *Domestic and International Trials 1700–2000—The Trial in History, vol II* (Manchester: Manchester University Press, 2003) ch 6, 109.

[129] For one, it will slow down proceedings to a speed that is not politically acceptable. The hearsay rule, Rule 90(A) of the original Rules of Procedure and Evidence of the International Criminal Tribunal for the Former Yugoslavia, provided that 'witnesses shall, in principle, be heard directly'. This rule had subsequently to be repealed as pressure mounted on the tribunal to expedite its proceedings: Megan A Fairlie, 'Due Process Erosion: The Diminution of Live Testimony at the ICTY' (2003) 34 California Western Intl LJ 47.

[130] Rodrigues and Tournaye (n 127) 296.

[131] ibid.

[132] All the more so when suitable safeguards are installed. For examples of safeguards, see Rules 92 bis, ter and quarter of the current version of the Rules of Procedure and Evidence of the International Criminal Tribunal for the Former Yugoslavia, IT/32/Rev 39, 22 September 2006, available at: <http://www.un.org/icty/legaldoc-e/basic/rpe/IT032Rev39e.pdf>.

[133] Decision on the Defence Motion on Hearsay, Case No IT-94-I-T, 5 August 1996 (decision of Trial Chamber). This ruling was approved by the Appeals Chamber in *Prosecutor v Aleksovski*, Decision on Prosecutor's Appeal on Admissibility of Evidence, Case No IT-95–14/1-AR73, 16 February 1999 (decision of Appeals Chamber) para 15, which in turn has been cited on many occasions: see eg *Prosecutor v Martić*, Case No IT-95–11-T, Judgment of the Trial Chamber I, 12 June 2007 at para 24; *Prosecutor v Martić*, Case No IT-95–11-T, Decision Adopting Guidelines on the Standards Governing the Admission of Evidence, 19 January 2006, Trial Chamber I, para 8.

ruled inadmissible.[134] Even if the hearsay evidence is admitted, 'the weight or probative value to be afforded to [it] will usually be less than that given to the testimony of a witness who has given it under a form of oath and who has been cross-examined'.[135] All of these add up to a very clear recognition by the Tribunal for caution to be exercised when relying on hearsay evidence. For these four reasons, it would be foolhardy to treat the absence of the hearsay exclusionary rule in international criminal proceedings as an argument for allowing hearsay evidence to be freely used in the domestic context.

2.1.8 Duty of judgment

There is, however, more to the hearsay rule than the testimonial argument suggests. The argument justifies the ban on the hearsay inference only insofar as, by reason of S's absence, the trier of fact lacks justification for relying testimonially on her statement. But it is not always true that where S does not testify in court, there will be no evidence of her trustworthiness, and it is clear that, at common law, the hearsay rule may operate even where such evidence is available—indeed, that is principally why the rule has attracted criticisms. Can the testimonial argument be defended against this criticism? One answer is that, even where someone is available to testify to S's trustworthiness, it would still be unjustifiable for the fact-finder to accept that p; this is because she would have to defer to that person's assessment of S's trustworthiness and she would, in doing so, breach her duty to exercise (critical and personal) judgment on the issue.

Let p be a proposition material to the case being tried. Suppose W testifies in court: 'I know that p because S told me that she saw p. We have been close friends for many years; she is an utterly honest person. I could tell by her demeanour that she was speaking the truth. I am absolutely confident of it.' W is testifying that p: by claiming knowledge, she is herself vouching for the truth of p. She is prepared to do so not because she has direct grounds for asserting that p, but because she believes she has sufficient reason to believe S in this instance. W's belief in p is derivative of her belief in S. Does W's testimony violate the 'personal knowledge' rule (that is, the rule requiring a witness to testify only to what she had directly perceived)? It is surely common sense that we can gain knowledge through the statements of others. If a police officer tells me that the police station is just round the corner, it could hardly be denied that I can, through her testimony, claim to know where it is. The information may of course be wrong. But if infallibility is a condition for knowledge, and knowledge cannot be communicated by

[134] *Prosecutor v Kordic*, Decision on Appeal Regarding Statement of a Deceased Witness, 21 July 2000 (decision of Appeals Chamber) (Case No IT-95–14/2) para 24.

[135] *Prosecutor v Aleksovski*, Decision on Prosecutor's Appeal on Admissibility of Evidence, Case No IT-95–14/1-AR73, 16 February 1999 (decision of Appeals Chamber) para 15.

testimony, we would know little of what we think we do: no one can even claim to know who her parents are nor the day one was born.[136]

Common sense grants that, in our example, W is entitled to say she knows p if she is justified in finding S trustworthy on the matter. Even so, at law, the knowledge that W is required to possess must, as a general rule, have been gained by direct perception rather than by the say-so of others. On the surface, this seems odd. Why is testimony treated as a legitimate source of knowledge for the fact-finder (or at least a legitimate source of justification for her belief) but not for W? The very idea of a trial as a truth-seeking enterprise supposes that the fact-finder can acquire truth 'at second-hand': it seems inconsistent to deny that W, too, can know at second-hand.

If W is allowed to testify to the statement of another, the testimony will be 'third-hand' when it reaches the fact-finder. Does this, on general principles, disqualify W's testimony from being a potential source of knowledge for the fact-finder (or at least of justification for her belief about the facts of the case)? It is difficult to see why it should. Surely we can know p (or at least be justified in believing p) from being told p by the speaker who has acquired her knowledge through the testimony of another; a student, for example, can know from her teacher that there was a first world war even though the teacher knows it only on the authority of others.[137] Why should it be different at a trial?

It is arguable that it ought to be different because our approach to fact-finding is grounded in a distinctive intellectual tradition that is sometimes called 'epistemic individualism'.[138] The fact-finder is expected to assert epistemic autonomy in assessing S's trustworthiness. On this matter, he must be the judge; it will not do for him to defer to W's judgment. We expect the fact-finder to be able to justify and defend his belief in the propositions of fact he finds to be true. He 'should know whatever it is off his own bat; he must be the authority; he must have discovered it or worked it out'.[139] Knowledge of this kind can be acquired through testimony 'only if the knower somehow checks, for himself, the credibility of the witnesses'.[140] What this intellectual tradition resists, as Ross observed:[141]

> is the idea that the judgment of others, as expressed in what they say, has in itself some claim on an individual's judgment. Such a claim can arise only via the hearer's own

[136] A D Woozley, *Theory of Knowledge—An Introduction* (London: Hutchinson's University Library, 1949) 184–185. Nicholas Rescher, *Dialectics—A Controversy-Oriented Approach to the Theory of Knowledge* (Albany: State University of New York Press, 1977) 90: 'To be sure we must be certain of what we know, but the "certainty" that must attach to knowledge-claims need not be absolutistic in some way that is in principle unrealizable. It must be construed in the sense of *as certain as can reasonably be expected in the circumstance.*'

[137] Anscombe (n 53) 146–147.

[138] Angus Ross, 'Why Do We Believe What We Are Told?' (1986) 28 *Ratio* 69, 70.

[139] J L Mackie, 'The Possibility of Innate Knowledge' (1970) 70 *Proceedings of the Aristotelian Society* 245, 254.

[140] ibid 254.

[141] Ross (n 138) 70.

assessment of the evidence for regarding the speaker as a reliable authority on the matter in question. For the hearer to adopt any other attitude to the opinions of others would involve a surrender of his autonomy, an abandonment of his own responsibility for the truth of his beliefs.

It is highly doubtful, especially in ordinary dealings, that one does, can or ought to always abide by this principle.[142] Ross, for instance, thinks this is untenable in relation to the 'everyday sort of communication whose purpose is simply to impart information'.[143] Nevertheless, he acknowledges that it does reflect our attitude to testimony in special contexts 'as for example, when witnesses give evidence in court'.[144] At a trial, the fact-finder's willingness to believe witnesses must be 'based on an assessment of the evidence for supposing them to be truthful and reliable'.[145]

The idea of epistemic individualism underpins much of our fact-finding system. It is exhibited in many ways. The point is driven home in these specimen directions to the jury:

[I]t has always been your responsibility to judge the evidence and decide all the relevant facts of this case, and when you come to consider your verdict you, and you alone, must do that...

The facts of this case are your responsibility... When it comes to the facts of this case, it is your judgement alone that counts.[146]

When it comes to determining the facts, the contested facts,... that is your job. Determining the contested facts in each and every jury case is solely and exclusively the function, the duty, and,... the very grave responsibility of the jury.[147]

The law says you members of the jury—and you alone—... are the sole and exclusive judges of the facts, the sole and exclusive judges of whether what each and every witness says is true or false, and the sole and final judges of the guilt or innocence of the defendant.[148]

The opinion rule is another example. Non-expert witnesses are forbidden, in their testimony, to extrapolate from their observations; they are told to stick to the 'facts' and not attempt to 'usurp' the fact-finder's role. It is for the latter to decide what inferences to draw from those facts. The argument has it that it is not only pointless for the non-expert witness to proffer her opinion, it is also

142 Frederick Schmitt, 'On the Road to Social Epistemic Interdependence' (1988) 2 *Social Epistemology* 297.

143 Ross (n 138) 80.

144 ibid 71.

145 ibid.

146 Judicial Studies Board, Criminal Bench Book, specimen direction 1, available at: <http://www.jsboard.co.uk/criminal_law/cbb/index.htm>.

147 Massachusetts Jury Instructions, Civil, 1.14(b) (1999) (Available on lexis).

148 Charges to the Jury and Requests to Charge in a Criminal Case in New York (Available on Westlaw; database updated August 2003) § 4.56 ('Jury as Triers of Facts').

dangerous: it might tempt the fact-finder away, or distract her, from the epistemic labour which it is her duty to undertake.[149]

In the scenario set out at the beginning of this section, W is seeking through her testimony to transmit to the fact-finder S's purported knowledge of the accused's commission of the crime. The fact-finder acquires knowledge through this transmission only if S, the first in the chain, has, indeed, knowledge of that fact, and only if the fact-finder is justified in believing that S had such knowledge. She is not justified in believing this unless she is justified in believing that S is trustworthy on the subject. It is not enough for the fact-finder to be satisfied that W found S to be trustworthy: she must personally judge S to be so and must not pass as her own W's judgment of the same. Why not?

Rational beings may reasonably differ in their evaluation and interpretation of evidence. A central purpose of a trial is to settle a dispute of fact by bringing it to 'closure'. If there is to be finality, someone must have the ultimate say on where the truth lies. That person, by political arrangement, is the fact-finder; her decision must be accepted, unless and until an appeal from it succeeds. But what the parties are obligated to accept is *her* decision. The fact-finder's role is to judge the dispute. To judge is, by definition, to judge critically and personally. The fact-finder must evaluate (for herself) whether S is trustworthy, and only her judgment, not W's or anyone else's, counts. For the fact-finder to defer to W's assessment of S's trustworthiness is a failure of duty: she has not done what she was appointed to do. When this happens, the trial is not merely defective; it has, in a fundamental sense, not taken place: the parties have been denied an essential part of what it means to have their case legally tried, namely, for evidence to be scrutinized and weighed by the arbiter authorized and entrusted to perform that task. The hearsay rule prevents W's testimony from being used as evidence of p because the fact-finder is not in a position to judge (critically and personally) whether S is trustworthy with respect to p.[150]

While this argument is powerful, it applies only to cases at the core of the hearsay rule. It is true that the fact-finder fails in her duty to assert epistemic autonomy if she simply defers to W's assessment of S's trustworthiness. But it is not the case that every acceptance by the fact-finder of W's assessment constitutes a failure to exercise (critical and personal) judgment. Sometimes, evidence may be available to provide a basis on which the fact-finder can make up her own mind as

[149] As Kingsmill Moore J puts it in a case before the Supreme Court of Ireland: 'If the tribunal is swayed by the opinion of the witness it is to that extent surrendering its privilege and duty of independent judgment... [I]n theory at least, the expression of an opinion by a non-expert must be either otiose or dangerous': *Attorney General (Ruddy) v Kenny* (1960) 94 Irish Law Times Reports 185, 191. It is controversial how far this argument can be pushed: eg *Christopher James Stockwell* (1993) 97 Cr App R 260, 265–6 (Court of Appeal, England); *Sherrard v Jacob* [1965] Northern Ireland Law Reports 151, 156, 170 (Court of Appeal, Northern Ireland); *Graat v The Queen* (1982) 144 Dominion Law Reports (3d) 268, 281–2 (Supreme Court of Canada).

[150] cf Mortimer R Kadish and Michael Davis, 'Defending the Hearsay Rule' (1989) 8 Law and Philosophy 333, 348–350.

to whether W's view on S's trustworthiness is itself trustworthy. Apart from the evidential significance of W's willingness to swear to S's trustworthiness, W may explain in her testimony why she believes that S was speaking the truth. Here, the fact-finder is not asked to defer to W's evaluation in the sense of adopting it blindly; rather, she is to accept it only if she personally and critically judges the reasons given by W good enough to support that evaluation. Furthermore, evidence of S's trustworthiness may not come in the form of another person's assessment of the same. It may take the form of direct evidence of the circumstances in which S made her statement; *Myers v DPP*,[151] discussed in Part 2.2.4 below, is a classic example. The scope of the hearsay rule extends even to the situations just described. Hence, the epistemic argument does not fully account for the law. Should it, perhaps, be accepted as a prescriptive principle instead?

2.1.9 Testimonial argument as a prescriptive principle

To treat it as a prescriptive principle is to claim that the rule ought to be reformed such as only to exclude hearsay evidence on which there lacks epistemic justification for reliance.[152] Adherence to this principle is, to some degree, already reflected in a number of exceptions.[153] They were apparently created in the belief (rightly or wrongly) that the circumstances in which S gave her testimony* justify believing it.[154] Some have argued that the logical way of rationalizing the law on hearsay evidence is to formulate the rule in terms of the epistemic principle which is already implicit in those exceptions.[155] The argument, then, is that hearsay evidence should generally be admissible if and so long as evidence is available on which the fact-finder can evaluate the trustworthiness of S with respect to p.[156]

[151] [1965] AC 1001.

[152] English judges seem to have, covertly, taken steps in this direction: Andrew Ashworth and Rosemary Pattenden, 'Reliability, Hearsay Evidence and the English Criminal Trial' (1986) 102 LQR 292; D J Birch, 'Hearsay-logic and Hearsay-fiddles: *Blastland* Revisited' in Peter Smith (ed), *Essays in Honour of J C Smith* (London: Sweet & Maxwell, 1987) 24.

[153] But not all: Spencer, 'Orality and the Evidence of Absent Witnesses' (n 117) 633.

[154] Morton (n 37) 1309; Coady (n 42) 206–207. That the thinking which created the exceptions may now be out of fashion does not detract from the influence which they had in the past: Roger C Park, 'The Hearsay Rule and the Stability of Verdicts: A Response to Professor Nesson' (1986) 70 Minnesota L Rev 1057, 1069.

[155] Morgan *et al*, *The Law of Evidence—Some Proposals for Its Reform* (New Haven: Yale UP, 1927) 39; James Allan, 'The Working and Rationale of the Hearsay Rule and the Implications of Modern Psychological Knowledge' (1991) 44 CLP 217, 221–222. The existence of 'circumstantial guarantee (or probability) of trustworthiness' is accepted as a general reason for not applying the hearsay rule in jurisdictions such as the United States (Wigmore (n 25) 202–203, 204–205; Rule 807 (previously Rules 803(24) and 804(5)) of the Federal Rules of Evidence, and see note to Rule 803 by the Advisory Committee on Rules) and Canada (*R v Khan* (1990) 59 CCC (3d) 92; *R v Smith* (1992) 75 CCC (3d) 257; *R v B (KG)* (1993) 79 CCC (3d) 257). In Australia, s 65 (2) of the Evidence Act 1995 (Commonwealth Act No 2 of 1995) provides for exceptions to the hearsay rule in criminal proceedings where S is unavailable; these exceptions, too, seem to be based on the existence of possible grounds for treating S's statement as trustworthy.

[156] For a proposal along this line, see Eleanor Swift, 'A Foundation Approach to Hearsay' (1987) 75 California L Rev 1339.

However, the epistemic justification is inadequate even as a prescriptive principle. It is insufficient that, notwithstanding S's absence, the court has evidence which provides possible grounds for believing that she may be trusted on her testimony*. We need to consider whether, if S were to testify in court, her evidence is likely to yield any argument that would defeat those grounds. This consideration has, again, to do with justice.

2.2 The defeasibility argument

It is said that the hearsay rule 'enshrines an important principle of justice'.[157] In what follows, an attempt will be made to show that this principle of justice is intrinsically connected to the epistemic basis of the hearsay rule, and that any articulation of the principle that fails to make this connection holds little promise.

The hearsay rule is sometimes criticized for hindering the ascertainment of truth by keeping out evidence which appears to serve that end. This criticism is pressed especially against exclusion of evidence of 'implied hearsay' for it is in that context that the tension seems greatest. If the rule is at all defensible, so we might think, it must be by virtue of some value or principle that outweighs our interest in getting the facts right. It is only natural then to conceive of the principle of justice that is 'enshrined' in the hearsay rule, whatever that principle may be, as a counterweight to our interests in uncovering truth, addressing a point of ethics rather than any epistemological concerns. We might be tempted, for example, to seize on the idea of justice as fairness, and to explain the hearsay rule, if only partly, as a vindication of fair play in an adversarial setting.[158]

2.2.1 The fairness argument

How might such a case be built? Is it a convincing one? The first question is addressed here; the second in the next section. The case might be made as follows: The justifiability of testimonial reliance on S's statement is only one part of the hearsay problem; the other is that it is typically unfair, in an adversarial trial, to allow a party to use S as a 'source of proof' without calling S to the witness box. The unfairness arises from the inequality in the treatment of the parties, or more specifically, from the unequal distribution of the risk of an adverse finding; to allow one side to rely on hearsay evidence is, in some sense, to give her an

[157] *R v Kearley* [1992] 2 AC 228, 259.

[158] It is frequently suggested that the hearsay rule is related to the adversary system of trial, or more specifically, to fairness within the framework of such a system: eg Morgan (n 15) 181–185; Swift (n 156) 1369–1375; Stephan Landsman, 'The Rise of the Contentious Spirit: Adversary Procedure in Eighteenth Century England' (1990) 75 Cornell L Rev 497, 564–572; Damaška (n 11) 80; Ho, 'A Theory of Hearsay' (1999) 19 OJLS 403; Alex Stein, *Foundations of Evidence Law* (Oxford: OUP, 2005) 228–231.

improper advantage over the other. The Supreme Court South Africa gestured towards this argument in *S v Ndlovu & Anor*[159] when it remarked:

> Not only is hearsay evidence... not subject to the reliability checks applied to first-hand testimony... but its reception exposes the party opposing its proof to the procedural unfairness of not being able to counter effectively inferences that may be drawn from it.

The argument hinted at in this passage is unpacked in this section and criticized in the next. Trials of the Anglo-American tradition conform to what has been called the principle of party-presentation.[160] It is generally the responsibility of the parties to provide proof for their respective cases; the court will not pursue and collect evidence on their behalf,[161] will not 'dictate to a litigant what evidence he should tender',[162] nor rely on personal knowledge of matters on which neither party has formally introduced evidence.[163]

Where one side ('the proponent') makes an allegation of fact (p) in support of her case, and the other side ('the opponent') disputes the truth of that allegation, the judge of fact must decide whether to accept that p. If she accepts that p, she is deciding in favour of the proponent and against the opponent, and, contrariwise, if she does not accept that p, she is deciding in favour of the opponent and against the proponent. The risk of an adverse decision is delicately balanced between the two sides within the framework of the testimonial procedure to which we have referred. Reliance on hearsay evidence undermines two procedural principles intended for the benefit of the opponent and, consequently, distorts the spread of the risk unfairly against her.

The fact-finder must decide according to the principle that it is for the proponent to prove p. This is captured in the evidential maxim that 'he who asserts must prove'. To succeed in proof, the proponent must, to begin with, produce evidence capable of supporting the belief that p.[164] If she fails to do this, the opponent is entitled to a decision in her favour—that is, the fact-finder *must* decide against finding that p. Unless the proponent produces some such evidence, the

159 (1993) (2) SACR 69 (A) at pg 10, para [13], available at: <http://www.supremecourtofappeal.gov.za/judgments/sca_judg/sca_2002/32701.pdf>.

160 Robert W Millar, 'The Formative Principles of Civil Procedure—I' (1923) 18 Illinois L Rev 1, 16–18. This principle is distinctive of the adversarial trial: J A Jolowicz, *On Civil Procedure* (Cambridge: Cambridge UP, 2000) 221, 217, 218; Landsman (n 158) 501 (an 'element of adversarial justice... is litigant responsibility for the production and quality of the proof upon which the case is decided'); Richard Eggleston, 'What is Wrong with the Adversary System?' (1975) 49 Australian LJ 428, 429; G L Certoma, 'The Accusatory System v The Inquisitorial System: Procedural Truth v Fact?' (1982) 56 Australian LJ 288, 288–289.

161 *Jones v National Coal Board* [1957] 2 QB 55, 63–4; Frederick Pollock, *The Expansion of the Common Law* (London: Stevens and Sons Ltd, 1904) 33–34; John Henry Wigmore, *A Treatise on the Anglo-American System of Evidence in Trials at Common Law*, vol 9 (3rd edn, Boston: Little, Brown & Co, 1940) 266.

162 *Tay Bok Choon v Tahansan Sdn Bhd* [1987] 1 Malayan LJ 433, 436 (PC).

163 *Goold v Evans & Co* [1951] TLR 1189.

164 The evidence must be such as 'if believed and if left uncontradicted and unexplained, could be accepted... as proof': *Jayasena v R* [1970] AC 618, 624.

opponent faces no risk at all of the adverse finding that p; the opponent has 'no case to answer' on that point.

The general way for the proponent to produce evidence of p is to call a witness (S) to testify that p. To do this, she must get S to enter the witness box and, from there, state that p. S may, for various reasons, be reluctant to appear as a witness. And when she is brought to the witness box, whether voluntarily or by compulsion, she may fail to 'come up to proof' for a variety of reasons; to list a few of them: her demeanour may show her to be untrustworthy, or she may refuse, for whatever reasons, to assert that p,[165] or she may be deterred by the penalty of perjury or the added responsibility of testifying in court to repeat what she had said out of it, or she may display such hesitation or equivocation in her testimony as to make it worthless, and so on. This is the first procedural principle on which the hearsay rule rests: Where the proponent wishes to rely on S as the source of proof, she must produce S in court and face the risk of failing to get S to come up to proof.

When the proponent succeeds in eliciting evidence from S in support of p, the question of the probative value of the evidence arises. The fact-finder may, depending on her assessment of S's testimony, find that p, and the opponent faces the risk that she will do so. It is only when the proponent has overcome the risk of her evidence not coming up to proof that the risk of an adverse decision (the finding that p) falls on the opponent; there is at this point a shift in the so-called tactical burden of proof. To avoid this adverse decision, the opponent will wish to dissuade the fact-finder from accepting that p. To that end, the law gives her, amongst other things, the right to cross-examine S with a view to undermining her evidence. This right is the basis of the second procedural principle that, on the present argument, underpins the hearsay rule. According to Morgan, 'the [opponent] has a right that the trier shall not be influenced by testimony which the [opponent] has had no opportunity to cross-examine'.[166]

In the situation that the hearsay rule seeks to avoid, the proponent does not call S as a witness but calls W to testify that S asserted that p. W is not recognized at law as a direct source of proof that p: as said earlier, she is not allowed to testify that p because she lacks personal knowledge of it. The hearsay rule prevents the proponent from relying on S as the source of proof without getting S into the witness box. If we allow her to take this step in establishing proof, and permit the fact-finder to infer from W's testimony that p is true, we would be allowing her to evade completely the risks of S not agreeing to give evidence or not coming up to proof. This alters, to the opponent's disadvantage, the allocation of risks that is characteristic of an adversarial trial.

[165] As Blackstone said, 'a witness may frequently depose... in private' that 'which he will be ashamed to testify in a public and solemn tribunal': William Blackstone, *Commentaries on the Laws of England*, vol 3 (London: Dawsons of Pall Mall, 1966) ch 23, 373.

[166] Edmund M Morgan, 'The Hearsay Rule' (1937) 12 Washington L Rev 1, 4.

The opponent would be disadvantaged in a second way. She would have to try to overcome the risk of the fact-finder accepting that p with a serious handicap. A party is normally equipped to challenge the evidence adduced by her adversary with two major means of undermining it. First, she is entitled to attack, by cross-examining, the source of evidence, S, in an attempt to dissuade the fact-finder from believing her testimony that p. Secondly, she is entitled to produce her own evidence to show that p is false. If we permit the proponent to use S as a source of proof without calling her as a witness, the opponent would be deprived of the first means of fighting her case. The more difficult it is for the opponent to procure and produce her own evidence against p, the more seriously is she disadvantaged in being denied the opportunity to cross-examine S.

On both counts, the distribution of risks inherent in the testimonial procedure is distorted. In consequence, the trial is not fully what it is meant to be, a contest on terms that defines an adversarial proceeding. The higher the risk that S might not come up to proof, and the more vital the opportunity of cross-examination is as a means of dissuasion, the greater is the force of the opponent's complaint of unfair disadvantage in defending or advancing her case.[167] The trier of fact is enjoined from relying on the hearsay inference out of our recognition of the legitimacy of this complaint.[168]

2.2.2 *Critique of the fairness argument*

There are difficulties with the argument just presented. Neither of the two procedural principles upon which the argument is founded withstands scrutiny. The first principle, as we may recall, requires the proponent who wants to rely on S as a source of proof to call S as a witness and bear the risk of S not coming up to proof. This principle does not follow from the principle of party presentation: it is not entailed by that feature of the common law system of trial which puts on the proponent of p the responsibility to find and produce evidence in support of p. While one can accept that it is an essential characteristic of an adversarial trial that it is for a party to produce evidence to back up her allegation of fact, it is another question altogether what qualifies as 'evidence'. It does not follow

[167] cf Morgan (n 15) 184 (the hearsay rule offers 'protection not of Trier but of Adversary'); Kenneth W Graham Jr, 'The Right of Confrontation and the Hearsay Rule: Sir Walter Raleigh Loses Another One' (1972) 8 Criminal Law Bulletin 99, 132–133 (right of cross-examination is a symbol of fairness); Jack B Weinstein, 'Some Difficulties in Devising Rules for Determining Truth in Judicial Trials' (1966) 66 Columbia L Rev 223, 245 (noting the 'psychic value' to litigants of being able to confront those who bear witness against them). In *Randall v R* [2002] UKPC 19; [2002] 1 WLR 2237, 2241, the Privy Council observed that the 'adversarial format' is 'directed to ensuring a fair opportunity for' each side to put forward its case.

[168] This recognition is implicit in the view of the Law Commission that the admission of hearsay evidence under its recommended inclusionary discretion should be based on the interests of justice, in the consideration of which, the court must take into account the extent to which the accused can controvert the hearsay statement and the risks of unfairness to her: Law Commission, *Evidence in Criminal Proceedings: Hearsay and Related Topics*, Report No 245 (London: HMSO, 1997) paras 8.141–8.142. See s 114(2)(h)(i) Criminal Justice Act 2003.

from the proponent's responsibility to produce evidence in support of her factual claims that the evidence she produces cannot take the form of hearsay. There is a gap in the argument. The first procedural principle, in the end, merely states the effect of the hearsay rule; it assumes what it is supposed to explain.

There is similarly a gap in the reasoning based on the second procedural principle. Undoubtedly, a party in an adversarial setting [the opponent] has a right to cross-examine witnesses called by the other side [the proponent]. But this does not in itself tell us why the proponent is not allowed to call someone [W] to give evidence of an out-of-court statement made by another person [S]. The opponent will have the opportunity to exercise her right of cross-examination insofar as W is concerned. It is true that she will not be able to cross-examine S. But her complaint then is not that her right to cross-examine S has been violated; it is that the proponent should call S as a witness so that she (the opponent) will *acquire* the right to cross-examine S. This begs the very question the fairness argument seeks to, but does not, answer: why should the proponent have to call S as a witness? At a criminal trial, the defendant may indeed have the legal right to insist on having S called as a witness so that she can 'confront' or examine S in court. This right is entrenched as a basic standard of fair trial in many constitutional and human rights documents[169] and one strand of its foundations may lie in some version of the fairness argument.[170] However, this right can exist without, and should not be taken for, the hearsay rule.

2.2.3 The defeasibility argument

The argument from fairness fails to provide an adequate explanation for the hearsay rule. Missing from it is a crucial step that links the dynamics of adversarial proof to the process of deliberation, a step that forges a connection between the principle of justice embodied in the rule and the epistemology of fact-finding.

Justice and truth are not separate and competing goals but integrated and concurrent aims. It is in the nature of her task that the fact-finder must strive to get the facts right. As explained in Chapter 1, Part 2, to find that p is to assert that p, and a primary concern is that where she finds that p, p is true. Sometimes, p is a proposition that casts a litigant or an accused person in a negative light. The finding that p may involve ascribing publicly to her responsibility for a blameworthy act. She suffers injustice if p is false. To find that p is also to declare that p. This declaration carries practical consequences for the parties. It may lead to punishment or financial loss. The defendant stands, therefore, to suffer various kinds of undeserved harm, of both the consequential and non-consequential type, when a

[169] Such as the Sixth Amendment of the United States Constitution, article 6(3)(d) of the European Convention on Human Rights, and Article 14(3)(e) of the International Convenant on Civil and Political Rights.

[170] eg *Kostovski v The Netherlands* (1990) 12 EHRR 434, paras 42 and 44; *Windisch v Austria* (1991) 13 EHRR 281 at para 28; *Birutis & Ors v Lithuania*, 28 March 2002, Application nos 47698/99 and 48115/99, para 29.

finding is made wrongly against her. Justice as empathic care demands the exercise of caution in trial deliberation. The trier of fact must ensure that the finding she makes against a person does not inflict on him undeserved harm. This obligation is grounded in his right to be accorded due respect and concern and the hearsay rule may be seen as expressing this obligation.[171] On the present argument, the ethical consideration is located *within* the epistemology of fact-finding: justice must be done *in* the pursuit of truth.

Thus far, our discussion has centred on the logic of epistemology. A static view was taken of proof where the focus was on the structure of the kind of argument that supports the claim of knowledge or at least justified belief through testimony. An argument may be construed 'as a set of sentences or propositions, abstractly considered'.[172] The goodness of an argument, as so construed, may be judged in the weak sense by the extent to which the conclusion follows, deductively or otherwise, from the premises, and in the strong sense by considering as well whether the premises are true.[173] The gist of what was said before is that it is invalid, in the trial context, to reason:

S testifies* that p.
Therefore, p is true.

The conclusion does not follow from the premise. For the argument to be valid, a second premise must be added thus:[174]

S testifies* that p.
S is trustworthy on the matter of p.
Therefore, p is true.

If this argument is to be sound, and not just valid, it must be true that S is trustworthy on the matter of p. The thrust of the testimonial argument was that, where the proponent does not call S as a witness and seeks to rely instead on W's legal testimony of S's testimony*, justification may be lacking for accepting the truth of the second premise.

[171] The suggested ethical basis of the hearsay rule is not founded on some wider moral objection to reliance on gossips or rumours. Coady sees rumours and gossips as pathologies of testimony, 'distortions of or diseases of the normal case of telling and relying on what is told': C A J Coady, 'Pathologies of Testimony' in Lackey and Sosa (n 43) ch 11, 253. Cf Paul Roberts and Adrian Zuckerman, *Criminal Evidence* (Oxford: OUP, 2004) 668.

[172] Alvin I Goldman, 'Argumentation and Social Epistemology' (1994) 91 *The Journal of Philosophy* 27 at 27.

[173] ibid.

[174] There are other ways of varying or expanding the steps of reasoning. For example, the reasoning may be formulated as an 'abductive' reasoning:

S reports that p.
That S perceived p best explains why S is reporting that p.
That p was the case best explains why S perceived p.
Therefore, p is probably true.

For the second thread to our theory of the hearsay rule, we must look beyond the *logic* of epistemology to the *practice* of epistemology. This requires a shift in focus from the validity and soundness of an *argument* to the dynamic process of *argumentation*. By 'argumentation' is meant what Goldman calls the 'interpersonal or social sense of "argument" '.[175] Of relevance for our purposes is that kind of argumentative discourse which is called a 'disputation'. This 'consists of argumentative exchange between two or more speakers addressed to a nonparticipating audience... [where] the chief aim of the speakers is to persuade the audience, not one another'.[176] An adversarial trial fits exactly this description; in the typical case, two sides engage in argumentation addressed to a neutral party, the trier of fact. The proponent is expected to produce evidence and rational argument in support of her allegation while the opponent will try either to rebut the argument by showing the allegation to be false or to undercut the argument by showing that the evidence does not support the allegation.[177] Arguments supporting factual claims are met with challenges and counter-arguments to those claims, which may in turn come up against counter-challenges and so forth.

The hearsay rule does not allow the opponent full opportunity to engage in argumentation. As previously noted, that she cannot cross-examine the original maker of the hearsay statement (S) deprives her of one important means of challenging the case the proponent is mounting on the strength of that statement. While the opponent may rightly feel aggrieved by this, the validity of that grievance cannot, as discussed earlier, be adequately explained on the ground that she was denied a 'fair fight'.

The explanation must be sought in the notion of just treatment seen from the perspective of the fact-finder as a moral agent. To deny the opponent the opportunity to cross-examine S is at the same time to deprive the fact-finder of a level of fortification in the justification of her finding of fact. The parties' engagement in disputation mirrors the way the fact-finder conducts her deliberation. Defeasible reasoning plays a major role in rational deliberation. Reasoning is defeasible in this sense:[178] we may find ourselves adopting a belief, and having subsequently to retract or, later still, reinstate that belief in the course of

[175] Goldman (n 172) 27.

[176] ibid 31.

[177] For more on the difference between rebutting and undercutting an argument, see the following by John L Pollock: 'Epistemology and Probability' (1983) 55 *Synthese* 231, 233; *Contemporary Theories Of Knowledge* (Totowa, New Jersey: Rowman & Littlefield, 1986) 38–39; 'Defeasible Reasoning' (1987) 11 *Cognitive Science* 481, 485; 'A Theory of Defeasible Reasoning' (1991) 6 *Intl J of Intelligent Systems* 33, 34; 'How to Reason Defeasibly' (1992) 57 *Artificial Intelligence* 1, 2–3.

[178] On defeasible reasoning, see the literature cited in (n 177); also John L Pollock, 'Procedural Epistemology' in Terrell Ward Bynum and James H Moor (eds), *The Digital Phoenix—How Computers are Changing Philosophy* (Oxford: Blackwell, 1998) 17, and 'The Building of Oscar' (1988) 2 *Philosophical Perspectives* 315.

reasoning. We may be justified in holding a particular belief on the basis of what we know, and of an argument we recognize as supporting our conclusion, at a particular moment. But we may come to lose that justification when, for example, we are fed new information which 'defeats' our original argument.[179] This 'defeater' may in turn be defeated, thus leading to the reinstatement of our original belief. And so on.

It is easy to see how this can happen at an adversarial trial. A witness may give the fact-finder good reasons to believe her testimony during examination in chief only to have those reasons defeated by what emerges during cross-examination, and justification for the belief will surface yet again if her evidence is adequately 'repaired' in re-examination.

The disputational framework within which parties in an adversarial trial engage in argumentation mirrors the way reasoning is conducted by the fact-finder. The public exchange of arguments and counter-arguments mirrors and informs the thinking process, whereby the fact-finder first forms a tentative belief about a matter in dispute, considers the support it receives on the evidence, explores how that support might be defeated, and searches for plausible answers to those challenges.[180] The parties make claims and challenges in court on the evidence they present before it with the view that they should be taken into account by the fact-finder during her deliberation. The more the parties are hampered in their presentment of proof and argumentation, the less the fact-finder has to work with in her deliberation.

Cross-examination has a significance that is internal to the trial as a mode of inquiry. Such findings of fact as are reached at the end of deliberation should be defensible with reference to what occurred during the trial. A finding should be made that p only if the assertion that p (is true) is defensible and the degree to which it is defensible increases with the extent and rigour of the challenges it has withstood. Cross-examination is the principal stage of the inquiry which allows such challenges to be made.

That the opponent, in a hearsay situation, is not able to cross-examine the original maker of the statement weakens the justifiability of accepting the inference the proponent is urging the court to draw from the evidence. The more it appears that the inference is vulnerable to defeat in cross-examination, the less it is defensible to accept the inference. As was argued in Chapter 3, to find that p is partly to assert that p, and one is justified in finding p only if one would be justified in believing p within the terms of BAF*. So far as truth is a standard of correctness for a positive finding, it may be said that the ultimate aim of trial deliberation is knowledge. In general, for a person to know that p she must

179 Pollock refers to this as 'synchronic defeasibility': eg 'Procedural Epistemology' (n 178) 30.

180 This point is made in a general context by Rescher (n 136) especially ch 3.

have the right to be sure that p.[181] When is the claim of knowledge justified? According to Rescher:[182]

> A claim to knowledge extends an assurance that all due care and caution has been exercised to ensure that any real possibility of error can be written off: it issues a guarantee that every proper safeguard has been exercised.

The basic idea is a familiar one and was brought up in Chapter 3, Part 3, in our discussion of the relevant alternatives theory of knowledge, Shackle's model of categorical belief, and the relative plausibility theory of fact-finding. The general objection to reliance on hearsay evidence is that the 'real possibility of error' in the inference that p cannot be written off without examining S. It is usually safer to hear it from S herself on the matter of p, rather than to rely on W's testimony of what S said as the basis for an inference to p. There may be information obtainable only from examining S which would defeat the inference which can otherwise be drawn from W's testimony. The opponent has a right to a reasonable level of protection from the harm which, as mentioned, she stands to suffer if a finding of fact is made wrongly against her. The court should undertake deliberation on the verdict with the seriousness that does justice to her personal dignity.[183] To consider her worthy of respect and concern is to insist on sufficient assurance that every inference drawn in support of holding her liable or guilty is true. Where there is a real possibility that examination of S will rebut or undercut the basis for inferring that p from W's testimony, it would be unjust to draw that inference against the opponent without examining S and without allowing the opponent the opportunity to cross-examine S; to draw the inference in those circumstances would be to reveal our indifference to her and her welfare, that she does not matter much to us.[184] The more it seems that cross-examination of S may lead to defeat of the justification for the inference, the greater the reason not to use W's testimony as the basis for the inference. The decision to allow use of a hearsay inference requires an exercise of judgment and value choices must be made; the answer cannot be deduced from mere conceptual analysis.

It is not claimed that the ethical concern pervades the whole of the law on hearsay. For instance, it is difficult to see how the argument of just treatment can apply when the hearsay evidence is sought to be adduced by an accused person. It can hardly be said that the drawing of the hearsay inference would, in the circumstances, betray lack of respect and concern for the prosecution. This does not

[181] A J Ayer, *The Problem of Knowledge* (London: Macmillan & Co, 1956) 28–34.

[182] Rescher (n 136) 91 (italics removed).

[183] As J R Lucas, *On Justice* (Oxford: Clarendon Press, 1980) 7 says: 'Injustice betokens an absence of respect, and manifests a lack of concern. It is important, therefore, not simply on account of its undesirable outcome but as a manifestation of an uncaring and unfavourable attitude of mind; and to understand it properly we have to construe it as an affront which belittles the worth of the man who suffers it.'

[184] But, of course, this criticism cannot be made if the opponent is given the opportunity to cross-examine S but chooses not to do so.

necessarily mean, as some writers have suggested, that the hearsay rule therefore ought not to apply (with full rigour) to the defence.[185] Nothing in the present account rules out the possibility that the exclusion of hearsay adduced by the defence may be explained on other grounds, for example, in terms of our interests in not making it too easy for the guilty to fabricate exculpatory evidence.

2.2.4 Limits of the defeasibility argument

There are limits to the applicability of the defeasibility argument. First, it is not unjust to use W's testimony against the opponent if she had wrongfully brought about or contributed to the non-availability of S.[186] This is recognized in Rule 804(b)(6) of the United States Federal Rules of Evidence. It provides an exception to the hearsay rule where the person against whom the evidence is tendered 'has engaged or acquiesced in wrongdoing that was intended to, and did, procure the unavailability of the declarant as a witness'. Another example is section 116(2)(e) of the Criminal Justice Act 2003 that applies in England and Wales. Broadly speaking, hearsay evidence may be admitted under that provision subject to the leave of the court if, amongst other conditions, the original maker of the statement does not give oral evidence in the proceedings through fear. Leave will be given by the court only if it considers the statement ought to be admitted 'in the interests of justice'.[187] According to the Law Commission, on whose recommendations this provision was based,[188] a factor to consider is whether the accused or someone acting on his behalf was involved in causing the fear. If there was such involvement, 'it is likely that the statement would be admitted. Conversely, if the witness's fear has no connection with the accused, it may not be fair to allow the statement to be admitted without the accused having a chance to cross-examine.'[189]

Secondly, the defeasibility argument supposes that S does not give evidence in court. Is it not against the argument that an issue of hearsay may arise even

[185] eg Stein (n 158) 193 (on his theory, 'the hearsay rule operates in a one-sided fashion by imposing its constraints on the prosecution, but not on the accused') and ibid 195 ('A defendant is... entitled to adduce in his or her defence any evidence—hearsay and non-hearsay—if that evidence is the best evidence available'); Katherine Goldwasser, 'Vindicating the Right to Trial by Jury and the Requirement of Proof Beyond a Reasonable Doubt: A Critique of the Conventional Wisdom About Excluding Defense Evidence' (1998) 86 Georgetown LJ 621. For a contrary argument: Larry Laudan, *Truth, Error, and Criminal Law* (Cambridge: CUP, 2006) 128- 136. In Canada, the law allows 'the accused to call hearsay evidence in some cases where it would be denied to the Crown', and 'judges can be satisfied with a less exacting reliability inquiry for defence evidence than they must impose on Crown evidence': David M Paciocco, 'Balancing the Rights of the Individual and Society in Matters of Truth and Proof: Part II—Evidence about Innocence' (2002) 81 Canadian Bar Rev 39, 49.

[186] Richard D Friedman, 'Confrontation and the Definition of Chutzpa' (1997) 31 Israel L Rev 506.

[187] Criminal Justice Act 2003, s 116(4).

[188] Law Commission Report No 245 (n 168) paras 8.48–8.70, and see cl 5(6)-(8) of the draft Bill attached thereto.

[189] ibid para 8.60.

if she does? This question is generated by the wider application of the common law hearsay rule. In the strict sense, the rule prevents a witness from testifying to what another person asserted on a previous occasion as evidence of the truth of her assertion. In the wider sense, it prevents a court witness from giving evidence of what *she herself* had said on a previous occasion.[190] The rule in the strict sense is based principally on concerns arising from the unavailability of S for courtroom examination. Such concerns cannot be said to underlie the wider application of the rule since the maker, in that situation, *is* available to be cross-examined.[191] But it is sometimes argued, to the contrary, that what is crucial is the opportunity for *contemporaneous* cross-examination, and that it is this opportunity that is lacking where a witness seeks to testify to what she had previously said. Thus the Supreme Court of Minnesota held in *State v Nathan Saporen*:[192]

> The Chief merit of cross-examination is not that at some future time it gives the party opponent the right to dissect adverse testimony. Its principal virtue is in its immediate application of the testing process. Its strokes fall while the iron is hot. False testimony is apt to harden and become unyielding to the blows of truth in proportion as the witness has opportunity for reconsideration and influence by the suggestions of others, whose interest may be, and often is, to maintain falsehood rather than truth.

The risk of falsehood is not unique to evidence of one's previous statement; it is a risk that, in theory, applies to every testimony, whatever its content. It seems to be the assumption in the above passage that the best time to test S's trustworthiness on her claim that p is when or immediately after she asserts p. But the same argument could be stretched to apply to direct (non-hearsay) testimony: by parity of reasoning, the best time to test, say, an eye-witness's observation of an accident should be at or immediately after she saw it happening: as time passes, she likewise would have 'opportunity for reconsideration and influence by the suggestions of others'. This is surely not a reason to exclude her testimony. If the 'wider' application of the hearsay rule is at all justifiable (which is doubtful[193]), the justification must be found elsewhere, possibly on the practical necessity of preventing excessive 'enlargement of the field of inquiry'.[194]

Thirdly, if the defeasibility argument is right, and the lack of opportunity to cross-examine S raises an issue of justice, what is critical to the judgment on that issue is not a clear definition of the concept of hearsay but sensitivity to what is at stake. Generally speaking, the more adverse the finding that p is to the opponent,

[190] *Cross and Tapper on Evidence* (n 72) 58, 588; Law Reform Committee, Thirteenth Report (n 14) 3. The common law position is modified in Rule 801(1)(d) of the US Federal Rules of Evidence.

[191] John Henry Wigmore, *A Treatise on the Anglo-American System of Evidence in Trials at Common Law*, vol 3A, James H Chadbourn revision (Boston: Little, Brown and Co, 1970) 996, § 1018.

[192] (1939) 285 NW 898, 901.

[193] eg *McCormick on Evidence* (n 64) vol 2, 148–150.

[194] *State v Nathan Saporen* (n 192) 901.

or the more damning it is of her, the greater the caution that must be exercised in inferring that p from W's testimony. The risk of injustice must be taken into account. That risk depends on the likelihood that examination of S will defeat the available justification for the disputed inference. A vivid illustration of this point can be found in the much criticized case of *Myers v DPP*.[195] The appellant was convicted, with another, of several counts relating to the theft of cars. His mode of operation was to steal cars, buy wrecked cars, and modify each stolen car so that it corresponds to the description in the log book of a wrecked car. The modification involved switching between each pair of cars the number plates and the plates containing the chassis and engine numbers. The stolen cars were then sold under the assumed identities. But the attempt at passing off did not wholly succeed. Each of the stolen cars had a unique and indelible cylinder block number. The prosecution sought to prove the discrepancy in the numbers to support their claim that the cars sold by the appellant were stolen and not, as he had alleged, reconstructed wrecks. Towards that end, the prosecution called an employee of the car manufacturer, Legg, to give evidence. He was in charge of the manufacturing records and described in evidence how the numbers of the components fitted in each car were written by workmen on a card which accompanied the car as it went down the assembly line.[196] The workmen who had made the relevant entries could not be identified. In addition to the testimony of Legg, the prosecution sought to adduce documentary evidence of the records.[197]

The documentary evidence was held by the majority of the House of Lords to be hearsay. According to Lord Reid, each record was an assertion by the unidentified man who had made it that he had entered numbers which he had seen on the car,[198] and the purpose of adducing evidence of the record was to prove that the numbers on the card were in fact the numbers on the car when it was made.[199] This must be right; the prosecution was seeking testimonial reliance on each record. E (record) was produced to prove that S (unidentified workman) had testified* that p ('these are relevant numbers on this car') and the fact-finder was asked to believe S that p.

But the fact-finder was not asked to infer that the block numbers of the cars were such and such simply because unknown persons had said so. It was not disputed that the records were made by workmen, whose duty was to make accurate entries and who were disinterested parties. Furthermore, there was evidence given by someone competent to give it of the system under which the workmen compiled the records. This was a situation where, despite the absence of S, there was ample evidence on which the fact-finder could evaluate S's trustworthiness with respect to p. Furthermore, there was no reason to think that calling S to give

195 [1965] AC 1001.
196 ibid 1004.
197 ibid 1035.
198 ibid 1022.
199 ibid 1019.

evidence and cross-examining him is likely to defeat the existing justification for the inference. In the circumstances, it would seem 'redundant, verging on the neurotic, to insist on checking with' S before believing what he wrote.[200] As Lord Pearce said so persuasively in his dissenting judgment:[201]

> It would be no advantage, if [the relevant workman] could have been identified, to put him on oath and cross-examine him about one out of many hundreds of repetitious and routine entries made three years before. He could say that to the best of his belief the number was correct; but everybody already knows that. If he pretends to any memory in the matter, he is untruthful; but, even if he is, that in no way reflects on whether he copied down a number correctly in the day's work three years before. Nor is it of importance how he answers the routine question in cross-examination: 'You may have made a mistake?' Everybody knows that he may have made a mistake.

2.2.5 Implied hearsay

The defeasibility argument supplements the testimonial argument in explaining the hearsay rule. At common law, the rule excludes evidence not only of 'express assertions' but also of 'implied assertions'. This can only be explained by the defeasibility argument; often the testimonial argument alone cannot tell us why such evidence is excluded. A classic example of implied hearsay was given by Baron Parke in *Wright v Tatham*.[202] To prove the seaworthiness of a vessel, it is proposed to adduce evidence that the captain set sail in it with his family after he had given it a thorough inspection. According to the judge, this evidence must be excluded as hearsay.

The captain did not *tell* anyone that the vessel was sound. For his conduct to constitute a testimony*, the captain must have acted with the intention that someone (i) sees that he believes, and intends him to believe, and (ii), on that basis, believe that the vessel is seaworthy.[203] This intention cannot plausibly be read into the captain's action. A lot more background circumstances would have to be postulated. Perhaps the captain was putting on a show for his crew; he wanted to shore up their confidence and acted with the intention that they recognize in his action an assertion that the ship was sound and that they believe him that it was so. But this is fanciful; usually, acts do not (and are not meant to) speak.[204] Baron Parke would have supplied more information in the hypothetical if he had such an unusual case in mind.

[200] C A J Coady, 'Pathologies of Testimony' in Lackey and Sosa (n 43) 261. Cf Rescher (n 136) 91: 'The evidential basis for effective certainty need not be "all the evidence there conceivably might be," but simply "all the evidence that might reasonably be asked for." It envisages that a stage could be reached when, even though further evidence might possibly be accumulated, there are no counterindications to suggest that this theoretically feasible prospect is practically desirable: there is *no reason* to think that further accumulation might be fruitful and *no reason* to believe that additional evidence might alter the situation.'

[201] (n 195) 1036.

[202] (1837) 7 Ad & E 313, 388.

[203] Grice (n 43) 151.

[204] Mellor (n 42) 94.

On the ordinary reading of the example, there was no testimony* in the captain's conduct that called for belief. Since the captain did not give his word, the issue of justifying reliance on his word does not arise. It is singularly misleading to call this a case of implied assertion; there was no assertion, express or implied.[205] At most, we can say that the captain's belief was revealed or implicit in his conduct. Arguably, in every finding of an 'implied assertion' in non-assertive conduct is a finding of some (prima facie) rational justification for an inference to the proposition said to have been 'asserted'. (The quotation marks serve as a reminder of the misuse of language.)[206] We think that the 'assertion' p is possibly 'implied' by S's conduct only when we have reason to believe that there is potentially a rational connection between p and S's behaviour. In Baron Parke's example, the fact-finder is not invited to believe any testimony* by the captain, but rather to judge the significance of his non-testimonial conduct. The claim that his conduct 'implied an assertion' that p is really an acknowledgement that there is a prima facie basis for inferring that he believed p from his action.

Although the captain was not, by his action, testifying* to the structural soundness of the ship, his non-assertive conduct does provide some justification for believing, prima facie, that the ship was sound. This is not a case where evidence is adduced of 'S testified* that p', from which the fact-finder is invited to believe S and, for that reason, accept that p is true. Rather, it is evidence of q from which the fact-finder is invited to draw, through an intermediate step (r), the inference that p. In the absence of evidence suggesting the contrary, it is reasonable for the fact-finder to infer from the captain's conduct (q) that he believed that the ship was seaworthy (r). This rests on the background belief that no reasonable person would knowingly risk the lives of himself and his family members. The fact-finder may further infer from the captain's belief (r) that the belief was true: that the vessel was seaworthy (p). It is reasonable to suppose that the captain was competent on the subject; given his profession and rank, he could be expected to have the expertise to judge whether the ship was in good condition, and he was in a position to apply that expertise to the vessel in question for he had, if we believe the witness, thoroughly inspected it. Thus the evidence, such as is available, supplies a basis on which the fact-finder can, with the aid of her background knowledge, judge that the ship is seaworthy. In short, *on such evidence as is available*, the inference is epistemically justifiable. (We will see in a moment the significance of the words in italics.)

Baron Parke's view on this matter has attracted widespread criticisms. Even if those criticisms are deserved, it is nevertheless fruitful to ask what prompted the judge to hold the view that he did. Although, in the example, the proponent is

[205] Stephen Guest: 'The Scope of the Hearsay Rule' (1985) 101 LQR 385, 398; 'Hearsay Revisited' [1988] 41 CLP 33, 41; 'Implied Assertions Under the English Rule Against Hearsay' in W E Butler (ed), *Justice and Comparative Law* (Dordretch: Martinus Nijhoff, 1987) 77, 81.

[206] This misuse of 'implied assertion' is noted by the Law Commission of England and Wales, Report No 245, *Hearsay in Criminal Proceedings: Hearsay and Related Topics* (n 168) para 2.4.

not relying on the captain's conduct testimonially, he is nevertheless seeking to use a chain of reasoning that also figures in an argument of testimonial reliance; in both situations, the fact-finder is asked to accept that p because S believed that p and S was right on the matter of p. While there may be prima facie justification for accepting this argument, the risk of defeat that the justification faces is greater where hearsay is 'implied' than where it is express: we can be more sure that S believes that p where he had, on a previous occasion, explicitly asserted that p than where his belief that p is merely an inference we are drawing from an interpretation of his conduct. There is, in the latter case, a greater danger of misinterpretation. It is often claimed that 'implied assertions' carry little risk of insincerity.[207] But our main concern is with the lack of the opportunity of cross-examination and the principal value of cross-examination lies 'in testing accuracy rather than veracity'.[208]

Baron Parke was aware that it was, prima facie, epistemically justifiable to infer from the captain's conduct that the ship was probably sound. He acknowledged that the 'inference no doubt would be raised in the conduct of the ordinary affairs of life' but insisted that 'it cannot be raised in a judicial inquiry'.[209] What might have troubled him was this possibility: examining the captain in court might show the truth to be otherwise. As we saw in Chapter 3, Part 3.5, the support a body of evidence gives a hypothesis is a function of, amongst other things, its weight. The epistemic stability of an inference depends not just on the evidence available to us, but also on the evidence that we know we do not have; it depends on how well tested the inference is, the rigour of the challenges it has managed to survive. The crucial question is: how likely is it that the captain, if called, would have given such evidence as would defeat the justification we presently have for the inference we want to draw from his conduct? Is it an unreal possibility, for example, that he would testify that he did not believe the vessel was fully seaworthy? Could it be that an urgency to set sail forced him to take a risk? Or would cross-examination reveal his incompetence or a fatal omission in his inspection? Critics of Baron Parke must think that these or such like possibilities are just too fanciful to worry about. Could it be that Baron Parke was more cautious than his critics and was not prepared to dismiss those alternative hypotheses without questioning the captain? On this analysis, their disagreement was not over a conceptual point.

The view taken in *Wright v Tatham* that implied assertions are also caught by the common law hearsay rule was affirmed by the House of Lords in *R v Kearley*.[210] The accused was on trial for drug dealing. According to the testimony of the

[207] eg Notes of Advisory Committee, Note to Rule 801(a) of the US Federal Rules of Evidence; David Ormerod, 'Reform of Implied Assertions' (1996) 60 Journal of Criminal Law 201, 204–205.

[208] Allan (n 155) 231. Also: Morgan (n 166) 4.

[209] (1837) 7 Ad & E 313, 387.

[210] [1992] 2 AC 228; subject of a symposium, papers of which are published in (1995) 16 Mississippi College L Rev 1–213.

police officers who had raided his house, in the few hours that they were there, and while the accused was absent, seventeen persons called (in person or by phone), asking to speak with the accused and for drugs. This evidence was pivotal to the prosecution's case.[211] Contrast this with an imagined scenario. Suppose someone (S) says: 'If you want amphetamine, go to Y.' S is telling the listener, by implication, that Y distributes the drug. Her testimonial intention is clear. There is no reason why this implied assertion should be treated differently to an explicit statement by S that Y is a dealer in amphetamine. If one should be considered hearsay, so should the other. Led by this logic, the majority of the House of Lords held in *R v Kearley*[212] that that the hearsay rule extends to 'implied assertions' as well.

For ease of discussion, the encounters in *Kearley* may be stripped of details and reduced to this essential form: S called at a house and was met by W. S asked to see Y and asked for drugs. In this transaction, S might or might not have testified* to W that Y was a dealer. S had not if, when talking to W, he had assumed that W was Y's housemate and already knew what Y was up to. On the other hand, S would have testified* to that fact if he had given it as the reason for wanting to see Y. The report of the case did not disclose fully the circumstances or background of the dialogue in which S had allegedly made his request.[213] The Court of Appeal[214] and some judges in the House of Lords[215] held that S's request did not amount to an assertion of fact or a narrative, or, to employ our terminology, S had not testified* to W of Y's drug dealing. However, the majority of the law lords thought that implied assertions were involved;[216] in any event, so they held, the hearsay rule was applicable even if S did not intend to assert that Y dealt in the drug[217]—it is enough that the proposition could be 'inferred' from S's speech, or more accurately, from S's belief in it.[218] If this is right, Lord Wilberforce's view, alluded to earlier, that a 'question of hearsay only arises when the words are relied on "testimonially"', must be qualified. Given the wide application of the hearsay rule, it cannot be concerned solely with the soundness of the argument advanced to support belief in S's testimony*.

The majority of the House of Lords held that the evidence was hearsay and, hence, inadmissible to prove that the accused was a drug dealer, even though it

211 Drugs were found on the accused's premises but, to quote from the judgments, they were 'a relatively small amount' (n 210) 259–260) and 'not in such quantities as to raise the irresistible inference that [he] was a dealer as opposed to having the drugs for his own consumption' (ibid 236). Unless the prosecution could rely on the evidence of the calls, their case was clearly too weak to warrant a conviction.

212 (n 210) 255 and 264.

213 Courts usually do not analyse this issue well: Paul F Kirgis, 'Meaning, Intention, and the Hearsay Rule' (2001) 43 William and Mary Law Review 275, 309.

214 (1991) 93 Cr App R 222, 225.

215 (n 210) 238 (Lord Griffiths, minority judge), 254 (Lord Ackner, majority judge).

216 ibid 243 (Lord Bridge). Cf Rosemary Pattenden, 'Conceptual Versus Pragmatic Approaches to Hearsay' (1993) 56 MLR 138, 140.

217 (n 210) 249–250.

218 ibid 277.

had probative value.[219] The convergence of so many similar incidents provided prima facie rational support for accepting that each caller believed, and believed rightly, that the accused was a drug dealer. This decision has been roundly condemned by writers.[220] Sharp criticisms came as well from Lord Griffiths in *Kearley*; in his dissenting judgment, he remarked: 'I believe that most laymen if told that the criminal law of evidence forbade them even to consider such evidence as we are debating in this appeal would reply "Then the law is an ass." '[221]

A reconstruction of the general thinking behind the majority position will help us to engage in meaningful debate even if we cannot agree with the majority on the conclusion. We need to penetrate the conceptual analysis to get to the substantive concerns, the values which were thought to be at stake. While not the legal grounds given for the exclusion, these considerations could have motivated the majority view: although there was prima facie justification for drawing the inference against the accused, the defeasibility of that justification was a legitimate concern. Nothing was disclosed of the identities of the callers, and it is not clear how much, if anything, the police knew of and about them. The statements they made were apparently no more than brief and fleeting enquiries. Surprisingly, and we are not told why, the prosecution did not produce any of the seventeen alleged callers as a witness. Lord Griffiths observed generally that it is 'notoriously difficult to persuade a user of drugs to give evidence against his supplier' and that this may be due to the 'fear of violent physical reprisals'.[222] But he expressly disavowed knowledge of the reason for not producing the callers at the trial. Had it been established that fear of retaliation by the accused (or his associates) had deterred the callers from testifying, in principle and as previously discussed, it would not be unjust to use the evidence against him in the manner proposed by the prosecution. However, in *Kearley*, there was no allegation that this was in fact the case.

The court was in the dark as to who the alleged callers were, their background and relationship with the accused, what led them to believe, if they did believe, that the accused could supply them with drugs, and so forth. It could be that, for the majority, the risk was not fanciful that there was more than met the eye, and what more there was could only be known by examining the callers. Given that they were not produced as witnesses, the evidence, as it stood, was not safe enough to be the primary basis for the inference of guilt. The majority might have thought that a court which cares sufficiently to protect the accused from wrongful conviction would not permit the adverse inference to be drawn in those circumstances. Examination of the person whose word is being used to convict another

[219] This was particularly emphasized by the minority: ibid 236, 287.

[220] eg Tapper, 'Hearsay and Implied Assertions' (1992) 108 LQR 524; J R Spencer, 'Hearsay, Relevance and Implied Assertions' (1993) 52 CLJ 40, and 'Orality and the Evidence of Absent Witnesses' (n 117) 633–634.

[221] (n 210) 236–237.

[222] ibid 236.

is not 'merely a desirable check which one would like to apply if possible';[223] the failure to insist on examination can, in itself, be a failure of justice—an instance of denying a person the due measure of respect and concern.

The minority judges were aware of the possibility of alternative explanations. For instance, Lord Griffiths acknowledged that this could be a case of 'a mistaken belief or even a deliberate attempt to frame the appellant'. But, he quickly added, 'there are very few factual situations from which different inferences cannot be drawn and it is for the jury to decide which inference they believe they can safely draw'.[224] Lord Griffiths found it safe enough to invite the jury to draw the inference; in the light of the number of similar calls, the alternative hypotheses were too speculative to cause worry.[225] For the minority, the majority were overcautious in protecting the accused from wrongful conviction and not as mindful as they should be of our interests in convicting the truly guilty. On the other hand, for the majority, the minority were not cautious enough. Thus Lord Ackner, who was a member of the majority, reminded his fellow judges: 'Some recent appeals, well known to your Lordships, regretfully demonstrate that currently [the] anxiety [over the possibility of police fabrication] rather than being unnecessarily morbid, is fully justified.'[226] Without having the callers examined in court, there was insufficient assurance that such fears were misplaced.

Which side is right cannot be established by pure conceptual analysis. Substantive concerns are at play. Behind the technical disagreements, which have the unfortunate veneer of sterility, is a debate on justice. The statutory response to the problem of 'implied hearsay' in a number of jurisdictions has been to redefine the hearsay rule so that it applies only where a fact is *intended* to be asserted by a statement[227] or to redefine the operative term 'statement' to mean an *intended* assertion.[228] This may have achieved conceptual clarity: it is, so it was earlier claimed, confused and confusing to interpret the conduct of the sea captain as an assertion (or testimony*), and a similar criticism could arguably be made of any attempt to read the relevant assertion into the callers' statements in *Kearley*. However to the extreme end these two cases may fall, and however clear we are as to the view we should take of them, they do raise a general problem of justice.

[223] Glanville Williams, *The Proof of Guilt* (3rd edn, London: Stevens & Sons, 1963) 199.

[224] (n 210) 238.

[225] Lord Griffiths, ibid 242: 'If there had been only one or two calls made to the premises offering to buy drugs they would carry little weight; they might be the result of mistake or even malice, but as the number of calls increases so these possibilities recede till the point is reached when any man of sense will be confident that any inference other than that the accused was a dealer can be safely rejected.'

[226] ibid 258. Expressing the same concern: John Jackson, 'Discussion: Character Evidence; United Kingdom Perspectives' (1995) 16 Mississippi C L Rev 185, 186–187. This risk is also noted by Roderick Munday, *Evidence* (4th edn, Oxford: OUP, 2007) 392, but he quickly adds that this 'was not the ground upon which the majority excluded the evidence'.

[227] See ss 59(1), 60 Australian Evidence Act 1995.

[228] See Rule 801(a) of the United States Federal Rules of Evidence and s 115(3) of the Criminal Justice Act 2003.

This problem cannot be solved by mere redefinitions. Bringing 'implied assertion' outside of the hearsay rule may have the merit of flexibility; however, it risks blunting our sensitivity to the need for caution, especially in cases which are much nearer the borderline than *Kearley* and the sea-captain example.

Conclusion

On the conventional view, hearsay evidence is excluded in the interest of protecting the correctness of the verdict. The exclusion is founded principally on two general assumptions of fact: first, that the jury is incompetent at evaluating hearsay evidence; and secondly, that the statement of a person who has not been cross-examined is unreliable. This external mode of analysis fails to capture the value of the rule which is internal to a conception of trial deliberation as a search for justified belief and ultimately of knowledge. Hearsay evidence presents epistemological problems at two levels, one of the logic of argument, the other of the dynamics of argumentation. The first is the problem of testimonial reliance. The trier of fact is justified in believing S that p only if she possesses positive evidence which enables her to judge, personally and critically, that S is trustworthy in relation to p. She may not be in a position to exercise that judgment where the proponent does not call S as a witness but seeks, instead, to call W to testify to what S said. The second problem is additional to the first. Even if the evidence adduced by the proponent supplies some prima facie epistemic justification for inferring that p from S's word or conduct, S's non-availability for courtroom examination may give rise to legitimate concern about the defeasibility of that justification.

The demand for positive epistemic justification and for assurance of its non-defeasibility is morally motivated. Although it is sometimes recognized that reliance on the hearsay inference raises an issue of justice,[229] the underlying interests have not been clearly articulated, nor have they been explored from the angle adopted here. Justice in the law of evidence can be explained in terms of care and caution and meaningfully understood as references to the cognitive and affective attitudes of the fact-finder. The court cares to know the truth about an allegation because it cares about the party to whom acceptance of the allegation is harmful.

[229] *R v Kearley* (n 210) 259 (the hearsay rule 'enshrines an important principle of justice'). See also A A S Zuckerman, *The Principles of Criminal Evidence* (Oxford: Clarendon Press, 1989) 221: 'The legislature would have done better to establish, as a general principle, that if the prosecution wishes to adduce hearsay evidence it must convince the court that it is of such probative weight that no injustice will be caused to the accused by being deprived of the opportunity of cross-examination. As regards hearsay adduced by the accused, the general principle should be that it will be admissible whenever exclusion would undermine the interests of justice.' The 'interests of justice' is now used as a criterion of admissibility in some hearsay statutes: eg ss 114(1)(d) and 116(4) Criminal Justice Act 2003 (England and Wales) and s 3(1)(c) Law of Evidence Amendment Act 45 of 1988 (South Africa; discussed in D T Zeffertt, A P Paizes and A St Q Skeen, *The South African Law of Evidence* (Durban: LexisNexis Butterworths, 2003) 365 *et seq*).

The degree of caution it exercises in accepting the allegation is reflective of the measure of respect and concern it has for that person. Underlying the hearsay rule is the belief that justice must be done in the search for truth.

The trial may be seen as a process of acquiring the moral authority to insist that the person whose case is before the court accepts its decision. To ground the decision on a hearsay inference undermines the claim of moral authority where the inference is drawn incautiously, without judgment or in the absence of epistemic justification, or when sufficient assurance of its non-defeasibility is lacking. The rationale for preventing use of the hearsay inference is not because we value fairness more than truth[230] but because it is, in certain circumstances, both unjust and epistemically unjustifiable to draw that inference. Fact-finding must satisfy the concomitant demands of justice and epistemic justification.

[230] cf Spencer, 'Hearsay, Relevance and Implied Assertions' (n 220) 42.

6

Similar Fact Evidence

Introduction

This chapter ventures into an area of evidence law in which the moral dimension is strong. It is stronger than is the case with the topics (standard of proof and hearsay evidence) covered in the last two chapters. Justice in the sense discussed in Chapter 2, Part 3.3, will figure most prominently in our discussion. This is the sense of justice which demands full acknowledgement of the humanity in our fellow beings. Here, as in previous chapters, we will find no antithesis between truth and justice: rather, the two values act in concert to secure the legitimacy of legal fact-finding. Part 1 deals with the law in criminal cases. The civil counterpart is considered in Part 2. A comparison of the two approaches will be made and an account given for a less forceful application of the law on the civil side.

1 Criminal Cases[1]

1.1 Introduction

The prosecution may want to adduce, as part of its case in chief, evidence of a previous conviction of the accused or of his discreditable conduct on an occasion other than that cited in the charge for which he is standing trial. Admissibility of the evidence is governed at common law by the 'similar facts rule'. For convenience, the evidence covered by this rule will be called 'evidence of previous misconduct', 'evidence of bad character', or 'propensity evidence'. These names are used merely as convenient tags and not as technical terms.

According to the modern common law test formulated by the House of Lords in *DPP v P*,[2] the evidence is admissible only if 'its *probative force* in support of the allegation that an accused person committed a crime is sufficiently great to make it *just* to admit the evidence, notwithstanding that it is *prejudicial* to the accused

[1] This part is a modified version of my article, 'Justice in the Pursuit of Truth: A Moral Defense of the Similar Facts Rule' (2006) 35 Common L World Rev 51.

[2] [1991] 2 AC 447.

in tending to show that he was guilty of another crime'.[3] Many other common law countries (but not all[4]) take the same approach, including Canada,[5] New Zealand,[6] Singapore,[7] and Malaysia.[8] On this test, the probative force must be balanced against the prejudicial effect of the evidence. While the focus has traditionally been on the opposing factors to be weighed, it should not be overlooked that 'justice' provides the fulcrum.

In England and Wales, the common law on similar fact evidence was abolished under the Criminal Justice Act 2003 ('CJA 2003').[9] Nevertheless, the present discussion remains of relevance in England and Wales. This is not only because understanding the changes effected by the statute requires knowledge of the position at common law;[10] more importantly, it is also because both the statute and the common law address the same problem, and this chapter is concerned with the essential nature of that problem and the normative response to it.

Under the CJA 2003, bad character evidence[11] is admissible by a number of routes. Amongst these, the 'core gateway, designed to replace the major part of... the similar fact rule' is section 101(1)(d).[12] This provision allows evidence

[3] ibid 460. Emphasis added.

[4] The old 'categories approach' associated with *Makin v Attorney-General for New South Wales* [1894] AC 57, under which admissibility is dependent on the evidence being adduced for one of the recognized purposes, is reflected in r 404(b) of the United States Federal Rules of Evidence. Although evidence that falls under r 404(b) may still be objected to on the ground that 'its probative value is substantially outweighed by the danger of unfair prejudice' under r 403, thus suggesting a need for balancing, the latter rule is, in practice, 'seldom a barrier to the admissibility of specific acts evidence': Ronald J Allen, Richard B Kuhns, Eleanor Swift and David S Schwartz, *Evidence—Text, Problems, and Cases* (NY: Aspen, 2006) 241. In Australia, the hurdle of admissibility appears to be unusually high: the evidence must have 'a particular probative value or cogency such that, if accepted, it bears no reasonable explanation other than inculpation of the accused in the offence charged': *Pfennig v The Queen* (1995) 182 CLR 461, 481, Australian High Court.

[5] *R v Handy* (2002) 213 DLR (4th) 385, 405, Supreme Court of Canada: 'The onus is on the prosecution to satisfy the trial judge on a balance of probabilities that in the context of the particular case the probative value of the evidence in relation to a particular issue outweighs its potential prejudice and thereby justifies its reception.'

[6] *R v Holtz* [2003] 1 NZLR 667, para 35, New Zealand Court of Appeal: 'to be admissible the evidence must be such that its probative value outweighs illegitimate prejudice to the accused in having adduced evidence of past conduct that might be given undue weight or used improperly in reasoning towards guilt of the crime charged'.

[7] *Tan Meng Jee v PP* [1996] 2 Singapore LR 422, 433, Singapore Court of Appeal (adopting the common law approach of balancing 'the probative value of the evidence against its prejudicial effect').

[8] *Azahan Bin Mohd Aminallah v Public Prosecutor* [2005] 5 Malayan LJ 334, 345, Malaysian Court of Appeal: 'A court when deciding whether to admit similar fact evidence must carry out a balancing exercise by weighing the probative value of such evidence... The court would be justified in admitting the evidence where its probative value is outweighed by its prejudicial effect.'

[9] CJA 2003, s 99(1). The provisions on bad character evidence were brought into force by the CJA 2003 (Commencement No 6 and Transitional Provisions) Order 2004 (SI 2004 No 3033).

[10] As pointed out by Paul Roberts and Adrian Zuckerman, *Criminal Evidence* (Oxford: OUP, 2004) 517.

[11] On the meaning of 'bad character': CJA 2003, ss 98, 112(1).

[12] Colin Tapper, 'The Criminal Justice Act 2003—(3) Evidence of Bad Character' [2004] Crim LR 533, 546.

of the defendant's bad character to be admitted where 'it is *relevant* to an important matter in issue between the defendant and the prosecution'.[13] Evidence is so relevant where, *inter alia*, the question is 'whether the defendant has a propensity to commit offences of the kind with which he is charged'.[14] Relevance, however, is not determinative of admissibility. Under section 101(3), the evidence *must* be excluded if it appears to the court that its admission 'would have such an adverse effect on the fairness of the proceeding that the court ought not to admit it'. This provision applies only on the application by the defendant for exclusion. But, according to Murphy, 'if the circumstances were sufficiently compelling, . . . the judge might properly take it upon himself to invite the defence to make the application'.[15] The word 'must' is significant as it suggests that the court has a duty, and not merely a discretion, to exclude the evidence where fairness so requires;[16] in other words, section 101(3) provides for 'a rule of inadmissibility'[17] and not merely an exclusionary discretion. This provision is supplemented by section 103(3) which further restricts proof of previous misconduct.[18] It qualifies section 103(2)[19] and disallows the defendant's propensity to be established by evidence of conviction of an offence of the same description or category as the one with which he is charged where it would be '*unjust*' to do so.[20]

Hence, both at common law and under the statute, probative value is not the ultimate criterion. In both cases, evidence of previous misconduct is excluded avowedly for ethical reasons, which have to do with considerations of justice or fairness. In principle, an essential factor that ought to be taken into account in deciding on the justice or fairness of admitting evidence of bad character under the CJA 2003, as at common law, is its prejudicial effect.[21] Mirfield,

[13] CJA 2003, s 101(1)(d).

[14] '[E]xcept where his having such propensity makes it no more likely that he is guilty of the offence': CJA 2003, s 103(1)(a). Tapper (n 12) 543, 547 notes that this lowers the common law probative hurdle and makes it much easier for the prosecution to adduce similar fact evidence; see also Colin Tapper (ed), *Cross and Tapper on Evidence* (11th edn, Oxford: OUP, 2007) 434–435. Other problems with this provision are raised by Roderick Munday, 'Bad Character Rules and Riddles: "Explanatory Notes" and True Meaning of s 103(1) of the Criminal Justice Act 2003' [2004] Crim LR 533, 338–339.

[15] Peter Murphy, *Murphy on Evidence* (9th edn, Oxford: OUP, 2005) 173; cf *R v Highton & Ors* [2005] EWCA Crim 1985, para 23.

[16] See *R v Somanathan*, reported in *R v Weir* [2005] EWCA Crim 2866; [2006] 2 All ER 570, para 46; *R v Hanson & Ors* [2005] EWCA Crim 824, 169 JP 250, para 10; Murphy (n 15) 171, 172.

[17] Hodge M Malek *et al* (eds), *Phipson on Evidence* (16th edn, London: Sweet & Maxwell, 2005) paras 19–35.

[18] In *R v Hanson & Ors* (n 16) para 10, Rose VP described s 101(3) and s 103(3) as closely related and calling for similar considerations.

[19] Elaborated in CJA 2003, ss 103(4), (5).

[20] It may be considered unjust 'by reason of the length of time since the conviction or for any other reason': CJA 2003, s 103(3).

[21] See *R v Benguit* [2005] EWCA Crim 1953 at paras 27–32. In deciding whether it is fair to admit the evidence, the court 'must have regard, in particular, to the length of time between

writing in *Phipson on Evidence*, describes section 101(3) as having 'embraced the *DPP v P* rule of exclusion'[22] and, similarly, Roberts and Zuckerman suggest that the effect of the provision 'may well be to place *DPP v P* on a statutory footing'.[23] However, Spencer reports that judges applying CJA 2003 are much more willing to admit bad character evidence compared to the situation under the previous law.[24] It is true that in *R v Weir*, the Court of Appeal declared: 'the pre-existing one-stage test which balanced probative value against prejudicial effect is obsolete'.[25] But this was said in the context where the court explicitly supposed the absence of application to exclude the evidence for unfairness under section 101(2). In a recent survey of post-CJA 2003 cases, two writers found in them vestiges of *DPP v P* approach and observe that there exists 'some sort of, as yet not defined, half-way position between the old principles and the new'.[26] Until the matter is resolved by the House of Lords, the application of the statute in this area is likely to remain uncertain. This chapter concentrates on the common law in the form in which it has been accepted across many parts of the Commonwealth.

1.2 External analysis

The ethical basis of the similar facts rule can be clarified only through an internal analysis of the objections to the prosecution's reliance on propensity evidence. There are inadequacies in the traditional attempts to explain or justify exclusion of the evidence from an external perspective. This section discusses the traditional views by first setting out the main grounds they identify for the exclusion. Following that, it goes on to show that (i) these accounts stand on empirical premises that are contestable, conceptually vague, or not easy to verify, and, in any event, (ii) they are in need of deeper explanations.

the matters to which that evidence relates and the matters which form the subject of the offence charged': CJA 2003, s 101(4). As Munday rightly points out, this provision 'does not prevent the court from considering other issues', which 'may be just as important', such as the prejudicial character of the previous misconduct: Roderick Munday, *Evidence* (Oxford: OUP, 2005) 286. Similarly, Murphy (n 15) 173–174.

[22] *Phipson on Evidence* (n 17) paras 19–35. Mirfield, ibid, further suggests that 'the only really significant change made to this branch of the law of bad character is that, whereas, under the common law, the prosecution had to show that probative value exceeded prejudicial effect, under s.101(3), the defence must show that prejudicial effect exceeds probative value'. However, s 101(3) does not allocate the burden of proof. It only obligates the court to rule on the issue of justice when the defence makes an application for exclusion; it does not say who carries the burden of persuasion on that issue. Also, if it is right that prejudice is a normative rather than factual enquiry, it may be misplaced to talk about the burden of proof.

[23] Roberts and Zuckerman (n 10) 517.

[24] J R Spencer, *Evidence of Bad Character* (Oxford: Hart, 2006) 64–66.

[25] *R v Weir* (n 16) para 36.

[26] Adrian Waterman and Tina Dempster, 'Bad Character: Feeling Our Way One Year On' [2006] Crim LR 614, 625.

1.2.1 *Account of external justifications*

On the external approach, the key question is this: how does the rule impact on the probabilities of getting the facts right in the end? The rule is assessed in terms of its contribution to the frequency of correct outcomes produced by the trial system. Empirical claims are made about the consequences of admitting evidence of previous misconduct and about how the rule affects reliability.

The impact on reliability is complicated by this perceived tension. Evidence of previous misconduct is often thought to have probative value. Depriving the fact-finder of it may lead to acquittal of the truly guilty. Most people would regard as relevant that the defendant had previously committed crimes of the same kind as that for which he now stands trial. They would think that a person with that record is more likely than someone without it to be guilty as presently charged. To accept that the evidence is relevant is to admit that it is of some use in ascertaining the facts under enquiry. If we are interested in the truth, we should admit the evidence. That, of course, is not to say that the evidence is conclusive; it is merely to say it should be taken into account in the overall assessment.

But it is also recognized that the evidence is potentially prejudicial. This is taken to mean that the evidence is capable of leading the fact-finder away from the correct factual conclusion.[27] Where the prejudicial effect of the evidence outweighs its probative force, admitting the evidence is more likely to obstruct than aid the discovery of truth. In such a case, it is justifiable to exclude the evidence for that is the course of action most conducive to the desired outcome.[28] This judgment is based on a prediction of how the fact-finder will respond mentally to the evidence. Two major factors are commonly cited for believing that admission of the evidence will probably hinder more than facilitate the pursuit of truth.[29]

[27] Thus Richard O Lempert treats 'prejudicial evidence' as 'any evidence that influences jury verdicts without relating logically to the issue of guilt or innocence' ('Modeling Relevance' (1977) 75 Michigan L Rev 1021, 1036) and Suzanne Scotchmer defines it as evidence which 'makes the jury more willing to convict without changing the posterior probability ratio of guilt to innocence' ('Rules of Evidence and Statistical Reasoning in Court' in Peter Newman (ed), *The New Palgrave Dictionary of Economics and the Law*, vol 3 (London: Macmillan, 1998) 390).

[28] Geoffrey R Stone, 'The Rules of Evidence and the Rules of Public Debate' [1993] U of Chicago Legal Forum 127, 141–142.

[29] The distinction that is being drawn between these two factors corresponds generally to that maintained by those who separate 'reasoning prejudice' from 'moral prejudice' (see eg Law Commission, *Evidence in Criminal Proceedings: Previous Misconduct of a Defendant* (Consultation Paper No 141, 1996) para 9.92, and Law Commission, *Evidence of Bad Character in Criminal Proceedings* (Law Com No 273, Cm 5257, 2001) para 7.23; Andrew Palmer, 'The Scope of the Similar Fact Rule' (1994) 16 Adelaide L Rev 161); 'inferential error prejudice' from 'nullification prejudice' (Roger C Park, 'Character at the Crossroads' (1998) 49 Hastings LJ 717, 720; David P Leonard, 'In Defense of the Character Evidence Prohibition: Foundations of the Rule Against Trial by Character' (1998) 73 Indiana LJ 1161, 1184); and, 'disposition prejudice' from 'bad person prejudice' (*Phipson on Evidence* (n 17) paras [19–46]-[19–47]).

First, there is a danger that the fact-finder will treat the evidence of previous misconduct as more damning than it actually is.[30] Commonsense assessment of the evidence, even though made in good faith, may be off the mark. Call this the *risk of cognitive error*. The cause is ignorance. Ignorance and irrationality are not the same. Those who believe 'that whales are fish need [not be] irrational; they may simply be ill-informed'.[31] It is common for those urging the reality of the risk of cognitive error to point to studies suggesting that the layperson is prone to overestimate recidivism rates, that the perception of criminal specialization—that criminals tend to recommit the same sorts of crime—is not wholly supported by empirical data,[32] and that people have a tendency to draw stronger inferences from evidence of past acts than is actually warranted,[33] in particular, that they tend to put too much store on character traits, exaggerating their consistency and failing to take sufficient account of situational factors.[34] We are told that evidence of the accused's criminal record is not as accurate as many suppose it to be, and not as telling as it appears on the face of criminal statistics.[35] The statistics can be misleading, especially to people without inside knowledge of the workings of the criminal justice system. It is said, for instance, that the likelihood of a person with a criminal past being investigated and charged does not truly reflect the objective likelihood of his guilt. This is because the police get leads from criminal files and, understandably, their investigation is usually 'biased' against persons who have had brushes with the law, especially those with records relating to the kind of offence under investigation.[36] It has also been pointed out that accused persons with criminal records have various incentives to plead guilty and that those who are not enticed by such incentives and insist on going to trial are more likely to be innocent than their criminal past might, at first blush, suggest.[37]

Secondly, it is believed that evidence of the accused's bad character has the potential to sway the fact-finder unduly against him. Let this be called the *risk of*

[30] *R v Boardman* [1975] AC 421, 456; *R v Isleworth Crown Court, ex p Marland* (1998) 162 JP 251, 255 and 258; Roberts and Zuckerman (n 10) 505–506.

[31] D H Mellor, *Probability—A Philosophical Introduction* (London: Routledge, 2005) 73.

[32] eg Julian V Roberts and Loretta J Stalans, *Public Opinion, Crime, and Criminal Justice* (Oxford: Westview, 1997) 30–32, 191–193.

[33] Donald A Dripps, 'Relevant but Prejudicial Exculpatory Evidence: Rationality versus Jury Trial and the Right to Put on a Defense' (1996) 69 Southern California L Rev 1389, 1401. The tendency to overestimate the probative value of character evidence has been explained in terms of the 'halo effect' of the evidence, or what Méndez prefers to call the 'devil's horns effect'; according to this theory, people are prone to oversimplify and judge others on the basis of one outstanding good or bad quality: Miguel Angel Méndez, 'California's New Law on Character Evidence: Evidence Code Section 352 and the Impact of Recent Psychological Studies' (1984) 31 U California, Los Angeles L Rev 1003, 1047.

[34] *B R S v The Queen* (1997) 191 CLR 275 at 322.

[35] John Jackson and Martin Wasik, 'Character Evidence and Criminal Procedure' in David Hayton (ed), *Law's Future—British Legal Development in the 21st Century* (Oxford: Hart, 2000) 352–354.

[36] Law Commission Consultation Paper 141 (n 29) paras 7.8 and 7.23.

[37] Richard O Lempert and Stephen A Saltzburg, *A Modern Approach to Evidence* (2nd edn, Minnesota: West Publishing, 1982) 216–217.

emotivism.[38] Unlike a cognitive error, there is an element of irrationality involved in emotivism. The fear is of the evidence creating in the fact-finder such antipathy towards the accused that she feels that he should be punished in any event, regardless of his guilt in respect of the crime with which he is charged.[39] In consequence, the fact-finder may convict the accused even though she does not really believe that he committed the present crime or, she may deny him the benefit of reasonable doubt to which he is entitled.[40] The latter occurs when the fact-finder allows herself to be persuaded too quickly of guilt;[41] is biased against the accused and fails to be objective and dispassionate in the evaluation of evidence;[42] or does not look with sufficient care for facts which are consistent with the accused's innocence.[43] According to a psychological explanation for this behaviour, knowledge of the accused's bad character tends to lower the fact-finder's anticipation of regret at wrongful conviction.[44]

1.2.2 Critique of external justifications

On the external account, neither cognitive error nor emotivism is intrinsically objectionable; both are objectionable because they are likely to lead the trier of fact to the wrong verdict. The first justification (the need to guard against the risk of cognitive error) is based on empirical assertions that are themselves not free of controversy amongst social scientists and psychologists. The claim that the jury is likely to overestimate the probative value of bad character evidence is contested by a number of writers.[45] Davies, for instance, has argued that '[c]urrent psychological literature strongly supports the commonsense intuition that people act predictably according to their characters'[46] and also that 'the psychological literature does not indicate that character evidence is unduly prejudicial'.[47]

[38] John Henry Wigmore, *A Treatise on the Anglo-American System of Evidence in Trials at Common Law*, vol 1 (3rd edn, Boston: Little, Brown & Co, 1940) 454–456, para 57. More generally, on the many roles emotions play in jury deliberation, see Reid Hastie, 'Emotions in Jurors' Decisions' (2001) 66 Brooklyn L Rev 991.

[39] *Thompson v The King* [1918] AC 221, 233.

[40] *Noor Mohamed v The King* [1949] AC 182, 193; Roberts and Zuckerman (n 10) 506–507.

[41] 'The more hateful the defendant, the more readily will judges find a causal connection between the defendant and the injury complained of': Felix S Cohen, 'Field Theory and Judicial Logic' (1950) 59 Yale LJ 238, 242.

[42] James Landon, 'Character Evidence: Getting to the Root of the Problem Through Comparison' (1997) 24 American J of Crim L 581, 590–591.

[43] Alfred Bucknill, *The Nature of Evidence* (London: Skeffington, 1953) 33–34.

[44] See Lempert (n 27) 1034–1036; Lempert and Saltzburg (n 37) 162–165.

[45] Mirko Bagaric and Kumar Amarasekara, 'The Prejudice Against Similar Fact Evidence' (2001) 5 E & P 71, 81: 'it seems that the dangers of a jury decision being influenced by feelings of bias or prejudice have been overstated'.

[46] Susan Marlene Davies, 'Evidence of Character to Prove Conduct: A Reassessment of Relevancy' (1991) 27 Crim L Bulletin 504, 506.

[47] ibid 533. See also Park (n 29) 730: on the issue of whether similar fact evidence ('specific-act evidence') should be admissible to prove guilt, he noted that 'the literature from social psychology and personality psychology does not point strongly to one conclusion or the other'. The Law Commission in its Consultation Paper 141 (n 29) para 6.11 urged caution in relying on

According to a popular view, evidence showing 'that a defendant has committed offences of a similar type before statistically and logically suggests that he is more likely than those without such a record to commit such offences again'.[48] Even so, it is critical to note that the traditional justification for exclusion under the similar facts rule is not that the evidence is irrelevant but that the fact-finder tends to give it greater weight than it actually has.[49] It is difficult to understand what is meant by the claim that the fact-finder has been *unduly* influenced, for, as Dripps notes, this claim 'depends on a background judgment of rationality that is difficult to verify or to falsify empirically'.[50] One cannot conclude merely from data suggesting that disclosure of the accused's criminal record increases the chances of conviction that fact-finders are inclined to *over*-value evidence of past convictions. This allegation implies that the evidence has an objectively 'correct' weight. But in what sense have fact-finders given, and how are we to tell (save in extreme cases) that they have given, 'too much' weight to the evidence?[51] If the evidence is of a previous criminal conviction, it has been argued that a rough sense of its objective probative value may be derived from the relevant crime statistics and recidivism figures; but the interpretation and use of such data are fraught with difficulties.[52] The first line of justification seems speculative, if not conceptually vague.

psychological studies: 'Psychologists are far from formulating a single, definitive explanation of the causes of human behaviour, or of the concept of personality, and their findings need to be treated with some care.' It noted that the various studies conducted in the United Kingdom and the United States 'do not give a uniform answer to the question whether [the disclosure of a criminal] record is prejudicial' (ibid at para 7.6, words in brackets added). But in their Report No 273 (n 29) para 6.41, they preferred to err on the side of caution. For a summary of psychological research findings and competing theses in this field, see Mike Redmayne, 'The Relevance of Bad Character' (2002) 61 CLJ 684, 687–690.

[48] Lord Justice Auld, *Review of the Criminal Courts of England and Wales* (London: HMSO 2001) 566.

[49] *DPP v Kilbourne* [1973] AC 729, 757; *R v Boardman* (n 30) 456; *R v Isleworth Crown Court ex p Marland* (n 30) 255. Cf suggestions that the evidence is irrelevant: *Thompson v R* [1918] AC 221, 232; *Miller* [1952] 2 All ER 667, 668H; James Fitzjames Stephen, *A General View of the Criminal Law of England* (London: Macmillan, 1863) 309–310.

[50] Dripps (n 33) 1401. Some have argued that studies claiming to show that people are prone to fallacious reasoning actually show no such thing, that the researchers have misconstrued the data or made questionable assumptions in analysing it: eg Nicholas Rescher, *Rationality—A Philosophical Inquiry into the Nature and the Rationale of Reason* (Oxford: Clarendon, 1988) 194–196.

[51] Referring to those who called for empirical verification, Rupert Cross rightly asked: 'But would they have been any wiser with regard to the crucial question whether the disclosure of the record increases the risk of the conviction of an innocent man?': 'Clause 3 of the Draft Criminal Evidence Bill, Research and Codification' [1973] Crim LR 400, 403.

[52] See Mike Redmayne, 'The Law Commission's Character Convictions' (2002) 6 Intl J of Evidence and Proof 71, and 'The Relevance of Bad Character' (2002) 61 CLJ 684. The author argued, based on a sampling of criminal and recidivism statistics, that the studies on which the Law Commission Report No 273 (n 29) relied for its claim that similar fact evidence has an unduly prejudicial effect on fact-finders do not in fact support the claim; indeed, he suggested that the studies showed the reverse: that the subjects gave too little rather than too much weight to the evidence. (On the studies, see Sally Lloyd-Bostock, 'The Effects on Juries of Hearing about the Defendant's Previous Criminal Record: A Simulation Study' [2000] Crim LR 734, and 'The Effects

But let it be that laypeople do tend to find past convictions and prior misconduct more incriminating that they actually are. The first line of justification, as mentioned, attributes the cognitive error to ignorance: the fact-finder relies, in her deliberation, on beliefs and reasoning which, unknown to her, are false or invalid. But if ignorance is the problem, and if bad character evidence is deemed probative, and therefore acknowledged to be truth-revealing to some degree, would not the most appropriate response be to guide the fact-finder in the evaluation of it?[53] Why does the law not treat it the same way it treats other evidence that carries the risk of cognitive error?[54] For example, evidence of (eye-witness) identification, as it has come to be accepted, is not as trustworthy as it is widely believed to be. Nevertheless, the law admits the evidence subject to 'advice' on its evaluation. The fact-finder is told about the aspects in which the testimony might be unreliable and urged to be cautious in believing it.

The law controls bad character evidence by the techniques of 'exclusion' and 'regulation' instead. The evidence is excluded from deliberation altogether if it is adduced for the purpose that offends the similar facts rule. If that purpose does not offend the rule, but the evidence might nevertheless attract a line of reasoning that offends it, the evidence is admitted subject to regulation on how it cannot be used; the jury will be warned not to rely on the so-called 'forbidden chain of reasoning'.[55] 'Advice' is a weaker form of controlling deliberation than 'exclusion' or 'regulation'. It is understandable why, in the present context, the law prefers one or the other of the last two options. To choose either is to take a categorical stand on the underlying objection. A categorical stand is the proper response because moral principles are at stake. To understand the similar facts rule, we have to explore its ethical basis. This will be done in the next section.

The second line of justification (the need to safeguard the accused against the risk of emotivism) is also inadequate. In determining the reality and degree of this risk, we have to predict how the trier of fact is likely to react to the evidence.

on Magistrates of Knowing of a Defendant's Criminal Record', summarized in the said Report (n 29) 241–9.) But, as the author himself acknowledged, there are many difficulties in interpreting the statistics on which he relied: 'The Relevance of Bad Character' (2002) 61 CLJ 684, 700–713.

[53] The question is raised also by A A S Zuckerman, *The Principles of Criminal Evidence* (Oxford: Clarendon, 1989) 231–232, and Bagaric and Amarasekara (n 45) 81–82.

[54] As Chris William Sanchirico, 'Character Evidence and the Object of Trial' (2001) 101 Columbia L Rev 1227, 1246, has pointed out: 'What is needed and what has never been provided is a comprehensive argument that judging conduct from character is susceptible to errors that are systematically different from and substantially worse than those affecting tasks that we currently assign to the jury.'

[55] *R v Boardman* (n 30) 453; *B R S v The Queen* (n 34) 294–295, 302–303, 326–327, 329–330; *R v Carrington* [1990] Crim LR 330; cf *R v Rance and R v Herron* (1975) 62 Cr App R 118, 122; *R v Roy* [1992] Crim LR 185; Philip McNamara, 'Dissimilar Judgments on Similar Facts' (1984) 58 Aust LJ 74 (Part I) at 77–78, and (1984) 58 Aust LJ 143 (Part II) at 154; Rajiv Nair, 'Weighing Similar Fact and Avoiding Prejudice' (1996) 112 LQR 262; Roberts and Zuckerman (n 10) 532, 534. The need for careful jury instruction is stressed in several post-CJA 2003 cases: eg *R v Hanson & Ors* (n 16) para 18; *R v Edwards & Ors* [2005] EWCA Crim 1813, para 3; for further discussion, see J R Spencer, *Evidence of Bad Character* (Oxford: Hart, 2006) 116–117 and 147–150.

As will be argued later, this idea makes little sense of the application of the similar facts rule at a bench trial. A deeper analysis of the second line of justification is needed to uncover its normative roots. What is risky about exposing the fact-finder to bad character evidence, we are told, is that it may cause her to convict the accused without the necessary belief in his guilt on the present charge, or to cause her to settle too quickly upon that belief, for example, by being biased in the evaluation of the evidence. But what sentiments is the evidence capable of invoking in the trier of fact that could induce her to behave thus? It is, broadly speaking, the belief that a leopard never changes its spots. In the words of the New Zealand Law Commission: 'The concern is that the jury might make unwarranted and dangerous assumptions along the lines of "once a thief, always a thief."'[56] Our moral intuition against the prejudice contained in such assumptions is captured in the proverb not to 'give a dog a bad name and hang him'.[57] The underlying ethical concerns remain even when the trial is by judge alone. They must be carefully articulated from the standpoint of the fact-finder as a moral agent. In the final analysis, it is not psychological weaknesses but our commitment to certain moral values underpinning the trial process that give meaning and importance to the similar facts rule.

1.3 Internal analysis

1.3.1 Moral constraints on evidential reasoning

The internal approach focuses on the process of deliberation rather than outcome of fact-finding. It seeks justification for the rule by arguing in particular from the moral import of finding facts establishing criminal guilt. This kind of justification relies on a priori principles and is not contingent on the validity of empirical claims. Whereas the emphasis of the external approach is on the potential that bad character evidence has in evoking certain mental responses from the fact-finder, the internal approach focuses on the normative bounds of reasoning on such evidence. The system engineer is primarily interested in how the similar facts rule contributes to the reliability of trial findings. But the rule has moral underpinnings and to understand them fully, we must take the perspective of the person, the fact-finder, on whom the rule binds; we must appreciate the expressive function and gravity of holding the accused responsible for a crime and reflect on the epistemic justification for, and the justice of the reasoning used to support, beliefs about his guilt.

It was, for long, the orthodoxy that the similar facts rule strictly prohibits the trier of fact from reasoning in a certain way towards the conclusion of guilt. The idea that there is a strictly 'forbidden chain of reasoning' is no longer fashionable,

[56] The New Zealand Law Commission, *Evidence—Reform of the Law*, Report 55, Vol 1 (1999) 48.

[57] *George Ballantine & Son v Dixon & Son* [1974] 1 WLR 1125, 1132.

but, as we will see, it is possible to interpret the idea in a manner reconcilable with the view which claims to oppose it. It was held in *Makin v Attorney-General for New South Wales*[58] that the court may not, from the fact that 'the accused had been guilty of criminal [or discreditable] acts other than those covered by the indictment', infer that he 'is a person likely from his criminal [or discreditable] conduct or character to have committed the offence for which he is being tried'. The law is largely the same under Rule 404(b) of the United States' Federal Rules of Evidence; it provides, subject to exceptions, that '[e]vidence of other crimes, wrongs or acts is not admissible to prove the character of a person in order to show action in conformity therewith'.[59] To arrive at a guilty verdict by the forbidden chain of reasoning would, according to Lord Sankey in *Maxwell v DPP*, offend 'one of the most deeply rooted and jealously guarded principles of our criminal law'.[60] The first task is to delineate the principles on which the rule rests.

The rule must be examined in the context of the purpose for which facts require proof. When the prosecution seeks to prove facts at a trial, they do so for the purpose of showing that the accused is guilty on the specified charge. To find that the accused has committed the alleged crime is at once to convict him of it, to condemn and blame him, not generally for the person that he is, but specifically for the act which constitutes the crime. Given the moral import of a conviction, the ascription of criminal responsibility has to be subjected to certain moral constraints. Two of them, as traditionally understood, are reflected in the similar facts rule. Although not free from challenges (as is to be expected in such a controversial field), they are familiar enough and possess sufficient orthodoxy to be used as our starting points.

The first moral constraint, broadly stated, is this: the court ought not, because it is unfair, to hold a person responsible for his action if he lacks the capacity of reflective self-control—where, although he did it, he can genuinely[61] protest, 'I could not help it.'[62] To be morally responsible for a crime, the agent must possess, at the time of its alleged commission, the normal capacity of understanding and control with respect to his action. The 'powers of reflective self-control' consist of two kinds of rational powers: the power to grasp and apply moral reasons, and the power to govern one's behaviour by the light of such reasons.[63]

[58] [1894] AC 57, 65 (words within square brackets added).

[59] But see the relatively new Rules 413 and 414 of the Federal Rules of Evidence which allow evidence of similar crimes to be admitted in sexual assault and child molestation cases respectively. They are criticized by Aviva Orenstein, 'Deviance, Due Process, the False Promise of Federal Rule of Evidence 403' (2005) 90 Cornell L Rev 1487 for compromising trial fairness.

[60] [1935] AC 309, 317.

[61] Stressing the importance of establishing the truth of this protest: Herbert Fingarette, 'Addiction and Criminal Responsibilities' (1975) 84 Yale LJ 413, 426–444.

[62] Underlying the criminal law, according to H L A Hart, is the 'fundamental principle of morality that a person is not to be blamed for what he has done if he could not help doing it': *Punishment and Responsibility—Essays in the Philosophy of Law* (revised edn, London: Clarendon, 1970) 174. See also ibid, 39–40.

[63] R Jay Wallace, *Responsibility and the Moral Sentiments* (Massachusetts: Harvard UP, 1994) 7.

According to Wallace, to hold a person morally responsible is to hold him to the moral obligations that we accept, and we hold him morally responsible for an action when we believe that he has, in so acting, violated those obligations. However, it is unfair to hold someone to such obligations if he is incapable of meeting our moral expectations:[64] 'it is unreasonable to demand that people do something—in a way that potentially exposes them to the harms of moral sanction—if they lack the general power to grasp and comply with the reasons that support the demand'.[65]

The second moral constraint comes from this settled principle of criminal justice: the accused is to be tried specifically on his responsibility for the criminal act the prosecution alleges he has committed; it is not the point of the trial to judge him generally for the person that he is, on the life that he has lived. '[A] defendant must be tried for what he did, not for who he is.'[66] As Gross elaborates:[67]

> [C]riminal justice requires us to determine the culpability of a person's conduct, not the culpability of a person... Judgments sometimes are rendered about what a person is rather than about what a person has done. At times it is a conclusion about him based on what he has done in the past. At other times it is a conclusion about him based on certain conduct he has engaged in that is assumed to be representative of what he is disposed to do... When determining criminal liability, the criminal law confines its concern with culpability to specific conduct that is alleged to constitute a crime, placing these other matters entirely out of bounds.

In *Phillips v The Queen*,[68] the Australian High Court cited exactly the same principle as a general reason for excluding evidence of previous misconduct:

> Criminal trials... are ordinarily focused with high particularity upon specified offences. They are not, as such, a trial of the accused's character or propensity towards criminal conduct.

The similar facts rule forbids reliance on reasoning in support of a conviction that violates either of the two moral constraints above. Of the two, the second stands in greater danger of violation. Suppose the court has to decide whether the accused is guilty of a particular crime. There is evidence of his previous engagements in that kind of criminal activity. One may seek to reason from his bad character along this line:

[64] For elaborated defence of this point: ibid 157 *et seq*.

[65] ibid 161.

[66] *US v Meyers* (1977) 550 F 2d 1036, 1044 (5th Cir), describing this principle as a 'concomitant of the presumption of innocence'. The same was held to be 'fundamental to American jurisprudence' in *US v Foskey* (1980) 636 F 2d 517, 523 (DC Cir).

[67] Hyman Gross, *A Theory Of Criminal Justice* (New York: OUP, 1979) 76–77; and see also ibid 9.

[68] (2006) 224 ALR 216, 236. Similarly, *United States v Hodges* (1985) 770 F 2d 1475, 1479; *United States v Mothershed* (1988) 859 F 2d 585, 589.

It is likely that the accused is guilty because his past shows that he is the *sort of person* likely to have committed this crime.

This general form of reasoning may rely on one of two generalizations about 'the sort of person' the accused is believed to be. We may think that:

G1: he is the sort of person who *cannot help doing* this kind of criminal act (under certain conditions); or
G2: he is the sort of person who *tends to commit* this kind of criminal act (under certain conditions).

Each of these generalizations (G1 and G2) can, in turn, be based on one of two conceptions of the accused as a person. That, under certain conditions (such as the availability of relevant opportunity or presence of sufficiently strong temptation), the accused cannot help committing the kind of criminal act in question (G1) may be explained by one of two possible characterizations of his moral personality. According to the first, he lacks the power of critical moral reflection. He was in each case guided by his basic, or first-order, desire to commit that kind of act. He is incapable of making higher-order evaluations, of reflecting on the rightness or wrongness of his conduct, and consequently of wanting to change.[69] According to the second, he lacks the power of self-control. He is unable to guide his life by the light of his critical judgments. While he understands that what he had done was wrong and, at a higher level, desires not to do it again, he is incapable, in certain circumstances, of self-restraint. His actions, while intentional, were involuntary. On each occasion, he truly could not help doing it and did it against his better judgment.[70]

Both conceptions of him may be objectionable on empirical or logical ground: often, the previous incidents of similar misconduct are not strong enough to show that the accused lacks the capacity to act otherwise than he allegedly did. In theory, there will come a point when the number of antecedents makes either conception of him plausible. But there is another independent objection, a moral one, to blaming him for the alleged crime on either of those conceptions. A finding of guilt not only asserts facts constitutive of the crime in question, it also (at least in the typical criminal case and if only implicitly) condemns the accused for committing it. According to the first moral constraint, a person does not merit blame for his action when he does not have the capacity of reflective self-control. In the present version of the reasoning (G1), the accused is treated precisely as such a person; he is thought either to lack the power to grasp and apply moral reasons, or to lack the capacity to control his behaviour by the light of such reasons.

[69] See Harry G Frankfurt's description of someone lacking 'second-order volitions': 'Freedom of the Will and the Concept of a Person' (1971) 68 *J of Philosophy* 5.

[70] Following Bernard Gert and Timothy Duggan, he may be said to lack the 'ability to will' in respect of committing the crime as a kind of action: 'Free Will as the Ability to Will' (1979) 13 *Noûs* 197.

The concept of character employed here has no ethical connotation. It is analogous to the kind attributed to non-moral entities. To say that sugar is soluble is to say that it will dissolve ('cannot help but dissolve') under the condition of being placed in water. It is unintelligible to hold sugar 'responsible' for 'behaving' as it is disposed to do.[71] If we accept the first moral constraint on the ascription of criminal responsibility, we cannot, without a lack of integrity, rely on the 'cannot help it' argument as a reason for a guilty verdict: if the accused's character is truly such that he could not help committing the crime, then he is not morally accountable for it and therefore ought not to be found guilty of it. G1 breaches this constraint covertly, under the guise of evidential reasoning, where an inference is drawn towards guilt from a conception of his character that ought, in principle, to exclude him from accountability.[72]

Breach of the first moral constraint is unlikely to occur since the personal characterization in G1 is extreme and will rarely be employed by the fact-finder. But there is a more problematic and worrying way in which the criminal past of the accused may be held against him, and it is on this that we will henceforth concentrate. One might be tempted to reason that he is the *sort of person* likely to have committed this crime because he is the sort of person who *tends to commit* this kind of criminal act under certain conditions (G2). Here, we do not think that he lacks the powers of reflective self-control. But we believe that his exercise of those powers is deviant or falls short of expectation. He may be a wicked man who does not think it is wrong to act in the way he did. Or he may be a moral weakling. He understands that it is wrong to commit the crime but gives in too easily. His will or power of self-control is weak.[73] In both cases, one might reason that it is likely that he will repeat what he did where the conditions which tend to elicit that kind of behaviour are present. However, the nature and form of this reasoning needs careful study.

1.3.2 Use and abuse of evidence of previous misconduct

Plainly, it cannot be inferred solely from the fact that the accused had committed this type of crime in the past that he is likely to be guilty of the instant crime.

[71] Example taken from Gilbert Ryle, *The Concept of Mind* (London: Hutchinson's University Library, 1949) 123.

[72] It is not suggested that the fact-finder is never allowed to find as a fact, were it a legal issue in the case, that the accused lacks the powers of reflective self-control. What the fact-finder is not allowed to do is to infer this fact from the accused's record of criminal or discreditable conduct and use it as a basis for finding that he is guilty where his incapacity is not presented as an issue in dispute at his trial.

[73] Action performed against one's better judgment is not necessarily involuntary. We are here supposing a case where judged by 'ordinary everyday criteria', we would say that he could have avoided acting as he had done (David Pears, *Motivated Irrationality* (Oxford: Clarendon, 1984) 229). As Pears points out (ibid 232), 'capitulation to... mild addiction would not be a case of compulsion'. The second conception of G2 (the case of the moral weakling) is different from the second conception of G1 (the case where the actor lacks the power of self-control); in the first, the person is 'weak-willed' and in the second, 'will-less': on the conceptual difference, see: Thomas E Hill, Jr, 'Weakness of Will and Character' (1986) 14 *Philosophical Topics* 93.

There is much debate between those who advocate the significance of character in controlling human behaviour and those who take as determinative the situation in which the actor found himself. Doris has warned against needlessly polarizing this debate. Whether character or situation has greater influence, it can scarcely be denied that both contribute to a person's conduct.[74] Attribution of a disposition does not *entail* action in conformity with it.[75] That a person has a disposition to do X does not mean that he will 'constantly, on every occasion, do things of sort X'; much will turn on 'the situation that is immediately present'.[76]

There are two ways in which one may account for the role that character and situation play in influencing behaviour.[77] This translates, in the present context, into two ways of conceptualizing, and reasoning from, the bad character of the accused. First, his bad character may be seen as the direct[78] cause of his behaviour. This account views people 'as objects which are passively affected by events in their environment'.[79] While they are treated as capable of making choices in their behaviour, their choices are thought to be dictated by their fixed psychological properties. This mechanical conception of human character, like the characterizations of moral personality assumed in G1, does not sufficiently accommodate moral agency. On a deterministic account of human behaviour, that a person behaves 'in character' (however badly) can provide as little basis for condemnation as when a rattlesnake bites out of instinct.[80] Given the moral aspect of ascribing criminal responsibility, a motivational conception of character is needed to justify reliance on it to explain criminal conduct.

The deterministic conception of human character encourages one to apply to human conduct a mode of prediction that is based on behavioural trends. One

[74] John M Doris, *Lack of Character—Personality and Moral Behavior* (Cambridge: CUP, 2002) 25–26. See also John A Johnson, 'Persons in Situations: Distinguishing New Wine from Old Wine in New Bottles' (1999) 13 *Eur J of Personality* 443, 444–445.

[75] 'To attribute a disposition to someone is never to preclude that he may on some occasion act, or have acted, in some way contrary to his general tendency or disposition... It is typical of human character... that it allows of lapses, and that people sometimes behave in a way which is not in accordance with their character.' Stuart Hampshire, 'Dispositions' (1953) 14 *Analysis* 5, 7.

[76] Joel J Kupperman, *Character* (Oxford: OUP, 1991) 59.

[77] The vast body of relevant literature includes William P Alston, 'Traits, Consistency and Conceptual Alternatives for Personality Theory' (1975) 5 *J of the Theory of Social Behaviour* 17; Richard B Brandt, 'Traits of Character: A Conceptual Analysis' (1970) 7 *American Philosophical Quarterly* 23; Walter Mischel and Yuichi Shoda, 'A Cognitive-Affective System Theory of Personality: Reconceptualizing Situations, Dispositions, Dynamics, and Invariance in Personality Structure' (1995) 102 *Psychological Rev* 246; Yuichi Shoda and Walter Mischel, 'Reconciling Contextualism with the Core Assumptions of Personality Psychology' (2000) 14 *Eur J of Personality* 407; Jerome C Wakefield, 'Levels of Explanation in Personality Theory' in David M Buss and Nancy Cantor (eds), *Personality Psychology—Recent Trends and Emerging Directions* (New York: Springer, 1989) ch 25.

[78] James R Averill, 'The Dis-Position of Psychological Dispositions' (1973) 6 *J of Experimental Research in Personality* 275, 278–279.

[79] R Harré and P F Secord, *The Explanation of Social Behaviour* (New York: Rowman and Littlefield, 1972) 30.

[80] Example given by Thomas Nagel, *The View From Nowhere* (New York: OUP, 1986) 121.

may, for example, take the accused's previous theft conviction as evidence of a propensity to steal. Relying on crime statistics on reoffending, he is placed in the reference class of persons presumably impressed with the same disposition. On purely statistical or 'actuarial grounds',[81] some weight is then attributed to his previous conviction as evidence of his guilt on the present charge. On this analysis, his previous conviction alone, apart from other evidence presented in the case, has some probative value: or, more accurately, his previous conviction of itself adds to the incriminating force of the collection of other evidence. It is assumed that he has a property, a certain propensity to steal, that he shares the (stereo)typical thief. That property is then used as the direct basis of a causal inference. Feinberg describes the underlying unfairness (in the different context of legislative discrimination) thus:

> Prejudice is a kind of unfairness that is literally 'pre-judging,' that is attributing a property to an individual person, and acting accordingly, in the absence of any direct evidence that he or she has that property, but only the very indirect evidence that other persons who share some resemblance to that person have it...[82]
>
> The correlation between statistical class membership and a specified type of behavior... does not connect that behavior to any causally relevant factor operating in each member of the class. That a given person is a member of the statistically dangerous class is a ground for suspecting that he might have a property that is causally connected with danger, but that class membership itself is not that property.[83]

Feinberg's claim, it must be noted, is not that class membership is always irrelevant but only that something more must be established to make it probative. The discussion below on the legitimate use of bad character evidence offers suggestions as to why this is so and what else must be shown.

Although statistical reasoning certainly has a place in legal fact-finding, the court should not rely upon it directly, in the manner just described. To do so is morally objectionable. Respect for the accused requires that the court must not be dismissive of his capacity to revise, or act against, his bad character. This is best interpreted as the point of the ban on the 'forbidden chain of reasoning'. It prohibits the court from drawing any probability of guilt, however slight, simply and immediately from his discreditable life history. His past, standing on its own, should not be used directly against him on the assumption of probability that he

[81] David M Buss and Kenneth H Craik, 'The Act Frequency Approach to Personality' (1983) 90 *Psychological Rev* 105, 107.

[82] Joel Feinberg, *Harm to Others* (Oxford: OUP, 1984) at 199.

[83] ibid 201. See also Mark Colyvan, Helen M Regan and Scott Ferson, 'Is it a Crime to Belong to a Reference Class?' (2001) 9 *J of Political Philosophy* 168, 172, observing that a person's '[m]embership in reference classes... does little to establish anything about [her] own behavior'. See Chapter 3, n 124 for further literature on the reference class problem.

is still the evil man or the moral weakling that he was. This offends the second of our two moral constraints. As Cardozo CJ said:[84]

If a... propensity may be proved against a defendant as one of the tokens of his guilt, a rule of criminal evidence, long believed to be of fundamental importance for the protection of the innocent, must be first declared away... In a very real sense a defendant starts his life afresh when he stands before a jury, a prisoner at the bar.

An aspect of autonomy is the ability to engage in the rational 'process of self-*re*-creation';[85] as autonomous beings, we 'always retain the possibility of stepping back and judging where we are and where we want to be'[86]—of 'starting life afresh', as Cardozo CJ says. Hampshire identifies 'the sense of freedom that men undoubtedly have... with their power of reflection and with the self-modifying power of thought'; when we think of someone as a thinking being, we are excluding deterministic explanations of his performances.[87] So far as one is free, one is able, through self-knowledge, to withdraw from one's 'situation and... character, assess them afresh and attempt a new response'.[88]

The freedom crucial to the accused's status as a person, not a thing, is denied in 'the crushing view that his mistakes constitute for him a destiny'.[89] We fail to respect him fully as a person when we are dismissive of the possibility of moral redemption, of him learning from his mistakes or developing moral fortitude to resist the kind of temptation to which he had previously fallen. When the accused's previous bad record is *in itself* treated as *a* (even if inconclusive) reason for believing in his guilt, as *in itself* contributing *some* (however slight) weight to that conclusion, his dignity is to that extent insulted. The full force of that insult is well captured by Sartre:[90]

Who can not see how offensive to the Other and how reassuring for me is a statement such as, 'He's just a paederast,' which removes a disturbing freedom from a trait and

[84] *People v Zackowitz* (1930) 172 NE 466, 468. The internal argument that the making of the forbidden assumption against the accused is intrinsically unjust to him is different from the consequentialist argument that it might discourage his rehabilitation: on the latter, see eg *R v Handy* (n 5) 401.

[85] Joel Feinberg, 'Autonomy' in John Christman (ed), *The Inner Citadel—Essays on Individual Autonomy* (Oxford: OUP, 1989) 34.

[86] Gerald Dworkin, 'Autonomy and Behaviour Control' (1976) 6 Hastings Center Report 23, 25.

[87] Stuart Hampshire, *Freedom of the Individual* (London: Chatto & Windus, 1975) at 142 (the sentence after the semi-colon is a paraphrase of the original sentence following that quoted); see also at 105, 112.

[88] See also Gerald A Cohen, 'Beliefs and Roles' (1967) 67 *Proceedings of the Aristotelian Society* (New Series) 17, 17.

[89] Jean-Paul Sartre, *Being and Nothingness: A Phenomenological Essay on Ontology*, translated by Hazel E Barnes (London: Methuen, 1957) 64.

[90] ibid 64.

which aims at henceforth constituting all the acts of the Other as consequences following strictly from his essence.

To think of a person in this fashion is to caricature his existence; it involves a flattening of his character, a refusal to acknowledge the complexity of his mind and hence the humanity in him.[91] Reliance on evidential reasoning that expresses such insult is objectionable apart from whatever bad consequences to which it might lead. A court cannot claim moral authority to demand of the accused acceptance of its verdict if the verdict was reached by a reasoning that treats him unjustly, as less of an autonomous moral agent than he has a right to be presumed to be.[92]

There is also, arguably, an internal connection between the similar facts rule and a purpose of the criminal trial. The trial, as some have persuasively argued, resembles a process of moral criticism; it 'seeks to persuade the person whose conduct is under scrutiny of the truth and justice of its conclusions'.[93] This supposes that the person is open to persuasion. There is an element of inconsistency, perhaps even a sense of incoherence, in trying a person for a crime, seeking outwardly to elicit from him moral contrition, and, at the same time, dismissing inwardly his capacity for moral reform. In the absence of hope that the person is capable of such reform, the trial loses much of its point as a moral dialogue aimed at getting him to see the wrongness of his action.

There is a legitimate alternative to the objectionable way of using bad character evidence. It is the availability of this alternative that makes it possible to reconcile the traditional view that the rule imposes a strict ban on a 'forbidden chain of reasoning' with the current view[94] that the reasoning is permissible if the probative force of the evidence is strong enough. The alternative view adopts an internal perspective and conceptualizes character in terms of an individual's set of relatively enduring motivational or cognitive-purposive structures, comprising of stable, but not un-revisable, higher-order desires, needs, motives, wants, aversions, beliefs, and such inner states. Here, we adopt the perspective of the person whose action is under examination. 'From the standpoint of the actor or agent who consciously controls his performance, desires, emotions or passions are not linked to behaviour like blind mechanical pushes, but are factors in determining

[91] E M Forster, *Aspects of the Novel* (London: Edward Arnold, 1949) 65 and 68.

[92] R A Duff, *Trials and Punishments* (Cambridge: CUP, 1986) 131. This internal demand of justice is distinct from such external concerns as fear of the consequential loss of public confidence in the trial system (Law Commission Report No 273 (n 29) para 6.52) and of incurring the resentment of the defendant (ibid para 6.46).

[93] Duff (n 92) 116. A view that is shared by others: eg T R S Allan, *Constitutional Justice—A Liberal Theory of the Rule of Law* (Oxford: OUP, 2001) 81 *et seq*.

[94] See the suggestions made by Lord Cross in *R v Boardman* (n 30) 456–457 and the clear acceptance of this view in *R v Randall* [2003] UKHL 69 at para 26, [2004] 1 All ER 467. In criminal cases, there is now explicit provisions on propensity reasoning in CJA 2003, ss 101(1)(d) and 103(1)(a).

what the agent takes himself to be doing.'[95] A person is not merely an object that is acted upon by the forces of circumstances, to whom things only happen. On the contrary, it is precisely on account of his capacity of reflective self-control that we hold him responsible for his intentional action.[96] The present conception of character allows for a person's disposition to serve as the key to an interpretation of the body of evidence brought by the prosecution that explains why he committed the crime with which he is charged. Importantly, the disposition has no role to play if there is nothing in the body of evidence to unlock. The explanation must be cast in terms of reasons, encompassing beliefs and desires, which motivated the specific action under enquiry.[97]

To the extent that it is true of an adult that his internal motivational structures, system of basic beliefs, and outlook of life are relatively stable, it is rational to believe that he will be disposed to a relatively stable pattern of experiencing needs and aversions that generates reasons (good or bad) that drive his conduct.[98] On this account, human action is voluntary, a response 'in judgment, feeling and action . . . to one's situation'.[99] How a person chooses to act in the circumstances depends on the 'set of motivations, including the person's desires, beliefs about the world, and ultimate goals and values'.[100] This set of motivations, if sufficiently integrated and enduring, informs a person's character.

However, action is under-determined by character. There are at least four sources of uncertainties in inferring specific action from the agent's traits. First, change in character is possible, reflecting fundamental shifts in beliefs, goals, and motivational system; it is thus that a person can turn over a new leaf, come to repent of his crime, when he finally realizes the true gravity of his action. Secondly, even if there is no 'global' change of the sort just mentioned, one may, on occasions, act against character.[101] Thirdly, the agent's motivational constitution will need specification if it is to have any strong explanatory power.[102] For example, the disposition to commit rape may consist of a latent higher-order

[95] Harré and Secord (n 79) 37.

[96] See Nagel (n 80) 120–121; Michele Moody-Adams, 'On the Old Saw That Character Is Destiny' in Owen Flanagan and Amélie Oksenberg Rorty (eds), *Identity, Character, and Morality—Essays in Moral Psychology* (Cambridge, Massachusetts: MIT Press, 1990) ch 5.

[97] That character traits indirectly explain human agency, see Brandt (n 77) 31; Wakefield (n 77) 338; Robert R McCrae and Paul T Costa, Jr, 'Trait Explanations in Personality Psychology' 9 (1995) *Eur J of Personality* 231, 247, 248.

[98] cf Zuckerman (n 53) 227; Kupperman (n 76) 15.

[99] Rachana Kamtekar, 'Situationism and Virtue Ethics on the Content of Our Character' (2004) 114 *Ethics* 458, 477.

[100] ibid 460.

[101] Moody-Adams (n 96).

[102] This point relies on the 'widely accepted' form of analysing character dispositions as subjunctive conditionals. On this view: 'To say that P is courageous means, among other things, that if P were in a situation of great danger that required action rather than inaction or passivity, P would be disposed to act' (Owen Flanagan, *Varieties of Moral Personality—Ethics and Psychological Realism* (Massachusetts: Harvard UP, 1991) 279). For theories of disposition along this line, see Ryle (n 71) ch v, and Brandt (n 77).

desire to forcibly violate prostitutes sexually and of the distorted belief that 'such people' somehow deserve to be so treated. If the victim is not believed by the accused to be a prostitute, this disposition loses much of its probative value.[103]

Fourthly, whether a disposition is activated on a particular occasion is dependent on many other variables, including the person's other (counter) traits. As Webber has pointed out, a particular situation may have many features eliciting different inclinations, all of which cannot be acted upon by the agent simultaneously. How the agent responds to the situation cannot then be the direct result of any single trait but the outcome of a complex interaction of his many dispositions.[104] To return to our example: suppose a man, in addition to having the trait described above, is very cautious by nature and highly averse to getting caught. An opportunity to commit rape on a prostitute presents itself to him but the circumstances are such that the chances of getting caught are high. How he reacts to this set of environmental stimuli would depend on the relative strengths of his conflicting inclinations. If the victim is known to the accused to be a prostitute but the crime was committed with incredible daring, the character of the accused, understood as a complex of interacting internal states, will not point us in any clear direction unless we know how he is likely to resolve his internal conflict.

To summarize: the probative value of the accused's disposition depends on the availability of evidence, not only of its existence and precise nature, but also of the presence of conditions in the circumstances of the case that would activate the first-order desire to act in the alleged manner.[105] It also depends on the existence of other relevant traits that might be elicited by the situational features and of the effect they have on each other. The demand that the evidence must have enough of the relevant details, and the motivational account be sensitive to the multi-dimensionality of character, is arguably how we should read the law's insistence that similar fact evidence must have sufficiently high probative value.[106] As the

[103] This was perhaps the point of the discussion on 'situation-specific propensity' in *R v Handy* (n 5) especially 413–415, criticized by Mike Redmayne, 'Similar Facts, Familiar Obfuscation' (2002) 6 Intl J of Evidence and Proof 243.

[104] Jonathan Webber, 'Virtue, Character and Situation' (2006) 3 *J of Moral Philosophy* 193.

[105] cf *R v Handy* (n 5) 398; *R v Shearing* (2002) 214 DLR (4th) 215, 232 (the Supreme Court of Canada found the cogency of similar fact evidence to lie in a 'double inference': first, that the accused has a situation-specific propensity to commit a particular crime in a particular way and, secondly, that his character or propensity gives rise to the further inference that he proceeded in that way with the victim on the charge under consideration).

[106] For an argument that takes the same direction, see A E Acorn, 'Similar Fact Evidence and the Principle of Inductive Reasoning: Makin Sense' (1991) 11 OJLS 63, 91, arguing that 'the proper method of assessing the degree of relevance... of similar fact evidence is to isolate the precise form of the generalization that it suggests and then to assess the extent of the inductive warrant for that generalization'. The general thesis is so stated by the author: 'Admissibility depends not just upon the generalization being of sufficient specificity but also upon the evidence which supports the generalization providing the inductive warrant to sustain its adoption as a major premise in an argument leading to a conclusion of guilt' (ibid 74). Bearing slight resemblance to this thesis but approaching the justification for exclusion of character evidence from a completely different angle

Court of Appeal held in *R v Cowie*,[107] 'the resolution of a dispute over the admissibility of allegedly similar fact evidence can be achieved only by considering the circumstances of a particular case. It is a contextual question.'

On the forbidden mode of using the evidence, previous misconduct *of its own* adds to the probability of guilt. It may do so, as mentioned earlier, in the statistical sense which relies on empirical generalizations about the class of persons to which the accused is said to belong. On the present view, similar fact evidence supports the inference of guilt only *indirectly* by offering an *explanation* for the alleged action that is grounded in the situation of the crime and in the *reasons* which motivated the agent. By way of illustration, consider the well-known case of *R v Ball*.[108] A pair of siblings was charged with incest, which was then recently criminalized. According to Lord Loreburn, the evidence showed that:

> there was ample opportunity for this offence, and that there were circumstances which, to say the least, were very suggestive of incest. Also these two persons lived together and occupied the same bedroom and the same bed.

When the police visited the house, the sister opened the door wearing her nightdress and when they accompanied her upstairs, they met the brother coming out of the bedroom fastening up his trousers.[109] Ordinarily, if a man and a woman live together in the way the defendants did, it is reasonable to infer that they are in a sexual relation. But the stumbling block to this inference was that the two were siblings. Usually, we would dismiss out of hand the possibility that a pair of siblings would be sexually attracted to each other. But there was evidence, the admissibility of which was the issue before the court, of their history of incest. The value of this evidence was to show that the siblings—siblings although they were—were sexually drawn to each other.[110] This made sense of their situation, particularly, of their living and sleeping arrangements.[111]

is the theory advanced by Alex Stein, *Foundations of Evidence Law* (Oxford: OUP, 2005) 183–186 (locating the crucial objection, ibid 184, in the fact that the evidence 'is not susceptible to individualized testing by the defendant').

107 [2003] EWCA Crim 3522, para 26. See also *R v Barney* [2005] EWCA Crim 1385.

108 [1911] AC 47. Although *Ball* is often cited in support of the contrary view, it was in fact emphasized in that case that the ban on the 'forbidden line of reasoning' is strict: ibid 64–65 (argument), 71 (per Lord Loreburn LC).

109 ibid 50.

110 As Lord Loreburn said, 'the existence of a sexual passion between them' was an element 'in proving that they had illicit connection in fact on or between the dates charged': ibid, 71. Unless this 'passion' was shown, opportunity to commit the alleged misconduct would have been neither here nor there: cf *Ross v Ross* [1930] AC 1, 21.

111 This approach is similar to that taken by historians in seeking explanation for human action: Herbert Burhenn, 'Historical Evidence and the Explanation of Actions' (1976) 10 *Southern Humanities Rev* 65, 68: 'If the historian can show that an action was reasonable, he will ordinarily not attempt to find some other kind of explanation for the action. He will rest content to have shown that the action is not puzzling... [I]t is primarily in those cases where an action does not make sense that the historian will press on to find further information.'

This interpretation of the evidence is based on our understanding of their desire for each other, and of the strength and relative durability of that desire. It is also predicated on the belief that their mutual feeling was so intense as to silence whatever inhibiting counter-dispositions they might have to comply with existing social and legal norms against incestuous relationship. The interpretation offers an explanation for their incestuous acts which relies in part on an internal construction of 'the kind of person' that the defendants are believed to be; personality, in the present context, refers to 'conceptions of disposition that involve motives, needs, beliefs and desires that energize, direct, and select behaviors as a function of the individual's values, capacities, and situational opportunities'.[112]

We do not take the siblings' previous sexual intercourse as a factor that, *in itself*, contributes directly some weight to the finding of guilt. On the contrary, in itself, and without more, it must count for nothing. What it can be allowed to do is to serve as evidence of the intense sexual attraction they must have felt for each other in the past, as the key to making sense of the other evidence adduced by the prosecution. The probative value of the couple's past turns on the belief that the kind of attraction they experienced is relatively durable. Statistical evidence may show the reasonableness or otherwise of this belief, and the potential usefulness of statistical reasoning in this connection is freely acknowledged. But, however reasonable the belief is, we cannot in fairness to the siblings dismiss their capacity to change the way they view each other or to resist the old urges to which they had previously succumbed. For that reason, we should allow evidence of their discreditable past to be used only to support a purposive interpretation of the body of other evidence brought by the prosecution to establish their guilt. Similar fact evidence should serve only, very loosely speaking, a 'corroborative' function.[113]

1.3.3 Reinterpretation of balancing test

If, as claimed, the similar facts rule is about dispensing justice or fairness to the accused, how should we read the test of admissibility? The common law test as set out in *DPP v P*[114] and as applied in many jurisdictions requires the probative force of the evidence to be weighed against its prejudicial effect. Traditionally, it is thought that the competing considerations spring from a common concern. Bad character evidence can potentially impede the objective ascertainment of the material facts. At the same time, it is often probative and can aid the search

[112] Jack Block, 'Critique of the Act Frequency Approach to Personality' (1989) 56 *J of Personality and Social Psychology* 234, 238.

[113] cf the suggestion that has been made that the similar facts rule operates 'as a sort of corroboration rule: it ensures that the defendant will not be convicted on the propensity inference alone, that there will always be other evidence... to back it up': Mike Redmayne, 'Drugs, Money and Relevance: R v. Yalman and R v. Guney' (1999) 3 Intl J of Evidence and Proof 128, 134, discussing the requirement that evidence be relevant to a specific issue.

[114] [1991] 2 AC 447, 460. The Law Commission had recommended essentially the same test, but wanted 'structured guidelines' on how it is to be applied: Report 273 (n 29) Part XI, especially paras 11.42–11.45.

for truth. These considerations are focused on the same end: the correct verdict. They are engaged, so to speak, in a tug-of-war; although they pull in opposite directions, their forces are exerted along the same (cognitive) plane. If the court predicts that, on balance, admission is more likely to benefit the search for truth than to harm it, it should admit the evidence; if the balance tips the other way, the court should exclude the evidence. Exclusion is a prudential measure, arising from distrust in the fact-finder's ability to assess the evidence 'logically', 'rationally', 'objectively'. In this respect, the trained judge is often deemed more trustworthy than the lay juror.

This traditional analysis of the balancing exercise raises many difficulties and overlooks fundamental principles that are at stake. To begin with, many commentators have pointed out that the considerations to be weighed lack a common measure, and that the court is, in effect, asked to balance incommensurable factors.[115] Also, the danger of the evidence being prejudicial, in the sense of it being overly influential, does not disappear just because, or whenever, the evidence has high probative value. The two factors do not stand in a logical relation of correlated variation. To say that the evidence is potentially prejudicial is to acknowledge the danger of the fact-finder giving the evidence more weight than it objectively has, *however much weight we think it objectively has*.[116]

Furthermore, on the psychological explanation of the rule, it is conceptually incoherent to apply the balancing test at a bench trial. First, on a literal application, the judge has to predict whether she has the psychological fortitude to stop herself from being influenced unduly by the evidence. If she answers negatively (and it must be hard to find a judge willing to admit to a weakness that amounts to professional incompetence), she must exclude the evidence. But, for exactly the same reason (the admitted lack of fortitude), the exclusion would, on the present account, be pointless since the judge has been exposed to the evidence. The shocking result is that, at a bench trial, the precaution can be taken only after the harm is done. Secondly, if the judge decides to exclude the evidence, she must not allow it to influence her deliberation on the verdict. We trust the judge to comply with the law and ignore the evidence completely.[117] But should not the same faith in the judge's ability to control her mental processes make us admit the evidence

[115] A A S Zuckerman, 'Similar Fact Evidence—The Unobservable Rule' [1987] 103 LQR 187, 196; Colin Tapper, 'Trends and Techniques in the Law of Evidence' in Peter Birks (ed), *Criminal Justice and Human Rights* (Oxford: OUP, 1995) 29; *Pfennig v R* (n 4) 528. Cf Roberts and Zuckerman (n 10) 526–527.

[116] Nair (n 55) 263.

[117] Critics argue that this trust in judges, and of their superiority in this regard over juries, is largely misplaced. See also Roderick Munday, 'Case Management, Similar Fact Evidence in Civil Cases, and a Divided Law of Evidence' (2006) 10 Intl J of Evidence and Proof 81; Andrew J Wistrich, Chris Guthrie and Jeffrey J Rachlinski, 'Can Judges Ignore Inadmissible Information? The Difficulty of Deliberately Disregarding' (2005) 153 U of Pennsylvania L Rev 1251.

instead? As the Privy Council held in *Attorney-General of Hong Kong v Siu Yak-Shing*:[118]

> If the judge having ruled it inadmissible is to be trusted to put the evidence out of his mind he can surely be trusted to give it only its probative, rather than its prejudicial, weight if he rules that it is admissible.

The conventional view of the balancing exercise sets up an opposition between truth and fairness. Admission of bad character evidence is unfair to the accused to the extent that it can potentially prejudice him. However, the unfairness is excusable if there is a greater countervailing interest in getting to the truth of his guilt. This way of thinking weakens the right to a fair trial, for it suggests that it is permissible to give the accused a less than fair trial whenever there is sufficiently great interest in securing his conviction.[119]

As noted earlier, it is acknowledged at common law, and under the new regime established by the CJA 2003, that the exclusion of bad character evidence is for reasons of justice or fairness. Criticisms of the balancing test can be met if it is seen, as it should be, as an operation of justice, manifesting in its application respect for the person standing trial. Contrary to the impression created by the metaphor of 'balancing', there is not an antithesis between truth and fairness; they are not on opposing sides of the scales such that every concession to one is a sacrifice of the other.

The balancing exercise is not about predicting the likely reaction of the fact-finder to the evidence. Exclusion of evidence of previous misconduct expresses in an emphatic fashion the law's particular concern about the moral legitimacy of the reasoning the State offers in its quest for a person's conviction. It displays a commitment, founded on respect for his moral autonomy, not to take his discreditable past against him unless it can lend coherence to a body of available evidence that shows his guilt in relation to the charge under trial. Similar fact evidence can serve this role only where there is sufficiently strong evidence, not only of the alleged disposition, but also of conditions that were present in the case which, given his disposition and in spite of such other counter-traits as might then be operating, would tend to motivate him to commit the alleged crime. How strong and detailed this body of evidence must be to satisfy the test of admissibility is a question of degree.[120] It would be naïve to expect a formulaic solution to this (or indeed any) moral problem. But this does not diminish the point that is being made: to take the accused's past *directly* against him, on the assumption of probability that he will repeat his error, is to insult his personal dignity. The exclusion of evidence in such a case is of significance even when the trial is by judge

[118] [1989] 1 WLR 236, 241.

[119] Contrast *Pfennig v R* (n 4) 528–529.

[120] *DPP v P* (n 2) 461; *R v H* [1995] 2 AC 596, 621; *Makin v Attorney-General for New South Wales* (n 4) 65.

alone.[121] It expresses the importance attached to finding the truth in a manner that, at the same time, does justice to the accused as a person.[122]

1.3.4 Ethics of belief

It is easy enough to comprehend the indignation the accused must feel and can rightly feel when the forbidden assumption is advanced publicly in support of or as a basis for believing him guilty on the charge at hand. In the absence of the similar facts rule, one can imagine use of the assumption by counsels during examination of witnesses or in submissions before the court, or by judges when delivering jury instructions or in their grounds of judgment. The injustice of these acts lies in a public characterization of the accused that denigrates an essential aspect of his dignity as a free individual. So far as the law allows or endorses use of this characterization against him, it is duplicitous in the injustice.

The law upholds justice by enjoining this offensive characterization. What is enjoined is not merely the public assertion of the objectionable belief about the accused ('once a thief, always a thief') or external manifestation of reliance on the reasoning that 'he must have done it again'. More than that, the law bars the forbidden assumption from entering the deliberative process. It does not follow from the fact that the various forms of external action described in the previous paragraph are subject to moral criticisms that trial deliberation is likewise open to moral evaluation. Is it immoral in itself to think an insult? Is it unethical just to judge a person unfairly in one's mind? After all, the jury does not disclose how they have reasoned. In a general verdict, they simply declare that the defendant is guilty or not. At a bench trial, the judge may hide the real reason for her decision to convict the accused. But the fact-finder (whether judge or jury) has committed a moral wrong against the accused just in leaping to the conclusion that he is guilty on the back of the forbidden assumption and by not bothering to engage in a situation-sensitive and fine-grained analysis of the probative value of his previous misconduct. She has done wrong even if she tells no one the truth about how she arrived at her verdict. How can this be?

[121] The value of the rule even in a trial without a jury is acknowledged by Mr Justice Schofield, 'Should Juries Know of a Defendant's Convictions?' (1992) 142 NLJ 1499.

[122] M C Slough and J William Knightly claim that the rule is 'born of fairness and sobriety' and 'based upon the precepts of a civilized society': 'Other Vices, Other Crimes' (1956) 41 Iowa L Rev 325, 349, 350. It has come to be widely accepted that the law ought equally to care about protecting the dignity of the sexual victim. This has led to restrictions on admissibility of evidence of her sexual history in many jurisdictions. For instance, such evidence is admissible under s 276 (2) of the Canadian Criminal Code only if, inter alia, it has 'significant probative value that is not outweighed by the danger of prejudice to the proper administration of justice'. (The constitutionality of this provision was upheld by the Supreme Court in *R v Darrach* (2000) 191 DLR (4th) 539.) This test is virtually identical to the modern common law test for the admissibility of similar fact evidence. In the United States, an argument for symmetry in the treatment of 'other crimes, wrongs, or acts' of the accused and the victim's sexual past was advanced by Harriett R Galvin in her influential article, 'Shielding Rape Victims in the State and Federal Courts: A Proposal for the Second Decade' (1986) 70 Minnesota L Rev 763.

What follows is no more than suggestive of possible answers. The wrong may be explicated at different levels. At one level, the object of moral evaluation is the public declaration of guilt. Since this is plainly an action, it is clearly subject to the constraints of morality. On a virtue theory of justice, the declaration of guilt is immoral insofar as it issues from a morally corrupt motivational source, in this case, from a disrespectful attitude towards the personal status of the accused and a careless disregard for his welfare (through a careless disregard of the relevant truths).[123] At a deeper level, the object of moral evaluation is the holding of a belief. Three possible lines of thought may be developed in this connection. First, one might argue that it is morally wrong to hold the belief about the accused that fuels the forbidden reasoning. It is morally wrong because the belief is prejudicial and enhances the risk that the fact-finder will commit the injustice of convicting the accused even though the evidence does not justify a guilty verdict. On this view, it is instrumentally bad to hold the belief. Secondly, one could go further and claim that it is intrinsically bad for the fact-finder to hold the prejudicial belief about the accused; in and of itself, it constitutes a form of morally defective or insufficient regard of the accused as a person. As Blum says:[124]

> Beliefs are typically part of our forms of regard for other persons. I may disrespect or do someone an injustice by thinking ill of her... Respect for other persons, an appreciation of others' humanity and their full individuality is inconsistent with certain beliefs about them. So false beliefs can be bad even if they do not contribute to harm to their targets.

Thirdly, one could view the forbidden reasoning as an immoral route to belief in the defendant's guilt. Take two different fact-finders, X and Y. X learns about the accused's criminal past and comes to loathe him for the person that his history shows him to be. She concludes that the accused is guilty as charged on the assumption that 'he is the sort of person who would do this sort of thing'. In contrast, Y looks carefully at the evidence, with open mind and dispassionately. She returns a guilty verdict only because she 'could draw no other reasonable conclusion'.[125] Both come to believe that the accused is guilty. Yet, there is a clear moral distinction in their *holding* of that belief. X's *believing* that the defendant is guilty is morally wrong, even if the *belief* that the accused is guilty is true. A belief that is driven by ill will and pre-judgment is, just for that reason, wrongly held. As Cox and Levine put it, an 'immoral process of belief acquisition leads to

[123] This ethical view falls into the class of what Garcia calls the '"infection" (or "input-centered" or backward-looking) models of wrongdoing, in contrast to the more familiar consequentialist and other result-driven approaches'. According to such models 'an action is wrong because of the moral disvalue of what goes into it rather than the nonmoral value of what comes out of it': J L A Garcia, 'The Heart of Racism' (1996) 27 *J of Social Philosophy* 5, 11.

[124] Lawrence Blum, 'Stereotypes and Stereotyping: A Moral Analysis' (2004) 33 *Philosophical Papers* 251, 262–263.

[125] This quote and the example are taken from Damian Cox and Michael Levine, 'Believing Badly' (2004) 33 *Philosophical Papers* 209, 225.

an immoral instance of believing quite directly'.[126] In the example, the reasoning was animated by ill will. But, following the second view, the disregard that is contained in the forbidden assumption is offensive even if it was not so animated.[127] The accused's sense of indignation does not dissipate upon learning that the fact-finder's belief that the accused 'is just a paederast' or some other bad stereotype was held out of laziness or disconcern or even simple ignorance.

It is critical to each of the three views that the fact-finder is, at least to some extent, in command of the beliefs that she holds. If beliefs are involuntary, it is difficult to criticize one for holding the beliefs that one does. This could be countered in a number of ways. First, the contention that beliefs are involuntary was addressed in Chapter 3, Part 1.4. This contention, as we saw, is compatible with the capacity to make up one's mind what to believe. It is also consistent with the possibility highlighted in Chapter 1, Part 3.4.4, of meta-level critical reflection on one's own thoughts. This is buttressed by studies which have shown that 'persons are capable of recognizing the operation of stereotypical associations in their own minds, and of deciding whether to personally endorse them—that is, whether to incorporate them as personal beliefs'.[128]

To those two observations, a third may be added. Some beliefs have a motivational source, and we are in charge of our state of motivation, at least to a degree. Consider again the previous example. The fact-finder believed that the accused is 'that sort of person' and, on the assumption that 'he has done it again', concluded that he is guilty. When we say that the belief was held (and the assumption applied) out of ill will or a morally defective regard for the accused, we do not mean that the ill will or disregard accompanied the belief. Neither is it accurate to say that the belief was held *with* ill will or disregard, as if the belief was in some sense being exploited in the service of ill will or disregard. Rather, the accusation is that the belief was held *from* ill will or disregard. It was the ill will or disregard which produced the belief (which in turn led to the conclusion). We are morally responsible for holding certain beliefs in virtue of their volitional roots.

1.3.5 Inquisitorial systems and international criminal trials

If the similar facts rule is founded on as basic a feature of criminal justice as we have portrayed, why is it found only in common law systems? While the exclusionary rule does not exist as such in civilian jurisdictions, it is not true that their judges are oblivious to the sentiment of justice expressed in the rule. In Continental legal systems, discussion in this area tends to concentrate on previous convictions; 'misconduct which has not resulted in a criminal conviction

126 ibid 226.

127 This is one of many important points made by Ward E Jones, 'Indignation, Immodesty, and Immoral Believing', draft paper. I am grateful to the author for allowing me to have a copy.

128 Blum (n 124) 269, citing the writings of Patricia G Devine; for an example of the latter, see her article 'Stereotypes and Prejudice: Their Automatic and Controlled Components' (1989) 56 *J of Personality and Social Psychology* 5.

seldom receives any separate scrutiny'.[129] There is no exclusionary rule for character or propensity evidence. Damaška offers a number of structural reasons for this. For one, guilt and sentencing are decided at the same stage and '[b]efore the court retires to deliberate and decide a case, all evidence relevant for sentencing purposes must be presented'.[130] Further, Continental trials are typically unitary in character. The judge decides both questions of fact and questions of law, including admissibility. In these circumstances, it is artificial to apply an exclusionary rule. The safeguard against the risk 'of uncritical acceptance of propensity evidence' assumes instead the form of an 'obligation of trial judges to write a reasoned opinion demonstrating that their factual findings have a firm basis in evidence and a solid support in rational inference'.[131]

Although the exclusionary rule is absent, concerns about the legitimacy of relying on previous offences are very much alive in inquisitorial systems. According to Damaška: 'It is generally acknowledged on the Continent to be improper to assume that just because a person has a criminal record that person is more likely to have committed the crime.'[132] In countries such as Germany and Italy, the view is expressed that 'prior convictions have no bearing whatsoever on the finding of criminal liability'.[133] Damaška cites German cases which have held that 'collateral misconduct can only serve to corroborate evidence linking an individual directly to the crime charged'[134] and that '[i]n the absence of... background information,... the prior prosecutions [of the accused can only generate] a "mere suspicion" incapable of providing adequate support for a...conviction'.[135] Spencer reports the same from his conversations with German, Belgian, French, Italian, and Dutch lawyers: 'continental lawyers seem to assume that, in so far as they have to explain what evidence convinced them, it would be improper to give this fact [that the accused has a criminal record] as one of the matters that decided them to convict, but it would be otherwise if the previous offences were very similar to the one for which he is currently on trial'.[136] There appears no substantial disagreement between common law and civilian law on the injustice of assuming guilt simply from the accused's previous bad record; the moral sensibility of the two traditions is not as different as one might think.

Further support for the universality of the standard of justice expressed by the similar facts rule comes from international legal fora. The structure of international criminal trials contains a 'unique amalgam of civil and common law

[129] Mirjan Damaška, 'Propensity Evidence in Continental Legal Systems' (1994) Chicago-Kent L Rev 55, 57–58.

[130] ibid 56.

[131] ibid 66.

[132] ibid 58.

[133] ibid 58. Damaška, however, is doubtful that such statements can be taken literally.

[134] ibid 62.

[135] ibid 63.

[136] J R Spencer, 'Evidence' in Mireille Delmas-Marty and J R Spencer (eds), *European Criminal Procedures* (Cambridge: CUP, 2002) ch 11 at 616.

features'.[137] Strict exclusionary rules of evidence are avoided. In that sense, there is affinity to the civilian tradition of 'a free system of evidence, both with regard to admissibility and evaluation'.[138] The Rules of Procedure and Evidence of the International Criminal Tribunal for Rwanda ('ICTR') are similar to the corresponding rules for the sister tribunal for the Former Yugoslavia ('ICTY'); and there are broad resemblances between these rules and those governing the International Criminal Court. Since we will be citing cases decided by the ICTR, we will focus on its statute and rules. It is provided in Rule 89(c) of the Rules of Procedure and Evidence of the ICTR that the tribunal 'may admit any relevant evidence which it deems to have probative value'. This provision appears to embrace the Continental principle of free admissibility. However, the permissive term 'may' is used instead of a mandatory term such as 'must' or 'shall'. The ICTR has read Rule 89(c) to confer on itself the discretion not to admit evidence even where it is relevant and probative. The evidence must be excluded if its admission undermines the fairness of the trial, as article 19 of ICTR statute states that the tribunal 'shall ensure that a trial is fair'. In *Prosecutor v Bagosora*,[139] the Trial Chamber I of the ICTR noted that both ICTR and ICTY have adopted the 'long-standing principle of common law' that 'evidence as to the character of an accused is generally inadmissible to show the accused's propensity to act in conformity therewith'. The Trial Chamber was greatly influenced by an opinion delivered in the earlier case of *Prosecutor v Nahimana*, where Judge Shahabuddeen endorsed this common law principle as one that was equally applicable to proceedings before the ICTR:[140]

> [I]f the evidence of the other offence or offences goes beyond showing a mere disposition to commit crime or a particular kind of crime and points in some other way to the commission of the offence in question, then it will be admissible if its probative value for that purpose outweighs or transcends its merely prejudicial effect.

While Rule 83(c) points the ICTR to the Continental approach of 'free proof', in practice, the tribunal has chosen to adhere to the spirit of the common law similar facts rule. This is remarkable because the similar facts rule is not explicitly

[137] *Prosecutor v Tadić*, Decision of the Trial Chamber on the Defence Motion on Hearsay, Case No IT-94-I-T, (1996) 1 Judicial Rep of the Intl Crim Tribunal for the Former Yugoslavia 106, para 14.

[138] Almiro Rodrigues and Cécile Tournaye, 'Hearsay Evidence' in Richard May *et al* (eds), *Essays on ICTY Procedure and Evidence in Honour of Gabrielle Kirk McDonald* (The Hague: Kluwer, 2001) ch 23, 296.

[139] *Prosecutor v Bagosora et al*, Decision on Admissibility of Proposed Testimony of Witness DBY, Case No ICTR-98-41-T, 18 September 2003, para 17. This decision was upheld on appeal: *Prosecutor v Bagosora et al*, Decision on Prosecutor's Interlocutory Appeals Regarding Exclusion of Evidence, Case Nos ICTR-98-41-AR93 & ICTR-98-41-AR93.2, 19 December 2003 (decision of Appeals Chamber), paras 12–14.

[140] Separate opinion of Judge Shahabuddeen delivered on 5 September 2000 in the appeal from *Prosecutor v Nahimana*, ICR-96-11-T, para 20, quoting from *Thompson v R* (1989) 169 CLR 1, 16 (Australian High Court).

stated in the Rules of Procedure and Evidence of the ICTR. The ICTR does not have to follow the common law: Rule 89(A) states clearly that the Tribunal 'shall not be bound by national rules of evidence'. The tribunal felt compelled to follow the common law principle on similar fact evidence because it sees it as critical to the fairness of a trial, which the tribunal has a duty to uphold under article 19 of its statute.[141] This should give pause to those who are quick to dismiss the similar facts rule as an unnecessary technicality.

1.3.6 Limitations of scope of theory

The theory proposed in this chapter is modest in two senses. First, it has no imperialistic ambition. The claim is merely that the suggested way of looking at the rule, through the eyes of the fact-finder as a moral agent, reveals an important facet of its intrinsic value. It is no part of the claim that this is the *only* way of analysing the rule or that the rule has *only* the function and value that are revealed by this mode of analysis. The external analyst might be right that there are wider systemic benefits to be had from having a rule that excludes evidence of the accused's unsavoury past; it may force 'the police to conduct more thorough investigations'[142] or give a person with a bad criminal record an incentive to exercise restraint.[143] Even if all that is true, these benefits are not all that can be said for the rule.

[141] As against this, it might be noted that r 93 of the Rules of Procedure and Evidence of both the ICTR and ICTY explicitly provides that 'evidence of a consistent pattern of conduct relevant to serious violations of international humanitarian law... may be admissible in the interests of justice'. However, in *Prosecutor v Bagosora et al*, Decision on Prosecutor's Interlocutory Appeals Regarding Exclusion of Evidence (n 139) para 13, the Appeals Chamber held that 'pattern evidence' falling under Rule 93 might still be excluded 'in the interests of justice when its admission could lead to unfairness in the trial proceedings, such as when the probative value of the proposed evidence is outweighed by its prejudicial effect, pursuant to the Chamber's duty to ensure a fair and expeditious trial as required by Article 19(1) of the Statute'. The need for this special provision is explained in the First Annual Report to the UN Security Council and General Assembly by the ICTY, 29 August 1994, para 76, available at: <http://www.un.org/icty/rappannu-e/1994/AR94e.pdf>. Rule 93 is a necessitated by the special nature of the crimes tried before the ICTR and ICTY. Such crimes 'do not concern isolated offences: the scale of events, in space and in time, is unknown to normal municipal adjudication': Opinion of Judge Shahabuddeen delivered in *Prosecutor v Nahimana* (n 140) para 24. Trials of crimes against humanity involve more than investigation into the conduct of specific individuals; it requires the attempt to connect specific incidents and events with a view to identifying an underlying policy to intentionally engage in a systematic practice. The rationale behind Rule 93 carries no significance for the ordinary criminal trial.

[142] Richard O Lempert, Samuel R Gross and James S Liebman, *A Modern Approach to Evidence: Text, Problems, Transcripts and Cases* (3rd edn, St Paul, Minnesota: West Publishing, 2000) 329, quoted in Sanchirico (n 54) 1250, note 58.

[143] See Joel Schrag and Suzanne Scotchmer, 'Crime and Prejudice: The Use of Character Evidence in Criminal Trials' (1994) 10 J of L, Economics, and Organization 319. The authors examine the effect of restricting character evidence on the *ex ante* deterrence of the criminal law. They claim that 'allowing character evidence to be considered can make the jury too punitive toward habitual criminals, and that withholding character evidence can improve deterrence by making the jury more lenient' (ibid 323); 'a prejudiced jury can be "too punitive" in the sense of being willing to convict a habitual criminal irrespective of the evidence linking that person to the crime. If that is what the habitual criminal expects, he or she has little incentive to avoid

Secondly, as the title of this chapter indicates, what it offers is only an account of the similar facts rule; it does not offer a theory of the law on character evidence of which the similar facts rule forms merely a part. It is highly doubtful that a unified theory of the larger area of law can be constructed. For instance, the accused is permitted at common law to adduce evidence of his good character. This has been criticized on the ground that 'it is illogical for the law to allow a defendant to put in his good character to indicate lack of propensity but to deny the prosecution the opportunity to establish the converse when he has a bad one'.[144] If, as is suggested, the similar facts rule emanates from respect for the accused and is meant to protect his personal dignity, the reason for exclusion delineated in this explanation is absent when the accused seeks to adduce evidence of his good character.[145] But this is not in itself a reason for admitting such evidence. That reason must be sought outside of the present theory; for instance, one might argue, as Zuckerman has done, that evidence of the accused's good character is admitted 'as a gesture of humanity'.[146] Or consider the statutory rules which allow evidence of the accused's bad character to be admitted should he attack the character of another person or portray himself as a person of good character.[147] These rules cannot be justified by logical extension of the proposed account of the law on similar facts; if they can be defended at all, they have to be defended on distinct and independent grounds such as the so-called tit-for-tat argument[148] and the 'justice of enabling the defendant's bad character to be displayed in order to correct a false impression'.[149]

1.4 Conclusion

Discourse on the law of evidence is usually conducted from an external perspective. The arguments are cast in consequentialist form. An instrumental interpretation is taken of the role of evidential rules. Those who take this approach tend to

crime' (ibid 341). A similar contention is advanced by Sanchirico (n 54); for critical discussion of his thesis: Roger C Park and Michael J Saks, 'Evidence Scholarship Reconsidered: Results of the Interdisciplinary Turn' (2006) 47 Boston College L Rev 949, 1014–1017.

[144] Auld (n 48) 566. Similarly, Jenny McEwan, 'Previous Misconduct at the Crossroads: Which "Way Ahead"?' [2002] Crim LR 180, 187.

[145] It is also absent when the defence seeks to proffer character evidence of a third party to show that he, and not the accused, is guilty of the crime: *R v Arcangioli* [1994] 1 SCR 129, 139–142; Andrew Ligertwood, *Australian Evidence* (3rd edn, Sydney: Butterworths, 1998) 163–164; John H Blume, Sheri L Johnson and Emily C Paavola, 'Every Juror Wants a Story: Narrative Relevance, Third Party Guilt and the Right to Present a Defense' (2007) 44 American Crim L Rev 1069 at 1107–1108.

[146] Zuckerman (n 53) 234. Cf Roberts and Zuckerman (n 10) 551–554.

[147] Criminal Justice Act 2003, s 101 (1)(f), (g).

[148] Roberts and Zuckerman (n 10) 559 (the authors find this rationale 'less respectable' than the argument which advances 'considerations of evidential completeness and transparency of proof').

[149] J R Spencer, *Evidence of Bad Character* (Oxford: Hart, 2006) at 82.

concentrate on the logical aspect of the trial, seeing it as a system engineered to get to the truth of a factual dispute, and their recommendations on the methodology of fact-finding are informed and moved chiefly by the desire to increase the chances of a correct verdict in the instant case or to maximize the ratio of correct verdicts in the long run. The external observer is chiefly interested in seeking out causal connections between the structures of fact-finding and reliability of the outcome.

We must take an internal perspective if we are to appreciate the moral significance of many aspects of evidence law. From this angle, the relevant issues appear in the deliberative context: given what fact-finding is about and entails, how ought the person with the responsibility of the task consider the evidence in her deliberation? Just as fact-finding is not a pure cognitive enterprise, the principles on which such questions must be answered are not wholly of a logical nature. Moral considerations are crucially and inextricably at play.

These general themes were illustrated by our examination of the similar facts rule in criminal cases. The rule regulates trial deliberations in two ways. First, it does not allow the court to reason that it is likely that the accused is guilty because his past shows that he is the sort of person who, in appropriate circumstances, cannot help committing the kind of crime in question. There is a lack of integrity in using this reasoning covertly to secure a guilty verdict; if it is true that the accused 'could not help doing what he did', he is not morally responsible for his action and, in general, ought not to be convicted of the crime. Most fact-finders would recognize and accept this normative objection and, for that reason, the risk of its violation is low. Secondly, the court must not hold the accused's discreditable past directly against him for to do so is to be dismissive of his moral autonomy. His bad history can be used against him only indirectly, as evidence of his motivational disposition, to support an explanation of his action that is suggested by other available evidence. It can be so used only when there is sufficiently strong evidence that the circumstances of the case were such as would engage his alleged trait and generate in him reasons or desires to commit the crime in question; further, there must be ground for believing that those reasons and desires were strong enough to overcome whatever counter-dispositions his environment might have triggered in him. The similar facts rule is founded ultimately on the demand that the court do justice to the accused in the pursuit of truth. It imposes ethical constraints on the kind of reasoning that may be used to support a guilty verdict. While it is special to the common law that those ethical constraints are enforced in the form of an exclusionary rule, the constraints are also recognized in Continental and international systems of trial; indeed, they must be recognized in any just system of criminal proof.

2 Civil Cases[150]

2.1 Introduction

Until recently, the leading English authorities on similar fact evidence in civil proceedings consisted of a 'trilogy of modern reported cases'.[151] To that trilogy must now be added *O'Brien v Chief Constable of South Wales Police* ('*O'Brien*'). In *O'Brien*, the Court of Appeal reviewed and restated the law in this area.[152] It sets out a new approach that was later upheld by the House of Lords.[153] There are difficulties with the new approach. They stem ultimately from the failure to grasp fully the moral foundation of the similar facts doctrine. Much about the doctrine, particularly the differences in its civil and criminal operations, can be adequately explained and justified only from the ethical perspective. To assess the impact of *O'Brien*, it is necessary to begin by examining the law as was to be found in the trilogy of modern authorities.

2.2 The law as it was: the trilogy of leading cases

The first case is *Mood Music Publishing Co v De Wolfe Ltd* ('*Mood Music*').[154] It is well known for this classic passage from the judgment of Lord Denning:[155]

> The criminal courts have been very careful not to admit [similar fact] evidence unless its probative value is so strong that it should be received in the interests of justice: and its admission will not operate unfairly to the accused. In civil cases the courts have followed a similar line but have not been so chary of admitting it. In civil cases the courts will admit evidence of similar facts if it is logically probative, that is, if it is logically relevant in determining the matter which is in issue: provided that it is not oppressive or unfair to the other side: and also that the other side has fair notice of it and is able to deal with it.

The suggestion that civil courts have 'followed a similar line' to the admission of similar fact evidence in criminal cases implies that the test of admissibility is broadly the same in civil and criminal trials. Hence, when Lord Denning further remarked that civil judges are less chary than criminal judges of admitting such evidence, he probably did not mean that different tests apply in the two contexts; more likely, he meant that the same test applies but the test, in its application,

150 This part is based on my article, 'Similar Facts in Civil Cases' (2006) 26 OJLS 131.

151 *O'Brien v Chief Constable of South Wales Police* [2003] EWCA Civ 1085 at [57]; The Times, 22 August 2003; [2003] All ER (D) 381 (July) (Court of Appeal).

152 ibid.

153 *O'Brien v Chief Constable of South Wales Police* [2005] UKHL 26; [2005] 2 AC 534 (House of Lords).

154 [1976] 1 Ch 119.

155 ibid at 127.

will naturally lead to exclusion of evidence more frequently in criminal than in civil cases.[156] The reason for this disparity is hinted in the passage itself. As his Lordship saw it, the similar facts rule is grounded on principles of 'justice' and 'fairness', and what 'justice' and 'fairness' demand in a criminal prosecution are different from what they require in a civil trial. This is an important point to which we must return.

Lord Denning cited *DPP v Boardman*[157] as authority for the proposition that similar fact evidence is inadmissible in criminal cases unless 'its probative value is so strong that it should be received in the interests of justice'. Soon after *Boardman* was decided, it was widely hailed as a legal landmark. For one commentator, the House of Lords achieved an 'intellectual breakthrough'.[158] It finally debunked the 'categories approach' associated with the earlier case of *Makin v Attorney-General for New South Wales*.[159] Under that approach, similar fact evidence is admissible only if it falls under a recognized category of relevance, for example, where it goes to the issue of whether the alleged act was 'designed or accidental' or is relied upon 'to rebut a defence which would otherwise be open to the accused'.[160] In *Boardman*, the law took a 'principled' turn. But there were differences in the judgments of the law lords. It needs a considerable degree of abstraction to draw from the various judgments the elegant principle Lord Denning attributed to the case as a whole.[161]

It was only in *DPP v P*[162] that the House of Lords endorsed a test that was explicitly formulated as the general principle of justice already examined in Part 1. To repeat it: the prosecution may adduce similar fact evidence in support of its case only if 'its probative force in support of the allegation that an accused person committed a crime is sufficiently great to make it just to admit the evidence, notwithstanding that it is prejudicial to the accused in tending to show that he was guilty of another crime'.[163] The House of Lords also held, contrary to suggestions made in earlier cases, that this probative force need not be derived from 'striking similarities' in the various incidents in which the accused is alleged to have been involved.[164]

[156] Von Doussa J expressed such a view in *Sheldon v Sun Alliance Limited* (1988) 50 ALR 236, 246: 'This is not to say that the test to be applied is different. It is a case of the same test producing different results in its application in different trial settings.'

[157] [1975] AC 421.

[158] L H Hoffmann, 'Similar Facts After Boardman' (1975) 91 LQR 193, 193. See also Rupert Cross, 'Fourth Time Lucky—Similar Fact Evidence in the House of Lords' [1975] Crim LR 62. Some, however, were critical of the case: eg Adrian A S Zuckerman, 'Similar Fact Evidence—The Unobservable Rule' (1987) 103 LQR 187.

[159] [1894] AC 57.

[160] ibid 65.

[161] The judgments of Lord Cross, (n 157) 456, and Lord Wilberforce, (n 157) 442, came closest to supporting the principle. That the test for admissibility was differently stated by the law lords in *Boardman* is noted by Lord Phillips in *O'Brien v Chief Constable of South Wales* (n 153) para 28.

[162] [1991] 2 AC 447.

[163] ibid at 460.

[164] ibid at 462.

The criminal law principle as stated in *P* is different from the civil version offered by Lord Denning. At a criminal trial, probative force of the evidence must be weighed against its potential prejudicial effect whereas, in the civil context, the countervailing consideration is described as 'fairness' and not 'prejudice'. As will be argued, 'fairness' bears on the similar facts rule as an ethical demand for equal treatment of litigants. This carries implications deeper than the practical requirements emphasized by Lord Denning of giving 'fair notice' and avoiding 'oppression' in litigation.

Berger v Raymond Sun Ltd ('*Berger*')[165] is the second of the trilogy. There, Warner J held, without the nuance in Lord Denning's carefully qualified affirmation, that 'the test of admissibility of evidence of similar facts... is the same in civil and in criminal cases'.[166] Although Warner J purported to follow *Mood Music*, he departed from it in at least two ways. First, surprisingly, Warner J cited and applied *Makin* without mentioning *Boardman*; the 'categories approach' was adopted without reference to the fact that, in criminal law, it had been replaced by the 'principled approach'.[167] Secondly, the judge held that the court has an overriding discretion to exclude (otherwise) admissible similar fact evidence. In the exercise of this discretion, the court is to consider the factors mentioned by Lord Denning, such as the oppressiveness of admitting the evidence and the ability of the party against whom the evidence is tendered to deal adequately with it. The better view is that, *pace* Warner J, Lord Denning intended that these considerations *must* be taken into account in deciding admissibility of similar fact evidence *as a matter of legal rule*; otherwise put, they operate *in* the test of admissibility, and not at the stage of exercising discretion *after* the evidence is found to be admissible.[168] The judicial discretion to which Warner J referred is described by one commentator as having 'dubious pedigree'.[169]

In the third case of the trilogy, *Thorpe v Chief Constable of Greater Manchester Police* ('*Thorpe*'),[170] it is again affirmed that the 'test of the admissibility of evidence of similar facts is in general the same in civil and in criminal cases'.[171] Two further points are noteworthy about this decision of the Court of the Appeal. First, according to Dillon LJ, when Lord Denning observed in *Mood Music* that courts are less hesitant in admitting similar fact evidence in civil than in criminal cases, he must have had in mind civil cases tried by judge alone. The jury, unlike

165 [1984] 1 WLR 625.

166 ibid at 630.

167 This was at least true in theory. However, there are some indications that, in reality, the 'categories approach' continued to hold sway in criminal trials long after *Boardman*: see Roderick Munday, 'Law Reports, Transcripts, and the Fabric of the Criminal Law—A Speculation' (2004) 68 J of the Criminal Law 227.

168 eg Colin Tapper (ed), *Cross and Tapper on Evidence* (9th edn, London: Butterworths, 1999) 381; cf (11th edn, 2007) 355–356.

169 Rosemary Pattenden, 'The Discretionary Exclusion of Relevant Evidence in English Civil Proceedings' (1997) 1 Intl J of Evidence and Proof 361, 367.

170 [1989] 2 All ER 627.

171 ibid 830.

the judge, cannot be fully trusted to evaluate similar fact evidence correctly.[172] Presumably, at a civil trial where a jury is empanelled, as great a caution must be exercised in admitting similar fact evidence as it is done at a criminal trial.

Secondly, *Makin* received apparent endorsement by Neill LJ although the case itself was not cited. Ironically, this endorsement came immediately after his quotation of the passage in *Mood Music* where Lord Denning, citing *Boardman*, drew attention to the recent adoption of a 'principled approach' in the criminal law. Neill LJ held, without mentioning *Makin*, that '[e]vidence of "similar facts" is relevant both in criminal and civil cases to rebut defences such as accident or coincidence or sometimes to prove a system of conduct. Such evidence is not admissible, however, merely to show that the party concerned has a disposition to commit the conduct alleged.'[173] This suggests that it is the purpose for which the evidence is adduced that is decisive. In contrast, on the 'principled approach' supported by *Boardman* and *P*, admissibility must be decided by weighing the probative value of the evidence against its prejudicial effect and not by ascertaining the category of relevance into which the evidence falls.

In what state did this modern trilogy of leading cases leave the law? First, a distinct ambivalence is discernible; there is both a desire and a reluctance to extend the similar facts rule as it applies in criminal proceedings to civil trials. As we have seen, in *Mood Music*, Lord Denning claimed that civil and criminal courts 'have followed a similar line' only to add immediately that, actually, they have not, inasmuch as the former are less chary than the latter of admitting similar fact evidence; and, in *Berger*, Warner J adopted the criminal formulation of the rule only to subject it to a discretion to exclude the evidence in spite of its admissibility under the criminal test.[174] Both views have the same overall effect of making the scope of exclusion wider in criminal than in civil cases. This is as it should be, so Dillon LJ explained in *Thorpe*, because criminal cases are usually tried by jury whereas civil cases are not, and jurors are less able than judges at proper evaluation of similar fact evidence. Secondly, if and to the extent that a civil judge must follow the criminal courts in applying the similar facts rule, she should at least be mindful of the latest common law development on the criminal side. It is hard to justify the influence that *Makin* has had in the civil context, and unfortunate that the 'categories approach' was applied or endorsed in *Berger* and *Thorpe* without indication of awareness that it was no longer the law in criminal cases.

O'Brien does not put the law in a much better state. On the first point, the case manifests the same ambivalence that was evident in the earlier decisions, and there is still no convincing account for that ambivalence. On the second point, while *O'Brien* has drawn the civil law closer to the criminal by clearly rejecting

[172] ibid 830–831.

[173] ibid 834.

[174] Although the test of admissibility of evidence of similar facts is the same in civil and criminal cases, 'the criteria according to which the court should exercise its discretion to exclude such evidence' are different: (n 165) 630.

the 'categories approach',[175] it has created an asymmetry between them by introducing a two-stage analysis special to civil cases. It is hard to claim, for the reasons that appear below, that the law has been made clearer or placed in a better light.

2.3 O'Brien: facts and decision

The claimant was convicted with two others of murder and was given a life sentence. After having served more than eleven years of imprisonment, an appeal against his conviction was brought on a reference by the Criminal Cases Review Commission under section 9 of the Criminal Appeal Act 1995. The appeal was allowed and his conviction was quashed. Following this, the claimant sued the Chief Constable of the South Wales Police for malicious prosecution and misfeasance in public office. He alleged acts of police malpractice against the two detectives who had charge of investigating his case. The allegations were made principally against the detective who ran the 'day to day' investigation (Detective Inspector Lewis). His action, it was claimed, was expressly or tacitly approved by the other detective, the senior colleague (Detective Chief Superintendent Carlsey). In support of these allegations, the claimant sought permission, at a case management conference, to adduce evidence at the trial of similar acts of police malpractice committed in two other cases by the same detectives. Jones J granted the claimant permission to do so.

The judge reached his decision in two steps. First, he held that the evidence was admissible in law as there were sufficient similarities in the incidents. For example, in each of them, the interrogating officer alleged that the suspect had made an admission to him when no one else was present but failed to produce genuine contemporaneous record of the admission. Also, in each case, it was claimed that the investigating officer applied improper pressure on the suspect to make untrue statements by engaging in similar tactics. These tactics included acts of bullying and prolonged interrogation, and the denial of proper access to a solicitor. Secondly, Jones J held that the circumstances did not justify the exercise of discretion to exclude the admissible evidence. Lengthening of the trial as a result of introducing the evidence would not be excessive; the issues raised were clear and unlikely to distract the jury; and the 'importance and seriousness of [the] case to [the claimant] and... wider public interest strongly favoured admission'.[176]

The appeal against this decision was dismissed by the Court of Appeal. Brooke LJ gave the judgment of the court. He endorsed the approach taken by Jones J of separating the issues of admissibility and discretion. At the first stage, the judge must consider the admissibility of the evidence. If she comes to the conclusion that the evidence is admissible, she must move on to the second stage. At the

[175] See in the Court of Appeal (n 151) para 59, and in the House of Lords (n 153) para 48, per Lord Phillips.

[176] (n 151) para 29.

second stage, the judge decides whether to exercise her discretion to exclude the evidence despite it being admissible. On further appeal, this two-staged approach was endorsed fully by the House of Lords.

2.4 Stage 1: admissibility

The Court of Appeal formulated the test applicable at the first stage as follows:[177]

> To be admissible, [the evidence] must be logically probative of an issue in the case, and the first part of the House of Lords' test in *P* must be applied to exclude the evidence which is not sufficiently similar to the evidence in the case before the court.

One difficulty with this passage is the suggestion that admissibility depends on 'sufficient similarity' between the facts which are sought to be proved by the evidence and the facts alleged in the case at hand. If the Court of Appeal intended 'sufficient similarity' as a condition of admissibility, and did not see it merely as one of various ways in which probative force may be derived, it would have committed the error criticized by Lord Mackay in *P* of restricting 'the operation of the principle in a way which gives too much effect to a particular manner of stating it, and is not justified in principle'.[178]

There is another difficulty with the passage. In determining admissibility, the judge is supposed to apply 'the first part of the House of Lords' test in *P*'. This is odd because that test did not, strictly speaking, contain parts. The 'test' laid down by Lord Mackay in *P* was, in truth, a single principle:[179] for the evidence to be admissible, its probative force in support of the prosecution's allegation must be sufficiently great to make it just to admit the evidence even though it is prejudicial to the accused. The reference by the Court of Appeal to the 'first part' of the test in *P* was, in all likelihood, to that aspect of the balancing exercise which involves the evaluation of probative strength. Further, in mentioning only the 'first part' of the test, the Court of Appeal was presumably of the view that the prejudicial effect of the evidence is not a factor that bears on its admissibility as a matter of law in civil proceedings. While the test in *P* calls for a balancing of probative value of the evidence against its prejudicial effect, the test in *O'Brien* does not call for any such comparison. All that matters is whether the evidence is 'logically probative of an issue in the case'.

In the House of Lords, it was argued that the Court of Appeal had used too lenient a test of admissibility as 'there is a rule of law which prevents the admission of similar fact evidence in a civil trial unless it has an enhanced probative value'.[180] This argument was unanimously rejected by the law lords. It was held

[177] ibid para 70.

[178] (n 162) 460. Ironically, this very statement was quoted by the Court of Appeal: (n 151) para 37.

[179] As recognized by Lord Carswell in *O'Brien* (n 153) paras 68 and 71.

[180] (n 153) para 15.

that legal admissibility of such evidence depends only on its relevance, understood in the ordinary sense as defined by Lord Simon in *R v Kilbourne*[181] of being 'logically probative or disprobative of some matter which requires proof'.[182]

2.4.1 *Relevance and probative force*

Sometimes, judges explain the exclusion of similar fact evidence on the ground that it is irrelevant. For example, in *Sattin v National Union Bank*,[183] Lawton LJ claimed that 'in general if there [is] an allegation that *A* did a particular act on a particular day the fact that he did the same act on another day [is] not relevant'. The underlying thinking appears to be that 'the past is not an invariable guide to the future'.[184] It is certainly true that the past does not provide 'invariable' guidance. However, insofar as human beings have character traits, consisting of relatively stable dispositions to behave in certain ways under certain conditions, a person's past may cast some light on her conduct at a particular time and place; hence, some guidance may be obtained if there is adequate knowledge of the relevant disposition and conditions, and of the circumstances of her alleged action on that occasion.

It grates on common sense to deny this. In *Thorpe*, Dillon LJ could not see how evidence that 'police officers used excessive violence in effecting an arrest of some other person in some other circumstance, can be probative that... they used excessive violence against the plaintiff on 1 March 1985'.[185] That a person has a disposition to act in a certain way implies neither total constancy nor perfect uniformity of that behaviour. It is difficult to imagine a violent person being violent in the same way to everyone all the time. Whether she will exhibit violence of a particular form will depend on the many factors discussed in Part 1.3.2 above. They include the situation she is in and whether that situation is of a kind prone to trigger off her disposition to behave in that way; further, the disposition must be strong enough to overcome such counter-tendencies as she may also be experiencing. Hence, it cannot be assumed just from a person having a violent disposition that she must have committed violence on a specific occasion. This is the essential point expressed in statements such as that evidence is insufficiently relevant or (perhaps, more accurately) insufficiently probative[186] if it goes '*merely* to show that the party concerned has a disposition to commit the conduct

[181] [1973] AC 729, 756.

[182] (n 153) paras 3–4, 15, 57, and 75.

[183] (1978) 122 SJ 367, 368. See also *R v Miller* [1952] 2 All ER 667, 668; *Inglis v The National Bank of Scotland, Limited* [1909] SC 1038, 1040. Cf *R v Randall* [2003] UKHL 69, paras 20–22; [2004] 1 WLR 56.

[184] John Peysner, 'Being Civil to Similar Fact Evidence' (1993) Civil Justice Quarterly 188, 189.

[185] (n 170) 831.

[186] Lord Hailsham probably overstated the point in *Boardman* (n 30) 451 when he said that the probative value of such evidence is nil. See Redmayne (n 47) 710–713.

alleged'.[187] Much more needs to be known to justify—and, often, more is known from the evidence adduced in the case as a whole which would justify—drawing an inference of some weight from a person's particular disposition to his action in conformity therewith.[188] If a police officer is known to have acted violently in his official role, towards persons over whom he was trying to exert authority, and in the face of pressure created by resistance to arrest, surely his past conduct has some rational bearing on his likely behaviour on an occasion that meets closely those detailed specifications. The fact that he has that disposition is relevant insofar as it makes him more likely than a person without that disposition to behave in that way on that occasion.[189] Evidence of his disposition will rarely be conclusive proof of his alleged conduct but, obviously, it need not be conclusive to be relevant.[190] It is therefore open to doubt that Dillon LJ was right to have found the evidence irrelevant.

That evidence of disposition can be relevant was explicitly accepted by Lord Carswell in *O'Brien*.[191] But there is a fundamental problem in resting admissibility of similar fact evidence on relevance alone. For evidence—not just of similar facts but *any* evidence—to be admissible, it must be probative of an issue in the case. It is a basic rule that relevance is the preliminary condition of admissibility. The test of admissibility at the first stage of the analysis is not only banal but would effectively mean that there is no similar facts rule in civil cases (understood as a rule distinct from that of relevance) unless the evidence is required to be, not just probative, but probative to a *sufficiently high degree*.[192] And since the

[187] *Thorpe* (n 170) 834 (emphasis added).

[188] This view accords with that discussed in Law Commission, *Evidence of Bad Character in Criminal Proceedings* (n 29) para 4.10: While propensity alone is not sufficiently probative, it can become so 'if combined with other features of the case'.

[189] Rachana Kamtekar, 'Situationism and Virtue Ethics on the Content of Our Character' (2004) 114 *Ethics* 458, 475–476.

[190] That similar fact evidence need not be conclusive to be admissible, see *R v Handy* (n 5) 415–416. An argument to the contrary was made before the House of Lords in *O'Brien*, but it was rightly rejected as being based on a misinterpretation of *Metropolitan Asylum District Managers v Hill* (1882) 47 LT 29: see (n 153) paras 46 and 71. Cf *Pfennig v R* (n 4) 485: propensity evidence 'ought not to be admitted if... there is a reasonable view of it which is consistent with innocence'. This test was further endorsed by the Australian High Court in *Phillips v The Queen* (2006) 224 ALR 216; the test and its application in *Phillips* is criticized by David Hamer, 'Similar Fact Reasoning in Phillips: Artificial, Disjointed and Pernicious', forthcoming in (2007) 30 University of New South Wales LJ.

[191] (n 153) para 73; similar statement was made by Lord Bingham, ibid para 4.

[192] The Supreme Court of South Australia held in *Sheldon v Sun Alliance Australia Ltd* (1989) 53 SASR 97, 148 that similar fact evidence is admissible at common law so long as it is 'logically probative'. However, the position is different under section 97(1) of the Australian Evidence Act 1995: it is not enough for the evidence to be relevant; it must have 'significant probative value': see *Jacara v Perpetual Trustees* (2000) 180 ALR 569, 586 (decision of the Federal Court of Australia). Contrast s 101(1)(d) of the UK Criminal Justice Act 2003, in which relevance is the test of admissibility. The Law Commission had proposed a higher standard, that evidence of bad character must not only be relevant but must have 'substantial' probative value to be admissible: see clause 8(2) of the draft Criminal Evidence Bill in *Evidence of Bad Character in Criminal Proceedings* (n 29).

requirement for enhanced probative value was explicitly rejected by the House of Lords, we seem forced to the conclusion that the rule is gone.

However, a vestige of it remains. It seems that the court *may* exclude similar fact evidence for lack of sufficient probative strength at the second stage of analysis. Indications of this can be found at both levels of appeal: in the Court of Appeal, it was held that the discretion to exclude admissible similar fact evidence should be guided by the principle that '... the stronger the probative force..., the more willing the court should be not to exclude it';[193] and in the House of Lords, Lord Carswell suggested that, at the second stage of the analysis, 'it may be necessary to look for enhanced relevance or substantial probative value, for that may be necessary to offset the degree of prejudice caused',[194] and Lord Phillips similarly held that where the prejudicial effect of similar fact evidence is 'disproportionate to its relevance', the judge, in the exercise of her discretion, 'will be astute to see that the probative cogency of the evidence justifies this risk of prejudice in the interests of a fair trial'.[195] Here then is another display of the ambivalence noted earlier, the tension between convergent and divergent inclinations; the criminal rule of exclusion is rejected only to be brought back in the weakened form of a discretionary power of exclusion. This has the effect of making similar fact evidence easier to admit in civil than in criminal litigation. Why should we want this disparity?

2.4.2 Psychological prejudice

After *O'Brien*, the court may still reject evidence of similar facts if it lacks sufficient probative strength to offset potential prejudice. Why is it important to retain the discretionary power to do so? How is it that the usual threshold of relevance may not be good enough where the evidence is of similar facts? There must be some danger peculiar to this kind of evidence that sometimes requires greater than normal caution to be exercised in admitting it. This danger is traditionally understood in the criminal context as one of likely prejudicial effect. The fact-finder, so it is said, might give the evidence more weight than it deserves and infer too hastily that the defendant is guilty of the crime with which she is charged. On the conventional view, this exclusionary rule exists because such value as the evidence has in helping to establish the truth may be outweighed by the risk of it leading the jury astray.

Has this argument any purchase in civil cases? The argument, in its conventional form, is essentially psychological. It is based on empirical claims about how the fact-finder's mind is likely to respond to the evidence while deliberating on the verdict. Civil litigation is normally conducted before a judge without jury

[193] (n 151) para 71.

[194] (n 153) para 75; similarly, ibid para 73: 'The probative strength of the evidence may be a material factor in balancing the factors in the second stage of the process... in civil cases.'

[195] ibid para 55.

involvement. According to Lord Phillips in *O'Brien*, members of the jury 'are not experienced as are judges in putting aside irrational prejudice';[196] and Dillon LJ assured us in *Thorpe* that judges are 'trained to distinguish between what is probative and what is not'.[197] Since most civil cases are tried by judge alone, and since there is little risk of the judge putting too much weight on similar fact evidence, there is, so the explanation goes, less reason against admitting similar fact evidence in civil than in criminal trials.

Logical development of this explanation points us to more drastic conclusions. As we already saw in the discussion of the rule in criminal cases, if the true foundation of the rule is indeed psychological, it is conceptually incoherent to apply it at a bench trial. First, in deciding on admissibility, the judge must, on a literal reading of the conventional theory, predict whether she has the psychological fortitude to guard herself against being swayed unduly by the evidence. If the answer is 'no', it must be excluded. But, for the very same reason, the exclusion would be largely pointless since the judge has been exposed to the evidence.[198] Secondly, if the judge decides to exclude the evidence, she must not allow it to influence her deliberation on the verdict. We put faith in the judge's willingness to comply with the law and in her ability to banish completely the excluded evidence from her mind. But that same faith in the judge's ability ought to lead us to admit, rather than exclude, the evidence.[199]

2.4.3 Moral prejudice

The argument against excluding similar fact evidence in trials without jury appears compelling *only if* we accept the argument on its own terms and suppose that the rule aims at averting logical errors in evidential evaluation. It is submitted that the rationale can be traced to a deeper level of normative justification. For reasons discussed later, this normative justification has much greater force in criminal than in civil cases, and this in turn explains why we would want the admissibility of similar fact evidence to be more circumscribed when it is adduced by the prosecution. What is risky about exposing the fact-finder to similar fact evidence, according to the traditional view, is that she might become biased against the person of whose conduct the evidence is about. But what exactly is the nature of the bias that we fear might taint trial deliberation? Broadly speaking, the fear is that, in reaching the verdict, the fact-finder might think that the

[196] (n 153) para 11.

[197] (n 170) 831.

[198] Contrast the response of the Singapore Court of Appeal in *Tan Meng Jee v PP* [1996] 2 Singapore L Rep 422, 434: '[W]e think ingenious the argument that a strict enforcement of the similar fact rule is futile if the evidence has already been allowed to infiltrate the mind of the trial judge. All we say in response is that we are far more confident in the ability of judges to disregard prejudicial evidence when the need arises.'

[199] *Attorney-General of Hong Kong v Siu Yak-Shing* [1989] 1 WLR 236, 241. See also Robert A Margolis, 'Evidence of Similar Facts, the Evidence Act, and the Judge of Law as Trier-of-fact' (1988) 9 Singapore L Rev 103, 106–107.

person stands to be judged, not for what she is specifically alleged to have done, but for and according to the sort of person that she is. The fact-finder might reason that the person must have acted in a certain bad way *just because* she is the sort of person who would commit this kind of act. This reasoning involves an assumption or a prejudgment. We assume that the person must have acted thus and so in the light of a background conception of her bad character; and, to the extent that there is no adequate evidence to support the inference from her disposition to the conclusion that she must have done it again in the incident at hand, we prejudge her responsibility for it.

The ban enforced by the similar facts rule on the so-called 'forbidden chain of reasoning'[200] should be understood as a moral injunction against making this assumption in trial deliberation. It must be stressed that what is strictly forbidden, as 'an irrefragable rule',[201] is the making of this assumption. The moral injunction is infringed only if the conclusion that the person acted in a certain bad way on a specific occasion is drawn too quickly from the premise that she is the sort of person who would do such a thing.[202] It is not infringed if the conclusion is supported by further and adequate evidence that the circumstances surrounding the incident were likely to elicit from her the kind of behaviour towards which she is said to be disposed. Where such supporting evidence is presented before and taken into account by the fact-finder, her deliberation is free of the forbidden prejudgment. The traditional understanding of the rule as having the effect of imposing a strict ban on a 'forbidden chain of reasoning' is, in this way, reconcilable with the modern view[203] that, where the probative force of the evidence is exceptionally strong, it is permissible to draw an inference from a person's disposition to her likely conduct in the instant case.

It is not psychological weaknesses as such or alone, but, more importantly, our commitment to the moral legitimacy of evidential reasoning that gives meaning and importance to the rule. This normative concern remains in full force even where the fact-finding is conducted by a judge. A finding of fact against a person acquires legitimacy from the justice of the process by which it is reached. Application of the similar facts rule does not call (or, at any rate, does not call merely) for a prediction of how the fact-finder will respond psychologically to information about someone's discreditable record. If all we see in the exclusion of evidence is the judge shepherding the jury—or even more unconvincingly, herself—to the correct outcome, we would have failed to

[200] *Makin v Attorney-General for New South Wales* (n 4) 65.

[201] *R v Straffen* [1952] 2 QB 911, 914.

[202] This is, arguably, how we should read statements such as 'similar fact evidence may be admissible if, *but only if*, it goes beyond showing general propensity' (*R v Handy* (n 5) para 71, original emphasis) and '[e]vidence is not to be excluded merely because it tends to show the accused to be of a bad disposition, but only if it shows nothing more' (*R v Sims* [1946] 1 All ER 697, 700).

[203] On the modern view: *Boardman* (n 30) 456–457; *R v Randall* (n 183) para 26, endorsed by Lord Carswell in *O'Brien* (n 153) para 73. In criminal cases, there is now explicit provisions for reliance on propensity reasoning in the Criminal Justice Act 2003, s 101(1)(d) and s 103(1)(a).

appreciate the significance of the measure in itself, and missed the point that in excluding the evidence, the court is making a moral statement, a statement that is profoundly significant even when the trial is by judge alone. In excluding evidence that violates the rule, the judge is declaring that she will not allow a verdict against a person to be supported by a form of reasoning that insults her personal dignity; and in paying and drawing attention to the moral defensibility of the reasoning used in deliberation on the verdict, the court seeks to assure and persuade that person, and the public, of the legitimacy of the verdict that is finally reached. Implicit in the exclusion is an acknowledgement by the judge that the person is entitled to respect as an autonomous moral being. If she is not given due respect at the trial, the trial loses, to the degree corresponding to the extent of its show of disrespect, its moral claim on her to accept the adverse verdict. The exclusion of evidence is, for these reasons, valuable; and it is valuable whether the trial is by jury or by judge alone.

2.4.4 Dissimilarities in the operation of the rule in civil and criminal proceedings

This argument is consistent with the conception of a trial as a process in which the grounds for an adverse judgment is communicated to the person against whom it is made, with an invitation for dialogue on the justification of those grounds. In seeking her participation in the process, the court expresses respect for her as a responsible agent; it recognizes that she is 'not merely an object to be acted upon',[204] but someone to be engaged with in the process of demonstrating the basis for drawing findings which are critical of her or harmful to her interests. This conception of a trial is put forward typically in the criminal context. Moral criticism figures strongly in most criminal prosecutions but is absent in many civil disputes.[205] It is generally thought that civil liability is about compensating someone for the breach of a personal obligation owed to her, which may not be fault-based, whereas a criminal conviction paradigmatically condemns an individual for acting in violation of some community standard or social interest.[206]

But the distinction should not be overstretched. Findings made in a civil case can also sometimes be critical of the party against whom they are drawn (in the

[204] Herbert L Packer, *The Limits of the Criminal Sanction* (Stanford: Stanford UP, 1968) 157.

[205] According to Henry M Hart, 'What distinguishes a criminal from a civil sanction and all that distinguishes it... is the judgment of community condemnation which accompanies and justifies its imposition': 'The Aims of The Criminal Law' (1958) 23 *Law and Contemporary Problems* 401, 404. Similarly, see Peter Brett, *An Inquiry into Criminal Guilt* (London: Sweet & Maxwell, 1963) 36, 50.

[206] The complexity of the distinction cannot be pursued here, but see generally Paul H Robinson, 'The Criminal-Civil Distinction and the Utility of Desert' (1996) 76 Boston U L Rev 201; Andrew Ashworth, 'Punishment and Compensation: Victims, Offenders and the State' (1986) 6 OJLS 86, 87–99; A P Simester and W J Brookbanks, *Principles of Criminal Law* (2nd edn, Wellington: Brookers, 2002) 2–5.

sense of casting blame on her) and they are usually harmful to her interest (by resulting, for example, in liability to pay damages). There is a similar need for the civil court to justify its findings to the party they badly affect and be concerned with the morality of the reasoning used in support of those findings. It is true however that there is less likely to be a moral issue with the reasoning used in the civil case than in the criminal; and when such an issue surfaces in the civil context, it tends not to be as great as those which commonly arise in the criminal context. For that reason, it is understandable why civil judges are decidedly shy of mentioning 'prejudice' in this area. As we saw, Lord Denning in *Mood Music* chose to speak of 'fairness', 'oppression', and 'fair notice' instead. And as we will see, the Court of Appeal in *O'Brien* urges the substitution of '*Mood Music* language' with the modern terminology of the Civil Procedure Rules, with the emphasis now on the need to deal with cases 'justly'.[207] In *Steel v Commissioner of Police for the Metropolis*,[208] Beldam LJ remarked: 'Whether Lord Denning's concept of fairness to the defendant in civil proceedings included the concept of prejudice to a defendant which is applied in criminal cases is a matter which may need to be considered in future.'

This aversion to use of the term 'prejudice' is partly because, as Pattenden has noted, 'similar fact evidence adduced in civil proceedings frequently does not disclose bad character'.[209] But, as she is also careful to acknowledge, sometimes, it does.[210] More to the point, allegations made in civil litigation do occasionally carry moral indictments. When they do, they tend not to be as serious as are allegations made in criminal cases. However, the extent to which the problem of moral prejudice is posed by similar fact evidence in civil cases should not be underestimated. The problem can arise in civil actions of a class as common as negligence claims. It is a moral failure to have acted negligently in the commission of a harm-producing or death-causing tort, even if it is less of a moral failure than to have committed assault or murder.[211] In *Hales v Kerr*,[212] Channell J thought that the similar facts rule has 'not dissimilar' operation in both civil and criminal cases. Respect for the personal autonomy of the defendant, as displayed

[207] (n 151) para 75.

[208] Unreported judgment of the Court of Appeal (Civil Division) dated 18 February 1993.

[209] Pattenden (n 169) 384.

[210] ibid, 384–385 (occasionally, similar fact evidence does 'show one of the parties ... in such a bad light as to be likely to bias anyone against him'). See also J R S Forbes, *Similar Facts* (Sydney: Law Book Co, 1987) 170: 'There are minor criminal cases which attract little opprobrium; on the other hand there are civil charges, such as fraud, breach of trust or even gross negligence which are capable of arousing strong disapproval of the alleged wrongdoer.'

[211] In *Brown v Eastern and Midlands Railway Co* (1889) 22 QBD 391, 393, Stephen J found it just as objectionable to rely on other instances of negligent conduct as it is to rely on other instances of criminal conduct: 'You must not prove ... that a particular engine driver is a careless man in order to prove that a particular accident was caused by his negligence on a particular occasion; nor that a person accused of a crime is an habitual criminal.'

[212] [1908] 2 KB 601.

in a refusal to be dismissive of his capacity for moral reform, is evident in this *obiter dictum* of the judge:[213]

It is not legitimate to charge a man with an act of negligence on a day in October and to ask a jury to infer that he was negligent on that day because he was negligent on every day in September. The defendant may have mended his ways before the day named in October.

It would be wrong, for the reasons given earlier, to claim that a person's disposition can never be relevant. This passage is better read in line with our previous argument to mean only that a person's general disposition to be careless cannot, *of its own*, justify the inference that he acted negligently on a particular occasion. His disposition is *sufficiently* relevant if and only insofar as there is evidence to show that the circumstances of the event in question were conducive to eliciting the kind of behaviour to which he is said to be disposed. As we will see, reliance on similar facts does not present the problem of moral prejudice in many civil cases. However, where moral prejudice is an issue, the judge must—or, as we must now say in view of *O'Brien*, the judge should, in the exercise of her discretion—look for evidence of the conditions which tend to elicit action in accordance with the alleged disposition before allowing similar facts to be proved. On the other hand, where moral prejudice is not an issue, relevance suffices for admissibility.

Concern for the moral legitimacy of evidential reasoning was also expressed in *George Ballantine & Son v Dixon & Son*.[214] The plaintiffs were well-known blenders and exporters of Scotch whisky. They sued the defendants for passing off goods as Scotch whisky which had been diluted with spirits produced locally in five countries outside of Scotland. The plaintiffs wanted information of 'parallel transactions' conducted by the defendants and sought discovery of 'documents relating to [the defendants'] trade in all countries of the world, and not merely in the five countries'. Walton J denied the application, which was unsurprising given its extremely wide scope. What is interesting is that the decision was based not only on the unfairness of allowing the plaintiffs to conduct a 'fishing expedition' against the defendants, but also on the injustice of using evidence of the latter's discreditable conduct generally to prove that they must have acted in the same way on the pleaded transactions. As the judge explained, the discovery application:[215]

is directed solely to credit, since it is simply and solely directed towards putting the plaintiffs in a position to say: 'You did a wicked act in Ecuador (or wherever), ergo you are a person who would do a dirty deed in the five countries with which the action is specifically concerned.' In other words, give a dog a bad name and hang him.

[213] ibid at 604–605.
[214] (n 57).
[215] ibid at 1132.

This passage treats 'prejudice', not as a psychological phenomenon, but as an ethical problem. The legitimacy of an ascription of responsibility is undermined where it is reached by a line of reasoning that fails to respect the personal autonomy of the subject. Similar fact evidence is more readily admitted in the civil than in the criminal context partly because prejudice is much less of a problem in the former. First, civil liability may not be contingent directly on human agency. In a claim for damages to a building caused by the roots of an oak tree, no question of morality is raised when evidence is admitted of similar wreckage inflicted by the tree on other houses in the vicinity.[216] Furthermore, even if the evidence is of the previous conduct of a person, it may not cast her in a poor moral light.[217] For example, in *McWilliams v William Arrol & Co*,[218] a workman had, in the past, consistently refused to wear the safety belt provided by his employers. He fell on a day when, by chance, all belts had been removed to another worksite. There was some evidence that the belts were 'cumbersome and... might be dangerous in certain circumstances'.[219] It is difficult to see what moral censure is expressed in the finding that the workman would not have worn the belt even had it been made available to him on the day of the accident; indeed, the finding may even speak well of him—perhaps he was a conscientious employee and did not want the belt to slow him down.

Thus one reason why we should be more willing to allow proof of similar facts in civil proceedings is that it often poses no or little problem of moral prejudice. There is, arguably, another reason. Where reliance on the evidence does pose that problem, its exclusion is not as easily justified in a civil dispute as in a criminal prosecution. 'Justice' in the civil context requires more delicate adjustments of competing interests than does 'justice' in the criminal context. In a criminal trial, the predominant interest is in protecting the innocent from conviction, and the court takes a 'protective attitude' towards the accused.[220] In a civil case, on the other hand, justice requires equal treatment of parties in the sense of equal respect for them and equal concern for their interests.[221] Given the primacy of the value of equality in civil adjudication, Lord Denning's emphasis on 'fairness'

[216] *Malewski & Anor v Ealing London Borough Council* [2003] EWHC 763 (TCC), 89 Construction L Rev 1.

[217] In *Joy v Phillips, Mills & Co, Limited* [1916] 1 KB 849, 853, Lord Cozens-Hardy MR asked: 'If you are required to inquire into the habits of [a] horse in order to consider whether the horse was vicious and likely to kick out, are you not entitled to inquire what were the habits of the boy?' Unsurprisingly, the judge did not see any moral obstacle to admitting the similar fact evidence since it showed no grave immoral conduct but only natural mischievousness on the part of the child.

[218] [1962] 1 WLR 295. This case is cited in J D Heydon (ed), *Cross on Evidence* (5th Australian edn, Sydney: Butterworths, 1996) 604 for this proposition: 'When there is no question of prejudice to an accused person, as in the case of a civil proceeding, it may be said that the rule has no place.'

[219] (n 218) 304.

[220] Zuckerman (n 53) 4–6 and, above, Chapter 4, Part 2.3.3.

[221] As Smith J puts it pithily in *R v Isleworth Crown Court, ex p Marland* (n 30) 262: 'Justice means justice to both parties.'

in *Mood Music* was entirely apt. The disparity in the operation of the similar facts rule reflects the difference in value orientation of civil and criminal trials. As Smith J said in *R v Isleworth Crown Court, ex p Marland*:[222]

> The circumstances in which similar fact evidence will be admitted are closely circumscribed for the protection of the accused. In civil cases the rules are less circumscribed because the underlying intention is not to protect one side but to be fair to both sides.

In what sense does the similar facts rule become 'less circumscribed'? Why does the need 'to be fair to both sides' require that it be 'less circumscribed'? In most cases, evidence adduced before the court suggests not just (i) that the person whose conduct in question has the disposition to behave in a certain manner, but, further, (ii) that there existed in the circumstances of the case conditions that tended at the relevant time to elicit conduct in conformity with that disposition. It is a question of degree how strongly the evidence supports (ii), and 'a matter of individual judgment'[223] how strong the support must be to justify admission of evidence relating to (i). This may be illustrated by comparing two cases.

In *R v Isleworth Crown Court, ex p Marland*,[224] the applicant, a Dutch resident, was stopped at Heathrow airport and found to have a large sum of money with him. His explanation for holding the money was that he had intended to buy 'classic' motorcars in the United Kingdom for export to Holland but had subsequently changed his mind. The money was seized under section 42 of the Drug Trafficking Act 1994 on the basis of reasonable grounds for suspecting that the money represented the proceeds of drug trafficking or was intended for use in drug trafficking. An order for forfeiture was subsequently made under section 43(1) of the same Act after the Crown Court was satisfied that the money was in fact connected with drug trafficking. The court applied the civil standard of proof as it was required to do under section 43(3). In arriving at its verdict, the court relied mainly on evidence of the applicant's two previous convictions on drug trafficking charges. This was treated as evidence of propensity to engage in drug trafficking.

It infringes the moral injunction contained in the similar facts rule to simply reason: 'he must have engaged in drug trafficking again because he is the sort of person who would do this kind of thing'. We need assurance that the

[222] ibid 258. The same view is reflected in other cases, including *Hurst v Evans* (1916) 1 KB 352, 357 ('In a prosecution the Court is not adjusting rights between two persons, and the judge often tells the jury that, though there is some evidence against the prisoner, it would not be safe to convict; but that cannot be done in a civil case'); *Berger* (n 165) 633 ('the potential injustice to the plaintiff if I exclude the evidence outweighs the greater burden on the defendants if I admit it'); *W Alexander v Dundee Corporation* [1950] SC 123, 133 ('to ignore all proof of the sort suggested here would not be to do justice between the parties').

[223] *R v H* (n 120) 621, per Lord Mustill. See also *Reza v General Medical Council* [1991] 2 WLR 939, 957 ('The decision [on admissibility of similar fact evidence] has been rightly called a question of degree').

[224] (1998) 162 JP 251.

circumstances of the case were such as to lead him into the error of his past. It is difficult to detect evidence of this in the judgment. The focus was on his possession of money, for which he had provided an innocent explanation; it would be wrong to doubt that he is telling the truth just because of his unsavoury past. The strength of the assurance we seek as a condition to allowing his past to be held against him reflects the degree of our respect for him as a person, capable of 'starting life afresh' as Cardozo CJ once put it.[225] Although the High Court upheld the admission of evidence of past convictions, it was not wholly comfortable with the decision, describing it as a borderline case.[226] The feeling of unease comes from this: to the extent that the court had jumped to the conclusion that Marland 'had done it again', a response that defines his destiny by his past, the court had treated Marland with less than the respect to which he was entitled.

The justification for admitting similar fact evidence was stronger in *O'Brien*. The claimant was allowed to adduce evidence of acts of malpractice allegedly committed by Detective Inspector Lewis in two other cases. It would have been wrong to reason that Lewis must have ill-treated O'Brien because he is the sort of person who would ill-treat suspects and he will always be the bad police officer that he is. But the argument from disposition was supported by evidence of relevant circumstances. In each case, Lewis was presented with similar opportunity or temptation to act on his alleged disposition to extract false admissions. For example, on each occasion, Lewis was in a position of power over the suspect; the suspect was in isolated confinement and did not have his lawyer with him; and he had no reason to fear being held accountable for the way in which he handled the suspect because he had, supposedly, the backing of his superior to employ the tactics which he allegedly used. Furthermore, the pressure on Lewis to fabricate evidence was equally great in each case as the crimes had attracted publicity and the investigation was not progressing well. The court did not simply assume that Lewis had acted in conformity with his alleged disposition to fabricate evidence; the circumstances in *O'Brien* suggested that Lewis was placed in a situation which made possible, and was likely to elicit from him, display of that disposition. In searching out those circumstances with care, the court shows its refusal to prejudge Lewis on a sweeping conception of him as a black sheep of the police force. It takes seriously his personal autonomy by recognizing that his actions issued from moral choices which he was free to make anew on each occasion.

Just treatment requires proportionality. What due respect and concern for a person requires is determined by the gravity of the charges made against her. The higher the gravity of the alleged conduct, the greater the caution the court must exercise in accepting it as true. The allegations tend to be more serious in criminal than in civil cases. It is therefore understandable why stronger assurance

[225] *People v Zackowitz* (n 84) 468. See also *R v Handy* (n 5) 401 (one objection to 'propensity evidence' is that it fails to take seriously the person's capacity 'of turning the page and starting a new life').

[226] (1998) 162 JP 251, 262.

is usually demanded by criminal law that the person did act 'in character' on the pleaded occasion. In conventional language, one would expect the probative threshold to be generally higher in criminal proceedings.

Pressure to lower the civil threshold emanates from the need to be 'fair to both sides'. Just as the court has a moral duty to show respect and concern to the party against whom similar fact evidence is adduced, it has a moral duty to treat likewise the party seeking to rely on the evidence. The latter duty yields countervailing moral pressure to admit the evidence.[227] In civil litigation, the court ought to be receptive to such evidence and arguments as a party may wish to put forward.[228] Unreasonable restraint of the development of her case undermines the legitimacy of the trial. As Hoffmann LJ explained in *Vernon v Bosley*:[229]

> It is an important aspect of an adversary system of justice that a party should so far as possible be allowed to decide how to present his case. If he or his counsel thinks that an item of evidence... may be relevant, the court is generally very reluctant to shut it out. He should not be left with a feeling that he might have won if only he had been allowed to adduce evidence... which the judge refused to hear.

Our receptiveness to what a party wishes us to hear and see, on a matter affecting her rights or interests, reflects our respect and concern for her. We express respect and concern by being serious in our desire to understand, to appreciate, to grasp more fully her case; and so the law grants her the general freedom to develop it. The greater the rights or interests she has at stake, the more she ought to be allowed the freedom to present evidence in support of her claim. Insofar as similar fact evidence has probative value, there is, for this reason, moral pressure to allow a civil party to use it in her favour. This kind of additional pressure is absent when it is the prosecution which is seeking to rely on the evidence to prove a criminal charge; it is unintelligible to speak of respect and concern for the prosecution.[230] In *O'Brien*, the pressure to allow the claimant reliance on the similar fact evidence was particularly great due to the gravity of the injustice alleged in his claim. The Court of Appeal was clearly sensitive to this pressure. The case, it emphasized, had 'exceptional features'.[231] Full account was taken of O'Brien

[227] For a display of judicial effort at weighing justice to one party against justice to the other, see *Berger* (n 165) 633 ('the potential injustice to the plaintiff if I exclude the evidence outweighs the greater burden on the defendants if I admit it'); *Perrin v Drennan* [1991] FSR 81, 87–88.

[228] James Fitzjames Stephen, *The Indian Evidence Act, With an Introduction on the Principles of Judicial Evidence* (Calcutta: Thacker, Spink & Co, 1872) 33: 'judicial enquiries... in all civilised countries are, or at least ought to be, conducted in such a manner as to give every person interested in the result the fullest possible opportunity of establishing the conclusion which he wishes to establish'.

[229] [1994] PIQR P337, P339.

[230] See, generally, Ronald Dworkin, 'Hard Cases' in *Taking Rights Seriously* (London: Duckworth, 1991) 81, 100, noting that there is a symmetry of rights in the standard civil case which does not exist in the criminal case: 'The accused... has a right to a decision in his favor if he is innocent, but the state has no parallel right to a conviction if he is guilty.'

[231] (n 151) para 80.

having 'been in prison for 11 years, convicted of a murder which he says he did not commit and in respect of which his conviction has now been quashed',[232] and also of the fact that if his 'case is proved at trial, he will be shown to have suffered a grievous wrong at the hands of the police'.[233] These same factors were similarly taken into account by the House of Lords.[234]

2.5 Stage 2: discretion

Under the two-stage analysis set out in *O'Brien*, '[o]nce it is decided that the evidence is admissible, the court must then ask itself whether it ought, in its discretion, to refuse to allow it to be admitted'.[235] This was essentially the approach taken by Warner J in the earlier case of *Berger*. As noted, it is doubtful that the judge was right in claiming the existence of a judicial discretion to exclude admissible evidence at common law. But this problem is circumvented with the introduction of the Civil Procedure Rules (CPR). CPR 32.1(2) confers on the court the general jurisdiction to exclude otherwise admissible evidence.[236] This provision applies to all kinds of evidence. It is not specifically aimed at similar facts. What is new about *O'Brien* is its founding of the civil discretion to exclude similar fact evidence in the general discretion conferred by CPR 32.1(2). When *Mood Music* and *Berger* were decided, 'the modern "cards on the table" approach to civil litigation was still in its infancy'.[237] Now that witness statements have to be exchanged before the trial, fear of evidence causing 'unfair surprise' or being 'oppressive' become less relevant. 'Today, it is the language of the CPR... that governs the exercise of the discretion.'[238]

The CPR provides that, in exercising this general discretion, the court must give effect to the overriding objective of achieving justice in the handling of the case.[239] A non-exhaustive list of relevant factors to be taken into account for this purpose is provided in CPR 1.1(2):[240] for example, it is provided that the court must ensure, so far as is practicable, that the case is dealt with expeditiously and fairly and in a way that is proportionate to the importance of the dispute. According to the Court of Appeal in *O'Brien*, the admission of similar fact evidence must be guided by the spirit of the CPR: 'the court should have a tendency to refuse to allow similar fact evidence to be called if it would tend to lengthen

[232] ibid para 80.
[233] ibid para 86.
[234] (n 153) para 60.
[235] (n 151) para 71.
[236] As held by the Court of Appeal in *Grobbelaar v Sun Newspapers Ltd*, The Times, 12 August 1999.
[237] (n 151) para 56.
[238] ibid para 75.
[239] CPR 1.2(a) and 1.1(1).
[240] 'In deciding how to exercise its discretion, the matters listed in CPR 1(2) must loom large in the court's deliberations': (n 151) para 71.

the proceedings and add to their cost or complexity unless there are strong countervailing arguments the other way'.[241] In the House of Lords, the same sort of language was used: for example, Lord Phillips held that judges must exercise their discretion 'in a way which is proportionate to what is involved in the case, and in a manner which is expeditious and fair';[242] and Lord Carswell emphasized that 'the lengthening of the trial and increase of costs to which the calling of similar fact evidence will give rise must not be disproportionate'.[243]

There is a danger in treating the discretion to exclude similar fact evidence as merely an instance of the discretion to exclude evidence in general. It may encourage the belief that similar fact evidence presents no more than a problem of efficiency, only needing analysis 'in case management terms'.[244] Undoubtedly, the introduction of such evidence may create problems that the introduction of other kinds of evidence may also create, such as undue lengthening of the trial or 'oppression' of the opponent when he is called upon to meet an unreasonably wide range of allegations.[245] Even so, if the similar facts rule is a distinct rule, with an independent sphere of operation, it must be addressing a special normative concern. What the rule protects is the legitimacy of trial deliberation. It excludes from that deliberation a form of reasoning that disrespects the moral autonomy of the person against whom the verdict is given. The exclusion should be a matter of legal right, and not a matter of judicial discretion.[246]

Conclusion

As we saw in Part I, a supposedly simplified regime in England and Wales for the admission of similar fact evidence in criminal cases is now set out in the Criminal Justice Act of 2003. Under that statute, evidence of the accused's bad character is admissible if 'relevant to an important matter in issue between the defendant and the prosecution';[247] but the court must not admit the evidence if doing so would undermine the 'fairness of the proceedings'.[248] Admissibility in criminal law is thus made dependent on relevance and controlled by considerations of fairness. *O'Brien* has adopted largely the same framework for civil cases. It has laid down an approach that appears simple: similar fact evidence is admissible so long as it is

241 ibid.
242 (n 153) para 54.
243 ibid para 77.
244 ibid para 65, per Lord Rodger.
245 eg *Kennedy v Dobson* [1895] 1 Ch 334, 338–339; *Metropolitan Asylum District Managers v Hill* (n 190) 31; *Hollingham v Head* (1858) 4 CB (NS) 388, 392–393. It seems that the need to avoid these problems was regarded in the early history of the rule as its main rationale: John H Langbein, *The Origins of Adversary Criminal Trial* (Oxford: Oxford University Press, 2003) 191.
246 *Boardman* (n 30) 457; *R v Gurney* [1994] Crim LR 116.
247 s 101(1)(d).
248 s 101(3).

logically probative; but the judge has discretion to exclude it nonetheless if justice so requires.

The simplicity is only superficial. All of the most important questions are begged. What are the issues of justice or fairness that are uniquely raised by evidence of bad character? Of what nature are these problems? On what principles should they be dealt with? Logic cannot, on its own, explain or justify the common law similar facts rule. However else it may also be seen, it has moral roots. It expresses due respect and concern for the person whose action is sought to be judged by her discreditable life history; on this view, the rule is grounded in the moral imperative of respect for personal autonomy. It can only appear as a mere technicality, prompting the desire to restrict or abolish it, if this ethical perspective is overlooked.

Adoption of that perspective helps to explain the ambivalence discernible in this area of the common law. On the one hand, it is felt that the similar facts rule has a role to play in both civil and criminal cases. This must be right if, as it is here argued, the rule protects the moral legitimacy of evidential reasoning, and reliance on evidence of previous misconduct can undermine the legitimacy in both kinds of proceedings. On the other hand, civil judges are less 'chary' of admitting similar fact evidence than are judges in the criminal courts. This, again, is explicable from the ethical point of view. The raising of the moral issue addressed by the rule is neither as frequent nor often as great in civil as in criminal trials; and there is a countervailing moral pressure to admit the evidence in the former that is absent in the latter. *O'Brien* rightly warns us to be 'conscious of important differences between criminal and civil proceedings'.[249] Contrary to the received wisdom, the most significant of those differences has not to do with the absence or presence of a jury. If the arguments advanced here are right, the critical differences are normative rather than structural.

[249] (n 151) para 35.

Epilogue

As the title indicates, this book offers a philosophy of the law of evidence. Its ambitions are much more modest that the title perhaps suggests. In the preceding chapters, no attempt was made to develop a theory of the law, understood as a unified and comprehensive account of the vast stock of relevant rules and doctrines. Instead, the aim has been to capture a humane way of looking at the trial and to exemplify, through examination of a few selected rules, a value-centred method of analysis; in short: to promote a particular philosophical attitude. This attitude is motivated by the fundamental concern that the court does justice in the search for the truth. To be distinguished from this claim is the markedly different idea that truth must be found in order to do justice; on that conventional view, justice is formally done when the law is correctly applied to the true facts of the case. However, it is important to recognize that justice imposes demands on the manner in which the facts are found. There is nothing novel in this claim of course. But the tendency has been to apply this claim only to rules which impose side-constraints on truth-seeking (such as evidential privileges) and consequently to think of the demands of justice as qualifying or opposing our interests in getting the truth. This study has tried to show that the claim runs deeper than that. It extends to rules which operate at the centre of the main enterprise: those selected for analysis here—the standard of proof and the rules on hearsay and similar facts—go to the heart of the trial's truth-seeking function. Behind their exclusionary form, such rules in substance reflect ethical demands of justice. They require the fact-finder to manifest empathic care for the parties by exercising appropriate caution and to treat them with respect and concern.

This insistence on justice does not ask for a reduction in the court's commitment to the pursuit of truth. That commitment, so it has been argued, is a heavy one from the internal point of view. In general, the fact-finder must make a positive finding only if she is justified in judging that one would be justified in believing that it is true. In making that judgment, she is bound by rules of evidence. For many, those rules run against common sense and that, in turn, has generated pressure for abolition. But the constraints imposed by the rules (at least all of those chosen for this study) do not appear irrational at all once we appreciate the special context in which they operate.

Closely tied to the substantive messages is a methodological contribution. Arguments about the merits of evidentiary rules need not turn on controversial empirical assumptions; indeed, the usefulness and relevance of empirical data can only be judged against a prior understanding of the value and purpose of the rule under investigation. For instance, empirical verification (or refutation) of the hypothesis that lay persons are cognitively incompetent supports the theory that a particular rule is (not) defensible in a jury system. But that is only if the rule is based on nothing more than distrust in their cognitive capacity. An alternative account was offered in this book. Many parts of the law of evidence express normative constraints that apply to the fact-finder, whether she is a judge or a lay juror. We can evaluate the normative arguments without relying on any controversial empirical assumptions. The primary norm that underlies the law of evidence, so this book has argued, is the demand that justice be done in the search for truth.

Index